The History of The Decline and Fall of the Roman Empire by Edward Gibbon

Volume III (of VI)

For decades, perhaps centuries, the standard work of reference on Roman History has been courtesy of Edward Gibbon. In its original printing it was a best-seller and a publishing sensation. History was brought to the masses in vivid detail.

Within its massive six volumes Gibbon put into context the entire sweep of this huge and complex Empire. We visit its far-flung regions, its most charismatic characters as we travel through centuries of its existence and its eternal influence on Western and, most probably, World culture.

Considering the times and the resources at his disposal it quite incredible what Gibbon has been able to put together, to distil, to formulate and precisely plot in this most seducing of histories.

Index of Contents
CHAPTER XXVII - Civil Wars, Reign of Theodosius
CHAPTER XXVIII - Destruction of Paganism
CHAPTER XXIX - Division of Roman Empire Between Sons of Theodosius
CHAPTER XXX - Revolt of The Goths
CHAPTER XXXI - Invasion of Italy, Occupation of Territories by the Barbarians
CHAPTER XXXII - Emperors Arcadius, Eutropius, Theodosius II
CHAPTER XXXIII - Conquest of Africa By the Vandals
CHAPTER XXXIV - Attila
CHAPTER XXXV - Invasion
CHAPTER XXXVI - Total Extinction of The Western Empireon by Attila
CHAPTER XXXVII - Conversion of the Barbarians to Christianity
CHAPTER XXXVIII - Reign of Clovis

CHAPTER XXVII

CIVIL WARS, REIGN OF THEODOSIUS

PART I

DEATH OF GRATIAN—RUIN OR ARIANISM—ST. AMBROSE—FIRST CIVIL WAR, AGAINST MAXIMUS—CHARACTER, ADMINISTRATION, AND PENANCE OF THEODOSIUS—DEATH OF VALENTINIAN II—SECOND CIVIL WAR, AGAINST EUGENIUS—DEATH OF THEODOSIUS

The fame of Gratian, before he had accomplished the twentieth year of his age, was equal to that of the most celebrated princes. His gentle and amiable disposition endeared him to his private friends, the graceful affability of his manners engaged the affection of the people: the men of letters, who enjoyed the liberality, acknowledged the taste and eloquence, of their sovereign; his valor and dexterity in arms were equally applauded by the soldiers; and the clergy considered the humble piety of Gratian as the first and most useful of his virtues. The victory of Colmar had delivered the West from a formidable invasion; and the grateful provinces of the East ascribed the merits of Theodosius to the author of his greatness, and of the public safety. Gratian survived those memorable events only four or five years; but he survived his reputation; and, before he fell a victim to rebellion, he had lost, in a great measure, the respect and confidence of the Roman world.

The remarkable alteration of his character or conduct may not be imputed to the arts of flattery, which had besieged the son of Valentinian from his infancy; nor to the headstrong passions which the that gentle youth appears to have escaped. A more attentive view of the life of Gratian may perhaps suggest the true cause of the disappointment of the public hopes. His apparent virtues, instead of being the hardy productions of experience and adversity, were the premature and artificial fruits of a royal education. The anxious tenderness of his father was continually employed to bestow on him those advantages, which he might perhaps esteem the more highly, as he himself had been deprived of them; and the most skilful masters of every science, and of every art, had labored to form the mind and body of the young prince. [1] The knowledge which they painfully communicated was displayed with ostentation, and celebrated with lavish praise. His soft and tractable disposition received the fair impression of their judicious precepts, and the absence of passion might easily be mistaken for the strength of reason. His preceptors gradually rose to the rank and consequence of ministers of state: [2] and, as they wisely dissembled their secret authority, he seemed to act with firmness, with propriety, and with judgment, on the most important occasions of his life and reign. But the influence of this elaborate instruction did not penetrate beyond the surface; and the skilful preceptors, who so accurately guided the steps of their royal pupil, could not infuse into his feeble and indolent character the vigorous and independent principle of action which renders the laborious pursuit of glory essentially necessary to the happiness, and almost to the existence, of the hero. As soon as time and accident had removed those faithful counsellors from the throne, the emperor of the West insensibly descended to the level of his natural genius; abandoned the reins of government to the ambitious hands which were stretched forwards to grasp them; and amused his leisure with the most frivolous gratifications. A public sale of favor and injustice was instituted, both in the court and in the provinces, by the worthless delegates of his power, whose merit it was made sacrilege to question. [3] The conscience of the credulous prince was directed by saints and bishops; [4] who procured an Imperial edict to punish, as a capital offence, the violation, the neglect, or even the ignorance, of the divine law. [5] Among the various arts which had exercised the youth of Gratian, he had applied himself, with singular inclination and success, to manage the horse, to draw the bow, and to dart the javelin; and these qualifications, which might be useful to a soldier, were prostituted to the viler purposes of hunting. Large parks were enclosed for the Imperial pleasures, and plentifully stocked with every species of wild beasts; and Gratian neglected the duties, and even the dignity, of his rank, to consume whole days in the vain display of his dexterity and boldness in the chase. The pride and wish of the Roman emperor to excel in an art, in which he might be surpassed by the meanest of his slaves, reminded the numerous spectators of the examples of Nero and Commodus, but the chaste and temperate Gratian was a stranger to their monstrous vices; and his hands were stained only with the blood of animals. [6] The behavior of Gratian, which degraded his character in the eyes of mankind, could not have disturbed the security of his reign, if the army had not been provoked to resent their peculiar injuries. As long as the young emperor was guided by the instructions of his masters, he professed himself the friend and pupil of the soldiers; many of his hours were spent in the familiar conversation of the camp; and the health, the comforts, the rewards, the honors, of his faithful troops, appeared to be the objects of his attentive concern. But, after Gratian more freely indulged his prevailing taste for hunting and shooting, he naturally connected himself with the most dexterous ministers of his favorite amusement. A body of the Alani was received into the military and domestic service of the palace; and the admirable skill, which they were accustomed to display in the unbounded plains of Scythia, was exercised, on a more narrow theatre, in the parks and enclosures of Gaul. Gratian admired the talents and customs of these favorite guards, to whom alone he intrusted the defence of his person; and, as if he meant to insult the public opinion, he frequently showed himself to the soldiers and people, with the dress and arms, the long bow, the sounding quiver, and the fur garments of a Scythian warrior. The unworthy spectacle of a Roman prince, who had renounced the dress and manners of his country, filled the minds of the legions with grief and indignation. [7] Even the Germans, so strong and formidable in the armies of the empire, affected to disdain the strange and horrid appearance of the savages of the North, who, in the space of a few years, had wandered from the banks of the Volga to those of the Seine. A loud and licentious murmur was echoed through the camps and garrisons of the West; and as the mild indolence of Gratian neglected to extinguish the first symptoms of discontent, the want of love and respect was not supplied by the influence of fear. But the subversion of an established government is always a work of some real, and of much apparent, difficulty; and the throne of Gratian was protected by the sanctions of custom, law, religion, and the nice balance of the civil and military powers, which had been established by the policy of Constantine. It is not very important to inquire from what cause the revolt of Britain was produced. Accident is commonly the parent of disorder; the seeds of rebellion happened to fall on a soil which was supposed to be more fruitful than any other in tyrants and usurpers; [8] the legions of that sequestered island had been long famous for a spirit of presumption and arrogance; [9] and the name of Maximus was proclaimed, by the tumultuary, but unanimous voice, both of the soldiers and of the provincials. The emperor, or the rebel,—for this title was not yet ascertained by fortune,—was a native of Spain, the countryman, the fellow-soldier, and the rival of Theodosius whose elevation he had not seen without some emotions of envy and resentment: the events of his life had long since fixed him in Britain; and I should not be unwilling to find some evidence for the marriage, which he is said to have contracted with the daughter of a wealthy lord of Caernarvonshire. [10] But this provincial rank might justly be considered as a state of exile and obscurity; and if Maximus had obtained any civil or military office, he was not invested with the authority either of governor or general. [11] His abilities, and even his integrity, are acknowledged by the partial writers of the age; and the merit must indeed have been conspicuous that could extort such a confession in favor of the vanquished enemy of Theodosius. The discontent of Maximus might incline him to censure the conduct of his sovereign, and to encourage, perhaps, without any views of ambition, the murmurs of the troops. But in the midst of the tumult, he artfully, or modestly, refused to ascend the throne; and some credit appears to have been given to his own positive declaration, that he was compelled to accept the dangerous present of the Imperial purple. [12]

[Footnote 1: Valentinian was less attentive to the religion of his son; since he intrusted the education of Gratian to Ausonius, a professed Pagan. (Mem. de l'Academie des Inscriptions, tom. xv. p. 125-138). The poetical fame of Ausonius condemns the taste of his age.]

[Footnote 2: Ausonius was successively promoted to the Praetorian praefecture of Italy, (A.D. 377,) and of Gaul, (A.D. 378;) and was at length invested with the consulship, (A.D. 379.) He expressed his gratitude in a servile and insipid piece of flattery, (Actio Gratiarum, p. 699-736,) which has survived more worthy productions.]

[Footnote 3: Disputare de principali judicio non oportet. Sacrilegii enim instar est dubitare, an is dignus sit, quem elegerit imperator. Codex Justinian, l. ix. tit. xxix. leg. 3. This convenient law was revived and promulgated, after the death of Gratian, by the feeble court of Milan.]

[Footnote 4: Ambrose composed, for his instruction, a theological treatise on the faith of the Trinity: and Tillemont, (Hist. des Empereurs, tom. v. p. 158, 169,) ascribes to the archbishop the merit of Gratian's intolerant laws.]

[Footnote 5: Qui divinae legis sanctitatem nesciendo omittunt, aut negligende violant, et offendunt, sacrilegium committunt. Codex Justinian. l. ix. tit. xxix. leg. 1. Theodosius indeed may claim his share in the merit of this comprehensive law.]

[Footnote 6: Ammianus (xxxi. 10) and the younger Victor acknowledge the virtues of Gratian; and accuse, or rather lament, his degenerate taste. The odious parallel of Commodus is saved by "licet incruentus;" and perhaps Philostorgius (l. x. c. 10, and Godefroy, p. 41) had guarded with some similar reserve, the comparison of Nero.]

[Footnote 7: Zosimus (l. iv. p. 247) and the younger Victor ascribe the revolution to the favor of the Alani, and the discontent of the Roman troops Dum exercitum negligeret, et paucos ex Alanis, quos ingenti auro ad sa transtulerat, anteferret veteri ac Romano militi.]

[Footnote 8: Britannia fertilis provincia tyrannorum, is a memorable expression, used by Jerom in the Pelagian controversy, and variously tortured in the disputes of our national antiquaries. The revolutions of the last age appeared to justify the image of the sublime Bossuet, "sette ile, plus orageuse que les mers qui l'environment."]

[Footnote 9: Zosimus says of the British soldiers.]

[Footnote 10: Helena, the daughter of Eudda. Her chapel may still be seen at Caer-segont, now Caer-narvon. (Carte's Hist. of England, vol. i. p. 168, from Rowland's Mona Antiqua.) The prudent reader may not perhaps be satisfied with such Welsh evidence.]

[Footnote 11: Camden (vol. i. introduct. p. ci.) appoints him governor at Britain; and the father of our antiquities is followed, as usual, by his blind progeny. Pacatus and Zosimus had taken some pains to prevent this error, or fable; and I shall protect myself by their decisive testimonies. Regali habitu exulem suum, illi exules orbis induerunt, (in Panegyr. Vet. xii. 23,) and the Greek historian still less equivocally, (Maximus) (l. iv. p. 248.)]

[Footnote 12: Sulpicius Severus, Dialog. ii. 7. Orosius, l. vii. c. 34. p. 556. They both acknowledge (Sulpicius had been his subject) his innocence and merit. It is singular enough, that Maximus should be less favorably treated by Zosimus, the partial adversary of his rival.]

But there was danger likewise in refusing the empire; and from the moment that Maximus had violated his allegiance to his lawful sovereign, he could not hope to reign, or even to live, if he confined his moderate ambition within the narrow limits of Britain. He boldly and wisely resolved to prevent the designs of Gratian; the youth of the island crowded to his standard, and he invaded Gaul with a fleet and army, which were long afterwards remembered, as the emigration of a considerable part of the British nation. [13] The emperor, in his peaceful residence of Paris, was alarmed by their hostile approach; and the darts which he idly wasted on lions and bears, might have been employed more honorably against the rebels. But his feeble efforts announced his degenerate spirit and desperate situation; and deprived him of the resources, which he still might have found, in the support of his subjects and allies. The armies of Gaul, instead of opposing the march of Maximus, received him with joyful and loyal acclamations; and the shame of the desertion was transferred from the people to the prince. The troops, whose station more immediately attached them to the service of the palace, abandoned the standard of Gratian the first time that it was displayed in the neighborhood of Paris. The emperor of the West fled towards Lyons, with a train of only three hundred horse; and, in the cities along the road, where he hoped to find refuge, or at least a passage, he was taught, by cruel experience, that every gate is shut against the unfortunate. Yet he might still have reached, in safety, the dominions of his brother; and soon have returned with the forces of Italy and the East; if he had not suffered himself to be fatally deceived by the perfidious governor of the Lyonnese province. Gratian was amused by protestations of doubtful fidelity, and the hopes of a support, which could not be effectual; till the arrival of Andragathius, the general of the cavalry of Maximus, put an end to his suspense. That resolute officer executed, without remorse, the orders or the intention of the usurper. Gratian, as he rose from supper, was delivered into the hands of the assassin: and his body was denied to the pious and pressing entreaties of his brother Valentinian. [14] The death of the emperor was followed by that of his powerful general Mellobaudes, the king of the Franks; who maintained, to the last moment of his life, the ambiguous reputation, which is the just recompense of obscure and subtle policy. [15] These executions might be necessary to the public safety: but the successful usurper, whose power was acknowledged by all the provinces of the West, had the merit, and the satisfaction, of boasting, that, except those who had perished by the chance of war, his triumph was not stained by the blood of the Romans. [16]

[Footnote 13: Archbishop Usher (Antiquat. Britan. Eccles. p. 107, 108) has diligently collected the legends of the island, and the continent. The whole emigration consisted of 30,000 soldiers, and 100,000 plebeians, who settled in Bretagne. Their destined brides, St. Ursula with 11,000 noble, and 60,000 plebeian, virgins, mistook their way; landed at Cologne, and were all most cruelly murdered by the Huns. But the plebeian sisters have been defrauded of their equal honors; and what is still harder, John Trithemius presumes to mention the children of these British virgins.]

[Footnote 14: Zosimus (l. iv. p. 248, 249) has transported the death of Gratian from Lugdunum in Gaul (Lyons) to Singidunum in Moesia. Some hints may be extracted from the Chronicles; some lies may be detected in Sozomen (l. vii. c. 13) and Socrates, (l. v. c. 11.) Ambrose is our most authentic evidence, (tom. i. Enarrat. in Psalm lxi. p. 961, tom ii. epist. xxiv. p. 888 &c., and de Obitu Valentinian Consolat. Ner. 28, p. 1182.)]

[Footnote 15: Pacatus (xii. 28) celebrates his fidelity; while his treachery is marked in Prosper's Chronicle, as the cause of the ruin of Gratian. Ambrose, who has occasion to exculpate himself, only condemns the death of Vallio, a faithful servant of Gratian, (tom. ii. epist. xxiv. p. 891, edit. Benedict.) Note: Le Beau contests the reading in the chronicle of Prosper upon which this charge rests. Le Beau, iv. 232—M. Note: According to Pacatus, the Count Valilo, who commanded the army, was carried to Chalons to be burnt alive; but Maximus, dreading the imputation of cruelty, caused him to be secretly strangled by his Bretons. Macedonius also, master of the offices, suffered the death which he merited. Le Beau, iv. 244—M.]

[Footnote 16: He protested, nullum ex adversariis nisi in acissie occubu. Sulp. Jeverus in Vit. B. Martin, c. 23. The orator Theodosius bestows reluctant, and therefore weighty, praise on his clemency. Si cui ille, pro ceteris sceleribus suis, minus crudelis fuisse videtur, (Panegyr. Vet. xii. 28.)]

The events of this revolution had passed in such rapid succession, that it would have been impossible for Theodosius to march to the relief of his benefactor, before he received the intelligence of his defeat and death. During the season of sincere grief, or ostentatious mourning, the Eastern emperor was interrupted by the arrival of the principal chamberlain of Maximus; and the choice of a venerable old man, for an office which was usually exercised by eunuchs, announced to the court of Constantinople the gravity and temperance of the British usurper.

The ambassador condescended to justify, or excuse, the conduct of his master; and to protest, in specious language, that the murder of Gratian had been perpetrated, without his knowledge or consent, by the precipitate zeal of the soldiers. But he proceeded, in a firm and equal tone, to offer Theodosius the alternative of peace, or war. The speech of the ambassador concluded with a spirited declaration, that although Maximus, as a Roman, and as the father of his people, would choose rather to employ his forces in the common defence of the republic, he was armed and prepared, if his friendship should be rejected, to dispute, in a field of battle, the empire of the world. An immediate and peremptory answer was required; but it was extremely difficult for Theodosius to satisfy, on this important occasion, either the feelings of his own mind, or the expectations of the public. The imperious voice of honor and gratitude called aloud for revenge. From the liberality of Gratian, he had received the Imperial diadem; his patience would encourage the odious suspicion, that he was more deeply sensible of former injuries, than of recent obligations; and if he accepted the friendship, he must seem to share the guilt, of the assassin. Even the principles of justice, and the interest of society, would receive a fatal blow from the impunity of Maximus; and the example of successful usurpation would tend to dissolve the artificial fabric of government, and once more to replunge the empire in the crimes and calamities of the preceding age. But, as the sentiments of gratitude and honor should invariably regulate the conduct of an individual, they may be overbalanced in the mind of a sovereign, by the sense of superior duties; and the maxims both of justice and humanity must permit the escape of an atrocious criminal, if an innocent people would be involved in the consequences of his punishment. The assassin of Gratian had usurped, but he actually possessed, the most warlike provinces of the empire: the East was exhausted by the misfortunes, and even by the success, of the Gothic war; and it was seriously to be apprehended, that, after the vital strength of the republic had been wasted in a doubtful and destructive contest, the feeble conqueror would remain an easy prey to the Barbarians of the North. These weighty considerations engaged Theodosius to dissemble his resentment, and to accept the alliance of the tyrant. But he stipulated, that Maximus should content himself with the possession of the countries beyond the Alps. The brother of Gratian was confirmed and secured in the sovereignty of Italy, Africa, and the Western Illyricum; and some honorable conditions were inserted in the treaty, to protect the memory, and the laws, of the deceased emperor. [17] According to the custom of the age, the images of the three Imperial colleagues were exhibited to the veneration of the people; nor should it be lightly supposed, that, in the moment of a solemn reconciliation, Theodosius secretly cherished the intention of perfidy and revenge. [18]

[Footnote 17: Ambrose mentions the laws of Gratian, quas non abrogavit hostia (tom. ii epist. xvii. p. 827.)]

[Footnote 18: Zosimus, l. iv. p. 251, 252. We may disclaim his odious suspicions; but we cannot reject the treaty of peace which the friends of Theodosius have absolutely forgotten, or slightly mentioned.]

The contempt of Gratian for the Roman soldiers had exposed him to the fatal effects of their resentment. His profound veneration for the Christian clergy was rewarded by the applause and gratitude of a powerful order, which has claimed, in every age, the privilege of dispensing honors, both on earth and in heaven. [19] The orthodox bishops bewailed his death, and their own irreparable loss; but they were soon comforted by the discovery, that Gratian had committed the sceptre of the East to the hands of a prince, whose humble faith and fervent zeal, were supported by the spirit and abilities of a more vigorous character. Among the benefactors of the church, the fame of Constantine has been rivalled by the glory of Theodosius. If Constantine had the advantage of erecting the standard of the cross, the emulation of his successor assumed the merit of subduing the Arian heresy, and of abolishing the worship of idols in the Roman world. Theodosius was the first of the emperors baptized in the true faith of the Trinity. Although he was born of a Christian family, the maxims, or at least the practice, of the age, encouraged him to delay the ceremony of his initiation; till he was admonished of the danger of delay, by the serious illness which threatened his life, towards the end of the first year of his reign. Before he again took the field against the Goths, he received the sacrament of baptism [20] from Acholius, the orthodox bishop of Thessalonica: [21] and, as the emperor ascended from the holy font, still glowing with the warm feelings of regeneration, he dictated a solemn edict, which proclaimed his own faith, and prescribed the religion of his subjects. "It is our pleasure (such is the Imperial style) that all the nations, which are governed by our clemency and moderation, should steadfastly adhere to the religion which was taught by St. Peter to the Romans; which faithful tradition has preserved; and which is now professed by the pontiff Damasus, and by Peter, bishop of Alexandria, a man of apostolic holiness. According to the discipline of the apostles, and the doctrine of the gospel, let us believe the sole deity of the Father, the Son, and the Holy Ghost; under an equal majesty, and a pious Trinity. We authorize the followers of this doctrine to assume the title of Catholic Christians; and as we judge, that all others are extravagant madmen, we brand them with the infamous name of Heretics; and declare that their conventicles shall no longer usurp the respectable appellation of churches. Besides the condemnation of divine justice, they must expect to suffer the severe penalties, which our authority, guided by heavenly wisdom, shall think proper to inflict upon them." [22] The faith of a soldier is commonly the fruit of instruction, rather than of inquiry; but as the emperor always fixed his eyes on the visible landmarks of orthodoxy, which he had so prudently constituted, his religious opinions were never affected by the specious texts, the subtle arguments, and the ambiguous creeds of the Arian doctors. Once indeed he expressed a faint inclination to converse with the eloquent and learned Eunomius, who lived in retirement at a small distance from Constantinople. But the dangerous interview was prevented by the prayers of the empress Flaccilla, who trembled for the salvation of her husband; and the mind of Theodosius was confirmed by a theological argument, adapted to the rudest capacity. He had lately bestowed on his eldest son, Arcadius, the name and honors of Augustus, and the two princes were seated on a stately throne to receive the homage of their subjects. A bishop, Amphilochius of Iconium, approached the throne, and after saluting, with due reverence, the person of his sovereign, he accosted the royal youth with the same familiar tenderness which he might have used towards a plebeian child. Provoked by this insolent behavior, the monarch gave orders, that the rustic priest should be instantly driven from his presence. But while the guards were forcing him to the door, the dexterous polemic had time to execute his design, by exclaiming, with a loud voice, "Such is the treatment, O emperor! which the King of heaven has prepared for those impious men, who affect to worship the Father, but refuse to acknowledge the equal majesty of his divine Son." Theodosius immediately embraced the bishop of Iconium, and never forgot the important lesson, which he had received from this dramatic parable. [23]

[Footnote 19: Their oracle, the archbishop of Milan, assigns to his pupil Gratian, a high and respectable place in heaven, (tom. ii. de Obit. Val. Consol p. 1193.)]

[Footnote 20: For the baptism of Theodosius, see Sozomen, (l. vii. c. 4,) Socrates, (l. v. c. 6,) and Tillemont, (Hist. des Empereurs, tom. v. p. 728.)]

[Footnote 21: Ascolius, or Acholius, was honored by the friendship, and the praises, of Ambrose; who styles him murus fidei atque sanctitatis, (tom. ii. epist. xv. p. 820;) and afterwards celebrates his speed and diligence in running to Constantinople, Italy, &c., (epist. xvi. p. 822.) a virtue which does not appertain either to a wall, or a bishop.]

[Footnote 22: Codex Theodos. l. xvi. tit. i. leg. 2, with Godefroy's Commentary, tom. vi. p. 5-9. Such an edict deserved the warmest praises of Baronius, auream sanctionem, edictum pium et salutare—Sic itua ad astra.]

[Footnote 23: Sozomen, l. vii. c. 6. Theodoret, l. v. c. 16. Tillemont is displeased (Mem. Eccles. tom. vi. p. 627, 628) with the terms of "rustic bishop," "obscure city." Yet I must take leave to think, that both Amphilochius and Iconium were objects of inconsiderable magnitude in the Roman empire.]

PART II

Constantinople was the principal seat and fortress of Arianism; and, in a long interval of forty years, [24] the faith of the princes and prelates, who reigned in the capital of the East, was rejected in the purer schools of Rome and Alexandria. The archiepiscopal throne of Macedonius, which had been polluted with so much Christian blood, was successively filled by Eudoxus and Damophilus. Their diocese enjoyed a free importation of vice and error from every province of the empire; the eager pursuit of religious controversy afforded a new occupation to the busy idleness of the metropolis; and we may credit the assertion of an intelligent observer, who describes, with some pleasantry, the effects of their loquacious zeal. "This city," says he, "is full of mechanics and slaves, who are all of them profound theologians; and preach in the shops, and in the streets. If you desire a man to change a piece of silver, he informs you, wherein the Son differs from the Father; if you ask the price of a loaf, you are told by way of reply, that the Son is inferior to the Father; and if you inquire, whether the bath is ready, the answer is, that the Son was made out of nothing." [25] The heretics, of various denominations, subsisted in peace under the protection of the Arians of Constantinople; who endeavored to secure the attachment of those obscure sectaries, while they abused, with unrelenting severity, the victory which they had obtained over the followers of the council of Nice. During the partial reigns of Constantius and Valens, the feeble remnant of the Homoousians was deprived of the public and private exercise of their religion; and it has been observed, in pathetic language, that the scattered flock was left without a shepherd to wander on the mountains, or to be devoured by rapacious wolves. [26] But, as their zeal, instead of being subdued, derived strength and vigor from oppression, they seized the first moments of imperfect freedom, which they had acquired by the death of Valens, to form themselves into a regular congregation, under the conduct of an episcopal pastor. Two natives of Cappadocia, Basil, and Gregory Nazianzen, [27] were distinguished above all their contemporaries, [28] by the rare union of profane eloquence and of orthodox piety.

These orators, who might sometimes be compared, by themselves, and by the public, to the most celebrated of the ancient Greeks, were united by the ties of the strictest friendship. They had cultivated, with equal ardor, the same liberal studies in the schools of Athens; they had retired, with equal devotion, to the same solitude in the deserts of Pontus; and every spark of emulation, or envy, appeared to be totally extinguished in the holy and ingenuous breasts of Gregory and Basil. But the exaltation of Basil, from a private life to the archiepiscopal throne of Caesarea, discovered to the world, and perhaps to himself, the pride of his character; and the first favor which he condescended to bestow on his friend, was received, and perhaps was intended, as a cruel insult. [29] Instead of employing the superior talents of Gregory in some useful and conspicuous station, the haughty prelate selected, among the fifty bishoprics of his extensive province, the wretched village of Sasima, [30] without water, without verdure, without society, situate at the junction of three highways, and frequented only by the incessant passage of rude and clamorous wagoners. Gregory submitted with reluctance to this humiliating exile; he was ordained bishop of Sasima; but he solemnly protests, that he never consummated his spiritual marriage with this disgusting bride. He afterwards consented to undertake the government of his native church of Nazianzus, [31] of which his father had been bishop above five-and-forty years. But as he was still conscious that he deserved another audience, and another theatre, he accepted, with no unworthy ambition, the honorable invitation, which was addressed to him from the orthodox party of Constantinople. On his arrival in the capital, Gregory was entertained in the house of a pious and charitable kinsman; the most spacious room was consecrated to the uses of religious worship; and the name of Anastasia was chosen to express the resurrection of the Nicene faith. This private conventicle was afterwards converted into a magnificent church; and the credulity of the succeeding age was prepared to believe the miracles and visions, which attested the presence, or at least the protection, of the Mother of God. [32] The pulpit of the Anastasia was the scene of the labors and triumphs of Gregory Nazianzen; and, in the space of two years, he experienced all the spiritual adventures which constitute the prosperous or adverse fortunes of a missionary. [33] The Arians, who were provoked by the boldness of his enterprise, represented his doctrine, as if he had preached three distinct and equal Deities; and the devout populace was excited to suppress, by violence and tumult, the irregular assemblies of the Athanasian heretics. From the cathedral of St. Sophia there issued a motley crowd "of common beggars, who had forfeited their claim to pity; of monks, who had the appearance of goats or satyrs; and of women, more terrible than so many Jezebels." The doors of the Anastasia were broke open; much mischief was perpetrated, or attempted, with sticks, stones, and firebrands; and as a man lost his life in the affray, Gregory, who was summoned the next morning before the magistrate, had the satisfaction of supposing, that he publicly confessed the name of Christ. After he was delivered from the fear and danger of a foreign enemy, his infant church was disgraced and distracted by intestine faction. A stranger who assumed the name of Maximus, [34] and the cloak of a Cynic philosopher, insinuated himself into the confidence of Gregory; deceived and abused his favorable opinion; and forming a secret connection with some bishops of Egypt, attempted, by a clandestine ordination, to supplant his patron in the episcopal seat of Constantinople. These mortifications might sometimes tempt the Cappadocian missionary to regret his obscure solitude. But his fatigues were rewarded by the daily increase of his fame and his congregation; and he enjoyed the pleasure of observing, that the greater part of his numerous audience retired from his sermons satisfied with the eloquence of the preacher, [35] or dissatisfied with the manifold imperfections of their faith and practice. [36]

[Footnote 24: Sozomen, l. vii. c. v. Socrates, l. v. c. 7. Marcellin. in Chron. The account of forty years must be dated from the election or intrusion of Eusebius, who wisely exchanged the bishopric of Nicomedia for the throne of Constantinople.]

[Footnote 25: See Jortin's Remarks on Ecclesiastical History, vol. iv. p. 71. The thirty-third Oration of Gregory Nazianzen affords indeed some similar ideas, even some still more ridiculous; but I have not yet found the words of this remarkable passage, which I allege on the faith of a correct and liberal scholar.]

[Footnote 26: See the thirty-second Oration of Gregory Nazianzen, and the account of his own life, which he has composed in 1800 iambics. Yet every physician is prone to exaggerate the inveterate nature of the disease which he has cured.]

[Footnote 27: I confess myself deeply indebted to the two lives of Gregory Nazianzen, composed, with very different views, by Tillemont (Mem. Eccles. tom. ix. p. 305-560, 692-731) and Le Clerc, (Bibliotheque Universelle, tom. xviii. p. 1-128.)]

[Footnote 28: Unless Gregory Nazianzen mistook thirty years in his own age, he was born, as well as his friend Basil, about the year 329. The preposterous chronology of Suidas has been graciously received, because it removes the scandal of Gregory's father, a saint likewise, begetting children after he became a bishop, (Tillemont, Mem. Eccles. tom. ix. p. 693-697.)]

[Footnote 29: Gregory's Poem on his own Life contains some beautiful lines, (tom. ii. p. 8,) which burst from the heart, and speak the pangs of injured and lost friendship. —In the Midsummer Night's Dream, Helena addresses the same pathetic complaint to her friend Hermia:—Is all the counsel that we two have shared. The sister's vows, &c. Shakspeare had never read the poems of Gregory Nazianzen; he was ignorant of the Greek language; but his mother tongue, the language of Nature, is the same in Cappadocia and in Britain.]

[Footnote 30: This unfavorable portrait of Sasimae is drawn by Gregory Nazianzen, (tom. ii. de Vita sua, p. 7, 8.) Its precise situation, forty-nine miles from Archelais, and thirty-two from Tyana, is fixed in the Itinerary of Antoninus, (p. 144, edit. Wesseling.)]

[Footnote 31: The name of Nazianzus has been immortalized by Gregory; but his native town, under the Greek or Roman title of Diocaesarea, (Tillemont, Mem. Eccles. tom. ix. p. 692,) is mentioned by Pliny, (vi. 3,) Ptolemy, and Hierocles, (Itinerar. Wesseling, p. 709). It appears to have been situate on the edge of Isauria.]

[Footnote 32: See Ducange, Constant. Christiana, l. iv. p. 141, 142. The Sozomen (l. vii. c. 5) is interpreted to mean the Virgin Mary.]

[Footnote 33: Tillemont (Mem. Eccles. tom. ix. p. 432, &c.) diligently collects, enlarges, and explains, the oratorical and poetical hints of Gregory himself.]

[Footnote 34: He pronounced an oration (tom. i. Orat. xxiii. p. 409) in his praise; but after their quarrel, the name of Maximus was changed into that of Heron, (see Jerom, tom. i. in Catalog. Script. Eccles. p. 301). I touch slightly on these obscure and personal squabbles.]

[Footnote 35: Under the modest emblem of a dream, Gregory (tom. ii. Carmen ix. p. 78) describes his own success with some human complacency. Yet it should seem, from his familiar conversation with his auditor St. Jerom, (tom. i. Epist. ad Nepotian. p. 14,) that the preacher understood the true value of popular applause.]

[Footnote 36: Lachrymae auditorum laudes tuae sint, is the lively and judicious advice of St. Jerom.]

The Catholics of Constantinople were animated with joyful confidence by the baptism and edict of Theodosius; and they impatiently waited the effects of his gracious promise. Their hopes were speedily accomplished; and the emperor, as soon as he had finished the operations of the campaign, made his public entry into the capital at the head of a victorious army. The next day after his arrival, he summoned Damophilus to his presence, and offered that Arian prelate the hard alternative of subscribing the Nicene creed, or of instantly resigning, to the orthodox believers, the use and possession of the episcopal palace, the cathedral of St. Sophia, and all the churches of Constantinople. The zeal of Damophilus, which in a Catholic saint would have been justly applauded, embraced, without hesitation, a life of poverty and exile, [37] and his removal was immediately followed by the purification of the Imperial city. The Arians might complain, with some appearance of justice, that an inconsiderable congregation of sectaries should usurp the hundred churches, which they were insufficient to fill; whilst the far greater part of the people was cruelly excluded from every place of religious worship. Theodosius was still inexorable; but as the angels who protected the Catholic cause were only visible to the eyes of faith, he prudently reenforced those heavenly legions with the more effectual aid of temporal and carnal weapons; and the church of St. Sophia was occupied by a large body of the Imperial guards. If the mind of Gregory was susceptible of pride, he must have felt a very lively satisfaction, when the emperor conducted him through the streets in solemn triumph; and, with his own hand, respectfully placed him on the archiepiscopal throne of Constantinople. But the saint (who had not subdued the imperfections of human virtue) was deeply affected by the mortifying consideration, that his entrance into the fold was that of a wolf, rather than of a shepherd; that the glittering arms which surrounded his person, were necessary for his safety; and that he alone was the object of the imprecations of a great party, whom, as men and citizens, it was impossible for him to despise. He beheld the innumerable multitude of either sex, and of every age, who crowded the streets, the windows, and the roofs of the houses; he heard the tumultuous voice of rage, grief, astonishment, and despair; and Gregory fairly confesses, that on the memorable day of his installation, the capital of the East wore the appearance of a city taken by storm, and in the hands of a Barbarian conqueror. [38] About six weeks afterwards, Theodosius declared his resolution of expelling from all the churches of his dominions the bishops and their clergy who should obstinately refuse to believe, or at least to profess, the doctrine of the council of Nice. His lieutenant, Sapor, was armed with the ample powers of a general law, a special commission, and a military force; [39] and this ecclesiastical revolution was conducted with so much discretion and vigor, that the religion of the emperor was established, without tumult or bloodshed, in all the provinces of the East. The writings of the Arians, if they had been permitted to exist, [40] would perhaps contain the lamentable story of the persecution, which afflicted the church under the reign of the impious Theodosius; and the sufferings of their holy confessors might claim the pity of the disinterested reader. Yet there is reason to imagine, that the violence of zeal and revenge was, in some measure, eluded by the want of resistance; and that, in their adversity, the Arians displayed much less firmness than had been exerted by the orthodox party under the reigns of Constantius and Valens. The moral character and conduct of the hostile sects appear to have been governed by the same common principles of nature and religion: but a very material circumstance may be discovered, which tended to distinguish the degrees of their theological faith. Both parties, in the schools, as well as in the temples, acknowledged and worshipped the divine majesty of Christ; and, as we are always prone to impute our own sentiments and passions to the Deity, it would be deemed more prudent and respectful to exaggerate, than to circumscribe, the adorable perfections of the Son of God. The disciple of Athanasius exulted in the proud confidence, that he had entitled himself to the divine favor; while the follower of Arius must have been tormented by the secret apprehension, that he was guilty, perhaps, of an unpardonable offence, by the scanty praise, and parsimonious honors, which he bestowed on the Judge of the World. The opinions of Arianism might satisfy a cold and speculative mind: but the doctrine of the Nicene creed, most powerfully recommended by the merits of faith and devotion, was much better adapted to become popular and successful in a believing age.

[Footnote 37: Socrates (l. v. c. 7) and Sozomen (l. vii. c. 5) relate the evangelical words and actions of Damophilus without a word of approbation. He considered, says Socrates, that it is difficult to resist the powerful, but it was easy, and would have been profitable, to submit.]

[Footnote 38: See Gregory Nazianzen, tom. ii. de Vita sua, p. 21, 22. For the sake of posterity, the bishop of Constantinople records a stupendous prodigy. In the month of November, it was a cloudy morning, but the sun broke forth when the procession entered the church.]

[Footnote 39: Of the three ecclesiastical historians, Theodoret alone (l. v. c. 2) has mentioned this important commission of Sapor, which Tillemont (Hist. des Empereurs, tom. v. p. 728) judiciously removes from the reign of Gratian to that of Theodosius.]

[Footnote 40: I do not reckon Philostorgius, though he mentions (l. ix. c. 19) the explosion of Damophilus. The Eunomian historian has been carefully strained through an orthodox sieve.]

The hope, that truth and wisdom would be found in the assemblies of the orthodox clergy, induced the emperor to convene, at Constantinople, a synod of one hundred and fifty bishops, who proceeded, without much difficulty or delay, to complete the theological system which had been established in the council of Nice. The vehement disputes of the fourth century had been chiefly employed on the nature of the Son of God; and the various opinions which were embraced, concerning the Second, were extended and transferred, by a natural analogy, to the Third person of the Trinity. [41] Yet it was found, or it was thought, necessary, by the victorious adversaries of Arianism, to explain the ambiguous language of some respectable doctors; to confirm the faith of the Catholics; and to condemn an unpopular and inconsistent sect of Macedonians; who freely admitted that the Son was consubstantial to the Father, while they were fearful of seeming to acknowledge the existence of Three Gods. A final and unanimous sentence was pronounced to ratify the equal Deity of the Holy Ghost: the mysterious doctrine has been received by all the nations, and all the churches of the Christian world; and their grateful reverence has assigned to the bishops of Theodosius the second rank among the general councils. [42] Their knowledge of religious truth may have been preserved by tradition, or it may have been communicated by inspiration; but the sober evidence of history will not allow much weight to the personal authority of the Fathers of Constantinople. In an age when the ecclesiastics had scandalously degenerated from the model of apostolic purity, the most worthless and corrupt were always the most eager to frequent, and disturb, the episcopal assemblies. The conflict and fermentation of so many opposite interests and tempers inflamed the passions of the bishops: and their ruling passions were, the love of gold, and the love of dispute. Many of the same prelates who now applauded the orthodox piety of Theodosius, had repeatedly changed, with prudent flexibility, their creeds and opinions; and in the various revolutions of the church and state, the religion of their sovereign was the rule of their obsequious faith. When the emperor suspended his prevailing influence, the turbulent synod was blindly impelled by the absurd or selfish motives of pride, hatred, or resentment. The death of Meletius, which happened at the council of Constantinople, presented the most favorable opportunity of terminating the schism of Antioch, by suffering his aged rival, Paulinus, peaceably to end his days in the episcopal chair. The faith and virtues of Paulinus were unblemished. But his cause was supported by the Western churches; and the bishops of the synod resolved to perpetuate the mischiefs of discord, by the hasty ordination of a perjured candidate, [43] rather than to betray the imagined dignity of the East, which had been illustrated by the birth and death of the Son of God. Such unjust and disorderly proceedings forced the gravest members of the assembly to dissent and to secede; and the clamorous majority which remained masters of the field of battle, could be compared only to wasps or magpies, to a flight of cranes, or to a flock of geese. [44]

[Footnote 41: Le Clerc has given a curious extract (Bibliotheque Universelle, tom. xviii. p. 91-105) of the theological sermons which Gregory Nazianzen pronounced at Constantinople against the Arians, Eunomians, Macedonians, &c. He tells the Macedonians, who deified the Father and the Son without the

Holy Ghost, that they might as well be styled Tritheists as Ditheists. Gregory himself was almost a Tritheist; and his monarchy of heaven resembles a well-regulated aristocracy.]

[Footnote 42: The first general council of Constantinople now triumphs in the Vatican; but the popes had long hesitated, and their hesitation perplexes, and almost staggers, the humble Tillemont, (Mem. Eccles. tom. ix. p. 499, 500.)]

[Footnote 43: Before the death of Meletius, six or eight of his most popular ecclesiastics, among whom was Flavian, had abjured, for the sake of peace, the bishopric of Antioch, (Sozomen, l. vii. c. 3, 11. Socrates, l. v. c. v.) Tillemont thinks it his duty to disbelieve the story; but he owns that there are many circumstances in the life of Flavian which seem inconsistent with the praises of Chrysostom, and the character of a saint, (Mem. Eccles. tom. x. p. 541.)]

[Footnote 44: Consult Gregory Nazianzen, de Vita sua, tom. ii. p. 25-28. His general and particular opinion of the clergy and their assemblies may be seen in verse and prose, (tom. i. Orat. i. p. 33. Epist. lv. p. 814, tom. ii. Carmen x. p. 81.) Such passages are faintly marked by Tillemont, and fairly produced by Le Clerc.]

A suspicion may possibly arise, that so unfavorable a picture of ecclesiastical synods has been drawn by the partial hand of some obstinate heretic, or some malicious infidel. But the name of the sincere historian who has conveyed this instructive lesson to the knowledge of posterity, must silence the impotent murmurs of superstition and bigotry. He was one of the most pious and eloquent bishops of the age; a saint, and a doctor of the church; the scourge of Arianism, and the pillar of the orthodox faith; a distinguished member of the council of Constantinople, in which, after the death of Meletius, he exercised the functions of president; in a word—Gregory Nazianzen himself. The harsh and ungenerous treatment which he experienced, [45] instead of derogating from the truth of his evidence, affords an additional proof of the spirit which actuated the deliberations of the synod. Their unanimous suffrage had confirmed the pretensions which the bishop of Constantinople derived from the choice of the people, and the approbation of the emperor. But Gregory soon became the victim of malice and envy. The bishops of the East, his strenuous adherents, provoked by his moderation in the affairs of Antioch, abandoned him, without support, to the adverse faction of the Egyptians; who disputed the validity of his election, and rigorously asserted the obsolete canon, that prohibited the licentious practice of episcopal translations. The pride, or the humility, of Gregory prompted him to decline a contest which might have been imputed to ambition and avarice; and he publicly offered, not without some mixture of indignation, to renounce the government of a church which had been restored, and almost created, by his labors. His resignation was accepted by the synod, and by the emperor, with more readiness than he seems to have expected. At the time when he might have hoped to enjoy the fruits of his victory, his episcopal throne was filled by the senator Nectarius; and the new archbishop, accidentally recommended by his easy temper and venerable aspect, was obliged to delay the ceremony of his consecration, till he had previously despatched the rites of his baptism. [46] After this remarkable experience of the ingratitude of princes and prelates, Gregory retired once more to his obscure solitude of Cappadocia; where he employed the remainder of his life, about eight years, in the exercises of poetry and devotion. The title of Saint has been added to his name: but the tenderness of his heart, [47] and the elegance of his genius, reflect a more pleasing lustre on the memory of Gregory Nazianzen.

[Footnote 45: See Gregory, tom. ii. de Vita sua, p. 28-31. The fourteenth, twenty-seventh, and thirty-second Orations were pronounced in the several stages of this business. The peroration of the last, (tom.

i. p. 528,) in which he takes a solemn leave of men and angels, the city and the emperor, the East and the West, &c., is pathetic, and almost sublime.]

[Footnote 46: The whimsical ordination of Nectarius is attested by Sozomen, (l. vii. c. 8;) but Tillemont observes, (Mem. Eccles. tom. ix. p. 719,) Apres tout, ce narre de Sozomene est si honteux, pour tous ceux qu'il y mele, et surtout pour Theodose, qu'il vaut mieux travailler a le detruire, qu'a le soutenir; an admirable canon of criticism!]

[Footnote 47: I can only be understood to mean, that such was his natural temper when it was not hardened, or inflamed, by religious zeal. From his retirement, he exhorts Nectarius to prosecute the heretics of Constantinople.]

It was not enough that Theodosius had suppressed the insolent reign of Arianism, or that he had abundantly revenged the injuries which the Catholics sustained from the zeal of Constantius and Valens. The orthodox emperor considered every heretic as a rebel against the supreme powers of heaven and of earth; and each of those powers might exercise their peculiar jurisdiction over the soul and body of the guilty. The decrees of the council of Constantinople had ascertained the true standard of the faith; and the ecclesiastics, who governed the conscience of Theodosius, suggested the most effectual methods of persecution. In the space of fifteen years, he promulgated at least fifteen severe edicts against the heretics; [48] more especially against those who rejected the doctrine of the Trinity; and to deprive them of every hope of escape, he sternly enacted, that if any laws or rescripts should be alleged in their favor, the judges should consider them as the illegal productions either of fraud or forgery. The penal statutes were directed against the ministers, the assemblies, and the persons of the heretics; and the passions of the legislator were expressed in the language of declamation and invective. I. The heretical teachers, who usurped the sacred titles of Bishops, or Presbyters, were not only excluded from the privileges and emoluments so liberally granted to the orthodox clergy, but they were exposed to the heavy penalties of exile and confiscation, if they presumed to preach the doctrine, or to practise the rites, of their accursed sects. A fine of ten pounds of gold (above four hundred pounds sterling) was imposed on every person who should dare to confer, or receive, or promote, an heretical ordination: and it was reasonably expected, that if the race of pastors could be extinguished, their helpless flocks would be compelled, by ignorance and hunger, to return within the pale of the Catholic church. II. The rigorous prohibition of conventicles was carefully extended to every possible circumstance, in which the heretics could assemble with the intention of worshipping God and Christ according to the dictates of their conscience. Their religious meetings, whether public or secret, by day or by night, in cities or in the country, were equally proscribed by the edicts of Theodosius; and the building, or ground, which had been used for that illegal purpose, was forfeited to the Imperial domain. III. It was supposed, that the error of the heretics could proceed only from the obstinate temper of their minds; and that such a temper was a fit object of censure and punishment. The anathemas of the church were fortified by a sort of civil excommunication; which separated them from their fellow-citizens, by a peculiar brand of infamy; and this declaration of the supreme magistrate tended to justify, or at least to excuse, the insults of a fanatic populace. The sectaries were gradually disqualified from the possession of honorable or lucrative employments; and Theodosius was satisfied with his own justice, when he decreed, that, as the Eunomians distinguished the nature of the Son from that of the Father, they should be incapable of making their wills or of receiving any advantage from testamentary donations. The guilt of the Manichaean heresy was esteemed of such magnitude, that it could be expiated only by the death of the offender; and the same capital punishment was inflicted on the Audians, or Quartodecimans, [49] who should dare to perpetrate the atrocious crime of celebrating on an improper day the festival of Easter. Every Roman might exercise the right of public accusation; but the office of Inquisitors of the Faith, a name so deservedly abhorred, was first instituted under the reign of Theodosius. Yet we are assured, that the execution of his penal edicts was seldom enforced; and that the pious emperor appeared less desirous to punish, than to reclaim, or terrify, his refractory subjects. [50]

[Footnote 48: See the Theodosian Code, l. xvi. tit. v. leg. 6—23, with Godefroy's commentary on each law, and his general summary, or Paratitlon, tom vi. p. 104-110.]

[Footnote 49: They always kept their Easter, like the Jewish Passover, on the fourteenth day of the first moon after the vernal equinox; and thus pertinaciously opposed the Roman Church and Nicene synod, which had fixed Easter to a Sunday. Bingham's Antiquities, l. xx. c. 5, vol. ii. p. 309, fol. edit.]

[Footnote 50: Sozomen, l. vii. c. 12.]

The theory of persecution was established by Theodosius, whose justice and piety have been applauded by the saints: but the practice of it, in the fullest extent, was reserved for his rival and colleague, Maximus, the first, among the Christian princes, who shed the blood of his Christian subjects on account of their religious opinions. The cause of the Priscillianists, [51] a recent sect of heretics, who disturbed the provinces of Spain, was transferred, by appeal, from the synod of Bordeaux to the Imperial consistory of Treves; and by the sentence of the Praetorian praefect, seven persons were tortured, condemned, and executed. The first of these was Priscillian [52] himself, bishop of Avila, in Spain; who adorned the advantages of birth and fortune, by the accomplishments of eloquence and learning. Two presbyters, and two deacons, accompanied their beloved master in his death, which they esteemed as a glorious martyrdom; and the number of religious victims was completed by the execution of Latronian, a poet, who rivalled the fame of the ancients; and of Euchrocia, a noble matron of Bordeaux, the widow of the orator Delphidius. [54] Two bishops who had embraced the sentiments of Priscillian, were condemned to a distant and dreary exile; [55] and some indulgence was shown to the meaner criminals, who assumed the merit of an early repentance. If any credit could be allowed to confessions extorted by fear or pain, and to vague reports, the offspring of malice and credulity, the heresy of the Priscillianists would be found to include the various abominations of magic, of impiety, and of lewdness. [56] Priscillian, who wandered about the world in the company of his spiritual sisters, was accused of praying stark naked in the midst of the congregation; and it was confidently asserted, that the effects of his criminal intercourse with the daughter of Euchrocia had been suppressed, by means still more odious and criminal. But an accurate, or rather a candid, inquiry will discover, that if the Priscillianists violated the laws of nature, it was not by the licentiousness, but by the austerity, of their lives. They absolutely condemned the use of the marriage-bed; and the peace of families was often disturbed by indiscreet separations. They enjoyed, or recommended, a total abstinence from all anima food; and their continual prayers, fasts, and vigils, inculcated a rule of strict and perfect devotion. The speculative tenets of the sect, concerning the person of Christ, and the nature of the human soul, were derived from the Gnostic and Manichaean system; and this vain philosophy, which had been transported from Egypt to Spain, was ill adapted to the grosser spirits of the West. The obscure disciples of Priscillian suffered languished, and gradually disappeared: his tenets were rejected by the clergy and people, but his death was the subject of a long and vehement controversy; while some arraigned, and others applauded, the justice of his sentence. It is with pleasure that we can observe the humane inconsistency of the most illustrious saints and bishops, Ambrose of Milan, [57] and Martin of Tours, [58] who, on this occasion, asserted the cause of toleration. They pitied the unhappy men, who had been executed at Treves; they refused to hold communion with their episcopal murderers; and if Martin deviated from that generous resolution, his motives were laudable, and his repentance was exemplary. The bishops of Tours and Milan pronounced, without hesitation, the eternal damnation of heretics; but they were surprised, and shocked, by the bloody image of their temporal death, and the honest feelings of nature resisted the artificial prejudices of theology. The humanity of Ambrose and Martin was confirmed by the scandalous irregularity of the proceedings against Priscillian and his adherents. The civil and ecclesiastical ministers had transgressed the limits of their respective provinces. The secular judge had presumed to receive an appeal, and to pronounce a definitive sentence, in a matter of faith, and episcopal jurisdiction. The bishops had disgraced themselves, by exercising the functions of accusers in a criminal prosecution. The cruelty of Ithacius, [59] who beheld the tortures, and solicited the death, of the heretics, provoked the just indignation of mankind; and the vices of that profligate bishop were admitted as a proof, that his zeal was instigated by the sordid motives of interest. Since the death of Priscillian, the rude attempts of persecution have been refined and methodized in the holy office, which assigns their distinct parts to the ecclesiastical and secular powers. The devoted victim is regularly delivered by the priest to the magistrate, and by the magistrate to the executioner; and the inexorable sentence of the church, which declares the spiritual guilt of the offender, is expressed in the mild language of pity and intercession.

[Footnote 51: See the Sacred History of Sulpicius Severus, (l. ii. p. 437-452, edit. Ludg. Bat. 1647,) a correct and original writer. Dr. Lardner (Credibility, &c., part ii. vol. ix. p. 256-350) has labored this article with pure learning, good sense, and moderation. Tillemont (Mem. Eccles. tom. viii. p. 491-527) has raked together all the dirt of the fathers; a useful scavenger!]

[Footnote 52: Severus Sulpicius mentions the arch-heretic with esteem and pity Faelix profecto, si non pravo studio corrupisset optimum ingenium prorsus multa in eo animi et corporis bona cerneres. (Hist. Sacra, l ii. p. 439.) Even Jerom (tom. i. in Script. Eccles. p. 302) speaks with temper of Priscillian and Latronian.]

[Footnote 53: The bishopric (in Old Castile) is now worth 20,000 ducats a year, (Busching's Geography, vol. ii. p. 308,) and is therefore much less likely to produce the author of a new heresy.]

[Footnote 54: Exprobrabatur mulieri viduae nimia religio, et diligentius culta divinitas, (Pacat. in Panegyr. Vet. xii. 29.) Such was the idea of a humane, though ignorant, polytheist.]

[Footnote 55: One of them was sent in Sillinam insulam quae ultra Britannianest. What must have been the ancient condition of the rocks of Scilly? (Camden's Britannia, vol. ii. p. 1519.)]

[Footnote 56: The scandalous calumnies of Augustin, Pope Leo, &c., which Tillemont swallows like a child, and Lardner refutes like a man, may suggest some candid suspicions in favor of the older Gnostics.]

[Footnote 57: Ambros. tom. ii. Epist. xxiv. p. 891.]

[Footnote 58: In the Sacred History, and the Life of St. Martin, Sulpicius Severus uses some caution; but he declares himself more freely in the Dialogues, (iii. 15.) Martin was reproved, however, by his own conscience, and by an angel; nor could he afterwards perform miracles with so much ease.]

[Footnote 59: The Catholic Presbyter (Sulp. Sever. l. ii. p. 448) and the Pagan Orator (Pacat. in Panegyr. Vet. xii. 29) reprobate, with equal indignation, the character and conduct of Ithacius.]

Among the ecclesiastics, who illustrated the reign of Theodosius, Gregory Nazianzen was distinguished by the talents of an eloquent preacher; the reputation of miraculous gifts added weight and dignity to the monastic virtues of Martin of Tours; [60] but the palm of episcopal vigor and ability was justly claimed by the intrepid Ambrose. [61] He was descended from a noble family of Romans; his father had exercised the important office of Praetorian praefect of Gaul; and the son, after passing through the studies of a liberal education, attained, in the regular gradation of civil honors, the station of consular of Liguria, a province which included the Imperial residence of Milan. At the age of thirty-four, and before he had received the sacrament of baptism, Ambrose, to his own surprise, and to that of the world, was suddenly transformed from a governor to an archbishop. Without the least mixture, as it is said, of art or intrigue, the whole body of the people unanimously saluted him with the episcopal title; the concord and perseverance of their acclamations were ascribed to a praeternatural impulse; and the reluctant magistrate was compelled to undertake a spiritual office, for which he was not prepared by the habits and occupations of his former life. But the active force of his genius soon qualified him to exercise, with zeal and prudence, the duties of his ecclesiastical jurisdiction; and while he cheerfully renounced the vain and splendid trappings of temporal greatness, he condescended, for the good of the church, to direct the conscience of the emperors, and to control the administration of the empire. Gratian loved and revered him as a father; and the elaborate treatise on the faith of the Trinity was designed for the instruction of the young prince. After his tragic death, at a time when the empress Justina trembled for her own safety, and for that of her son Valentinian, the archbishop of Milan was despatched, on two different embassies, to the court of Treves. He exercised, with equal firmness and dexterity, the powers of his spiritual and political characters; and perhaps contributed, by his authority and eloquence, to check the ambition of Maximus, and to protect the peace of Italy. [62] Ambrose had devoted his life, and his abilities, to the service of the church. Wealth was the object of his contempt; he had renounced his private patrimony; and he sold, without hesitation, the consecrated plate, for the redemption of captives. The clergy and people of Milan were attached to their archbishop; and he deserved the esteem, without soliciting the favor, or apprehending the displeasure, of his feeble sovereigns.

[Footnote 60: *The Life of St. Martin, and the Dialogues concerning his miracles contain facts adapted to the grossest barbarism, in a style not unworthy of the Augustan age. So natural is the alliance between good taste and good sense, that I am always astonished by this contrast.*]

[Footnote 61: *The short and superficial Life of St. Ambrose, by his deacon Paulinus, (Appendix ad edit. Benedict. p. i—xv.,) has the merit of original evidence. Tillemont (Mem. Eccles. tom. x. p. 78-306) and the Benedictine editors (p. xxxi—lxiii.) have labored with their usual diligence.*]

[Footnote 62: *Ambrose himself (tom. ii. Epist. xxiv. p. 888—891) gives the emperor a very spirited account of his own embassy.*]

The government of Italy, and of the young emperor, naturally devolved to his mother Justina, a woman of beauty and spirit, but who, in the midst of an orthodox people, had the misfortune of professing the Arian heresy, which she endeavored to instil into the mind of her son. Justina was persuaded, that a Roman emperor might claim, in his own dominions, the public exercise of his religion; and she proposed to the archbishop, as a moderate and reasonable concession, that he should resign the use of a single church, either in the city or the suburbs of Milan. But the conduct of Ambrose was governed by very different principles. [63] The palaces of the earth might indeed belong to Caesar; but the churches were the houses of God; and, within the limits of his diocese, he himself, as the lawful successor of the apostles, was the only minister of God. The privileges of Christianity, temporal as well as spiritual, were confined to the true believers; and the mind of Ambrose was satisfied, that his own theological opinions were the standard of truth and orthodoxy. The archbishop, who refused to hold any conference, or negotiation, with the instruments of Satan, declared, with modest firmness, his resolution to die a martyr, rather than to yield to the impious sacrilege; and Justina, who resented the refusal as an act of insolence and rebellion, hastily determined to exert the Imperial prerogative of her son. As she desired to perform her public devotions on the approaching festival of Easter, Ambrose was ordered to appear before the council. He obeyed the summons with the respect of a faithful subject, but he was followed, without his consent, by an innumerable people they pressed, with impetuous zeal, against the gates of the palace; and the affrighted ministers of Valentinian, instead of pronouncing a sentence of exile on the archbishop of Milan, humbly requested that he would interpose his authority, to protect the person of the emperor, and to restore the tranquility of the capital. But the promises which Ambrose received and communicated were soon violated by a perfidious court; and, during six of the most solemn days, which Christian piety had set apart for the exercise of religion, the city was agitated by the irregular convulsions of tumult and fanaticism. The officers of the household were directed to prepare, first, the Portian, and afterwards, the new, Basilica, for the immediate reception of the emperor and his mother. The splendid canopy and hangings of the royal seat were arranged in the customary manner; but it was found necessary to defend them. by a strong guard, from the insults of the populace. The Arian ecclesiastics, who ventured to show themselves in the streets, were exposed to the most imminent danger of their lives; and Ambrose enjoyed the merit and reputation of rescuing his personal enemies from the hands of the enraged multitude.

[Footnote 63: *His own representation of his principles and conduct (tom. ii. Epist. xx xxi. xxii. p. 852-880) is one of the curious monuments of ecclesiastical antiquity. It contains two letters to his sister Marcellina, with a petition to Valentinian and the sermon de Basilicis non madendis.*]

But while he labored to restrain the effects of their zeal, the pathetic vehemence of his sermons continually inflamed the angry and seditious temper of the people of Milan. The characters of Eve, of the wife of Job, of Jezebel, of Herodias, were indecently applied to the mother of the emperor; and her desire to obtain a church for the Arians was compared to the most cruel persecutions which Christianity had endured under the reign of Paganism. The measures of the court served only to expose the magnitude of the evil. A fine of two hundred pounds of gold was imposed on the corporate body of merchants and manufacturers: an order was signified, in the name of the emperor, to all the officers, and inferior servants, of the courts of justice, that, during the continuance of the public disorders, they should strictly confine themselves to their houses; and the ministers of Valentinian imprudently confessed, that the most respectable part of the citizens of Milan was attached to the cause of their archbishop. He was again solicited to restore peace to his country, by timely compliance with the will of his sovereign. The reply of Ambrose was couched in the most humble and respectful terms, which might, however, be interpreted as a serious declaration of civil war. "His life and fortune were in the hands of the emperor; but he would never betray the church of Christ, or degrade the dignity of the episcopal character. In such a cause he was prepared to suffer whatever the malice of the daemon could inflict; and he only wished to die in the presence of his faithful flock, and at the foot of the altar; he had not contributed to excite, but it was in the power of God alone to appease, the rage of the people: he deprecated the scenes of blood and confusion which were likely to ensue; and it was his fervent prayer, that he might not survive to behold the ruin of a flourishing city, and perhaps the desolation of all Italy." [64] The obstinate bigotry of Justina would have endangered the empire of her son, if, in this contest with the church and people of Milan, she could have depended on the active obedience of the troops of the palace. A large body of Goths had marched to occupy the Basilica, which was the object of the dispute: and it might be expected from the Arian principles, and barbarous manners, of these foreign mercenaries, that they would not entertain any scruples in the execution of the most sanguinary orders. They were encountered, on the sacred threshold, by the archbishop, who, thundering against them a sentence of excommunication, asked them, in the tone of a father and a master, whether it was to invade the house of God, that they had implored the hospitable protection of the republic. The suspense of the Barbarians allowed some hours for a more effectual negotiation; and the empress was persuaded, by the advice of her wisest counsellors, to leave the Catholics in possession of all the churches of Milan; and to dissemble, till a more convenient season, her intentions of revenge. The mother of Valentinian could never forgive the triumph of Ambrose; and the royal youth uttered a passionate exclamation, that his own servants were ready to betray him into the hands of an insolent priest.

[Footnote 64: *Retz had a similar message from the queen, to request that he would appease the tumult of Paris. It was no longer in his power, &c. A quoi j'ajoutai tout ce que vous pouvez vous imaginer de respect de douleur, de regret, et de soumission, &c. (Memoires, tom. i. p. 140.) Certainly I do not compare either the causes or the men yet the coadjutor himself had some idea (p. 84) of imitating St. Ambrose*]

The laws of the empire, some of which were inscribed with the name of Valentinian, still condemned the Arian heresy, and seemed to excuse the resistance of the Catholics. By the influence of Justina, an edict of toleration was promulgated in all the provinces which were subject to the court of Milan; the free exercise of their religion was granted to those who professed the faith of Rimini; and the emperor declared, that all persons who should infringe this sacred and salutary constitution, should be capitally punished, as the enemies of the public peace. [65] The character and language of the archbishop of Milan may justify the suspicion, that his conduct soon afforded a reasonable ground, or at least a specious pretence, to the Arian ministers; who watched the opportunity of surprising him in some act of disobedience to a law which he strangely represents as a law of blood and tyranny. A sentence of easy and honorable banishment was pronounced, which enjoined Ambrose to depart from Milan without delay; whilst it permitted him to choose the place of his exile, and the number of his companions. But the authority of the saints, who have preached and practised the maxims of passive loyalty, appeared to Ambrose of less moment than the extreme and pressing danger of the church. He boldly refused to obey; and his refusal was supported by the unanimous consent of his faithful people. [66] They guarded by turns the person of their archbishop; the gates of the cathedral and the episcopal palace were strongly secured; and the Imperial troops, who had formed the blockade, were unwilling to risk the attack, of that impregnable fortress. The numerous poor, who had been relieved by the liberality of Ambrose, embraced the fair occasion of signalizing their zeal and gratitude; and as the patience of the multitude might have been exhausted by the length and uniformity of nocturnal vigils, he prudently introduced into the church of Milan the useful institution of a loud and regular psalmody. While he maintained this arduous contest, he was instructed, by a dream, to open the earth in a place where the remains of two martyrs, Gervasius and Protasius, [67] had been deposited above three hundred years. Immediately under the pavement of the church two perfect skeletons were found, [68] with the heads separated from their bodies, and a plentiful effusion of blood. The holy relics were presented, in solemn pomp, to the veneration of the people; and every circumstance of this fortunate discovery was admirably adapted to promote the designs of Ambrose. The bones of the martyrs, their blood, their garments, were supposed to contain a healing power; and the praeternatural influence was communicated to the most distant objects, without losing any part of its original virtue. The extraordinary cure of a blind man, [69] and the reluctant confessions of several daemoniacs, appeared to justify the faith and sanctity of Ambrose; and the truth of those miracles is attested by Ambrose himself, by his secretary Paulinus, and by his proselyte, the celebrated Augustin, who, at that time, professed the art of rhetoric in Milan. The reason of the present age may possibly approve the incredulity of Justina and her Arian court; who derided the theatrical representations which were exhibited by the contrivance, and at the expense, of the archbishop. [70] Their effect, however, on the minds of the people, was rapid and irresistible; and the feeble sovereign of Italy found himself unable to contend with the favorite of Heaven. The powers likewise of the earth interposed in the defence of Ambrose: the disinterested advice of Theodosius was the genuine result of piety and friendship; and the mask of religious zeal concealed the hostile and ambitious designs of the tyrant of Gaul. [71]

[Footnote 65: Sozomen alone (l. vii. c. 13) throws this luminous fact into a dark and perplexed narrative.]

[Footnote 66: Excubabat pia plebs in ecclesia, mori parata cum episcopo suo.... Nos, adhuc frigidi, excitabamur tamen civitate attonita atque curbata. Augustin. Confession. l. ix. c. 7]

[Footnote 67: Tillemont, Mem. Eccles. tom. ii. p. 78, 498. Many churches in Italy, Gaul, &c., were dedicated to these unknown martyrs, of whom St. Gervaise seems to have been more fortunate than his companion.]

[Footnote 68: Invenimus mirae magnitudinis viros duos, ut prisca aetas ferebat, tom. ii. Epist. xxii. p. 875. The size of these skeletons was fortunately, or skillfully, suited to the popular prejudice of the gradual decrease of the human stature, which has prevailed in every age since the time of Homer—Grandiaque effossis mirabitur ossa sepulchris.]

[Footnote 69: Ambros. tom. ii. Epist. xxii. p. 875. Augustin. Confes, l. ix. c. 7, de Civitat. Dei, l. xxii. c. 8. Paulin. in Vita St. Ambros. c. 14, in Append. Benedict. p. 4. The blind man's name was Severus; he touched the holy garment, recovered his sight, and devoted the rest of his life (at least twenty-five years) to the service of the church. I should recommend this miracle to our divines, if it did not prove the worship of relics, as well as the Nicene creed.]

[Footnote 70: Paulin, in Tit. St. Ambros. c. 5, in Append. Benedict. p. 5.]

[Footnote 71: Tillemont, Mem. Eccles. tom. x. p. 190, 750. He partially allow the mediation of Theodosius, and capriciously rejects that of Maximus, though it is attested by Prosper, Sozomen, and Theodoret.]

The reign of Maximus might have ended in peace and prosperity, could he have contented himself with the possession of three ample countries, which now constitute the three most flourishing kingdoms of modern Europe. But the aspiring usurper, whose sordid ambition was not dignified by the love of glory and of arms, considered his actual forces as the instruments only of his future greatness, and his success was the immediate cause of his destruction. The wealth which he extorted [72] from the oppressed provinces of Gaul, Spain, and Britain, was employed in levying and maintaining a formidable army of Barbarians, collected, for the most part, from the fiercest nations of Germany. The conquest of Italy was the object of his hopes and preparations: and he secretly meditated the ruin of an innocent youth, whose government was abhorred and despised by his Catholic subjects. But as Maximus wished to occupy, without resistance, the passes of the Alps, he received, with perfidious smiles, Domninus of Syria, the ambassador of Valentinian, and pressed him to accept the aid of a considerable body of troops, for the service of a Pannonian war. The penetration of Ambrose had discovered the snares of an enemy under the professions of friendship; [73] but the Syrian Domninus was corrupted, or deceived, by the liberal favor of the court of Treves; and the council of Milan obstinately rejected the suspicion of danger, with a blind confidence, which was the effect, not of courage, but of fear. The march of the auxiliaries was guided by the ambassador; and they were admitted, without distrust, into the fortresses of the Alps. But the crafty tyrant followed, with hasty and silent footsteps, in the rear; and, as he diligently intercepted all intelligence of his motions, the gleam of armor, and the dust excited by the troops of cavalry, first announced the hostile approach of a stranger to the gates of Milan. In this extremity, Justina and her son might accuse their own imprudence, and the perfidious arts of Maximus; but they wanted time, and force, and resolution, to stand against the Gauls and Germans, either in the field, or within the walls of a large and disaffected city. Flight was their only hope, Aquileia their only refuge; and as Maximus now displayed his genuine character, the brother of Gratian might expect the same fate from the hands of the same assassin. Maximus entered Milan in triumph; and if the wise archbishop refused a dangerous and criminal connection with the usurper, he might indirectly contribute to the success of his arms, by inculcating, from the pulpit, the duty of resignation, rather than that of resistance. [74] The unfortunate Justina reached Aquileia in safety; but she distrusted the strength of the fortifications: she dreaded the event of a siege; and she resolved to implore the protection of the great Theodosius, whose power and virtue were celebrated in all the countries of the West. A vessel was secretly provided to transport the Imperial family; they embarked with precipitation in one of the obscure harbors of Venetia, or Istria; traversed the whole extent of the Adriatic and Ionian Seas; turned the extreme promontory of Peloponnesus; and, after a long, but successful navigation, reposed themselves in the port of Thessalonica. All the subjects of Valentinian deserted the cause of a prince, who, by his abdication, had absolved them from the duty of allegiance; and if the little city of Aemona, on the verge of Italy, had not presumed to stop the career of his inglorious victory, Maximus would have obtained, without a struggle, the sole possession of the Western empire.

[Footnote 72: The modest censure of Sulpicius (Dialog. iii. 15) inflicts a much deeper wound than the declamation of Pacatus, (xii. 25, 26.)]

[Footnote 73: Esto tutior adversus hominem, pacis involurco tegentem, was the wise caution of Ambrose (tom. ii. p. 891) after his return from his second embassy.]

[Footnote 74: Baronius (A.D. 387, No. 63) applies to this season of public distress some of the penitential sermons of the archbishop.]

Instead of inviting his royal guests to take the palace of Constantinople, Theodosius had some unknown reasons to fix their residence at Thessalonica; but these reasons did not proceed from contempt or indifference, as he speedily made a visit to that city, accompanied by the greatest part of his court and senate. After the first tender expressions of friendship and sympathy, the pious emperor of the East gently admonished Justina, that the guilt of heresy was sometimes punished in this world, as well as in the next; and that the public profession of the Nicene faith would be the most efficacious step to promote the restoration of her son, by the satisfaction which it must occasion both on earth and in heaven. The momentous question of peace or war was referred, by Theodosius, to the deliberation of his council; and the arguments which might be alleged on the side of honor and justice, had acquired, since the death of Gratian, a considerable degree of additional weight. The persecution of the Imperial family, to which Theodosius himself had been indebted for his fortune, was now aggravated by recent and repeated injuries. Neither oaths nor treaties could restrain the boundless ambition of Maximus; and the delay of vigorous and decisive measures, instead of prolonging the blessings of peace, would expose the Eastern empire to the danger of a hostile invasion. The Barbarians, who had passed the Danube, had lately assumed the character of soldiers and subjects, but their native fierceness was yet untamed: and the operations of a war, which would exercise their valor, and diminish their numbers, might tend to relieve the provinces from an intolerable oppression. Notwithstanding these specious and solid reasons, which were approved by a majority of the council, Theodosius still hesitated whether he should draw the sword in a contest which could no longer admit any terms of reconciliation; and his magnanimous character was not disgraced by the apprehensions which he felt for the safety of his infant sons, and the welfare of his exhausted people. In this moment of anxious doubt, while the fate of the Roman world depended on the resolution of a single man, the charms of the princess Galla most powerfully pleaded the cause of her brother Valentinian. [75] The heart of Theodosius wa softened by the tears of beauty; his affections were insensibly engaged by the graces of youth and innocence: the art of Justina managed and directed the impulse of passion; and the celebration of the royal nuptials was the assurance and signal of the civil war. The unfeeling critics, who consider every amorous weakness as an indelible stain on the memory of a great and orthodox emperor, are inclined, on this occasion, to dispute the suspicious evidence of the historian Zosimus. For my own part, I shall frankly confess, that I am willing to find, or even to seek, in the revolutions of the world, some traces of the mild and tender sentiments of domestic life; and amidst the crowd of fierce and ambitious conquerors, I can distinguish, with peculiar complacency, a gentle hero, who may be supposed to receive his armor from the hands of love. The alliance of the Persian king was secured by the faith of treaties; the martial Barbarians were persuaded to follow the standard, or to respect the frontiers, of an active and liberal monarch; and the dominions of Theodosius, from the Euphrates to the Adriatic, resounded with the preparations of war both by land and sea. The skilful disposition of the forces of the East seemed to multiply their numbers, and distracted the attention of Maximus. He had reason to fear, that a chosen body of troops, under the command of the intrepid Arbogastes, would direct their march along the banks of the Danube, and boldly penetrate through the Rhaetian provinces into the centre of Gaul. A powerful fleet was equipped in the harbors of Greece and Epirus, with an apparent design, that, as soon as the passage had been opened by a naval victory, Valentinian and his mother should land in Italy, proceed, without delay, to Rome, and occupy the majestic seat of religion and empire. In the mean while, Theodosius himself advanced at the head of a brave and disciplined army, to encounter his unworthy rival, who, after the siege of Aemona, [7511] had fixed his camp in the neighborhood of Siscia, a city of Pannonia, strongly fortified by the broad and rapid stream of the Save.

[Footnote 75: The flight of Valentinian, and the love of Theodosius for his sister, are related by Zosimus, (l. iv. p. 263, 264.) Tillemont produces some weak and ambiguous evidence to antedate the second marriage of Theodosius, (Hist. des Empereurs, to. v. p. 740,) and consequently to refute ces contes de Zosime, qui seroient trop contraires a la piete de Theodose.]

[Footnote 7511: Aemonah, Laybach. Siscia Sciszek—M.]

PART IV

The veterans, who still remembered the long resistance, and successive resources, of the tyrant Magnentius, might prepare themselves for the labors of three bloody campaigns. But the contest with his successor, who, like him, had usurped the throne of the West, was easily decided in the term of two months, [76] and within the space of two hundred miles. The superior genius of the emperor of the East might prevail over the feeble Maximus, who, in this important crisis, showed himself destitute of military skill, or personal courage; but the abilities of Theodosius were seconded by the advantage which he possessed of a numerous and active cavalry. The Huns, the Alani, and, after their example, the Goths themselves, were formed into squadrons of archers; who fought on horseback, and confounded the steady valor of the Gauls and Germans, by the rapid motions of a Tartar war. After the fatigue of a long march, in the heat of summer, they spurred their foaming horses into the waters of the Save, swam the river in the presence of the enemy, and instantly charged and routed the troops who guarded the high ground on the opposite side. Marcellinus, the tyrant's brother, advanced to support them with the select cohorts, which were considered as the hope and strength of the army. The action, which had been interrupted by the approach of night, was renewed in the morning; and, after a sharp conflict, the surviving remnant of the bravest soldiers of Maximus threw down their arms at the feet of the conqueror. Without suspending his march, to receive the loyal acclamations of the citizens of Aemona, Theodosius pressed forwards to terminate the war by the death or captivity of his rival, who fled before him with the diligence of fear. From the summit of the Julian Alps, he descended with such incredible speed into the plain of Italy, that he reached Aquileia on the evening of the first day; and Maximus, who found himself encompassed on all sides, had scarcely time to shut the gates of the city. But the gates could not long resist the effort of a victorious enemy; and the despair, the disaffection, the indifference of the soldiers and people, hastened the downfall of the wretched Maximus. He was dragged from his throne, rudely stripped of the Imperial ornaments, the robe, the diadem, and the purple slippers; and conducted, like a malefactor, to the camp and presence of Theodosius, at a place about three miles from Aquileia. The behavior of the emperor was not intended to insult, and he showed disposition to pity and forgive, the tyrant of the West, who had never been his personal enemy, and was now become the object of his contempt. Our sympathy is the most forcibly excited by the misfortunes to which we are exposed; and the spectacle of a proud competitor, now prostrate at his feet, could not fail of producing very serious and solemn thoughts in the mind of the victorious emperor. But the feeble emotion of involuntary pity was checked by his regard for public justice, and the memory of Gratian; and he abandoned the victim to the pious zeal of the soldiers, who drew him out of the Imperial presence, and instantly separated his head from his body. The intelligence of his defeat and death was received with sincere or well-dissembled joy: his son Victor, on whom he had conferred the title of Augustus, died by the order, perhaps by the hand, of the bold Arbogastes; and all the military plans of Theodosius were successfully executed. When he had thus terminated the civil war, with less difficulty and bloodshed than he might naturally expect, he employed the winter months of his residence at Milan, to restore the state of the afflicted provinces; and early in the spring he made, after the example of Constantine and Constantius, his triumphal entry into the ancient capital of the Roman empire. [77]

[Footnote 76: See Godefroy's Chronology of the Laws, Cod. Theodos, tom l. p. cxix.]

[Footnote 77: Besides the hints which may be gathered from chronicles and ecclesiastical history, Zosimus (l. iv. p. 259—267,) Orosius, (l. vii. c. 35,) and Pacatus, (in Panegyr. Vet. xii. 30-47,) supply the loose and scanty materials of this civil war. Ambrose (tom. ii. Epist. xl. p. 952, 953) darkly alludes to the well-known events of a magazine surprised, an action at Petovio, a Sicilian, perhaps a naval, victory, &c., Ausonius (p. 256, edit. Toll.) applauds the peculiar merit and good fortune of Aquileia.] The orator, who may be silent without danger, may praise without difficulty, and without reluctance; [78] and posterity will confess, that the character of Theodosius [79] might furnish the subject of a sincere and ample panegyric. The wisdom of his laws, and the success of his arms, rendered his administration respectable in the eyes both of his subjects and of his enemies. He loved and practised the virtues of domestic life, which seldom hold their residence in the palaces of kings. Theodosius was chaste and temperate; he enjoyed, without excess, the sensual and social pleasures of the table; and the warmth of his amorous passions was never diverted from their lawful objects. The proud titles of Imperial greatness were adorned by the tender names of a faithful husband, an indulgent father; his uncle was raised, by his affectionate esteem, to the rank of a second parent: Theodosius embraced, as his own, the children of his brother and sister; and the expressions of his regard were extended to the most distant and obscure branches of his numerous kindred. His familiar friends were judiciously selected from among those persons, who, in the equal intercourse of private life, had appeared before his eyes without a mask; the consciousness of personal and superior merit enabled him to despise the accidental distinction of the purple; and he proved by his conduct, that he had forgotten all the injuries, while he most gratefully remembered all the favors and services, which he had received before he ascended the throne of the Roman empire. The serious or lively tone of his conversation was adapted to the age, the rank, or the character of his subjects, whom he admitted into his society; and the affability of his manners displayed the image of his mind. Theodosius respected the simplicity of the good and virtuous: every art, every talent, of a useful, or even of an innocent nature, was rewarded by his judicious liberality; and, except the heretics, whom he persecuted with implacable hatred, the diffusive circle of his benevolence was circumscribed only by the limits of the human race. The government of a mighty empire may assuredly suffice to occupy the time, and the abilities, of a mortal: yet the diligent prince, without aspiring to the unsuitable reputation of profound learning, always reserved some moments of his leisure for the instructive amusement of reading. History, which enlarged his experience, was his favorite study. The annals of Rome, in the long period of eleven hundred years, presented him with a various and splendid picture of human life: and it has been particularly observed, that whenever he perused the cruel acts of Cinna, of Marius, or of Sylla, he warmly expressed his generous detestation of those enemies of humanity and freedom. His disinterested opinion of past events was usefully applied as the rule of his own actions; and Theodosius has deserved the singular commendation, that his virtues always seemed to expand with his fortune: the season of his prosperity was that of his moderation; and his clemency appeared the most conspicuous after the danger and success of a civil war. The Moorish guards of the tyrant had been massacred in the first heat of the victory, and a small number of the most obnoxious criminals suffered the punishment of the law. But the emperor showed himself much more attentive to relieve the innocent than to chastise the guilty. The oppressed subjects of the West, who would have deemed themselves happy in the restoration of their lands, were astonished to receive a sum of money equivalent to their losses; and the liberality of the conqueror supported the aged mother, and educated the orphan daughters, of Maximus. [80] A character thus accomplished might almost excuse the extravagant supposition of the orator Pacatus; that, if the elder Brutus could be permitted to revisit the earth, the stern republican would abjure, at the feet of Theodosius, his hatred of kings; and ingenuously confess, that such a monarch was the most faithful guardian of the happiness and dignity of the Roman people. [81]

[Footnote 78: Quam promptum laudare principem, tam tutum siluisse de principe, (Pacat. in Panegyr. Vet. xii. 2.) Latinus Pacatus Drepanius, a native of Gaul, pronounced this oration at Rome, (A.D. 388.) He was afterwards proconsul of Africa; and his friend Ausonius praises him as a poet second only to Virgil. See Tillemont, Hist. des Empereurs, tom. v. p. 303.]

[Footnote 79: See the fair portrait of Theodosius, by the younger Victor; the strokes are distinct, and the colors are mixed. The praise of Pacatus is too vague; and Claudian always seems afraid of exalting the father above the son.]

[Footnote 80: Ambros. tom. ii. Epist. xl. p. 55. Pacatus, from the want of skill or of courage, omits this glorious circumstance.]

[Footnote 81: Pacat. in Panegyr. Vet. xii. 20.]

Yet the piercing eye of the founder of the republic must have discerned two essential imperfections, which might, perhaps, have abated his recent love of despotism. The virtuous mind of Theodosius was often relaxed by indolence, [82] and it was sometimes inflamed by passion. [83] In the pursuit of an important object, his active courage was capable of the most vigorous exertions; but, as soon as the design was accomplished, or the danger was surmounted, the hero sunk into inglorious repose; and, forgetful that the time of a prince is the property of his people, resigned himself to the enjoyment of the innocent, but trifling, pleasures of a luxurious court. The natural disposition of Theodosius was hasty and choleric; and, in a station where none could resist, and few would dissuade, the fatal consequence of his resentment, the humane monarch was justly alarmed by the consciousness of his infirmity and of his power. It was the constant study of his life to suppress, or regulate, the intemperate sallies of passion and the success of his efforts enhanced the merit of his clemency. But the painful virtue which claims the merit of victory, is exposed to the danger of defeat; and the reign of a wise and merciful prince was polluted by an act of cruelty which would stain the annals of Nero or Domitian. Within the space of three years, the inconsistent historian of Theodosius must relate the generous pardon of the citizens of Antioch, and the inhuman massacre of the people of Thessalonica.

[Footnote 82: Zosimus, l. iv. p. 271, 272. His partial evidence is marked by an air of candor and truth. He observes these vicissitudes of sloth and activity, not as a vice, but as a singularity in the character of Theodosius.]

[Footnote 83: This choleric temper is acknowledged and excused by Victor Sed habes (says Ambrose, in decent and many language, to his sovereign) nature impetum, quem si quis lenire velit, cito vertes ad misericordiam: si quis stimulet, in magis exsuscitas, ut eum revocare vix possis, (tom. ii. Epist. li. p. 998.) Theodosius (Claud. in iv. Hon. 266, &c.) exhorts his son to moderate his anger.]

The lively impatience of the inhabitants of Antioch was never satisfied with their own situation, or with the character and conduct of their successive sovereigns. The Arian subjects of Theodosius deplored the loss of their churches; and as three rival bishops disputed the throne of Antioch, the sentence which decided their pretensions excited the murmurs of the two unsuccessful congregations. The exigencies of the Gothic war, and the inevitable expense that accompanied the conclusion of the peace, had constrained the emperor to aggravate the weight of the public impositions; and the provinces of Asia, as they had not been involved in the distress were the less inclined to contribute to the relief, of Europe. The auspicious period now approached of the tenth year of his reign; a festival more grateful to the soldiers, who received a liberal donative, than to the subjects, whose voluntary offerings had been long since converted into an extraordinary and oppressive burden. The edicts of taxation interrupted the repose, and pleasures, of Antioch; and the tribunal of the magistrate was besieged by a suppliant crowd; who, in pathetic, but, at first, in respectful language, solicited the redress of their grievances. They were gradually incensed by the pride of their haughty rulers, who treated their complaints as a criminal resistance; their satirical wit degenerated into sharp and angry invectives; and, from the subordinate powers of government, the invectives of the people insensibly rose to attack the sacred character of the emperor himself. Their fury, provoked by a feeble opposition, discharged itself on the images of the Imperial family, which were erected, as objects of public veneration, in the most conspicuous places of the city. The statues of Theodosius, of his father, of his wife Flaccilla, of his two sons, Arcadius and Honorius, were insolently thrown down from their pedestals, broken in pieces, or dragged with contempt through the streets; and the indignities which were offered to the representations of Imperial majesty, sufficiently declared the impious and treasonable wishes of the populace. The tumult was almost immediately suppressed by the arrival of a body of archers: and Antioch had leisure to reflect on the nature and consequences of her crime. [84] According to the duty of his office, the governor of the province despatched a faithful narrative of the whole transaction: while the trembling citizens intrusted the confession of their crime, and the assurances of their repentance, to the zeal of Flavian, their bishop, and to the eloquence of the senator Hilarius, the friend, and most probably the disciple, of Libanius;

whose genius, on this melancholy occasion, was not useless to his country. [85] But the two capitals, Antioch and Constantinople, were separated by the distance of eight hundred miles; and, notwithstanding the diligence of the Imperial posts, the guilty city was severely punished by a long and dreadful interval of suspense. Every rumor agitated the hopes and fears of the Antiochians, and they heard with terror, that their sovereign, exasperated by the insult which had been offered to his own statues, and more especially, to those of his beloved wife, had resolved to level with the ground the offending city; and to massacre, without distinction of age or sex, the criminal inhabitants; [86] many of whom were actually driven, by their apprehensions, to seek a refuge in the mountains of Syria, and the adjacent desert. At length, twenty-four days after the sedition, the general Hellebicus and Caesarius, master of the offices, declared the will of the emperor, and the sentence of Antioch. That proud capital was degraded from the rank of a city; and the metropolis of the East, stripped of its lands, its privileges, and its revenues, was subjected, under the humiliating denomination of a village, to the jurisdiction of Laodicea. [87] The baths, the Circus, and the theatres were shut: and, that every source of plenty and pleasure might at the same time be intercepted, the distribution of corn was abolished, by the severe instructions of Theodosius. His commissioners then proceeded to inquire into the guilt of individuals; of those who had perpetrated, and of those who had not prevented, the destruction of the sacred statues. The tribunal of Hellebicus and Caesarius, encompassed with armed soldiers, was erected in the midst of the Forum. The noblest, and most wealthy, of the citizens of Antioch appeared before them in chains; the examination was assisted by the use of torture, and their sentence was pronounced or suspended, according to the judgment of these extraordinary magistrates. The houses of the criminals were exposed to sale, their wives and children were suddenly reduced, from affluence and luxury, to the most abject distress; and a bloody execution was expected to conclude the horrors of the day, [88] which the preacher of Antioch, the eloquent Chrysostom, has represented as a lively image of the last and universal judgment of the world. But the ministers of Theodosius performed, with reluctance, the cruel task which had been assigned them; they dropped a gentle tear over the calamities of the people; and they listened with reverence to the pressing solicitations of the monks and hermits, who descended in swarms from the mountains. [89] Hellebicus and Caesarius were persuaded to suspend the execution of their sentence; and it was agreed that the former should remain at Antioch, while the latter returned, with all possible speed, to Constantinople; and presumed once more to consult the will of his sovereign. The resentment of Theodosius had already subsided; the deputies of the people, both the bishop and the orator, had obtained a favorable audience; and the reproaches of the emperor were the complaints of injured friendship, rather than the stern menaces of pride and power. A free and general pardon was granted to the city and citizens of Antioch; the prison doors were thrown open; the senators, who despaired of their lives, recovered the possession of their houses and estates; and the capital of the East was restored to the enjoyment of her ancient dignity and splendor. Theodosius condescended to praise the senate of Constantinople, who had generously interceded for their distressed brethren: he rewarded the eloquence of Hilarius with the government of Palestine; and dismissed the bishop of Antioch with the warmest expressions of his respect and gratitude. A thousand new statues arose to the clemency of Theodosius; the applause of his subjects was ratified by the approbation of his own heart; and the emperor confessed, that, if the exercise of justice is the most important duty, the indulgence of mercy is the most exquisite pleasure, of a sovereign. [90]

[Footnote 84: The Christians and Pagans agreed in believing that the sedition of Antioch was excited by the daemons. A gigantic woman (says Sozomen, l. vii. c. 23) paraded the streets with a scourge in her hand. An old man, says Libanius, (Orat. xii. p. 396,) transformed himself into a youth, then a boy, &c.]

[Footnote 85: Zosimus, in his short and disingenuous account, (l. iv. p. 258, 259,) is certainly mistaken in sending Libanius himself to Constantinople. His own orations fix him at Antioch.]

[Footnote 86: Libanius (Orat. i. p. 6, edit. Venet.) declares, that under such a reign the fear of a massacre was groundless and absurd, especially in the emperor's absence, for his presence, according to the eloquent slave, might have given a sanction to the most bloody acts.]

[Footnote 87: Laodicea, on the sea-coast, sixty-five miles from Antioch, (see Noris Epoch. Syro-Maced. Dissert. iii. p. 230.) The Antiochians were offended, that the dependent city of Seleucia should presume to intercede for them.]

[Footnote 88: As the days of the tumult depend on the movable festival of Easter, they can only be determined by the previous determination of the year. The year 387 has been preferred, after a laborious inquiry, by Tillemont (Hist. des. Emp. tom. v. p. 741-744) and Montfaucon, (Chrysostom, tom. xiii. p. 105-110.)]

[Footnote 89: Chrysostom opposes their courage, which was not attended with much risk, to the cowardly flight of the Cynics.]

[Footnote 90: The sedition of Antioch is represented in a lively, and almost dramatic, manner by two orators, who had their respective shares of interest and merit. See Libanius (Orat. xiv. xv. p. 389-420, edit. Morel. Orat. i. p. 1-14, Venet. 1754) and the twenty orations of St. John Chrysostom, de Statuis, (tom. ii. p. 1-225, edit. Montfaucon.) I do not pretend to much personal acquaintance with Chrysostom but Tillemont (Hist. des Empereurs, tom. v. p. 263-283) and Hermant (Vie de St. Chrysostome, tom. i. p. 137-224) had read him with pious curiosity and diligence.]

The sedition of Thessalonica is ascribed to a more shameful cause, and was productive of much more dreadful consequences. That great city, the metropolis of all the Illyrian provinces, had been protected from the dangers of the Gothic war by strong fortifications and a numerous garrison. Botheric, the general of those troops, and, as it should seem from his name, a Barbarian, had among his slaves a beautiful boy, who excited the impure desires of one of the charioteers of the Circus. The insolent and brutal lover was thrown into prison by the order of Botheric; and he sternly rejected the importunate clamors of the multitude, who, on the day of the public games, lamented the absence of their favorite; and considered the skill of a charioteer as an object of more importance than his virtue. The resentment of the people was imbittered by some previous disputes; and, as the strength of the garrison had been drawn away for the service of the Italian war, the feeble remnant, whose numbers were reduced by desertion, could not save the unhappy general from their licentious fury. Botheric, and several of his principal officers, were inhumanly murdered; their mangled bodies were dragged about the streets; and the emperor, who then resided at Milan, was surprised by the intelligence of the audacious and wanton cruelty of the people of Thessalonica. The sentence of a dispassionate judge would have inflicted a severe punishment on the authors of the crime; and the merit of Botheric might contribute to exasperate the grief and indignation of his master.

The fiery and choleric temper of Theodosius was impatient of the dilatory forms of a judicial inquiry; and he hastily resolved, that the blood of his lieutenant should be expiated by the blood of the guilty people. Yet his mind still fluctuated between the counsels of clemency and of revenge; the zeal of the bishops had almost extorted from the reluctant emperor the promise of a general pardon; his passion was again inflamed by the flattering suggestions of his minister Rufinus; and, after Theodosius had despatched the messengers of death, he attempted, when it was too late, to prevent the execution of his orders. The punishment of a Roman city was blindly committed to the undistinguishing sword of the Barbarians; and the hostile preparations were concerted with the dark and perfidious artifice of an illegal conspiracy. The people of Thessalonica were treacherously invited, in the name of their sovereign, to the games of the Circus; and such was their insatiate avidity for those amusements, that every consideration of fear, or suspicion, was disregarded by the numerous spectators. As soon as the assembly was complete, the soldiers, who had secretly been posted round the Circus, received the signal, not of the races, but of a general massacre. The promiscuous carnage continued three hours, without discrimination of strangers or natives, of age or sex, of innocence or guilt; the most moderate accounts state the number of the slain at seven thousand; and it is affirmed by some writers that more than fifteen thousand victims were sacrificed to the names of Botheric. A foreign merchant, who had probably no concern in his murder, offered his own life, and all his wealth, to supply the place of one of his two sons; but, while the father hesitated with equal tenderness, while he was doubtful to choose, and unwilling to condemn, the soldiers determined his suspense, by plunging their daggers at the same moment into the breasts of the defenceless youths. The apology of the assassins, that they were obliged to produce the prescribed number of heads, serves only to increase, by an appearance of order and design, the horrors of the massacre, which was executed by the commands of Theodosius. The guilt of the emperor is aggravated by his long and frequent residence at Thessalonica. The situation of the unfortunate city, the aspect of the streets and buildings, the dress and faces of the inhabitants, were familiar, and even present, to his imagination; and Theodosius possessed a quick and lively sense of the existence of the people whom he destroyed. [91]

[Footnote 91: The original evidence of Ambrose, (tom. ii. Epist. li. p. 998.) Augustin, (de Civitat. Dei, v. 26,) and Paulinus, (in Vit. Ambros. c. 24,) is delivered in vague expressions of horror and pity. It is illustrated by the subsequent and unequal testimonies of Sozomen, (l. vii. c. 25,) Theodoret, (l. v. c. 17,) Theophanes, (Chronograph. p. 62,) Cedrenus, (p. 317,) and Zonaras, (tom. ii. l. xiii. p. 34.) Zosimus alone, the partial enemy of Theodosius, most unaccountably passes over in silence the worst of his actions.]

The respectful attachment of the emperor for the orthodox clergy, had disposed him to love and admire the character of Ambrose; who united all the episcopal virtues in the most eminent degree. The friends and ministers of Theodosius imitated the example of their sovereign; and he observed, with more surprise than displeasure, that all his secret counsels were immediately communicated to the archbishop; who acted from the laudable persuasion, that every measure of civil government may have some connection with the glory of God, and the interest of the true religion. The monks and populace of Callinicum, [91/1] an obscure town on the frontier of Persia, excited by their own fanaticism, and by that of their bishop, had tumultuously burnt a conventicle of the Valentinians, and a synagogue of the Jews. The seditious prelate was condemned, by the magistrate of the province, either to rebuild the synagogue, or to repay the damage; and this moderate sentence was confirmed by the emperor. But it was not confirmed by the archbishop of Milan. [92] He dictated an epistle of censure and reproach, more suitable, perhaps, if the emperor had received the mark of circumcision, and renounced the faith of his baptism. Ambrose considers the toleration of the Jewish, as the persecution of the Christian, religion; boldly declares that he himself, and every true believer, would eagerly dispute with the bishop of Callinicum the merit of the deed, and the crown of martyrdom; and laments, in the most pathetic terms, that the execution of the sentence would be fatal to the fame and salvation of Theodosius. As this private admonition did not produce an immediate effect, the archbishop, from his pulpit, [93] publicly addressed the emperor on his throne; [94] nor would he consent to offer the oblation of the altar, till he had obtained from Theodosius a solemn and positive declaration, which secured the impunity of the bishop and monks of Callinicum. The recantation of Theodosius was sincere; [95] and, during the term of his residence at Milan, his affection for Ambrose was continually increased by the habits of pious and familiar conversation.

[Footnote 91/1: Raeca, on the Euphrates—M.]

[Footnote 92: See the whole transaction in Ambrose, (tom. ii. Epist. xl. xli. p. 950-956,) and his biographer Paulinus, (c. 23.) Bayle and Barbeyrac (Morales des Peres, c. xvii. p. 325, &c.) have justly condemned the archbishop.]

[Footnote 93: His sermon is a strange allegory of Jeremiah's rod, of an almond tree, of the woman who washed and anointed the feet of Christ. But the peroration is direct and personal.]

[Footnote 94: Hodie, Episcope, de me proposuisti. Ambrose modestly confessed it; but he sternly reprimanded Timasius, general of the horse and foot, who had presumed to say that the monks of Callinicum deserved punishment.]

[Footnote 95: Yet, five years afterwards, when Theodosius was absent from his spiritual guide, he tolerated the Jews, and condemned the destruction of their synagogues. Cod. Theodos. l. xvi. tit. viii. leg. 9, with Godefroy's Commentary, tom. vi. p. 225.]

When Ambrose was informed of the massacre of Thessalonica, his mind was filled with horror and anguish. He retired into the country to indulge his grief, and to avoid the presence of Theodosius. But as the archbishop was satisfied that a timid silence would render him the accomplice of his guilt, he represented, in a private letter, the enormity of the crime; which could only be effaced by the tears of penitence. The episcopal vigor of Ambrose was tempered by prudence; and he contented himself with signifying [96] an indirect sort of excommunication, by the assurance, that he had been warned in a vision not to offer the oblation in the name, or in the presence, of Theodosius; and by the advice, that he would confine himself to the use of prayer, without presuming to approach the altar of Christ, or to receive the holy eucharist with those hands that were still polluted with the blood of an innocent people. The emperor was deeply affected by his own reproaches, and by those of his spiritual father; and after he had bewailed the mischievous and irreparable consequences of his rash fury, he proceeded, in the accustomed manner, to perform his devotions in the great church of Milan. He was stopped in the porch by the archbishop; who, in the tone and language of an ambassador of Heaven, declared to his sovereign, that private contrition was not sufficient to atone for a public fault, or to appease the justice of the offended Deity. Theodosius humbly represented, that if he had contracted the guilt of homicide, David, the man after God's own heart, had been guilty, not only of murder, but of adultery. "You have imitated David in his crime, imitate then his repentance," was the reply of the undaunted Ambrose. The rigorous conditions of peace and pardon were accepted; and the public penance of the emperor Theodosius has been recorded as one of the most honorable events in the annals of the church. According to the mildest rules of ecclesiastical discipline, which were established in the fourth century, the crime of homicide was expiated by the penitence of twenty years: [97] and as it was impossible, in the period of human life, to purge the accumulated guilt of the massacre of Thessalonica, the murderer should have been excluded from the holy communion till the hour of his death. But the archbishop, consulting the maxims of religious policy, granted some indulgence to the rank of his illustrious penitent, who humbled in the dust the pride of the diadem; and the public edification might be admitted as a weighty reason to abridge the duration of his punishment. It was sufficient, that the emperor of the Romans, stripped of the ensigns of royalty, should appear in a mournful and suppliant posture; and that, in the midst of the church of Milan, he should humbly solicit, with sighs and tears, the pardon of his sins. [98] In this spiritual cure, Ambrose employed the various methods of mildness and severity. After a delay of about eight months, Theodosius was restored to the communion of the faithful; and the edict which interposes a salutary interval of thirty days between the sentence and the execution, may be accepted as the worthy fruits of his repentance. [99] Posterity has applauded the virtuous firmness of the archbishop; and the example of Theodosius may prove the beneficial influence of those principles, which could force a monarch, exalted above the apprehension of human punishment, to respect the laws, and ministers, of an invisible Judge. "The prince," says Montesquieu, "who is actuated by the hopes and fears of religion, may be compared to a lion, docile only to the voice, and tractable to the hand, of his keeper." [100] The motions of the royal animal will therefore depend on the inclination, and interest, of the man who has acquired such dangerous authority over him; and the priest, who holds in his hands the conscience of a king, may inflame, or moderate, his sanguinary passions. The cause of humanity, and that of persecution, have been asserted, by the same Ambrose, with equal energy, and with equal success.

[Footnote 96: Ambros. tom. ii. Epist. li. p. 997-1001. His epistle is a miserable rhapsody on a noble subject. Ambrose could act better than he could write. His compositions are destitute of taste, or genius; without the spirit of Tertullian, the copious elegance of Lactantius the lively wit of Jerom, or the grave energy of Augustin.]

[Footnote 97: According to the discipline of St. Basil, (Canon lvi.,) the voluntary homicide was four years a mourner; five a hearer; seven in a prostrate state; and four in a standing posture. I have the original (Beveridge, Pandect. tom. ii. p. 47-151) and a translation (Chardon, Hist. des Sacremens, tom. iv. p. 219-277) of the Canonical Epistles of St. Basil.]

[Footnote 98: The penance of Theodosius is authenticated by Ambrose, (tom. vi. de Obit. Theodos. c. 34, p. 1207,) Augustin, (de Civitat. Dei, v. 26,) and Paulinus, (in Vit. Ambros. c. 24.) Socrates is ignorant; Sozomen (l. vii. c. 25) concise; and the copious narrative of Theodoret (l. v. c. 18) must be used with precaution.]

[Footnote 99: Codex Theodos. l. ix. tit. xl. leg. 13. The date and circumstances of this law are perplexed with difficulties; but I feel myself inclined to favor the honest efforts of Tillemont (Hist. des Emp. tom. v. p. 721) and Pagi, (Critica, tom. i. p. 578.)]

[Footnote 100: Un prince qui aime la religion, et qui la craint, est un lion qui cede a la main qui le flatte, ou a la voix qui l'appaise. Esprit des Loix, l. xxiv. c. 2.]

PART V

After the defeat and death of the tyrant of Gaul, the Roman world was in the possession of Theodosius. He derived from the choice of Gratian his honorable title to the provinces of the East: he had acquired the West by the right of conquest; and the three years which he spent in Italy were usefully employed to restore the authority of the laws, and to correct the abuses which had prevailed with impunity under the usurpation of Maximus, and the minority of Valentinian. The name of Valentinian was regularly inserted in the public acts: but the tender age, and doubtful faith, of the son of Justina, appeared to require the prudent care of an orthodox guardian; and his specious ambition might have excluded the unfortunate youth, without a struggle, and almost without a murmur, from the administration, and even from the inheritance, of the empire. If Theodosius had consulted the rigid maxims of interest and policy, his conduct would have been justified by his friends; but the generosity of his behavior on this memorable occasion has extorted the applause of his most inveterate enemies. He seated Valentinian on the throne of Milan; and, without stipulating any present or future advantages, restored him to the absolute dominion of all the provinces, from which he had been driven by the arms of Maximus. To the restitution of his ample patrimony, Theodosius added the free and generous gift of the countries beyond the Alps, which his successful valor had recovered from the assassin of Gratian. [101] Satisfied with the glory which he had acquired, by revenging the death of his benefactor, and delivering the West from the yoke of tyranny, the emperor returned from Milan to Constantinople; and, in the peaceful possession of the East, insensibly relapsed into his former habits of luxury and indolence. Theodosius discharged his obligation to the brother, he indulged his conjugal tenderness to the sister, of Valentinian; and posterity, which admires the pure and singular glory of his elevation, must applaud his unrivalled generosity in the use of victory.

[Footnote 101: It is the niggard praise of Zosimus himself, (l. iv. p. 267.) Augustin says, with some happiness of expression, Valentinianum.... misericordissima veneratione restituit.]

The empress Justina did not long survive her return to Italy; and, though she beheld the triumph of Theodosius, she was not allowed to influence the government of her son. [102] The pernicious attachment to the Arian sect, which Valentinian had imbibed from her example and instructions, was soon erased by the lessons of a more orthodox education. His growing zeal for the faith of Nice, and his filial reverence for the character and authority of Ambrose, disposed the Catholics to entertain the most favorable opinion of the virtues of the young emperor of the West. [103] They applauded his chastity and temperance, his contempt of pleasure, his application to business, and his tender affection for his two sisters; which could not, however, seduce his impartial equity to pronounce an unjust sentence against the meanest of his subjects. But this amiable youth, before he had accomplished the twentieth year of his age, was oppressed by domestic treason; and the empire was again involved in the horrors of a civil war. Arbogastes, [104] a gallant soldier of the nation of the Franks, held the second rank in the service of Gratian. On the death of his master he joined the standard of Theodosius; contributed, by his valor and military conduct, to the destruction of the tyrant; and was appointed, after the victory, master-general of the armies of Gaul. His real merit, and apparent fidelity, had gained the confidence both of the prince and people; his boundless liberality corrupted the allegiance of the troops; and, whilst he was universally esteemed as the pillar of the state, the bold and crafty Barbarian was secretly determined either to rule, or to ruin, the empire of the West. The important commands of the army were distributed among the Franks; the creatures of Arbogastes were promoted to all the honors and offices of the civil government; the progress of the conspiracy removed every faithful servant from the presence of Valentinian; and the emperor, without power and without intelligence, insensibly sunk into the precarious and dependent condition of a captive. [105] The indignation which he expressed, though it might arise only from the rash and impatient temper of youth, may be candidly ascribed to the generous spirit of a prince, who felt that he was not unworthy to reign. He secretly invited the archbishop of Milan to undertake the office of a mediator; as the pledge of his sincerity, and the guardian of his safety. He contrived to apprise the emperor of the East of his helpless situation, and he declared, that, unless Theodosius could speedily march to his assistance, he must attempt to escape from the palace, or rather prison, of Vienna in Gaul, where he had imprudently fixed his residence in the midst of the hostile faction. But the hopes of relief were distant, and doubtful: and, as every day furnished some new provocation, the emperor, without strength or counsel, too hastily resolved to risk an immediate contest with his powerful general. He received Arbogastes on the throne; and, as the count approached with some appearance of respect, delivered to him a paper, which dismissed him from all his employments. "My authority," replied Arbogastes, with insulting coolness, "does not depend on the smile or the frown of a monarch;" and he contemptuously threw the paper on the ground. The indignant monarch snatched at the sword of one of the guards, which he struggled to draw from its scabbard; and it was not without some degree of violence that he was prevented from using the deadly weapon against his enemy, or against himself. A few days after this extraordinary quarrel, in which he had exposed his resentment and his weakness, the unfortunate Valentinian was found strangled in his apartment; and some pains were employed to disguise the manifest guilt of Arbogastes, and to persuade the world, that the death of the young emperor had been the voluntary effect of his own despair. [106] His body was conducted with decent pomp to the sepulchre of Milan; and the archbishop pronounced a funeral oration to commemorate his virtues and his misfortunes. [107] On this occasion the humanity of Ambrose tempted him to make a singular breach in his theological system; and to comfort the weeping sisters of Valentinian, by the firm assurance, that their pious brother, though he had not received the sacrament of baptism, was introduced, without difficulty, into the mansions of eternal bliss. [108]

[Footnote 102: Sozomen, l. vii. c. 14. His chronology is very irregular.]

[Footnote 103: See Ambrose, (tom. ii. de Obit. Valentinian. c. 15, &c. p. 1178. c. 36, &c. p. 1184.) When the young emperor gave an entertainment, he fasted himself; he refused to see a handsome actress, &c. Since he ordered his wild beasts to to be killed, it is ungenerous in Philostor (l. xi. c. 1) to reproach him with the love of that amusement.]

[Footnote 104: Zosimus (l. iv. p. 275) praises the enemy of Theodosius. But he is detested by Socrates (l. v. c. 25) and Orosius, (l. vii. c. 35.)]

[Footnote 105: Gregory of Tours (l. ii. c. 9, p. 165, in the second volume of the Historians of France) has preserved a curious fragment of Sulpicius Alexander, an historian far more valuable than himself.]

[Footnote 106: Godefroy (Dissertat. ad. Philostorg. p. 429-434) has diligently collected all the circumstances of the death of Valentinian II. The variations, and the ignorance, of contemporary writers, prove that it was secret.]

[Footnote 107: De Obitu Valentinian. tom. ii. p. 1173-1196. He is forced to speak a discreet and obscure language: yet he is much bolder than any layman, or perhaps any other ecclesiastic, would have dared to be.]

[Footnote 108: See c. 51, p. 1188, c. 75, p. 1193. Dom Chardon, (Hist. des Sacramens, tom. i. p. 86,) who owns that St. Ambrose most strenuously maintains the indispensable necessity of baptism, labors to reconcile the contradiction.]

The prudence of Arbogastes had prepared the success of his ambitious designs: and the provincials, in whose breast every sentiment of patriotism or loyalty was extinguished, expected, with tame resignation, the unknown master, whom the choice of a Frank might place on the Imperial throne. But some remains of pride and prejudice still opposed the elevation of Arbogastes himself; and the judicious Barbarian thought it more advisable to reign under the name of some dependent Roman. He bestowed the purple on the rhetorician Eugenius; [109] whom he had already raised from the place of his domestic secretary to the rank of master of the offices. In the course, both of his private and public service, the count had always approved the attachment and abilities of Eugenius; his learning and eloquence, supported by the gravity of his manners, recommended him to the esteem of the people; and the reluctance with which he seemed to ascend the throne, may inspire a favorable prejudice of his virtue and moderation. The ambassadors of the new emperor were immediately despatched to the court of Theodosius, to communicate, with affected grief, the unfortunate accident of the death of Valentinian; and, without mentioning the name of Arbogastes, to request, that the monarch of the East would embrace, as his lawful colleague, the respectable citizen, who had obtained the unanimous suffrage of the armies and provinces of the West. [110] Theodosius was justly provoked, that the perfidy of a Barbarian, should have destroyed, in a moment, the labors, and the fruit, of his former victory; and he was excited by the tears of his beloved wife, [111] to revenge the fate of her unhappy brother, and once more to assert by arms the violated majesty of the throne. But as the second conquest of the West was a task of difficulty and danger, he dismissed, with splendid presents, and an ambiguous answer, the ambassadors of Eugenius; and almost two years were consumed in the preparations of the civil war. Before he formed any decisive resolution, the pious emperor was anxious to discover the will of Heaven; and as the progress of Christianity had silenced the oracles of Delphi and Dodona, he consulted an Egyptian monk, who possessed, in the opinion of the age, the gift of miracles, and the knowledge of futurity. Eutropius, one of the favorite eunuchs of the palace of Constantinople, embarked for Alexandria, from whence he sailed up the Nile, as far as the city of Lycopolis, or of Wolves, in the remote province of Thebais. [112] In the neighborhood of that city, and on the summit of a lofty mountain, the holy John [113] had constructed, with his own hands, an humble cell, in which he had dwelt above fifty years, without opening his door, without seeing the face of a woman, and without tasting any food that had been prepared by fire, or any human art. Five days of the week he spent in prayer and meditation; but on Saturdays and Sundays he regularly opened a small window, and gave audience to the crowd of suppliants who successively flowed from every part of the Christian world. The eunuch of Theodosius approached the window with respectful steps, proposed his questions concerning the event of the civil war, and soon returned with a favorable oracle, which animated the courage of the emperor by the assurance of a bloody, but infallible victory. [114] The accomplishment of the prediction was forwarded by all the means that human prudence could supply. The industry of the two master-generals, Stilicho and Timasius, was directed to recruit the numbers, and to revive the discipline of the Roman legions. The formidable troops of Barbarians marched under the ensigns of their national chieftains. The Iberian, the Arab, and the Goth, who gazed on each other with mutual astonishment, were enlisted in the service of the same prince; [1141] and the renowned Alaric acquired, in the school of Theodosius, the knowledge of the art of war, which he afterwards so fatally exerted for the destruction of Rome. [115]

[Footnote 109: Quem sibi Germanus famulam delegerat exul, is the contemptuous expression of Claudian, (iv. Cons. Hon. 74.) Eugenius professed Christianity; but his secret attachment to Paganism (Sozomen, l. vii. c. 22, Philostorg. l. xi. c. 2) is probable in a grammarian, and would secure the friendship of Zosimus, (l. iv. p. 276, 277.)]

[Footnote 110: Zosimus (l. iv. p. 278) mentions this embassy; but he is diverted by another story from relating the event.]

[Footnote 111: Zosim. l. iv. p. 277. He afterwards says (p. 280) that Galla died in childbed; and intimates, that the affliction of her husband was extreme but short.]

[Footnote 112: Lycopolis is the modern Siut, or Osiot, a town of Said, about the size of St. Denys, which drives a profitable trade with the kingdom of Senaar, and has a very convenient fountain, "cujus potu signa virgini tatis eripiuntur." See D'Anville, Description de l'Egypte, p. 181 Abulfeda, Descript. Egypt. p. 14, and the curious Annotations, p. 25, 92, of his editor Michaelis.]

[Footnote 113: The Life of John of Lycopolis is described by his two friends, Rufinus (l. ii. c. i. p. 449) and Palladius, (Hist. Lausiac. c. 43, p. 738,) in Rosweyde's great Collection of the Vitae Patrum. Tillemont (Mem. Eccles. tom. x. p. 718, 720) has settled the chronology.]

[Footnote 114: Sozomen, l. vii. c. 22. Claudian (in Eutrop. l. i. 312) mentions the eunuch's journey; but he most contemptuously derides the Egyptian dreams, and the oracles of the Nile.]

[Footnote 1141]: Gibbon has embodied the picturesque verses of Claudian:—

.... Nec tantis dissona linguis Turba, nec armorum cultu diversion unquam]

[Footnote 115: Zosimus, l. iv. p. 280. Socrates, l. vii. 10. Alaric himself (de Bell. Getico, 524) dwells with more complacency on his early exploits against the Romans.

.... Tot Augustos Hebro qui teste fugavi.

Yet his vanity could scarcely have proved this plurality of flying emperors.]

The emperor of the West, or, to speak more properly, his general Arbogastes, was instructed by the misconduct and misfortune of Maximus, how dangerous it might prove to extend the line of defence against a skilful antagonist, who was free to press, or to suspend, to contract, or to multiply, his various methods of attack. [116] Arbogastes fixed his station on the confines of Italy; the troops of Theodosius were permitted to occupy, without resistance, the provinces of Pannonia, as far as the foot of the Julian Alps; and even the passes of the mountains were negligently, or perhaps artfully, abandoned to the bold invader. He descended from the hills, and beheld, with some astonishment, the formidable camp of the Gauls and Germans, that covered with arms and tents the open country which extends to the walls of Aquileia, and the banks of the Frigidus, [117] or Cold River. [118] This narrow theatre of the war, circumscribed by the Alps and the Adriatic, did not allow much room for the operations of military skill; the spirit of Arbogastes would have disdained a pardon; his guilt extinguished the hope of a negotiation; and Theodosius was impatient to satisfy his glory and revenge, by the chastisement of the assassins of Valentinian. Without weighing the natural and artificial obstacles that opposed his efforts, the emperor of the East immediately attacked the fortifications of his rivals, assigned the post of honorable danger to the Goths, and cherished a secret wish, that the bloody conflict might diminish the pride and numbers of the conquerors. Ten thousand of those auxiliaries, and Bacurius, general of the Iberians, died bravely on the field of battle. But the victory was not purchased by their blood; the Gauls maintained their advantage; and the approach of night protected the disorderly flight, or retreat, of the troops of Theodosius. The emperor retired to the adjacent hills; where he passed a disconsolate night, without sleep, without provisions, and without hopes; [119] except that strong assurance, which, under the most desperate circumstances, the independent mind may derive from the contempt of fortune and of life. The triumph of Eugenius was celebrated by the insolent and dissolute joy of his camp; whilst the active and vigilant Arbogastes secretly detached a considerable body of troops to occupy the passes of the mountains, and to encompass the rear of the Eastern army. The dawn of day discovered to the eyes of Theodosius the extent and the extremity of his danger; but his apprehensions were soon dispelled, by a friendly message from the leaders of those troops who expressed their inclination to desert the standard of the tyrant. The honorable and lucrative rewards, which they stipulated as the price of their perfidy, were granted without hesitation; and as ink and paper could not easily be procured, the emperor subscribed, on his own tablets, the ratification of the treaty. The spirit of his soldiers was revived by this seasonable reenforcement; and they again marched, with confidence, to surprise the camp of a tyrant, whose principal officers appeared to distrust, either the justice or the success of his arms. In the heat of the battle, a violent tempest, [120] such as is often felt among the Alps, suddenly arose from the East. The army of Theodosius was sheltered by their position from the impetuosity of the wind, which blew a cloud of dust in the faces of the enemy, disordered their ranks, wrested their weapons from their hands, and diverted, or repelled, their ineffectual javelins. This accidental advantage was skilfully improved, the violence of the storm was magnified by the superstitious terrors of the Gauls; and they yielded without shame to the invisible powers of heaven, who seemed to militate on the side of the pious emperor. His victory was decisive; and the deaths of his two rivals were distinguished only by the difference of their characters. The rhetorician Eugenius, who had almost acquired the dominion of the world, was reduced to implore the mercy of the conqueror; and the unrelenting soldiers separated his head from his body as he lay prostrate at the feet of Theodosius. Arbogastes, after the loss of a battle, in which he had discharged the duties of a soldier and a general, wandered several days among the mountains. But when he was convinced that his cause was desperate, and his escape impracticable, the intrepid Barbarian imitated the example of the ancient Romans, and turned his sword against his own breast. The fate of the empire was determined in a narrow corner of Italy; and the legitimate successor of the house of Valentinian embraced the archbishop of Milan, and graciously received the submission of the provinces of the West. Those provinces were involved in the guilt of rebellion; while the inflexible courage of Ambrose alone had resisted the claims of successful usurpation. With a manly freedom, which might have been fatal to any other subject, the archbishop rejected the gifts of Eugenius, [120/1] declined his correspondence, and withdrew himself from Milan, to avoid the odious presence of a tyrant, whose downfall he predicted in discreet and ambiguous language. The merit of Ambrose was applauded by the conqueror, who secured the attachment of the people by his alliance with the church; and the clemency of Theodosius is ascribed to the humane intercession of the archbishop of Milan. [121]

[Footnote 116: Claudian (in iv. Cons. Honor. 77, &c.) contrasts the military plans of the two usurpers:—

.... Novitas audere priorem Suadebat; cautumque dabant exempla sequentem. Hic nova moliri praeceps: hic quaerere tuta Providus. Hic fusis; colectis viribus ille. Hic vagus excurrens; hic claustra reductus Dissimiles, sed morte pares......]

[Footnote 117: The Frigidus, a small, though memorable, stream in the country of Goretz, now called the Vipao, falls into the Sontius, or Lisonzo, above Aquileia, some miles from the Adriatic. See D'Anville's ancient and modern maps, and the Italia Antiqua of Cluverius, (tom. i. c. 188.)]

[Footnote 118: Claudian's wit is intolerable: the snow was dyed red; the cold ver smoked; and the channel must have been choked with carcasses the current had not been swelled with blood. Confluxit populus: totam pater undique secum Moverat Auroren; mixtis hic Colchus Iberis, Hic mitra velatus Arabs, hic crine decoro Armenius, hic picta Saces, fucataque Medus, Hic gemmata tiger tentoria fixerat Indus—De Laud. Stil. l. 145—M.]

[Footnote 119: Theodoret affirms, that St. John, and St. Philip, appeared to the waking, or sleeping, emperor, on horseback, &c. This is the first instance of apostolic chivalry, which afterwards became so popular in Spain, and in the Crusades.]

[Footnote 120: Te propter, gelidis Aquilo de monte procellis

Obruit adversas acies; revolutaque tela Vertit in auctores, et turbine reppulit hastas

O nimium dilecte Deo, cui fundit ab antris Aeolus armatas hyemes; cui militat Aether, Et conjurati veniunt ad classica venti.

These famous lines of Claudian (in iii. Cons. Honor. 93, &c. A.D. 396) are alleged by his contemporaries, Augustin and Orosius; who suppress the Pagan deity of Aeolus, and add some circumstances from the information of eye-witnesses. Within four months after the victory, it was compared by Ambrose to the miraculous victories of Moses and Joshua.]

[Footnote 120/1: Arbogastes and his emperor had openly espoused the Pagan party, according to Ambrose and Augustin. See Le Beau, v. 40. Beugnot (Histoire de la Destruction du Paganisme) is more full, and perhaps somewhat fanciful, on this remarkable reaction in favor of Paganism, but compare p 116—M.]

[Footnote 121: The events of this civil war are gathered from Ambrose, (tom. ii. Epist. lxii. p. 1022,) Paulinus, (in Vit. Ambros. c. 26-34,) Augustin, (de Civitat. Dei, v. 26,) Orosius, (l. vii. c. 35,) Sozomen, (l. vii. c. 24,) Theodoret, (l. v. c. 24,) Zosimus, (l. iv. p. 281, 282,) Claudian, (in iii. Cons. Hon. 63-105, in iv. Cons. Hon. 70-117,) and the Chronicles published by Scaliger.]

After the defeat of Eugenius, the merit, as well as the authority, of Theodosius was cheerfully acknowledged by all the inhabitants of the Roman world. The experience of his past conduct encouraged the most pleasing expectations of his future reign; and the age of the emperor, which did not exceed fifty years, seemed to extend the prospect of the public felicity. His death, only four months after his victory, was considered by the people as an unforeseen and fatal event, which destroyed, in a moment, the hopes of the rising generation. But the indulgence of ease and luxury had secretly nourished the principles of disease. [122] The strength of Theodosius was unable to support the sudden and violent transition from the palace to the camp; and the increasing symptoms of a dropsy announced the speedy dissolution of the emperor. The opinion, and perhaps the interest, of the public had confirmed the division of the Eastern and Western empires; and the two royal youths, Arcadius and Honorius, who had already obtained, from the tenderness of their father, the title of Augustus, were destined to fill the thrones of Constantinople and of Rome. Those princes were not permitted to share the danger and glory of the civil war; [123] but as soon as Theodosius had triumphed over his unworthy rivals, he called his younger son, Honorius, to enjoy the fruits of the victory, and to receive the sceptre of the West from the hands of his dying father. The arrival of Honorius at Milan was welcomed by a splendid exhibition of the games of the Circus; and the emperor, though he was oppressed by the weight of his disorder, contributed by his presence to the public joy. But the remains of his strength were exhausted by the painful effort which he made to assist at the spectacles of the morning. Honorius supplied, during the rest of the day, the place of his father; and the great Theodosius expired in the ensuing night. Notwithstanding the recent animosities of a civil war, his death was universally lamented. The Barbarians, whom he had vanquished and the churchmen, by whom he had been subdued, celebrated, with loud and sincere applause, the qualities of the deceased emperor, which appeared the most valuable in their eyes. The Romans were terrified by the impending dangers of a feeble and divided administration, and every disgraceful moment of the unfortunate reigns of Arcadius and Honorius revived the memory of their irreparable loss.

[Footnote 122: This disease, ascribed by Socrates (l. v. c. 26) to the fatigues of war, is represented by Philostorgius (l. xi. c. 2) as the effect of sloth and intemperance; for which Photius calls him an impudent liar, (Godefroy, Dissert. p. 438.)]

[Footnote 123: Zosimus supposes, that the boy Honorius accompanied his father, (l. iv. p. 280.) Yet the quanto flagrabrant pectora voto is all that flattery would allow to a contemporary poet; who clearly describes the emperor's refusal, and the journey of Honorius, after the victory (Claudian in iii. Cons. 78-125.)]

In the faithful picture of the virtues of Theodosius, his imperfections have not been dissembled; the act of cruelty, and the habits of indolence, which tarnished the glory of one of the greatest of the Roman princes. An historian, perpetually adverse to the fame of Theodosius, has exaggerated his vices, and their pernicious effects; he boldly asserts, that every rank of subjects imitated the effeminate manners of their sovereign; and that every species of corruption polluted the course of public and private life; and that the feeble restraints of order and decency were insufficient to resist the progress of that degenerate spirit, which sacrifices, without a blush, the consideration of duty and interest to the base indulgence of sloth and appetite. [124] The complaints of contemporary writers, who deplore the increase of luxury, and depravation of manners, are commonly expressive of their peculiar temper and situation. There are few observers, who possess a clear and comprehensive view of the revolutions of society; and who are capable of discovering the nice and secret springs of action, which impel, in the same uniform direction, the blind and capricious passions of a multitude of individuals. If it can be affirmed, with any degree of truth, that the luxury of the Romans was more shameless and dissolute in the reign of Theodosius than in the age of Constantine, perhaps, or of Augustus, the alteration cannot be ascribed to any beneficial improvements, which had gradually increased the stock of national riches. A long period of calamity or decay must have checked the industry, and diminished the wealth, of the people; and their profuse luxury must have been the result of that indolent despair, which enjoys the present hour, and declines the thoughts of futurity. The uncertain condition of their property discouraged the subjects of Theodosius from engaging in those useful and laborious undertakings which require an immediate expense, and promise a slow and distant advantage. The frequent examples of ruin and desolation tempted them not to spare the remains of a patrimony, which might, every hour, become the prey of the rapacious Goth. And the mad prodigality which prevails in the confusion of a shipwreck, or a siege, may serve to explain the progress of luxury amidst the misfortunes and terrors of a sinking nation.

[Footnote 124: Zosimus, l. iv. p. 244.]

The effeminate luxury, which infected the manners of courts and cities, had instilled a secret and destructive poison into the camps of the legions; and their degeneracy has been marked by the pen of a military writer, who had accurately studied the genuine and ancient principles of Roman discipline. It is the just and important observation of Vegetius, that the infantry was invariably covered with defensive armor, from the foundation of the city, to the reign of the emperor Gratian. The relaxation of discipline, and the disuse of exercise, rendered the soldiers less able, and less willing, to support the fatigues of the service; they complained of the weight of the armor, which they seldom wore; and they successively obtained the permission of laying aside both their cuirasses and their helmets. The heavy weapons of their ancestors, the short sword, and the formidable pilum, which had subdued the world, insensibly dropped from their feeble hands. As the use of the shield is incompatible with that of the bow, they reluctantly marched into the field; condemned to suffer either the pain of wounds, or the ignominy of flight, and always disposed to prefer the more shameful alternative. The cavalry of the Goths, the Huns, and the Alani, had felt the benefits, and adopted the use, of defensive armor; and, as they excelled in the management of missile weapons, they easily overwhelmed the naked and trembling legions, whose heads and breasts were exposed, without defence, to the arrows of the Barbarians. The loss of armies, the destruction of cities, and the dishonor of the Roman name, ineffectually solicited the successors of Gratian to restore the helmets and the cuirasses of the infantry. The enervated soldiers abandoned their own and the public defence; and their pusillanimous indolence may be considered as the immediate cause of the downfall of the empire. [125]

[Footnote 125: Vegetius, de Re Militari, l. i. c. 10. The series of calamities which he marks, compel us to believe, that the Hero, to whom he dedicates his book, is the last and most inglorious of the Valentinians.]

CHAPTER XXVIII

DESTRUCTION OF PAGANISM

PART I

FINAL DESTRUCTION OF PAGANISM—INTRODUCTION OF THE WORSHIP OF SAINTS, AND RELICS, AMONG THE CHRISTIANS

The ruin of Paganism, in the age of Theodosius, is perhaps the only example of the total extirpation of any ancient and popular superstition; and may therefore deserve to be considered as a singular event in the history of the human mind. The Christians, more especially the clergy, had impatiently supported the prudent delays of Constantine, and the equal toleration of the elder Valentinian; nor could they deem their conquest perfect or secure, as long as their adversaries were permitted to exist. The influence which Ambrose and his brethren had acquired over the youth of Gratian, and the piety of Theodosius, was employed to infuse the maxims of persecution into the breasts of their Imperial proselytes. Two specious principles of religious jurisprudence were established, from whence they deduced a direct and rigorous conclusion, against the subjects of the empire who still adhered to the ceremonies of their ancestors: that the magistrate is, in some measure, guilty of the crimes which he neglects to prohibit, or to punish; and, that the idolatrous worship of fabulous deities, and real daemons, is the most abominable crime against the supreme majesty of the Creator. The laws of Moses, and the examples of Jewish history, [1] were hastily, perhaps erroneously, applied, by the clergy, to the mild and universal reign of Christianity. [2] The zeal of the emperors was excited to vindicate their own honor, and that of the Deity: and the temples of the Roman world were subverted, about sixty years after the conversion of Constantine.

[Footnote 1: St. Ambrose (tom. ii. de Obit. Theodos. p. 1208) expressly praises and recommends the zeal of Josiah in the destruction of idolatry The language of Julius Firmicus Maternus on the same subject (de Errore Profan. Relig. p. 467, edit. Gronov.) is piously inhuman. Nec filio jubet (the Mosaic Law) parci, nec fratri, et per amatam conjugera gladium vindicem ducit, &c.]

[Footnote 2: Bayle (tom. ii. p. 406, in his Commentaire Philosophique) justifies, and limits, these intolerant laws by the temporal reign of Jehovah over the Jews. The attempt is laudable.]

From the age of Numa to the reign of Gratian, the Romans preserved the regular succession of the several colleges of the sacerdotal order. [3] Fifteen Pontiffs exercised their supreme jurisdiction over all things, and persons, that were consecrated to the service of the gods; and the various questions which perpetually arose in a loose and traditionary system, were submitted to the judgment of their holy tribunal Fifteen grave and learned Augurs observed the face of the heavens, and prescribed the actions of heroes, according to the flight of birds. Fifteen keepers of the Sibylline books (their name of Quindecemvirs was derived from their number) occasionally consulted the history of future, and, as it should seem, of contingent, events. Six Vestals devoted their virginity to the guard of the sacred fire, and of the unknown pledges of the duration of Rome; which no mortal had been suffered to behold with impunity. [4] Seven Epulos prepared the table of the gods, conducted the solemn procession, and regulated the ceremonies of the annual festival. The three Flamens of Jupiter, of Mars, and of Quirinus, were considered as the peculiar ministers of the three most powerful deities, who watched over the fate of Rome and of the universe. The King of the Sacrifices represented the person of Numa, and of his successors, in the religious functions, which could be performed only by royal hands. The confraternities of the Salians, the Lupercals, &c., practised such rites as might extort a smile of contempt from every reasonable man, with a lively confidence of recommending themselves to the favor of the immortal gods. The authority, which the Roman priests had formerly obtained in the counsels of the republic, was gradually abolished by the establishment of monarchy, and the removal of the seat of empire. But the dignity of their sacred character was still protected by the laws, and manners of their country; and they still continued, more especially the college of pontiffs, to exercise in the capital, and sometimes in the provinces, the rights of their ecclesiastical and civil jurisdiction. Their robes of purple, chariotz of state, and sumptuous entertainments, attracted the admiration of the people; and they received, from the consecrated lands, and the public revenue, an ample stipend, which liberally supported the splendor of the priesthood, and all the expenses of the religious worship of the state. As the service of the altar was not incompatible with the command of armies, the Romans, after their consulships and triumphs, aspired to the place of pontiff, or of augur; the seats of Cicero [5] and Pompey were filled, in the fourth century, by the most illustrious members of the senate; and the dignity of their birth reflected additional splendor on their sacerdotal character. The fifteen priests, who composed the college of pontiffs, enjoyed a more distinguished rank as the companions of their sovereign; and the Christian emperors condescended to accept the robe and ensigns, which were appropriated to the office of supreme pontiff. But when Gratian ascended the throne, more scrupulous or more enlightened, he sternly rejected those profane symbols; [6] applied to the service of the state, or of the church, the revenues of the priests and vestals; abolished their honors and immunities; and dissolved the ancient fabric of Roman superstition, which was supported by the opinions and habits of eleven hundred years. Paganism was still the constitutional religion of the senate. The hall, or temple, in which they assembled, was adorned by the statue and altar of Victory; [7] a majestic female standing on a globe, with flowing garments, expanded wings, and a crown of laurel in her outstretched hand. [8] The senators were sworn on the altar of the goddess to observe the laws of the emperor and of the empire: and a solemn offering of wine and incense was the ordinary prelude of their public deliberations. The removal of this ancient monument was the only injury which Constantius had offered to the superstition of the Romans. The altar of Victory was again restored by Julian, tolerated by Valentinian, and once more banished from the senate by the zeal of Gratian. [10] But the emperor yet spared the statues of the gods which were exposed to the public veneration: four hundred and twenty-four temples, or chapels, still remained to satisfy the devotion of the people; and in every quarter of Rome the delicacy of the Christians was offended by the fumes of idolatrous sacrifice. [11]

[Footnote 3: See the outlines of the Roman hierarchy in Cicero, (de Legibus, ii. 7, 8,) Livy, (i. 20,) Dionysius Halicarnassensis, (l. ii. p. 119-129, edit. Hudson,) Beaufort, (Republique Romaine, tom. i. p. 1-90,) and Moyle, (vol. i. p. 10-55.) The last is the work of an English whig, as well as of a Roman antiquary.]

[Footnote 4: These mystic, and perhaps imaginary, symbols have given birth to various fables and conjectures. It seems probable, that the Palladium was a small statue (three cubits and a half high) of Minerva, with a lance and distaff; that it was usually enclosed in a seria, or barrel; and that a similar barrel was placed by its side to disconcert curiosity, or sacrilege. See Mezeriac (Comment. sur les Epitres d'Ovide, tom i. p. 60—66) and Lipsius, (tom. iii. p. 610 de Vesta, &c. c 10.)]

[Footnote 5: Cicero frankly (ad Atticum, l. ii. Epist. 5) or indirectly (ad Familiar. l. xv. Epist. 4) confesses that the Augurate is the supreme object of his wishes. Pliny is proud to tread in the footsteps of Cicero, (l. iv. Epist. 8,) and the chain of tradition might be continued from history and marbles.]

[Footnote 6: Zosimus, l. iv. p. 249, 250. I have suppressed the foolish pun about Pontifex and Maximus.]

[Footnote 7: This statue was transported from Tarentum to Rome, placed in the Curia Julia by Caesar, and decorated by Augustus with the spoils of Egypt.]

[Footnote 8: Prudentius (l. ii. in initio) has drawn a very awkward portrait of Victory; but the curious reader will obtain more satisfaction from Montfaucon's Antiquities, (tom. i. p. 341.)]

[Footnote 9: See Suetonius (in August. c. 35) and the Exordium of Pliny's Panegyric.]

[Footnote 10: These facts are mutually allowed by the two advocates, Symmachus and Ambrose.]

[Footnote 11: The Notitia Urbis, more recent than Constantine, does not find one Christian church worthy to be named among the edifices of the city. Ambrose (tom. ii. Epist. xvii. p. 825) deplores the public scandals of Rome, which continually offended the eyes, the ears, and the nostrils of the faithful.]

But the Christians formed the least numerous party in the senate of Rome: [12] and it was only by their absence, that they could express their dissent from the legal, though profane, acts of a Pagan majority. In that assembly, the dying embers of freedom were, for a moment, revived and inflamed by the breath of fanaticism. Four respectable deputations were successively voted to the Imperial court, [13] to represent the grievances of the priesthood and the senate, and to solicit the restoration of the altar of Victory. The conduct of this important business was intrusted to the eloquent Symmachus, [14] a wealthy and noble senator, who united the sacred characters of pontiff and augur with the civil dignities of proconsul of Africa and praefect of the city. The breast of Symmachus was animated by the warmest zeal for the cause of expiring Paganism; and his religious antagonists lamented the abuse of his genius, and the inefficacy of his moral virtues. [15] The orator, whose petition is extant to the emperor Valentinian, was conscious of the difficulty and danger of the office which he had assumed. He cautiously avoids every topic which might appear to reflect on the religion of his sovereign; humbly declares, that prayers and entreaties are his only arms; and artfully draws his arguments from the schools of rhetoric, rather than from those of philosophy. Symmachus endeavors to seduce the imagination of a young prince, by displaying the attributes of the goddess of victory; he insinuates, that the confiscation of the revenues, which were consecrated to the service of the gods, was a measure unworthy of his liberal and disinterested character; and he maintains, that the Roman sacrifices would be deprived of their force and energy, if they were no longer celebrated at the expense, as well as in the name, of the republic. Even scepticism is made to supply an apology for superstition. The great and incomprehensible secret of the universe eludes the inquiry of man. Where reason cannot instruct, custom may be permitted to guide; and every nation seems to consult the dictates of prudence, by a faithful attachment to those rites and opinions, which have received the sanction of ages. If those ages have been crowned with glory and prosperity, if the devout people have frequently obtained the blessings which they have solicited at the altars of the gods, it must appear still more advisable to persist in the same salutary practice; and not to risk the unknown perils that may attend any rash innovations. The test of antiquity and success was applied with singular advantage to the religion of Numa; and Rome herself, the celestial genius that presided over the fates of the city, is introduced by the orator to plead her own cause before the tribunal of the emperors. "Most excellent princes," says the venerable matron, "fathers of your country! pity and respect my age, which has hitherto flowed in an uninterrupted course of piety. Since I do not repent, permit me to continue in the practice of my ancient rites. Since I am born free, allow me to enjoy my domestic institutions. This religion has reduced the world under my laws. These rites have repelled Hannibal from the city, and the Gauls from the Capitol. Were my gray hairs reserved for such intolerable disgrace? I am ignorant of the new system that I am required to adopt; but I am well assured, that the correction of old age is always an ungrateful and ignominious office." [16] The fears of the people supplied what the discretion of the orator had suppressed; and the calamities, which afflicted, or threatened, the declining empire, were unanimously imputed, by the Pagans, to the new religion of Christ and of Constantine.

[Footnote 12: *Ambrose repeatedly affirms, in contradiction to common sense (Moyle's Works, vol. ii. p. 147,) that the Christians had a majority in the senate.*]

[Footnote 13: *The first (A.D. 382) to Gratian, who refused them audience; the second (A.D. 384) to Valentinian, when the field was disputed by Symmachus and Ambrose; the third (A.D. 388) to Theodosius; and the fourth (A.D. 392) to Valentinian. Lardner (Heathen Testimonies, vol. iv. p. 372-399) fairly represents the whole transaction.*]

[Footnote 14: *Symmachus, who was invested with all the civil and sacerdotal honors, represented the emperor under the two characters of Pontifex Maximus, and Princeps Senatus. See the proud inscription at the head of his works. Note: Mr. Beugnot has made it doubtful whether Symmachus was more than Pontifex Major. Destruction du Paganisme, vol. i. p. 459—M.*]

[Footnote 15: *As if any one, says Prudentius (in Symmach. i. 639) should dig in the mud with an instrument of gold and ivory. Even saints, and polemic saints, treat this adversary with respect and civility.*]

[Footnote 16: *See the fifty-fourth Epistle of the tenth book of Symmachus. In the form and disposition of his ten books of Epistles, he imitated the younger Pliny; whose rich and florid style he was supposed, by his friends, to equal or excel, (Macrob. Saturnal. l. v. c. i.) But the luxcriancy of Symmachus consists of barren leaves, without fruits, and even without flowers. Few facts, and few sentiments, can be extracted from his verbose correspondence.*]

But the hopes of Symmachus were repeatedly baffled by the firm and dexterous opposition of the archbishop of Milan, who fortified the emperors against the fallacious eloquence of the advocate of Rome. In this controversy, Ambrose condescends to speak the language of a philosopher, and to ask, with some contempt, why it should be thought necessary to introduce an imaginary and invisible power, as the cause of those victories, which were sufficiently explained by the valor and discipline of the legions. He justly derides the absurd reverence for antiquity, which could only tend to discourage the improvements of art, and to replunge the human race into their original barbarism. From thence, gradually rising to a more lofty and theological tone, he pronounces, that Christianity alone is the doctrine of truth and salvation; and that every mode of Polytheism conducts its deluded votaries, through the paths of error, to the abyss of eternal perdition. [17] Arguments like these, when they were suggested by a favorite bishop, had power to prevent the restoration of the altar of Victory; but the same arguments fell, with much more energy and effect, from the mouth of a conqueror; and the gods of antiquity were dragged in triumph at the chariot-wheels of Theodosius. [18] In a full meeting of the senate, the emperor proposed, according to the forms of the republic, the important question, Whether the worship of Jupiter, or that of Christ, should be the religion of the Romans. [18/1] The liberty of suffrages, which he affected to allow, was destroyed by the hopes and fears that his presence inspired; and the arbitrary exile of Symmachus was a recent admonition, that it might be dangerous to oppose the wishes of the monarch. On a regular division of the senate, Jupiter was condemned and degraded by the sense of a very large majority; and it is rather surprising, that any members should be found bold enough to declare, by their speeches and votes, that they were still attached to the interest of an abdicated deity. [19] The hasty conversion of the senate must be attributed either to supernatural or to sordid motives; and many of these reluctant proselytes betrayed, on every favorable occasion, their secret disposition to throw aside the mask of odious dissimulation. But they were gradually fixed in the new religion, as the cause of the ancient became more hopeless; they yielded to the authority of the emperor, to the fashion of the times, and to the entreaties of their wives and children, [20] who were instigated and governed by the clergy of Rome and the monks of the East. The edifying example of the Anician family was soon imitated by the rest of the nobility: the Bassi, the Paullini, the Gracchi, embraced the Christian religion; and "the luminaries of the world, the venerable assembly of Catos (such are the high-flown expressions of Prudentius) were impatient to strip themselves of their pontifical garment; to cast the skin of the old serpent; to assume the snowy robes of baptismal innocence, and to humble the pride of the consular fasces before tombs of the martyrs." [21] The citizens, who subsisted by their own industry, and the populace, who were supported by the public liberality, filled the churches of the Lateran, and Vatican, with an incessant throng of devout proselytes. The decrees of the senate, which proscribed the worship of idols, were ratified by the general consent of the Romans; [22] the splendor of the Capitol was defaced, and the solitary temples were abandoned to ruin and contempt. [23] Rome submitted to the yoke of the Gospel; and the vanquished provinces had not yet lost their reverence for the name and authority of Rome. [23/1]

[Footnote 17: See Ambrose, (tom. ii. Epist. xvii. xviii. p. 825-833.) The former of these epistles is a short caution; the latter is a formal reply of the petition or libel of Symmachus. The same ideas are more copiously expressed in the poetry, if it may deserve that name, of Prudentius; who composed his two books against Symmachus (A.D. 404) while that senator was still alive. It is whimsical enough that Montesquieu (Considerations, &c. c. xix. tom. iii. p. 487) should overlook the two professed antagonists of Symmachus, and amuse himself with descanting on the more remote and indirect confutations of Orosius, St. Augustin, and Salvian.]

[Footnote 18: See Prudentius (in Symmach. l. i. 545, &c.) The Christian agrees with the Pagan Zosimus (l. iv. p. 283) in placing this visit of Theodosius after the second civil war, gemini bis victor caede Tyranni, (l. i. 410.) But the time and circumstances are better suited to his first triumph.]

[Footnote 18/1: M. Beugnot (in his Histoire de la Destruction du Paganisme en Occident, i. p. 483-488) questions, altogether, the truth of this statement. It is very remarkable that Zosimus and Prudentius concur in asserting the fact of the question being solemnly deliberated by the senate, though with directly opposite results. Zosimus declares that the majority of the assembly adhered to the ancient religion of Rome; Gibbon has adopted the authority of Prudentius, who, as a Latin writer, though a poet, deserves more credit than the Greek historian. Both concur in placing this scene after the second triumph of Theodosius; but it has been almost demonstrated (and Gibbon—see the preceding note—seems to

have acknowledged this) by Pagi and Tillemont, that Theodosius did not visit Rome after the defeat of Eugenius. M. Beugnot urges, with much force, the improbability that the Christian emperor would submit such a question to the senate, whose authority was nearly obsolete, except on one occasion, which was almost hailed as an epoch in the restoration of her ancient privileges. The silence of Ambrose and of Jerom on an event so striking, and redounding so much to the honor of Christianity, is of considerable weight. M. Beugnot would ascribe the whole scene to the poetic imagination of Prudentius; but I must observe, that, however Prudentius is sometimes elevated by the grandeur of his subject to vivid and eloquent language, this flight of invention would be so much bolder and more vigorous than usual with this poet, that I cannot but suppose there must have been some foundation for the story, though it may have been exaggerated by the poet, or misrepresented by the historian—M]

[Footnote 19: Prudentius, after proving that the sense of the senate is declared by a legal majority, proceeds to say, (609, &c.)—

Adspice quam pleno subsellia nostra Senatu Decernant infame Jovis pulvinar, et omne Idolum longe purgata ex urbe fugandum, Qua vocat egregii sententia Principis, illuc Libera, cum pedibus, tum corde, frequentia transit.

Zosimus ascribes to the conscript feathers a heathenish courage, which few of them are found to possess.]

[Footnote 20: Jerom specifies the pontiff Albinus, who was surrounded with such a believing family of children and grandchildren, as would have been sufficient to convert even Jupiter himself; an extraordinary proselyted (tom. i. ad Laetam, p. 54.)]

[Footnote 21:
Exultare Patres videas, pulcherrima mundi Lumina; Conciliumque senum gestire Catonum Candidiore toga niveum pietatis amictum Sumere; et exuvias deponere pontificales.

The fancy of Prudentius is warmed and elevated by victory]

[Footnote 22: Prudentius, after he has described the conversion of the senate and people, asks, with some truth and confidence,

Et dubitamus adhuc Romam, tibi, Christe, dicatam In leges transisse tuas?]

[Footnote 23: Jerom exults in the desolation of the Capitol, and the other temples of Rome, (tom. i. p. 54, tom. ii. p. 95.)]

[Footnote 23/1: M. Beugnot is more correct in his general estimate of the measures enforced by Theodosius for the abolition of Paganism. He seized (according to Zosimus) the funds bestowed by the public for the expense of sacrifices. The public sacrifices ceased, not because they were positively prohibited, but because the public treasury would no longer bear the expense. The public and the private sacrifices in the provinces, which were not under the same regulations with those of the capital, continued to take place. In Rome itself, many pagan ceremonies, which were without sacrifice, remained in full force. The gods, therefore, were invoked, the temples were frequented, the pontificates inscribed, according to ancient usage, among the family titles of honor; and it cannot be asserted that idolatry was completely destroyed by Theodosius. See Beugnot, p. 491—M.]

PART II

The filial piety of the emperors themselves engaged them to proceed, with some caution and tenderness, in the reformation of the eternal city. Those absolute monarchs acted with less regard to the prejudices of the provincials. The pious labor which had been suspended near twenty years since the death of Constantius, [24] was vigorously resumed, and finally accomplished, by the zeal of Theodosius. Whilst that warlike prince yet struggled with the Goths, not for the glory, but for the safety, of the republic, he ventured to offend a considerable party of his subjects, by some acts which might perhaps secure the protection of Heaven, but which must seem rash and unseasonable in the eye of human prudence. The success of his first experiments against the Pagans encouraged the pious emperor to reiterate and enforce his edicts of proscription: the same laws which had been originally published in the provinces of the East, were applied, after the defeat of Maximus, to the whole extent of the Western empire; and every victory of the orthodox Theodosius contributed to the triumph of the Christian and Catholic faith. [25] He attacked superstition in her most vital part, by prohibiting the use of sacrifices, which he declared to be criminal as well as infamous; and if the terms of his edicts more strictly condemned the impious curiosity which examined the entrails of the victim, [26] every subsequent explanation tended to involve in the same guilt the general practice of immolation, which essentially constituted the religion of the Pagans. As the temples had been erected for the purpose of sacrifice, it was the duty of a benevolent prince to remove from his subjects the dangerous temptation of offending against the laws which he had enacted. A special commission was granted to Cynegius, the Praetorian praefect of the East, and afterwards to the counts Jovius and Gaudentius, two officers of distinguished rank in the West; by which they were directed to shut the temples, to seize or destroy the instruments of idolatry, to abolish the privileges of the priests, and to confiscate the consecrated property for the benefit of the emperor, of the church, or of the army. [27] Here the desolation might have stopped: and the naked edifices, which were no longer employed in the service of idolatry, might have been protected from the destructive rage of fanaticism. Many of those temples were the most splendid and beautiful monuments of Grecian architecture; and the emperor himself was interested not to deface the splendor of his own cities, or to diminish the value of his own possessions. Those stately edifices might be suffered to remain, as so many lasting trophies of the victory of Christ. In the decline of the arts they might be usefully converted into magazines, manufactures, or places of public assembly: and perhaps, when the walls of the temple had been sufficiently purified by holy rites, the worship of the true Deity might be allowed to expiate the ancient guilt of idolatry. But as long as they subsisted, the Pagans fondly cherished the secret hope, that an auspicious revolution, a second Julian, might again restore the altars of the gods: and the earnestness with which they addressed their unavailing prayers to the throne, [28] increased the zeal of the Christian reformers to extirpate, without mercy, the root of superstition. The laws of the emperors exhibit some symptoms of a milder disposition: [29] but their cold and languid efforts were insufficient to stem the torrent of enthusiasm and rapine, which was conducted, or rather impelled, by the spiritual rulers of the church. In Gaul, the holy Martin, bishop of Tours, [30] marched at the head of his faithful monks to destroy the idols, the temples, and the consecrated trees of his extensive diocese; and, in the execution of this arduous task, the prudent reader will judge whether Martin was supported by the aid of miraculous powers, or of carnal weapons. In Syria, the divine and excellent Marcellus, [31] as he is styled by Theodoret, a bishop animated with apostolic fervor, resolved to level with the ground the stately temples within the diocese of Apamea. His attack was resisted by the skill and solidity with which the temple of Jupiter had been constructed. The building was seated on an eminence: on each of the four sides, the lofty roof was supported by fifteen massy columns, sixteen feet in circumference; and the large stone, of which they were composed, were firmly cemented with lead and iron. The force of the strongest and sharpest tools had been tried without effect. It was found necessary to undermine the foundations of the columns, which fell down as soon as the temporary wooden props had been consumed with fire; and the difficulties of the enterprise are described under the allegory of a black daemon, who retarded, though he could not defeat, the operations of the Christian engineers. Elated with victory, Marcellus took the field in person against the powers of darkness; a numerous troop of soldiers and gladiators marched under the episcopal banner, and he successively attacked the villages and country temples of the diocese of Apamea. Whenever any resistance or danger was apprehended, the champion of the faith, whose lameness would not allow him either to fight or fly, placed himself at a convenient distance, beyond the reach of darts. But this prudence was the occasion of his death: he was surprised and slain by a body of exasperated rustics; and the synod of the province pronounced, without hesitation, that the holy Marcellus had sacrificed his life in the cause of God. In the support of this cause, the monks, who rushed with tumultuous fury from the desert, distinguished themselves by their zeal and diligence. They deserved the enmity of the Pagans; and some of them might deserve the reproaches of avarice and intemperance; of avarice, which they gratified with holy plunder, and of intemperance, which they indulged at the expense of the people, who foolishly admired their tattered garments, loud psalmody, and artificial paleness. [32] A small number of temples was protected by the fears, the venality, the taste, or the prudence, of the civil and ecclesiastical governors. The temple of the Celestial Venus at Carthage, whose sacred precincts formed a circumference of two miles, was judiciously converted into a Christian church; [33] and a similar consecration has preserved inviolate the majestic dome of the Pantheon at Rome. [34] But in almost every province of the Roman world, an army of fanatics, without authority, and without discipline, invaded the peaceful inhabitants; and the ruin of the fairest structures of antiquity still displays the ravages of those Barbarians, who alone had time and inclination to execute such laborious destruction.

[Footnote 24: Libanius (Orat. pro Templis, p. 10, Genev. 1634, published by James Godefroy, and now extremely scarce) accuses Valentinian and Valens of prohibiting sacrifices. Some partial order may have been issued by the Eastern emperor; but the idea of any general law is contradicted by the silence of the Code, and the evidence of ecclesiastical history. Note: See in Reiske's edition of Libanius, tom. ii. p. 155. Sacrific was prohibited by Valens, but not the offering of incense—M.]

[Footnote 25: See his laws in the Theodosian Code, l. xvi. tit. x. leg. 7-11.]

[Footnote 26: Homer's sacrifices are not accompanied with any inquisition of entrails, (see Feithius, Antiquitat. Homer. l. i. c. 10, 16.) The Tuscans, who produced the first Haruspices, subdued both the Greeks and the Romans, (Cicero de Divinatione, ii. 23.)]

[Footnote 27: Zosimus, l. iv. p. 245, 249. Theodoret. l. v. c. 21. Idatius in Chron. Prosper. Aquitan. l. iii. c. 38, apud Baronium, Annal. Eccles. A.D. 389, No. 52. Libanius (pro Templis, p. 10) labors to prove that the commands of Theodosius were not direct and positive. Note: Libanius appears to be the best authority for the East, where, under Theodosius, the work of devastation was carried on with very different degrees of violence, according to the temper of the local authorities and of the clergy; and more especially the neighborhood of the more fanatican monks. Neander well observes, that the prohibition of sacrifice would be easily misinterpreted into an authority for the destruction of the buildings in which sacrifices were performed. (Geschichte der Christlichen religion ii. p. 156.) An abuse of this kind led to this remarkable oration of Libanius. Neander, however, justly doubts whether this bold vindication or at least exculpation, of Paganism was ever delivered before, or even placed in the hands of the Christian emperor—M.]

[Footnote 28: Cod. Theodos, l. xvi. tit. x. leg. 8, 18. There is room to believe, that this temple of Edessa, which Theodosius wished to save for civil uses, was soon afterwards a heap of ruins, (Libanius pro Templis, p. 26, 27, and Godefroy's notes, p. 59.)]

[Footnote 29: See this curious oration of Libanius pro Templis, pronounced, or rather composed, about the year 390. I have consulted, with advantage, Dr. Lardner's version and remarks, (Heathen Testimonies, vol. iv. p. 135-163.)]

[Footnote 30: See the Life of Martin by Sulpicius Severus, c. 9-14. The saint once mistook (as Don Quixote might have done) a harmless funeral for an idolatrous procession, and imprudently committed a miracle.]

[Footnote 31: Compare Sozomen, (l. vii. c. 15) with Theodoret, (l. v. c. 21.) Between them, they relate the crusade and death of Marcellus.]

[Footnote 32: Libanius, pro Templis, p. 10-13. He rails at these black-garbed men, the Christian monks, who eat more than elephants. Poor elephants! they are temperate animals.]

[Footnote 33: Prosper. Aquitan. l. iii. c. 38, apud Baronium; Annal. Eccles. A.D. 389, No. 58, &c. The temple had been shut some time, and the access to it was overgrown with brambles.]

[Footnote 34: Donatus, Roma Antiqua et Nova, l. iv. c. 4, p. 468. This consecration was performed by Pope Boniface IV. I am ignorant of the favorable circumstances which had preserved the Pantheon above two hundred years after the reign of Theodosius.]

In this wide and various prospect of devastation, the spectator may distinguish the ruins of the temple of Serapis, at Alexandria. [35] Serapis does not appear to have been one of the native gods, or monsters, who sprung from the fruitful soil of superstitious Egypt. [36] The first of the Ptolemies had been commanded, by a dream, to import the mysterious stranger from the coast of Pontus, where he had been long adored by the inhabitants of Sinope; but his attributes and his reign were so imperfectly understood, that it became a subject of dispute, whether he represented the bright orb of day, or the gloomy monarch of the subterraneous regions. [37] The Egyptians, who were obstinately devoted to the religion of their fathers, refused to admit this foreign deity within the walls of their cities. [38] But the obsequious priests, who were seduced by the liberality of the Ptolemies, submitted, without resistance, to the power of the god of Pontus: an honorable and domestic genealogy was provided; and this fortunate usurper was introduced into the throne and bed of Osiris, [39] the husband of Isis, and the celestial monarch of Egypt. Alexandria, which claimed his peculiar protection, gloried in the name of the city of Serapis. His temple, [40] which rivalled the pride and magnificence of the Capitol, was erected on the spacious summit of an artificial mount, raised one hundred steps above the level of the adjacent parts of the city; and the interior cavity was strongly supported by arches, and distributed into vaults and subterraneous apartments. The consecrated buildings were surrounded by a quadrangular portico; the stately halls, and exquisite statues, displayed the triumph of the arts; and the treasures of ancient learning were preserved in the famous Alexandrian library, which had arisen with new splendor from its ashes. [41] After the edicts of Theodosius had severely prohibited the sacrifices of the Pagans, they were still tolerated in the city and temple of Serapis; and this singular indulgence was imprudently ascribed to the superstitious terrors of the Christians themselves; as if they had feared to abolish those ancient rites, which could alone secure the inundations of the Nile, the harvests of Egypt, and the subsistence of Constantinople. [42]

[Footnote 35: Sophronius composed a recent and separate history, (Jerom, in Script. Eccles. tom. i. p. 303,) which has furnished materials to Socrates, (l. v. c. 16.) Theodoret, (l. v. c. 22,) and Rufinus, (l. ii. c. 22.) Yet the last, who had been at Alexandria before and after the event, may deserve the credit of an original witness.]

[Footnote 36: Gerard Vossius (Opera, tom. v. p. 80, and de Idoloaltria, l. i. c. 29) strives to support the strange notion of the Fathers; that the patriarch Joseph was adored in Egypt, as the bull Apis, and the god Serapis. Note: Consult du Dieu Serapis et son Origine, par J D. Guigniaut, (the translator of Creuzer's Symbolique,) Paris, 1828; and in the fifth volume of Bournouf's translation of Tacitus—M.]

[Footnote 37: Origo dei nondum nostris celebrata. Aegyptiorum antistites sic memorant, &c., Tacit. Hist. iv. 83. The Greeks, who had travelled into Egypt, were alike ignorant of this new deity.]

[Footnote 38: Macrobius, Saturnal, l. i. c. 7. Such a living fact decisively proves his foreign extraction.]

[Footnote 39: At Rome, Isis and Serapis were united in the same temple. The precedency which the queen assumed, may seem to betray her unequal alliance with the stranger of Pontus. But the superiority of the female sex was established in Egypt as a civil and religious institution, (Diodor. Sicul. tom. i. l. i. p. 31, edit. Wesseling,) and the same order is observed in Plutarch's Treatise of Isis and Osiris; whom he identifies with Serapis.]

[Footnote 40: Ammianus, (xxii. 16.) The Expositio totius Mundi, (p. 8, in Hudson's Geograph. Minor. tom. iii.,) and Rufinus, (l. ii. c. 22,) celebrate the Serapeum, as one of the wonders of the world.]

[Footnote 41: See Memoires de l'Acad. des Inscriptions, tom. ix. p. 397-416. The old library of the Ptolemies was totally consumed in Caesar's Alexandrian war. Marc Antony gave the whole collection of Pergamus (200,000 volumes) to Cleopatra, as the foundation of the new library of Alexandria.]

[Footnote 42: Libanius (pro Templis, p. 21) indiscreetly provokes his Christian masters by this insulting remark.]

At that time [43] the archiepiscopal throne of Alexandria was filled by Theophilus, [44] the perpetual enemy of peace and virtue; a bold, bad man, whose hands were alternately polluted with gold and with blood. His pious indignation was excited by the honors of Serapis; and the insults which he offered to an ancient temple of Bacchus, [44/1] convinced the Pagans that he meditated a more important and dangerous enterprise. In the tumultuous capital of Egypt, the slightest provocation was sufficient to inflame a civil war. The votaries of Serapis, whose strength and numbers were much inferior to those of their antagonists, rose in arms at the instigation of the philosopher Olympius, [45] who exhorted them to die in the defence of the altars of the gods. These Pagan fanatics fortified themselves in the temple, or rather fortress, of Serapis; repelled the besiegers by daring sallies, and a resolute defence; and, by the inhuman cruelties which they exercised on their Christian prisoners, obtained the last consolation of despair. The efforts of the prudent magistrate were usefully exerted for the establishment of a truce, till the answer of Theodosius should determine the fate of Serapis. The two parties assembled, without arms, in the principal square; and the Imperial rescript was publicly read. But when a sentence of destruction against the idols of Alexandria was pronounced, the Christians set up a shout of joy and exultation, whilst the unfortunate Pagans, whose fury had given way to consternation, retired with hasty and silent steps, and eluded, by their flight or obscurity, the resentment of their enemies. Theophilus proceeded to demolish the temple of Serapis, without any other difficulties, than those which he found in the weight and solidity of the materials: but these obstacles proved so insuperable, that he was obliged to leave the foundations; and to content himself with reducing the edifice itself to a heap of rubbish, a part of which was soon afterwards cleared away, to make room for a church, erected in honor of the Christian martyrs. The valuable library of Alexandria was pillaged or destroyed; and near twenty years afterwards, the appearance of the empty shelves excited the regret and indignation of every spectator, whose mind was not totally darkened by religious prejudice. [46] The compositions of ancient genius, so many of which have irretrievably perished, might surely have been excepted from the wreck of idolatry, for the amusement and instruction of succeeding ages; and either the zeal or the avarice of the archbishop, [47] might have been satiated with the rich spoils, which were the reward of his victory. While the images and vases of gold and silver were carefully melted, and those of a less valuable metal were contemptuously broken, and cast into the streets, Theophilus labored to expose the frauds and vices of the ministers of the idols; their dexterity in the management of the loadstone; their secret methods of introducing a human actor into a hollow statue; [47/1] and their scandalous abuse of the confidence of devout husbands and unsuspecting females. [48] Charges like these may seem to deserve some degree of credit, as they are not repugnant to the crafty and interested spirit of superstition. But the same spirit is equally prone to the base practice of insulting and calumniating a fallen enemy; and our belief is naturally checked by the reflection, that it is much less difficult to invent a fictitious story, than to support a practical fraud. The colossal statue of Serapis [49] was involved in the ruin of his temple and religion. A great number of plates of different metals, artificially joined together, composed the majestic figure of the deity, who touched on either side the walls of the sanctuary. The aspect of Serapis, his sitting posture, and the sceptre, which he bore in his left hand, were extremely similar to the ordinary representations of Jupiter. He was distinguished from Jupiter by the basket, or bushel, which was placed on his head; and by the emblematic monster which he held in his right hand; the head and body of a serpent branching into three tails, which were again terminated by the triple heads of a dog, a lion, and a wolf. It was confidently affirmed, that if any impious hand should dare to violate the majesty of the god, the heavens and the earth would instantly return to their original chaos. An intrepid soldier, animated by zeal, and armed with a weighty battle-axe, ascended the ladder; and even the Christian multitude expected, with some anxiety, the event of the combat. [50] He aimed a vigorous stroke against the cheek of Serapis; the cheek fell to the ground; the thunder was still silent, and both the heavens and the earth continued to preserve their accustomed order and tranquillity. The victorious soldier repeated his blows: the huge idol was overthrown, and broken in pieces; and the limbs of Serapis were ignominiously dragged through the streets of Alexandria. His mangled carcass was burnt in the Amphitheatre, amidst the shouts of the populace; and many persons attributed their conversion to this discovery of the impotence of their tutelar deity. The popular modes of religion, that propose any visible and material objects of worship, have the advantage of adapting and familiarizing themselves to the senses of mankind: but this advantage is counterbalanced by the various and inevitable accidents to which the faith of the idolater is exposed. It is scarcely possible, that, in every disposition of mind, he should preserve his implicit reverence for the idols, or the relics, which the naked eye, and the profane hand, are unable to distinguish from the most common productions of art or nature; and if, in the hour of danger, their secret and miraculous virtue does not operate for their own preservation, he scorns the vain apologies of his priests, and justly derides the object, and the folly, of his superstitious attachment. [51] After the fall of Serapis, some hopes were still entertained by the Pagans, that the Nile would refuse his annual supply to the impious masters of Egypt; and the extraordinary delay of the inundation seemed to announce the displeasure of the river-god. But this delay was soon compensated by the rapid swell of the waters. They suddenly rose to such an unusual height, as to comfort the discontented party with the pleasing expectation of a deluge; till the peaceful river again subsided to the well-known and fertilizing level of sixteen cubits, or about thirty English feet. [52]

[Footnote 43: We may choose between the date of Marcellinus (A.D. 389) or that of Prosper, (A.D. 391.) Tillemont (Hist. des Emp. tom. v. p. 310, 756) prefers the former, and Pagi the latter.]

[Footnote 44: Tillemont, Mem. Eccles. tom. xi. p. 441-500. The ambiguous situation of Theophilus—a saint, as the friend of Jerom a devil, as the enemy of Chrysostom—produces a sort of impartiality; yet, upon the whole, the balance is justly inclined against him.]

[Footnote 44/1: No doubt a temple of Osiris. St. Martin, iv 398-M.]

[Footnote 45: Lardner (Heathen Testimonies, vol. iv. p. 411) has alleged beautiful passage from Suidas, or rather from Damascius, which show the devout and virtuous Olympius, not in the light of a warrior, but of a prophet.]

[Footnote 46: Nos vidimus armaria librorum, quibus direptis, exinanita ea a nostris hominibus, nostris temporibus memorant. Orosius, l. vi. c. 15, p. 421, edit. Havercamp. Though a bigot, and a controversial writer. Orosius seems to blush.]

[Footnote 47: Eunapius, in the Lives of Antoninus and Aedesius, execrates the sacrilegious rapine of Theophilus. Tillemont (Mem. Eccles. tom. xiii. p. 453) quotes an epistle of Isidore of Pelusium, which reproaches the primate with the idolatrous worship of gold, the auri sacra fames.]

[Footnote 47/1: An English traveller, Mr. Wilkinson, has discovered the secret of the vocal Memnon. There was a cavity in which a person was concealed, and struck a stone, which gave a ringing sound like brass. The Arabs, who stood below when Mr. Wilkinson performed the miracle, described sound just as the author of the epigram—M.]

[Footnote 48: Rufinus names the priest of Saturn, who, in the character of the god, familiarly conversed with many pious ladies of quality, till he betrayed himself, in a moment of transport, when he could not disguise the tone of his voice. The authentic and impartial narrative of Aeschines, (see Bayle, Dictionnaire Critique, Scamandre,) and the adventure of Mudus, (Joseph. Antiquitat. Judaic. l. xviii. c. 3, p. 877 edit. Havercamp,) may prove that such amorous frauds have been practised with success.]

[Footnote 49: See the images of Serapis, in Montfaucon, (tom. ii. p. 297:) but the description of Macrobius (Saturnal. l. i. c. 20) is much more picturesque and satisfactory.]

[Footnote 50:
Sed fortes tremuere manus, motique verenda Majestate loci, si robora sacra ferirent In sua credebant redituras membra secures.

(Lucan. iii. 429.) "Is it true," (said Augustus to a veteran of Italy, at whose house he supped) "that the man who gave the first blow to the golden statue of Anaitis, was instantly deprived of his eyes, and of his life?"—"I was that man, (replied the clear-sighted veteran,) and you now sup on one of the legs of the goddess." (Plin. Hist. Natur. xxxiii. 24)]

[Footnote 51: The history of the reformation affords frequent examples of the sudden change from superstition to contempt.]

[Footnote 52: Sozomen, l. vii. c. 20. I have supplied the measure. The same standard, of the inundation, and consequently of the cubit, has uniformly subsisted since the time of Herodotus. See Freret, in the Mem. de l'Academie des Inscriptions, tom. xvi. p. 344-353. Greaves's Miscellaneous Works, vol. i. p. 233. The Egyptian cubit is about twenty-two inches of the English measure. Note: Compare Wilkinson's Thebes and Egypt, p. 313—M.]

The temples of the Roman empire were deserted, or destroyed; but the ingenious superstition of the Pagans still attempted to elude the laws of Theodosius, by which all sacrifices had been severely prohibited. The inhabitants of the country, whose conduct was less opposed to the eye of malicious curiosity, disguised their religious, under the appearance of convivial, meetings. On the days of solemn festivals, they assembled in great numbers under the spreading shade of some consecrated trees; sheep and oxen were slaughtered and roasted; and this rural entertainment was sanctified by the use of incense, and by the hymns which were sung in honor of the gods. But it was alleged, that, as no part of the animal was made a burnt-offering, as no altar was provided to receive the blood, and as the previous oblation of salt cakes, and the concluding ceremony of libations, were carefully omitted, these festal meetings did not involve the guests in the guilt, or penalty, of an illegal sacrifice. [53] Whatever might be the truth of the facts, or the merit of the distinction, [54] these vain pretences were swept away by the last edict of Theodosius, which inflicted a deadly wound on the superstition of the Pagans. [55] [55/1] This prohibitory law is expressed in the most absolute and comprehensive terms. "It is our will and pleasure," says the emperor, "that none of our subjects, whether magistrates or private citizens, however exalted or however humble may be their rank and condition, shall presume, in any city or in any place, to worship an inanimate idol, by the sacrifice of a guiltless victim." The act of sacrificing, and the practice of divination by the entrails of the victim, are declared (without any regard to the object of the inquiry) a crime of high treason against the state, which can be expiated only by the death of the guilty. The rites of Pagan superstition, which might seem less bloody and atrocious, are abolished, as highly injurious to the truth and honor of religion; luminaries, garlands, frankincense, and libations of wine, are specially enumerated and condemned; and the harmless claims of the domestic genius, of the household gods, are included in this rigorous proscription. The use of any of these profane and illegal ceremonies, subjects the offender to the forfeiture of the house or estate, where they have been performed; and if he has artfully chosen the property of another for the scene of his impiety, he is compelled to discharge, without delay, a heavy fine of twenty-five pounds of gold, or more than one thousand pounds sterling. A fine, not less considerable, is imposed on the connivance of the secret enemies of religion, who shall neglect the duty of their respective stations, either to reveal, or to punish, the guilt of idolatry. Such was the persecuting spirit of the laws of Theodosius, which were repeatedly enforced by his sons and grandsons, with the loud and unanimous applause of the Christian world. [56]

[Footnote 53: Libanius (pro Templis, p. 15, 16, 17) pleads their cause with gentle and insinuating rhetoric. From the earliest age, such feasts had enlivened the country: and those of Bacchus (Georgic. ii. 380) had produced the theatre of Athens. See Godefroy, ad loc. Liban. and Codex Theodos. tom. vi. p. 284.]

[Footnote 54: Honorius tolerated these rustic festivals, (A.D. 399.) "Absque ullo sacrificio, atque ulla superstitione damnabili." But nine years afterwards he found it necessary to reiterate and enforce the same proviso, (Codex Theodos. l. xvi. tit. x. leg. 17, 19.)]

[Footnote 55: Cod. Theodos. l. xvi. tit. x. leg. 12. Jortin (Remarks on Eccles. History, vol. iv. p. 134) censures, with becoming asperity, the style and sentiments of this intolerant law.]

[Footnote 55/1: Paganism maintained its ground for a considerable time in the rural districts. Endelechius, a poet who lived at the beginning of the fifth century, speaks of the cross as Signum quod perhibent esse crucis Dei, Magnis qui colitur solus inurbibus. In the middle of the same century, Maximus, bishop of Turin, writes against the heathen deities as if their worship was still in full vigor in the neighborhood of his city. Augustine complains of the encouragement of the Pagan rites by heathen landowners; and Zeno of Verona, still later, reproves the apathy of the Christian proprietors in conniving at this abuse. (Compare Neander, ii. p. 169.) M. Beugnot shows that this was the case throughout the north and centre of Italy and in Sicily. But neither of these authors has adverted to one fact, which must have tended greatly to retard the progress of Christianity in these quarters. It was still chiefly a slave population which cultivated the soil; and however, in the towns, the better class of Christians might be eager to communicate "the blessed liberty of the gospel" to this class of mankind; however their condition could not but be silently ameliorated by the humanizing influence of Christianity; yet, on the whole, no doubt the servile class would be the least fitted to receive the gospel; and its general propagation among them would be embarrassed by many peculiar difficulties. The rural population was probably not entirely converted before the general establishment of the monastic institutions. Compare Quarterly Review of Beugnot. vol lvii. p. 52—M.]

[Footnote 56: Such a charge should not be lightly made; but it may surely be justified by the authority of St. Augustin, who thus addresses the Donatists: "Quis nostrum, quis vestrum non laudat leges ab Imperatoribus datas adversus sacrificia Paganorum? Et certe longe ibi poera severior constituta est; illius quippe impietatis capitale supplicium est." Epist. xciii. No. 10, quoted by Le Clerc, (Bibliotheque Choisie, tom. viii. p. 277,) who adds some judicious reflections on the intolerance of the victorious Christians. Note: Yet Augustine, with laudable inconsistency, disapproved of the forcible demolition of the temples. "Let us first extirpate the idolatry of the hearts of the heathen, and they will either themselves invite us or anticipate us in the execution of this good work," tom. v. p. 62. Compare Neander, ii. 169, and, in p. 155, a beautiful passage from Chrysostom against all violent means of propagating Christianity—M.]

PART III

In the cruel reigns of Decius and Dioclesian, Christianity had been proscribed, as a revolt from the ancient and hereditary religion of the empire; and the unjust suspicions which were entertained of a dark and dangerous faction, were, in some measure, countenanced by the inseparable union and rapid conquests of the Catholic church. But the same excuses of fear and ignorance cannot be applied to the Christian emperors who violated the precepts of humanity and of the Gospel. The experience of ages had betrayed the weakness, as well as folly, of Paganism; the light of reason and of faith had already exposed, to the greatest part of mankind, the vanity of idols; and the declining sect, which still adhered to their worship, might have been permitted to enjoy, in peace and obscurity, the religious costumes of their ancestors. Had the Pagans been animated by the undaunted zeal which possessed the minds of the primitive believers, the triumph of the Church must have been stained with blood; and the martyrs of Jupiter and Apollo might have embraced the glorious opportunity of devoting their lives and fortunes at the foot of their altars. But such obstinate zeal was not congenial to the loose and careless temper of Polytheism. The violent and repeated strokes of the orthodox princes were broken by the soft and yielding substance against which they were directed; and the ready obedience of the Pagans protected them from the pains and penalties of the Theodosian Code. [57] Instead of asserting, that the authority of the gods was superior to that of the emperor, they desisted, with a plaintive murmur, from the use of those sacred rites which their sovereign had condemned. If they were sometimes tempted by a sally of passion, or by the hopes of concealment, to indulge their favorite superstition, their humble repentance disarmed the severity of the Christian magistrate, and they seldom refused to atone for their rashness, by submitting, with some secret reluctance, to the yoke of the Gospel. The churches were filled with the increasing multitude of these unworthy proselytes, who had conformed, from temporal motives, to the reigning religion; and whilst they devoutly imitated the postures, and recited the prayers, of the faithful, they satisfied their conscience by the silent and sincere invocation of the gods of antiquity. [58] If the Pagans wanted patience to suffer they wanted spirit to resist; and the scattered myriads, who deplored the ruin of the temples, yielded, without a contest, to the fortune of their adversaries. The disorderly opposition [59] of the peasants of Syria, and the populace of Alexandria, to the rage of private fanaticism, was silenced by the name and authority of the emperor. The Pagans of the West, without contributing to the elevation of Eugenius, disgraced, by their partial attachment, the cause and character of the usurper. The clergy vehemently exclaimed, that he aggravated the crime of rebellion by the guilt of apostasy; that, by his permission, the altar of victory was again restored; and that the idolatrous symbols of Jupiter and Hercules were displayed in the field, against the invincible standard of the cross. But the vain hopes of the Pagans were soon annihilated by the defeat of Eugenius; and they were left exposed to the resentment of the conqueror, who labored to deserve the favor of Heaven by the extirpation of idolatry. [60]

[Footnote 57: Orosius, l. vii. c. 28, p. 537. Augustin (Enarrat. in Psalm cxl apud Lardner, Heathen Testimonies, vol. iv. p. 458) insults their cowardice. "Quis eorum comprehensus est in sacrificio (cum his legibus sta prohiberentur) et non negavit?"]

[Footnote 58: Libanius (pro Templis, p. 17, 18) mentions, without censure the occasional conformity, and as it were theatrical play, of these hypocrites.]

[Footnote 59: Libanius concludes his apology (p. 32) by declaring to the emperor, that unless he expressly warrants the destruction of the temples, the proprietors will defend themselves and the laws.]

[Footnote 60: Paulinus, in Vit. Ambros. c. 26. Augustin de Civitat. Dei, l. v. c. 26. Theodoret, l. v. c. 24.]

A nation of slaves is always prepared to applaud the clemency of their master, who, in the abuse of absolute power, does not proceed to the last extremes of injustice and oppression. Theodosius might undoubtedly have proposed to his Pagan subjects the alternative of baptism or of death; and the eloquent Libanius has praised the moderation of a prince, who never enacted, by any positive law, that all his subjects should immediately embrace and practise the religion of their sovereign. [61] The profession of Christianity was not made an essential qualification for the enjoyment of the civil rights of society, nor were any peculiar hardships imposed on the sectaries, who credulously received the fables of Ovid, and obstinately rejected the miracles of the Gospel. The palace, the schools, the army, and the senate, were filled with declared and devout Pagans; they obtained, without distinction, the civil and military honors of the empire. [6111] Theodosius distinguished his liberal regard for virtue and genius by the consular dignity, which he bestowed on Symmachus; [62] and by the personal friendship which he expressed to Libanius; [63] and the two eloquent apologists of Paganism were never required either to change or to dissemble their religious opinions. The Pagans were indulged in the most licentious freedom of speech and writing; the historical and philosophic remains of Eunapius, Zosimus, [64] and the fanatic teachers of the school of Plato, betray the most furious animosity, and contain the sharpest invectives, against the sentiments and conduct of their victorious adversaries. If these audacious libels were publicly known, we must applaud the good sense of the Christian princes, who viewed, with a smile of contempt, the last struggles of superstition and despair. [65] But the Imperial laws, which prohibited the sacrifices and ceremonies of Paganism, were rigidly executed; and every hour contributed to destroy the influence of a religion, which was supported by custom, rather than by argument. The devotion or the poet, or the philosopher, may be secretly nourished by prayer, meditation, and study; but the exercise of public worship appears to be the only solid foundation of the religious sentiments of the people, which derive their force from imitation and habit. The interruption of that public exercise may consummate, in the period of a few years, the important work of a national revolution. The memory of theological opinions cannot long be preserved, without the artificial helps of priests, of temples, and of books. [66] The ignorant vulgar, whose minds are still agitated by the blind hopes and terrors of superstition, will be soon persuaded by their superiors to direct their vows to the reigning deities of the age; and will insensibly imbibe an ardent zeal for the support and propagation of the new doctrine, which spiritual hunger at first compelled them to accept. The generation that arose in the world after the promulgation of the Imperial laws, was attracted within the pale of the Catholic church: and so rapid, yet so gentle, was the fall of Paganism, that only twenty-eight years after the death of Theodosius, the faint and minute vestiges were no longer visible to the eye of the legislator. [67]

[Footnote 61: Libanius suggests the form of a persecuting edict, which Theodosius might enact, (pro Templis, p. 32;) a rash joke, and a dangerous experiment. Some princes would have taken his advice.]

[Footnote 61/1: The most remarkable instance of this, at a much later period, occurs in the person of Merobaudes, a general and a poet, who flourished in the first half of the fifth century. A statue in honor of Merobaudes was placed in the Forum of Trajan, of which the inscription is still extant. Fragments of his poems have been recovered by the industry and sagacity of Niebuhr. In one passage, Merobaudes, in the genuine heathen spirit, attributes the ruin of the empire to the abolition of Paganism, and almost renews the old accusation of Atheism against Christianity. He impersonates some deity, probably Discord, who summons Bellona to take arms for the destruction of Rome; and in a strain of fierce irony recommends to her other fatal measures, to extirpate the gods of Rome:—

Roma, ipsique tremant furialia murmura reges. Jam superos terris atque hospita numina pelle: Romanos populare Deos, et nullus in aris Vestoe exoratoe fotus strue palleat ignis. Ilis instructa dolis palatia celsa subibo; Majorum mores, et pectora prisca fugabo Funditus; atque simul, nullo discrimine rerum, Spernantur fortes, nec sic reverentia justis. Attica neglecto pereat facundia Phoebo: Indignis contingat honos, et pondera rerum; Non virtus sed casus agat; tristique cupido; Pectoribus saevi demens furor aestuet aevi; Omniaque hoec sine mente Jovis, sine numine sumimo.

Merobaudes in Niebuhr's edit. of the Byzantines, p. 14—M.]

[Footnote 62: Denique pro meritis terrestribus aequa rependens

Munera, sacricolis summos impertit honores.

Dux bonus, et certare sinit cum laude suorum, Nec pago implicitos per debita culmina mundi Ire viros prohibet. Ipse magistratum tibi consulis, ipse tribunal

Contulit. Prudent. in Symmach. i. 617, &c.

Note: I have inserted some lines omitted by Gibbon—M.]

[Footnote 63: Libanius (pro Templis, p. 32) is proud that Theodosius should thus distinguish a man, who even in his presence would swear by Jupiter. Yet this presence seems to be no more than a figure of rhetoric.]

[Footnote 64: Zosimus, who styles himself Count and Ex-advocate of the Treasury, reviles, with partial and indecent bigotry, the Christian princes, and even the father of his sovereign. His work must have been privately circulated, since it escaped the invectives of the ecclesiastical historians prior to Evagrius, (l. iii. c. 40-42,) who lived towards the end of the sixth century. Note: Heyne in his Disquisitio in Zosimum Ejusque Fidem. places Zosimum towards the close of the fifth century. Zosim. Heynii, p. xvii—M.]

[Footnote 65: Yet the Pagans of Africa complained, that the times would not allow them to answer with freedom the City of God; nor does St. Augustin (v. 26) deny the charge.]

[Footnote 66: The Moors of Spain, who secretly preserved the Mahometan religion above a century, under the tyranny of the Inquisition, possessed the Koran, with the peculiar use of the Arabic tongue. See the curious and honest story of their expulsion in Geddes, (Miscellanies, vol. i. p. 1-198.)]

[Footnote 67: Paganos qui supersunt, quanquam jam nullos esse credamus, &c. Cod. Theodos. l. xvi. tit. x. leg. 22, A.D. 423. The younger Theodosius was afterwards satisfied, that his judgment had been somewhat premature. Note: The statement of Gibbon is much too strongly worded. M. Beugnot has traced the vestiges of Paganism in the West, after this period, in monuments and inscriptions with curious industry. Compare likewise note, p. 112, on the more tardy progress of Christianity in the rural districts—M.]

The ruin of the Pagan religion is described by the sophists as a dreadful and amazing prodigy, which covered the earth with darkness, and restored the ancient dominion of chaos and of night. They relate, in solemn and pathetic strains, that the temples were converted into sepulchres, and that the holy places, which had been adorned by the statues of the gods, were basely polluted by the relics of Christian martyrs. "The monks" (a race of filthy animals, to whom Eunapius is tempted to refuse the name of men) "are the authors of the new worship, which, in the place of those deities who are conceived by the understanding, has substituted the meanest and most contemptible slaves. The heads, salted and pickled, of those infamous malefactors, who for the multitude of their crimes have suffered a just and ignominious death; their bodies still marked by the impression of the lash, and the scars of those tortures which were inflicted by the sentence of the magistrate; such" (continues Eunapius) "are the gods which the earth produces in our days; such are the martyrs, the supreme arbitrators of our prayers and petitions to the Deity, whose tombs are now consecrated as the objects of the veneration of the people." [68] Without approving the malice, it is natural enough to share the surprise of the sophist, the spectator of a revolution, which raised those obscure victims of the laws of Rome to the rank of celestial and invisible protectors of the Roman empire. The grateful respect of the Christians for the martyrs of the faith, was exalted, by time and victory, into religious adoration; and the most illustrious of the saints and prophets were deservedly associated to the honors of the martyrs. One hundred and fifty years after the glorious deaths of St. Peter and St. Paul, the Vatican and the Ostian road were distinguished by the tombs, or rather by the trophies, of those spiritual heroes. [69] In the age which followed the conversion of Constantine, the emperors, the consuls, and the generals of armies, devoutly visited the sepulchres of a tentmaker and a fisherman; [70] and their venerable bones were deposited under the altars of Christ, on which the bishops of the royal city continually offered the unbloody sacrifice. [71] The new capital of the Eastern world, unable to produce any ancient and domestic trophies, was enriched by the spoils of dependent provinces. The bodies of St. Andrew, St. Luke, and St. Timothy, had reposed near three hundred years in the obscure graves, from whence they were transported, in solemn pomp, to the church of the apostles, which the magnificence of Constantine had founded on the banks of the Thracian Bosphorus. [72] About fifty years afterwards, the same banks were honored by the presence of Samuel, the judge and prophet of the people of Israel. His ashes, deposited in a golden vase, and covered with a silken veil, were delivered by the bishops into each other's hands. The relics of Samuel were received by the people with the same joy and reverence which they would have shown to the living prophet; the highways, from Palestine to the gates of Constantinople, were filled with an uninterrupted procession; and the emperor Arcadius himself, at the head of the most illustrious members of the clergy and senate, advanced to meet his extraordinary guest, who had always deserved and claimed the homage of kings. [73] The example of Rome and Constantinople confirmed the faith and discipline of the Catholic world. The honors of the saints and martyrs, after a feeble and ineffectual murmur of profane reason, [74] were universally established; and in the age of Ambrose and Jerom, something was still deemed wanting to the sanctity of a Christian church, till it had been consecrated by some portion of holy relics, which fixed and inflamed the devotion of the faithful.

[Footnote 68: See Eunapius, in the Life of the sophist Aedesius; in that of Eustathius he foretells the ruin of Paganism.]

[Footnote 69: Caius, (apud Euseb. Hist. Eccles. l. ii. c. 25,) a Roman presbyter, who lived in the time of Zephyrinus, (A.D. 202-219,) is an early witness of this superstitious practice.]

[Footnote 70: Chrysostom. Quod Christus sit Deus. Tom. i. nov. edit. No. 9. I am indebted for this quotation to Benedict the XIVth's pastoral letter on the Jubilee of the year 1759. See the curious and entertaining letters of M. Chais, tom. iii.]

[Footnote 71: Male facit ergo Romanus episcopus? qui, super mortuorum hominum, Petri & Pauli, secundum nos, ossa veneranda ... offeri Domino sacrificia, et tumulos eorum, Christi arbitratur altaria. Jerom. tom. ii. advers. Vigilant. p. 183.]

[Footnote 72: Jerom (tom. ii. p. 122) bears witness to these translations, which are neglected by the ecclesiastical historians. The passion of St. Andrew at Patrae is described in an epistle from the clergy of Achaia, which Baronius (Annal. Eccles. A.D. 60, No. 34) wishes to believe, and Tillemont is forced to reject. St. Andrew was adopted as the spiritual founder of Constantinople, (Mem. Eccles. tom. i. p. 317-323, 588-594.)]

[Footnote 73: Jerom (tom. ii. p. 122) pompously describes the translation of Samuel, which is noticed in all the chronicles of the times.]

[Footnote 74: The presbyter Vigilantius, the Protestant of his age, firmly, though ineffectually, withstood the superstition of monks, relics, saints, fasts, &c., for which Jerom compares him to the Hydra, Cerberus, the Centaurs, &c., and considers him only as the organ of the Daemon, (tom. ii. p. 120-126.) Whoever will peruse the controversy of St. Jerom and Vigilantius, and St. Augustin's account of the miracles of St. Stephen, may speedily gain some idea of the spirit of the Fathers.]

In the long period of twelve hundred years, which elapsed between the reign of Constantine and the reformation of Luther, the worship of saints and relics corrupted the pure and perfect simplicity of the Christian model: and some symptoms of degeneracy may be observed even in the first generations which adopted and cherished this pernicious innovation.

I. The satisfactory experience, that the relics of saints were more valuable than gold or precious stones, [75] stimulated the clergy to multiply the treasures of the church. Without much regard for truth or probability, they invented names for skeletons, and actions for names. The fame of the apostles, and of the holy men who had imitated their virtues, was darkened by religious fiction. To the invincible band of genuine and primitive martyrs, they added myriads of imaginary heroes, who had never existed, except in the fancy of crafty or credulous legendaries; and there is reason to suspect, that Tours might not be the only diocese in which the bones of a malefactor were adored, instead of those of a saint. [76] A superstitious practice, which tended to increase the temptations of fraud, and credulity, insensibly extinguished the light of history, and of reason, in the Christian world.

[Footnote 75: M. de Beausobre (Hist. du Manicheisme, tom. ii. p. 648) has applied a worldly sense to the pious observation of the clergy of Smyrna, who carefully preserved the relics of St. Polycarp the martyr.]

[Footnote 76: Martin of Tours (see his Life, c. 8, by Sulpicius Severus) extorted this confession from the mouth of the dead man. The error is allowed to be natural; the discovery is supposed to be miraculous. Which of the two was likely to happen most frequently?]

II. But the progress of superstition would have been much less rapid and victorious, if the faith of the people had not been assisted by the seasonable aid of visions and miracles, to ascertain the authenticity and virtue of the most suspicious relics. In the reign of the younger Theodosius, Lucian, [77] a presbyter of Jerusalem, and the ecclesiastical minister of the village of Caphargamala, about twenty miles from the city, related a very singular dream, which, to remove his doubts, had been repeated on three successive Saturdays. A venerable figure stood before him, in the silence of the night, with a long beard, a white robe, and a gold rod; announced himself by the name of Gamaliel, and revealed to the astonished presbyter, that his own corpse, with the bodies of his son Abibas, his friend Nicodemus, and the illustrious Stephen, the first martyr of the Christian faith, were secretly buried in the adjacent field. He added, with some impatience, that it was time to release himself and his companions from their obscure prison; that their appearance would be salutary to a distressed world; and that they had made choice of Lucian to inform the bishop of Jerusalem of their situation and their wishes. The doubts and difficulties which still retarded this important discovery were successively removed by new visions; and the ground was opened by the bishop, in the presence of an innumerable multitude. The coffins of Gamaliel, of his son, and of his friend, were found in regular order; but when the fourth coffin, which contained the remains of Stephen, was shown to the light, the earth trembled, and an odor, such as that of paradise, was smelt, which instantly cured the various diseases of seventy-three of the assistants. The companions of Stephen were left in their peaceful residence of Caphargamala: but the relics of the first martyr were transported, in solemn procession, to a church constructed in their honor on Mount Sion; and the minute particles of those relics, a drop of blood, [78] or the scrapings of a bone, were acknowledged, in almost every province of the Roman world, to possess a divine and miraculous virtue. The grave and learned Augustin, [79] whose understanding scarcely admits the excuse of credulity, has attested the innumerable prodigies which were performed in Africa by the relics of St. Stephen; and this marvellous narrative is inserted in the elaborate work of the City of God, which the bishop of Hippo designed as a solid and immortal proof of the truth of Christianity. Augustin solemnly declares, that he has selected those miracles only which were publicly certified by the persons who were either the objects, or the spectators, of the power of the martyr. Many prodigies were omitted, or forgotten; and Hippo had been less favorably treated than the other cities of the province. And yet the bishop enumerates above seventy miracles, of which three were resurrections from the dead, in the space of two years, and within the limits of his own diocese. [80] If we enlarge our view to all the dioceses, and all the saints, of the Christian world, it will not be easy to calculate the fables, and the errors, which issued from this inexhaustible source. But we may surely be allowed to observe, that a miracle, in that age of superstition and credulity, lost its name and its merit, since it could scarcely be considered as a deviation from the ordinary and established laws of nature.

[Footnote 77: Lucian composed in Greek his original narrative, which has been translated by Avitus, and published by Baronius, (Annal. Eccles. A.D. 415, No. 7-16.) The Benedictine editors of St. Augustin have given (at the end of the work de Civitate Dei) two several copies, with many various readings. It is the character of falsehood to be loose and inconsistent. The most incredible parts of the legend are smoothed and softened by Tillemont, (Mem. Eccles. tom. ii. p. 9, &c.)]

[Footnote 78: A phial of St. Stephen's blood was annually liquefied at Naples, till he was superseded by St. Jamarius, (Ruinart. Hist. Persecut. Vandal p. 529.)]

[Footnote 79: Augustin composed the two-and-twenty books de Civitate Dei in the space of thirteen years, A.D. 413-426. Tillemont, (Mem. Eccles. tom. xiv. p. 608, &c.) His learning is too often borrowed, and his arguments are too often his own; but the whole work claims the merit of a magnificent design, vigorously, and not unskilfully, executed.]

[Footnote 80: See Augustin de Civitat. Dei, l. xxii. c. 22, and the Appendix, which contains two books of St. Stephen's miracles, by Evodius, bishop of Uzalis. Freculphus (apud Basnage, Hist. des Juifs, tom. vii. p. 249) has preserved a Gallic or a Spanish proverb, "Whoever pretends to have read all the miracles of St. Stephen, he lies."]

III. The innumerable miracles, of which the tombs of the martyrs were the perpetual theatre, revealed to the pious believer the actual state and constitution of the invisible world; and his religious speculations appeared to be founded on the firm basis of fact and experience. Whatever might be the condition of vulgar souls, in the long interval between the dissolution and the resurrection of their bodies, it was evident that the superior spirits of the saints and martyrs did not consume that portion of their existence in silent and inglorious sleep. [81] It was evident (without presuming to determine the place of their habitation, or the nature of their felicity) that they enjoyed the lively and active consciousness of their happiness, their virtue, and their powers; and that they had already secured the possession of their eternal reward. The enlargement of their intellectual faculties surpassed the measure of the human imagination; since it was proved by experience, that they were capable of hearing and understanding the various petitions of their numerous votaries; who, in the same moment of time, but in the most distant parts of the world, invoked the name and assistance of Stephen or of Martin. [82] The confidence of their petitioners was founded on the persuasion, that the saints, who reigned with Christ, cast an eye of pity upon earth; that they were warmly interested in the prosperity of the Catholic Church; and that the individuals, who imitated the example of their faith and piety, were the peculiar and favorite objects of their most tender regard. Sometimes, indeed, their friendship might be influenced by considerations of a less exalted kind: they viewed with partial affection the places which had been consecrated by their birth, their residence, their death, their burial, or the possession of their relics. The meaner passions of pride, avarice, and revenge, may be deemed unworthy of a celestial breast; yet the saints themselves condescended to testify their grateful approbation of the liberality of their votaries; and the sharpest bolts of punishment were hurled against those impious wretches, who violated their magnificent shrines, or disbelieved their supernatural power. [83] Atrocious, indeed, must have been the guilt, and strange would have been the scepticism, of those men, if they had obstinately resisted the proofs of a divine agency, which the elements, the whole range of the animal creation, and even the subtle and invisible operations of the human mind, were compelled to obey. [84] The immediate, and almost instantaneous, effects that were supposed to follow the prayer, or the offence, satisfied the Christians of the ample measure of favor and authority which the saints enjoyed in the presence of the Supreme God; and it seemed almost superfluous to inquire whether they were continually obliged to intercede before the throne of grace; or whether they might not be permitted to exercise, according to the dictates of their benevolence and justice, the delegated powers of their subordinate ministry. The imagination, which had been raised by a painful effort to the contemplation and worship of the Universal Cause, eagerly embraced such inferior objects of adoration as were more proportioned to its gross conceptions and imperfect faculties. The sublime and simple theology of the primitive Christians was gradually corrupted; and the Monarchy of heaven, already clouded by metaphysical subtleties, was degraded by the introduction of a popular mythology, which tended to restore the reign of polytheism. [85]

[Footnote 81: Burnet (de Statu Mortuorum, p. 56-84) collects the opinions of the Fathers, as far as they assert the sleep, or repose, of human souls till the day of judgment. He afterwards exposes (p. 91, &c.) the inconveniences which must arise, if they possessed a more active and sensible existence.]

[Footnote 82: Vigilantius placed the souls of the prophets and martyrs, either in the bosom of Abraham, (in loco refrigerii,) or else under the altar of God. Nec posse suis tumulis et ubi voluerunt adesse praesentes. But Jerom (tom. ii. p. 122) sternly refutes this blasphemy. Tu Deo leges pones? Tu apostolis vincula injicies, ut usque ad diem judicii teneantur custodia, nec sint cum Domino suo; de quibus scriptum est, Sequuntur Agnum quocunque vadit. Si Agnus ubique, ergo, et hi, qui cum Agno sunt, ubique esse credendi sunt. Et cum diabolus et daemones tote vagentur in orbe, &c.]

[Footnote 83: Fleury Discours sur l'Hist. Ecclesiastique, iii p. 80.]

[Footnote 84: At Minorca, the relics of St. Stephen converted, in eight days, 540 Jews; with the help, indeed, of some wholesome severities, such as burning the synagogue, driving the obstinate infidels to starve among the rocks, &c. See the original letter of Severus, bishop of Minorca (ad calcem St. Augustin. de Civ. Dei,) and the judicious remarks of Basnage, (tom. viii. p. 245-251.)]

[Footnote 85: Mr. Hume (Essays, vol. ii. p. 434) observes, like a philosopher, the natural flux and reflux of polytheism and theism.]

IV. As the objects of religion were gradually reduced to the standard of the imagination, the rites and ceremonies were introduced that seemed most powerfully to affect the senses of the vulgar. If, in the beginning of the fifth century, [86] Tertullian, or Lactantius, [87] had been suddenly raised from the dead, to assist at the festival of some popular saint, or martyr, [88] they would have gazed with astonishment, and indignation, on the profane spectacle, which had succeeded to the pure and spiritual worship of a Christian congregation. As soon as the doors of the church were thrown open, they must have been offended by the smoke of incense, the perfume of flowers, and the glare of lamps and tapers, which diffused, at noonday, a gaudy, superfluous, and, in their opinion, a sacrilegious light. If they approached the balustrade of the altar, they made their way through the prostrate crowd, consisting, for the most part, of strangers and pilgrims, who resorted to the city on the vigil of the feast; and who already felt the strong intoxication of fanaticism, and, perhaps, of wine. Their devout kisses were imprinted on the walls and pavement of the sacred edifice; and their fervent prayers were directed, whatever might be the language of their church, to the bones, the blood, or the ashes of the saint, which were usually concealed, by a linen or silken veil, from the eyes of the vulgar. The Christians frequented the tombs of the martyrs, in the hope of obtaining, from their powerful intercession, every sort of spiritual, but more especially of temporal, blessings. They implored the preservation of their health, or the cure of their infirmities; the fruitfulness of their barren wives, or the safety and happiness of their children. Whenever they undertook any distant or dangerous journey, they requested, that the holy martyrs would be their guides and protectors on the road; and if they returned without having experienced any misfortune, they again hastened to the tombs of the martyrs, to celebrate, with grateful thanksgivings, their obligations to the memory and relics of those heavenly patrons. The walls were hung round with symbols of the favors which they had received; eyes, and hands, and feet, of gold and silver: and edifying pictures, which could not long escape the abuse of indiscreet or idolatrous devotion, represented the image, the attributes, and the miracles of the tutelar saint. The same uniform original spirit of superstition might suggest, in the most distant ages and countries, the same methods of deceiving the credulity, and of affecting the senses of mankind: [89] but it must ingenuously be confessed, that the ministers of the Catholic church imitated the profane model, which they were impatient to destroy. The most respectable bishops had persuaded themselves that the ignorant rustics would more cheerfully renounce the superstitions of Paganism, if they found some resemblance, some compensation, in the bosom of Christianity. The religion of Constantine achieved, in less than a century, the final conquest of the Roman empire: but the victors themselves were insensibly subdued by the arts of their vanquished rivals. [90] [90/1]

[Footnote 86: D'Aubigne (see his own Memoires, p. 156-160) frankly offered, with the consent of the Huguenot ministers, to allow the first 400 years as the rule of faith. The Cardinal du Perron haggled for forty years more, which were indiscreetly given. Yet neither party would have found their account in this foolish bargain.]

[Footnote 87: The worship practised and inculcated by Tertullian, Lactantius Arnobius, &c., is so extremely pure and spiritual, that their declamations against the Pagan sometimes glance against the Jewish, ceremonies.]

[Footnote 88: Faustus the Manichaean accuses the Catholics of idolatry. Vertitis idola in martyres.... quos votis similibus colitis. M. de Beausobre, (Hist. Critique du Manicheisme, tom. ii. p. 629-700,) a Protestant, but a philosopher, has represented, with candor and learning, the introduction of Christian idolatry in the fourth and fifth centuries.]

[Footnote 89: The resemblance of superstition, which could not be imitated, might be traced from Japan to Mexico. Warburton has seized this idea, which he distorts, by rendering it too general and absolute, (Divine Legation, vol. iv. p. 126, &c.)]

[Footnote 90: The imitation of Paganism is the subject of Dr. Middleton's agreeable letter from Rome. Warburton's animadversions obliged him to connect (vol. iii. p. 120-132,) the history of the two religions, and to prove the antiquity of the Christian copy.]

[Footnote 90/1: But there was always this important difference between Christian and heathen Polytheism. In Paganism this was the whole religion; in the darkest ages of Christianity, some, however *obscure and vague, Christian notions of future retribution, of the life after death, lurked at the bottom, and operated, to a certain extent, on the thoughts and feelings, sometimes on the actions—M.]*

CHAPTER XXIX

DIVISION OF ROMAN EMPIRE BETWEEN SONS OF THEODOSIUS

PART I

FINAL DIVISION OF THE ROMAN EMPIRE BETWEEN THE SONS OF THEODOSIUS—REIGN OF ARCADIUS AND HONORIUS—ADMINISTRATION OF RUFINUS AND STILCHO—REVOLT AND DEFEAT OF GILDO IN AFRICA

The genius of Rome expired with Theodosius; the last of the successors of Augustus and Constantine, who appeared in the field at the head of their armies, and whose authority was universally acknowledged throughout the whole extent of the empire. The memory of his virtues still continued, however, to protect the feeble and inexperienced youth of his two sons. After the death of their father, Arcadius and Honorius were saluted, by the unanimous consent of mankind, as the lawful emperors of the East, and of the West; and the oath of fidelity was eagerly taken by every order of the state; the senates of old and new Rome, the clergy, the magistrates, the soldiers, and the people. Arcadius, who was then about eighteen years of age, was born in Spain, in the humble habitation of a private family. But he received a princely education in the palace of Constantinople; and his inglorious life was spent in that peaceful and splendid seat of royalty, from whence he appeared to reign over the provinces of Thrace, Asia Minor, Syria, and Egypt, from the Lower Danube to the confines of Persia and Aethiopia. His younger brother Honorius, assumed, in the eleventh year of his age, the nominal government of Italy, Africa, Gaul, Spain, and Britain; and the troops, which guarded the frontiers of his kingdom, were opposed, on one side, to the Caledonians, and on the other, to the Moors. The great and martial praefecture of Illyricum was divided between the two princes: the defence and possession of the provinces of Noricum, Pannonia, and Dalmatia still belonged to the Western empire; but the two large dioceses of Dacia and Macedonia, which Gratian had intrusted to the valor of Theodosius, were forever united to the empire of the East. The boundary in Europe was not very different from the line which now separates the Germans and the Turks; and the respective advantages of territory, riches, populousness, and military strength, were fairly balanced and compensated, in this final and permanent division of the Roman empire. The hereditary sceptre of the sons of Theodosius appeared to be the gift of nature, and of their father; the generals and ministers had been accustomed to adore the majesty of the royal infants; and the army and people were not admonished of their rights, and of their power, by the dangerous example of a recent election. The gradual discovery of the weakness of Arcadius and Honorius, and the repeated calamities of their reign, were not sufficient to obliterate the deep and early impressions of loyalty. The subjects of Rome, who still reverenced the persons, or rather the names, of their sovereigns, beheld, with equal abhorrence, the rebels who opposed, and the ministers who abused, the authority of the throne.

Theodosius had tarnished the glory of his reign by the elevation of Rufinus; an odious favorite, who, in an age of civil and religious faction, has deserved, from every party, the imputation of every crime. The strong impulse of ambition and avarice [1] had urged Rufinus to abandon his native country, an obscure corner of Gaul, [2] to advance his fortune in the capital of the East: the talent of bold and ready elocution, [3] qualified him to succeed in the lucrative profession of the law; and his success in that profession was a regular step to the most honorable and important employments of the state. He was raised, by just degrees, to the station of master of the offices. In the exercise of his various functions, so essentially connected with the whole system of civil government, he acquired the confidence of a monarch, who soon discovered his diligence and capacity in business, and who long remained ignorant of the pride, the malice, and the covetousness of his disposition. These vices were concealed beneath the mask of profound dissimulation; [4] his passions were subservient only to the passions of his master; yet in the horrid massacre of Thessalonica, the cruel Rufinus inflamed the fury, without imitating the repentance, of Theodosius. The minister, who viewed with proud indifference the rest of mankind, never forgave the appearance of an injury; and his personal enemies had forfeited, in his opinion, the merit of all public services. Promotus, the master-general of the infantry, had saved the empire from the invasion of the Ostrogoths; but he indignantly supported the preeminence of a rival, whose character and profession he despised; and in the midst of a public council, the impatient soldier was provoked to chastise with a blow the indecent pride of the favorite. This act of violence was represented to the emperor as an insult, which it was incumbent on his dignity to resent. The disgrace and exile of Promotus were signified by a peremptory order, to repair, without delay, to a military station on the banks of the Danube; and the death of that general (though he was slain in a skirmish with the Barbarians) was imputed to the perfidious arts of Rufinus. [5] The sacrifice of a hero gratified his revenge; the honors of the consulship elated his vanity; but his power was still imperfect and precarious, as long as the important posts of praefect of the East, and of praefect of Constantinople, were filled by Tatian, [6] and his son Proculus; whose united authority balanced, for some time, the ambition and favor of the master of the offices. The two praefects were accused of rapine and corruption in the administration of the laws and finances. For the trial of these illustrious offenders, the emperor constituted a special commission: several judges were named to share the guilt and reproach of injustice; but the right of pronouncing sentence was reserved to the president alone, and that president was Rufinus himself. The father, stripped of the praefecture of the East, was thrown into a dungeon; but the son, conscious that few ministers can be found innocent, where an enemy is their judge, had secretly escaped; and Rufinus must have been satisfied with the least obnoxious victim, if despotism had not condescended to employ the basest and most ungenerous artifice. The prosecution was conducted with an appearance of equity and moderation, which flattered Tatian with the hope of a favorable event: his confidence was fortified by the solemn assurances, and perfidious oaths, of the president, who presumed to interpose the sacred name of Theodosius himself; and the unhappy father was at last persuaded to recall, by a private letter, the fugitive Proculus. He was instantly seized, examined, condemned, and beheaded, in one of the suburbs of Constantinople, with a precipitation which disappointed the clemency of the emperor. Without respecting the misfortunes of a consular senator, the cruel judges of Tatian compelled him to behold the execution of his son: the fatal cord was fastened round his own neck; but in the moment when he expected. and perhaps desired, the relief of a speedy death, he was permitted to consume the miserable remnant of his old age in poverty and exile. [7] The punishment of the two praefects might, perhaps, be excused by the exceptionable parts of their own conduct; the enmity of Rufinus might be palliated by the jealous and unsociable nature of ambition. But he indulged a spirit of revenge equally repugnant to prudence and to justice, when he degraded their native country of Lycia from the rank of Roman provinces; stigmatized a guiltless people with a mark of ignominy; and declared, that the countrymen of Tatian and Proculus should forever remain incapable of holding any employment of honor or advantage under the Imperial government. [8] The new praefect of the East (for Rufinus instantly succeeded to the vacant honors of his adversary) was not diverted, however, by the most criminal pursuits, from the performance of the religious duties, which in that age were considered as the most essential to salvation. In the suburb of Chalcedon, surnamed the Oak, he had built a magnificent villa; to which he devoutly added a stately church, consecrated to the apostles

St. Peter and St. Paul, and continually sanctified by the prayers and penance of a regular society of monks. A numerous, and almost general, synod of the bishops of the Eastern empire, was summoned to celebrate, at the same time, the dedication of the church, and the baptism of the founder. This double ceremony was performed with extraordinary pomp; and when Rufinus was purified, in the holy font, from all the sins that he had hitherto committed, a venerable hermit of Egypt rashly proposed himself as the sponsor of a proud and ambitious statesman. [9]

[Footnote 1: Alecto, envious of the public felicity, convenes an infernal synod Megaera recommends her pupil Rufinus, and excites him to deeds of mischief, &c. But there is as much difference between Claudian's fury and that of Virgil, as between the characters of Turnus and Rufinus.]

[Footnote 2: It is evident, (Tillemont, Hist. des Emp. tom. v. p. 770,) though De Marca is ashamed of his countryman, that Rufinus was born at Elusa, the metropolis of Novempopulania, now a small village of Gassony, (D'Anville, Notice de l'Ancienne Gaule, p. 289.)]

[Footnote 3: Philostorgius, l. xi c. 3, with Godefroy's Dissert. p. 440.]

[Footnote 4: A passage of Suidas is expressive of his profound dissimulation.]

[Footnote 5: Zosimus, l. iv. p. 272, 273.]

[Footnote 6: Zosimus, who describes the fall of Tatian and his son, (l. iv. p. 273, 274,) asserts their innocence; and even his testimony may outweigh the charges of their enemies, (Cod. Theod. tom. iv. p. 489,) who accuse them of oppressing the Curiae. The connection of Tatian with the Arians, while he was praefect of Egypt, (A.D. 373,) inclines Tillemont to believe that he was guilty of every crime, (Hist. des Emp. tom. v. p. 360. Mem. Eccles. tom vi. p. 589.)]

[Footnote 7:—Juvenum rorantia colla Ante patrum vultus stricta cecidere securi.

Ibat grandaevus nato moriente superstes Post trabeas exsul. —In Rufin. i. 248.

The facts of Zosimus explain the allusions of Claudian; but his classic interpreters were ignorant of the fourth century. The fatal cord, I found, with the help of Tillemont, in a sermon of St. Asterius of Amasea.]

[Footnote 8: This odious law is recited and repealed by Arcadius, (A.D. 296,) on the Theodosian Code, l. ix. tit. xxxviii. leg. 9. The sense as it is explained by Claudian, (in Rufin. i. 234,) and Godefroy, (tom. iii. p. 279,) is perfectly clear.

—Exscindere cives Funditus; et nomen gentis delere laborat.

The scruples of Pagi and Tillemont can arise only from their zeal for the glory of Theodosius.]

[Footnote 9: Ammonius.... Rufinum propriis manibus suscepit sacro fonte mundatum. See Rosweyde's Vitae Patrum, p. 947. Sozomen (l. viii. c. 17) mentions the church and monastery; and Tillemont (Mem. Eccles. tom. ix. p. 593) records this synod, in which St. Gregory of Nyssa performed a conspicuous part.]

The character of Theodosius imposed on his minister the task of hypocrisy, which disguised, and sometimes restrained, the abuse of power; and Rufinus was apprehensive of disturbing the indolent slumber of a prince still capable of exerting the abilities and the virtue, which had raised him to the throne. [10] But the absence, and, soon afterwards, the death, of the emperor, confirmed the absolute authority of Rufinus over the person and dominions of Arcadius; a feeble youth, whom the imperious praefect considered as his pupil, rather than his sovereign. Regardless of the public opinion, he indulged his passions without remorse, and without resistance; and his malignant and rapacious spirit rejected every passion that might have contributed to his own glory, or the happiness of the people. His avarice, [11] which seems to have prevailed, in his corrupt mind, over every other sentiment, attracted the wealth of the East, by the various arts of partial and general extortion; oppressive taxes, scandalous bribery, immoderate fines, unjust confiscations, forced or fictitious testaments, by which the tyrant despoiled of their lawful inheritance the children of strangers, or enemies; and the public sale of justice, as well as of favor, which he instituted in the palace of Constantinople. The ambitious candidate eagerly solicited, at the expense of the fairest part of his patrimony, the honors and emoluments of some provincial government; the lives and fortunes of the unhappy people were abandoned to the most liberal purchaser; and the public discontent was sometimes appeased by the sacrifice of an unpopular criminal, whose punishment was profitable only to the praefect of the East, his accomplice and his judge. If avarice were not the blindest of the human passions, the motives of Rufinus might excite our curiosity; and we might be tempted to inquire with what view he violated every principle of humanity and justice, to accumulate those immense treasures, which he could not spend without folly, nor possess without danger. Perhaps he vainly imagined, that he labored for the interest of an only daughter, on whom he intended to bestow his royal pupil, and the august rank of Empress of the East. Perhaps he deceived himself by the opinion, that his avarice was the instrument of his ambition. He aspired to place his fortune on a secure and independent basis, which should no longer depend on the caprice of the young emperor; yet he neglected to conciliate the hearts of the soldiers and people, by the liberal distribution of those riches, which he had acquired with so much toil, and with so much guilt. The extreme parsimony of Rufinus left him only the reproach and envy of ill-gotten wealth; his dependants served him without attachment; the universal hatred of mankind was repressed only by the influence of servile fear. The fate of Lucian proclaimed to the East, that the praefect, whose industry was much abated in the despatch of ordinary business, was active and indefatigable in the pursuit of revenge. Lucian, the son of the praefect Florentius, the oppressor of Gaul, and the enemy of Julian, had employed a considerable part of his inheritance, the fruit of rapine and corruption, to purchase the friendship of Rufinus, and the high office of Count of the East. But the new magistrate imprudently departed from the maxims of the court, and of the times; disgraced his benefactor by the contrast of a virtuous and temperate administration; and presumed to refuse an act of injustice, which might have tended to the profit of the emperor's uncle. Arcadius was easily persuaded to resent the supposed insult; and the praefect of the East resolved to execute in person the cruel vengeance, which he meditated against this ungrateful delegate of his power. He performed with incessant speed the journey of seven or eight hundred miles, from Constantinople to Antioch, entered the capital of Syria at the dead of night, and spread universal consternation among a people ignorant of his design, but not ignorant of his character. The Count of the fifteen provinces of the East was dragged, like the vilest malefactor, before the arbitrary tribunal of Rufinus. Notwithstanding the clearest evidence of his integrity, which was not impeached even by the voice of an accuser, Lucian was condemned, almost with out a trial, to suffer a cruel and ignominious punishment. The ministers of the tyrant, by the orders, and in the presence, of their master, beat him on the neck with leather thongs armed at the extremities with lead; and when he fainted under the violence of the pain, he was removed in a close litter, to conceal his dying agonies from the eyes of the indignant city. No sooner had Rufinus perpetrated this inhuman act, the sole object of his expedition, than he returned, amidst the deep and silent curses of a trembling people, from Antioch to Constantinople; and his diligence was accelerated by the hope of accomplishing, without delay, the nuptials of his daughter with the emperor of the East. [12]

[Footnote 10: Montesquieu (Esprit des Loix, l. xii. c. 12) praises one of the laws of Theodosius addressed to the praefect Rufinus, (l. ix. tit. iv. leg. unic.,) to discourage the prosecution of treasonable, or sacrilegious, words. A tyrannical statute always proves the existence of tyranny; but a laudable edict may only contain the specious professions, or ineffectual wishes, of the prince, or his ministers. This, I am afraid, is a just, though mortifying, canon of criticism.]

[Footnote 11:
—*fluctibus auri Expleri sitis ista nequit—Congestae cumulantur opes; orbisque ruinas Accipit una domus.*

This character (Claudian, in. Rufin. i. 184-220) is confirmed by Jerom, a disinterested witness, (dedecus insatiabilis avaritiae, tom. i. ad Heliodor. p. 26,) by Zosimus, (l. v. p. 286,) and by Suidas, who copied the history of Eunapius.]

[Footnote 12:
—*Caetera segnis; Ad facinus velox; penitus regione remotas Impiger ire vias.*

This allusion of Claudian (in Rufin. i. 241) is again explained by the circumstantial narrative of Zosimus, (l. v. p. 288, 289.)]

But Rufinus soon experienced, that a prudent minister should constantly secure his royal captive by the strong, though invisible chain of habit; and that the merit, and much more easily the favor, of the absent, are obliterated in a short time from the mind of a weak and capricious sovereign. While the praefect satiated his revenge at Antioch, a secret conspiracy of the favorite eunuchs, directed by the great chamberlain Eutropius, undermined his power in the palace of Constantinople. They discovered that Arcadius was not inclined to love the daughter of Rufinus, who had been chosen, without his consent, for his bride; and they contrived to substitute in her place the fair Eudoxia, the daughter of Bauto, [13] a general of the Franks in the service of Rome; and who was educated, since the death of her father, in the family of the sons of Promotus. The young emperor, whose chastity had been strictly guarded by the pious care of his tutor Arsenius, [14] eagerly listened to the artful and flattering descriptions of the charms of Eudoxia: he gazed with impatient ardor on her picture, and he understood the necessity of concealing his amorous designs from the knowledge of a minister who was so deeply interested to oppose the consummation of his happiness. Soon after the return of Rufinus, the approaching ceremony of the royal nuptials was announced to the people of Constantinople, who prepared to celebrate, with false and hollow acclamations, the fortune of his daughter. A splendid train of eunuchs and officers issued, in hymeneal pomp, from the gates of the palace; bearing aloft the diadem, the robes, and the inestimable ornaments, of the future empress. The solemn procession passed through the streets of the city, which were adorned with garlands, and filled with spectators; but when it reached the house of the sons of Promotus, the principal eunuch respectfully entered the mansion, invested the fair Eudoxia with the Imperial robes, and conducted her in triumph to the palace and bed of Arcadius. [15] The secrecy and success with which this conspiracy against Rufinus had been conducted, imprinted a mark of indelible ridicule on the character of a minister, who had suffered himself to be deceived, in a post where the arts of deceit and dissimulation constitute the most distinguished merit. He considered, with a mixture of indignation and fear, the victory of an aspiring eunuch, who had secretly captivated the favor of his sovereign; and the disgrace of his daughter, whose interest was inseparably connected with his own, wounded the tenderness, or, at least, the pride of Rufinus. At the moment when he flattered himself that he should become the father of a line of kings, a foreign maid, who had been educated in the house of his implacable enemies, was introduced into the

Imperial bed; and Eudoxia soon displayed a superiority of sense and spirit, to improve the ascendant which her beauty must acquire over the mind of a fond and youthful husband. The emperor would soon be instructed to hate, to fear, and to destroy the powerful subject, whom he had injured; and the consciousness of guilt deprived Rufinus of every hope, either of safety or comfort, in the retirement of a private life. But he still possessed the most effectual means of defending his dignity, and perhaps of oppressing his enemies. The praefect still exercised an uncontrolled authority over the civil and military government of the East; and his treasures, if he could resolve to use them, might be employed to procure proper instruments for the execution of the blackest designs, that pride, ambition, and revenge could suggest to a desperate statesman. The character of Rufinus seemed to justify the accusations that he conspired against the person of his sovereign, to seat himself on the vacant throne; and that he had secretly invited the Huns and the Goths to invade the provinces of the empire, and to increase the public confusion. The subtle praefect, whose life had been spent in the intrigues of the palace, opposed, with equal arms, the artful measures of the eunuch Eutropius; but the timid soul of Rufinus was astonished by the hostile approach of a more formidable rival, of the great Stilicho, the general, or rather the master, of the empire of the West. [16]

[Footnote 13: Zosimus (l. iv. p. 243) praises the valor, prudence, and integrity of Bauto the Frank. See Tillemont, Hist. des Empereurs, tom. v. p. 771.]

[Footnote 14: Arsenius escaped from the palace of Constantinople, and passed fifty-five years in rigid penance in the monasteries of Egypt. See Tillemont, Mem. Eccles. tom. xiv. p. 676-702; and Fleury, Hist Eccles. tom. v. p. 1, &c.; but the latter, for want of authentic materials, has given too much credit to the legend of Metaphrastes.]

[Footnote 15: This story (Zosimus, l. v. p. 290) proves that the hymeneal rites of antiquity were still practised, without idolatry, by the Christians of the East; and the bride was forcibly conducted from the house of her parents to that of her husband. Our form of marriage requires, with less delicacy, the express and public consent of a virgin.]

[Footnote 16: Zosimus, (l. v. p. 290,) Orosius, (l. vii. c. 37,) and the Chronicle of Marcellinus. Claudian (in Rufin. ii. 7-100) paints, in lively colors, the distress and guilt of the praefect.]

The celestial gift, which Achilles obtained, and Alexander envied, of a poet worthy to celebrate the actions of heroes has been enjoyed by Stilicho, in a much higher degree than might have been expected from the declining state of genius, and of art. The muse of Claudian, [17] devoted to his service, was always prepared to stigmatize his adversaries, Rufinus, or Eutropius, with eternal infamy; or to paint, in the most splendid colors, the victories and virtues of a powerful benefactor. In the review of a period indifferently supplied with authentic materials, we cannot refuse to illustrate the annals of Honorius, from the invectives, or the panegyrics, of a contemporary writer; but as Claudian appears to have indulged the most ample privilege of a poet and a courtier, some criticism will be requisite to translate the language of fiction or exaggeration, into the truth and simplicity of historic prose. His silence concerning the family of Stilicho may be admitted as a proof, that his patron was neither able, nor desirous, to boast of a long series of illustrious progenitors; and the slight mention of his father, an officer of Barbarian cavalry in the service of Valens, seems to countenance the assertion, that the general, who so long commanded the armies of Rome, was descended from the savage and perfidious race of the Vandals. [18] If Stilicho had not possessed the external advantages of strength and stature, the most flattering bard, in the presence of so many thousand spectators, would have hesitated to affirm, that he surpassed the measure of the demi-gods of antiquity; and that whenever he moved, with lofty steps, through the streets of the capital, the astonished crowd made room for the stranger, who displayed, in a private condition, the awful majesty of a hero. From his earliest youth he embraced the profession of arms; his prudence and valor were soon distinguished in the field; the horsemen and archers of the East admired his superior dexterity; and in each degree of his military promotions, the public judgment always prevented and approved the choice of the sovereign. He was named, by Theodosius, to ratify a solemn treaty with the monarch of Persia; he supported, during that important embassy, the dignity of the Roman name; and after he return to Constantinople, his merit was rewarded by an intimate and honorable alliance with the Imperial family. Theodosius had been prompted, by a pious motive of fraternal affection, to adopt, for his own, the daughter of his brother Honorius; the beauty and accomplishments of Serena [19] were universally admired by the obsequious court; and Stilicho obtained the preference over a crowd of rivals, who ambitiously disputed the hand of the princess, and the favor of her adopted father. [20] The assurance that the husband of Serena would be faithful to the throne, which he was permitted to approach, engaged the emperor to exalt the fortunes, and to employ the abilities, of the sagacious and intrepid Stilicho. He rose, through the successive steps of master of the horse, and count of the domestics, to the supreme rank of master-general of all the cavalry and infantry of the Roman, or at least of the Western, empire; [21] and his enemies confessed, that he invariably disdained to barter for gold the rewards of merit, or to defraud the soldiers of the pay and gratifications which they deserved or claimed, from the liberality of the state. [22] The valor and conduct which he afterwards displayed, in the defence of Italy, against the arms of Alaric and Radagaisus, may justify the fame of his early achievements and in an age less attentive to the laws of honor, or of pride, the Roman generals might yield the preeminence of rank, to the ascendant of superior genius. [23] He lamented, and revenged, the murder of Promotus, his rival and his friend; and the massacre of many thousands of the flying Bastarnae is represented by the poet as a bloody sacrifice, which the Roman Achilles offered to the manes of another Patroclus. The virtues and victories of Stilicho deserved the hatred of Rufinus: and the arts of calumny might have been successful if the tender and vigilant Serena had not protected her husband against his domestic foes, whilst he vanquished in the field the enemies of the empire. [24] Theodosius continued to support an unworthy minister, to whose diligence he delegated the government of the palace, and of the East; but when he marched against the tyrant Eugenius, he associated his faithful general to the labors and glories of the civil war; and in the last moments of his life, the dying monarch recommended to Stilicho the care of his sons, and of the republic. [25] The ambition and the abilities of Stilicho were not unequal to the important trust; and he claimed the guardianship of the two empires, during the minority of Arcadius and Honorius. [26] The first measure of his administration, or rather of his reign, displayed to the nations the vigor and activity of a spirit worthy to command. He passed the Alps in the depth of winter; descended the stream of the Rhine, from the fortress of Basil to the marshes of Batavia; reviewed the state of the garrisons; repressed the enterprises of the Germans; and, after establishing along the banks a firm and honorable peace, returned, with incredible speed, to the palace of Milan. [27] The person and court of Honorius were subject to the master-general of the West; and the armies and provinces of Europe obeyed, without hesitation, a regular authority, which was exercised in the name of their young sovereign. Two rivals only remained to dispute the claims, and to provoke the vengeance, of Stilicho. Within the limits of Africa, Gildo, the Moor, maintained a proud and dangerous independence; and the minister of Constantinople asserted his equal reign over the emperor, and the empire, of the East.

[Footnote 17: Stilicho, directly or indirectly, is the perpetual theme of Claudian. The youth and private life of the hero are vaguely expressed in the poem on his first consulship, 35-140.]

[Footnote 18: Vandalorum, imbellis, avarae, perfidae, et dolosae, gentis, genere editus. Orosius, l. vii. c. 38. Jerom (tom. i. ad Gerontiam, p. 93) call him a Semi-Barbarian.]

[Footnote 19: Claudian, in an imperfect poem, has drawn a fair, perhaps a flattering, portrait of Serena. That favorite niece of Theodosius was born, as well as here sister Thermantia, in Spain; from whence, in their earliest youth, they were honorably conducted to the palace of Constantinople.]

[Footnote 20: Some doubt may be entertained, whether this adoption was legal or only metaphorical, (see Ducange, Fam. Byzant. p. 75.) An old inscription gives Stilicho the singular title of Pro-gener Divi Theodosius]

[Footnote 21: Claudian (Laus Serenae, 190, 193) expresses, in poetic language "the dilectus equorum," and the "gemino mox idem culmine duxit agmina." The inscription adds, "count of the domestics," an important command, which Stilicho, in the height of his grandeur, might prudently retain.]

[Footnote 22: The beautiful lines of Claudian (in i. Cons. Stilich. ii. 113) displays his genius; but the integrity of Stilicho (in the military administration) is much more firmly established by the unwilling evidence of Zosimus, (l. v. p. 345.)]

[Footnote 23:
Si bellica moles Ingrueret, quamvis annis et jure minori,
Cedere grandaevos equitum peditumque magistros
Adspiceres. Claudian, Laus Seren. p. 196, &c.
A modern general would deem their submission either heroic patriotism or abject servility.]

[Footnote 24: Compare the poem on the first consulship (i. 95-115) with the Laus Serenoe (227-237, where it unfortunately breaks off.) We may perceive the deep, inveterate malice of Rufinus.]

[Footnote 25:—Quem fratribus ipse Discedens, clypeum defensoremque dedisti. Yet the nomination (iv. Cons. Hon. 432) was private, (iii. Cons. Hon. 142,) cunctos discedere... jubet; and may therefore be suspected. Zosimus and Suidas apply to Stilicho and Rufinus the same equal title of guardians, or procurators.]

[Footnote 26: The Roman law distinguishes two sorts of minority, which expired at the age of fourteen, and of twenty-five. The one was subject to the tutor, or guardian, of the person; the other, to the curator, or trustee, of the estate, (Heineccius, Antiquitat. Rom. ad Jurisprudent. pertinent. l. i. tit. xxii. xxiii. p. 218-232.) But these legal ideas were never accurately transferred into the constitution of an elective monarchy.]

[Footnote 27: See Claudian, (i. Cons. Stilich. i. 188-242,) but he must allow more than fifteen days for the journey and return between Milan and Leyden.]

PART II

The impartiality which Stilicho affected, as the common guardian of the royal brothers, engaged him to regulate the equal division of the arms, the jewels, and the magnificent wardrobe and furniture of the deceased emperor. [28] But the most important object of the inheritance consisted of the numerous legions, cohorts, and squadrons, of Romans, or Barbarians, whom the event of the civil war had united under the standard of Theodosius. The various multitudes of Europe and Asia, exasperated by recent animosities, were overawed by the authority of a single man; and the rigid discipline of Stilicho protected the lands of the citizens from the rapine of the licentious soldier. [29] Anxious, however, and impatient, to relieve Italy from the presence of this formidable host, which could be useful only on the frontiers of the empire, he listened to the just requisition of the minister of Arcadius, declared his intention of reconducting in person the troops of the East, and dexterously employed the rumor of a Gothic tumult to conceal his private designs of ambition and revenge. [30] The guilty soul of Rufinus was alarmed by the approach of a warrior and a rival, whose enmity he deserved; he computed, with increasing terror, the narrow space of his life and greatness; and, as the last hope of safety, he interposed the authority of the emperor Arcadius. Stilicho, who appears to have directed his march along the sea-coast of the Adriatic, was not far distant from the city of Thessalonica, when he received a peremptory message, to recall the troops of the East, and to declare, that his nearer approach would be considered, by the Byzantine court, as an act of hostility. The prompt and unexpected obedience of the general of the West, convinced the vulgar of his loyalty and moderation; and, as he had already engaged the affection of the Eastern troops, he recommended to their zeal the execution of his bloody design, which might be accomplished in his absence, with less danger, perhaps, and with less reproach. Stilicho left the command of the troops of the East to Gainas, the Goth, on whose fidelity he firmly relied, with an assurance, at least, that the hardy Barbarians would never be diverted from his purpose by any consideration of fear or remorse. The soldiers were easily persuaded to punish the enemy of Stilicho and of Rome; and such was the general hatred which Rufinus had excited, that the fatal secret, communicated to thousands, was faithfully preserved during the long march from Thessalonica to the gates of Constantinople. As soon as they had resolved his death, they condescended to flatter his pride; the ambitious praefect was seduced to believe, that those powerful auxiliaries might be tempted to place the diadem on his head; and the treasures which he distributed, with a tardy and reluctant hand, were accepted by the indignant multitude as an insult, rather than as a gift. At the distance of a mile from the capital, in the field of Mars, before the palace of Hebdomon, the troops halted: and the emperor, as well as his minister, advanced, according to ancient custom, respectfully to salute the power which supported their throne. As Rufinus passed along the ranks, and disguised, with studied courtesy, his innate haughtiness, the wings insensibly wheeled from the right and left, and enclosed the devoted victim within the circle of their arms. Before he could reflect on the danger of his situation, Gainas gave the signal of death; a daring and forward soldier plunged his sword into the breast of the guilty praefect, and Rufinus fell, groaned, and expired, at the feet of the affrighted emperor. If the agonies of a moment could expiate the crimes of a whole life, or if the outrages inflicted on a breathless corpse could be the object of pity, our humanity might perhaps be affected by the horrid circumstances which accompanied the murder of Rufinus. His mangled body was abandoned to the brutal fury of the populace of either sex, who hastened in crowds, from every quarter of the city, to trample on the remains of the haughty minister, at whose frown they had so lately trembled. His right hand was cut off, and carried through the streets of Constantinople, in cruel mockery, to extort contributions for the avaricious tyrant, whose head was publicly exposed, borne aloft on the point of a long lance. [31] According to the savage maxims of the Greek republics, his innocent family would have shared the punishment of his crimes. The wife and daughter of Rufinus were indebted for their safety to the influence of religion. Her sanctuary protected them from the raging madness of the people; and they were permitted to spend the remainder of their lives in the exercise of Christian devotions, in the peaceful retirement of Jerusalem. [32]

[Footnote 28: l. Cons. Stilich. ii. 88-94. Not only the robes and diadems of the deceased emperor, but even the helmets, sword-hilts, belts, rasses, &c., were enriched with pearls, emeralds, and diamonds.]

[Footnote 29:—Tantoque remoto Principe, mutatas orbis non sensit habenas. This high commendation (i. Cons. Stil. i. 149) may be justified by the fears of the dying emperor, (de Bell. Gildon. 292-301;) and the peace and good order which were enjoyed after his death, (i. Cons. Stil i. 150-168.)]

[Footnote 30: Stilicho's march, and the death of Rufinus, are described by Claudian, (in Rufin. l. ii. 101-453, Zosimus, l. v. p. 296, 297,) Sozomen (l. viii. c. 1,) Socrates, l. vi. c. 1,) Philostorgius, (l. xi c. 3, with Godefory, p. 441,) and the Chronicle of Marcellinus.]

[Footnote 31: The dissection of Rufinus, which Claudian performs with the savage coolness of an anatomist, (in Rufin. ii. 405-415,) is likewise specified by Zosimus and Jerom, (tom. i. p. 26.)]

[Footnote 32: The Pagan Zosimus mentions their sanctuary and pilgrimage. The sister of Rufinus, Sylvania, who passed her life at Jerusalem, is famous in monastic history. 1. The studious virgin had diligently, and even repeatedly, perused the commentators on the Bible, Origen, Gregory, Basil, &c., to the amount of five millions of lines. 2. At the age of threescore, she could boast, that she had never washed her hands, face, or any part of her whole body, except the tips of her fingers to receive the communion. See the Vitae Patrum, p. 779, 977.] The servile poet of Stilicho applauds, with ferocious joy, this horrid deed, which, in the execution, perhaps, of justice, violated every law of nature and society, profaned the majesty of the prince, and renewed the dangerous examples of military license. The contemplation of the universal order and harmony had satisfied Claudian of the existence of the Deity; but the prosperous impunity of vice appeared to contradict his moral attributes; and the fate of Rufinus was the only event which could dispel the religious doubts of the poet. [33] Such an act might vindicate the honor of Providence, but it did not much contribute to the happiness of the people. In less than three months they were informed of the maxims of the new administration, by a singular edict, which established the exclusive right of the treasury over the spoils of Rufinus; and silenced, under heavy penalties, the presumptuous claims of the subjects of the Eastern empire, who had been injured by his rapacious tyranny. [34] Even Stilicho did not derive from the murder of his rival the fruit which he had proposed; and though he gratified his revenge, his ambition was disappointed. Under the name of a favorite, the weakness of Arcadius required a master, but he naturally preferred the obsequious arts of the eunuch Eutropius, who had obtained his domestic confidence: and the emperor contemplated, with terror and aversion, the stern genius of a foreign warrior. Till they were divided by the jealousy of power, the sword of Gainas, and the charms of Eudoxia, supported the favor of the great chamberlain of the palace: the perfidious Goth, who was appointed master-general of the East, betrayed, without scruple, the interest of his benefactor; and the same troops, who had so lately massacred the enemy of Stilicho, were engaged to support, against him, the independence of the throne of Constantinople. The favorites of Arcadius fomented a secret and irreconcilable war against a formidable hero, who aspired to govern, and to defend, the two empires of Rome, and the two sons of Theodosius. They incessantly labored, by dark and treacherous machinations, to deprive him of the esteem of the prince, the respect of the people, and the friendship of the Barbarians. The life of Stilicho was repeatedly attempted by the dagger of hired assassins; and a decree was obtained from the senate of Constantinople, to declare him an enemy of the republic, and to confiscate his ample possessions in the provinces of the East. At a time when the only hope of delaying the ruin of the Roman name depended on the firm union, and reciprocal aid, of all the nations to whom it had been gradually communicated, the subjects of Arcadius and Honorius were instructed, by their respective masters, to view each other in a foreign, and even hostile, light; to rejoice in their mutual calamities, and to embrace, as their faithful allies, the Barbarians, whom they excited to invade the territories of their countrymen. [35] The natives of Italy affected to despise the servile and effeminate Greeks of Byzantium, who presumed to imitate the dress, and to usurp the dignity, of Roman senators; [36] and the Greeks had not yet forgot the sentiments of hatred and contempt, which their polished ancestors had so long entertained for the rude inhabitants of the West. The distinction of two governments, which soon produced the separation of two nations, will justify my design of suspending the series of the Byzantine history, to prosecute, without interruption, the disgraceful, but memorable, reign of Honorius.

[Footnote 33: See the beautiful exordium of his invective against Rufinus, which is curiously discussed by the sceptic Bayle, Dictionnaire Critique, Rufin. Not. E.]

[Footnote 34: See the Theodosian Code, l. ix. tit. xlii. leg. 14, 15. The new ministers attempted, with inconsistent avarice, to seize the spoils of their predecessor, and to provide for their own future security.]

[Footnote 35: See Claudian, (i. Cons. Stilich, l. i. 275, 292, 296, l. ii. 83,) and Zosimus, (l. v. p. 302.)]

[Footnote 36: Claudian turns the consulship of the eunuch Eutropius into a national reflection, (l. ii. 134):—
—Plaudentem cerne senatum,
Et Byzantinos proceres Graiosque Quirites:
O patribus plebes, O digni consule patres.

It is curious to observe the first symptoms of jealousy and schism between old and new Rome, between the Greeks and Latins.]

The prudent Stilicho, instead of persisting to force the inclinations of a prince, and people, who rejected his government, wisely abandoned Arcadius to his unworthy favorites; and his reluctance to involve the two empires in a civil war displayed the moderation of a minister, who had so often signalized his military spirit and abilities. But if Stilicho had any longer endured the revolt of Africa, he would have betrayed the security of the capital, and the majesty of the Western emperor, to the capricious insolence of a Moorish rebel. Gildo, [37] the brother of the tyrant Firmus, had preserved and obtained, as the reward of his apparent fidelity, the immense patrimony which was forfeited by treason: long and meritorious service, in the armies of Rome, raised him to the dignity of a military count; the narrow policy of the court of Theodosius had adopted the mischievous expedient of supporting a legal government by the interest of a powerful family; and the brother of Firmus was invested with the command of Africa. His ambition soon usurped the administration of justice, and of the finances, without account, and without control; and he maintained, during a reign of twelve years, the possession of an office, from which it was impossible to remove him, without the danger of a civil war. During those twelve years, the provinces of Africa groaned under the dominion of a tyrant, who seemed to unite the unfeeling temper of a stranger with the partial resentments of domestic faction. The forms of law were often superseded by the use of poison; and if the trembling guests, who were invited to the table of Gildo, presumed to express fears, the insolent suspicion served only to excite his fury, and he loudly summoned the ministers of death. Gildo alternately indulged the passions of avarice and lust; [38] and if his days were terrible to the rich, his nights were not less dreadful to husbands and parents. The fairest of their wives and daughters were prostituted to the embraces of the tyrant; and afterwards abandoned to a ferocious troop of Barbarians and assassins, the black, or swarthy, natives of the desert; whom Gildo considered as the only of his throne. In the civil war between Theodosius and Eugenius, the count, or rather the sovereign, of Africa, maintained a haughty and suspicious neutrality; refused to assist either of the contending parties with troops or vessels, expected the declaration of fortune, and reserved for the conqueror the vain professions of his allegiance. Such professions would not have satisfied the master of the Roman world; but the death of Theodosius, and the weakness and discord of his sons, confirmed the power of the Moor; who condescended, as a proof of his moderation, to abstain from the use of the diadem, and to supply Rome with the customary tribute, or rather subsidy, of corn. In every division of the empire, the five provinces of Africa were invariably assigned to the West; and Gildo had to govern that extensive country in the name of Honorius, but his knowledge of the character and designs of Stilicho soon engaged him to address his homage to a more distant and feeble sovereign. The ministers of Arcadius embraced the cause of a perfidious rebel; and the delusive hope of adding the numerous cities of Africa to the empire of the East, tempted them to assert a claim, which they were incapable of supporting, either by reason or by arms. [39]

[Footnote 37: Claudian may have exaggerated the vices of Gildo; but his Moorish extraction, his notorious actions, and the complaints of St. Augustin, may justify the poet's invectives. Baronius (Annal. Eccles. A.D. 398, No. 35-56) has treated the African rebellion with skill and learning.]

[Footnote 38:
Instat terribilis vivis, morientibus haeres, Virginibus raptor, thalamis obscoenus adulter. Nulla quies: oritur praeda cessante libido, Divitibusque dies, et nox metuenda maritis. Mauris clarissima quaeque Fastidita datur. —De Bello Gildonico, 165, 189.

Baronius condemns, still more severely, the licentiousness of Gildo; as his wife, his daughter, and his sister, were examples of perfect chastity. The adulteries of the African soldiers are checked by one of the Imperial laws.]

[Footnote 39: Inque tuam sortem numerosas transtulit urbes. Claudian (de Bell. Gildonico, 230-324) has touched, with political delicacy, the intrigues of the Byzantine court, which are likewise mentioned by Zosimus, (l. v. p. 302.)]

When Stilicho had given a firm and decisive answer to the pretensions of the Byzantine court, he solemnly accused the tyrant of Africa before the tribunal, which had formerly judged the kings and nations of the earth; and the image of the republic was revived, after a long interval, under the reign of Honorius. The emperor transmitted an accurate and ample detail of the complaints of the provincials, and the crimes of Gildo, to the Roman senate; and the members of that venerable assembly were required to pronounce the condemnation of the rebel. Their unanimous suffrage declared him the enemy of the republic; and the decree of the senate added a sacred and legitimate sanction to the Roman arms. [40] A people, who still remembered that their ancestors had been the masters of the world, would have applauded, with conscious pride, the representation of ancient freedom; if they had not since been accustomed to prefer the solid assurance of bread to the unsubstantial visions of liberty and greatness. The subsistence of Rome depended on the harvests of Africa; and it was evident, that a declaration of war would be the signal of famine. The praefect Symmachus, who presided in the deliberations of the senate, admonished the minister of his just apprehension, that as soon as the revengeful Moor should prohibit the exportation of corn, the and perhaps the safety, of the capital would be threatened by the hungry rage of a turbulent multitude. [41] The prudence of Stilicho conceived and executed, without delay, the most effectual measure for the relief of the Roman people. A large and seasonable supply of corn, collected in the inland provinces of Gaul, was embarked on the rapid stream of the Rhone, and transported, by an easy navigation, from the Rhone to the Tyber. During the whole term of the African war, the granaries of Rome were continually filled, her dignity was vindicated from the humiliating dependence, and the minds of an immense people were quieted by the calm confidence of peace and plenty. [42]

[Footnote 40: Symmachus (l. iv. epist. 4) expresses the judicial forms of the senate; and Claudian (i. Cons. Stilich. l. i. 325, &c.) seems to feel the spirit of a Roman.]

[Footnote 41: Claudian finely displays these complaints of Symmachus, in a speech of the goddess of Rome, before the throne of Jupiter, (de Bell Gildon. 28-128.)]

[Footnote 42: See Claudian (in Eutrop. l. i 401, &c. i. Cons. Stil. l. i. 306, &c. i. Cons. Stilich. 91, &c.)]

The cause of Rome, and the conduct of the African war, were intrusted by Stilicho to a general, active and ardent to avenge his private injuries on the head of the tyrant. The spirit of discord which prevailed in the house of Nabal, had excited a deadly quarrel between two of his sons, Gildo and Mascezel. [43] The usurper pursued, with implacable rage, the life of his younger brother, whose courage and abilities he feared; and Mascezel, oppressed by superior power, refuge in the court of Milan, where he soon received the cruel intelligence that his two innocent and helpless children had been murdered by their inhuman uncle. The affliction of the father was suspended only by the desire of revenge. The vigilant Stilicho already prepared to collect the naval and military force of the Western empire; and he had resolved, if the tyrant should be able to wage an equal and doubtful war, to march against him in person. But as Italy required his presence, and as it might be dangerous to weaken the of the frontier, he judged it more advisable, that Mascezel should attempt this arduous adventure at the head of a chosen body of Gallic veterans, who had lately served exhorted to convince the world that they could subvert, as well as defend the throne of a usurper, consisted of the Jovian, the Herculian, and the Augustan legions; of the Nervian auxiliaries; of the soldiers who displayed in their banners the symbol of a lion, and of the troops which were distinguished by the auspicious names of Fortunate, and Invincible. Yet such was the smallness of their establishments, or the difficulty of recruiting, that these seven bands, [44] of high dignity and reputation in the service of Rome, amounted to no more than five thousand effective men. [45] The fleet of galleys and transports sailed in tempestuous weather from the port of Pisa, in Tuscany, and steered their course to the little island of Capraria; which had borrowed that name from the wild goats, its original inhabitants, whose place was occupied by a new colony of a strange and savage appearance. "The whole island (says an ingenious traveller of those times) is filled, or rather defiled, by men who fly from the light. They call themselves Monks, or solitaries, because they choose to live alone, without any witnesses of their actions. They fear the gifts of fortune, from the apprehension of losing them; and, lest they should be miserable, they embrace a life of voluntary wretchedness. How absurd is their choice! how perverse their understanding! to dread the evils, without being able to support the blessings, of the human condition. Either this melancholy madness is the effect of disease, or exercise on their own bodies the tortures which are inflicted on fugitive slaves by the hand of justice." [46] Such was the contempt of a profane magistrate for the monks as the chosen servants of God. [47] Some of them were persuaded, by his entreaties, to embark on board the fleet; and it is observed, to the praise of the Roman general, that his days and nights were employed in prayer, fasting, and the occupation of singing psalms. The devout leader, who, with such a reenforcement, appeared confident of victory, avoided the dangerous rocks of Corsica, coasted along the eastern side of Sardinia, and secured his ships against the violence of the south wind, by casting anchor in the and capacious harbor of Cagliari, at the distance of one hundred and forty miles from the African shores. [48]

[Footnote 43: He was of a mature age; since he had formerly (A.D. 373) served against his brother Firmus (Ammian. xxix. 5.) Claudian, who understood the court of Milan, dwells on the injuries, rather than the merits, of Mascezel, (de Bell. Gild. 389-414.) The Moorish war was not worthy of Honorius, or Stilicho, &c.]

[Footnote 44: Claudian, Bell. Gild. 415-423. The change of discipline allowed him to use indifferently the names of Legio Cohors, Manipulus. See Notitia Imperii, S. 38, 40.]

[Footnote 45: Orosius (l. vii. c. 36, p. 565) qualifies this account with an expression of doubt, (ut aiunt;) and it scarcely coincides with Zosimus, (l. v. p. 303.) Yet Claudian, after some declamation about Cadmus, soldiers, frankly owns that Stilicho sent a small army lest the rebels should fly, ne timeare times, (i. Cons. Stilich. l. i. 314 &c.)]

[Footnote 46: Claud. Rutil. Numatian. Itinerar. i. 439-448. He afterwards (515-526) mentions a religious madman on the Isle of Gorgona. For such profane remarks, Rutilius and his accomplices are styled, by his commentator, Barthius, rabiosi canes diaboli. Tillemont (Mem. Eccles com. xii. p. 471) more calmly observes, that the unbelieving poet praises where he means to censure.]

[Footnote 47: Orosius, l. vii. c. 36, p. 564. Augustin commends two of these savage saints of the Isle of Goats, (epist. lxxxi. apud Tillemont, Mem. Eccles. tom. xiii. p. 317, and Baronius, Annal Eccles. A.D. 398 No. 51.)]

[Footnote 48: Here the first book of the Gildonic war is terminated. The rest of Claudian's poem has been lost; and we are ignorant how or where the army made good their landing in Afica.]

Gildo was prepared to resist the invasion with all the forces of Africa. By the liberality of his gifts and promises, he endeavored to secure the doubtful allegiance of the Roman soldiers, whilst he attracted to his standard the distant tribes of Gaetulia and Aethiopia. He proudly reviewed an army of seventy thousand men, and boasted, with the rash presumption which is the forerunner of disgrace, that his numerous cavalry would trample under their horses' feet the troops of Mascezel, and involve, in a cloud of burning sand, the natives of the cold regions of Gaul and Germany. [49] But the Moor, who commanded the legions of Honorius, was too well acquainted with the manners of his countrymen, to entertain any serious apprehension of a naked and disorderly host of Barbarians; whose left arm, instead of a shield, was protected only by mantle; who were totally disarmed as soon as they had darted their javelin from their right hand; and whose horses had never He fixed his camp of five thousand veterans in the face of a superior enemy, and, after the delay of three days, gave the signal of a general engagement. [50] As Mascezel advanced before the front with fair offers of peace and pardon, he encountered one of the foremost standard-bearers of the Africans, and, on his refusal to yield, struck him on the arm with his sword. The arm, and the standard, sunk under the weight of the blow; and the imaginary act of submission was hastily repeated by all the standards of the line. At this the disaffected cohorts proclaimed the name of their lawful sovereign; the Barbarians, astonished by the defection of their Roman allies, dispersed, according to their custom, in tumultuary flight; and Mascezel obtained the of an easy, and almost bloodless, victory. [51] The tyrant escaped from the field of battle to the sea-shore; and threw himself into a small vessel, with the hope of reaching in safety some friendly port of the empire of the East; but the obstinacy of the wind drove him back into the harbor of Tabraca, [52] which had acknowledged, with the rest of the province, the dominion of Honorius, and the authority of his lieutenant. The inhabitants, as a proof of their repentance and loyalty, seized and confined the person of Gildo in a dungeon; and his own despair saved him from the intolerable torture of supporting the presence of an injured and victorious brother. [53] The captives and the spoils of Africa were laid at the feet of the emperor; but more sincere, in the midst of prosperity, still affected to consult the laws of the republic; and referred to the senate and people of Rome the judgment of the most illustrious criminals. [54] Their trial was public and solemn; but the judges, in the exercise of this obsolete and precarious jurisdiction, were impatient to punish the African magistrates, who had intercepted the subsistence of the Roman people. The rich and guilty province was oppressed by the Imperial ministers, who had a visible interest to multiply the number of the accomplices of Gildo; and if an edict of Honorius seems to check the malicious industry of informers, a subsequent edict, at the distance of ten years, continues and renews the prosecution of the which had been committed in the time of the general rebellion. [55] The adherents of the tyrant who escaped the first fury of the soldiers, and the judges, might derive some consolation from the tragic fate of his brother, who could never obtain his pardon for the extraordinary services which he had performed. After he had finished an important war in the space of a single winter, Mascezel was received at the court of Milan with loud applause, affected gratitude, and secret jealousy; [56] and his death, which, perhaps, was the effect of passage of a bridge, the Moorish prince, who accompanied the master-general of the West, was suddenly thrown from his horse into the river; the officious haste of the attendants was on the countenance of Stilicho; and while they delayed the necessary assistance, the unfortunate Mascezel was irrecoverably drowned. [57]

[Footnote 49: Orosius must be responsible for the account. The presumption of Gildo and his various train of Barbarians is celebrated by Claudian, Cons. Stil. l. i. 345-355.]

[Footnote 50: St. Ambrose, who had been dead about a year, revealed, in a vision, the time and place of the victory. Mascezel afterwards related his dream to Paulinus, the original biographer of the saint, from whom it might easily pass to Orosius.]

[Footnote 51: Zosimus (l. v. p. 303) supposes an obstinate combat; but the narrative of Orosius appears to conceal a real fact, under the disguise of a miracle.]

[Footnote 52: Tabraca lay between the two Hippos, (Cellarius, tom. ii. p. 112; D'Anville, tom. iii. p. 84.) Orosius has distinctly named the field of battle, but our ignorance cannot define the precise situation.]

[Footnote 53: The death of Gildo is expressed by Claudian (i. Cons. Stil. 357) and his best interpreters, Zosimus and Orosius.]

[Footnote 54: Claudian (ii. Cons. Stilich. 99-119) describes their trial (tremuit quos Africa nuper, cernunt rostra reos,) and applauds the restoration of the ancient constitution. It is here that he introduces the famous sentence, so familiar to the friends of despotism:

—Nunquam libertas gratior exstat, Quam sub rege pio.

But the freedom which depends on royal piety, scarcely deserves appellation]

[Footnote 55: See the Theodosian Code, l. ix. tit. xxxix. leg. 3, tit. xl. leg. 19.]

[Footnote 56: Stilicho, who claimed an equal share in all the victories of Theodosius and his son, particularly asserts, that Africa was recovered by the wisdom of his counsels, (see an inscription produced by Baronius.)]

[Footnote 57: I have softened the narrative of Zosimus, which, in its crude simplicity, is almost incredible, (l. v. p. 303.) Orosius damns the victorious general (p. 538) for violating the right of sanctuary.]

The joy of the African triumph was happily connected with the nuptials of the emperor Honorius, and of his cousin Maria, the daughter of Stilicho: and this equal and honorable alliance seemed to invest the powerful minister with the authority of a parent over his submissive pupil. The muse of Claudian was not silent on this propitious day; [58] he sung, in various and lively strains, the happiness of the royal pair; and the glory of the hero, who confirmed their union, and supported their throne. The ancient fables of Greece, which had almost ceased to be the object of religious faith, were saved from oblivion by the genius of poetry. The picture of the Cyprian grove, the seat of harmony and love; the triumphant progress of Venus over her native seas, and the mild influence which her presence diffused in the palace of Milan, express to every age the natural sentiments of the heart, in the just and pleasing language of allegorical fiction. But the amorous impatience which Claudian attributes to the young prince, [59] must excite the smiles of the court; and his beauteous spouse (if she deserved the praise of beauty) had not much to fear or to hope from the passions of her lover. Honorius was only in the fourteenth year of his age; Serena, the mother of his bride, deferred, by art of persuasion, the consummation of the royal nuptials; Maria died a virgin, after she had been ten years a wife; and the chastity of the emperor was secured by the coldness, perhaps, the debility,of his constitution. [60] His subjects, who attentively studied the character of their young sovereign, discovered that Honorius was without passions, and consequently without talents; and that his feeble and languid disposition was alike incapable of discharging the duties of his rank, or of enjoying the pleasures of his age. In his early youth he made some progress in the exercises of riding and drawing the bow: but he soon relinquished these fatiguing occupations, and the amusement of feeding poultry became the serious and daily care of the monarch of the West, [61] who resigned the reins of empire to the firm and skilful hand of his guardian Stilicho. The experience of history will countenance the suspicion that a prince who was born in the purple, received a worse education than the meanest peasant of his dominions; and that the ambitious minister suffered him to attain the age of manhood, without attempting to excite his courage, or to enlighten his under standing. [62] The predecessors of Honorius were accustomed to animate by their example, or at least by their presence, the valor of the legions; and the dates of their laws attest the perpetual activity of their motions through the provinces of the Roman world. But the son of Theodosius passed the slumber of his life, a captive in his palace, a stranger in his country, and the patient, almost the indifferent, spectator of the ruin of the Western empire, which was repeatedly attacked, and finally subverted, by the arms of the Barbarians. In the eventful history of a reign of twenty-eight years, it will seldom be necessary to mention the name of the emperor Honorius.

[Footnote 58: Claudian,as the poet laureate, composed a serious and elaborate epithalamium of 340 lines; besides some gay Fescennines, which were sung, in a more licentious tone, on the wedding night.]

[Footnote 59:
Calet obvius ire Jam princeps, tardumque cupit discedere solem. Nobilis haud aliter sonipes.

(De Nuptiis Honor. et Mariae, and more freely in the Fescennines 112-116)

Dices, O quoties,hoc mihi dulcius Quam flavos decics vincere Sarmatas. .... Tum victor madido prosilias toro, Nocturni referens vulnera proelii.]

[Footnote 60: See Zosimus, l. v. p. 333.]

[Footnote 61: Procopius de Bell. Gothico, l. i. c. 2. I have borrowed the general practice of Honorius, without adopting the singular, and indeed improbable tale, which is related by the Greek historian.]

[Footnote 62: The lessons of Theodosius, or rather Claudian, (iv. Cons. Honor 214-418,) might compose a fine institution for the future prince of a great and free nation. It was far above Honorius, and his degenerate subjects.]

CHAPTER XXX

REVOLT OF THE GOTHS

PART I

REVOLT OF THE GOTHS—THEY PLUNDER GREECE—TWO GREAT INVASIONS OF ITALY BY ALARIC AND RADAGAISUS—THEY ARE REPULSED BY STILICHO—THE GERMANS OVERRUN GAUL—USURPATION OF CONSTANTINE IN THE WEST—DISGRACE AND DEATH OF STILCHO

If the subjects of Rome could be ignorant of their obligations to the great Theodosius, they were too soon convinced, how painfully the spirit and abilities of their deceased emperor had supported the frail and mouldering edifice of the republic. He died in the month of January; and before the end of the winter of the same year, the Gothic nation was in arms. [1] The Barbarian auxiliaries erected their independent standard; and boldly avowed the hostile designs, which they had long cherished in their ferocious minds. Their countrymen, who had been condemned, by the conditions of the last treaty, to a life of tranquility and labor, deserted their farms at the first sound of the trumpet; and eagerly resumed the weapons which they had reluctantly laid down. The barriers of the Danube were thrown open; the savage warriors of Scythia issued from their forests; and the uncommon severity of the winter allowed the poet to remark, "that they rolled their ponderous wagons over the broad and icy back of the indignant river." [2] The unhappy natives of the provinces to the south of the Danube submitted to the calamities, which, in the course of twenty years, were almost grown familiar to their imagination; and the various troops of Barbarians, who gloried in the Gothic name, were irregularly spread from woody shores of Dalmatia, to the walls of Constantinople. [3] The interruption, or at least the diminution, of the subsidy, which the Goths had received from the prudent liberality of Theodosius, was the specious pretence of their revolt: the affront was imbittered by their contempt for the unwarlike sons of Theodosius; and their resentment was inflamed by the weakness, or treachery, of the minister of Arcadius. The frequent visits of Rufinus to the camp of the Barbarians whose arms and apparel he affected to imitate, were considered as a sufficient evidence of his guilty correspondence, and the public enemy, from a motive either of gratitude or of policy, was attentive, amidst the general devastation, to spare the private estates of the unpopular praefect. The Goths, instead of being impelled by the blind and headstrong passions of their chiefs, were now directed by the bold and artful genius of Alaric. That renowned leader was descended from the noble race of the Balti; [4] which yielded only to the royal dignity of the Amali: he had solicited the command of the Roman armies; and the Imperial court provoked him to demonstrate the folly of their refusal, and the importance of their loss. Whatever hopes might be entertained of the conquest of Constantinople, the judicious general soon abandoned an impracticable enterprise. In the midst of a divided court and a discontented people, the emperor Arcadius was terrified by the aspect of the Gothic arms; but the want of wisdom and valor was supplied by the strength of the city; and the fortifications, both of the sea and land, might securely brave the impotent and random darts of the Barbarians. Alaric disdained to trample any longer on the prostrate and ruined countries of Thrace and Dacia, and he resolved to seek a plentiful harvest of fame and riches in a province which had hitherto escaped the ravages of war. [5]

[Footnote 1: The revolt of the Goths, and the blockade of Constantinople, are distinctly mentioned by Claudian, (in Rufin. l. ii. 7-100,) Zosimus, (l. v. 292,) and Jornandes, (de Rebus Geticis, c. 29.)]

[Footnote 2:—
Alii per toga ferocis Danubii solidata ruunt; expertaque remis Frangunt stagna rotis.

Claudian and Ovid often amuse their fancy by interchanging the metaphors and properties of liquid water, and solid ice. Much false wit has been expended in this easy exercise.]

[Footnote 3: Jerom, tom. i. p. 26. He endeavors to comfort his friend Heliodorus, bishop of Altinum, for the loss of his nephew, Nepotian, by a curious recapitulation of all the public and private misfortunes of the times. See Tillemont, Mem. Eccles. tom. xii. p. 200, &c.]

[Footnote 4: Baltha or bold: origo mirifica, says Jornandes, (c. 29.) This illustrious race long continued to flourish in France, in the Gothic province of Septimania, or Languedoc; under the corrupted appellation of Boax; and a branch of that family afterwards settled in the kingdom of Naples (Grotius in Prolegom. ad Hist. Gothic. p. 53.) The lords of Baux, near Arles, and of seventy-nine subordinate places, were independent of the counts of Provence, (Longuerue, Description de la France, tom. i. p. 357).]

[Footnote 5: Zosimus (l. v. p. 293-295) is our best guide for the conquest of Greece: but the hints and allusion of Claudian are so many rays of historic light.]

The character of the civil and military officers, on whom Rufinus had devolved the government of Greece, confirmed the public suspicion, that he had betrayed the ancient seat of freedom and learning to the Gothic invader. The proconsul Antiochus was the unworthy son of a respectable father; and Gerontius, who commanded the provincial troops, was much better qualified to execute the oppressive orders of a tyrant, than to defend, with courage and ability, a country most remarkably fortified by the hand of nature. Alaric had traversed, without resistance, the plains of Macedonia and Thessaly, as far as the foot of Mount Oeta, a steep and woody range of hills, almost impervious to his cavalry. They stretched from east to west, to the edge of the sea-shore; and left, between the precipice and the Malian Gulf, an interval of three hundred feet, which, in some places, was contracted to a road capable of admitting only a single carriage. [6] In this narrow pass of Thermopylae, where Leonidas and the three hundred Spartans had gloriously devoted their lives, the Goths might have been stopped, or destroyed, by a skilful general; and perhaps the view of that sacred spot might have kindled some sparks of military ardor in the breasts of the degenerate Greeks. The troops which had been posted to defend the Straits of Thermopylae, retired, as they were directed, without attempting to disturb the secure and rapid passage of Alaric, [7] and the fertile fields of Phocis and Boeotia were instantly covered by a deluge of Barbarians who massacred the males of an age to bear arms, and drove away the beautiful females, with the spoil and cattle of the flaming villages. The travellers, who visited Greece several years afterwards, could easily discover the deep and bloody traces of the march of the Goths; and Thebes was less indebted for her preservation to the strength of her seven gates, than to the eager haste of Alaric, who advanced to occupy the city of Athens, and the important harbor of the Piraeus. The same impatience urged him to prevent the delay and danger of a siege, by the offer of a capitulation; and as soon as the Athenians heard the voice of the Gothic herald, they were easily persuaded to deliver the greatest part of their wealth, as the ransom of the city of Minerva and its inhabitants. The treaty was ratified by solemn oaths, and observed with mutual fidelity. The Gothic prince, with a small and select train, was admitted within the walls; he indulged himself in the refreshment of the bath, accepted a splendid banquet, which was provided by the magistrate, and affected to show that he was not ignorant of the manners of civilized nations. [8] But the whole territory of Attica, from the promontory of Sunium to the town of Megara, was blasted by his baleful presence; and, if we may use the comparison of a contemporary philosopher, Athens itself resembled the bleeding and empty skin of a slaughtered victim. The distance between Megara and Corinth could not much exceed thirty miles; but the bad road, an expressive name, which it still bears among the Greeks, was, or might easily have been made, impassable for the march of an enemy. The thick and gloomy woods of Mount Cithaeron covered the inland country; the Scironian rocks approached the water's edge, and hung over the narrow and winding path, which was confined above six miles along the sea-shore. [9] The passage of those rocks, so infamous in every age, was terminated by the Isthmus of Corinth; and a small a body of firm and intrepid soldiers might have successfully defended a temporary intrenchment of five or six miles from the Ionian to the Aegean Sea. The confidence of the cities of Peloponnesus in their natural rampart, had tempted them to neglect the care of their antique walls; and the avarice of the Roman governors had exhausted and betrayed the unhappy province. [10] Corinth, Argos, Sparta, yielded without resistance to the arms of the Goths; and the most fortunate of the inhabitants were saved, by death, from beholding the slavery of their families and the conflagration of their cities. [11] The vases and statues were distributed among the Barbarians, with more regard to the value of the materials, than to the elegance of the workmanship; the female captives submitted to the laws of war; the enjoyment of beauty was the reward of valor; and the Greeks could not reasonably complain of an abuse which was justified by the example of the heroic times. [12] The descendants of that extraordinary people, who had considered valor and discipline as the walls of Sparta, no longer remembered the generous reply of their ancestors to an invader more formidable than Alaric. "If thou art a god, thou wilt not hurt those who have never injured thee; if thou art a man, advance:—and thou wilt find men equal to thyself." [13] From Thermopylae to Sparta, the leader of the Goths pursued his victorious march without encountering any mortal antagonists: but one of the advocates of expiring Paganism has confidently asserted, that the walls of Athens were guarded by the goddess Minerva, with her formidable Aegis, and by the angry phantom of Achilles; [14] and that the conqueror was dismayed by the presence of the hostile deities of Greece. In an age of miracles, it would perhaps be unjust to dispute the claim of the historian Zosimus to the common benefit: yet it cannot be dissembled, that the mind of Alaric was ill prepared to receive, either in sleeping or waking visions, the impressions of Greek superstition. The songs of Homer, and the fame of Achilles, had probably never reached the ear of the illiterate Barbarian; and the Christian faith, which he had devoutly embraced, taught him to despise the imaginary deities of Rome and Athens. The invasion of the Goths, instead of vindicating the honor, contributed, at least accidentally, to extirpate the last remains of Paganism: and the mysteries of Ceres, which had subsisted eighteen hundred years, did not survive the destruction of Eleusis, and the calamities of Greece. [15]

[Footnote 6: Compare Herodotus (l. vii. c. 176) and Livy, (xxxvi. 15.) The narrow entrance of Greece was probably enlarged by each successive ravisher.]

[Footnote 7: He passed, says Eunapius, (in Vit. Philosoph. p. 93, edit. Commelin, 1596,) through the straits, of Thermopylae.]

[Footnote 8: In obedience to Jerom and Claudian, (in Rufin. l. ii. 191,) I have mixed some darker colors in the mild representation of Zosimus, who wished to soften the calamities of Athens.

Nec fera Cecropias traxissent vincula matres.

Synesius (Epist. clvi. p. 272, edit. Petav.) observes, that Athens, whose sufferings he imputes to the proconsul's avarice, was at that time less famous for her schools of philosophy than for her trade of honey.]

[Footnote 9:—

Vallata mari Scironia rupes, Et duo continuo connectens aequora muro Isthmos. —Claudian de Bel. Getico, 188.

The Scironian rocks are described by Pausanias, (l. i. c. 44, p. 107, edit. Kuhn,) and our modern travellers, Wheeler (p. 436) and Chandler, (p. 298.) Hadrian made the road passable for two carriages.]

[Footnote 10: Claudian (in Rufin. l. ii. 186, and de Bello Getico, 611, &c.) vaguely, though forcibly, delineates the scene of rapine and destruction.]

[Footnote 11: These generous lines of Homer (Odyss. l. v. 306) were transcribed by one of the captive youths of Corinth: and the tears of Mummius may prove that the rude conqueror, though he was ignorant of the value of an original picture, possessed the purest source of good taste, a benevolent heart, (Plutarch, Symposiac. l. ix. tom. ii. p. 737, edit. Wechel.)]

[Footnote 12: Homer perpetually describes the exemplary patience of those female captives, who gave their charms, and even their hearts, to the murderers of their fathers, brothers, &c. Such a passion (of Eriphile for Achilles) is touched with admirable delicacy by Racine.]

[Footnote 13: Plutarch (in Pyrrho, tom. ii. p. 474, edit. Brian) gives the genuine answer in the Laconic dialect. Pyrrhus attacked Sparta with 25,000 foot, 2000 horse, and 24 elephants, and the defence of that open town is a fine comment on the laws of Lycurgus, even in the last stage of decay.]

[Footnote 14: Such, perhaps, as Homer (Iliad, xx. 164) had so nobly painted him.]

[Footnote 15: Eunapius (in Vit. Philosoph. p. 90-93) intimates that a troop of monks betrayed Greece, and followed the Gothic camp. Note: The expression is curious: Vit. Max. t. i. p. 53, edit. Boissonade—M.]

The last hope of a people who could no longer depend on their arms, their gods, or their sovereign, was placed in the powerful assistance of the general of the West; and Stilicho, who had not been permitted to repulse, advanced to chastise, the invaders of Greece. [16] A numerous fleet was equipped in the ports of Italy; and the troops, after a short and prosperous navigation over the Ionian Sea, were safely disembarked on the isthmus, near the ruins of Corinth. The woody and mountainous country of Arcadia, the fabulous residence of Pan and the Dryads, became the scene of a long and doubtful conflict between the two generals not unworthy of each other. The skill and perseverance of the Roman at length prevailed; and the Goths, after sustaining a considerable loss from disease and desertion, gradually retreated to the lofty mountain of Pholoe, near the sources of the Peneus, and on the frontiers of Elis; a sacred country, which had formerly been exempted from the calamities of war. [17] The camp of the Barbarians was immediately besieged; the waters of the river [18] were diverted into another channel; and while they labored under the intolerable pressure of thirst and hunger, a strong line of circumvallation was formed to prevent their escape. After these precautions, Stilicho, too confident of victory, retired to enjoy his triumph, in the theatrical games, and lascivious dances, of the Greeks; his soldiers, deserting their standards, spread themselves over the country of their allies, which they stripped of all that had been saved from the rapacious hands of the enemy. Alaric appears to have seized the favorable moment to execute one of those hardy enterprises, in which the abilities of a general are displayed with more genuine lustre, than in the tumult of a day of battle. To extricate himself from the prison of Peloponnesus, it was necessary that he should pierce the intrenchments which surrounded his camp; that he should perform a difficult and dangerous march of thirty miles, as far as the Gulf of Corinth; and that he should transport his troops, his captives, and his spoil, over an arm of the sea, which, in the narrow interval between Rhium and the opposite shore, is at least half a mile in breadth. [19] The operations of Alaric must have been secret, prudent, and rapid; since the Roman general was confounded by the intelligence, that the Goths, who had eluded his efforts, were in full possession of the important province of Epirus. This unfortunate delay allowed Alaric sufficient time to conclude the treaty, which he secretly negotiated, with the ministers of Constantinople. The apprehension of a civil war compelled Stilicho to retire, at the haughty mandate of his rivals, from the dominions of Arcadius; and he respected, in the enemy of Rome, the honorable character of the ally and servant of the emperor of the East.

[Footnote 16: For Stilicho's Greek war, compare the honest narrative of Zosimus (l. v. p. 295, 296) with the curious circumstantial flattery of Claudian, (i. Cons. Stilich. l. i. 172-186, iv. Cons. Hon. 459-487.) As the event was not glorious, it is artfully thrown into the shade.]

[Footnote 17: The troops who marched through Elis delivered up their arms. This security enriched the Eleans, who were lovers of a rural life. Riches begat pride: they disdained their privilege, and they suffered. Polybius advises them to retire once more within their magic circle. See a learned and judicious discourse on the Olympic games, which Mr. West has prefixed to his translation of Pindar.]

[Footnote 18: Claudian (in iv. Cons. Hon. 480) alludes to the fact without naming the river; perhaps the Alpheus, (i. Cons. Stil. l. i. 185.)

—Et Alpheus Geticis angustus acervis Tardior ad Siculos etiamnum pergit amores.

Yet I should prefer the Peneus, a shallow stream in a wide and deep bed, which runs through Elis, and falls into the sea below Cyllene. It had been joined with the Alpheus to cleanse the Augean stable. (Cellarius, tom. i. p. 760. Chandler's Travels, p. 286.)]

[Footnote 19: Strabo, l. viii. p. 517. Plin. Hist. Natur. iv. 3.

Wheeler, p. 308. Chandler, p. 275. They measured from different points the distance between the two lands.]

A Grecian philosopher, [20] who visited Constantinople soon after the death of Theodosius, published his liberal opinions concerning the duties of kings, and the state of the Roman republic. Synesius observes, and deplores, the fatal abuse, which the imprudent bounty of the late emperor had introduced into the military service. The citizens and subjects had purchased an exemption from the indispensable duty of defending their country; which was supported by the arms of Barbarian mercenaries. The fugitives of Scythia were permitted to disgrace the illustrious dignities of the empire; their ferocious youth, who disdained the salutary restraint of laws, were more anxious to acquire the riches, than to imitate the arts, of a people, the object of their contempt and hatred; and the power of the Goths was the stone of Tantalus, perpetually suspended over the peace and safety of the devoted state. The measures which Synesius recommends, are the dictates of a bold and generous patriot. He exhorts the emperor to revive the courage of his subjects, by the example of manly virtue; to banish luxury from the court and from the camp; to substitute, in the place of the Barbarian mercenaries, an army of men, interested in the defence of their laws and of their property; to force, in such a moment of public danger, the mechanic from his shop, and the philosopher from his school; to rouse the indolent citizen from his dream of pleasure, and to arm, for the protection of agriculture, the hands of the laborious husbandman. At the head of such troops, who might deserve the name, and would display the spirit, of Romans, he animates the son of Theodosius to encounter a race of Barbarians, who were destitute of any real courage; and never to lay down his arms, till he had chased them far away into the solitudes of Scythia; or had reduced them to the state of ignominious servitude, which the Lacedaemonians formerly imposed on the captive Helots. [21] The court of Arcadius indulged the zeal, applauded the eloquence, and neglected the advice, of Synesius. Perhaps the philosopher who addresses the emperor of the East in the language of reason and virtue, which he might have used to a Spartan king, had not condescended to form a practicable scheme, consistent with the temper, and circumstances, of a degenerate age. Perhaps the pride of the ministers, whose business was seldom interrupted by reflection, might reject, as wild and visionary, every proposal, which exceeded the measure of their capacity, and deviated from the forms and precedents of office. While the oration of Synesius, and the downfall of the Barbarians, were the topics of popular conversation, an edict was published at Constantinople, which declared the promotion of Alaric to the rank of master-general of the Eastern Illyricum. The Roman provincials, and the allies, who had respected the faith of treaties, were justly indignant, that the ruin of Greece and Epirus should be so liberally rewarded. The Gothic conqueror was received as a lawful magistrate, in the cities which he had so lately besieged. The fathers, whose sons he had massacred, the husbands, whose wives he had violated, were subject to his authority; and the success of his rebellion encouraged the ambition of every leader of the foreign mercenaries. The use to which Alaric applied his new command, distinguishes the firm and judicious character of his policy. He issued his orders to the four magazines and manufactures of offensive and defensive arms, Margus, Ratiaria, Naissus, and Thessalonica, to provide his troops with an extraordinary supply of shields, helmets, swords, and spears; the unhappy provincials were compelled to forge the instruments of their own destruction; and the Barbarians removed the only defect which had sometimes disappointed the efforts of their courage. [22] The birth of Alaric, the glory of his past exploits, and the confidence in his future designs, insensibly united the body of the nation under his victorious standard; and, with the unanimous consent of the Barbarian chieftains, the master-general of Illyricum was elevated, according to ancient custom, on a shield, and solemnly proclaimed king of the Visigoths. [23] Armed with this double power, seated on the verge of the two empires, he alternately sold his deceitful promises to the courts of Arcadius and Honorius; [24] till he declared and executed his resolution of invading the dominions of the West. The provinces of Europe which belonged to the Eastern emperor, were already exhausted; those of Asia were inaccessible; and the strength of Constantinople had resisted his attack. But he was tempted by the fame, the beauty, the wealth of Italy, which he had twice visited, and he secretly aspired to plant the Gothic standard on the walls of Rome, and to enrich his army with the accumulated spoils of three hundred triumphs. [25]

[Footnote 20: Synesius passed three years (A.D. 397-400) at Constantinople, as deputy from Cyrene to the emperor Arcadius. He presented him with a crown of gold, and pronounced before him the instructive oration de Regno, (p. 1-32, edit. Petav. Paris, 1612.) The philosopher was made bishop of Ptolemais, A.D. 410, and died about 430. See Tillemont, Mem. Eccles. tom. xii. p. 490, 554, 683-685.]

[Footnote 21: Synesius de Regno, p. 21-26.]

[Footnote 22:—qui foedera rumpit

Ditatur: qui servat, eget: vastator Achivae Gentis, et Epirum nuper populatus inultam, Praesidet Illyrico: jam, quos obsedit, amicos Ingreditur muros; illis responsa daturus, Quorum conjugibus potitur, natosque peremit.

Claudian in Eutrop. l. ii. 212. Alaric applauds his own policy (de Bell Getic. 533-543) in the use which he had made of this Illyrian jurisdiction.]

[Footnote 23: Jornandes, c. 29, p. 651. The Gothic historian adds, with unusual spirit, Cum suis deliberans suasit suo labore quaerere regna, quam alienis per otium subjacere.

Discors odiisque anceps civilibus orbis, Non sua vis tutata diu, dum foedera fallax Ludit, et alternae perjuria venditat aulae. —Claudian de Bell. Get. 565]

[Footnote 25: Alpibus Italiae ruptis penetrabis ad Urbem. This authentic prediction was announced by Alaric, or at least by Claudian, (de Bell. Getico, 547,) seven years before the event. But as it was not accomplished within the term which has been rashly fixed the interpreters escaped through an ambiguous meaning.]

The scarcity of facts, [26] and the uncertainty of dates, [27] oppose our attempts to describe the circumstances of the first invasion of Italy by the arms of Alaric. His march, perhaps from Thessalonica, through the warlike and hostile country of Pannonia, as far as the foot of the Julian Alps; his passage of those mountains, which were strongly guarded by troops and intrenchments; the siege of Aquileia, and the conquest of the provinces of Istria and Venetia, appear to have employed a considerable time. Unless his operations were extremely cautious and slow, the length of the interval would suggest a probable suspicion, that the Gothic king retreated towards the banks of the Danube; and reenforced his army with fresh swarms of Barbarians, before he again attempted to penetrate into the heart of Italy. Since the public and important events escape the diligence of the historian, he may amuse himself with contemplating, for a moment, the influence of the arms of Alaric on the fortunes of two obscure individuals, a presbyter of Aquileia and a husbandman of Verona. The learned Rufinus, who was summoned by his enemies to appear before a Roman synod, [28] wisely preferred the dangers of a besieged city; and the Barbarians, who furiously shook the walls of Aquileia, might save him from the cruel sentence of another heretic, who, at the request of the same bishops, was severely whipped, and condemned to perpetual exile on a desert island. [29] The old man, [30] who had passed his simple and innocent life in the neighborhood of Verona, was a stranger to the quarrels both of kings and of bishops; his pleasures, his desires, his knowledge, were confined within the little circle of his paternal farm; and a staff supported his aged steps, on the same ground where he had sported in his infancy. Yet even this humble and rustic felicity (which Claudian describes with so much truth and feeling) was still exposed to the undistinguishing rage of war. His trees, his old contemporary trees, [31] must blaze in the conflagration of the whole country; a detachment of Gothic cavalry might sweep away his cottage and his family; and the power of Alaric could destroy this happiness, which he was not able either to taste or to bestow. "Fame," says the poet, "encircling with terror her gloomy wings, proclaimed the march of the Barbarian army, and filled Italy with consternation:" the apprehensions of each individual were increased in just proportion to the measure of his fortune: and the most timid, who had already embarked their valuable effects, meditated their escape to the Island of Sicily, or the African coast. The public distress was aggravated by the fears and reproaches of superstition. [32] Every hour produced some horrid tale of strange and portentous accidents; the Pagans deplored the neglect of omens, and the interruption of sacrifices; but the Christians still derived some comfort from the powerful intercession of the saints and martyrs. [33]

[Footnote 26: Our best materials are 970 verses of Claudian in the poem on the Getic war, and the beginning of that which celebrates the sixth consulship of Honorius. Zosimus is totally silent; and we are reduced to such scraps, or rather crumbs, as we can pick from Orosius and the Chronicles.]

[Footnote 27: Notwithstanding the gross errors of Jornandes, who confounds the Italian wars of Alaric, (c. 29,) his date of the consulship of Stilicho and Aurelian (A.D. 400) is firm and respectable. It is certain from Claudian (Tillemont, Hist. des Emp. tom. v. p. 804) that the battle of Polentia was fought A.D. 403; but we cannot easily fill the interval.]

[Footnote 28: Tantum Romanae urbis judicium fugis, ut magis obsidionem barbaricam, quam pacatoe urbis judicium velis sustinere. Jerom, tom. ii. p. 239. Rufinus understood his own danger; the peaceful city was inflamed by the beldam Marcella, and the rest of Jerom's faction.]

[Footnote 29: Jovinian, the enemy of fasts and of celibacy, who was persecuted and insulted by the furious Jerom, (Jortin's Remarks, vol. iv. p. 104, &c.) See the original edict of banishment in the Theodosian Code, xvi. tit. v. leg. 43.]

[Footnote 30: This epigram (de Sene Veronensi qui suburbium nusquam egres sus est) is one of the earliest and most pleasing compositions of Claudian. Cowley's imitation (Hurd's edition, vol. ii. p. 241) has some natural and happy strokes: but it is much inferior to the original portrait, which is evidently drawn from the life.]

[Footnote 31:
Ingentem meminit parvo qui germine quercum Aequaevumque videt consenuisse nemus.

A neighboring wood born with himself he sees, And loves his old contemporary trees.

In this passage, Cowley is perhaps superior to his original; and the English poet, who was a good botanist, has concealed the oaks under a more general expression.]

[Footnote 32: Claudian de Bell. Get. 199-266. He may seem prolix: but fear and superstition occupied as large a space in the minds of the Italians.]

[Footnote 33: From the passages of Paulinus, which Baronius has produced, (Annal. Eccles. A.D. 403, No. 51,) it is manifest that the general alarm had pervaded all Italy, as far as Nola in Campania, where that famous penitent had fixed his abode.]

PART II

The emperor Honorius was distinguished, above his subjects, by the preeminence of fear, as well as of rank. The pride and luxury in which he was educated, had not allowed him to suspect, that there existed on the earth any power presumptuous enough to invade the repose of the successor of Augustus. The arts of flattery concealed the impending danger, till Alaric approached the palace of Milan. But when the sound of war had awakened the young emperor, instead of flying to arms with the spirit, or even the rashness, of his age, he eagerly listened to those timid counsellors, who proposed to convey his sacred person, and his faithful attendants, to some secure and distant station in the provinces of Gaul. Stilicho alone [34] had courage and authority to resist his disgraceful measure, which would have abandoned Rome and Italy to the Barbarians; but as the troops of the palace had been lately detached to the Rhaetian frontier, and as the resource of new levies was slow and precarious, the general of the West could only promise, that if the court of Milan would maintain their ground during his absence, he would soon return with an army equal to the encounter of the Gothic king. Without losing a moment, (while each moment was so important to the public safety,) Stilicho hastily embarked on the Larian Lake, ascended the mountains of ice and snow, amidst the severity of an Alpine winter, and suddenly repressed, by his unexpected presence, the enemy, who had disturbed the tranquillity of Rhaetia. [35] The Barbarians, perhaps some tribes of the Alemanni, respected the firmness of a chief, who still assumed the language of command; and the choice which he condescended to make, of a select number of their bravest youth, was considered as a mark of his esteem and favor. The cohorts, who were delivered from the neighboring foe, diligently repaired to the Imperial standard; and Stilicho issued his orders to the most remote troops of the West, to advance, by rapid marches, to the defence of Honorius and of Italy. The fortresses of the Rhine were abandoned; and the safety of Gaul was protected only by the faith of the Germans, and the ancient terror of the Roman name. Even the legion, which had been stationed to guard the wall of Britain against the Caledonians of the North, was hastily recalled; [36] and a numerous body of the cavalry of the Alani was persuaded to engage in the service of the emperor, who anxiously expected the return of his general. The prudence and vigor of Stilicho were conspicuous on this occasion, which revealed, at the same time, the weakness of the falling empire. The legions of Rome, which had long since languished in the gradual decay of discipline and courage, were exterminated by the Gothic and civil wars; and it was found impossible, without exhausting and exposing the provinces, to assemble an army for the defence of Italy.

[Footnote 34: Solus erat Stilicho, &c., is the exclusive commendation which Claudian bestows, (del Bell. Get. 267,) without condescending to except the emperor. How insignificant must Honorius have appeared in his own court.]

[Footnote 35: The face of the country, and the hardiness of Stilicho, are finely described, (de Bell. Get. 340-363.)]

[Footnote 36:
Venit et extremis legio praetenta Britannis, Quae Scoto dat frena truci.—De Bell. Get. 416.

Yet the most rapid march from Edinburgh, or Newcastle, to Milan, must have required a longer space of time than Claudian seems willing to allow for the duration of the Gothic war.]

PART III

When Stilicho seemed to abandon his sovereign in the unguarded palace of Milan, he had probably calculated the term of his absence, the distance of the enemy, and the obstacles that might retard their march. He principally depended on the rivers of Italy, the Adige, the Mincius, the Oglio, and the Addua, which, in the winter or spring, by the fall of rains, or by the melting of the snows, are commonly swelled into broad and impetuous torrents. [37] But the season happened to be remarkably dry: and the Goths could traverse, without impediment, the wide and stony beds, whose centre was faintly marked by the course of a shallow stream. The bridge and passage of the Addua were secured by a strong detachment of the Gothic army; and as Alaric approached the walls, or rather the suburbs, of Milan, he enjoyed the proud satisfaction of seeing the emperor of the Romans fly before him. Honorius, accompanied by a feeble train of statesmen and eunuchs, hastily retreated towards the Alps, with a design of securing his person in the city of Arles, which had often been the royal residence of his predecessors. [37/1] But Honorius [38] had scarcely passed the Po, before he was overtaken by the speed of the Gothic cavalry; [39] since the urgency of the danger compelled him to seek a temporary shelter within the fortifications of Asta, a town of Liguria or Piemont, situate on the banks of the Tanarus. [40] The siege of an obscure place, which contained so rich a prize, and seemed incapable of a long resistance, was instantly formed, and indefatigably pressed, by the king of the Goths; and the bold declaration, which the emperor might afterwards make, that his breast had never been susceptible of fear, did not probably obtain much credit, even in his own court. [41] In the last, and almost hopeless extremity, after the Barbarians had already proposed the indignity of a capitulation, the Imperial captive was suddenly relieved by the fame, the approach, and at length the presence, of the hero, whom he had so long expected. At the head of a chosen and intrepid vanguard, Stilicho swam the stream of the Addua, to gain the time which he must have lost in the attack of the bridge; the passage of the Po was an enterprise of much less hazard and difficulty; and the successful action, in which he cut his way through the Gothic camp under the walls of Asta, revived the hopes, and vindicated the honor, of Rome. Instead of grasping the fruit of his victory, the Barbarian was gradually invested, on every side, by the troops of the West, who successively issued through all the passes of the Alps; his quarters were straitened; his convoys were intercepted; and the vigilance of the Romans prepared to form a chain of fortifications, and to besiege the lines of the besiegers. A military council was assembled of the long-haired chiefs of the Gothic nation; of aged warriors, whose bodies were wrapped in furs, and whose stern countenances were marked with honorable wounds. They weighed the glory of persisting in their attempt against the advantage of securing their plunder; and they recommended the prudent measure of a seasonable retreat. In this important debate, Alaric displayed the spirit of the conqueror of Rome; and after he had reminded his countrymen of their achievements and of their designs, he concluded his animating speech by the solemn and positive assurance that he was resolved to find in Italy either a kingdom or a grave. [42]

[Footnote 37: Every traveller must recollect the face of Lombardy, (see Fonvenelle, tom. v. p. 279,) which is often tormented by the capricious and irregular abundance of waters. The Austrians, before Genoa, were encamped in the dry bed of the Polcevera. "Ne sarebbe" (says Muratori) "mai passato per mente a que' buoni Alemanni, che quel picciolo torrente potesse, per cosi dire, in un instante cangiarsi in un terribil gigante." (Annali d'Italia, tom. xvi. p. 443, Milan, 1752, 8vo edit.)]

[Footnote 37/1: According to Le Beau and his commentator M. St. Martin, Honorius did not attempt to fly. Settlements were offered to the Goths in Lombardy, and they advanced from the Po towards the Alps to take possession of them. But it was a treacherous stratagem of Stilicho, who surprised them while they were reposing on the faith of this treaty. Le Beau, v. x.]

[Footnote 38: Claudian does not clearly answer our question, Where was Honorius himself? Yet the flight is marked by the pursuit; and my idea of the Gothic was is justified by the Italian critics, Sigonius (tom. P, ii. p. 369, de Imp. Occident. l. x.) and Muratori, (Annali d'Italia. tom. iv. p. 45.)]

[Footnote 39: One of the roads may be traced in the Itineraries, (p. 98, 288, 294, with Wesseling's Notes.) Asta lay some miles on the right hand.]

[Footnote 40: Asta, or Asti, a Roman colony, is now the capital of a pleasant country, which, in the sixteenth century, devolved to the dukes of Savoy, (Leandro Alberti Descrizzione d'Italia, p. 382.)]

[Footnote 41: Nec me timor impulit ullus. He might hold this proud language the next year at Rome, five hundred miles from the scene of danger (vi. Cons. Hon. 449.)]

[Footnote 42: Hanc ego vel victor regno, vel morte tenebo Victus, humum—The speeches (de Bell. Get. 479-549) of the Gothic Nestor, and Achilles, are strong, characteristic, adapted to the circumstances; and possibly not less genuine than those of Livy.]

The loose discipline of the Barbarians always exposed them to the danger of a surprise; but, instead of choosing the dissolute hours of riot and intemperance, Stilicho resolved to attack the Christian Goths, whilst they were devoutly employed in celebrating the festival of Easter. [43] The execution of the stratagem, or, as it was termed by the clergy of the sacrilege, was intrusted to Saul, a Barbarian and a Pagan, who had served, however, with distinguished reputation among the veteran generals of Theodosius. The camp of the Goths, which Alaric had pitched in the neighborhood of Pollentia, [44] was thrown into confusion by the sudden and impetuous charge of the Imperial cavalry; but, in a few moments, the undaunted genius of their leader gave them an order, and a field of battle; and, as soon as they had recovered from their astonishment, the pious confidence, that the God of the Christians would assert their cause, added new strength to their native valor. In this engagement, which was long maintained with equal courage and success, the chief of the Alani, whose diminutive and savage form concealed a magnanimous soul approved his suspected loyalty, by the zeal with which he fought, and fell, in the service of the republic; and the fame of this gallant Barbarian has been imperfectly preserved in the verses of Claudian, since the poet, who celebrates his virtue, has omitted the mention of his name. His death was followed by the flight and dismay of the squadrons which he commanded; and the defeat of the wing of cavalry might have decided the victory of Alaric, if Stilicho had not immediately led the Roman and Barbarian infantry to the attack. The skill of the general, and the bravery of the soldiers, surmounted every obstacle. In the evening of the bloody day, the Goths retreated from the field of battle; the intrenchments of their camp were forced, and the scene of rapine and slaughter made some atonement for the calamities which they had inflicted on the subjects of the empire. [45] The magnificent spoils of Corinth and Argos enriched the veterans of the West; the captive wife of Alaric, who had impatiently claimed his promise of Roman jewels and Patrician handmaids, [46] was reduced to implore the mercy of the insulting foe; and many thousand prisoners, released from the Gothic chains, dispersed through the provinces of Italy the praises of their heroic deliverer. The triumph of Stilicho [47] was compared by the poet, and perhaps by the public, to that of Marius; who, in the same part of Italy, had encountered and destroyed another army of Northern Barbarians. The huge bones, and the empty helmets, of the Cimbri and of the Goths, would easily be confounded by succeeding generations; and posterity might erect a common trophy to the memory of the two most illustrious generals, who had vanquished, on the same memorable ground, the two most formidable enemies of Rome. [48]

[Footnote 43: Orosius (l. vii. c. 37) is shocked at the impiety of the Romans, who attacked, on Easter Sunday, such pious Christians. Yet, at the same time, public prayers were offered at the shrine of St. Thomas of Edessa, for the destruction of the Arian robber. See Tillemont (Hist des Emp. tom. v. p. 529) who quotes a homily, which has been erroneously ascribed to St. Chrysostom.]

[Footnote 44: The vestiges of Pollentia are twenty-five miles to the south-east of Turin. Urbs, in the same neighborhood, was a royal chase of the kings of Lombardy, and a small river, which excused the prediction, "penetrabis ad urbem," (Cluver. Ital. Antiq tom. i. p. 83-85.)]

[Footnote 45: Orosius wishes, in doubtful words, to insinuate the defeat of the Romans. "Pugnantes vicimus, victores victi sumus." Prosper (in Chron.) makes it an equal and bloody battle, but the Gothic writers Cassiodorus (in Chron.) and Jornandes (de Reb. Get. c. 29) claim a decisive victory.]

[Footnote 46: Demens Ausonidum gemmata monilia matrum, Romanasque alta famulas cervice petebat. De Bell. Get. 627.]

[Footnote 47: Claudian (de Bell. Get. 580-647) and Prudentius (in Symmach. n. 694-719) celebrate, without ambiguity, the Roman victory of Pollentia. They are poetical and party writers; yet some credit is due to the most suspicious witnesses, who are checked by the recent notoriety of facts.]

[Footnote 48: Claudian's peroration is strong and elegant; but the identity of the Cimbric and Gothic fields must be understood (like Virgil's Philippi, Georgic i. 490) according to the loose geography of a poet. Verselle and Pollentia are sixty miles from each other; and the latitude is still greater, if the Cimbri were defeated in the wide and barren plain of Verona, (Maffei, Verona Illustrata, P. i. p. 54-62.)]

The eloquence of Claudian [49] has celebrated, with lavish applause, the victory of Pollentia, one of the most glorious days in the life of his patron; but his reluctant and partial muse bestows more genuine praise on the character of the Gothic king. His name is, indeed, branded with the reproachful epithets of pirate and robber, to which the conquerors of every age are so justly entitled; but the poet of Stilicho is compelled to acknowledge that Alaric possessed the invincible temper of mind, which rises superior to every misfortune, and derives new resources from adversity. After the total defeat of his infantry, he escaped, or rather withdrew, from the field of battle, with the greatest part of his cavalry entire and unbroken. Without wasting a moment to lament the irreparable loss of so many brave companions, he left his victorious enemy to bind in chains the captive images of a Gothic king; [50] and boldly resolved to break through the unguarded passes of the Apennine, to spread desolation over the fruitful face of Tuscany, and to conquer or die before the gates of Rome. The capital was saved by the active and incessant diligence of Stilicho; but he respected the despair of his enemy; and, instead of committing the fate of the republic to the chance of another battle, he proposed to purchase the absence of the Barbarians. The spirit of Alaric would have rejected such terms, the permission of a retreat, and the offer of a pension, with contempt and indignation; but he exercised a limited and precarious authority over the independent chieftains who had raised him, for their service, above the rank of his equals; they were still less disposed to follow an unsuccessful general, and many of them were tempted to consult their interest by a private negotiation with the minister of Honorius. The king submitted to the voice of his people, ratified the treaty with the empire of the West, and repassed the Po with the remains of the flourishing army which he had led into Italy. A considerable part of the Roman forces still continued to attend his motions; and Stilicho, who maintained a secret correspondence with some of the Barbarian chiefs, was punctually apprised of the designs that were formed in the camp and council of Alaric. The king of the Goths, ambitious to signalize his retreat by some splendid achievement, had resolved to occupy the important city of Verona, which commands the principal passage of the Rhaetian Alps; and, directing his march through the territories of those German tribes, whose alliance would restore his exhausted strength, to invade, on the side of the Rhine, the wealthy and unsuspecting provinces of Gaul. Ignorant of the treason which had already betrayed his bold and judicious enterprise, he advanced towards the passes of the mountains, already possessed by the Imperial troops; where he was exposed, almost at the same instant, to a general attack in the front, on his flanks, and in the rear. In this bloody action, at a small distance from the walls of Verona, the loss of the Goths was not less heavy than that which they had sustained in the defeat of Pollentia; and their valiant king, who escaped by the swiftness of his horse, must either have been slain or made prisoner, if the hasty rashness of the Alani had not disappointed the measures of the Roman general. Alaric secured the remains of his army on the adjacent rocks; and prepared himself, with undaunted resolution, to maintain a siege against the superior numbers of the enemy, who invested him on all sides. But he could not oppose the destructive progress of hunger and disease; nor was it possible for him to check the continual desertion of his impatient and capricious Barbarians. In this extremity he still found resources in his own courage, or in the moderation of his adversary; and the retreat of the Gothic king was considered as the deliverance of Italy. [51] Yet the people, and even the clergy, incapable of forming any rational judgment of the business of peace and war, presumed to arraign the policy of Stilicho, who so often vanquished, so often surrounded, and so often dismissed the implacable enemy of the republic. The first momen of the public safety is devoted to gratitude and joy; but the second is diligently occupied by envy and calumny. [52]

[Footnote 49: Claudian and Prudentius must be strictly examined, to reduce the figures, and extort the historic sense, of those poets.]

[Footnote 50:
Et gravant en airain ses freles avantages De mes etats conquis enchainer les images.

The practice of exposing in triumph the images of kings and provinces was familiar to the Romans. The bust of Mithridates himself was twelve feet high, of massy gold, (Freinshem. Supplement. Livian. ciii. 47.)]

[Footnote 51: The Getic war, and the sixth consulship of Honorius, obscurely connect the events of Alaric's retreat and losses.]

[Footnote 52: Taceo de Alarico... saepe visto, saepe concluso, semperque dimisso. Orosius, l. vii. c. 37, p. 567. Claudian (vi. Cons. Hon. 320) drops the curtain with a fine image.]

The citizens of Rome had been astonished by the approach of Alaric; and the diligence with which they labored to restore the walls of the capital, confessed their own fears, and the decline of the empire. After the retreat of the Barbarians, Honorius was directed to accept the dutiful invitation of the senate, and to celebrate, in the Imperial city, the auspicious aera of the Gothic victory, and of his sixth consulship. [53] The suburbs and the streets, from the Milvian bridge to the Palatine mount, were filled by the Roman people, who, in the space of a hundred years, had only thrice been honored with the presence of their sovereigns. While their eyes were fixed on the chariot where Stilicho was deservedly seated by the side of his royal pupil, they applauded the pomp of a triumph, which was not stained, like that of Constantine, or of Theodosius, with civil blood. The procession passed under a lofty arch, which had been purposely erected: but in less than seven years, the Gothic conquerors of Rome might read, if they were able to read, the superb inscription of that monument, which attested the total defeat and destruction of their nation. [54] The emperor resided several months in the capital, and every part of his behavior was regulated with care to conciliate the affection of the clergy, the senate, and the people of Rome. The clergy was edified by his frequent visits and liberal gifts to the shrines of the apostles. The senate, who, in the triumphal procession, had been excused from the humiliating ceremony of preceding on foot the Imperial chariot, was treated with the decent reverence which Stilicho always affected for that assembly. The people was repeatedly gratified by the attention and courtesy of Honorius in the public games, which were celebrated on that occasion with a magnificence not unworthy of the spectator. As soon as the appointed number of chariot-races was concluded, the decoration of the Circus was suddenly changed; the hunting of wild beasts afforded a various and splendid entertainment; and the chase was succeeded by a military dance, which seems, in the lively description of Claudian, to present the image of a modern tournament.

[Footnote 53: The remainder of Claudian's poem on the sixth consulship of Honorius, describes the journey, the triumph, and the games, (330-660.)]

[Footnote 54: See the inscription in Mascou's History of the Ancient Germans, viii. 12. The words are positive and indiscreet: Getarum nationem in omne aevum domitam, &c.]

In these games of Honorius, the inhuman combats of gladiators [55] polluted, for the last time, the amphitheater of Rome. The first Christian emperor may claim the honor of the first edict which condemned the art and amusement of shedding human blood; [56] but this benevolent law expressed the wishes of the prince, without reforming an inveterate abuse, which degraded a civilized nation below the condition of savage cannibals. Several hundred, perhaps several thousand, victims were annually slaughtered in the great cities of the empire; and the month of December, more peculiarly devoted to the combats of gladiators, still exhibited to the eyes of the Roman people a grateful spectacle of blood and cruelty. Amidst the general joy of the victory of Pollentia, a Christian poet exhorted the emperor to extirpate, by his authority, the horrid custom which had so long resisted the voice of humanity and religion. [57] The pathetic representations of Prudentius were less effectual than the generous boldness of Telemachus, and Asiatic monk, whose death was more useful to mankind than his life. [58] The Romans were provoked by the interruption of their pleasures; and the rash monk, who had descended into the arena to separate the gladiators, was overwhelmed under a shower of stones. But the madness of the people soon subsided; they respected the memory of Telemachus, who had deserved the honors of martyrdom; and they submitted, without a murmur, to the laws of Honorius, which abolished forever the human sacrifices of the amphitheater. [58/1] The citizens, who adhered to the manners of their ancestors, might perhaps insinuate that the last remains of a martial spirit were preserved in this school of fortitude, which accustomed the Romans to the sight of blood, and to the contempt of death; a vain and cruel prejudice, so nobly confuted by the valor of ancient Greece, and of modern Europe! [59]

[Footnote 55: On the curious, though horrid, subject of the gladiators, consult the two books of the Saturnalia of Lipsius, who, as an antiquarian, is inclined to excuse the practice of antiquity, (tom. iii. p. 483-545.)]

[Footnote 56: Cod. Theodos. l. xv. tit. xii. leg. i. The Commentary of Godefroy affords large materials (tom. v. p. 396) for the history of gladiators.]

[Footnote 57: See the peroration of Prudentius (in Symmach. l. II. 1121-1131) who had doubtless read the eloquent invective of Lactantius, (Divin. Institut. l. vi. c. 20.) The Christian apologists have not spared these bloody games, which were introduced in the religious festivals of Paganism.]

[Footnote 58: Theodoret, l. v. c. 26. I wish to believe the story of St. Telemachus. Yet no church has been dedicated, no altar has been erected, to the only monk who died a martyr in the cause of humanity.]

[Footnote 58/1: Muller, in his valuable Treatise, de Genio, moribus et luxu aevi Theodosiani, is disposed to question the effect produced by the heroic, or rather saintly, death of Telemachus. No prohibitory law of Honorius is to be found in the Theodosian Code, only the old and imperfect edict of Constantine. But Muller has produced no evidence or allusion to gladiatorial shows after this period. The combats with wild beasts certainly lasted till the fall of the Western empire; but the gladiatorial combats ceased either by common consent, or by Imperial edict—M.]

[Footnote 59: Crudele gladiatorum spectaculum et inhumanum nonnullis videri solet, et haud scio an ita sit, ut nunc fit. Cicero Tusculan. ii. 17. He faintly censures the abuse, and warmly defends the use, of these sports; oculis nulla poterat esse fortior contra dolorem et mortem disciplina. Seneca (epist. vii.) shows the feelings of a man.]

The recent danger, to which the person of the emperor had been exposed in the defenceless palace of Milan, urged him to seek a retreat in some inaccessible fortress of Italy, where he might securely remain, while the open country was covered by a deluge of Barbarians. On the coast of the Adriatic, about ten or twelve miles from the most southern of the seven mouths of the Po, the Thessalians had founded the ancient colony of Ravenna, [60] which they afterwards resigned to the natives of Umbria. Augustus, who had observed the opportunity of the place, prepared, at the distance of three miles from the old town, a capacious harbor, for the reception of two hundred and fifty ships of war. This naval establishment, which included the arsenals and magazines, the barracks of the troops, and the houses of the artificers, derived its origin and name from the permanent station of the Roman fleet; the intermediate space was soon filled with buildings and inhabitants, and the three extensive and populous quarters of Ravenna gradually contributed to form one of the most important cities of Italy. The principal canal of Augustus poured a copious stream of the waters of the Po through the midst of the city, to the entrance of the harbor; the same waters were introduced into the profound ditches that encompassed the walls; they were distributed by a thousand subordinate canals, into every part of the city, which they divided into a variety of small islands; the communication was maintained only by the use of boats and bridges; and the houses of Ravenna, whose appearance may be compared to that of Venice, were raised on the foundation of wooden piles. The adjacent country, to the distance of many miles, was a deep and impassable morass; and the artificial causeway, which connected Ravenna with the continent, might be easily guarded or destroyed, on the approach of a hostile army These morasses were interspersed, however, with vineyards: and though the soil was exhausted by four or five crops, the town enjoyed a more plentiful supply of wine than of fresh water. [61] The air, instead of receiving the sickly, and almost pestilential, exhalations of low and marshy grounds, was distinguished, like the neighborhood of Alexandria, as uncommonly pure and salubrious; and this singular advantage was ascribed to the regular tides of the Adriatic, which swept the canals, interrupted the unwholesome stagnation of the waters, and floated, every day, the vessels of the adjacent country into the heart of Ravenna. The gradual retreat of the sea has left the modern city at the distance of four miles from the Adriatic; and as early as the fifth or sixth century of the Christian aera, the port of Augustus was converted into pleasant orchards; and a lonely grove of pines covered the ground where the Roman fleet once rode at anchor. [62] Even this alteration contributed to increase the natural strength of the place, and the shallowness of the water was a sufficient barrier against the large ships of the enemy. This advantageous situation was fortified by art and labor; and in the twentieth year of his age, the emperor of the West, anxious only for his personal safety, retired to the perpetual confinement of the walls and morasses of Ravenna. The example of Honorius was imitated by his feeble successors, the Gothic kings, and afterwards the Exarchs, who occupied the throne and palace of the emperors; and till the middle of the eight century, Ravenna was considered as the seat of government, and the capital of Italy. [63]

[Footnote 60: This account of Ravenna is drawn from Strabo, (l. v. p. 327,) Pliny, (iii. 20,) Stephen of Byzantium, (sub voce, p. 651, edit. Berkel,) Claudian, (in vi. Cons. Honor. 494, &c.,) Sidonius Apollinaris, (l. i. epist. 5, 8,) Jornandes, (de Reb. Get. c. 29,) Procopius (de Bell, (lothic, l. i. c. i. p. 309, edit. Louvre,) and

Cluverius, (Ital. Antiq tom i. p. 301-307.) Yet I still want a local antiquarian and a good topographical map.]

[Footnote 61: *Martial (Epigram iii. 56, 57) plays on the trick of the knave, who had sold him wine instead of water; but he seriously declares that a cistern at Ravenna is more valuable than a vineyard. Sidonius complains that the town is destitute of fountains and aqueducts; and ranks the want of fresh water among the local evils, such as the croaking of frogs, the stinging of gnats, &c.]*

[Footnote 62: *The fable of Theodore and Honoria, which Dryden has so admirably transplanted from Boccaccio, (Giornata iii. novell. viii.,) was acted in the wood of Chiassi, a corrupt word from Classis, the naval station which, with the intermediate road, or suburb the Via Caesaris, constituted the triple city of Ravenna.]*

[Footnote 63: *From the year 404, the dates of the Theodosian Code become sedentary at Constantinople and Ravenna. See Godefroy's Chronology of the Laws, tom. i. p. cxlviii., &c.]*

The fears of Honorius were not without foundation, nor were his precautions without effect. While Italy rejoiced in her deliverance from the Goths, a furious tempest was excited among the nations of Germany, who yielded to the irresistible impulse that appears to have been gradually communicated from the eastern extremity of the continent of Asia. The Chinese annals, as they have been interpreted by the earned industry of the present age, may be usefully applied to reveal the secret and remote causes of the fall of the Roman empire. The extensive territory to the north of the great wall was possessed, after the flight of the Huns, by the victorious Sienpi, who were sometimes broken into independent tribes, and sometimes reunited under a supreme chief; till at length, styling themselves Topa, or masters of the earth, they acquired a more solid consistence, and a more formidable power. The Topa soon compelled the pastoral nations of the eastern desert to acknowledge the superiority of their arms; they invaded China in a period of weakness and intestine discord; and these fortunate Tartars, adopting the laws and manners of the vanquished people, founded an Imperial dynasty, which reigned near one hundred and sixty years over the northern provinces of the monarchy. Some generations before they ascended the throne of China, one of the Topa princes had enlisted in his cavalry a slave of the name of Moko, renowned for his valor, but who was tempted, by the fear of punishment, to desert his standard, and to range the desert at the head of a hundred followers. This gang of robbers and outlaws swelled into a camp, a tribe, a numerous people, distinguished by the appellation of Geougen; and their hereditary chieftains, the posterity of Moko the slave, assumed their rank among the Scythian monarchs. The youth of Toulun, the greatest of his descendants, was exercised by those misfortunes which are the school of heroes. He bravely struggled with adversity, broke the imperious yoke of the Topa, and became the legislator of his nation, and the conqueror of Tartary. His troops were distributed into regular bands of a hundred and of a thousand men; cowards were stoned to death; the most splendid honors were proposed as the reward of valor; and Toulun, who had knowledge enough to despise the learning of China, adopted only such arts and institutions as were favorable to the military spirit of his government. His tents, which he removed in the winter season to a more southern latitude, were pitched, during the summer, on the fruitful banks of the Selinga. His conquests stretched from Corea far beyond the River Irtish. He vanquished, in the country to the north of the Caspian Sea, the nation of the Huns; and the new title of Khan, or Cagan, expressed the fame and power which he derived from this memorable victory. [64]

[Footnote 64: *See M. de Guignes, Hist. des Huns, tom. i. p. 179-189, tom ii p. 295, 334-338.]*

The chain of events is interrupted, or rather is concealed, as it passes from the Volga to the Vistula, through the dark interval which separates the extreme limits of the Chinese, and of the Roman, geography. Yet the temper of the Barbarians, and the experience of successive emigrations, sufficiently declare, that the Huns, who were oppressed by the arms of the Geougen, soon withdrew from the presence of an insulting victor. The countries towards the Euxine were already occupied by their kindred tribes; and their hasty flight, which they soon converted into a bold attack, would more naturally be directed towards the rich and level plains, through which the Vistula gently flows into the Baltic Sea. The North must again have been alarmed, and agitated, by the invasion of the Huns; [64/1] and the nations who retreated before them must have pressed with incumbent weight on the confines of Germany. [65] The inhabitants of those regions, which the ancients have assigned to the Suevi, the Vandals, and the Burgundians, might embrace the resolution of abandoning to the fugitives of Sarmatia their woods and morasses; or at least of discharging their superfluous numbers on the provinces of the Roman empire. [66] About four years after the victorious Toulun had assumed the title of Khan of the Geougen, another Barbarian, the haughty Rhodogast, or Radagaisus, [67] marched from the northern extremities of Germany almost to the gates of Rome, and left the remains of his army to achieve the destruction of the West. The Vandals, the Suevi, and the Burgundians, formed the strength of this mighty host; but the Alani, who had found a hospitable reception in their new seats, added their active cavalry to the heavy infantry of the Germans; and the Gothic adventurers crowded so eagerly to the standard of Radagaisus, that by some historians, he has been styled the King of the Goths. Twelve thousand warriors, distinguished above the vulgar by their noble birth, or their valiant deeds, glittered in the van; [68] and the whole multitude, which was not less than two hundred thousand fighting men, might be increased, by the accession of women, of children, and of slaves, to the amount of four hundred thousand persons. This formidable emigration issued from the same coast of the Baltic, which had poured forth the myriads of the Cimbri and Teutones, to assault Rome and Italy in the vigor of the republic. After the departure of those Barbarians, their native country, which was marked by the vestiges of their greatness, long ramparts, and gigantic moles, [69] remained, during some ages, a vast and dreary solitude; till the human species was renewed by the powers of generation, and the vacancy was filled by the influx of new inhabitants. The nations who now usurp an extent of land which they are unable to cultivate, would soon be assisted by the industrious poverty of their neighbors, if the government of Europe did not protect the claims of dominion and property.

[Footnote 64/1: There is no authority which connects this inroad of the Teutonic tribes with the movements of the Huns. The Huns can hardly have reached the shores of the Baltic, and probably the greater part of the forces of Radagaisus, particularly the Vandals, had long occupied a more southern position—M.]

[Footnote 65: Procopius (de Bell. Vandal. l. i. c. iii. p. 182) has observed an emigration from the Palus Maeotis to the north of Germany, which he ascribes to famine. But his views of ancient history are strangely darkened by ignorance and error.]

[Footnote 66: Zosimus (l. v. p. 331) uses the general description of the nations beyond the Danube and the Rhine. Their situation, and consequently their names, are manifestly shown, even in the various epithets which each ancient writer may have casually added.]

[Footnote 67: The name of Rhadagast was that of a local deity of the Obotrites, (in Mecklenburg.) A hero might naturally assume the appellation of his tutelar god; but it is not probable that the Barbarians should worship an unsuccessful hero. See Mascou, Hist. of the Germans, viii. 14. Note: The god of war and of hospitality with the Vends and all the Sclavonian races of Germany bore the name of Radegast, *apparently the same with Rhadagaisus. His principal temple was at Rhetra in Mecklenburg. It was adorned with great magnificence. The statue of the gold was of gold. St. Martin, v. 255. A statue of Radegast, of much coarser materials, and of the rudest workmanship, was discovered between 1760 and 1770, with those of other Wendish deities, on the supposed site of Rhetra. The names of the gods were cut upon them in Runic characters. See the very curious volume on these antiquities—Die Gottesdienstliche Alterthumer der Obotriter—Masch and Wogen. Berlin, 1771—M.]*

[Footnote 68: Olympiodorus (apud Photium, p. 180), uses the Greek word which does not convey any precise idea. I suspect that they were the princes and nobles with their faithful companions; the knights with their squires, as they would have been styled some centuries afterwards.]

[Footnote 69: Tacit. de Moribus Germanorum, c. 37.]

PART IV

The correspondence of nations was, in that age, so imperfect and precarious, that the revolutions of the North might escape the knowledge of the court of Ravenna; till the dark cloud, which was collected along the coast of the Baltic, burst in thunder upon the banks of the Upper Danube. The emperor of the West, if his ministers disturbed his amusements by the news of the impending danger, was satisfied with being the occasion, and the spectator, of the war. [70] The safety of Rome was intrusted to the counsels, and the sword, of Stilicho; but such was the feeble and exhausted state of the empire, that it was impossible to restore the fortifications of the Danube, or to prevent, by a vigorous effort, the invasion of the Germans. [71] The hopes of the vigilant minister of Honorius were confined to the defence of Italy. He once more abandoned the provinces, recalled the troops, pressed the new levies, which were rigorously exacted, and pusillanimously eluded; employed the most efficacious means to arrest, or allure, the deserters; and offered the gift of freedom, and of two pieces of gold, to all the slaves who would enlist. [72] By these efforts he painfully collected, from the subjects of a great empire, an army of thirty or forty thousand men, which, in the days of Scipio or Camillus, would have been instantly furnished by the free citizens of the territory of Rome. [73] The thirty legions of Stilicho were reenforced by a large body of Barbarian auxiliaries; the faithful Alani were personally attached to his service; and the troops of Huns and of Goths, who marched under the banners of their native princes, Huldin and Sarus, were animated by interest and resentment to oppose the ambition of Radagaisus. The king of the confederate Germans passed, without resistance, the Alps, the Po, and the Apennine; leaving on one hand the inaccessible palace of Honorius, securely buried among the marshes of Ravenna; and, on the other, the camp of Stilicho, who had fixed his head-quarters at Ticinum, or Pavia, but who seems to have avoided a decisive battle, till he had assembled his distant forces. Many cities of Italy were pillaged, or destroyed; and the siege of Florence, [74] by Radagaisus, is one of the earliest events in the history of that celebrated republic; whose firmness checked and delayed the unskillful fury of the Barbarians. The senate and people trembled at their approached within a hundred and eighty miles of Rome; and anxiously compared the danger which they had escaped, with the new perils to which they were exposed. Alaric was a Christian and a soldier, the leader of a disciplined army; who understood the laws of war, who respected the sanctity of treaties, and who had familiarly conversed with the subjects of the empire in the same camps, and the same churches. The savage Radagaisus was a stranger to the manners, the religion, and even the language, of the civilized nations of the South. The fierceness of his temper was exasperated by cruel superstition; and it was universally believed, that he had bound himself, by a solemn vow, to reduce the city into a heap of stones and ashes, and to sacrifice the most illustrious of the Roman senators on the altars of those gods who were appeased by human blood. The public danger, which should have reconciled all domestic animosities, displayed the incurable madness of religious faction. The oppressed votaries of Jupiter and Mercury respected, in the implacable enemy of Rome, the character of a devout Pagan; loudly declared, that they were more apprehensive of the sacrifices, than of the arms, of Radagaisus; and secretly rejoiced in the calamities of their country, which condemned the faith of their Christian adversaries. [75] [75/1]

[Footnote 70:
Cujus agendi Spectator vel causa fui, —(Claudian, vi. Cons. Hon. 439,)

is the modest language of Honorius, in speaking of the Gothic war, which he had seen somewhat nearer.]

[Footnote 71: Zosimus (l. v. p. 331) transports the war, and the victory of Stilisho, beyond the Danube. A strange error, which is awkwardly and imperfectly cured (Tillemont, Hist. des Emp. tom. v. p. 807.) In good policy, we must use the service of Zosimus, without esteeming or trusting him.]

[Footnote 72: Codex Theodos. l. vii. tit. xiii. leg. 16. The date of this law A.D. 406. May 18 satisfies me, as it had done Godefroy, (tom. ii. p. 387,) of the true year of the invasion of Radagaisus. Tillemont, Pagi, and Muratori, prefer the preceding year; but they are bound, by certain obligations of civility and respect, to St. Paulinus of Nola.]

[Footnote 73: Soon after Rome had been taken by the Gauls, the senate, on a sudden emergency, armed ten legions, 3000 horse, and 42,000 foot; a force which the city could not have sent forth under Augustus, (Livy, xi. 25.) This declaration may puzzle an antiquary, but it is clearly explained by Montesquieu.]

[Footnote 74: Machiavel has explained, at least as a philosopher, the origin of Florence, which insensibly descended, for the benefit of trade, from the rock of Faesulae to the banks of the Arno, (Istoria Fiorentina, tom. i. p. 36. Londra, 1747.) The triumvirs sent a colony to Florence, which, under Tiberius, (Tacit. Annal. i. 79,) deserved the reputation and name of a flourishing city. See Cluver. Ital. Antiq. tom. i. p. 507, &c.]

[Footnote 75: Yet the Jupiter of Radagaisus, who worshipped Thor and Woden, was very different from the Olympic or Capitoline Jove. The accommodating temper of Polytheism might unite those various and remote deities; but the genuine Romans abhorred the human sacrifices of Gaul and Germany.]

[Footnote 75/1: Gibbon has rather softened the language of Augustine as to this threatened insurrection of the Pagans, in order to restore the prohibited rites and ceremonies of Paganism; and their treasonable hopes that the success of Radagaisus would be the triumph of idolatry. Compare ii. 25—M.]

Florence was reduced to the last extremity; and the fainting courage of the citizens was supported only by the authority of St. Ambrose; who had communicated, in a dream, the promise of a speedy deliverance. [76] On a sudden, they beheld, from their walls, the banners of Stilicho, who advanced, with his united force, to the relief of the faithful city; and who soon marked that fatal spot for the grave of the Barbarian host. The apparent contradictions of those writers who variously relate the defeat of Radagaisus, may be reconciled without offering much violence to their respective testimonies. Orosius and Augustin, who were intimately connected by friendship and religion, ascribed this miraculous victory to the providence of God, rather than to the valor of man. [77] They strictly exclude every idea of chance, or even of bloodshed; and positively affirm, that the Romans, whose camp was the scene of plenty and idleness, enjoyed the distress of the Barbarians, slowly expiring on the sharp and barren ridge of the hills of Faesulae, which rise above the city of Florence. Their extravagant assertion that not a single soldier of the Christian army was killed, or even wounded, may be dismissed with silent contempt; but the rest of the narrative of Augustin and Orosius is consistent with the state of the war, and the character of Stilicho. Conscious that he commanded the last army of the republic, his prudence would not expose it, in the open field, to the headstrong fury of the Germans. The method of surrounding the enemy with strong lines of circumvallation, which he had twice employed against the Gothic king, was repeated on a larger scale, and with more considerable effect. The examples of Caesar must have been familiar to the most illiterate of the Roman warriors; and the fortifications of Dyrrachium, which connected twenty-four castles, by a perpetual ditch and rampart of fifteen miles, afforded the model of an intrenchment which might confine, and starve, the most numerous host of Barbarians. [78] The Roman troops had less degenerated from the industry, than from the valor, of their ancestors; and if their servile and laborious work offended the pride of the soldiers, Tuscany could supply many thousand peasants, who would labor, though, perhaps, they would not fight, for the salvation of their native country. The imprisoned multitude of horses and men [79] was gradually destroyed, by famine rather than by the sword; but the Romans were exposed, during the progress of such an extensive work, to the frequent attacks of an impatient enemy. The despair of the hungry Barbarians would precipitate them against the fortifications of Stilicho; the general might sometimes indulge the ardor of his brave auxiliaries, who eagerly pressed to assault the camp of the Germans; and these various incidents might produce the sharp and bloody conflicts which dignify the narrative of Zosimus, and the Chronicles of Prosper and Marcellinus. [80] A seasonable supply of men and provisions had been introduced into the walls of Florence, and the famished host of Radagaisus was in its turn besieged. The proud monarch of so many warlike nations, after the loss of his bravest warriors, was reduced to confide either in the faith of a capitulation, or in the clemency of Stilicho. [81] But the death of the royal captive, who was ignominiously beheaded, disgraced the triumph of Rome and of Christianity; and the short delay of his execution was sufficient to brand the conqueror with the guilt of cool and deliberate cruelty. [82] The famished Germans, who escaped the fury of the auxiliaries, were sold as slaves, at the contemptible price of as many single pieces of gold; but the difference of food and climate swept away great numbers of those unhappy strangers; and it was observed, that the inhuman purchasers, instead of reaping the fruits of their labor were soon obliged to provide the expense of their interment Stilicho informed the emperor and the senate of his success; and deserved, a second time, the glorious title of Deliverer of Italy. [83]

[Footnote 76: Paulinus (in Vit. Ambros c. 50) relates this story, which he received from the mouth of Pansophia herself, a religious matron of Florence. Yet the archbishop soon ceased to take an active part in the business of the world, and never became a popular saint.]

[Footnote 77: Augustin de Civitat. Dei, v. 23. Orosius, l. vii. c. 37, p. 567-571. The two friends wrote in Africa, ten or twelve years after the victory; and their authority is implicitly followed by Isidore of Seville, (in Chron. p. 713, edit. Grot.) How many interesting facts might Orosius have inserted in the vacant space which is devoted to pious nonsense!]

[Footnote 78:
Franguntur montes, planumque per ardua Caesar Ducit opus: pandit fossas, turritaque summis Disponit castella jugis, magnoque necessu Amplexus fines, saltus, memorosaque tesqua Et silvas, vastaque feras indagine claudit.!

Yet the simplicity of truth (Caesar, de Bell. Civ. iii. 44) is far greater than the amplifications of Lucan, (Pharsal. l. vi. 29-63.)]

[Footnote 79: The rhetorical expressions of Orosius, "in arido et aspero montis jugo;" "in unum ac parvum verticem," are not very suitable to the encampment of a great army. But Faesulae, only three miles from Florence, might afford space for the head-quarters of Radagaisus, and would be comprehended within the circuit of the Roman lines.]

[Footnote 80: See Zosimus, l. v. p. 331, and the Chronicles of Prosper and Marcellinus.]

[Footnote 81: Olympiodorus (apud Photium, p. 180) uses an expression which would denote a strict and friendly alliance, and render Stilicho still more criminal. The paulisper detentus, deinde interfectus, of Orosius, is sufficiently odious. Note: Gibbon, by translating this passage of Olympiodorus, as if it had been good Greek, has probably fallen into an error. The natural order of the words is as Gibbon translates it; but it is almost clear, refers to the Gothic chiefs, "whom Stilicho, after he had defeated Radagaisus, attached to his army." So in the version corrected by Classen for Niebuhr's edition of the Byzantines, p. 450—M.]

[Footnote 82: Orosius, piously inhuman, sacrifices the king and people, Agag and the Amalekites, without a symptom of compassion. The bloody actor is less detestable than the cool, unfeeling historian—Note: Considering the vow, which he was universally believed to have made, to destroy Rome, and to sacrifice the senators on the altars, and that he is said to have immolated his prisoners to his gods, the execution of Radagaisus, if, as it appears, he was taken in arms, cannot deserve Gibbon's severe condemnation. Mr. Herbert (notes to his poem of Attila, p. 317) justly observes, that "Stilicho had probably authority for hanging him on the first tree." Marcellinus, adds Mr. Herbert, attributes the execution to the Gothic chiefs Sarus—M.]

[Footnote 83: And Claudian's muse, was she asleep? had she been ill paid! Methinks the seventh consulship of Honorius (A.D. 407) would have furnished the subject of a noble poem. Before it was discovered that the state could no longer be saved, Stilicho (after Romulus, Camillus and Marius) might have been worthily surnamed the fourth founder of Rome.]

The fame of the victory, and more especially of the miracle, has encouraged a vain persuasion, that the whole army, or rather nation, of Germans, who migrated from the shores of the Baltic, miserably perished under the walls of Florence. Such indeed was the fate of Radagaisus himself, of his brave and faithful companions, and of more than one third of the various multitude of Sueves and Vandals, of Alani and Burgundians, who adhered to the standard of their general. [84] The union of such an army might excite our surprise, but the causes of separation are obvious and forcible; the pride of birth, the insolence of valor, the jealousy of command, the impatience of subordination, and the obstinate conflict of opinions, of interests, and of passions, among so many kings and warriors, who were untaught to yield, or to obey. After the defeat of Radagaisus, two parts of the German host, which must have exceeded the number of one hundred thousand men, still remained in arms, between the Apennine and the Alps, or between the Alps and the Danube. It is uncertain whether they attempted to revenge the death of their general; but their irregular fury was soon diverted by the prudence and firmness of Stilicho, who opposed their march, and facilitated their retreat; who considered the safety of Rome and Italy as the great object of his care, and who sacrificed, with too much indifference, the wealth and tranquillity of the distant provinces. [85] The Barbarians acquired, from the junction of some Pannonian deserters, the knowledge of the country, and of the roads; and the invasion of Gaul, which Alaric had designed, was executed by the remains of the great army of Radagaisus. [86]

[Footnote 84: A luminous passage of Prosper's Chronicle, "In tres partes, pes diversos principes, diversus exercitus," reduces the miracle of Florence and connects the history of Italy, Gaul, and Germany.]

[Footnote 85: Orosius and Jerom positively charge him with instigating the in vasion. "Excitatae a Stilichone gentes," &c. They must mean a directly. He saved Italy at the expense of Gaul]

[Footnote 86: The Count de Buat is satisfied, that the Germans who invaded Gaul were the two thirds that yet remained of the army of Radagaisus. See the Histoire Ancienne des Peuples de l'Europe, (tom. vii. p. 87, 121. Paris, 1772;) an elaborate work, which I had not the advantage of perusing till the year 1777. As early as 1771, I find the same idea expressed in a rough draught of the present History. I have since observed a similar intimation in Mascou, (viii. 15.) Such agreement, without mutual communication, may add some weight to our common sentiment.]

Yet if they expected to derive any assistance from the tribes of Germany, who inhabited the banks of the Rhine, their hopes were disappointed. The Alemanni preserved a state of inactive neutrality; and the Franks distinguished their zeal and courage in the defence of the of the empire. In the rapid progress down the Rhine, which was the first act of the administration of Stilicho, he had applied himself, with peculiar attention, to secure the alliance of the warlike Franks, and to remove the irreconcilable enemies of peace and of the republic. Marcomir, one of their kings, was publicly convicted, before the tribunal of the Roman magistrate, of violating the faith of treaties. He was sentenced to a mild, but distant exile, in the province of Tuscany; and this degradation of the regal dignity was so far from exciting the resentment of his subjects, that they punished with death the turbulent Sunno, who attempted to revenge his brother; and maintained a dutiful allegiance to the princes, who were established on the throne by the choice of Stilicho. [87] When the limits of Gaul and Germany were shaken by the northern emigration, the Franks bravely encountered the single force of the Vandals; who, regardless of the lessons of adversity, had again separated their troops from the standard of their Barbarian allies. They paid the penalty of their rashness; and twenty thousand Vandals, with their king Godigisclus, were slain in the field of battle. The whole people must have been extirpated, if the squadrons of the Alani, advancing to their relief, had not trampled down the infantry of the Franks; who, after an honorable resistance, were compelled to relinquish the unequal contest. The victorious confederates pursued their march, and on the last day of the year, in a season when the waters of the Rhine were most probably frozen, they entered, without opposition, the defenceless provinces of Gaul. This memorable passage of the Suevi, the Vandals, the Alani, and the Burgundians, who never afterwards retreated, may be considered as the fall of the Roman empire in the countries beyond the Alps; and the barriers, which had so long separated the savage and the civilized nations of the earth, were from that fatal moment levelled with the ground. [88]

[Footnote 87:
Provincia missos Expellet citius fasces, quam Francia reges Quos dederis.

Claudian (i. Cons. Stil. l. i. 235, &c.) is clear and satisfactory. These kings of France are unknown to Gregory of Tours; but the author of the Gesta Francorum mentions both Sunno and Marcomir, and names the latter as the father of Pharamond, (in tom. ii. p. 543.) He seems to write from good materials, which he did not understand.]

[Footnote 88: See Zosimus, (l. vi. p. 373,) Orosius, (l. vii. c. 40, p. 576,) and the Chronicles. Gregory of Tours (l. ii. c. 9, p. 165, in the second volume of the Historians of France) has preserved a valuable fragment of Renatus Profuturus Frigeridus, whose three names denote a Christian, a Roman subject, and a Semi-Barbarian.]

While the peace of Germany was secured by the attachment of the Franks, and the neutrality of the Alemanni, the subjects of Rome, unconscious of their approaching calamities, enjoyed the state of quiet and prosperity, which had seldom blessed the frontiers of Gaul. Their flocks and herds were permitted to graze in the pastures of the Barbarians; their huntsmen penetrated, without fear or danger, into the darkest recesses of the Hercynian wood. [89] The banks of the Rhine were crowned, like those of the Tyber, with elegant houses, and well-cultivated farms; and if a poet descended the river, he might express his doubt, on which side was situated the territory of the Romans. [90] This scene of peace and plenty was suddenly changed into a desert; and the prospect of the smoking ruins could alone distinguish the solitude of nature from the desolation of man. The flourishing city of Mentz was surprised and destroyed; and many thousand Christians were inhumanly massacred in the church. Worms perished after a long and obstinate siege; Strasburgh, Spires, Rheims, Tournay, Arras, Amiens, experienced the cruel oppression of the German yoke; and the consuming flames of war spread from the banks of the Rhine over the greatest part of the seventeen provinces of Gaul. That rich and extensive country, as far as the ocean, the Alps, and the Pyrenees, was delivered to the Barbarians, who drove before them, in a promiscuous crowd, the bishop, the senator, and the virgin, laden with the spoils of their houses and altars. [91] The ecclesiastics, to whom we are indebted for this vague description of the public calamities, embraced the opportunity of exhorting the Christians to repent of the sins which had provoked the Divine Justice, and to renounce the perishable goods of a wretched and deceitful world. But as the Pelagian controversy, [92] which attempts to sound the abyss of grace and predestination, soon became the serious employment of the Latin clergy, the Providence which had decreed, or foreseen, or permitted, such a train of moral and natural evils, was rashly weighed in the imperfect and fallacious balance of reason. The crimes, and the misfortunes, of the suffering people, were presumptuously compared with those of their ancestors; and they arraigned the Divine Justice, which did not exempt from the common destruction the feeble, the guiltless, the infant portion of the human species. These idle disputants overlooked the invariable laws of nature, which have connected peace with innocence, plenty with industry, and safety with valor. The timid and selfish policy of the court of Ravenna might recall the Palatine legions for the protection of Italy; the remains of the stationary troops might be unequal to the arduous task; and the Barbarian auxiliaries might prefer the unbounded license of spoil to the benefits of a moderate and regular stipend. But the provinces of Gaul were filled with a numerous race of hardy and robust youth, who, in the defence of their houses, their families, and their altars, if they had dared to die, would have deserved to vanquish. The knowledge of their native country would have enabled them to oppose continual and insuperable obstacles to the progress of an invader; and the deficiency of the Barbarians, in arms, as well as in discipline, removed the only pretence which excuses the submission of a populous country to the inferior numbers of a veteran army. When France was invaded by Charles V., he inquired of a prisoner, how many days Paris might be distant from the frontier; "Perhaps twelve, but they will be days of battle:" [93] such was the gallant answer which checked the arrogance of that ambitious prince. The subjects of Honorius, and those of Francis I., were animated by a very different spirit; and in less than two years, the divided troops of the savages of the Baltic, whose numbers, were they fairly stated, would appear contemptible, advanced, without a combat, to the foot of the Pyrenean Mountains.

[Footnote 89: Claudian (i. Cons. Stil. l. i. 221, &c., l. ii. 186) describes the peace and prosperity of the Gallic frontier. The Abbe Dubos (Hist. Critique, &c., tom. i. p. 174) would read Alba (a nameless rivulet of the Ardennes) instead of Albis; and expatiates on the danger of the Gallic cattle grazing beyond the Elbe. Foolish enough! In poetical geography, the Elbe, and the Hercynian, signify any river, or any wood, in Germany. Claudian is not prepared for the strict examination of our antiquaries.]

[Footnote 90:—Germinasque viator Cum videat ripas, quae sit Romana requirat.]

[Footnote 91: Jerom, tom. i. p. 93. See in the 1st vol. of the Historians of France, p. 777, 782, the proper extracts from the Carmen de Providentil Divina, and Salvian. The anonymous poet was himself a captive, with his bishop and fellow-citizens.]

[Footnote 92: The Pelagian doctrine, which was first agitated A.D. 405, was condemned, in the space of ten years, at Rome and Carthage. St Augustin fought and conquered; but the Greek church was favorable to his adversaries; and (what is singular enough) the people did not take any part in a dispute which they could not understand.]

[Footnote 93: See the Memoires de Guillaume du Bellay, l. vi. In French, the original reproof is less obvious, and more pointed, from the double sense of the word journee, which alike signifies, a day's travel, or a battle.]

In the early part of the reign of Honorius, the vigilance of Stilicho had successfully guarded the remote island of Britain from her incessant enemies of the ocean, the mountains, and the Irish coast. [94] But those restless Barbarians could not neglect the fair opportunity of the Gothic war, when the walls and stations of the province were stripped of the Roman troops. If any of the legionaries were permitted to return from the Italian expedition, their faithful report of the court and character of Honorius must have tended to dissolve the bonds of allegiance, and to exasperate the seditious temper of the British army. The spirit of revolt, which had formerly disturbed the age of Gallienus, was revived by the capricious violence of the soldiers; and the unfortunate, perhaps the ambitious, candidates, who were the objects of their choice, were the instruments, and at length the victims, of their passion. [95] Marcus was the first whom they placed on the throne, as the lawful emperor of Britain and of the West. They violated, by the hasty murder of Marcus, the oath of fidelity which they had imposed on themselves; and their disapprobation of his manners may seem to inscribe an honorable epitaph on his tomb. Gratian was the next whom they adorned with the diadem and the purple; and, at the end of four months, Gratian experienced the fate of his predecessor. The memory of the great Constantine, whom the British legions had given to the church and to the empire, suggested the singular motive of their third choice. They discovered in the ranks a private soldier of the name of Constantine, and their impetuous levity had already seated him on the throne, before they perceived his incapacity to sustain the weight of that glorious appellation. [96] Yet the authority of Constantine was less precarious, and his government was more successful, than the transient reigns of Marcus and of Gratian. The danger of leaving his inactive troops in those camps, which had been twice polluted with blood and sedition, urged him to attempt the reduction of the Western provinces. He landed at Boulogne with an inconsiderable force; and after he had reposed himself some days, he summoned the cities of Gaul, which had escaped the yoke of the Barbarians, to acknowledge their lawful sovereign. They obeyed the summons without reluctance. The neglect of the court of Ravenna had absolved a deserted people from the duty of allegiance; their actual distress encouraged them to accept any circumstances of change, without apprehension, and, perhaps, with some degree of hope; and they might flatter themselves, that the troops, the authority, and even the name of a Roman emperor, who fixed his residence in Gaul, would protect the unhappy country from the rage of the Barbarians. The first successes of Constantine against the detached parties of the Germans, were magnified by the voice of adulation into splendid and decisive victories; which the reunion and insolence of the enemy soon reduced to their just value. His negotiations procured a short and precarious truce; and if some tribes of the Barbarians were engaged, by the liberality of his gifts and promises, to undertake the defence of the Rhine, these expensive and uncertain treaties, instead of restoring the pristine vigor of the Gallic frontier, served only to disgrace the majesty of the prince, and to exhaust what yet remained of the treasures of the republic. Elated, however, with this imaginary triumph, the vain deliverer of Gaul advanced into the provinces of the South, to encounter a more pressing and personal danger. Sarus the Goth was ordered to lay the head of the rebel at the feet of the emperor Honorius; and the forces of Britain and Italy were unworthily consumed in this domestic quarrel. After the loss of his two bravest generals, Justinian and Nevigastes, the former of whom was slain in the field of battle, the latter in a peaceful but treacherous interview, Constantine fortified himself within the walls of Vienna. The place was ineffectually attacked seven days; and the Imperial army supported, in a precipitate retreat, the ignominy of purchasing a secure passage from the freebooters and outlaws of the Alps. [97] Those mountains now separated the dominions of two rival monarchs; and the fortifications of the double frontier were guarded by the troops of the empire, whose arms would have been more usefully employed to maintain the Roman limits against the Barbarians of Germany and Scythia.

[Footnote 94: Claudian, (i. Cons. Stil. l. ii. 250.) It is supposed that the Scots of Ireland invaded, by sea, the whole western coast of Britain: and some slight credit may be given even to Nennius and the Irish traditions, (Carte's Hist. of England, vol. i. p. 169.) Whitaker's Genuine History of the Britons, p. 199. The sixty-six lives of St. Patrick, which were extant in the ninth century, must have contained as many thousand lies; yet we may believe, that, in one of these Irish inroads the future apostle was led away captive, (Usher, Antiquit. Eccles Britann. p. 431, and Tillemont, Mem. Eccles. tom. xvi. p. 45 782, &c.)]

[Footnote 95: The British usurpers are taken from Zosimus, (l. vi. p. 371-375,) Orosius, (l. vii. c. 40, p. 576, 577,) Olympiodorus, (apud Photium, p. 180, 181,) the ecclesiastical historians, and the Chronicles. The Latins are ignorant of Marcus.]

[Footnote 96: Cum in Constantino inconstantiam... execrarentur, (Sidonius Apollinaris, l. v. epist. 9, p. 139, edit. secund. Sirmond.) Yet Sidonius might be tempted, by so fair a pun, to stigmatize a prince who had disgraced his grandfather.]

[Footnote 97: Bagaudoe is the name which Zosimus applies to them; perhaps they deserved a less odious character, (see Dubos, Hist. Critique, tom. i. p. 203, and this History, vol. i. p. 407.) We shall hear of them again.]

PART V

On the side of the Pyrenees, the ambition of Constantine might be justified by the proximity of danger; but his throne was soon established by the conquest, or rather submission, of Spain; which yielded to the influence of regular and habitual subordination, and received the laws and magistrates of the Gallic praefecture. The only opposition which was made to the authority of Constantine proceeded not so much from the powers of government, or the spirit of the people, as from the private zeal and interest of the family of Theodosius. Four brothers [98] had obtained, by the favor of their kinsman, the deceased emperor, an honorable rank and ample possessions in their native country; and the grateful youths resolved to risk those advantages in the service of his son. After an unsuccessful effort to maintain their ground at the head of the stationary troops of Lusitania, they retired to their estates; where they armed and levied, at their own expense, a considerable body of slaves and dependants, and boldly marched to occupy the strong posts of the Pyrenean Mountains. This domestic insurrection alarmed and perplexed the sovereign of Gaul and Britain; and he was compelled to negotiate with some troops of Barbarian auxiliaries, for the service of the Spanish war. They were distinguished by the title of Honorians; [99] a name which might have reminded them of their fidelity to their lawful sovereign; and if it should candidly be allowed that the Scots were influenced by any partial affection for a British prince, the Moors and the Marcomanni could be tempted only by the profuse liberality of the usurper, who distributed among the Barbarians the military, and even the civil, honors of Spain. The nine bands of Honorians, which may be easily traced on the establishment of the Western empire, could not exceed the number of five thousand men: yet this inconsiderable force was sufficient to terminate a war, which had threatened the power and safety of Constantine. The rustic army of the Theodosian family was surrounded and destroyed in the Pyrenees: two of the brothers had the good fortune to escape by sea to Italy, or the East; the other two, after an interval of suspense, were executed at Arles; and if Honorius could remain insensible of the public disgrace, he might perhaps be affected by the personal misfortunes of his generous kinsmen. Such were the feeble arms which decided the possession of the Western provinces of Europe, from the wall of Antoninus to the columns of Hercules. The events of peace and war have undoubtedly been diminished by the narrow and imperfect view of the historians of the times, who were equally ignorant of the causes, and of the effects, of the most important revolutions. But the total decay of the national strength had annihilated even the last resource of a despotic government; and the revenue of exhausted provinces could no longer purchase the military service of a discontented and pusillanimous people.

[Footnote 98: Verinianus, Didymus, Theodosius, and Lagodius, who in modern courts would be styled princes of the blood, were not distinguished by any rank or privileges above the rest of their fellow-subjects.]

[Footnote 99: These Honoriani, or Honoriaci, consisted of two bands of Scots, or Attacotti, two of Moors, two of Marcomanni, the Victores, the Asca in, and the Gallicani, (Notitia Imperii, sect. xxxiii. edit. Lab.) They were part of the sixty-five Auxilia Palatina, and are properly styled by Zosimus, (l. vi. 374.)]

The poet, whose flattery has ascribed to the Roman eagle the victories of Pollentia and Verona, pursues the hasty retreat of Alaric, from the confines of Italy, with a horrid train of imaginary spectres, such as might hover over an army of Barbarians, which was almost exterminated by war, famine, and disease. [100] In the course of this unfortunate expedition, the king of the Goths must indeed have sustained a considerable loss; and his harassed forces required an interval of repose, to recruit their numbers and revive their confidence. Adversity had exercised and displayed the genius of Alaric; and the fame of his valor invited to the Gothic standard the bravest of the Barbarian warriors; who, from the Euxine to the Rhine, were agitated by the desire of rapine and conquest. He had deserved the esteem, and he soon accepted the friendship, of Stilicho himself. Renouncing the service of the emperor of the East, Alaric concluded, with the court of Ravenna, a treaty of peace and alliance, by which he was declared master-general of the Roman armies throughout the praefecture of Illyricum; as it was claimed, according to the true and ancient limits, by the minister of Honorius. [101] The execution of the ambitious design, which was either stipulated, or implied, in the articles of the treaty, appears to have been suspended by the formidable irruption of Radagaisus; and the neutrality of the Gothic king may perhaps be compared to the indifference of Caesar, who, in the conspiracy of Catiline, refused either to assist, or to oppose, the enemy of the republic. After the defeat of the Vandals, Stilicho resumed his pretensions to the provinces of the East; appointed civil magistrates for the administration of justice, and of the finances; and declared his impatience to lead to the gates of Constantinople the united armies of the Romans and of the Goths. The prudence, however, of Stilicho, his aversion to civil war, and his perfect knowledge of the weakness of the state, may countenance the suspicion, that domestic peace, rather than foreign conquest, was the object of his policy; and that his principal care was to employ the forces of Alaric at a distance from Italy. This design could not long escape the penetration of the Gothic king, who continued to hold a doubtful, and perhaps a treacherous, correspondence with the rival courts; who protracted, like a dissatisfied mercenary, his languid operations in Thessaly and Epirus, and who soon returned to claim the extravagant reward of his ineffectual services. From his camp near Aemona, [102] on the confines of Italy, he transmitted to the emperor of the West a long account of promises, of expenses, and of demands; called for immediate satisfaction, and clearly intimated the consequences of a refusal. Yet if his conduct was hostile, his language was decent and dutiful. He humbly professed himself the friend of Stilicho, and the soldier of Honorius; offered his person and his troops to march, without delay, against the usurper of Gaul; and solicited, as a permanent retreat for the Gothic nation, the possession of some vacant province of the Western empire.

[Footnote 100:
Comitatur euntem Pallor, et atra fames; et saucia lividus ora Luctus; et inferno stridentes agmine morbi. —Claudian in vi. Cons. Hon. 821, &c.]

[Footnote 101: These dark transactions are investigated by the Count de Bual (Hist. des Peuples de l'Europe, tom. vii. c. iii—viii. p. 69-206,) whose laborious accuracy may sometimes fatigue a superficial reader.]

[Footnote 102: See Zosimus, l. v. p. 334, 335. He interrupts his scanty narrative to relate the fable of Aemona, and of the ship Argo; which was drawn overland from that place to the Adriatic. Sozomen (l. viii. c. 25, l. ix. c. 4) and Socrates (l. vii. c. 10) cast a pale and doubtful light; and Orosius (l. vii. c. 38, p. 571) is abominably partial.]

The political and secret transactions of two statesmen, who labored to deceive each other and the world, must forever have been concealed in the impenetrable darkness of the cabinet, if the debates of a popular assembly had not thrown some rays of light on the correspondence of Alaric and Stilicho. The necessity of finding some artificial support for a government, which, from a principle, not of moderation, but of weakness, was reduced to negotiate with its own subjects, had insensibly revived the authority of the Roman senate; and the minister of Honorius respectfully consulted the legislative council of the republic. Stilicho assembled the senate in the palace of the Caesars; represented, in a studied oration, the actual state of affairs; proposed the demands of the Gothic king, and submitted to their consideration the choice of peace or war. The senators, as if they had been suddenly awakened from a dream of four hundred years, appeared, on this important occasion, to be inspired by the courage, rather than by the wisdom, of their predecessors. They loudly declared, in regular speeches, or in tumultuary acclamations, that it was unworthy of the majesty of Rome to purchase a precarious and disgraceful truce from a Barbarian king; and that, in the judgment of a magnanimous people, the chance of ruin was always preferable to the certainty of dishonor. The minister, whose pacific intentions were seconded only by the voice of a few servile and venal followers, attempted to allay the general ferment, by an apology for his own conduct, and even for the demands of the Gothic prince. "The payment of a subsidy, which had excited the indignation of the Romans, ought not (such was the language of Stilicho) to be considered in the odious light, either of a tribute, or of a ransom, extorted by the menaces of a Barbarian enemy. Alaric had faithfully asserted the just pretensions of the republic to the provinces which were usurped by the Greeks of Constantinople: he modestly required the fair and stipulated recompense of his services; and if he had desisted from the prosecution of his enterprise, he had obeyed, in his retreat, the peremptory, though private, letters of the emperor himself. These contradictory orders (he would not dissemble the errors of his own family) had been procured by the intercession of Serena. The tender piety of his wife had been too deeply affected by the discord of the royal brothers, the sons of her adopted father; and the sentiments of nature had too easily prevailed over the stern dictates of the public welfare." These ostensible reasons, which faintly disguise the obscure intrigues of the palace of Ravenna, were supported by the authority of Stilicho; and obtained, after a warm debate, the reluctant approbation of the senate. The tumult of virtue and freedom subsided; and the sum of four thousand pounds of gold was granted, under the name of a subsidy, to secure the peace of Italy, and to conciliate the friendship of the king of the Goths. Lampadius alone, one of the most illustrious members of the assembly, still persisted in his dissent; exclaimed, with a loud voice, "This is not a treaty of peace, but of servitude;" [103] and escaped the danger of such bold opposition by immediately retiring to the sanctuary of a Christian church. [See Palace Of The Caesars]

[Footnote 103: Zosimus, l. v. p. 338, 339. He repeats the words of Lampadius, as they were spoke in Latin, "Non est ista pax, sed pactio servi tutis," and then translates them into Greek for the benefit of his readers. Note: From Cicero's XIIth Philippic, 14—M.]

But the reign of Stilicho drew towards its end; and the proud minister might perceive the symptoms of his approaching disgrace. The generous boldness of Lampadius had been applauded; and the senate, so patiently resigned to a long servitude, rejected with disdain the offer of invidious and imaginary freedom. The troops, who still assumed the name and prerogatives of the Roman legions, were exasperated by the partial affection of Stilicho for the Barbarians: and the people imputed to the mischievous policy of the minister the public misfortunes, which were the natural consequence of their own degeneracy. Yet Stilicho might have continued to brave the clamors of the people, and even of the soldiers, if he could have maintained his dominion over the feeble mind of his pupil. But the respectful attachment of Honorius was converted into fear, suspicion, and hatred. The crafty Olympius, [104] who concealed his vices under the mask of Christian piety, had secretly undermined the benefactor, by whose favor he was promoted to the honorable offices of the Imperial palace. Olympius revealed to the unsuspecting emperor, who had attained the twenty-fifth year of his age, that he was without weight, or authority, in his own government; and artfully alarmed his timid and indolent disposition by a lively picture of the designs of Stilicho, who already meditated the death of his sovereign, with the ambitious hope of placing the diadem on the head of his son Eucherius. The emperor was instigated, by his new favorite, to assume the tone of independent dignity; and the minister was astonished to find, that secret resolutions were formed in the court and council, which were repugnant to his interest, or to his intentions. Instead of residing in the palace of Rome, Honorius declared that it was his pleasure to return to the secure fortress of Ravenna. On the first intelligence of the death of his brother Arcadius, he prepared to visit Constantinople, and to regulate, with the authority of a guardian, the provinces of the infant Theodosius. [105] The representation of the difficulty and expense of such a distant expedition, checked this strange and sudden sally of active diligence; but the dangerous project of showing the emperor to the camp of Pavia, which was composed of the Roman troops, the enemies of Stilicho, and his Barbarian auxiliaries, remained fixed and unalterable. The minister was pressed, by the advice of his confidant, Justinian, a Roman advocate, of a lively and penetrating genius, to oppose a journey so prejudicial to his reputation and safety. His strenuous but ineffectual efforts confirmed the triumph of Olympius; and the prudent lawyer withdrew himself from the impending ruin of his patron.

[Footnote 104: He came from the coast of the Euxine, and exercised a splendid office. His actions justify his character, which Zosimus (l. v. p. 340) exposes with visible satisfaction. Augustin revered the piety of

Olympius, whom he styles a true son of the church, (Baronius, Annal. Eccles, Eccles. A.D. 408, No. 19, &c. Tillemont, Mem. Eccles. tom. xiii. p. 467, 468.) But these praises, which the African saint so unworthily bestows, might proceed as well from ignorance as from adulation.]

[Footnote 105: Zosimus, l. v. p. 338, 339. Sozomen, l. ix. c. 4. Stilicho offered to undertake the journey to Constantinople, that he might divert Honorius from the vain attempt. The Eastern empire would not have obeyed, and could not have been conquered.]

In the passage of the emperor through Bologna, a mutiny of the guards was excited and appeased by the secret policy of Stilicho; who announced his instructions to decimate the guilty, and ascribed to his own intercession the merit of their pardon. After this tumult, Honorius embraced, for the last time, the minister whom he now considered as a tyrant, and proceeded on his way to the camp of Pavia; where he was received by the loyal acclamations of the troops who were assembled for the service of the Gallic war. On the morning of the fourth day, he pronounced, as he had been taught, a military oration in the presence of the soldiers, whom the charitable visits, and artful discourses, of Olympius had prepared to execute a dark and bloody conspiracy. At the first signal, they massacred the friends of Stilicho, the most illustrious officers of the empire; two Praetorian praefects, of Gaul and of Italy; two masters-general of the cavalry and infantry; the master of the offices; the quaestor, the treasurer, and the count of the domestics. Many lives were lost; many houses were plundered; the furious sedition continued to rage till the close of the evening; and the trembling emperor, who was seen in the streets of Pavia without his robes or diadem, yielded to the persuasions of his favorite; condemned the memory of the slain; and solemnly approved the innocence and fidelity of their assassins. The intelligence of the massacre of Pavia filled the mind of Stilicho with just and gloomy apprehensions; and he instantly summoned, in the camp of Bologna, a council of the confederate leaders, who were attached to his service, and would be involved in his ruin. The impetuous voice of the assembly called aloud for arms, and for revenge; to march, without a moment's delay, under the banners of a hero, whom they had so often followed to victory; to surprise, to oppress, to extirpate the guilty Olympius, and his degenerate Romans; and perhaps to fix the diadem on the head of their injured general. Instead of executing a resolution, which might have been justified by success, Stilicho hesitated till he was irrecoverably lost. He was still ignorant of the fate of the emperor; he distrusted the fidelity of his own party; and he viewed with horror the fatal consequences of arming a crowd of licentious Barbarians against the soldiers and people of Italy. The confederates, impatient of his timorous and doubtful delay, hastily retired, with fear and indignation. At the hour of midnight, Sarus, a Gothic warrior, renowned among the Barbarians themselves for his strength and valor, suddenly invaded the camp of his benefactor, plundered the baggage, cut in pieces the faithful Huns, who guarded his person, and penetrated to the tent, where the minister, pensive and sleepless, meditated on the dangers of his situation. Stilicho escaped with difficulty from the sword of the Goths and, after issuing a last and generous admonition to the cities of Italy, to shut their gates against the Barbarians, his confidence, or his despair, urged him to throw himself into Ravenna, which was already in the absolute possession of his enemies. Olympius, who had assumed the dominion of Honorius, was speedily informed, that his rival had embraced, as a suppliant the altar of the Christian church. The base and cruel disposition of the hypocrite was incapable of pity or remorse; but he piously affected to elude, rather than to violate, the privilege of the sanctuary. Count Heraclian, with a troop of soldiers, appeared, at the dawn of day, before the gates of the church of Ravenna. The bishop was satisfied by a solemn oath, that the Imperial mandate only directed them to secure the person of Stilicho: but as soon as the unfortunate minister had been tempted beyond the holy threshold, he produced the warrant for his instant execution. Stilicho supported, with calm resignation, the injurious names of traitor and parricide; repressed the unseasonable zeal of his followers, who were ready to attempt an ineffectual rescue; and, with a firmness not unworthy of the last of the Roman generals, submitted his neck to the sword of Heraclian. [106]

[Footnote 106: Zosimus (l. v. p. 336-345) has copiously, though not clearly, related the disgrace and death of Stilicho. Olympiodorus, (apud Phot. p. 177.) Orosius, (l. vii. c. 38, p. 571, 572,) Sozomen, (l. ix. c. 4,) and Philostorgius, (l. xi. c. 3, l. xii. c. 2,) afford supplemental hints.]

The servile crowd of the palace, who had so long adored the fortune of Stilicho, affected to insult his fall; and the most distant connection with the master-general of the West, which had so lately been a title to wealth and honors, was studiously denied, and rigorously punished. His family, united by a triple alliance with the family of Theodosius, might envy the condition of the meanest peasant. The flight of his son Eucherius was intercepted; and the death of that innocent youth soon followed the divorce of Thermantia, who filled the place of her sister Maria; and who, like Maria, had remained a virgin in the Imperial bed. [107] The friends of Stilicho, who had escaped the massacre of Pavia, were persecuted by the implacable revenge of Olympius; and the most exquisite cruelty was employed to extort the confession of a treasonable and sacrilegious conspiracy. They died in silence: their firmness justified the choice, [108] and perhaps absolved the innocence of their patron: and the despotic power, which could take his life without a trial, and stigmatize his memory without a proof, has no jurisdiction over the impartial suffrage of posterity. [109] The services of Stilicho are great and manifest; his crimes, as they are vaguely stated in the language of flattery and hatred, are obscure at least, and improbable. About four months after his death, an edict was published, in the name of Honorius, to restore the free communication of the two empires, which had been so long interrupted by the public enemy. [110] The minister, whose fame and fortune depended on the prosperity of the state, was accused of betraying Italy to the Barbarians; whom he repeatedly vanquished at Pollentia, at Verona, and before the walls of Florence. His pretended design of placing the diadem on the head of his son Eucherius, could not have been conducted without preparations or accomplices; and the ambitious father would not surely have left the future emperor, till the twentieth year of his age, in the humble station of tribune of the notaries. Even the religion of Stilicho was arraigned by the malice of his rival. The seasonable, and almost miraculous, deliverance was devoutly celebrated by the applause of the clergy; who asserted, that the restoration of idols, and the persecution of the church, would have been the first measure of the reign of Eucherius. The son of Stilicho, however, was educated in the bosom of Christianity, which his father had uniformly professed, and zealously supported. [111] [111/1] Serena had borrowed her magnificent necklace from the statue of Vesta; [112] and the Pagans execrated the memory of the sacrilegious minister, by whose order the Sibylline books, the oracles of Rome, had been committed to the flames. [113] The pride and power of Stilicho constituted his real guilt. An honorable reluctance to shed the blood of his countrymen appears to have contributed to the success of his unworthy rival; and it is the last humiliation of the character of Honorius, that posterity has not condescended to reproach him with his base ingratitude to the guardian of his youth, and the support of his empire.

[Footnote 107: Zosimus, l. v. p. 333. The marriage of a Christian with two sisters, scandalizes Tillemont, (Hist. des Empereurs, tom. v. p. 557;) who expects, in vain, that Pope Innocent I. should have done something in the way either of censure or of dispensation.]

[Footnote 108: Two of his friends are honorably mentioned, (Zosimus, l. v. p. 346:) Peter, chief of the school of notaries, and the great chamberlain Deuterius. Stilicho had secured the bed-chamber; and it is surprising that, under a feeble prince, the bed-chamber was not able to secure him.]

[Footnote 109: Orosius (l. vii. c. 38, p. 571, 572) seems to copy the false and furious manifestos, which were dispersed through the provinces by the new administration.]

[Footnote 110: See the Theodosian code, l. vii. tit. xvi. leg. 1, l. ix. tit. xlii. leg. 22. Stilicho is branded with the name of proedo publicus, who employed his wealth, ad omnem ditandam, inquietandamque Barbariem.]

[Footnote 111: Augustin himself is satisfied with the effectual laws, which Stilicho had enacted against heretics and idolaters; and which are still extant in the Code. He only applies to Olympius for their confirmation, (Baronius, Annal. Eccles. A.D. 408, No. 19.)]

[Footnote 112: Zosimus, l. v. p. 351. We may observe the bad taste of the age, in dressing their statues with such awkward finery.]

[Footnote 113: See Rutilius Numatianus, (Itinerar. l. ii. 41-60,) to whom religious enthusiasm has dictated some elegant and forcible lines. Stilicho likewise stripped the gold plates from the doors of the Capitol, and read a prophetic sentence which was engraven under them, (Zosimus, l. v. p. 352.) These are foolish stories: yet the charge of impiety adds weight and credit to the praise which Zosimus reluctantly bestows on his virtues. Note: One particular in the extorted praise of Zosimus, deserved the notice of the historian, as strongly opposed to the former imputations of Zosimus himself, and indicative of he corrupt practices of a declining age. "He had never bartered promotion in the army for bribes, nor peculated in the supplies of provisions for the army." l. v. c. xxxiv—M.]

[Footnote 111/1: Hence, perhaps, the accusation of treachery is countenanced by Hatilius:—

Quo magis est facinus diri Stilichonis iniquum Proditor arcani quod fuit imperii. Romano generi dum nititur esse superstes, Crudelis summis miscuit ima furor. Dumque timet, quicquid se fecerat ipso timeri, Immisit Latiae barbara tela neci. Rutil. Itin. II. 41—M.] Among the train of dependants whose wealth and dignity attracted the notice of their own times, our curiosity is excited by the celebrated name of the poet Claudian, who enjoyed the favor of Stilicho, and was overwhelmed in the ruin of his patron.

The titular offices of tribune and notary fixed his rank in the Imperial court: he was indebted to the powerful intercession of Serena for his marriage with a very rich heiress of the province of Africa; [114] and the statute of Claudian, erected in the forum of Trajan, was a monument of the taste and liberality of the Roman senate. [115] After the praises of Stilicho became offensive and criminal, Claudian was exposed to the enmity of a powerful and unforgiving courtier, whom he had provoked by the insolence of wit. He had compared, in a lively epigram, the opposite characters of two Praetorian praefects of Italy; he contrasts the innocent repose of a philosopher, who sometimes resigned the hours of business to slumber, perhaps to study, with the interesting diligence of a rapacious minister, indefatigable in the pursuit of unjust or sacrilegious, gain. "How happy," continues Claudian, "how happy might it be for the people of Italy, if Mallius could be constantly awake, and if Hadrian would always sleep!" [116] The repose of Mallius was not disturbed by this friendly and gentle admonition; but the cruel vigilance of Hadrian watched the opportunity of revenge, and easily obtained, from the enemies of Stilicho, the trifling sacrifice of an obnoxious poet. The poet concealed himself, however, during the tumult of the revolution; and, consulting the dictates of prudence rather than of honor, he addressed, in the form of an epistle, a suppliant and humble recantation to the offended praefect. He deplores, in mournful strains, the fatal indiscretion into which he had been hurried by passion and folly; submits to the imitation of his adversary the generous examples of the clemency of gods, of heroes, and of lions; and expresses his hope that the magnanimity of Hadrian will not trample on a defenceless and contemptible foe, already humbled by disgrace and poverty, and deeply wounded by the exile, the tortures, and the death of his dearest friends. [117] Whatever might be the success of his prayer, or the accidents of his future life, the period of a few years levelled in the grave the minister and the poet: but the name of Hadrian is almost sunk in oblivion, while Claudian is read with pleasure in every country which has retained, or acquired, the knowledge of the Latin language. If we fairly balance his merits and his defects, we shall acknowledge that Claudian does not either satisfy, or silence, our reason. It would not be easy to produce a passage that deserves the epithet of sublime or pathetic; to select a verse that melts the heart or enlarges the imagination. We should vainly seek, in the poems of Claudian, the happy invention, and artificial conduct, of an interesting fable; or the just and lively representation of the characters and situations of real life. For the service of his patron, he published occasional panegyrics and invectives: and the design of these slavish compositions encouraged his propensity to exceed the limits of truth and nature. These imperfections, however, are compensated in some degree by the poetical virtues of Claudian. He was endowed with the rare and precious talent of raising the meanest, of adorning the most barren, and of diversifying the most similar, topics: his coloring, more especially in descriptive poetry, is soft and splendid; and he seldom fails to display, and even to abuse, the advantages of a cultivated understanding, a copious fancy, an easy, and sometimes forcible, expression; and a perpetual flow of harmonious versification. To these commendations, independent of any accidents of time and place, we must add the peculiar merit which Claudian derived from the unfavorable circumstances of his birth. In the decline of arts, and of empire, a native of Egypt, [118] who had received the education of a Greek, assumed, in a mature age, the familiar use, and absolute command, of the Latin language; [119] soared above the heads of his feeble contemporaries; and placed himself, after an interval of three hundred years, among the poets of ancient Rome. [120]

[Footnote 114: At the nuptials of Orpheus (a modest comparison!) all the parts of animated nature contributed their various gifts; and the gods themselves enriched their favorite. Claudian had neither flocks, nor herds, nor vines, nor olives. His wealthy bride was heiress to them all. But he carried to Africa a recommendatory letter from Serena, his Juno, and was made happy, (Epist. ii. ad Serenam.)]

[Footnote 115: Claudian feels the honor like a man who deserved it, (in praefat Bell. Get.) The original inscription, on marble, was found at Rome, in the fifteenth century, in the house of Pomponius Laetus. The statue of a poet, far superior to Claudian, should have been erected, during his lifetime, by the men of letters, his countrymen and contemporaries. It was a noble design.]

[Footnote 116: See Epigram xxx.

Mallius indulget somno noctesque diesque: Insomnis Pharius sacra, profana, rapit. Omnibus, hoc, Italae gentes, exposcite votis; Mallius ut vigilet, dormiat ut Pharius.

Hadrian was a Pharian, (of Alexandrian.) See his public life in Godefroy, Cod. Theodos. tom. vi. p. 364. Mallius did not always sleep. He composed some elegant dialogues on the Greek systems of natural philosophy, (Claud, in Mall. Theodor. Cons. 61-112.)]

[Footnote 117: See Claudian's first Epistle. Yet, in some places, an air of irony and indiqnation betrays his secret reluctance. Note: M. Beugnot has pointed out one remarkable characteristic of Claudian's poetry, and of the times—his extraordinary religious indifference. Here is a poet writing at the actual crisis of the complete triumph of the new religion, the visible extinction of the old: if we may so speak, a strictly historical poet, whose works, excepting his Mythological poem on the rape of Proserpine, are confined to temporary subjects, and to the politics of his own eventful day; yet, excepting in one or two small and indifferent pieces, manifestly written by a Christian, and interpolated among his poems, there is no allusion whatever to the great religious strife. No one would know the existence of Christianity at that period of the world, by reading the works of Claudian. His panegyric and his satire preserve the same religious impartiality; award their most lavish praise or their bitterest invective on Christian or Pagan; he insults the fall of Eugenius, and glories in the victories of Theodosius. Under the child,—and Honorius never became more than a child,—Christianity continued to inflict wounds more and more deadly on expiring Paganism. Are the gods of Olympus agitated with apprehension at the birth of this new enemy? They are introduced as rejoicing at his appearance, and promising long years of glory. The whole prophetic choir of Paganism, all the oracles throughout the world, are summoned to predict the felicity of his reign. His birth is compared to that of Apollo, but the narrow limits of an island must not confine the new deity—

... Non littora nostro Sufficerent angusta Deo.

Augury and divination, the shrines of Ammon, and of Delphi, the Persian Magi, and the Etruscan seers, the Chaldean astrologers, the Sibyl herself, are described as still discharging their prophetic functions, and celebrating the natal day of this Christian prince. They are noble lines, as well as curious illustrations of the times:

... Quae tunc documenta futuri? Quae voces avium? quanti per inane volatus? Quis vatum discursus erat? Tibi corniger Ammon, Et dudum taciti rupere silentia Delphi. Te Persae cecinere Magi, te sensit Etruscus Augur, et inspectis Babylonius horruit astris; Chaldaei stupuere senes, Cumanaque rursus Itonuit rupes, rabidae delubra Sibyllae. —Claud. iv. Cons. Hon. 141.

From the Quarterly Review of Beugnot. Hist. de la Paganisme en Occident, Q. R. v. lvii. p. 61—M.]

[Footnote 118: National vanity has made him a Florentine, or a Spaniard. But the first Epistle of Claudian proves him a native of Alexandria, (Fabricius, Bibliot. Latin. tom. iii. p. 191-202, edit. Ernest.)]

[Footnote 119: His first Latin verses were composed during the consulship of Probinus, A.D. 395.

Romanos bibimus primum, te consule, fontes, Et Latiae cessit Graia Thalia togae.

Besides some Greek epigrams, which are still extant, the Latin poet had composed, in Greek, the Antiquities of Tarsus, Anazarbus, Berytus, Nice, &c. It is more easy to supply the loss of good poetry, than of authentic history.]

[Footnote 120: Strada (Prolusion v. vi.) allows him to contend with the five heroic poets, Lucretius, Virgil, Ovid, Lucan, and Statius. His patron is the accomplished courtier Balthazar Castiglione. His admirers are numerous and passionate. Yet the rigid critics reproach the exotic weeds, or flowers, which spring too luxuriantly in his Latian soil]

CHAPTER XXXI

INVASION OF ITALY, OCCUPATION OF TERRITORIES BY BARBARIANS

PART I

INVASION OF ITALY BY ALARIC—MANNERS OF THE ROMAN SENATE AND PEOPLE—ROME IS THRICE BESIEGED, AND AT LENGTH PILLAGED, BY THE GOTHS—DEATH OF ALARIC—THE GOTHS EVACUATE ITALY—FALL OF CONSTANTINE—GAUL AND SPAIN ARE OCCUPIED BY THE BARBARIANS—INDEPENDENCE OF BRITAIN

The incapacity of a weak and distracted government may often assume the appearance, and produce the effects, of a treasonable correspondence with the public enemy. If Alaric himself had been introduced into the council of Ravenna, he would probably have advised the same measures which were actually pursued by the ministers of Honorius. [1] The king of the Goths would have conspired, perhaps with some reluctance, to destroy the formidable adversary, by whose arms, in Italy, as well as in Greece, he had been twice overthrown. Their active and interested hatred laboriously accomplished the disgrace and ruin of the great Stilicho. The valor of Sarus, his fame in arms, and his personal, or hereditary, influence over the confederate Barbarians, could recommend him only to the friends of their country, who despised, or detested, the worthless characters of Turpilio, Varanes, and Vigilantius. By the pressing instances of the new favorites, these generals, unworthy as they had shown themselves of the names of soldiers, [2] were promoted to the command of the cavalry, of the infantry, and of the domestic troops. The Gothic prince would have subscribed with pleasure the edict which the fanaticism of Olympius dictated to the simple and devout emperor. Honorius excluded all persons, who were adverse to the Catholic church, from holding any office in the state; obstinately rejected the service of all those who dissented from his religion; and rashly disqualified many of his bravest and most skilful officers, who adhered to the Pagan worship, or who had imbibed the opinions of Arianism. [3] These measures, so advantageous to an enemy, Alaric would have approved, and might perhaps have suggested; but it may seem doubtful, whether the Barbarian would have promoted his interest at the expense of the inhuman and absurd cruelty which was perpetrated by the direction, or at least with the connivance of the Imperial ministers. The foreign auxiliaries, who had been attached to the person of Stilicho, lamented his death; but the desire of revenge was checked by a natural apprehension for the safety of their wives and children; who were detained as hostages in the strong cities of Italy, where they had likewise deposited their most valuable effects. At the same hour, and as if by a common signal, the cities of Italy were polluted by the same horrid scenes of universal massacre and pillage, which involved, in promiscuous destruction, the families and fortunes of the Barbarians. Exasperated by such an injury, which might have awakened the tamest and most servile spirit, they cast a look of indignation and hope towards the camp of Alaric, and unanimously swore to pursue, with just and implacable war, the perfidious nation who had so basely violated the laws of hospitality. By the imprudent conduct of the ministers of Honorius, the republic lost the assistance, and deserved the enmity, of thirty thousand of her bravest soldiers; and the weight of that formidable army, which alone might have determined the event of the war, was transferred from the scale of the Romans into that of the Goths.

[Footnote 1: The series of events, from the death of Stilicho to the arrival of Alaric before Rome, can only be found in Zosimus, l. v. p. 347-350.]

[Footnote 2: The expression of Zosimus is strong and lively, sufficient to excite the contempt of the enemy.]

[Footnote 3: Eos qui catholicae sectae sunt inimici, intra palatium militare pro hibemus. Nullus nobis sit aliqua ratione conjunctus, qui a nobis fidest religione discordat. Cod. Theodos. l. xvi. tit. v. leg. 42, and

Godefroy's Commentary, tom. vi. p. 164. This law was applied in the utmost latitude, and rigorously executed. Zosimus, l. v. p. 364.]

In the arts of negotiation, as well as in those of war, the Gothic king maintained his superior ascendant over an enemy, whose seeming changes proceeded from the total want of counsel and design. From his camp, on the confines of Italy, Alaric attentively observed the revolutions of the palace, watched the progress of faction and discontent, disguised the hostile aspect of a Barbarian invader, and assumed the more popular appearance of the friend and ally of the great Stilicho: to whose virtues, when they were no longer formidable, he could pay a just tribute of sincere praise and regret. The pressing invitation of the malecontents, who urged the king of the Goths to invade Italy, was enforced by a lively sense of his personal injuries; and he might especially complain, that the Imperial ministers still delayed and eluded the payment of the four thousand pounds of gold which had been granted by the Roman senate, either to reward his services, or to appease his fury. His decent firmness was supported by an artful moderation, which contributed to the success of his designs. He required a fair and reasonable satisfaction; but he gave the strongest assurances, that, as soon as he had obtained it, he would immediately retire. He refused to trust the faith of the Romans, unless Aetius and Jason, the sons of two great officers of state, were sent as hostages to his camp; but he offered to deliver, in exchange, several of the noblest youths of the Gothic nation. The modesty of Alaric was interpreted, by the ministers of Ravenna, as a sure evidence of his weakness and fear. They disdained either to negotiate a treaty, or to assemble an army; and with a rash confidence, derived only from their ignorance of the extreme danger, irretrievably wasted the decisive moments of peace and war. While they expected, in sullen silence, that the Barbarians would evacuate the confines of Italy, Alaric, with bold and rapid marches, passed the Alps and the Po; hastily pillaged the cities of Aquileia, Altinum, Concordia, and Cremona, which yielded to his arms; increased his forces by the accession of thirty thousand auxiliaries; and, without meeting a single enemy in the field, advanced as far as the edge of the morass which protected the impregnable residence of the emperor of the West. Instead of attempting the hopeless siege of Ravenna, the prudent leader of the Goths proceeded to Rimini, stretched his ravages along the sea-coast of the Hadriatic, and meditated the conquest of the ancient mistress of the world. An Italian hermit, whose zeal and sanctity were respected by the Barbarians themselves, encountered the victorious monarch, and boldly denounced the indignation of Heaven against the oppressors of the earth; but the saint himself was confounded by the solemn asseveration of Alaric, that he felt a secret and praeternatural impulse, which directed, and even compelled, his march to the gates of Rome. He felt, that his genius and his fortune were equal to the most arduous enterprises; and the enthusiasm which he communicated to the Goths, insensibly removed the popular, and almost superstitious, reverence of the nations for the majesty of the Roman name. His troops, animated by the hopes of spoil, followed the course of the Flaminian way, occupied the unguarded passes of the Apennine, [4] descended into the rich plains of Umbria; and, as they lay encamped on the banks of the Clitumnus, might wantonly slaughter and devour the milk-white oxen, which had been so long reserved for the use of Roman triumphs. [5] A lofty situation, and a seasonable tempest of thunder and lightning, preserved the little city of Narni; but the king of the Goths, despising the ignoble prey, still advanced with unabated vigor; and after he had passed through the stately arches, adorned with the spoils of Barbaric victories, he pitched his camp under the walls of Rome. [6]

[Footnote 4: Addison (see his Works, vol. ii. p. 54, edit. Baskerville) has given a very picturesque description of the road through the Apennine. The Goths were not at leisure to observe the beauties of the prospect; but they were pleased to find that the Saxa Intercisa, a narrow passage which Vespasian had cut through the rock, (Cluver. Italia Antiq. tom. i. p. 168,) was totally neglected.

Hine albi, Clitumne, greges, et maxima taurus Victima, saepe tuo perfusi flumine sacro, Romanos ad templa Deum duxere triumphos. —Georg. ii. 147.

Besides Virgil, most of the Latin poets, Propertius, Lucan, Silius Italicus, Claudian, &c., whose passages may be found in Cluverius and Addison, have celebrated the triumphal victims of the Clitumnus.]

[Footnote 6: Some ideas of the march of Alaric are borrowed from the journey of Honorius over the same ground. (See Claudian in vi. Cons. Hon. 494-522.) The measured distance between Ravenna and Rome was 254 Roman miles. Itinerar. Wesseling, p. 126.] During a period of six hundred and nineteen years, the seat of empire had never been violated by the presence of a foreign enemy. The unsuccessful expedition of Hannibal [7] served only to display the character of the senate and people; of a senate degraded, rather than ennobled, by the comparison of an assembly of kings; and of a people, to whom the ambassador of Pyrrhus ascribed the inexhaustible resources of the Hydra. [8] Each of the senators, in the time of the Punic war, had accomplished his term of the military service, either in a subordinate or a superior station; and the decree, which invested with temporary command all those who had been consuls, or censors, or dictators, gave the republic the immediate assistance of many brave and experienced generals. In the beginning of the war, the Roman people consisted of two hundred and fifty thousand citizens of an age to bear arms. [9] Fifty thousand had already died in the defence of their country; and the twenty-three legions which were employed in the different camps of Italy, Greece, Sardinia, Sicily, and Spain, required about one hundred thousand men. But there still remained an equal number in Rome, and the adjacent territory, who were animated by the same intrepid courage; and every citizen was trained, from his earliest youth, in the discipline and exercises of a soldier. Hannibal was astonished by the constancy of the senate, who, without raising the siege of Capua, or recalling their scattered forces, expected his approach. He encamped on the banks of the Anio, at the distance of three miles from the city; and he was soon informed, that the ground on which he had pitched his tent, was sold for an adequate price at a public auction; [911] and that a body of troops was dismissed by an opposite road, to reenforce the legions of Spain. [10] He led his Africans to the gates of Rome, where he found three armies in order of battle, prepared to receive him; but Hannibal dreaded the event of a combat, from which he could not hope to escape, unless he destroyed the last of his enemies; and his speedy retreat confessed the invincible courage of the Romans.

[Footnote 7: The march and retreat of Hannibal are described by Livy, l. xxvi. c. 7, 8, 9, 10, 11; and the reader is made a spectator of the interesting scene.]

[Footnote 8: These comparisons were used by Cyneas, the counsellor of Pyrrhus, after his return from his embassy, in which he had diligently studied the discipline and manners of Rome. See Plutarch in Pyrrho. tom. ii. p. 459.]

[Footnote 9: In the three census which were made of the Roman people, about the time of the second Punic war, the numbers stand as follows, (see Livy, Epitom. l. xx. Hist. l. xxvii. 36. xxix. 37:) 270,213, 137,108 214,000. The fall of the second, and the rise of the third, appears so enormous, that several critics, notwithstanding the unanimity of the Mss., have suspected some corruption of the text of Livy. (See Drakenborch ad xxvii. 36, and Beaufort, Republique Romaine, tom. i. p. 325.) They did not consider that the second census was taken only at Rome, and that the numbers were diminished, not only by the death, but likewise by the absence, of many soldiers. In the third census, Livy expressly affirms, that the legions were mustered by the care of particular commissaries. From the numbers on the list we must always deduct one twelfth above threescore, and incapable of bearing arms. See Population de la France, p. 72.]

[Footnote 9/1: Compare the remarkable transaction in Jeremiah xxxii. 6, to 44, where the prophet purchases his uncle's estate at the approach of the Babylonian captivity, in his undoubting confidence in the future restoration of the people. In the one case it is the triumph of religious faith, in the other of national pride—M.]

[Footnote 10: Livy considers these two incidents as the effects only of chance and courage. I suspect that they were both managed by the admirable policy of the senate.]

From the time of the Punic war, the uninterrupted succession of senators had preserved the name and image of the republic; and the degenerate subjects of Honorius ambitiously derived their descent from the heroes who had repulsed the arms of Hannibal, and subdued the nations of the earth. The temporal honors which the devout Paula [11] inherited and despised, are carefully recapitulated by Jerom, the guide of her conscience, and the historian of her life. The genealogy of her father, Rogatus, which ascended as high as Agamemnon, might seem to betray a Grecian origin; but her mother, Blaesilla, numbered the Scipios, Aemilius Paulus, and the Gracchi, in the list of her ancestors; and Toxotius, the husband of Paula, deduced his royal lineage from Aeneas, the father of the Julian line. The vanity of the rich, who desired to be noble, was gratified by these lofty pretensions. Encouraged by the applause of their parasites, they easily imposed on the credulity of the vulgar; and were countenanced, in some measure, by the custom of adopting the name of their patron, which had always prevailed among the freedmen and clients of illustrious families. Most of those families, however, attacked by so many causes of external violence or internal decay, were gradually extirpated; and it would be more reasonable to seek for a lineal descent of twenty generations, among the mountains of the Alps, or in the peaceful solitude of Apulia, than on the theatre of Rome, the seat of fortune, of danger, and of perpetual revolutions. Under each successive reign, and from every province of the empire, a crowd of hardy adventurers, rising to eminence by their talents or their vices, usurped the wealth, the honors, and the palaces of Rome; and oppressed, or protected, the poor and humble remains of consular families; who were ignorant, perhaps, of the glory of their ancestors. [12]

[Footnote 11: See Jerom, tom. i. p. 169, 170, ad Eustochium; he bestows on Paula the splendid titles of Gracchorum stirps, soboles Scipionum, Pauli haeres, cujus vocabulum trahit, Martiae Papyriae Matris Africani vera et germana propago. This particular description supposes a more solid title than the surname of Julius, which Toxotius shared with a thousand families of the western provinces. See the Index of Tacitus, of Gruter's Inscriptions, &c.]

[Footnote 12: Tacitus (Annal. iii. 55) affirms, that between the battle of Actium and the reign of Vespasian, the senate was gradually filled with new families from the Municipia and colonies of Italy.]

In the time of Jerom and Claudian, the senators unanimously yielded the preeminence to the Anician line; and a slight view of their history will serve to appreciate the rank and antiquity of the noble families, which contended only for the second place. [13] During the five first ages of the city, the name of the Anicians was unknown; they appear to have derived their origin from Praeneste; and the ambition of those new citizens was long satisfied with the Plebeian honors of tribunes of the people. [14] One hundred and sixty-eight years before the Christian aera, the family was ennobled by the Praetorship of Anicius, who gloriously terminated the Illyrian war, by the conquest of the nation, and the captivity of their king. [15] From the triumph of that general, three consulships, in distant periods, mark the succession of the Anician name. [16] From the reign of Diocletian to the final extinction of the Western empire, that name shone with a lustre which was not eclipsed, in the public estimation, by the majesty of the Imperial purple. [17] The several branches, to whom it was communicated, united, by marriage or inheritance, the wealth and titles of the Annian, the Petronian, and the Olybrian houses; and in each generation the number of consulships was multiplied by an hereditary claim. [18] The Anician family excelled in faith and in riches: they were the first of the Roman senate who embraced Christianity; and it is probable that Anicius Julian, who was afterwards consul and praefect of the city, atoned for his attachment to the party of Maxentius, by the readiness with which he accepted the religion of Constantine. [19] Their ample patrimony was increased by the industry of Probus, the chief of the Anician family; who shared with Gratian the honors of the consulship, and exercised, four times, the high office of Praetorian praefect. [20] His immense estates were scattered over the wide extent of the Roman world; and though the public might suspect or disapprove the methods by which they had been acquired, the generosity and magnificence of that fortunate statesman deserved the gratitude of his clients, and the admiration of strangers. [21] Such was the respect entertained for his memory, that the two sons of Probus, in their earliest youth, and at the request of the senate, were associated in the consular dignity; a memorable distinction, without example, in the annals of Rome. [22]

[Footnote 13:

Nec quisquam Procerum tentet (licet aere vetusto Floreat, et claro cingatur Roma senatu) Se jactare parem; sed prima sede relicta Aucheniis, de jure licet certare secundo. —Claud. in Prob. et Olybrii Coss. 18.

Such a compliment paid to the obscure name of the Auchenii has amazed the critics; but they all agree, that whatever may be the true reading, the sense of Claudian can be applied only to the Anician family.]

[Footnote 14: The earliest date in the annals of Pighius, is that of M. Anicius Gallus. Trib. Pl. A. U. C. 506. Another tribune, Q. Anicius, A. U. C. 508, is distinguished by the epithet of Praenestinus. Livy (xlv. 43) places the Anicii below the great families of Rome.]

[Footnote 15: Livy, xliv. 30, 31, xlv. 3, 26, 43. He fairly appreciates the merit of Anicius, and justly observes, that his fame was clouded by the superior lustre of the Macedonian, which preceded the Illyrian triumph.]

[Footnote 16: The dates of the three consulships are, A. U. C. 593, 818, 967 the two last under the reigns of Nero and Caracalla. The second of these consuls distinguished himself only by his infamous flattery, (Tacit. Annal. xv. 74;) but even the evidence of crimes, if they bear the stamp of greatness and antiquity, is admitted, without reluctance, to prove the genealogy of a noble house.]

[Footnote 17: In the sixth century, the nobility of the Anician name is mentioned (Cassiodor. Variar. l. x. Ep. 10, 12) with singular respect by the minister of a Gothic king of Italy.]

[Footnote 18:

Fixus in omnes Cognatos procedit honos; quemcumque requiras Hac de stirpe virum, certum est de Consule nasci. Per fasces numerantur Avi, semperque renata Nobilitate virent, et prolem fata sequuntur.

(Claudian in Prob. et Olyb. Consulat. 12, &c.) The Annii, whose name seems to have merged in the Anician, mark the Fasti with many consulships, from the time of Vespasian to the fourth century.]

[Footnote 19: The title of first Christian senator may be justified by the authority of Prudentius (in Symmach. i. 553) and the dislike of the Pagans to the Anician family. See Tillemont, Hist. des Empereurs, tom. iv. p. 183, v. p. 44. Baron. Annal. A.D. 312, No. 78, A.D. 322, No. 2.]

[Footnote 20: Probus... claritudine generis et potentia et opum magnitudine, cognitus Orbi Romano, per quem universum poene patrimonia sparsa possedit, juste an secus non judicioli est nostri. Ammian Marcellin. xxvii. 11. His children and widow erected for him a magnificent tomb in the Vatican, which was demolished in the time of Pope Nicholas V. to make room for the new church of St. Peter Baronius, who laments the ruin of this Christian monument, has diligently preserved the inscriptions and basso-relievos. See Annal. Eccles. A.D. 395, No. 5-17.]

[Footnote 21: Two Persian satraps travelled to Milan and Rome, to hear St. Ambrose, and to see Probus, (Paulin. in Vit. Ambros.) Claudian (in Cons. Probin. et Olybr. 30-60) seems at a loss how to express the glory of Probus.]

[Footnote 22: See the poem which Claudian addressed to the two noble youths.]

PART II

"The marbles of the Anician palace," were used as a proverbial expression of opulence and splendor; [23] but the nobles and senators of Rome aspired, in due gradation, to imitate that illustrious family. The accurate description of the city, which was composed in the Theodosian age, enumerates one thousand seven hundred and eighty houses, the residence of wealthy and honorable citizens. [24] Many of these stately mansions might almost excuse the exaggeration of the poet; that Rome contained a multitude of palaces, and that each palace was equal to a city: since it included within its own precincts every thing which could be subservient either to use or luxury; markets, hippodromes, temples, fountains, baths, porticos, shady groves, and artificial aviaries. [25] The historian Olympiodorus, who represents the state of Rome when it was besieged by the Goths, [26] continues to observe, that several of the richest senators received from their estates an annual income of four thousand pounds of gold, above one hundred and sixty thousand pounds sterling; without computing the stated provision of corn and wine, which, had they been sold, might have equalled in value one third of the money. Compared to this immoderate wealth, an ordinary revenue of a thousand or fifteen hundred pounds of gold might be considered as no more than adequate to the dignity of the senatorian rank, which required many expenses of a public and ostentatious kind. Several examples are recorded, in the age of Honorius, of vain and popular nobles, who celebrated the year of their praetorship by a festival, which lasted seven days, and cost above one hundred thousand pounds sterling. [27] The estates of the Roman senators, which so far exceeded the proportion of modern wealth, were not confined to the limits of Italy. Their possessions extended far beyond the Ionian and Aegean Seas, to the most distant provinces: the city of Nicopolis, which Augustus had founded as an eternal monument of the Actian victory, was the property of the devout Paula; [28] and it is observed by Seneca, that the rivers, which had divided hostile nations, now flowed through the lands of private citizens. [29] According to their temper and circumstances, the estates of the Romans were either cultivated by the labor of their slaves, or granted, for a certain and stipulated rent, to the industrious farmer. The economical writers of antiquity strenuously recommend the former method, wherever it may be practicable; but if the object should be removed, by its distance or magnitude, from the immediate eye of the master, they prefer the active care of an old hereditary tenant, attached to the soil, and interested in the produce, to the mercenary administration of a negligent, perhaps an unfaithful, steward. [30]

[Footnote 23: Secundinus, the Manichaean, ap. Baron. Annal. Eccles. A.D. 390, No. 34.]

[Footnote 24: See Nardini, Roma Antica, p. 89, 498, 500.]

[Footnote 25:

Quid loquar inclusas inter laquearia sylvas; Vernula queis vario carmine ludit avis.

Claud. Rutil. Numatian. Itinerar. ver. 111. The poet lived at the time of the Gothic invasion. A moderate palace would have covered Cincinnatus's farm of four acres (Val. Max. iv. 4.) In laxitatem ruris excurrunt, says Seneca, Epist. 114. See a judicious note of Mr. Hume, Essays, vol. i. p. 562, last 8vo edition.]

[Footnote 26: This curious account of Rome, in the reign of Honorius, is found in a fragment of the historian Olympiodorus, ap. Photium, p. 197.]

[Footnote 27: The sons of Alypius, of Symmachus, and of Maximus, spent, during their respective praetorships, twelve, or twenty, or forty, centenaries, (or hundred weight of gold.) See Olympiodor. ap. Phot. p. 197. This popular estimation allows some latitude; but it is difficult to explain a law in the Theodosian Code, (l. vi. leg. 5,) which fixes the expense of the first praetor at 25,000, of the second at 20,000, and of the third at 15,000 folles. The name of follis (see Mem. de l'Academie des Inscriptions, tom. xxviii. p. 727) was equally applied to a purse of 125 pieces of silver, and to a small copper coin of the value of 1/2625 part of that purse. In the former sense, the 25,000 folles would be equal to 150,000 L.; in the latter, to five or six ponuds sterling The one appears extravagant, the other is ridiculous. There must have existed some third and middle value, which is here understood; but ambiguity is an excusable fault in the language of laws.]

[Footnote 28: Nicopolis...... in Actiaco littore sita possessioris vestra nunc pars vel maxima est. Jerom. in Praefat. Comment. ad Epistol. ad Titum, tom. ix. p. 243. M. D. Tillemont supposes, strangely enough, that it was part of Agamemnon's inheritance. Mem. Eccles. tom. xii. p. 85.]

[Footnote 29: Seneca, Epist. lxxxix. His language is of the declamatory kind: but declamation could scarcely exaggerate the avarice and luxury of the Romans. The philosopher himself deserved some share of the reproach, if it be true that his rigorous exaction of Quadringenties, above three hundred thousand pounds which he had lent at high interest, provoked a rebellion in Britain, (Dion Cassius, l. lxii. p. 1003.) According to the conjecture of Gale (Antoninus's Itinerary in Britain, p. 92,) the same Faustinus possessed an estate near Bury, in Suffolk and another in the kingdom of Naples.]

[Footnote 30: Volusius, a wealthy senator, (Tacit. Annal. iii. 30,) always preferred tenants born on the estate. Columella, who received this maxim from him, argues very judiciously on the subject. De Re Rustica, l. i. c. 7, p. 408, edit. Gesner. Leipsig, 1735.]

The opulent nobles of an immense capital, who were never excited by the pursuit of military glory, and seldom engaged in the occupations of civil government, naturally resigned their leisure to the business and amusements of private life. At Rome, commerce was always held in contempt: but the senators, from the first age of the republic, increased their patrimony, and multiplied their clients, by the lucrative practice of usury; and the obselete laws were eluded, or violated, by the mutual inclinations and interest of both parties. [31] A considerable mass of treasure must always have existed at Rome, either in the current coin of the empire, or in the form of gold and silver plate; and there were many sideboards in the time of Pliny which contained more solid silver, than had been transported by Scipio from vanquished Carthage. [32] The greater part of the nobles, who dissipated their fortunes in profuse luxury, found themselves poor in the midst of wealth, and idle in a constant round of dissipation. Their desires were continually gratified by the labor of a thousand hands; of the numerous train of their domestic slaves, who were actuated by the fear of punishment; and of the various professions of artificers and merchants, who were more powerfully impelled by the hopes of gain. The ancients were destitute of many of the conveniences of life, which have been invented or improved by the progress of industry; and the plenty of glass and linen has diffused more real comforts among the modern nations of Europe, than the senators of Rome could derive from all the refinements of pompous or sensual luxury. [33] Their luxury, and their manners, have been the subject of minute and laborious disposition: but as such inquiries would divert me too long from the design of the present work, I shall produce an authentic state of Rome and its inhabitants, which is more peculiarly applicable to the period of the Gothic invasion. Ammianus Marcellinus, who prudently chose the capital of the empire as the residence the best adapted to the historian of his own times, has mixed with the narrative of public events a lively representation of the scenes with which he was familiarly conversant. The judicious reader will not always approve of the asperity of censure, the choice of circumstances, or the style of expression; he will perhaps detect the latent prejudices, and personal resentments, which soured the temper of Ammianus himself; but he will surely observe, with philosophic curiosity, the interesting and original picture of the manners of Rome. [34]

[Footnote 31: *Valesius (ad Ammian. xiv. 6) has proved, from Chrysostom and Augustin, that the senators were not allowed to lend money at usury. Yet it appears from the Theodosian Code, (see Godefroy ad l. ii. tit. xxxiii. tom. i. p. 230-289,) that they were permitted to take six percent., or one half of the legal interest; and, what is more singular, this permission was granted to the young senators.]*

[Footnote 32: *Plin. Hist. Natur. xxxiii. 50. He states the silver at only 4380 pounds, which is increased by Livy (xxx. 45) to 100,023: the former seems too little for an opulent city, the latter too much for any private sideboard.]*

[Footnote 33: *The learned Arbuthnot (Tables of Ancient Coins, &c. p. 153) has observed with humor, and I believe with truth, that Augustus had neither glass to his windows, nor a shirt to his back. Under the lower empire, the use of linen and glass became somewhat more common. Note: The discovery of glass in such common use at Pompeii, spoils the argument of Arbuthnot. See Sir W. Gell. Pompeiana, 2d ser. p. 98—M.]*

[Footnote 34: *It is incumbent on me to explain the liberties which I have taken with the text of Ammianus. 1. I have melted down into one piece the sixth chapter of the fourteenth and the fourth of the twenty-eighth book. 2. I have given order and connection to the confused mass of materials. 3. I have softened some extravagant hyperbeles, and pared away some superfluities of the original. 4. I have developed some observations which were insinuated rather than expressed. With these allowances, my version will be found, not literal indeed, but faithful and exact.]*

"The greatness of Rome"—such is the language of the historian—"was founded on the rare, and almost incredible, alliance of virtue and of fortune. The long period of her infancy was employed in a laborious struggle against the tribes of Italy, the neighbors and enemies of the rising city. In the strength and ardor of youth, she sustained the storms of war; carried her victorious arms beyond the seas and the mountains; and brought home triumphal laurels from every country of the globe. At length, verging towards old age, and sometimes conquering by the terror only of her name, she sought the blessings of ease and tranquillity. The venerable city, which had trampled on the necks of the fiercest nations, and established a system of laws, the perpetual guardians of justice and freedom, was content, like a wise and wealthy parent, to devolve on the Caesars, her favorite sons, the care of governing her ample patrimony. [35] A secure and profound peace, such as had been once enjoyed in the reign of Numa, succeeded to the tumults of a republic; while Rome was still adored as the queen of the earth; and the subject nations still reverenced the name of the people, and the majesty of the senate. But this native splendor," continues Ammianus, "is degraded, and sullied, by the conduct of some nobles, who, unmindful of their own dignity, and of that of their country, assume an unbounded license of vice and folly. They contend with each other in the empty vanity of titles and surnames; and curiously select, or invent, the most lofty and sonorous appellations, Reburrus, or Fabunius, Pagonius, or Tarasius, [36] which may impress the ears of the vulgar with astonishment and respect. From a vain ambition of perpetuating their memory, they affect to multiply their likeness, in statues of bronze and marble; nor are they satisfied, unless those statues are covered with plates of gold; an honorable distinction, first granted to Acilius the consul, after he had subdued, by his arms and counsels, the power of King Antiochus. The ostentation of displaying, of magnifying, perhaps, the rent-roll of the estates which they possess in all the provinces, from the rising to the setting sun, provokes the just resentment of every man, who recollects, that their poor and invincible ancestors were not distinguished from the meanest of the soldiers, by the delicacy of their food, or the splendor of their apparel. But the modern nobles measure their rank and consequence according to the loftiness of their chariots, [37] and the weighty magnificence of their dress. Their long robes of silk and purple float in the wind; and as they are agitated, by art or accident, they occasionally discover the under garments, the rich tunics, embroidered with the figures of various animals. [38] Followed by a train of fifty servants, and tearing up the pavement, they move along the streets with the same impetuous speed as if they travelled with post-horses; and the example of the senators is boldly imitated by the matrons and ladies, whose covered carriages are continually driving round the immense space of the city and suburbs. Whenever these persons of high distinction condescend to visit the public baths, they assume, on their entrance, a tone of loud and insolent command, and appropriate to their own use the conveniences which were designed for the Roman people. If, in these places of mixed and general resort, they meet any of the infamous ministers of their pleasures, they express their affection by a tender embrace; while they proudly decline the salutations of their fellow-citizens, who are not permitted to aspire above the honor of kissing their hands, or their knees. As soon as they have indulged themselves in the refreshment of the bath, they resume their rings, and the other ensigns of their dignity, select from their private wardrobe of the finest linen, such as might suffice for a dozen persons, the garments the most agreeable to their fancy, and maintain till their departure the same haughty demeanor; which perhaps might have been excused in the great Marcellus, after the conquest of Syracuse. Sometimes, indeed, these heroes undertake more arduous achievements; they visit their estates in Italy, and procure themselves, by the toil of servile hands, the amusements of the chase. [39] If at any time, but more especially on a hot day, they have courage to sail, in their painted galleys, from the Lucrine Lake [40] to their elegant villas on the seacoast of Puteoli and Cayeta, [41] they compare their own expeditions to the marches of Caesar and Alexander. Yet should a fly presume to settle on the silken folds of their gilded umbrellas; should a sunbeam penetrate through some unguarded and imperceptible chink, they deplore their intolerable hardships, and lament, in affected language, that they were not born in the land of the Cimmerians, [42] the regions of eternal darkness. In these journeys into the country, [43] the whole body of the household marches with their master. In the same manner as the cavalry and infantry, the heavy and the light armed troops, the advanced guard and the rear, are marshalled by the skill of their military leaders; so the domestic officers, who bear a rod, as an ensign of authority, distribute and arrange the numerous train of slaves and attendants. The baggage and wardrobe move in the front; and are immediately followed by a multitude of cooks, and inferior ministers, employed in the service of the kitchens, and of the table. The main body is composed of a promiscuous crowd of slaves, increased by the accidental concourse of idle or dependent plebeians. The rear is closed by the favorite band of eunuchs, distributed from age to youth, according to the order of seniority. Their numbers and their deformity excite the horror of the indignant spectators, who are ready to execrate the memory of Semiramis, for the cruel art which she invented, of frustrating the purposes of nature, and of blasting in the bud the hopes of future generations. In the exercise of domestic jurisdiction, the nobles of Rome express an exquisite sensibility for any personal injury, and a contemptuous indifference for the rest of the human species. When they have called for warm water, if a slave has been tardy in his obedience, he is instantly chastised with three hundred lashes: but should the same slave commit a wilful murder, the master will mildly observe, that he is a worthless fellow; but that, if he repeats the offence, he shall not escape punishment. Hospitality was formerly the virtue of the Romans; and every stranger, who could plead either merit or misfortune, was relieved, or rewarded by their generosity. At present, if a foreigner, perhaps of no contemptible rank, is introduced to one of the proud and wealthy senators, he is welcomed indeed in the first audience, with such warm professions, and such kind inquiries, that he retires, enchanted with the affability of his illustrious friend, and full of regret that he had so long delayed his journey to Rome, the active seat of manners, as well as of empire. Secure of a favorable reception, he repeats his visit the ensuing day, and is mortified by the discovery, that his person, his name, and his country, are already forgotten. If he still has resolution to persevere, he is gradually numbered in the train of dependants, and obtains the permission to pay his assiduous and unprofitable court to a haughty patron, incapable of gratitude or friendship; who scarcely deigns to remark his presence, his departure, or his return. Whenever the rich prepare a solemn and popular entertainment; [44] whenever they celebrate, with profuse and pernicious luxury, their private banquets; the choice of the guests is the subject of anxious deliberation. The modest, the sober, and the learned, are seldom preferred; and the nomenclators, who are commonly swayed by interested motives, have the address to insert, in the list of invitations, the obscure names of the most worthless of mankind. But the frequent and familiar companions of the great, are those parasites, who practise the most useful of all arts, the art of flattery; who eagerly applaud each word, and every action, of their immortal patron; gaze with rapture on his marble columns and variegated pavements; and strenuously praise the pomp and elegance which he is taught to consider as a part of his personal merit. At the Roman tables, the birds, the squirrels, [45] or the fish, which appear of an uncommon size, are contemplated with curious attention; a pair of scales is accurately applied, to ascertain their real weight; and, while the more rational guests are disgusted by the vain and tedious repetition, notaries are summoned to attest, by an authentic record, the truth of such a marvelous event. Another method of introduction into the houses and society of the great, is derived from the profession of gaming, or, as it is more politely styled, of play. The confederates are united by a strict and indissoluble bond of friendship, or rather of conspiracy; a superior degree of skill in the Tesserarian art (which may be interpreted the game of dice and tables) [46] is a sure road to wealth and reputation. A master of that sublime science, who in a supper, or assembly, is placed below a magistrate, displays in his countenance the surprise and indignation which Cato might be supposed to feel, when he was refused the praetorship by the votes of a capricious people. The acquisition of knowledge seldom engages the curiosity of nobles, who abhor the fatigue, and disdain the advantages, of study; and the only books which they peruse are the Satires of Juvenal, and the verbose and fabulous histories of Marius Maximus. [47] The libraries, which they have inherited from their fathers, are secluded, like dreary sepulchres, from the light of day. [48] But the costly instruments of the theatre, flutes, and enormous lyres, and hydraulic organs, are constructed for their use; and the harmony of vocal and instrumental music is incessantly repeated in the palaces of Rome. In those palaces, sound is preferred to sense, and the care of the body to that of the mind."

It is allowed as a salutary maxim, that the light and frivolous suspicion of a contagious malady, is of sufficient weight to excuse the visits of the most intimate friends; and even the servants, who are despatched to make the decent inquiries, are not suffered to return home, till they have undergone the ceremony of a previous ablution. Yet this selfish and unmanly delicacy occasionally yields to the more imperious passion of avarice. The prospect of gain will urge a rich and gouty senator as far as Spoleto; every sentiment of arrogance and dignity is subdued by the hopes of an inheritance, or even of a legacy; and a wealthy childless citizen is the most powerful of the Romans. The art of obtaining the signature of a favorable testament, and sometimes of hastening the moment of its execution, is perfectly understood; and it has happened, that in the same house, though in different apartments, a husband and a wife, with the laudable design of overreaching each other, have summoned their respective lawyers, to declare, at the same time, their mutual, but contradictory, intentions. The distress which follows and chastises extravagant luxury, often reduces the great to the use of the most humiliating expedients. When they desire to borrow, they employ the base and supplicating style of the slave in the comedy; but when they are called upon to pay, they assume the royal and tragic declamation of the grandsons of Hercules. If the demand is repeated, they readily procure some trusty sycophant, instructed to maintain a charge of poison, or magic, against the insolent creditor; who is seldom released from prison, till he has signed a discharge of the whole debt. These vices, which degrade the moral character of the Romans, are mixed with a puerile superstition, that disgraces their understanding. They listen with confidence to the predictions of haruspices, who pretend to read, in the entrails of victims, the signs of future greatness and prosperity; and there are many who do not presume either to bathe, or to dine, or to appear in public, till they have diligently consulted, according to the rules of astrology, the situation of Mercury, and the aspect of the moon. [49] It is singular enough, that this vain credulity may often be discovered among the profane sceptics, who impiously doubt, or deny, the existence of a celestial power."

[Footnote 35: *Claudian, who seems to have read the history of Ammianus, speaks of this great revolution in a much less courtly style:—*

Postquam jura ferox in se communia Caesar Transtulit; et lapsi mores; desuetaque priscis Artibus, in gremium pacis servile recessi. —De Be. Gildonico, p. 49.]

[Footnote 36: *The minute diligence of antiquarians has not been able to verify these extraordinary names. I am of opinion that they were invented by the historian himself, who was afraid of any personal satire or application. It is certain, however, that the simple denominations of the Romans were gradually lengthened to the number of four, five, or even seven, pompous surnames; as, for instance, Marcus Maecius Maemmius Furius Balburius Caecilianus Placidus. See Noris Cenotaph Piran Dissert. iv. p. 438.]*

[Footnote 37: *The or coaches of the romans, were often of solid silver, curiously carved and engraved; and the trappings of the mules, or horses, were embossed with gold. This magnificence continued from the reign of Nero to that of Honorius; and the Appian way was covered with the splendid equipages of the nobles, who came out to meet St. Melania, when she returned to Rome, six years before the Gothic siege, (Seneca, epist. lxxxvii. Plin. Hist. Natur. xxxiii. 49. Paulin. Nolan. apud Baron. Annal. Eccles. A.D. 397, No. 5.) Yet pomp is well exchange for convenience; and a plain modern coach, that is hung upon springs, is much preferable to the silver or gold carts of antiquity, which rolled on the axle-tree, and were exposed, for the most part, to the inclemency of the weather.]*

[Footnote 38: In a homily of Asterius, bishop of Amasia, M. de Valois has discovered (ad Ammian. xiv. 6) that this was a new fashion; that bears, wolves lions, and tigers, woods, hunting-matches, &c., were represented in embroidery: and that the more pious coxcombs substituted the figure or legend of some favorite saint.]

[Footnote 39: See Pliny's Epistles, i. 6. Three large wild boars were allured and taken in the toils without interrupting the studies of the philosophic sportsman.]

[Footnote 40: The change from the inauspicious word Avernus, which stands in the text, is immaterial. The two lakes, Avernus and Lucrinus, communicated with each other, and were fashioned by the stupendous moles of Agrippa into the Julian port, which opened, through a narrow entrance, into the Gulf of Puteoli. Virgil, who resided on the spot, has described (Georgic ii. 161) this work at the moment of its execution: and his commentators, especially Catrou, have derived much light from Strabo, Suetonius, and Dion. Earthquakes and volcanoes have changed the face of the country, and turned the Lucrine Lake, since the year 1538, into the Monte Nuovo. See Camillo Pellegrino Discorsi della Campania Felice, p. 239, 244, &c. Antonii Sanfelicii Campania, p. 13, 88—Note: Compare Lyell's Geology, ii. 72—M.]

[Footnote 41: The regna Cumana et Puteolana; loca caetiroqui valde expe tenda, interpellantium autem multitudine paene fugienda. Cicero ad Attic. xvi. 17.]

[Footnote 42: The proverbial expression of Cimmerian darkness was originally borrowed from the description of Homer, (in the eleventh book of the Odyssey,) which he applies to a remote and fabulous country on the shores of the ocean. See Erasmi Adagia, in his works, tom. ii. p. 593, the Leyden edition.]

[Footnote 43: We may learn from Seneca (epist. cxxiii.) three curious circumstances relative to the journeys of the Romans. 1. They were preceded by a troop of Numidian light horse, who announced, by a cloud of dust, the approach of a great man. 2. Their baggage mules transported not only the precious vases, but even the fragile vessels of crystal and murra, which last is almost proved, by the learned French translator of Seneca, (tom. iii. p. 402-422,) to mean the porcelain of China and Japan. 3. The beautiful faces of the young slaves were covered with a medicated crust, or ointment, which secured them against the effects of the sun and frost.]

[Footnote 44: Distributio solemnium sportularum. The sportuloe, or sportelloe, were small baskets, supposed to contain a quantity of hot provisions of the value of 100 quadrantes, or twelvepence halfpenny, which were ranged in order in the hall, and ostentatiously distributed to the hungry or servile crowd who waited at the door. This indelicate custom is very frequently mentioned in the epigrams of Martial, and the satires of Juvenal. See likewise Suetonius, in Claud. c. 21, in Neron. c. 16, in Domitian, c. 4, 7. These baskets of provisions were afterwards converted into large pieces of gold and silver coin, or plate, which were mutually given and accepted even by persons of the highest rank, (see Symmach. epist. iv. 55, ix. 124, and Miscell. p. 256,) on solemn occasions, of consulships, marriages, &c.]

[Footnote 45: The want of an English name obliges me to refer to the common genus of squirrels, the Latin glis, the French loir; a little animal, who inhabits the woods, and remains torpid in cold weather, (see Plin. Hist. Natur. viii. 82. Buffon, Hist. Naturelle, tom. viii. 153. Pennant's Synopsis of Quadrupeds, p. 289.) The art of rearing and fattening great numbers of glires was practised in Roman villas as a profitable article of rural economy, (Varro, de Re Rustica, iii. 15.) The excessive demand of them for luxurious tables was increased by the foolish prohibitions of the censors; and it is reported that they are *still esteemed in modern Rome, and are frequently sent as presents by the Colonna princes, (see Brotier, the last editor of Pliny tom. ii. p. 453. epud Barbou, 1779.)—Note: Is it not the dormouse?—M.]*

[Footnote 46: This game, which might be translated by the more familiar names of trictrac, or backgammon, was a favorite amusement of the gravest Romans; and old Mucius Scaevola, the lawyer, had the reputation of a very skilful player. It was called ludus duodecim scriptorum, from the twelve scripta, or lines, which equally divided the alvevolus or table. On these, the two armies, the white and the black, each consisting of fifteen men, or catculi, were regularly placed, and alternately moved according to the laws of the game, and the chances of the tesseroe, or dice. Dr. Hyde, who diligently traces the history and varieties of the nerdiludium (a name of Persic etymology) from Ireland to Japan, pours forth, on this trifling subject, a copious torrent of classic and Oriental learning. See Syntagma Dissertat. tom. ii. p. 217-405.]

[Footnote 47: Marius Maximus, homo omnium verbosissimus, qui, et mythistoricis se voluminibus implicavit. Vopiscus in Hist. August. p. 242. He wrote the lives of the emperors, from Trajan to Alexander Severus. See Gerard Vossius de Historicis Latin. l. ii. c. 3, in his works, vol. iv. p. 47.]

[Footnote 48: This satire is probably exaggerated. The Saturnalia of Macrobius, and the epistles of Jerom, afford satisfactory proofs, that Christian theology and classic literature were studiously cultivated by several Romans, of both sexes, and of the highest rank.]

[Footnote 49: Macrobius, the friend of these Roman nobles, considered the siara as the cause, or at least the signs, of future events, (de Somn. Scipion l. i. c 19. p. 68.)]

PART III

In populous cities, which are the seat of commerce and manufactures, the middle ranks of inhabitants, who derive their subsistence from the dexterity or labor of their hands, are commonly the most prolific, the most useful, and, in that sense, the most respectable part of the community. But the plebeians of Rome, who disdained such sedentary and servile arts, had been oppressed from the earliest times by the weight of debt and usury; and the husbandman, during the term of his military service, was obliged to abandon the cultivation of his farm. [50] The lands of Italy which had been originally divided among the families of free and indigent proprietors, were insensibly purchased or usurped by the avarice of the nobles; and in the age which preceded the fall of the republic, it was computed that only two thousand citizens were possessed of an independent substance. [51] Yet as long as the people bestowed, by their suffrages, the honors of the state, the command of the legions, and the administration of wealthy provinces, their conscious pride alleviated in some measure, the hardships of poverty; and their wants were seasonably supplied by the ambitious liberality of the candidates, who aspired to secure a venal majority in the thirty-five tribes, or the hundred and ninety-three centuries, of Rome. But when the prodigal commons had not only imprudently alienated the use, but the inheritance of power, they sunk, under the reign of the Caesars, into a vile and wretched populace, which must, in a few generations, have been totally extinguished, if it had not been continually recruited by the manumission of slaves, and the influx of strangers. As early as the time of Hadrian, it was the just complaint of the ingenuous natives, that the capital had attracted the vices of the universe, and the manners of the most opposite nations. The intemperance of the Gauls, the cunning and levity of the Greeks, the savage obstinacy of the Egyptians and Jews, the servile temper of the Asiatics, and the dissolute, effeminate prostitution of the Syrians, were mingled in the various multitude, which, under the proud and false denomination of Romans, presumed to despise their fellow-subjects, and even their sovereigns, who dwelt beyond the precincts of the Eternal City. [52]

[Footnote 50: The histories of Livy (see particularly vi. 36) are full of the extortions of the rich, and the sufferings of the poor debtors. The melancholy story of a brave old soldier (Dionys. Hal. l. vi. c. 26, p. 347, edit. Hudson, and Livy, ii. 23) must have been frequently repeated in those primitive times, which have been so undeservedly praised.]

[Footnote 51: Non esse in civitate duo millia hominum qui rem habereni. Cicero. Offic. ii. 21, and Comment. Paul. Manut. in edit. Graev. This vague computation was made A. U. C. 649, in a speech of the tribune Philippus, and it was his object, as well as that of the Gracchi, (see Plutarch,) to deplore, and perhaps to exaggerate, the misery of the common people.]

[Footnote 52: See the third Satire (60-125) of Juvenal, who indignantly complains,

Quamvis quota portio faecis Achaei! Jampridem Syrus in Tiberem defluxit Orontes; Et linguam et mores, &c.

Seneca, when he proposes to comfort his mother (Consolat. ad Helv. c. 6) by the reflection, that a great part of mankind were in a state of exile, reminds her how few of the inhabitants of Rome were born in the city.]

Yet the name of that city was still pronounced with respect: the frequent and capricious tumults of its inhabitants were indulged with impunity; and the successors of Constantine, instead of crushing the last remains of the democracy by the strong arm of military power, embraced the mild policy of Augustus, and studied to relieve the poverty, and to amuse the idleness, of an innumerable people. [53] I. For the convenience of the lazy plebeians, the monthly distributions of corn were converted into a daily allowance of bread; a great number of ovens were constructed and maintained at the public expense; and at the appointed hour, each citizen, who was furnished with a ticket, ascended the flight of steps, which had been assigned to his peculiar quarter or division, and received, either as a gift, or at a very low price, a loaf of bread of the weight of three pounds, for the use of his family. II. The forest of Lucania, whose acorns fattened large droves of wild hogs, [54] afforded, as a species of tribute, a plentiful supply of cheap and wholesome meat. During five months of the year, a regular allowance of bacon was distributed to the poorer citizens; and the annual consumption of the capital, at a time when it was much declined from its former lustre, was ascertained, by an edict from Valentinian the Third, at three millions six hundred and twenty-eight thousand pounds. [55] III. In the manners of antiquity, the use of oil was indispensable for the lamp, as well as for the bath; and the annual tax, which was imposed on Africa for the benefit of Rome, amounted to the weight of three millions of pounds, to the measure, perhaps, of three hundred thousand English gallons. IV. The anxiety of Augustus to provide the metropolis with sufficient plenty of corn, was not extended beyond that necessary article of human subsistence; and when the popular clamor accused the dearness and scarcity of wine, a proclamation was issued, by the grave reformer, to remind his subjects that no man could reasonably complain of thirst, since the aqueducts of Agrippa had introduced into the city so many copious streams of pure and salubrious water. [56] This rigid sobriety was insensibly relaxed; and, although the generous design of Aurelian [57] does not appear to have been executed in its full extent, the use of wine was allowed on very easy and liberal terms. The administration of the public cellars was delegated to a magistrate of honorable rank; and a considerable part of the vintage of Campania was reserved for the fortunate inhabitants of Rome.

[Footnote 53: Almost all that is said of the bread, bacon, oil, wine, &c., may be found in the fourteenth book of the Theodosian Code; which expressly treats of the police of the great cities. See particularly the titles iii. iv. xv. xvi. xvii. xxiv. The collateral testimonies are produced in Godefroy's Commentary, and it is needless to transcribe them. According to a law of Theodosius, which appreciates in money the military allowance, a piece of gold (eleven shillings) was equivalent to eighty pounds of bacon, or to eighty pounds of oil, or to twelve modii (or pecks) of salt, (Cod. Theod. l. viii. tit. iv. leg. 17.) This equation, compared with another of seventy pounds of bacon for an amphora, (Cod. Theod. l. xiv. tit. iv. leg. 4,) fixes the price of wine at about sixteenpence the gallon.]

[Footnote 54: The anonymous author of the Description of the World (p. 14. in tom. iii. Geograph. Minor. Hudson) observes of Lucania, in his barbarous Latin, Regio optima, et ipsa omnibus habundans, et lardum multum foras. Proptor quod est in montibus, cujus aescam animalium rariam, &c.]

[Footnote 55: See Novell. ad calcem Cod. Theod. D. Valent. l. i. tit. xv. This law was published at Rome, June 29th, A.D. 452.]

[Footnote 56: Sueton. in August. c. 42. The utmost debauch of the emperor himself, in his favorite wine of Rhaetia, never exceeded a sextarius, (an English pint.) Id. c. 77. Torrentius ad loc. and Arbuthnot's Tables, p. 86.]

[Footnote 57: His design was to plant vineyards along the sea-coast of Hetruria, (Vopiscus, in Hist. August. p. 225;) the dreary, unwholesome, uncultivated Maremme of modern Tuscany]

The stupendous aqueducts, so justly celebrated by the praises of Augustus himself, replenished the Thermoe, or baths, which had been constructed in every part of the city, with Imperial magnificence. The baths of Antoninus Caracalla, which were open, at stated hours, for the indiscriminate service of the senators and the people, contained above sixteen hundred seats of marble; and more than three thousand were reckoned in the baths of Diocletian. [58] The walls of the lofty apartments were covered with curious mosaics, that imitated the art of the pencil in the elegance of design, and the variety of colors. The Egyptian granite was beautifully encrusted with the precious green marble of Numidia; the perpetual stream of hot water was poured into the capacious basins, through so many wide mouths of bright and massy silver; and the meanest Roman could purchase, with a small copper coin, the daily enjoyment of a scene of pomp and luxury, which might excite the envy of the kings of Asia. [59] From these stately palaces issued a swarm of dirty and ragged plebeians, without shoes and without a mantle; who loitered away whole days in the street of Forum, to hear news and to hold disputes; who dissipated in extravagant gaming, the miserable pittance of their wives and children; and spent the hours of the night in the obscure taverns, and brothels, in the indulgence of gross and vulgar sensuality. [60]

[Footnote 58: Olympiodor. apud Phot. p. 197.]

[Footnote 59: Seneca (epistol. lxxxvi.) compares the baths of Scipio Africanus, at his villa of Liternum, with the magnificence (which was continually increasing) of the public baths of Rome, long before the stately Thermae of Antoninus and Diocletian were erected. The quadrans paid for admission was the quarter of the as, about one eighth of an English penny.]

[Footnote 60: Ammianus, (l. xiv. c. 6, and l. xxviii. c. 4,) after describing the luxury and pride of the nobles of Rome, exposes, with equal indignation, the vices and follies of the common people.]

But the most lively and splendid amusement of the idle multitude, depended on the frequent exhibition of public games and spectacles. The piety of Christian princes had suppressed the inhuman combats of gladiators; but the Roman people still considered the Circus as their home, their temple, and the seat of the republic. The impatient crowd rushed at the dawn of day to secure their places, and there were many who passed a sleepless and anxious night in the adjacent porticos. From the morning to the evening, careless of the sun, or of the rain, the spectators, who sometimes amounted to the number of four hundred thousand, remained in eager attention; their eyes fixed on the horses and charioteers, their minds agitated with hope and fear, for the success of the colors which they espoused: and the happiness of Rome appeared to hang on the event of a race. [61] The same immoderate ardor inspired their clamors and their applause, as often as they were entertained with the hunting of wild beasts, and the various modes of theatrical representation. These representations in modern capitals may deserve to be considered as a pure and elegant school of taste, and perhaps of virtue. But the Tragic and Comic Muse of the Romans, who seldom aspired beyond the imitation of Attic genius, [62] had been almost totally silent since the fall of the republic; [63] and their place was unworthily occupied by licentious farce, effeminate music, and splendid pageantry. The pantomimes, [64] who maintained their reputation from the age of Augustus to the sixth century, expressed, without the use of words, the various fables of the gods and heroes of antiquity; and the perfection of their art, which sometimes disarmed the gravity of the philosopher, always excited the applause and wonder of the people. The vast and magnificent theatres of Rome were filled by three thousand female dancers, and by three thousand singers, with the masters of the respective choruses. Such was the popular favor which they enjoyed, that, in a time of scarcity, when all strangers were banished from the city, the merit of contributing to the public pleasures exempted them from a law, which was strictly executed against the professors of the liberal arts. [65]

[Footnote 61: Juvenal. Satir. xi. 191, &c. The expressions of the historian Ammianus are not less strong and animated than those of the satirist and both the one and the other painted from the life. The numbers which the great Circus was capable of receiving are taken from the original Notitioe of the city. The differences between them prove that they did not transcribe each other; but the same may appear incredible, though the country on these occasions flocked to the city.]

[Footnote 62: Sometimes indeed they composed original pieces.

Vestigia Graeca Ausi deserere et celeb rare domestica facta.

Horat. Epistol. ad Pisones, 285, and the learned, though perplexed note of Dacier, who might have allowed the name of tragedies to the Brutus and the Decius of Pacuvius, or to the Cato of Maternus. The Octavia, ascribed to one of the Senecas, still remains a very unfavorable specimen of Roman tragedy.]

[Footnote 63: In the time of Quintilian and Pliny, a tragic poet was reduced to the imperfect method of hiring a great room, and reading his play to the company, whom he invited for that purpose. (See Dialog. de Oratoribus, c. 9, 11, and Plin. Epistol. vii. 17.)]

[Footnote 64: See the dialogue of Lucian, entitled the Saltatione, tom. ii. p. 265-317, edit. Reitz. The pantomimes obtained the honorable name; and it was required, that they should be conversant with *almost every art and science. Burette (in the Memoires de l'Academie des Inscriptions, tom. i. p. 127, &c.) has given a short history of the art of pantomimes.]*

[Footnote 65: Ammianus, l. xiv. c. 6. He complains, with decent indignation that the streets of Rome were filled with crowds of females, who might have given children to the state, but whose only occupation was to curl and dress their hair, and jactari volubilibus gyris, dum experimunt innumera simulacra, quae finxere fabulae theatrales.]

It is said, that the foolish curiosity of Elagabalus attempted to discover, from the quantity of spiders' webs, the number of the inhabitants of Rome. A more rational method of inquiry might not have been undeserving of the attention of the wisest princes, who could easily have resolved a question so important for the Roman government, and so interesting to succeeding ages. The births and deaths of the citizens were duly registered; and if any writer of antiquity had condescended to mention the annual amount, or the common average, we might now produce some satisfactory calculation, which would destroy the extravagant assertions of critics, and perhaps confirm the modest and probable conjectures of philosophers. [66] The most diligent researches have collected only the following circumstances; which, slight and imperfect as they are, may tend, in some degree, to illustrate the question of the populousness of ancient Rome. I. When the capital of the empire was besieged by the Goths, the circuit of the walls was accurately measured, by Ammonius, the mathematician, who found it equal to twenty-one miles. [67] It should not be forgotten that the form of the city was almost that of a circle; the geometrical figure which is known to contain the largest space within any given circumference. II. The architect Vitruvius, who flourished in the Augustan age, and whose evidence, on this occasion, has peculiar weight and authority, observes, that the innumerable habitations of the Roman people would have spread themselves far beyond the narrow limits of the city; and that the want of ground, which was probably contracted on every side by gardens and villas, suggested the common, though inconvenient, practice of raising the houses to a considerable height in the air. [68] But the loftiness of these buildings, which often consisted of hasty work and insufficient materials, was the cause of frequent and fatal accidents; and it was repeatedly enacted by Augustus, as well as by Nero, that the height of private edifices within the walls of Rome, should not exceed the measure of seventy feet from the ground. [69] III. Juvenal [70] laments, as it should seem from his own experience, the hardships of the poorer citizens, to whom he addresses the salutary advice of emigrating, without delay, from the smoke of Rome, since they might purchase, in the little towns of Italy, a cheerful commodious dwelling, at the same price which they annually paid for a dark and miserable lodging. House-rent was therefore immoderately dear: the rich acquired, at an enormous expense, the ground, which they covered with palaces and gardens; but the body of the Roman people was crowded into a narrow space; and the different floors, and apartments, of the same house, were divided, as it is still the custom of Paris, and other cities, among several families of plebeians. IV. The total number of houses in the fourteen regions of the city, is accurately stated in the description of Rome, composed under the reign of Theodosius, and they amount to forty-eight thousand three hundred and eighty-two. [71] The two classes of domus and of insuloe, into which they are divided, include all the habitations of the capital, of every rank and condition from the marble palace of the Anicii, with a numerous establishment of freedmen and slaves, to the lofty and narrow lodging-house, where the poet Codrus and his wife were permitted to hire a wretched garret immediately under the files. If we adopt the same average, which, under similar circumstances, has been found applicable to Paris, [72] and indifferently allow about twenty-five persons for each house, of every degree, we may fairly estimate the inhabitants of Rome at twelve hundred thousand: a number which cannot be thought excessive for the capital of a mighty empire, though it exceeds the populousness of the greatest cities of modern Europe. [73] [73/1]

[Footnote 66: Lipsius (tom. iii. p. 423, de Magnitud. Romana, l. iii. c. 3) and Isaac Vossius (Observant. Var. p. 26-34) have indulged strange dreams, of four, or eight, or fourteen, millions in Rome. Mr. Hume, (Essays, vol. i. p. 450-457,) with admirable good sense and scepticism betrays some secret disposition to extenuate the populousness of ancient times.]

[Footnote 67: Olympiodor. ap. Phot. p. 197. See Fabricius, Bibl. Graec. tom. ix. p. 400.]

[Footnote 68: In ea autem majestate urbis, et civium infinita frequentia, innumerabiles habitationes opus fuit explicare. Ergo cum recipero non posset area plana tantam multitudinem in urbe, ad auxilium altitudinis aedificiorum res ipsa coegit devenire. Vitruv. ii. 8. This passage, which I owe to Vossius, is clear, strong, and comprehensive.]

[Footnote 69: The successive testimonies of Pliny, Aristides, Claudian, Rutilius, &c., prove the insufficiency of these restrictive edicts. See Lipsius, de Magnitud. Romana, l. iii. c. 4.

Tabulata tibi jam tertia fumant; Tu nescis; nam si gradibus trepidatur ab imis Ultimus ardebit, quem tegula sola tuetur A pluvia. —Juvenal. Satir. iii. 199]

[Footnote 70: Read the whole third satire, but particularly 166, 223, &c. The description of a crowded insula, or lodging-house, in Petronius, (c. 95, 97,) perfectly tallies with the complaints of Juvenal; and we learn from legal authority, that, in the time of Augustus, (Heineccius, Hist. Juris. Roman. c. iv. p. 181,) the ordinary rent of the several coenacula, or apartments of an insula, annually produced forty thousand sesterces, between three and four hundred pounds sterling, (Pandect. l. xix. tit. ii. No. 30,) a sum which proves at once the large extent, and high value, of those common buildings.]

[Footnote 71: This sum total is composed of 1780 domus, or great houses of 46,602 insuloe, or plebeian habitations, (see Nardini, Roma Antica, l. iii. p. 88;) and these numbers are ascertained by the agreement of the texts of the different Notitioe. Nardini, l. viii. p. 498, 500.]

[Footnote 72: See that accurate writer M. de Messance, Recherches sur la Population, p. 175-187. From probable, or certain grounds, he assigns to Paris 23,565 houses, 71,114 families, and 576,630 inhabitants.]

[Footnote 73: This computation is not very different from that which M. Brotier, the last editor of Tacitus, (tom. ii. p. 380,) has assumed from similar principles; though he seems to aim at a degree of precision which it is neither possible nor important to obtain.]

[Footnote 73/1: M. Dureau de la Malle (Economic Politique des Romaines, t. i. p. 369) quotes a passage from the xvth chapter of Gibbon, in which he estimates the population of Rome at not less than a million, and adds (omitting any reference to this passage,) that he (Gibbon) could not have seriously studied the question. M. Dureau de la Malle proceeds to argue that Rome, as contained within the walls of Servius Tullius, occupying an area only one fifth of that of Paris, could not have contained 300,000 inhabitants; within those of Aurelian not more than 560,000, inclusive of soldiers and strangers. The suburbs, he endeavors to show, both up to the time of Aurelian, and after his reign, were neither so extensive, nor so populous, as generally supposed. M. Dureau de la Malle has but imperfectly quoted the important passage of Dionysius, that which proves that when he wrote (in the time of Augustus) the walls of Servius no longer marked the boundary of the city. In many places they were so built upon, that it was impossible to trace them. There was no certain limit, where the city ended and ceased to be the city; it *stretched out to so boundless an extent into the country. Ant. Rom. iv. 13. None of M. de la Malle's arguments appear to me to prove, against this statement, that these irregular suburbs did not extend so far in many parts, as to make it impossible to calculate accurately the inhabited area of the city. Though no doubt the city, as reconstructed by Nero, was much less closely built and with many more open spaces for palaces, temples, and other public edifices, yet many passages seem to prove that the laws respecting the height of houses were not rigidly enforced. A great part of the lower especially of the slave population, were very densely crowded, and lived, even more than in our modern towns, in cellars and subterranean dwellings under the public edifices. Nor do M. de la Malle's arguments, by which he would explain the insulae insulae (of which the Notitiae Urbis give us the number) as rows of shops, with a chamber or two within the domus, or houses of the wealthy, satisfy me as to their soundness of their scholarship. Some passages which he adduces directly contradict his theory; none, as appears to me, distinctly prove it. I must adhere to the old interpretation of the word, as chiefly dwellings for the middling or lower classes, or clusters of tenements, often perhaps, under the same roof. On this point, Zumpt, in the Dissertation before quoted, entirely disagrees with M. de la Malle. Zumpt has likewise detected the mistake of M. de la Malle as to the "canon" of corn, mentioned in the life of Septimius Severus by Spartianus. On this canon the French writer calculates the inhabitants of Rome at that time. But the "canon" was not the whole supply of Rome, but that quantity which the state required for the public granaries to supply the gratuitous distributions to the people, and the public officers and slaves; no doubt likewise to keep down the general price. M. Zumpt reckons the population of Rome at 2,000,000. After careful consideration, I should conceive the number in the text, 1,200,000, to be nearest the truth—M. 1845.]*

Such was the state of Rome under the reign of Honorius; at the time when the Gothic army formed the siege, or rather the blockade, of the city. [74] By a skilful disposition of his numerous forces, who impatiently watched the moment of an assault, Alaric encompassed the walls, commanded the twelve principal gates, intercepted all communication with the adjacent country, and vigilantly guarded the navigation of the Tyber, from which the Romans derived the surest and most plentiful supply of provisions. The first emotions of the nobles, and of the people, were those of surprise and indignation, that a vile Barbarian should dare to insult the capital of the world: but their arrogance was soon humbled by misfortune; and their unmanly rage, instead of being directed against an enemy in arms, was meanly exercised on a defenceless and innocent victim. Perhaps in the person of Serena, the Romans might have respected the niece of Theodosius, the aunt, nay, even the adoptive mother, of the reigning emperor: but they abhorred the widow of Stilicho; and they listened with credulous passion to the tale of calumny, which accused her of maintaining a secret and criminal correspondence with the Gothic invader. Actuated, or overawed, by the same popular frenzy, the senate, without requiring any evidence of his guilt, pronounced the sentence of her death. Serena was ignominiously strangled; and the infatuated multitude were astonished to find, that this cruel act of injustice did not immediately produce the retreat of the Barbarians, and the deliverance of the city. That unfortunate city gradually experienced the distress of scarcity, and at length the horrid calamities of famine. The daily allowance of three pounds of bread was reduced to one half, to one third, to nothing; and the price of corn still continued to rise in a rapid and extravagant proportion. The poorer citizens, who were unable to purchase the necessaries of life, solicited the precarious charity of the rich; and for a while the public misery was alleviated by the humanity of Laeta, the widow of the emperor Gratian, who had fixed her residence at Rome, and consecrated to the use of the indigent the princely revenue which she annually received from the grateful successors of her husband. [75] But these private and temporary donatives were insufficient to appease the hunger of a numerous people; and the progress of famine invaded the marble palaces of the senators themselves. The persons of both sexes, who had been educated in the enjoyment of ease and luxury, discovered how little is requisite to supply the demands of nature; and lavished their unavailing treasures of gold and silver, to obtain the coarse and scanty sustenance which they would formerly have rejected with disdain. The food the most repugnant to sense or imagination, the aliments the most unwholesome and pernicious to the constitution, were eagerly devoured, and fiercely disputed, by the rage of hunger. A dark suspicion was entertained, that some desperate wretches fed on the bodies of their fellow-creatures, whom they had secretly murdered; and even mothers, (such was the horrid conflict of the two most powerful instincts implanted by nature in the human breast,) even mothers are said to have tasted the flesh of their slaughtered infants! [76] Many thousands of the inhabitants of Rome expired in their houses, or in the streets, for want of sustenance; and as the public sepulchres without the walls were in the power of the enemy the stench, which arose from so many putrid and unburied carcasses, infected the air; and the miseries of famine were succeeded and aggravated by the contagion of a pestilential disease. The assurances of speedy and effectual relief, which were repeatedly transmitted from the court of Ravenna, supported for some time, the fainting resolution of the Romans, till at length the despair of any human aid tempted them to accept the offers of a praeternatural deliverance. Pompeianus, praefect of the city, had been persuaded, by the art or fanaticism of some Tuscan diviners, that, by the mysterious force of spells and sacrifices, they could extract the lightning from the clouds, and point those celestial fires against the camp of the Barbarians. [77] The important secret was communicated to Innocent, the bishop of Rome; and the successor of St. Peter is accused, perhaps without foundation, of preferring the safety of the republic to the rigid severity of the Christian worship. But when the question was agitated in the senate; when it was proposed, as an essential condition, that those sacrifices should be performed in the Capitol, by the authority, and in the presence, of the magistrates, the majority of that respectable assembly, apprehensive either of the Divine or of the Imperial displeasure, refused to join in an act, which appeared almost equivalent to the public restoration of Paganism. [78]

[Footnote 74: For the events of the first siege of Rome, which are often confounded with those of the second and third, see Zosimus, l. v. p. 350-354, Sozomen, l. ix. c. 6, Olympiodorus, ap. Phot. p. 180, Philostorgius, l. xii. c. 3, and Godefroy, Dissertat. p. 467-475.]

[Footnote 75: The mother of Laeta was named Pissumena. Her father, family, and country, are unknown. Ducange, Fam. Byzantium, p. 59.]

[Footnote 76: Ad nefandos cibos erupit esurientium rabies, et sua invicem membra laniarunt, dum mater non parcit lactenti infantiae; et recipit utero, quem paullo ante effuderat. Jerom. ad Principiam, tom. i. p. 121. The same horrid circumstance is likewise told of the sieges of Jerusalem and Paris. For the latter, compare the tenth book of the Henriade, and the Journal de Henri IV. tom. i. p. 47-83; and observe that a plain narrative of facts is much more pathetic, than the most labored descriptions of epic poetry]

[Footnote 77: Zosimus (l. v. p. 355, 356) speaks of these ceremonies like a Greek unacquainted with the national superstition of Rome and Tuscany. I suspect, that they consisted of two parts, the secret and the public; the former were probably an imitation of the arts and spells, by which Numa had drawn down Jupiter and his thunder on Mount Aventine.

Quid agant laqueis, quae carmine dicant, Quaque trahant superis sedibus arte Jovem, Scire nefas homini.

The ancilia, or shields of Mars, the pignora Imperii, which were carried in solemn procession on the calends of March, derived their origin from this mysterious event, (Ovid. Fast. iii. 259-398.) It was probably designed to revive this ancient festival, which had been suppressed by Theodosius. In that case, we recover a chronological date (March the 1st, A.D. 409) which has not hitherto been observed. Note:

On this curious question of the knowledge of conducting lightning, processed by the ancients, consult Eusebe Salverte, des Sciences Occultes, l. xxiv. Paris, 1829—M.]

[Footnote 78: Sozomen (l. ix. c. 6) insinuates that the experiment was actually, though unsuccessfully, made; but he does not mention the name of Innocent: and Tillemont, (Mem. Eccles. tom. x. p. 645) is determined not to believe, that a pope could be guilty of such impious condescension.]

The last resource of the Romans was in the clemency, or at least in the moderation, of the king of the Goths. The senate, who in this emergency assumed the supreme powers of government, appointed two ambassadors to negotiate with the enemy. This important trust was delegated to Basilius, a senator, of Spanish extraction, and already conspicuous in the administration of provinces; and to John, the first tribune of the notaries, who was peculiarly qualified, by his dexterity in business, as well as by his former intimacy with the Gothic prince. When they were introduced into his presence, they declared, perhaps in a more lofty style than became their abject condition, that the Romans were resolved to maintain their dignity, either in peace or war; and that, if Alaric refused them a fair and honorable capitulation, he might sound his trumpets, and prepare to give battle to an innumerable people, exercised in arms, and animated by despair. "The thicker the hay, the easier it is mowed," was the concise reply of the Barbarian; and this rustic metaphor was accompanied by a loud and insulting laugh, expressive of his contempt for the menaces of an unwarlike populace, enervated by luxury before they were emaciated by famine. He then condescended to fix the ransom, which he would accept as the price of his retreat from the walls of Rome: all the gold and silver in the city, whether it were the property of the state, or of individuals; all the rich and precious movables; and all the slaves that could prove their title to the name of Barbarians. The ministers of the senate presumed to ask, in a modest and suppliant tone, "If such, O king, are your demands, what do you intend to leave us?" "Your Lives!" replied the haughty conqueror: they trembled, and retired. Yet, before they retired, a short suspension of arms was granted, which allowed some time for a more temperate negotiation. The stern features of Alaric were insensibly relaxed; he abated much of the rigor of his terms; and at length consented to raise the siege, on the immediate payment of five thousand pounds of gold, of thirty thousand pounds of silver, of four thousand robes of silk, of three thousand pieces of fine scarlet cloth, and of three thousand pounds weight of pepper. [79] But the public treasury was exhausted; the annual rents of the great estates in Italy and the provinces, had been exchanged, during the famine, for the vilest sustenance; the hoards of secret wealth were still concealed by the obstinacy of avarice; and some remains of consecrated spoils afforded the only resource that could avert the impending ruin of the city. As soon as the Romans had satisfied the rapacious demands of Alaric, they were restored, in some measure, to the enjoyment of peace and plenty. Several of the gates were cautiously opened; the importation of provisions from the river and the adjacent country was no longer obstructed by the Goths; the citizens resorted in crowds to the free market, which was held during three days in the suburbs; and while the merchants who undertook this gainful trade made a considerable profit, the future subsistence of the city was secured by the ample magazines which were deposited in the public and private granaries. A more regular discipline than could have been expected, was maintained in the camp of Alaric; and the wise Barbarian justified his regard for the faith of treaties, by the just severity with which he chastised a party of licentious Goths, who had insulted some Roman citizens on the road to Ostia. His army, enriched by the contributions of the capital, slowly advanced into the fair and fruitful province of Tuscany, where he proposed to establish his winter quarters; and the Gothic standard became the refuge of forty thousand Barbarian slaves, who had broke their chains, and aspired, under the command of their great deliverer, to revenge the injuries and the disgrace of their cruel servitude. About the same time, he received a more honorable reenforcement of Goths and Huns, whom Adolphus, [80] the brother of his wife, had conducted, at his pressing invitation, from the banks of the Danube to those of the Tyber, and who had cut their way, with some difficulty and loss, through the superior number of the Imperial troops. A victorious leader, who united the daring spirit of a Barbarian with the art and discipline of a Roman general, was at the head of a hundred thousand fighting men; and Italy pronounced, with terror and respect, the formidable name of Alaric. [81]

[Footnote 79: Pepper was a favorite ingredient of the most expensive Roman cookery, and the best sort commonly sold for fifteen denarii, or ten shillings, the pound. See Pliny, Hist. Natur. xii. 14. It was brought from India; and the same country, the coast of Malabar, still affords the greatest plenty: but the improvement of trade and navigation has multiplied the quantity and reduced the price. See Histoire Politique et Philosophique, &c., tom. i. p. 457.]

[Footnote 80: This Gothic chieftain is called by Jornandes and Isidore, Athaulphus; by Zosimus and Orosius, Ataulphus; and by Olympiodorus, Adaoulphus. I have used the celebrated name of Adolphus, which seems to be authorized by the practice of the Swedes, the sons or brothers of the ancient Goths.]

[Footnote 81: The treaty between Alaric and the Romans, &c., is taken from Zosimus, l. v. p. 354, 355, 358, 359, 362, 363. The additional circumstances are too few and trifling to require any other quotation.]

PART IV

At the distance of fourteen centuries, we may be satisfied with relating the military exploits of the conquerors of Rome, without presuming to investigate the motives of their political conduct. In the midst of his apparent prosperity, Alaric was conscious, perhaps, of some secret weakness, some internal defect; or perhaps the moderation which he displayed, was intended only to deceive and disarm the easy credulity of the ministers of Honorius. The king of the Goths repeatedly declared, that it was his desire to be considered as the friend of peace, and of the Romans. Three senators, at his earnest request, were sent ambassadors to the court of Ravenna, to solicit the exchange of hostages, and the conclusion of the treaty; and the proposals, which he more clearly expressed during the course of the negotiations, could only inspire a doubt of his sincerity, as they might seem inadequate to the state of his fortune. The Barbarian still aspired to the rank of master-general of the armies of the West; he stipulated an annual subsidy of corn and money; and he chose the provinces of Dalmatia, Noricum, and Venetia, for the seat of his new kingdom, which would have commanded the important communication between Italy and the Danube. If these modest terms should be rejected, Alaric showed a disposition to relinquish his pecuniary demands, and even to content himself with the possession of Noricum; an exhausted and impoverished country, perpetually exposed to the inroads of the Barbarians of Germany. [82] But the hopes of peace were disappointed by the weak obstinacy, or interested views, of the minister Olympius. Without listening to the salutary remonstrances of the senate, he dismissed their ambassadors under the conduct of a military escort, too numerous for a retinue of honor, and too feeble for any army of defence. Six thousand Dalmatians, the flower of the Imperial legions, were ordered to march from Ravenna to Rome, through an open country which was occupied by the formidable myriads of the Barbarians. These brave legionaries, encompassed and betrayed, fell a sacrifice to ministerial folly; their general, Valens, with a hundred soldiers, escaped from the field of battle; and one of the ambassadors, who could no longer claim the protection of the law of nations, was obliged to purchase his freedom with a ransom of thirty thousand pieces of gold. Yet Alaric, instead of resenting this act of impotent hostility, immediately renewed his proposals of peace; and the second embassy of the Roman senate, which derived weight and dignity from the presence of Innocent, bishop of the city, was guarded from the dangers of the road by a detachment of Gothic soldiers. [83]

[Footnote 82: Zosimus, l. v. p. 367 368, 369.]

[Footnote 83: Zosimus, l. v. p. 360, 361, 362. The bishop, by remaining at Ravenna, escaped the impending calamities of the city. Orosius, l. vii. c. 39, p. 573.]

Olympius [84] might have continued to insult the just resentment of a people who loudly accused him as the author of the public calamities; but his power was undermined by the secret intrigues of the palace. The favorite eunuchs transferred the government of Honorius, and the empire, to Jovius, the Praetorian praefect; an unworthy servant, who did not atone, by the merit of personal attachment, for the errors and misfortunes of his administration. The exile, or escape, of the guilty Olympius, reserved him for more vicissitudes of fortune: he experienced the adventures of an obscure and wandering life; he again rose to power; he fell a second time into disgrace; his ears were cut off; he expired under the lash; and his ignominious death afforded a grateful spectacle to the friends of Stilicho. After the removal of Olympius, whose character was deeply tainted with religious fanaticism, the Pagans and heretics were delivered from the impolitic proscription, which excluded them from the dignities of the state. The brave Gennerid, [85] a soldier of Barbarian origin, who still adhered to the worship of his ancestors, had been obliged to lay aside the military belt: and though he was repeatedly assured by the emperor himself, that laws were not made for persons of his rank or merit, he refused to accept any partial dispensation, and persevered in honorable disgrace, till he had extorted a general act of justice from the distress of the Roman government. The conduct of Gennerid in the important station to which he was promoted or restored, of master-general of Dalmatia, Pannonia, Noricum, and Rhaetia, seemed to revive the discipline and spirit of the republic. From a life of idleness and want, his troops were soon habituated to severe exercise and plentiful subsistence; and his private generosity often supplied the rewards, which were denied by the avarice, or poverty, of the court of Ravenna. The valor of Gennerid, formidable to the adjacent Barbarians, was the firmest bulwark of the Illyrian frontier; and his vigilant care assisted the empire with a reenforcement of ten thousand Huns, who arrived on the confines of Italy, attended by such a convoy of provisions, and such a numerous train of sheep and oxen, as might have been sufficient, not only for the march of an army, but for the settlement of a colony. But the court and councils of Honorius still remained a scene of weakness and distraction, of corruption and anarchy. Instigated by the praefect Jovius, the guards rose in furious mutiny, and demanded the heads of two generals, and of the two principal eunuchs. The generals, under a perfidious promise of safety, were sent on shipboard, and privately executed; while the favor of the eunuchs procured them a mild and secure exile at Milan and Constantinople. Eusebius the eunuch, and the Barbarian Allobich, succeeded to the command of the bed-chamber and of the guards; and the mutual jealousy of these subordinate ministers was the cause of their mutual destruction. By the insolent order of the count of the domestics, the great chamberlain was shamefully beaten to death with sticks, before the eyes of the astonished emperor; and the subsequent assassination of Allobich, in the midst of a public procession, is the only circumstance of his life, in which Honorius discovered the faintest symptom of courage or resentment. Yet before they fell, Eusebius and Allobich had contributed their part to the ruin of the empire, by opposing the conclusion of a treaty which Jovius, from a selfish, and perhaps a criminal, motive, had negotiated with Alaric, in a personal interview under the walls of Rimini. During the absence of Jovius, the emperor was persuaded to assume a lofty tone of inflexible dignity, such as neither his situation, nor his character, could enable him to support; and a letter, signed with the name of Honorius, was immediately despatched to the Praetorian praefect, granting him a free permission to dispose of the public money, but sternly refusing to prostitute the military honors of Rome to the proud demands of a

Barbarian. This letter was imprudently communicated to Alaric himself; and the Goth, who in the whole transaction had behaved with temper and decency, expressed, in the most outrageous language, his lively sense of the insult so wantonly offered to his person and to his nation. The conference of Rimini was hastily interrupted; and the praefect Jovius, on his return to Ravenna, was compelled to adopt, and even to encourage, the fashionable opinions of the court. By his advice and example, the principal officers of the state and army were obliged to swear, that, without listening, in any circumstances, to any conditions of peace, they would still persevere in perpetual and implacable war against the enemy of the republic. This rash engagement opposed an insuperable bar to all future negotiation. The ministers of Honorius were heard to declare, that, if they had only in voked the name of the Deity, they would consult the public safety, and trust their souls to the mercy of Heaven: but they had sworn by the sacred head of the emperor himself; they had sworn by the sacred head of the emperor himself; they had touched, in solemn ceremony, that august seat of majesty and wisdom; and the violation of their oath would exposethem to the temporal penalties of sacrilege and rebellion. [86]

[Footnote 84: For the adventures of Olympius, and his successors in the ministry, see Zosimus, l. v. p. 363, 365, 366, and Olympiodor. ap. Phot. p. 180, 181.]

[Footnote 85: Zosimus (l. v. p. 364) relates this circumstance with visible complacency, and celebrates the character of Gennerid as the last glory of expiring Paganism. Very different were the sentiments of the council of Carthage, who deputed four bishops to the court of Ravenna to complain of the law, which had been just enacted, that all conversions to Christianity should be free and voluntary. See Baronius, Annal. Eccles. A.D. 409, No. 12, A.D. 410, No. 47, 48.]

[Footnote 86: Zosimus, l. v. p. 367, 368, 369. This custom of swearing by the head, or life, or safety, or genius, of the sovereign, was of the highest antiquity, both in Egypt (Genesis, xlii. 15) and Scythia. It was soon transferred, by flattery, to the Caesars; and Tertullian complains, that it was the only oath which the Romans of his time affected to reverence. See an elegant Dissertation of the Abbe Mossieu on the Oaths of the Ancients, in the Mem de l'Academie des Inscriptions, tom. i. p. 208, 209.]

While the emperor and his court enjoyed, with sullen pride, the security of the marches and fortifications of Ravenna, they abandoned Rome, almost without defence, to the resentment of Alaric. Yet such was the moderation which he still preserved, or affected, that, as he moved with his army along the Flaminian way, he successively despatched the bishops of the towns of Italy to reiterate his offers of peace, and to congradulate the emperor, that he would save the city and its inhabitants from hostile fire, and the sword of the Barbarians. [87] These impending calamities were, however, averted, not indeed by the wisdom of Honorius, but by the prudence or humanity of the Gothic king; who employed a milder, though not less effectual, method of conquest. Instead of assaulting the capital, he successfully directed his efforts against the Port of Ostia, one of the boldest and most stupendous works of Roman magnificence. [88] The accidents to which the precarious subsistence of the city was continually exposed in a winter navigation, and an open road, had suggested to the genius of the first Caesar the useful design, which was executed under the reign of Claudius. The artificial moles, which formed the narrow entrance, advanced far into the sea, and firmly repelled the fury of the waves, while the largest vessels securely rode at anchor within three deep and capacious basins, which received the northern branch of the Tyber, about two miles from the ancient colony of Ostia. [89] The Roman Port insensibly swelled to the size of an episcopal city, [90] where the corn of Africa was deposited in spacious granaries for the use of the capital. As soon as Alaric was in possession of that important place, he summoned the city to surrender at discretion; and his demands were enforced by the positive declaration, that a refusal, or even a delay, should be instantly followed by the destruction of the magazines, on which the life of the Roman people depended. The clamors of that people, and the terror of famine, subdued the pride of the senate; they listened, without reluctance, to the proposal of placing a new emperor on the throne of the unworthy Honorius; and the suffrage of the Gothic conqueror bestowed the purple on Attalus, praefect of the city. The grateful monarch immediately acknowledged his protector as master-general of the armies of the West; Adolphus, with the rank of count of the domestics, obtained the custody of the person of Attalus; and the two hostile nations seemed to be united in the closest bands of friendship and alliance. [91]

[Footnote 87: Zosimus, l. v. p. 368, 369. I have softened the expressions of Alaric, who expatiates, in too florid a manner, on the history of Rome]

[Footnote 88: See Sueton. in Claud. c. 20. Dion Cassius, l. lx. p. 949, edit Reimar, and the lively description of Juvenal, Satir. xii. 75, &c. In the sixteenth century, when the remains of this Augustan port were still visible, the antiquarians sketched the plan, (see D'Anville, Mem. de l'Academie des Inscriptions, tom. xxx. p. 198,) and declared, with enthusiasm, that all the monarchs of Europe would be unable to execute so great a work, (Bergier, Hist. des grands Chemins des Romains, tom. ii. p. 356.)]

[Footnote 89: The Ostia Tyberina, (see Cluver. Italia Antiq. l. iii. p. 870-879,) in the plural number, the two mouths of the Tyber, were separated by the Holy Island, an equilateral triangle, whose sides were each of them computed at about two miles. The colony of Ostia was founded immediately beyond the left, or southern, and the Port immediately beyond the right, or northern, branch of hte river; and the distance between their remains measures something more than two miles on Cingolani's map. In the time of Strabo, the sand and mud deposited by the Tyber had choked the harbor of Ostia; the progress of the same cause has added much to the size of the Holy Islands, and gradually left both Ostia and the Port at a considerable distance from the shore. The dry channels (fiumi morti) and the large estuaries (stagno di Ponente, di Levante) mark the changes of the river, and the efforts of the sea. Consult, for the present state of this dreary and desolate tract, the excellent map of the ecclesiastical state by the mathematicians of Benedict XIV.; an actual survey of the Agro Romano, in six sheets, by Cingolani, which contains 113,819 rubbia, (about 570,000 acres;) and the large topographical map of Ameti, in eight sheets.]

[Footnote 90: As early as the third, (Lardner's Credibility of the Gospel, part ii. vol. iii. p. 89-92,) or at least the fourth, century, (Carol. a Sancta Paulo, Notit. Eccles. p. 47,) the Port of Rome was an episcopal city, which was demolished, as it should seem in the ninth century, by Pope Gregory IV., during the incursions of the Arabs. It is now reduced to an inn, a church, and the house, or palace, of the bishop; who ranks as one of six cardinal-bishops of the Roman church. See Eschinard, Deserizione di Roman et dell' Agro Romano, p. 328. Note: Compare Sir W. Gell. Rome and its Vicinity vol. ii p. 134—M.]

[Footnote 91: For the elevation of Attalus, consult Zosimus, l. vi. 377-380, Sozomen, l. ix. c. 8, 9, Olympiodor. ap. Phot. p. 180, 181, Philostorg. l. xii. c. 3, and Godefroy's Dissertat. p. 470.]

The gates of the city were thrown open, and the new emperor of the Romans, encompassed on every side by the Gothic arms, was conducted, in tumultuous procession, to the palace of Augustus and Trajan. After he had distributed the civil and military dignities among his favorites and followers, Attalus convened an assembly of the senate; before whom, in a format and florid speech, he asserted his resolution of restoring the majesty of the republic, and of uniting to the empire the provinces of Egypt and the East, which had once acknowledged the sovereignty of Rome. Such extravagant promises inspired every reasonable citizen with a just contempt for the character of an unwarlike usurper, whose elevation was the deepest and most ignominious wound which the republic had yet sustained from the insolence of the Barbarians. But the populace, with their usual levity, applauded the change of masters. The public discontent was favorable to the rival of Honorius; and the sectaries, oppressed by his persecuting edicts, expected some degree of countenance, or at least of toleration, from a prince, who, in his native country of Ionia, had been educated in the Pagan superstition, and who had since received the sacrament of baptism from the hands of an Arian bishop. [92] The first days of the reign of Attalus were fair and prosperous. An officer of confidence was sent with an inconsiderable body of troops to secure the obedience of Africa; the greatest part of Italy submitted to the terror of the Gothic powers; and though the city of Bologna made a vigorous and effectual resistance, the people of Milan, dissatisfied perhaps with the absence of Honorius, accepted, with loud acclamations, the choice of the Roman senate. At the head of a formidable army, Alaric conducted his royal captive almost to the gates of Ravenna; and a solemn embassy of the principal ministers, of Jovius, the Praetorian praefect, of Valens, master of the cavalry and infantry, of the quaestor Potamius, and of Julian, the first of the notaries, was introduced, with martial pomp, into the Gothic camp. In the name of their sovereign, they consented to acknowledge the lawful election of his competitor, and to divide the provinces of Italy and the West between the two emperors. Their proposals were rejected with disdain; and the refusal was aggravated by the insulting clemency of Attalus, who condescended to promise, that, if Honorius would instantly resign the purple, he should be permitted to pass the remainder of his life in the peaceful exile of some remote island. [93] So desperate indeed did the situation of the son of Theodosius appear, to those who were the best acquainted with his strength and resources, that Jovius and Valens, his minister and his general, betrayed their trust, infamously deserted the sinking cause of their benefactor, and devoted their treacherous allegiance to the service of his more fortunate rival. Astonished by such examples of domestic treason, Honorius trembled at the approach of every servant, at the arrival of every messenger. He dreaded the secret enemies, who might lurk in his capital, his palace, his bed-chamber; and some ships lay ready in the harbor of Ravenna, to transport the abdicated monarch to the dominions of his infant nephew, the emperor of the East.

[Footnote 92: We may admit the evidence of Sozomen for the Arian baptism, and that of Philostorgius for the Pagan education, of Attalus. The visible joy of Zosimus, and the discontent which he imputes to the Anician family, are very unfavorable to the Christianity of the new emperor.]

[Footnote 93: He carried his insolence so far, as to declare that he should mutilate Honorius before he sent him into exile. But this assertion of Zosimus is destroyed by the more impartial testimony of Olympiodorus; who attributes the ungenerous proposal (which was absolutely rejected by Attalus) to the baseness, and perhaps the treachery, of Jovius.]

But there is a Providence (such at least was the opinion of the historian Procopius) [94] that watches over innocence and folly; and the pretensions of Honorius to its peculiar care cannot reasonably be disputed. At the moment when his despair, incapable of any wise or manly resolution, meditated a shameful flight, a seasonable reenforcement of four thousand veterans unexpectedly landed in the port of Ravenna. To these valiant strangers, whose fidelity had not been corrupted by the factions of the court, he committed the walls and gates of the city; and the slumbers of the emperor were no longer disturbed by the apprehension of imminent and internal danger. The favorable intelligence which was received from Africa suddenly changed the opinions of men, and the state of public affairs. The troops and officers, whom Attalus had sent into that province, were defeated and slain; and the active zeal of Heraclian maintained his own allegiance, and that of his people. The faithful count of Africa transmitted a large sum of money, which fixed the attachment of the Imperial guards; and his vigilance, in preventing the exportation of corn and oil, introduced famine, tumult, and discontent, into the walls of

Rome. The failure of the African expedition was the source of mutual complaint and recrimination in the party of Attalus; and the mind of his protector was insensibly alienated from the interest of a prince, who wanted spirit to command, or docility to obey. The most imprudent measures were adopted, without the knowledge, or against the advice, of Alaric; and the obstinate refusal of the senate, to allow, in the embarkation, the mixture even of five hundred Goths, betrayed a suspicious and distrustful temper, which, in their situation, was neither generous nor prudent. The resentment of the Gothic king was exasperated by the malicious arts of Jovius, who had been raised to the rank of patrician, and who afterwards excused his double perfidy, by declaring, without a blush, that he had only seemed to abandon the service of Honorius, more effectually to ruin the cause of the usurper. In a large plain near Rimini, and in the presence of an innumerable multitude of Romans and Barbarians, the wretched Attalus was publicly despoiled of the diadem and purple; and those ensigns of royalty were sent by Alaric, as the pledge of peace and friendship, to the son of Theodosius. [95] The officers who returned to their duty, were reinstated in their employments, and even the merit of a tardy repentance was graciously allowed; but the degraded emperor of the Romans, desirous of life, and insensible of disgrace, implored the permission of following the Gothic camp, in the train of a haughty and capricious Barbarian. [96]

[Footnote 94: Procop. de Bell. Vandal. l. i. c. 2.]

[Footnote 95: See the cause and circumstances of the fall of Attalus in Zosimus, l. vi. p. 380-383. Sozomen, l. ix. c. 8. Philostorg. l. xii. c. 3. The two acts of indemnity in the Theodosian Code, l. ix. tit. xxxviii. leg. 11, 12, which were published the 12th of February, and the 8th of August, A.D. 410, evidently relate to this usurper.]

[Footnote 96: In hoc, Alaricus, imperatore, facto, infecto, refecto, ac defecto... Mimum risit, et ludum spectavit imperii. Orosius, l. vii. c. 42, p. 582.]

The degradation of Attalus removed the only real obstacle to the conclusion of the peace; and Alaric advanced within three miles of Ravenna, to press the irresolution of the Imperial ministers, whose insolence soon returned with the return of fortune. His indignation was kindled by the report, that a rival chieftain, that Sarus, the personal enemy of Adolphus, and the hereditary foe of the house of Balti, had been received into the palace. At the head of three hundred followers, that fearless Barbarian immediately sallied from the gates of Ravenna; surprised, and cut in pieces, a considerable body of Goths; reentered the city in triumph; and was permitted to insult his adversary, by the voice of a herald, who publicly declared that the guilt of Alaric had forever excluded him from the friendship and alliance of the emperor. [97] The crime and folly of the court of Ravenna was expiated, a third time, by the calamities of Rome. The king of the Goths, who no longer dissembled his appetite for plunder and revenge, appeared in arms under the walls of the capital; and the trembling senate, without any hopes of relief, prepared, by a desperate resistance, to defray the ruin of their country. But they were unable to guard against the secret conspiracy of their slaves and domestics; who, either from birth or interest, were attached to the cause of the enemy. At the hour of midnight, the Salarian gate was silently opened, and the inhabitants were awakened by the tremendous sound of the Gothic trumpet. Eleven hundred and sixty-three years after the foundation of Rome, the Imperial city, which had subdued and civilized so considerable a part of mankind, was delivered to the licentious fury of the tribes of Germany and Scythia. [98]

[Footnote 97: Zosimus, l. vi. p. 384. Sozomen, l. ix. c. 9. Philostorgius, l. xii. c. 3. In this place the text of Zosimus is mutilated, and we have lost the remainder of his sixth and last book, which ended with the sack of Rome. Credulous and partial as he is, we must take our leave of that historian with some regret.]

[Footnote 98: Adest Alaricus, trepidam Romam obsidet, turbat, irrumpit. Orosius, l. vii. c. 39, p. 573. He despatches this great event in seven words; but he employs whole pages in celebrating the devotion of the Goths. I have extracted from an improbable story of Procopius, the circumstances which had an air of probability. Procop. de Bell. Vandal. l. i. c. 2. He supposes that the city was surprised while the senators slept in the afternoon; but Jerom, with more authority and more reason, affirms, that it was in the night, nocte Moab capta est. nocte cecidit murus ejus, tom. i. p. 121, ad Principiam.]

The proclamation of Alaric, when he forced his entrance into a vanquished city, discovered, however, some regard for the laws of humanity and religion. He encouraged his troops boldly to seize the rewards of valor, and to enrich themselves with the spoils of a wealthy and effeminate people: but he exhorted them, at the same time, to spare the lives of the unresisting citizens, and to respect the churches of the apostles, St. Peter and St. Paul, as holy and inviolable sanctuaries. Amidst the horrors of a nocturnal tumult, several of the Christian Goths displayed the fervor of a recent conversion; and some instances of their uncommon piety and moderation are related, and perhaps adorned, by the zeal of ecclesiastical writers. [99] While the Barbarians roamed through the city in quest of prey, the humble dwelling of an aged virgin, who had devoted her life to the service of the altar, was forced open by one of the powerful Goths. He immediately demanded, though in civil language, all the gold and silver in her possession; and was astonished at the readiness with which she conducted him to a splendid hoard of massy plate, of the richest materials, and the most curious workmanship. The Barbarian viewed with wonder and delight this valuable acquisition, till he was interrupted by a serious admonition, addressed to him in the following words: "These," said she, "are the consecrated vessels belonging to St. Peter: if you presume to touch them, the sacrilegious deed will remain on your conscience. For my part, I dare not keep what I am unable to defend." The Gothic captain, struck with reverential awe, despatched a messenger to inform the king of the treasure which he had discovered; and received a peremptory order from Alaric, that all the consecrated plate and ornaments should be transported, without damage or delay, to the church of the apostle. From the extremity, perhaps, of the Quirinal hill, to the distant quarter of the Vatican, a numerous detachment of Goths, marching in order of battle through the principal streets, protected, with glittering arms, the long train of their devout companions, who bore aloft, on their heads, the sacred vessels of gold and silver; and the martial shouts of the Barbarians were mingled with the sound of religious psalmody. From all the adjacent houses, a crowd of Christians hastened to join this edifying procession; and a multitude of fugitives, without distinction of age, or rank, or even of sect, had the good fortune to escape to the secure and hospitable sanctuary of the Vatican. The learned work, concerning the City of God, was professedly composed by St. Augustin, to justify the ways of Providence in the destruction of the Roman greatness. He celebrates, with peculiar satisfaction, this memorable triumph of Christ; and insults his adversaries, by challenging them to produce some similar example of a town taken by storm, in which the fabulous gods of antiquity had been able to protect either themselves or their deluded votaries. [100]

[Footnote 99: Orosius (l. vii. c. 39, p. 573-576) applauds the piety of the Christian Goths, without seeming to perceive that the greatest part of them were Arian heretics. Jornandes (c. 30, p. 653) and Isidore of Seville, (Chron. p. 417, edit. Grot.,) who were both attached to the Gothic cause, have repeated and embellished these edifying tales. According to Isidore, Alaric himself was heard to say, that he waged war with the Romans, and not with the apostles. Such was the style of the seventh century; two hundred years before, the fame and merit had been ascribed, not to the apostles, but to Christ.]

[Footnote 100: See Augustin, de Civitat. Dei, l. i. c. 1-6. He particularly appeals to the examples of Troy, Syracuse, and Tarentum.]

In the sack of Rome, some rare and extraordinary examples of Barbarian virtue have been deservedly applauded. But the holy precincts of the Vatican, and the apostolic churches, could receive a very small proportion of the Roman people; many thousand warriors, more especially of the Huns, who served under the standard of Alaric, were strangers to the name, or at least to the faith, of Christ; and we may suspect, without any breach of charity or candor, that in the hour of savage license, when every passion was inflamed, and every restraint was removed, the precepts of the Gospel seldom influenced the behavior of the Gothic Christians. The writers, the best disposed to exaggerate their clemency, have freely confessed, that a cruel slaughter was made of the Romans; [101] and that the streets of the city were filled with dead bodies, which remained without burial during the general consternation. The despair of the citizens was sometimes converted into fury: and whenever the Barbarians were provoked by opposition, they extended the promiscuous massacre to the feeble, the innocent, and the helpless. The private revenge of forty thousand slaves was exercised without pity or remorse; and the ignominious lashes, which they had formerly received, were washed away in the blood of the guilty, or obnoxious, families. The matrons and virgins of Rome were exposed to injuries more dreadful, in the apprehension of chastity, than death itself; and the ecclesiastical historian has selected an example of female virtue, for the admiration of future ages. [102] A Roman lady, of singular beauty and orthodox faith, had excited the impatient desires of a young Goth, who, according to the sagacious remark of Sozomen, was attached to the Arian heresy. Exasperated by her obstinate resistance, he drew his sword, and, with the anger of a lover, slightly wounded her neck. The bleeding heroine still continued to brave his resentment, and to repel his love, till the ravisher desisted from his unavailing efforts, respectfully conducted her to the sanctuary of the Vatican, and gave six pieces of gold to the guards of the church, on condition that they should restore her inviolate to the arms of her husband. Such instances of courage and generosity were not extremely common. The brutal soldiers satisfied their sensual appetites, without consulting either the inclination or the duties of their female captives: and a nice question of casuistry was seriously agitated, Whether those tender victims, who had inflexibly refused their consent to the violation which they sustained, had lost, by their misfortune, the glorious crown of virginity. [103] Their were other losses indeed of a more substantial kind, and more general concern. It cannot be presumed, that all the Barbarians were at all times capable of perpetrating such amorous outrages; and the want of youth, or beauty, or chastity, protected the greatest part of the Roman women from the danger of a rape. But avarice is an insatiate and universal passion; since the enjoyment of almost every object that can afford pleasure to the different tastes and tempers of mankind may be procured by the possession of wealth. In the pillage of Rome, a just preference was given to gold and jewels, which contain the greatest value in the smallest compass and weight: but, after these portable riches had been removed by the more diligent robbers, the palaces of Rome were rudely stripped of their splendid and costly furniture. The sideboards of massy plate, and the variegated wardrobes of silk and purple, were irregularly piled in the wagons, that always followed the march of a Gothic army. The most exquisite works of art were roughly handled, or wantonly destroyed; many a statue was melted for the sake of the precious materials; and many a vase, in the division of the spoil, was shivered into fragments by the stroke of a battle-axe.

The acquisition of riches served only to stimulate the avarice of the rapacious Barbarians, who proceeded, by threats, by blows, and by tortures, to force from their prisoners the confession of hidden treasure. [104] Visible splendor and expense were alleged as the proof of a plentiful fortune; the appearance of poverty was imputed to a parsimonious disposition; and the obstinacy of some misers, who endured the most cruel torments before they would discover the secret object of their affection, was fatal to many unhappy wretches, who expired under the lash, for refusing to reveal their imaginary treasures. The edifices of Rome, though the damage has been much exaggerated, received some injury from the violence of the Goths. At their entrance through the Salarian gate, they fired the adjacent houses to guide their march, and to distract the attention of the citizens; the flames, which encountered no obstacle in the disorder of the night, consumed many private and public buildings; and the ruins of the palace of Sallust [105] remained, in the age of Justinian, a stately monument of the Gothic conflagration. [106] Yet a contemporary historian has observed, that fire could scarcely consume the enormous beams of solid brass, and that the strength of man was insufficient to subvert the foundations of ancient structures. Some truth may possibly be concealed in his devout assertion, that the wrath of Heaven supplied the imperfections of hostile rage; and that the proud Forum of Rome, decorated with the statues of so many gods and heroes, was levelled in the dust by the stroke of lightning. [107]

[Footnote 101: Jerom (tom. i. p. 121, ad Principiam) has applied to the sack of Rome all the strong expressions of Virgil:—

Quis cladem illius noctis, quis funera fando, Explicet, &c.

Procopius (l. i. c. 2) positively affirms that great numbers were slain by the Goths. Augustin (de Civ. Dei, l. i. c. 12, 13) offers Christian comfort for the death of those whose bodies (multa corpora) had remained (in tanta strage) unburied. Baronius, from the different writings of the Fathers, has thrown some light on the sack of Rome. Annal. Eccles. A.D. 410, No. 16-34.]

[Footnote 102: Sozomen. l. ix. c. 10. Augustin (de Civitat. Dei, l. i. c. 17) intimates, that some virgins or matrons actually killed themselves to escape violation; and though he admires their spirit, he is obliged, by his theology, to condemn their rash presumption. Perhaps the good bishop of Hippo was too easy in the belief, as well as too rigid in the censure, of this act of female heroism. The twenty maidens (if they ever existed) who threw themselves into the Elbe, when Magdeburgh was taken by storm, have been multiplied to the number of twelve hundred. See Harte's History of Gustavus Adolphus, vol. i. p. 308.]

[Footnote 103: See Augustin de Civitat. Dei, l. i. c. 16, 18. He treats the subject with remarkable accuracy: and after admitting that there cannot be any crime where there is no consent, he adds, Sed quia non solum quod ad dolorem, verum etiam quod ad libidinem, pertinet, in corpore alieno pepetrari potest; quicquid tale factum fuerit, etsi retentam constantissimo animo pudicitiam non excutit, pudorem tamen incutit, ne credatur factum cum mentis etiam voluntate, quod fieri fortasse sine carnis aliqua voluptate non potuit. In c. 18 he makes some curious distinctions between moral and physical virginity.]

[Footnote 104: Marcella, a Roman lady, equally respectable for her rank, her age, and her piety, was thrown on the ground, and cruelly beaten and whipped, caesam fustibus flagellisque, &c. Jerom, tom. i. p. 121, ad Principiam. See Augustin, de Civ. Dei, l. c. 10. The modern Sacco di Roma, p. 208, gives an idea of the various methods of torturing prisoners for gold.]

[Footnote 105: The historian Sallust, who usefully practiced the vices which he has so eloquently censured, employed the plunder of Numidia to adorn his palace and gardens on the Quirinal hill. The spot where the house stood is now marked by the church of St. Susanna, separated only by a street from the baths of Diocletian, and not far distant from the Salarian gate. See Nardini, Roma Antica, p. 192, 193, and the great l'lan of Modern Rome, by Nolli.]

[Footnote 106: The expressions of Procopius are distinct and moderate, (de Bell. Vandal. l. i. c. 2.) The Chronicle of Marcellinus speaks too strongly partem urbis Romae cremavit; and the words of Philostorgius (l. xii. c. 3) convey a false and exaggerated idea. Bargaeus has composed a particular dissertation (see tom. iv. Antiquit. Rom. Graev.) to prove that the edifices of Rome were not subverted by the Goths and Vandals.]

[Footnote 107: Orosius, l. ii. c. 19, p. 143. He speaks as if he disapproved all statues; vel Deum vel hominem mentiuntur. They consisted of the kings of Alba and Rome from Aeneas, the Romans, illustrious either in arms or arts, and the deified Caesars. The expression which he uses of Forum is somewhat ambiguous, since there existed five principal Fora; but as they were all contiguous and adjacent, in the plain which is surrounded by the Capitoline, the Quirinal, the Esquiline, and the Palatine hills, they might fairly be considered as one. See the Roma Antiqua of Donatus, p. 162-201, and the Roma Antica of Nardini, p. 212-273. The former is more useful for the ancient descriptions, the latter for the actual topography.]

PART V

Whatever might be the numbers of equestrian or plebeian rank, who perished in the massacre of Rome, it is confidently affirmed that only one senator lost his life by the sword of the enemy. [108] But it was not easy to compute the multitudes, who, from an honorable station and a prosperous fortune, were suddenly reduced to the miserable condition of captives and exiles. As the Barbarians had more occasion for money than for slaves, they fixed at a moderate price the redemption of their indigent prisoners; and the ransom was often paid by the benevolence of their friends, or the charity of strangers. [109] The captives, who were regularly sold, either in open market, or by private contract, would have legally regained their native freedom, which it was impossible for a citizen to lose, or to alienate. [110] But as it was soon discovered that the vindication of their liberty would endanger their lives; and that the Goths, unless they were tempted to sell, might be provoked to murder, their useless prisoners; the civil jurisprudence had been already qualified by a wise regulation, that they should be obliged to serve the moderate term of five years, till they had discharged by their labor the price of their redemption. [111] The nations who invaded the Roman empire, had driven before them, into Italy, whole troops of hungry and affrighted provincials, less apprehensive of servitude than of famine. The calamities of Rome and Italy dispersed the inhabitants to the most lonely, the most secure, the most distant places of refuge. While the Gothic cavalry spread terror and desolation along the sea-coast of Campania and Tuscany, the little island of Igilium, separated by a narrow channel from the Argentarian promontory, repulsed, or eluded, their hostile attempts; and at so small a distance from Rome, great numbers of citizens were securely concealed in the thick woods of that sequestered spot. [112] The ample patrimonies, which many senatorian families possessed in Africa, invited them, if they had time, and prudence, to escape from the ruin of their country, to embrace the shelter of that hospitable province. The most illustrious of these fugitives was the noble and pious Proba, [113] the widow of the praefect Petronius. After the death of her husband, the most powerful subject of Rome, she had remained at the head of the Anician family, and successively supplied, from her private fortune, the expense of the consulships of her three sons. When the city was besieged and taken by the Goths, Proba supported, with Christian resignation, the loss of immense riches; embarked in a small vessel, from whence she beheld, at sea, the flames of her burning palace, and fled with her daughter Laeta, and her granddaughter, the celebrated virgin, Demetrias, to the coast of Africa. The benevolent profusion with which the matron distributed the fruits, or the price, of her estates, contributed to alleviate the misfortunes of exile and captivity. But even the family of Proba herself was not exempt from the rapacious oppression of Count Heraclian, who basely sold, in matrimonial prostitution, the noblest maidens of Rome to the lust or avarice of the Syrian merchants. The Italian fugitives were dispersed through the provinces, along the coast of Egypt and Asia, as far as Constantinople and Jerusalem; and the village of Bethlem, the solitary residence of St. Jerom and his female converts, was crowded with illustrious beggars of either sex, and every age, who excited the public compassion by the remembrance of their past fortune. [114] This awful catastrophe of Rome filled the astonished empire with grief and terror. So interesting a contrast of greatness and ruin, disposed the fond credulity of the people to deplore, and even to exaggerate, the afflictions of the queen of cities. The clergy, who applied to recent events the lofty metaphors of oriental prophecy, were sometimes tempted to confound the destruction of the capital and the dissolution of the globe.

[Footnote 108: *Orosius (l. ii. c. 19, p. 142) compares the cruelty of the Gauls and the clemency of the Goths. Ibi vix quemquam inventum senatorem, qui vel absens evaserit; hic vix quemquam requiri, qui forte ut latens perierit. But there is an air of rhetoric, and perhaps of falsehood, in this antithesis; and Socrates (l. vii. c. 10) affirms, perhaps by an opposite exaggeration, that many senators were put to death with various and exquisite tortures.*]

[Footnote 109: *Multi... Christiani incaptivitatem ducti sunt. Augustin, de Civ Dei, l. i. c. 14; and the Christians experienced no peculiar hardships.*]

[Footnote 110: *See Heineccius, Antiquitat. Juris Roman. tom. i. p. 96.*]

[Footnote 111: *Appendix Cod. Theodos. xvi. in Sirmond. Opera, tom. i. p. 735. This edict was published on the 11th of December, A.D. 408, and is more reasonable than properly belonged to the ministers of Honorius.*]

[Footnote 112: *Eminus Igilii sylvosa cacumina miror; Quem fraudare nefas laudis honore suae.*

Haec proprios nuper tutata est insula saltus;

Sive loci ingenio, seu Domini genio. Gurgite cum modico victricibus obstitit armis, Tanquam longinquo dissociata mari.

Haec multos lacera suscepit ab urbe fugates,

Hic fessis posito certa timore salus. Plurima terreno populaverat aequora bello,

Contra naturam classe timendus eques: Unum, mira fides, vario discrimine portum!

Tam prope Romanis, tam procul esse Getis.

—Rutilius, in Itinerar. l. i. 325

The island is now called Giglio. See Cluver. Ital. Antiq. l. ii.]

[Footnote 113: *As the adventures of Proba and her family are connected with the life of St. Augustin, they are diligently illustrated by Tillemont, Mem. Eccles. tom. xiii. p. 620-635. Some time after their* arrival in Africa, Demetrias took the veil, and made a vow of virginity; an event which was considered as of the highest importance to Rome and to the world. All the Saints wrote congratulatory letters to her; that of Jerom is still extant, (tom. i. p. 62-73, ad Demetriad. de servand Virginitat.,) and contains a mixture of absurd reasoning, spirited declamation, and curious facts, some of which relate to the siege and sack of Rome.]

[Footnote 114: See the pathetic complaint of Jerom, (tom. v. p. 400,) in his preface to the second book of his Commentaries on the Prophet Ezekiel.]

There exists in human nature a strong propensity to depreciate the advantages, and to magnify the evils, of the present times. Yet, when the first emotions had subsided, and a fair estimate was made of the real damage, the more learned and judicious contemporaries were forced to confess, that infant Rome had formerly received more essential injury from the Gauls, than she had now sustained from the Goths in her declining age. [115] The experience of eleven centuries has enabled posterity to produce a much more singular parallel; and to affirm with confidence, that the ravages of the Barbarians, whom Alaric had led from the banks of the Danube, were less destructive than the hostilities exercised by the troops of Charles the Fifth, a Catholic prince, who styled himself Emperor of the Romans. [116] The Goths evacuated the city at the end of six days, but Rome remained above nine months in the possession of the Imperialists; and every hour was stained by some atrocious act of cruelty, lust, and rapine. The authority of Alaric preserved some order and moderation among the ferocious multitude which acknowledged him for their leader and king; but the constable of Bourbon had gloriously fallen in the attack of the walls; and the death of the general removed every restraint of discipline from an army which consisted of three independent nations, the Italians, the Spaniards, and the Germans. In the beginning of the sixteenth century, the manners of Italy exhibited a remarkable scene of the depravity of mankind. They united the sanguinary crimes that prevail in an unsettled state of society, with the polished vices which spring from the abuse of art and luxury; and the loose adventurers, who had violated every prejudice of patriotism and superstition to assault the palace of the Roman pontiff, must deserve to be considered as the most profligate of the Italians. At the same aera, the Spaniards were the terror both of the Old and New World: but their high-spirited valor was disgraced by gloomy pride, rapacious avarice, and unrelenting cruelty. Indefatigable in the pursuit of fame and riches, they had improved, by repeated practice, the most exquisite and effectual methods of torturing their prisoners: many of the Castilians, who pillaged Rome, were familiars of the holy inquisition; and some volunteers, perhaps, were lately returned from the conquest of Mexico The Germans were less corrupt than the Italians, less cruel than the Spaniards; and the rustic, or even savage, aspect of those Tramontane warriors, often disguised a simple and merciful disposition. But they had imbibed, in the first fervor of the reformation, the spirit, as well as the principles of Luther. It was their favorite amusement to insult, or destroy, the consecrated objects of Catholic superstition; they indulged, without pity or remorse, a devout hatred against the clergy of every denomination and degree, who form so considerable a part of the inhabitants of modern Rome; and their fanatic zeal might aspire to subvert the throne of Anti-christ, to purify, with blood and fire, the abominations of the spiritual Babylon. [117]

[Footnote 115: Orosius, though with some theological partiality, states this comparison, l. ii. c. 19, p. 142, l. vii. c. 39, p. 575. But, in the history of the taking of Rome by the Gauls, every thing is uncertain, and perhaps fabulous. See Beaufort sur l'Incertitude, &c., de l'Histoire Romaine, p. 356; and Melot, in the Mem. de l'Academie des Inscript. tom. xv. p. 1-21.]

[Footnote 116: The reader who wishes to inform himself of the circumstances of his famous event, may peruse an admirable narrative in Dr. Robertson's History of Charles V. vol. ii. p. 283; or consult the Annali d'Italia of the learned Muratori, tom. xiv. p. 230-244, octavo edition. If he is desirous of examining the originals, he may have recourse to the eighteenth book of the great, but unfinished, history of Guicciardini. But the account which most truly deserves the name of authentic and original, is a little book, entitled, Il Sacco di Roma, composed, within less than a month after the assault of the city, by the brother of the historian Guicciardini, who appears to have been an able magistrate and a dispassionate writer.]

[Footnote 117: The furious spirit of Luther, the effect of temper and enthusiasm, has been forcibly attacked, (Bossuet, Hist. des Variations des Eglises Protestantes, livre i. p. 20-36,) and feebly defended, (Seckendorf. Comment. de Lutheranismo, especially l. i. No. 78, p. 120, and l. iii. No. 122, p. 556.)]

The retreat of the victorious Goths, who evacuated Rome on the sixth day, [118] might be the result of prudence; but it was not surely the effect of fear. [119] At the head of an army encumbered with rich and weighty spoils, their intrepid leader advanced along the Appian way into the southern provinces of Italy, destroying whatever dared to oppose his passage, and contenting himself with the plunder of the unresisting country. The fate of Capua, the proud and luxurious metropolis of Campania, and which was respected, even in its decay, as the eighth city of the empire, [120] is buried in oblivion; whilst the adjacent town of Nola [121] has been illustrated, on this occasion, by the sanctity of Paulinus, [122] who was successively a consul, a monk, and a bishop. At the age of forty, he renounced the enjoyment of wealth and honor, of society and literature, to embrace a life of solitude and penance; and the loud applause of the clergy encouraged him to despise the reproaches of his worldly friends, who ascribed this desperate act to some disorder of the mind or body. [123] An early and passionate attachment determined him to fix his humble dwelling in one of the suburbs of Nola, near the miraculous tomb of St. Faelix, which the public devotion had already surrounded with five large and populous churches. The remains of his fortune, and of his understanding, were dedicated to the service of the glorious martyr; whose praise, on the day of his festival, Paulinus never failed to celebrate by a solemn hymn; and in whose name he erected a sixth church, of superior elegance and beauty, which was decorated with many curious pictures, from the history of the Old and New Testament. Such assiduous zeal secured the favor of the saint, [124] or at least of the people; and, after fifteen years' retirement, the Roman consul was compelled to accept the bishopric of Nola, a few months before the city was invested by the Goths. During the siege, some religious persons were satisfied that they had seen, either in dreams or visions, the divine form of their tutelar patron; yet it soon appeared by the event, that Faelix wanted power, or inclination, to preserve the flock of which he had formerly been the shepherd. Nola was not saved from the general devastation; [125] and the captive bishop was protected only by the general opinion of his innocence and poverty. Above four years elapsed from the successful invasion of Italy by the arms of Alaric, to the voluntary retreat of the Goths under the conduct of his successor Adolphus; and, during the whole time, they reigned without control over a country, which, in the opinion of the ancients, had united all the various excellences of nature and art. The prosperity, indeed, which Italy had attained in the auspicious age of the Antonines, had gradually declined with the decline of the empire.

The fruits of a long peace perished under the rude grasp of the Barbarians; and they themselves were incapable of tasting the more elegant refinements of luxury, which had been prepared for the use of the soft and polished Italians. Each soldier, however, claimed an ample portion of the substantial plenty, the corn and cattle, oil and wine, that was daily collected and consumed in the Gothic camp; and the principal warriors insulted the villas and gardens, once inhabited by Lucullus and Cicero, along the beauteous coast of Campania. Their trembling captives, the sons and daughters of Roman senators, presented, in goblets of gold and gems, large draughts of Falernian wine to the haughty victors; who stretched their huge limbs under the shade of plane-trees, [126] artificially disposed to exclude the scorching rays, and to admit the genial warmth, of the sun. These delights were enhanced by the memory of past hardships: the comparison of their native soil, the bleak and barren hills of Scythia, and the frozen banks of the Elbe and Danube, added new charms to the felicity of the Italian climate. [127]

[Footnote 118: Marcellinus, in Chron. Orosius, (l. vii. c. 39, p. 575,) asserts, that he left Rome on the third day; but this difference is easily reconciled by the successive motions of great bodies of troops.]

[Footnote 119: Socrates (l. vii. c. 10) pretends, without any color of truth, or reason, that Alaric fled on the report that the armies of the Eastern empire were in full march to attack him.]

[Footnote 120: Ausonius de Claris Urbibus, p. 233, edit. Toll. The luxury of Capua had formerly surpassed that of Sybaris itself. See Athenaeus Deipnosophist. l. xii. p. 528, edit. Casaubon.]

[Footnote 121: Forty-eight years before the foundation of Rome, (about 800 before the Christian aera,) the Tuscans built Capua and Nola, at the distance of twenty-three miles from each other; but the latter of the two cities never emerged from a state of mediocrity.]

[Footnote 122: Tillemont (Mem. Eccles. tom. xiv. p. 1-46) has compiled, with his usual diligence, all that relates to the life and writings of Paulinus, whose retreat is celebrated by his own pen, and by the praises of St. Ambrose, St. Jerom, St. Augustin, Sulpicius Severus, &c., his Christian friends and contemporaries.]

[Footnote 123: See the affectionate letters of Ausonius (epist. xix—xxv. p. 650-698, edit. Toll.) to his colleague, his friend, and his disciple, Paulinus. The religion of Ausonius is still a problem, (see Mem. de l'Academie des Inscriptions, tom. xv. p. 123-138.) I believe that it was such in his own time, and, consequently, that in his heart he was a Pagan.]

[Footnote 124: The humble Paulinus once presumed to say, that he believed St. Faelix did love him; at least, as a master loves his little dog.]

[Footnote 125: See Jornandes, de Reb. Get. c. 30, p. 653. Philostorgius, l. xii. c. 3. Augustin. de Civ. Dei, l.i.c. 10. Baronius, Annal. Eccles. A.D. 410, No. 45, 46.]

[Footnote 126: The platanus, or plane-tree, was a favorite of the ancients, by whom it was propagated, for the sake of shade, from the East to Gaul. Plin. Hist. Natur. xii. 3, 4, 5. He mentions several of an enormous size; one in the Imperial villa, at Velitrae, which Caligula called his nest, as the branches were capable of holding a large table, the proper attendants, and the emperor himself, whom Pliny quaintly styles pars umbroe; an expression which might, with equal reason, be applied to Alaric]

[Footnote 127: The prostrate South to the destroyer yields

Her boasted titles, and her golden fields; With grim delight the brood of winter view A brighter day, and skies of azure hue; Scent the new fragrance of the opening rose, And quaff the pendent vintage as it grows.

See Gray's Poems, published by Mr. Mason, p. 197. Instead of compiling tables of chronology and natural history, why did not Mr. Gray apply the powers of his genius to finish the philosophic poem, of which he has left such an exquisite specimen?]

Whether fame, or conquest, or riches, were the object or Alaric, he pursued that object with an indefatigable ardor, which could neither be quelled by adversity nor satiated by success. No sooner had he reached the extreme land of Italy, than he was attracted by the neighboring prospect of a fertile and peaceful island. Yet even the possession of Sicily he considered only as an intermediate step to the important expedition, which he already meditated against the continent of Africa. The Straits of Rhegium and Messina [128] are twelve miles in length, and, in the narrowest passage, about one mile and a half broad; and the fabulous monsters of the deep, the rocks of Scylla, and the whirlpool of Charybdis, could terrify none but the most timid and unskilful mariners. Yet as soon as the first division of the Goths had embarked, a sudden tempest arose, which sunk, or scattered, many of the transports; their courage was daunted by the terrors of a new element; and the whole design was defeated by the premature death of Alaric, which fixed, after a short illness, the fatal term of his conquests. The ferocious character of the Barbarians was displayed in the funeral of a hero whose valor and fortune they celebrated with mournful applause. By the labor of a captive multitude, they forcibly diverted the course of the Busentinus, a small river that washes the walls of Consentia. The royal sepulchre, adorned with the splendid spoils and trophies of Rome, was constructed in the vacant bed; the waters were then restored to their natural channel; and the secret spot, where the remains of Alaric had been deposited, was forever concealed by the inhuman massacre of the prisoners, who had been employed to execute the work. [129]

[Footnote 128: For the perfect description of the Straits of Messina, Scylla, Clarybdis, &c., see Cluverius, (Ital. Antiq. l. iv. p. 1293, and Sicilia Antiq. l. i. p. 60-76), who had diligently studied the ancients, and surveyed with a curious eye the actual face of the country.]

[Footnote 129: Jornandes, de Reb Get. c. 30, p. 654.]

PART VI

The personal animosities and hereditary feuds of the Barbarians were suspended by the strong necessity of their affairs; and the brave Adolphus, the brother-in-law of the deceased monarch, was unanimously elected to succeed to his throne. The character and political system of the new king of the Goths may be best understood from his own conversation with an illustrious citizen of Narbonne; who afterwards, in a pilgrimage to the Holy Land, related it to St. Jerom, in the presence of the historian Orosius. "In the full confidence of valor and victory, I once aspired (said Adolphus) to change the face of the universe; to obliterate the name of Rome; to erect on its ruins the dominion of the Goths; and to acquire, like Augustus, the immortal fame of the founder of a new empire. By repeated experiments, I was gradually convinced, that laws are essentially necessary to maintain and regulate a well-constituted state; and that the fierce, untractable humor of the Goths was incapable of bearing the salutary yoke of laws and civil government. From that moment I proposed to myself a different object of glory and ambition; and it is now my sincere wish that the gratitude of future ages should acknowledge the merit of a stranger, who employed the sword of the Goths, not to subvert, but to restore and maintain, the prosperity of the Roman empire." [130] With these pacific views, the successor of Alaric suspended the operations of war; and seriously negotiated with the Imperial court a treaty of friendship and alliance. It was the interest of the ministers of Honorius, who were now released from the obligation of their extravagant oath, to deliver Italy from the intolerable weight of the Gothic powers; and they readily accepted their service against the tyrants and Barbarians who infested the provinces beyond the Alps. [131] Adolphus, assuming the character of a Roman general, directed his march from the extremity of Campania to the southern provinces of Gaul. His troops, either by force of agreement, immediately occupied the cities of Narbonne, Thoulouse, and Bordeaux; and though they were repulsed by Count Boniface from the walls of Marseilles, they soon extended their quarters from the Mediterranean to the Ocean.

The oppressed provincials might exclaim, that the miserable remnant, which the enemy had spared, was cruelly ravished by their pretended allies; yet some specious colors were not wanting to palliate, or justify the violence of the Goths. The cities of Gaul, which they attacked, might perhaps be considered as in a state of rebellion against the government of Honorius: the articles of the treaty, or the secret instructions of the court, might sometimes be alleged in favor of the seeming usurpations of Adolphus; and the guilt of any irregular, unsuccessful act of hostility might always be imputed, with an appearance of truth, to the ungovernable spirit of a Barbarian host, impatient of peace or discipline. The luxury of Italy had been less effectual to soften the temper, than to relax the courage, of the Goths; and they had imbibed the vices, without imitating the arts and institutions, of civilized society. [132]

[Footnote 130: Orosius, l. vii. c. 43, p. 584, 585. He was sent by St. Augustin in the year 415, from Africa to Palestine, to visit St. Jerom, and to consult with him on the subject of the Pelagian controversy.]

[Footnote 131: Jornandes supposes, without much probability, that Adolphus visited and plundered Rome a second time, (more locustarum erasit) Yet he agrees with Orosius in supposing that a treaty of peace was concluded between the Gothic prince and Honorius. See Oros. l. vii. c. 43 p. 584, 585. Jornandes, de Reb. Geticis, c. 31, p. 654, 655.]

[Footnote 132: The retreat of the Goths from Italy, and their first transactions in Gaul, are dark and doubtful. I have derived much assistance from Mascou, (Hist. of the Ancient Germans, l. viii. c. 29, 35, 36, 37,) who has illustrated, and connected, the broken chronicles and fragments of the times.]

The professions of Adolphus were probably sincere, and his attachment to the cause of the republic was secured by the ascendant which a Roman princess had acquired over the heart and understanding of the Barbarian king. Placidia, [133] the daughter of the great Theodosius, and of Galla, his second wife, had received a royal education in the palace of Constantinople; but the eventful story of her life is connected with the revolutions which agitated the Western empire under the reign of her brother Honorius. When Rome was first invested by the arms of Alaric, Placidia, who was then about twenty years of age, resided in the city; and her ready consent to the death of her cousin Serena has a cruel and ungrateful appearance, which, according to the circumstances of the action, may be aggravated, or excused, by the consideration of her tender age. [134] The victorious Barbarians detained, either as a hostage or a captive, [135] the sister of Honorius; but, while she was exposed to the disgrace of following round Italy the motions of a Gothic camp, she experienced, however, a decent and respectful treatment. The authority of Jornandes, who praises the beauty of Placidia, may perhaps be counterbalanced by the silence, the expressive silence, of her flatterers: yet the splendor of her birth, the bloom of youth, the elegance of manners, and the dexterous insinuation which she condescended to employ, made a deep impression on the mind of Adolphus; and the Gothic king aspired to call himself the brother of the emperor. The ministers of Honorius rejected with disdain the proposal of an alliance so injurious to every sentiment of Roman pride; and repeatedly urged the restitution of Placidia, as an indispensable condition of the treaty of peace. But the daughter of Theodosius submitted, without reluctance, to the desires of the conqueror, a young and valiant prince, who yielded to Alaric in loftiness of stature, but who excelled in the more attractive qualities of grace and beauty. The marriage of Adolphus and Placidia [136] was consummated before the Goths retired from Italy; and the solemn, perhaps the anniversary day of their nuptials was afterwards celebrated in the house of Ingenuus, one of the most illustrious citizens of Narbonne in Gaul. The bride, attired and adorned like a Roman empress, was placed on a throne of state; and the king of the Goths, who assumed, on this occasion, the Roman habit, contented himself with a less honorable seat by her side. The nuptial gift, which, according to the custom of his nation, [137] was offered to Placidia, consisted of the rare and magnificent spoils of her country. Fifty beautiful youths, in silken robes, carried a basin in each hand; and one of these basins was filled with pieces of gold, the other with precious stones of an inestimable value. Attalus, so long the sport of fortune, and of the Goths, was appointed to lead the chorus of the Hymeneal song; and the degraded emperor might aspire to the praise of a skilful musician. The Barbarians enjoyed the insolence of their triumph; and the provincials rejoiced in this alliance, which tempered, by the mild influence of love and reason, the fierce spirit of their Gothic lord. [138]

[Footnote 133: See an account of Placidia in Ducange Fam. Byzant. p. 72; and Tillemont, Hist. des Empereurs, tom. v. p. 260, 386, &c. tom. vi. p. 240.]

[Footnote 134: Zosim. l. v. p. 350.]

[Footnote 135: Zosim. l. vi. p. 383. Orosius, (l. vii. c. 40, p. 576,) and the Chronicles of Marcellinus and Idatius, seem to suppose, that the Goths did not carry away Placidia till after the last siege of Rome.]

[Footnote 136: See the pictures of Adolphus and Placidia, and the account of their marriage, in Jornandes, de Reb. Geticis, c. 31, p. 654, 655. With regard to the place where the nuptials were stipulated, or consummated, or celebrated, the Mss. of Jornandes vary between two neighboring cities, Forli and Imola, (Forum Livii and Forum Cornelii.) It is fair and easy to reconcile the Gothic historian with Olympiodorus, (see Mascou, l. viii. c. 46:) but Tillemont grows peevish, and swears that it is not worth while to try to conciliate Jornandes with any good authors.]

[Footnote 137: The Visigoths (the subjects of Adolphus) restrained by subsequent laws, the prodigality of conjugal love. It was illegal for a husband to make any gift or settlement for the benefit of his wife during the first year of their marriage; and his liberality could not at any time exceed the tenth part of his property. The Lombards were somewhat more indulgent: they allowed the morgingcap immediately after the wedding night; and this famous gift, the reward of virginity might equal the fourth part of the husband's substance. Some cautious maidens, indeed, were wise enough to stipulate beforehand a present, which they were too sure of not deserving. See Montesquieu, Esprit des Loix, l. xix. c. 25. Muratori, delle Antichita Italiane, tom. i. Dissertazion, xx. p. 243.]

[Footnote 138: We owe the curious detail of this nuptial feast to the historian Olympiodorus, ap. Photium, p. 185, 188.]

The hundred basins of gold and gems, presented to Placidia at her nuptial feast, formed an inconsiderable portion of the Gothic treasures; of which some extraordinary specimens may be selected from the history of the successors of Adolphus. Many curious and costly ornaments of pure gold, enriched with jewels, were found in their palace of Narbonne, when it was pillaged, in the sixth century, by the Franks: sixty cups, caps, or chalices; fifteen patens, or plates, for the use of the communion; twenty boxes, or cases, to hold the books of the Gospels: this consecrated wealth [139] was distributed by the son of Clovis among the churches of his dominions, and his pious liberality seems to upbraid some former sacrilege of the Goths. They possessed, with more security of conscience, the famous missorium, or great dish for the service of the table, of massy gold, of the weight of five hundred pounds, and of far superior value, from the precious stones, the exquisite workmanship, and the tradition, that it had been presented by Aetius, the patrician, to Torismond, king of the Goths. One of the successors of Torismond purchased the aid of the French monarch by the promise of this magnificent gift. When he was seated on the throne of Spain, he delivered it with reluctance to the ambassadors of Dagobert; despoiled them on the road; stipulated, after a long negotiation, the inadequate ransom of two hundred thousand pieces of gold; and preserved the missorium, as the pride of the Gothic treasury. [140] When that treasury, after the conquest of Spain, was plundered by the Arabs, they admired, and they have celebrated, another object still more remarkable; a table of considerable size, of one single piece of solid emerald, [141] encircled with three rows of fine pearls, supported by three hundred and sixty-five feet of gems and massy gold, and estimated at the price of five hundred thousand pieces of gold. [142] Some portion of the Gothic treasures might be the gift of friendship, or the tribute of obedience; but the far greater part had been the fruits of war and rapine, the spoils of the empire, and perhaps of Rome.

[Footnote 139: See in the great collection of the Historians of France by Dom Bouquet, tom. ii. Greg. Turonens. l. iii. c. 10, p. 191. Gesta Regum Francorum, c. 23, p. 557. The anonymous writer, with an ignorance worthy of his times, supposes that these instruments of Christian worship had belonged to the temple of Solomon. If he has any meaning it must be, that they were found in the sack of Rome.]

[Footnote 140: Consult the following original testimonies in the Historians of France, tom. ii. Fredegarii Scholastici Chron. c. 73, p. 441. Fredegar. Fragment. iii. p. 463. Gesta Regis Dagobert, c. 29, p. 587. The accession of Sisenand to the throne of Spain happened A.D. 631. The 200,000 pieces of gold were appropriated by Dagobert to the foundation of the church of St. Denys.]

[Footnote 141: The president Goguet (Origine des Loix, &c., tom. ii. p. 239) is of opinion, that the stupendous pieces of emerald, the statues and columns which antiquity has placed in Egypt, at Gades, at Constantinople, were in reality artificial compositions of colored glass. The famous emerald dish, which is shown at Genoa, is supposed to countenance the suspicion.]

[Footnote 142: Elmacin. Hist. Saracenica, l. i. p. 85. Roderic. Tolet. Hist. Arab. c. 9. Cardonne, Hist. de l'Afrique et de l'Espagne sous les Arabes tom. i. p. 83. It was called the Table of Solomon, according to the custom of the Orientals, who ascribe to that prince every ancient work of knowledge or magnificence.]

After the deliverance of Italy from the oppression of the Goths, some secret counsellor was permitted, amidst the factions of the palace, to heal the wounds of that afflicted country. [143] By a wise and humane regulation, the eight provinces which had been the most deeply injured, Campania, Tuscany, Picenum, Samnium, Apulia, Calabria, Bruttium, and Lucania, obtained an indulgence of five years: the ordinary tribute was reduced to one fifth, and even that fifth was destined to restore and support the useful institution of the public posts. By another law, the lands which had been left without inhabitants or cultivation, were granted, with some diminution of taxes, to the neighbors who should occupy, or the strangers who should solicit them; and the new possessors were secured against the future claims of the fugitive proprietors. About the same time a general amnesty was published in the name of Honorius, to abolish the guilt and memory of all the involuntary offences which had been committed by his unhappy subjects, during the term of the public disorder and calamity A decent and respectful attention was paid to the restoration of the capital; the citizens were encouraged to rebuild the edifices which had been destroyed or damaged by hostile fire; and extraordinary supplies of corn were imported from the coast of Africa. The crowds that so lately fled before the sword of the Barbarians, were soon recalled by the hopes of plenty and pleasure; and Albinus, praefect of Rome, informed the court, with some anxiety and surprise, that, in a single day, he had taken an account of the arrival of fourteen thousand strangers. [144] In less than seven years, the vestiges of the Gothic invasion were almost obliterated; and the city appeared to resume its former splendor and tranquillity. The venerable matron replaced her crown of laurel, which had been ruffled by the storms of war; and was still amused, in the last moment of her decay, with the prophecies of revenge, of victory, and of eternal dominion. [145]

[Footnote 143: His three laws are inserted in the Theodosian Code, l. xi. tit. xxviii. leg. 7. L. xiii. tit. xi. leg. 12. L. xv. tit. xiv. leg. 14 The expressions of the last are very remarkable; since they contain not only a pardon, but an apology.]

[Footnote 144: Olympiodorus ap. Phot. p. 188. Philostorgius (l. xii. c. 5) observes, that when Honorius made his triumphal entry, he encouraged the Romans, with his hand and voice, to rebuild their city; and the Chronicle of Prosper commends Heraclian, qui in Romanae urbis reparationem strenuum exhibuerat ministerium.]

[Footnote 145: The date of the voyage of Claudius Rutilius Numatianus is clogged with some difficulties; but Scaliger has deduced from astronomical characters, that he left Rome the 24th of September and embarked at Porto the 9th of October, A.D. 416. See Tillemont, Hist. des Empereurs, tom, v. p. 820. In this poetical Itinerary, Rutilius (l. i. 115, &c.) addresses Rome in a high strain of congratulation:—

Erige crinales lauros, seniumque sacrati Verticis in virides, Roma, recinge comas, &c.]

This apparent tranquillity was soon disturbed by the approach of a hostile armament from the country which afforded the daily subsistence of the Roman people. Heraclian, count of Africa, who, under the most difficult and distressful circumstances, had supported, with active loyalty, the cause of Honorius, was tempted, in the year of his consulship, to assume the character of a rebel, and the title of emperor. The ports of Africa were immediately filled with the naval forces, at the head of which he prepared to invade Italy: and his fleet, when it cast anchor at the mouth of the Tyber, indeed surpassed the fleets of Xerxes and Alexander, if all the vessels, including the royal galley, and the smallest boat, did actually amount to the incredible number of three thousand two hundred. [146] Yet with such an armament, which might have subverted, or restored, the greatest empires of the earth, the African usurper made a very faint and feeble impression on the provinces of his rival. As he marched from the port, along the road which leads to the gates of Rome, he was encountered, terrified, and routed, by one of the Imperial captains; and the lord of this mighty host, deserting his fortune and his friends, ignominiously fled with a single ship. [147] When Heraclian landed in the harbor of Carthage, he found that the whole province, disdaining such an unworthy ruler, had returned to their allegiance. The rebel was beheaded in the ancient temple of Memory his consulship was abolished: [148] and the remains of his private fortune, not exceeding the moderate sum of four thousand pounds of gold, were granted to the brave Constantius, who had already defended the throne, which he afterwards shared with his feeble sovereign. Honorius viewed, with supine indifference, the calamities of Rome and Italy; [149] but the rebellious attempts of Attalus and Heraclian, against his personal safety, awakened, for a moment, the torpid instinct of his nature. He was probably ignorant of the causes and events which preserved him from these impending dangers; and as Italy was no longer invaded by any foreign or domestic enemies, he peaceably existed in the palace of Ravenna, while the tyrants beyond the Alps were repeatedly vanquished in the name, and by the lieutenants, of the son of Theodosius. [150] In the course of a busy and interesting narrative I might possibly forget to mention the death of such a prince: and I shall therefore take the precaution of observing, in this place, that he survived the last siege of Rome about thirteen years.

[Footnote 146: Orosius composed his history in Africa, only two years after the event; yet his authority seems to be overbalanced by the improbability of the fact. The Chronicle of Marcellinus gives Heraclian 700 ships and 3000 men: the latter of these numbers is ridiculously corrupt; but the former would please me very much.]

[Footnote 147: The Chronicle of Idatius affirms, without the least appearance of truth, that he advanced as far as Otriculum, in Umbria, where he was overthrown in a great battle, with the loss of 50,000 men.]

[Footnote 148: See Cod. Theod. l. xv. tit. xiv. leg. 13. The legal acts performed in his name, even the manumission of slaves, were declared invalid, till they had been formally repeated.]

[Footnote 149: I have disdained to mention a very foolish, and probably a false, report, (Procop. de Bell. Vandal. l. i. c. 2,) that Honorius was alarmed by the loss of Rome, till he understood that it was not a favorite chicken of that name, but only the capital of the world, which had been lost. Yet even this story is some evidence of the public opinion.]

[Footnote 150: The materials for the lives of all these tyrants are taken from six contemporary historians, two Latins and four Greeks: Orosius, l. vii. c. 42, p. 581, 582, 583; Renatus Profuturus Frigeridus, apud Gregor Turon. l. ii. c. 9, in the Historians of France, tom. ii. p. 165, 166; Zosimus, l. v. p. 370, 371; Olympiodorus, apud Phot. p. 180, 181, 184, 185; Sozomen, l. ix. c. 12, 13, 14, 15; and Philostorgius, l. xii. c. 5, 6, with Godefroy's Dissertation, p. 477-481; besides the four Chronicles of Prosper Tyro, Prosper of Aquitain, Idatius, and Marcellinus.]

The usurpation of Constantine, who received the purple from the legions of Britain, had been successful, and seemed to be secure. His title was acknowledged, from the wall of Antoninus to the columns of Hercules; and, in the midst of the public disorder he shared the dominion, and the plunder, of Gaul and Spain, with the tribes of Barbarians, whose destructive progress was no longer checked by the Rhine or Pyrenees. Stained with the blood of the kinsmen of Honorius, he extorted, from the court of Ravenna, with which he secretly corresponded, the ratification of his rebellious claims Constantine engaged himself, by a solemn promise, to deliver Italy from the Goths; advanced as far as the banks of the Po; and after alarming, rather than assisting, his pusillanimous ally, hastily returned to the palace of Arles, to celebrate, with intemperate luxury, his vain and ostentatious triumph. But this transient prosperity was soon interrupted and destroyed by the revolt of Count Gerontius, the bravest of his generals; who, during the absence of his son Constans, a prince already invested with the Imperial purple, had been left to command in the provinces of Spain. From some reason, of which we are ignorant, Gerontius, instead of assuming the diadem, placed it on the head of his friend Maximus, who fixed his residence at Tarragona, while the active count pressed forwards, through the Pyrenees, to surprise the two emperors, Constantine and Constans, before they could prepare for their defence. The son was made prisoner at Vienna, and immediately put to death: and the unfortunate youth had scarcely leisure to deplore the elevation of his family; which had tempted, or compelled him, sacrilegiously to desert the peaceful obscurity of the monastic life. The father maintained a siege within the walls of Arles; but those walls must have yielded to the assailants, had not the city been unexpectedly relieved by the approach of an Italian army. The name of Honorius, the proclamation of a lawful emperor, astonished the contending parties of the rebels. Gerontius, abandoned by his own troops, escaped to the confines of Spain; and rescued his name from oblivion, by the Roman courage which appeared to animate the last moments of his life. In the middle of the night, a great body of his perfidious soldiers surrounded and attacked his house, which he had strongly barricaded. His wife, a valiant friend of the nation of the Alani, and some faithful slaves, were still attached to his person; and he used, with so much skill and resolution, a large magazine of darts and arrows, that above three hundred of the assailants lost their lives in the attempt. His slaves when all the missile weapons were spent, fled at the dawn of day; and Gerontius, if he had not been restrained by conjugal tenderness, might have imitated their example; till the soldiers, provoked by such obstinate resistance, applied fire on all sides to the house. In this fatal extremity, he complied with the request of his Barbarian friend, and cut off his head. The wife of Gerontius, who conjured him not to abandon her to a life of misery and disgrace, eagerly presented her neck to his sword; and the tragic scene was terminated by the death of the count himself, who, after three ineffectual strokes, drew a short dagger, and sheathed it in his heart. [151] The unprotected Maximus, whom he had invested with the purple, was indebted for his life to the contempt that was entertained of his power and abilities. The caprice of the Barbarians, who ravaged Spain, once more seated this Imperial phantom on the throne: but they soon resigned him to the justice of Honorius; and the tyrant Maximus, after he had been shown to the people of Ravenna and Rome, was publicly executed.

[Footnote 151: The praises which Sozomen has bestowed on this act of despair, appear strange and scandalous in the mouth of an ecclesiastical historian. He observes (p. 379) that the wife of Gerontius was a Christian; and that her death was worthy of her religion, and of immortal fame.]

The general, (Constantius was his name,) who raised by his approach the siege of Arles, and dissipated the troops of Gerontius, was born a Roman; and this remarkable distinction is strongly expressive of the decay of military spirit among the subjects of the empire. The strength and majesty which were conspicuous in the person of that general, [152] marked him, in the popular opinion, as a candidate worthy of the throne, which he afterwards ascended. In the familiar intercourse of private life, his manners were cheerful and engaging; nor would he sometimes disdain, in the license of convivial mirth, to vie with the pantomimes themselves, in the exercises of their ridiculous profession. But when the trumpet summoned him to arms; when he mounted his horse, and, bending down (for such was his singular practice) almost upon the neck, fiercely rolled his large animated eyes round the field, Constantius then struck terror into his foes, and inspired his soldiers with the assurance of victory. He had received from the court of Ravenna the important commission of extirpating rebellion in the provinces of the West; and the pretended emperor Constantine, after enjoying a short and anxious respite, was again besieged in his capital by the arms of a more formidable enemy. Yet this interval allowed time for a successful negotiation with the Franks and Alemanni and his ambassador, Edobic, soon returned at the head of an army, to disturb the operations of the siege of Arles. The Roman general, instead of expecting the attack in his lines, boldly and perhaps wisely, resolved to pass the Rhone, and to meet the Barbarians. His measures were conducted with so much skill and secrecy, that, while they engaged the infantry of Constantius in the front, they were suddenly attacked, surrounded, and destroyed, by the cavalry of his lieutenant Ulphilas, who had silently gained an advantageous post in their rear. The remains of the army of Edobic were preserved by flight or submission, and their leader escaped from the field of battle to the house of a faithless friend; who too clearly understood, that the head of his obnoxious guest would be an acceptable and lucrative present for the Imperial general. On this occasion, Constantius behaved with the magnanimity of a genuine Roman. Subduing, or suppressing, every sentiment of jealousy, he publicly acknowledged the merit and services of Ulphilas; but he turned with horror from the assassin of Edobic; and sternly intimated his commands, that the camp should no longer be polluted by the presence of an ungrateful wretch, who had violated the laws of friendship and hospitality. The usurper, who beheld, from the walls of Arles, the ruin of his last hopes, was tempted to place some confidence in so generous a conqueror. He required a solemn promise for his security; and after receiving, by the imposition of hands, the sacred character of a Christian

Presbyter, he ventured to open the gates of the city. But he soon experienced that the principles of honor and integrity, which might regulate the ordinary conduct of Constantius, were superseded by the loose doctrines of political morality. The Roman general, indeed, refused to sully his laurels with the blood of Constantine; but the abdicated emperor, and his son Julian, were sent under a strong guard into Italy; and before they reached the palace of Ravenna, they met the ministers of death.

[Footnote 152: It is the expression of Olympiodorus, which he seems to have borrowed from Aeolus, a tragedy of Euripides, of which some fragments only are now extant, (Euripid. Barnes, tom. ii. p. 443, ver 38.) This allusion may prove, that the ancient tragic poets were still familiar to the Greeks of the fifth century.]

At a time when it was universally confessed, that almost every man in the empire was superior in personal merit to the princes whom the accident of their birth had seated on the throne, a rapid succession of usurpers, regardless of the fate of their predecessors, still continued to arise. This mischief was peculiarly felt in the provinces of Spain and Gaul, where the principles of order and obedience had been extinguished by war and rebellion. Before Constantine resigned the purple, and in the fourth month of the siege of Arles, intelligence was received in the Imperial camp, that Jovinus has assumed the diadem at Mentz, in the Upper Germany, at the instigation of Goar, king of the Alani, and of Guntiarius, king of the Burgundians; and that the candidate, on whom they had bestowed the empire, advanced with a formidable host of Barbarians, from the banks of the Rhine to those of the Rhone. Every circumstance is dark and extraordinary in the short history of the reign of Jovinus. It was natural to expect, that a brave and skilful general, at the head of a victorious army, would have asserted, in a field of battle, the justice of the cause of Honorius. The hasty retreat of Constantius might be justified by weighty reasons; but he resigned, without a struggle, the possession of Gaul; and Dardanus, the Praetorian praefect, is recorded as the only magistrate who refused to yield obedience to the usurper. [153] When the Goths, two years after the siege of Rome, established their quarters in Gaul, it was natural to suppose that their inclinations could be divided only between the emperor Honorius, with whom they had formed a recent alliance, and the degraded Attalus, whom they reserved in their camp for the occasional purpose of acting the part of a musician or a monarch. Yet in a moment of disgust, (for which it is not easy to assign a cause, or a date,) Adolphus connected himself with the usurper of Gaul; and imposed on Attalus the ignominious task of negotiating the treaty, which ratified his own disgrace. We are again surprised to read, that, instead of considering the Gothic alliance as the firmest support of his throne, Jovinus upbraided, in dark and ambiguous language, the officious importunity of Attalus; that, scorning the advice of his great ally, he invested with the purple his brother Sebastian; and that he most imprudently accepted the service of Sarus, when that gallant chief, the soldier of Honorius, was provoked to desert the court of a prince, who knew not how to reward or punish. Adolphus, educated among a race of warriors, who esteemed the duty of revenge as the most precious and sacred portion of their inheritance, advanced with a body of ten thousand Goths to encounter the hereditary enemy of the house of Balti. He attacked Sarus at an unguarded moment, when he was accompanied only by eighteen or twenty of his valiant followers. United by friendship, animated by despair, but at length oppressed by multitudes, this band of heroes deserved the esteem, without exciting the compassion, of their enemies; and the lion was no sooner taken in the toils, [154] than he was instantly despatched. The death of Sarus dissolved the loose alliance which Adolphus still maintained with the usurpers of Gaul. He again listened to the dictates of love and prudence; and soon satisfied the brother of Placidia, by the assurance that he would immediately transmit to the palace of Ravenna the heads of the two tyrants, Jovinus and Sebastian. The king of the Goths executed his promise without difficulty or delay; the helpless brothers, unsupported by any personal merit, were abandoned by their Barbarian auxiliaries; and the short opposition of Valentia was expiated by the ruin of one of the noblest cities of

Gaul. The emperor, chosen by the Roman senate, who had been promoted, degraded, insulted, restored, again degraded, and again insulted, was finally abandoned to his fate; but when the Gothic king withdrew his protection, he was restrained, by pity or contempt, from offering any violence to the person of Attalus. The unfortunate Attalus, who was left without subjects or allies, embarked in one of the ports of Spain, in search of some secure and solitary retreat: but he was intercepted at sea, conducted to the presence of Honorius, led in triumph through the streets of Rome or Ravenna, and publicly exposed to the gazing multitude, on the second step of the throne of his invincible conqueror. The same measure of punishment, with which, in the days of his prosperity, he was accused of menacing his rival, was inflicted on Attalus himself; he was condemned, after the amputation of two fingers, to a perpetual exile in the Isle of Lipari, where he was supplied with the decent necessaries of life. The remainder of the reign of Honorius was undisturbed by rebellion; and it may be observed, that, in the space of five years, seven usurpers had yielded to the fortune of a prince, who was himself incapable either of counsel or of action.

[Footnote 153: Sidonius Apollinaris, (l. v. epist. 9, p. 139, and Not. Sirmond. p. 58,) after stigmatizing the inconstancy of Constantine, the facility of Jovinus, the perfidy of Gerontius, continues to observe, that all the vices of these tyrants were united in the person of Dardanus. Yet the praefect supported a respectable character in the world, and even in the church; held a devout correspondence with St. Augustin and St. Jerom; and was complimented by the latter (tom. iii. p. 66) with the epithets of Christianorum Nobilissime, and Nobilium Christianissime.]

[Footnote 154: The expression may be understood almost literally: Olympiodorus says a sack, or a loose garment; and this method of entangling and catching an enemy, laciniis contortis, was much practised by the Huns, (Ammian. xxxi. 2.) Il fut pris vif avec des filets, is the translation of Tillemont, Hist. des Empereurs, tom. v. p. 608. Note: Bekker in his Photius reads something, but in the new edition of the Bysantines, he retains the old version, which is translated Scutis, as if they protected him with their shields, in order to take him alive. Photius, Bekker, p. 58—M]

PART VII

The situation of Spain, separated, on all sides, from the enemies of Rome, by the sea, by the mountains, and by intermediate provinces, had secured the long tranquillity of that remote and sequestered country; and we may observe, as a sure symptom of domestic happiness, that, in a period of four hundred years, Spain furnished very few materials to the history of the Roman empire. The footsteps of the Barbarians, who, in the reign of Gallienus, had penetrated beyond the Pyrenees, were soon obliterated by the return of peace; and in the fourth century of the Christian aera, the cities of Emerita, or Merida, of Corduba, Seville, Bracara, and Tarragona, were numbered with the most illustrious of the Roman world. The various plenty of the animal, the vegetable, and the mineral kingdoms, was improved and manufactured by the skill of an industrious people; and the peculiar advantages of naval stores contributed to support an extensive and profitable trade. [155] The arts and sciences flourished under the protection of the emperors; and if the character of the Spaniards was enfeebled by peace and servitude, the hostile approach of the Germans, who had spread terror and desolation from the Rhine to the Pyrenees, seemed to rekindle some sparks of military ardor. As long as the defence of the mountains was intrusted to the hardy and faithful militia of the country, they successfully repelled the frequent attempts of the Barbarians. But no sooner had the national troops been compelled to resign their post to the Honorian bands, in the service of Constantine, than the gates of Spain were treacherously betrayed to the public enemy, about ten months before the sack of Rome by the Goths. [156] The consciousness of guilt, and the thirst of rapine, prompted the mercenary guards of the Pyrenees to desert their station; to invite the arms of the Suevi, the Vandals, and the Alani; and to swell the torrent which was poured with irresistible violence from the frontiers of Gaul to the sea of Africa. The misfortunes of Spain may be described in the language of its most eloquent historian, who has concisely expressed the passionate, and perhaps exaggerated, declamations of contemporary writers. [157] "The irruption of these nations was followed by the most dreadful calamities; as the Barbarians exercised their indiscriminate cruelty on the fortunes of the Romans and the Spaniards, and ravaged with equal fury the cities and the open country. The progress of famine reduced the miserable inhabitants to feed on the flesh of their fellow-creatures; and even the wild beasts, who multiplied, without control, in the desert, were exasperated, by the taste of blood, and the impatience of hunger, boldly to attack and devour their human prey. Pestilence soon appeared, the inseparable companion of famine; a large proportion of the people was swept away; and the groans of the dying excited only the envy of their surviving friends. At length the Barbarians, satiated with carnage and rapine, and afflicted by the contagious evils which they themselves had introduced, fixed their permanent seats in the depopulated country. The ancient Gallicia, whose limits included the kingdom of Old Castille, was divided between the Suevi and the Vandals; the Alani were scattered over the provinces of Carthagena and Lusitania, from the Mediterranean to the Atlantic Ocean; and the fruitful territory of Boetica was allotted to the Silingi, another branch of the Vandalic nation. After regulating this partition, the conquerors contracted with their new subjects some reciprocal engagements of protection and obedience: the lands were again cultivated; and the towns and villages were again occupied by a captive people. The greatest part of the Spaniards was even disposed to prefer this new condition of poverty and barbarism, to the severe oppressions of the Roman government; yet there were many who still asserted their native freedom; and who refused, more especially in the mountains of Gallicia, to submit to the Barbarian yoke." [158]

[Footnote 155: Without recurring to the more ancient writers, I shall quote three respectable testimonies which belong to the fourth and seventh centuries; the Expositio totius Mundi, (p. 16, in the third volume of Hudson's Minor Geographers,) Ausonius, (de Claris Urbibus, p. 242, edit. Toll.,) and Isidore of Seville, (Praefat. ad. Chron. ap. Grotium, Hist. Goth. 707.) Many particulars relative to the fertility and trade of Spain may be found in Nonnius, Hispania Illustrata; and in Huet, Hist. du Commerce des Anciens, c. 40. p. 228-234.]

[Footnote 156: The date is accurately fixed in the Fasti, and the Chronicle of Idatius. Orosius (l. vii. c. 40, p. 578) imputes the loss of Spain to the treachery of the Honorians; while Sozomen (l. ix. c. 12) accuses only their negligence.]

[Footnote 157: Idatius wishes to apply the prophecies of Daniel to these national calamities; and is therefore obliged to accommodate the circumstances of the event to the terms of the prediction.]

[Footnote 158: Mariana de Rebus Hispanicis, l. v. c. 1, tom. i. p. 148. Comit. 1733. He had read, in Orosius, (l. vii. c. 41, p. 579,) that the Barbarians had turned their swords into ploughshares; and that many of the Provincials had preferred inter Barbaros pauperem libertatem, quam inter Romanos tributariam solicitudinem, sustinere.]

The important present of the heads of Jovinus and Sebastian had approved the friendship of Adolphus, and restored Gaul to the obedience of his brother Honorius. Peace was incompatible with the situation and temper of the king of the Goths. He readily accepted the proposal of turning his victorious arms against the Barbarians of Spain; the troops of Constantius intercepted his communication with the seaports of Gaul, and gently pressed his march towards the Pyrenees: [159] he passed the mountains, and surprised, in the name of the emperor, the city of Barcelona. The fondness of Adolphus for his Roman bride, was not abated by time or possession: and the birth of a son, surnamed, from his illustrious grandsire, Theodosius, appeared to fix him forever in the interest of the republic. The loss of that infant, whose remains were deposited in a silver coffin in one of the churches near Barcelona, afflicted his parents; but the grief of the Gothic king was suspended by the labors of the field; and the course of his victories was soon interrupted by domestic treason.

He had imprudently received into his service one of the followers of Sarus; a Barbarian of a daring spirit, but of a diminutive stature; whose secret desire of revenging the death of his beloved patron was continually irritated by the sarcasms of his insolent master. Adolphus was assassinated in the palace of Barcelona; the laws of the succession were violated by a tumultuous faction; [160] and a stranger to the royal race, Singeric, the brother of Sarus himself, was seated on the Gothic throne. The first act of his reign was the inhuman murder of the six children of Adolphus, the issue of a former marriage, whom he tore, without pity, from the feeble arms of a venerable bishop. [161] The unfortunate Placidia, instead of the respectful compassion, which she might have excited in the most savage breasts, was treated with cruel and wanton insult. The daughter of the emperor Theodosius, confounded among a crowd of vulgar captives, was compelled to march on foot above twelve miles, before the horse of a Barbarian, the assassin of a husband whom Placidia loved and lamented. [162]

[Footnote 159: This mixture of force and persuasion may be fairly inferred from comparing Orosius and Jornandes, the Roman and the Gothic historian.]

[Footnote 160: According to the system of Jornandes, (c. 33, p. 659,) the true hereditary right to the Gothic sceptre was vested in the Amali; but those princes, who were the vassals of the Huns, commanded the tribes of the Ostrogoths in some distant parts of Germany or Scythia.]

[Footnote 161: The murder is related by Olympiodorus: but the number of the children is taken from an epitaph of suspected authority.]

[Footnote 162: The death of Adolphus was celebrated at Constantinople with illuminations and Circensian games. (See Chron. Alexandrin.) It may seem doubtful whether the Greeks were actuated, on this occasion, be their hatred of the Barbarians, or of the Latins.]

But Placidia soon obtained the pleasure of revenge, and the view of her ignominious sufferings might rouse an indignant people against the tyrant, who was assassinated on the seventh day of his usurpation. After the death of Singeric, the free choice of the nation bestowed the Gothic sceptre on Wallia; whose warlike and ambitious temper appeared, in the beginning of his reign, extremely hostile to the republic. He marched in arms from Barcelona to the shores of the Atlantic Ocean, which the ancients revered and dreaded as the boundary of the world. But when he reached the southern promontory of Spain, [163] and, from the rock now covered by the fortress of Gibraltar, contemplated the neighboring and fertile coast of Africa, Wallia resumed the designs of conquest, which had been interrupted by the death of Alaric. The winds and waves again disappointed the enterprise of the Goths; and the minds of a superstitious people were deeply affected by the repeated disasters of storms and shipwrecks. In this disposition the successor of Adolphus no longer refused to listen to a Roman ambassador, whose proposals were enforced by the real, or supposed, approach of a numerous army, under the conduct of the brave Constantius. A solemn treaty was stipulated and observed; Placidia was honorably restored to her brother; six hundred thousand measures of wheat were delivered to the hungry Goths; [164] and Wallia engaged to draw his sword in the service of the empire. A bloody war was instantly excited among the Barbarians of Spain; and the contending princes are said to have addressed their letters, their ambassadors, and their hostages, to the throne of the Western emperor, exhorting him to remain a tranquil spectator of their contest; the events of which must be favorable to the Romans, by the mutual slaughter of their common enemies. [165] The Spanish war was obstinately supported, during three campaigns, with desperate valor, and various success; and the martial achievements of Wallia diffused through the empire the superior renown of the Gothic hero. He exterminated the Silingi, who had irretrievably ruined the elegant plenty of the province of Boetica. He slew, in battle, the king of the Alani; and the remains of those Scythian wanderers, who escaped from the field, instead of choosing a new leader, humbly sought a refuge under the standard of the Vandals, with whom they were ever afterwards confounded. The Vandals themselves, and the Suevi, yielded to the efforts of the invincible Goths. The promiscuous multitude of Barbarians, whose retreat had been intercepted, were driven into the mountains of Gallicia; where they still continued, in a narrow compass and on a barren soil, to exercise their domestic and implacable hostilities. In the pride of victory, Wallia was faithful to his engagements: he restored his Spanish conquests to the obedience of Honorius; and the tyranny of the Imperial officers soon reduced an oppressed people to regret the time of their Barbarian servitude. While the event of the war was still doubtful, the first advantages obtained by the arms of Wallia had encouraged the court of Ravenna to decree the honors of a triumph to their feeble sovereign. He entered Rome like the ancient conquerors of nations; and if the monuments of servile corruption had not long since met with the fate which they deserved, we should probably find that a crowd of poets and orators, of magistrates and bishops, applauded the fortune, the wisdom, and the invincible courage, of the emperor Honorius. [166]

[Footnote 163:
Quod Tartessiacis avus hujus Vallia terris Vandalicas turmas, et juncti Martis Alanos Stravit, et occiduam texere cadavera Calpen.

Sidon. Apollinar. in Panegyr. Anthem. 363 p. 300, edit. Sirmond.]

[Footnote 164: This supply was very acceptable: the Goths were insulted by the Vandals of Spain with the epithet of Truli, because in their extreme distress, they had given a piece of gold for a trula, or about half a pound of flour. Olympiod. apud Phot. p. 189.]

[Footnote 165: Orosius inserts a copy of these pretended letters.

Tu cum omnibus pacem habe, omniumque obsides accipe; nos nobis confligimus nobis perimus, tibi vincimus; immortalis vero quaestus erit Reipublicae tuae, si utrique pereamus. The idea is just; but I cannot persuade myself that it was entertained or expressed by the Barbarians.]

[Footnote 166: Roman triumphans ingreditur, is the formal expression of Prosper's Chronicle. The facts which relate to the death of Adolphus, and the exploits of Wallia, are related from Olympiodorus, (ap. Phot. p. 188,) Orosius, (l. vii. c. 43 p. 584-587,) Jornandes, (de Rebus p. 31, 32,) and the chronicles of Idatius and Isidore.]

Such a triumph might have been justly claimed by the ally of Rome, if Wallia, before he repassed the Pyrenees, had extirpated the seeds of the Spanish war. His victorious Goths, forty-three years after they had passed the Danube, were established, according to the faith of treaties, in the possession of the second Aquitain; a maritime province between the Garonne and the Loire, under the civil and ecclesiastical jurisdiction of Bourdeaux. That metropolis, advantageously situated for the trade of the ocean, was built in a regular and elegant form; and its numerous inhabitants were distinguished among the Gauls by their wealth, their learning, and the politeness of their manners. The adjacent province, which has been fondly compared to the garden of Eden, is blessed with a fruitful soil, and a temperate climate; the face of the country displayed the arts and the rewards of industry; and the Goths, after their martial toils, luxuriously exhausted the rich vineyards of Aquitain. [167] The Gothic limits were enlarged by the additional gift of some neighboring dioceses; and the successors of Alaric fixed their royal residence at Thoulouse, which included five populous quarters, or cities, within the spacious circuit of its walls. About the same time, in the last years of the reign of Honorius, the Goths, the Burgundians, and the Franks, obtained a permanent seat and dominion in the provinces of Gaul. The liberal grant of the usurper Jovinus to his Burgundian allies, was confirmed by the lawful emperor; the lands of the First, or Upper, Germany, were ceded to those formidable Barbarians; and they gradually occupied, either by conquest or treaty, the two provinces which still retain, with the titles of Duchy and County, the national appellation of Burgundy. [168] The Franks, the valiant and faithful allies of the Roman republic, were soon tempted to imitate the invaders, whom they had so bravely resisted. Treves, the capital of Gaul, was pillaged by their lawless bands; and the humble colony, which they so long maintained in the district of Toxandia, in Brabant, insensibly multiplied along the banks of the Meuse and Scheld, till their independent power filled the whole extent of the Second, or Lower Germany. These facts may be sufficiently justified by historic evidence; but the foundation of the French monarchy by Pharamond, the conquests, the laws, and even the existence, of that hero, have been justly arraigned by the impartial severity of modern criticism. [169]

[Footnote 167: Ausonius (de Claris Urbibus, p. 257-262) celebrates Bourdeaux with the partial affection of a native. See in Salvian (de Gubern. Dei, p. 228. Paris, 1608) a florid description of the provinces of Aquitain and Novempopulania.]

[Footnote 168: Orosius (l. vii. c. 32, p. 550) commends the mildness and modesty of these Burgundians, who treated their subjects of Gaul as their Christian brethren. Mascou has illustrated the origin of their kingdom in the four first annotations at the end of his laborious History of the Ancient Germans, vol. ii. p. 555-572, of the English translation.]

[Footnote 169: See Mascou, l. viii. c. 43, 44, 45. Except in a short and suspicious line of the Chronicle of Prosper, (in tom. i. p. 638,) the name of Pharamond is never mentioned before the seventh century. The author of the Gesta Francorum (in tom. ii. p. 543) suggests, probably enough, that the choice of Pharamond, or at least of a king, was recommended to the Franks by his father Marcomir, who was an exile in Tuscany. Note: The first mention of Pharamond is in the Gesta Francorum, assigned to about the year 720. St. Martin, iv. 469. The modern French writers in general subscribe to the opinion of Thierry: Faramond fils de Markomir, quo que son nom soit bien germanique, et son regne possible, ne figure pas dans les histoires les plus dignes de foi. A. Thierry, Lettres l'Histoire de France, p. 90—M.]

The ruin of the opulent provinces of Gaul may be dated from the establishment of these Barbarians, whose alliance was dangerous and oppressive, and who were capriciously impelled, by interest or passion, to violate the public peace. A heavy and partial ransom was imposed on the surviving provincials, who had escaped the calamities of war; the fairest and most fertile lands were assigned to the rapacious strangers, for the use of their families, their slaves, and their cattle; and the trembling natives relinquished with a sigh the inheritance of their fathers. Yet these domestic misfortunes, which are seldom the lot of a vanquished people, had been felt and inflicted by the Romans themselves, not only in the insolence of foreign conquest, but in the madness of civil discord. The Triumvirs proscribed eighteen of the most flourishing colonies of Italy; and distributed their lands and houses to the veterans who revenged the death of Caesar, and oppressed the liberty of their country. Two poets of unequal fame have deplored, in similar circumstances, the loss of their patrimony; but the legionaries of Augustus appear to have surpassed, in violence and injustice, the Barbarians who invaded Gaul under the reign of Honorius. It was not without the utmost difficulty that Virgil escaped from the sword of the Centurion, who had usurped his farm in the neighborhood of Mantua; [170] but Paulinus of Bourdeaux received a sum of money from his Gothic purchaser, which he accepted with pleasure and surprise; and though it was much inferior to the real value of his estate, this act of rapine was disguised by some colors of moderation and equity. [171] The odious name of conquerors was softened into the mild and friendly appellation of the guests of the Romans; and the Barbarians of Gaul, more especially the Goths, repeatedly declared, that they were bound to the people by the ties of hospitality, and to the emperor by the duty of allegiance and military service. The title of Honorius and his successors, their laws, and their civil magistrates, were still respected in the provinces of Gaul, of which they had resigned the possession to the Barbarian allies; and the kings, who exercised a supreme and independent authority over their native subjects, ambitiously solicited the more honorable rank of master-generals of the Imperial armies. [172] Such was the involuntary reverence which the Roman name still impressed on the minds of those warriors, who had borne away in triumph the spoils of the Capitol.

[Footnote 170: O Lycida, vivi pervenimus: advena nostri (Quod nunquam veriti sumus) ut possessor agelli Diseret: Haec mea sunt; veteres migrate coloni. Nunc victi tristes, &c—See the whole of the ninth eclogue, with the useful Commentary of Servius. Fifteen miles of the Mantuan territory were assigned to the veterans, with a reservation, in favor of the inhabitants, of three miles round the city. Even in this favor they were cheated by Alfenus Varus, a famous lawyer, and one of the commissioners, who measured eight hundred paces of water and morass.]

[Footnote 171: See the remarkable passage of the Eucharisticon of Paulinus, 575, apud Mascou, l. viii. c. 42.]

[Footnote 172: This important truth is established by the accuracy of Tillemont, (Hist. des Emp. tom. v. p. 641,) and by the ingenuity of the Abbe Dubos, (Hist. de l'Etablissement de la Monarchie Francoise dans les Gaules, tom. i. p. 259.)]

Whilst Italy was ravaged by the Goths, and a succession of feeble tyrants oppressed the provinces beyond the Alps, the British island separated itself from the body of the Roman empire. The regular forces, which guarded that remote province, had been gradually withdrawn; and Britain was abandoned without defence to the Saxon pirates, and the savages of Ireland and Caledonia. The Britons, reduced to this extremity, no longer relied on the tardy and doubtful aid of a declining monarchy. They assembled in arms, repelled the invaders, and rejoiced in the important discovery of their own strength. [173] Afflicted by similar calamities, and actuated by the same spirit, the Armorican provinces (a name which comprehended the maritime countries of Gaul between the Seine and the Loire [174] resolved to imitate the example of the neighboring island. They expelled the Roman magistrates, who acted under the authority of the usurper Constantine; and a free government was established among a people who had so long been subject to the arbitrary will of a master. The independence of Britain and Armorica was soon confirmed by Honorius himself, the lawful emperor of the West; and the letters, by which he committed to the new states the care of their own safety, might be interpreted as an absolute and perpetual abdication of the exercise and rights of sovereignty. This interpretation was, in some measure, justified by the event.

After the usurpers of Gaul had successively fallen, the maritime provinces were restored to the empire. Yet their obedience was imperfect and precarious: the vain, inconstant, rebellious disposition of the people, was incompatible either with freedom or servitude; [175] and Armorica, though it could not long maintain the form of a republic, [176] was agitated by frequent and destructive revolts. Britain was irrecoverably lost. [177] But as the emperors wisely acquiesced in the independence of a remote province, the separation was not imbittered by the reproach of tyranny or rebellion; and the claims of allegiance and protection were succeeded by the mutual and voluntary offices of national friendship. [178]

[Footnote 173: Zosimus (l. vi. 376, 383) relates in a few words the revolt of Britain and Armorica. Our antiquarians, even the great Cambder himself, have been betrayed into many gross errors, by their imperfect knowledge of the history of the continent.]

[Footnote 174: The limits of Armorica are defined by two national geographers, Messieurs De Valois and D'Anville, in their Notitias of Ancient Gaul. The word had been used in a more extensive, and was afterwards contracted to a much narrower, signification.]

[Footnote 175: Gens inter geminos notissima clauditur amnes,

Armoricana prius veteri cognomine dicta. Torva, ferox, ventosa, procax, incauta, rebellis; Inconstans, disparque sibi novitatis amore; Prodiga verborum, sed non et prodiga facti.

Erricus, Monach. in Vit. St. Germani. l. v. apud Vales. Notit. Galliarum, p. 43. Valesius alleges several testimonies to confirm this character; to which I shall add the evidence of the presbyter Constantine, (A.D. 488,) who, in the life of St. Germain, calls the Armorican rebels mobilem et indisciplinatum populum. See the Historians of France, tom. i. p. 643.]

[Footnote 176: I thought it necessary to enter my protest against this part of the system of the Abbe Dubos, which Montesquieu has so vigorously opposed. See Esprit des Loix, l. xxx. c. 24. Note: See Memoires de Gallet sur l'Origine des Bretons, quoted by Daru Histoire de Bretagne, i. p. 57. According to the opinion of these authors, the government of Armorica was monarchical from the period of its independence on the Roman empire—M.]

[Footnote 177: The words of Procopius (de Bell. Vandal. l. i. c 2, p. 181, Louvre edition) in a very important passage, which has been too much neglected Even Bede (Hist. Gent. Anglican. l. i. c. 12, p. 50, edit. Smith) acknowledges that the Romans finally left Britain in the reign of Honorius. Yet our modern historians and antiquaries extend the term of their dominion; and there are some who allow only the interval of a few months between their departure and the arrival of the Saxons.]

[Footnote 178: Bede has not forgotten the occasional aid of the legions against the Scots and Picts; and more authentic proof will hereafter be produced, that the independent Britons raised 12,000 men for the service of the emperor Anthemius, in Gaul.]

This revolution dissolved the artificial fabric of civil and military government; and the independent country, during a period of forty years, till the descent of the Saxons, was ruled by the authority of the clergy, the nobles, and the municipal towns. [179] I. Zosimus, who alone has preserved the memory of this singular transaction, very accurately observes, that the letters of Honorius were addressed to the cities of Britain. [180] Under the protection of the Romans, ninety-two considerable towns had arisen in the several parts of that great province; and, among these, thirty-three cities were distinguished above the rest by their superior privileges and importance. [181] Each of these cities, as in all the other provinces of the empire, formed a legal corporation, for the purpose of regulating their domestic policy; and the powers of municipal government were distributed among annual magistrates, a select senate, and the assembly of the people, according to the original model of the Roman constitution. [182] The management of a common revenue, the exercise of civil and criminal jurisdiction, and the habits of public counsel and command, were inherent to these petty republics; and when they asserted their independence, the youth of the city, and of the adjacent districts, would naturally range themselves under the standard of the magistrate. But the desire of obtaining the advantages, and of escaping the burdens, of political society, is a perpetual and inexhaustible source of discord; nor can it reasonably be presumed, that the restoration of British freedom was exempt from tumult and faction. The preeminence of birth and fortune must have been frequently violated by bold and popular citizens; and the haughty nobles, who complained that they were become the subjects of their own servants, [183] would sometimes regret the reign of an arbitrary monarch.

II. The jurisdiction of each city over the adjacent country, was supported by the patrimonial influence of the principal senators; and the smaller towns, the villages, and the proprietors of land, consulted their own safety by adhering to the shelter of these rising republics. The sphere of their attraction was proportioned to the respective degrees of their wealth and populousness; but the hereditary lords of ample possessions, who were not oppressed by the neighborhood of any powerful city, aspired to the rank of independent princes, and boldly exercised the rights of peace and war. The gardens and villas, which exhibited some faint imitation of Italian elegance, would soon be converted into strong castles, the refuge, in time of danger, of the adjacent country: [184] the produce of the land was applied to purchase arms and horses; to maintain a military force of slaves, of peasants, and of licentious followers; and the chieftain might assume, within his own domain, the powers of a civil magistrate. Several of these British chiefs might be the genuine posterity of ancient kings; and many more would be tempted to adopt this honorable genealogy, and to vindicate their hereditary claims, which had been suspended by the usurpation of the Caesars. [185] Their situation and their hopes would dispose them to affect the dress, the language, and the customs of their ancestors. If the princes of Britain relapsed into barbarism, while the cities studiously preserved the laws and manners of Rome, the whole island must have been gradually divided by the distinction of two national parties; again broken into a thousand subdivisions of war and faction, by the various provocations of interest and resentment. The public strength, instead of being united against a foreign enemy, was consumed in obscure and intestine quarrels; and the personal merit which had placed a successful leader at the head of his equals, might enable him to subdue the freedom of some neighboring cities; and to claim a rank among the tyrants, [186] who infested Britain after the dissolution of the Roman government. III. The British church might be composed of thirty or forty bishops, [187] with an adequate proportion of the inferior clergy; and the want of riches (for they seem to have been poor [188] would compel them to deserve the public esteem, by a decent and exemplary behavior.

The interest, as well as the temper of the clergy, was favorable to the peace and union of their distracted country: those salutary lessons might be frequently inculcated in their popular discourses; and the episcopal synods were the only councils that could pretend to the weight and authority of a national assembly.

In such councils, where the princes and magistrates sat promiscuously with the bishops, the important affairs of the state, as well as of the church, might be freely debated; differences reconciled, alliances formed, contributions imposed, wise resolutions often concerted, and sometimes executed; and there is reason to believe, that, in moments of extreme danger, a Pendragon, or Dictator, was elected by the general consent of the Britons. These pastoral cares, so worthy of the episcopal character, were interrupted, however, by zeal and superstition; and the British clergy incessantly labored to eradicate the Pelagian heresy, which they abhorred, as the peculiar disgrace of their native country. [189]

[Footnote 179: I owe it to myself, and to historic truth, to declare, that some circumstances in this paragraph are founded only on conjecture and analogy. The stubbornness of our language has sometimes forced me to deviate from the conditional into the indicative mood.]

[Footnote 180: Zosimus, l. vi. p. 383.]

[Footnote 181: Two cities of Britain were municipia, nine colonies, ten Latii jure donatoe, twelve stipendiarioe of eminent note. This detail is taken from Richard of Cirencester, de Situ Britanniae, p. 36; and though it may not seem probable that he wrote from the Mss. of a Roman general, he shows a genuine knowledge of antiquity, very extraordinary for a monk of the fourteenth century.

Note: The names may be found in Whitaker's Hist. of Manchester vol. ii. 330, 379. Turner, Hist. Anglo-Saxons, i. 216—M.]

[Footnote 182: See Maffei Verona Illustrata, part i. l. v. p. 83-106.]

[Footnote 183: Leges restituit, libertatemque reducit, Et servos famulis non sinit esse suis. Itinerar. Rutil. l. i. 215.]

[Footnote 184: An inscription (apud Sirmond, Not. ad Sidon. Apollinar. p. 59) describes a castle, cum muris et portis, tutioni omnium, erected by Dardanus on his own estate, near Sisteron, in the second Narbonnese, and named by him Theopolis.]

[Footnote 185: The establishment of their power would have been easy indeed, if we could adopt the impracticable scheme of a lively and learned antiquarian; who supposes that the British monarchs of the several tribes continued to reign, though with subordinate jurisdiction, from the time of Claudius to that of Honorius. See Whitaker's History of Manchester, vol. i. p. 247-257.]

[Footnote 186: Procopius, de Bell. Vandal. l. i. c. 3, p. 181. Britannia fertilis provincia tyrannorum, was the expression of Jerom, in the year 415 (tom. ii. p. 255, ad Ctesiphont.) By the pilgrims, who resorted every year to the Holy Land, the monk of Bethlem received the earliest and most accurate intelligence.]

[Footnote 187: See Bingham's Eccles. Antiquities, vol. i. l. ix. c. 6, p. 394.]

[Footnote 188: It is reported of three British bishops who assisted at the council of Rimini, A.D. 359, tam pauperes fuisse ut nihil haberent. Sulpicius Severus, Hist. Sacra, l. ii. p. 420. Some of their brethren however, were in better circumstances.]

[Footnote 189: Consult Usher, de Antiq. Eccles. Britannicar. c. 8-12.] It is somewhat remarkable, or rather it is extremely natural, that the revolt of Britain and Armorica should have introduced an appearance of liberty into the obedient provinces of Gaul. In a solemn edict, [190] filled with the strongest assurances of that paternal affection which princes so often express, and so seldom feel, the emperor Honorius promulgated his intention of convening an annual assembly of the seven provinces: a name peculiarly appropriated to Aquitain and the ancient Narbonnese, which had long since exchanged their Celtic rudeness for the useful and elegant arts of Italy. [191] Arles, the seat of government and commerce, was appointed for the place of the assembly; which regularly continued twenty-eight days, from the fifteenth of August to the thirteenth of September, of every year. It consisted of the Praetorian praefect of the Gauls; of seven provincial governors, one consular, and six presidents; of the magistrates, and perhaps the bishops, of about sixty cities; and of a competent, though indefinite, number of the most honorable and opulent possessors of land, who might justly be considered as the representatives of their country. They were empowered to interpret and communicate the laws of their sovereign; to expose the grievances and wishes of their constituents; to moderate the excessive or unequal weight of taxes; and to deliberate on every subject of local or national importance, that could tend to the restoration of the peace and prosperity of the seven provinces. If such an institution, which gave the people an interest in their own government, had been universally established by Trajan or the Antonines, the seeds of public wisdom and virtue might have been cherished and propagated in the empire of Rome. The privileges of the subject would have secured the throne of the monarch; the abuses of an arbitrary administration might have been prevented, in some degree, or corrected, by the interposition of these representative assemblies; and the country would have been defended against a foreign enemy by the arms of natives and freemen. Under the mild and generous influence of liberty, the Roman empire might have remained invincible and immortal; or if its excessive magnitude, and the instability of human affairs, had opposed such perpetual continuance, its vital and constituent members might have separately preserved their vigor and independence. But in the decline of the empire, when every principle of health and life had been exhausted, the tardy application of this partial remedy was incapable of producing any important or salutary effects. The emperor Honorius expresses his surprise, that he must compel the reluctant provinces to accept a privilege which they should ardently have solicited. A fine of three, or even five, pounds of gold, was imposed on the absent representatives; who seem to have declined this imaginary gift of a free constitution, as the last and most cruel insult of their oppressors.

[Footnote 190: See the correct text of this edict, as published by Sirmond, (Not. ad Sidon. Apollin. p. 148.) Hincmar of Rheims, who assigns a place to the bishops, had probably seen (in the ninth century) a more perfect copy. Dubos, Hist. Critique de la Monarchie Francoise, tom. i. p. 241-255]

[Footnote 191: It is evident from the Notitia, that the seven provinces were the Viennensis, the maritime Alps, the first and second Narbonnese Novempopulania, and the first and second Aquitain. In the room of the first Aquitain, the Abbe Dubos, on the authority of Hincmar, desires to introduce the first Lugdunensis, or Lyonnese.]

CHAPTER XXXII

EMPERORS ARCADIUS, EUTROPIUS, THEODOSIUS II

PART I

ARCADIUS EMPEROR OF THE EAST—ADMINISTRATION AND DISGRACE OF EUTROPIUS—REVOLT OF GAINAS—PERSECUTION OF ST. JOHN CHRYSOTOM—THEODOSIUS II. EMPEROR OF THE EAST—HIS SISTER PULCHERIA—HIS WIFE EUDOCIA—THE PERSIAN WAR, AND DIVISION OF ARMENIA

The division of the Roman world between the sons of Theodosius marks the final establishment of the empire of the East, which, from the reign of Arcadius to the taking of Constantinople by the Turks, subsisted one thousand and fifty-eight years, in a state of premature and perpetual decay. The sovereign of that empire assumed, and obstinately retained, the vain, and at length fictitious, title of Emperor of the Romans; and the hereditary appellation of Caesar and Augustus continued to declare, that he was the legitimate successor of the first of men, who had reigned over the first of nations. The place of Constantinople rivalled, and perhaps excelled, the magnificence of Persia; and the eloquent sermons of St. Chrysostom [1] celebrate, while they condemn, the pompous luxury of the reign of Arcadius. "The emperor," says he, "wears on his head either a diadem, or a crown of gold, decorated with precious stones of inestimable value. These ornaments, and his purple garments, are reserved for his sacred person alone; and his robes of silk are embroidered with the figures of golden dragons. His throne is of massy gold. Whenever he appears in public, he is surrounded by his courtiers, his guards, and his attendants. Their spears, their shields, their cuirasses, the bridles and trappings of their horses, have either the substance or the appearance of gold; and the large splendid boss in the midst of their shield is encircled with smaller bosses, which represent the shape of the human eye. The two mules that drew the chariot of the monarch are perfectly white, and shining all over with gold. The chariot itself, of pure and solid gold, attracts the admiration of the spectators, who contemplate the purple curtains, the snowy carpet, the size of the precious stones, and the resplendent plates of gold, that glitter as they are agitated by the motion of the carriage. The Imperial pictures are white, on a blue ground; the emperor appears seated on his throne, with his arms, his horses, and his guards beside him; and his vanquished enemies in chains at his feet." The successors of Constantine established their perpetual residence in the royal city, which he had erected on the verge of Europe and Asia. Inaccessible to the menaces of their enemies, and perhaps to the complaints of their people, they received, with each wind, the tributary productions of every climate; while the impregnable strength of their capital continued for ages to defy the hostile attempts of the Barbarians. Their dominions were bounded by the Adriatic and the Tigris; and the whole interval of twenty-five days' navigation, which separated the extreme cold of Scythia from the torrid zone of Aethiopia, [2] was comprehended within the limits of the empire of the East. The populous countries of that empire were the seat of art and learning, of luxury and wealth; and the inhabitants, who had assumed the language and manners of Greeks, styled themselves, with some appearance of truth, the most enlightened and civilized portion of the human species. The form of government was a pure and simple monarchy; the name of the Roman Republic, which so long preserved a faint tradition of freedom, was confined to the Latin provinces; and the princes of Constantinople measured their greatness by the servile obedience of their people. They were ignorant how much this passive disposition enervates and degrades every faculty of the mind. The subjects, who had resigned their will to the absolute commands of a master, were equally incapable of guarding their lives and fortunes against the assaults of the Barbarians, or of defending their reason from the terrors of superstition.

[Footnote 1: Father Montfaucon, who, by the command of his Benedictine superiors, was compelled (see Longueruana, tom. i. p. 205) to execute the laborious edition of St. Chrysostom, in thirteen volumes in folio, (Paris, 1738,) amused himself with extracting from that immense collection of morals, some curious antiquities, which illustrate the manners of the Theodosian age, (see Chrysostom, Opera, tom. xiii. p. 192-196,) and his French Dissertation, in the Memoires de l'Acad. des Inscriptions, tom. xiii. p. 474-490.]

[Footnote 2: According to the loose reckoning, that a ship could sail, with a fair wind, 1000 stadia, or 125 miles, in the revolution of a day and night, Diodorus Siculus computes ten days from the Palus Moeotis to Rhodes, and four days from Rhodes to Alexandria. The navigation of the Nile from Alexandria to Syene, under the tropic of Cancer, required, as it was against the stream, ten days more. Diodor. Sicul. tom. i. l.

iii. p. 200, edit. Wesseling. He might, without much impropriety, measure the extreme heat from the verge of the torrid zone; but he speaks of the Moeotis in the 47th degree of northern latitude, as if it lay within the polar circle.]

The first events of the reign of Arcadius and Honorius are so intimately connected, that the rebellion of the Goths, and the fall of Rufinus, have already claimed a place in the history of the West. It has already been observed, that Eutropius, [3] one of the principal eunuchs of the palace of Constantinople, succeeded the haughty minister whose ruin he had accomplished, and whose vices he soon imitated. Every order of the state bowed to the new favorite; and their tame and obsequious submission encouraged him to insult the laws, and, what is still more difficult and dangerous, the manners of his country. Under the weakest of the predecessors of Arcadius, the reign of the eunuchs had been secret and almost invisible. They insinuated themselves into the confidence of the prince; but their ostensible functions were confined to the menial service of the wardrobe and Imperial bed-chamber. They might direct, in a whisper, the public counsels, and blast, by their malicious suggestions, the fame and fortunes of the most illustrious citizens; but they never presumed to stand forward in the front of empire, [4] or to profane the public honors of the state. Eutropius was the first of his artificial sex, who dared to assume the character of a Roman magistrate and general. [5] Sometimes, in the presence of the blushing senate, he ascended the tribunal to pronounce judgment, or to repeat elaborate harangues; and, sometimes, appeared on horseback, at the head of his troops, in the dress and armor of a hero. The disregard of custom and decency always betrays a weak and ill-regulated mind; nor does Eutropius seem to have compensated for the folly of the design by any superior merit or ability in the execution. His former habits of life had not introduced him to the study of the laws, or the exercises of the field; his awkward and unsuccessful attempts provoked the secret contempt of the spectators; the Goths expressed their wish that such a general might always command the armies of Rome; and the name of the minister was branded with ridicule, more pernicious, perhaps, than hatred, to a public character. The subjects of Arcadius were exasperated by the recollection, that this deformed and decrepit eunuch, [6] who so perversely mimicked the actions of a man, was born in the most abject condition of servitude; that before he entered the Imperial palace, he had been successively sold and purchased by a hundred masters, who had exhausted his youthful strength in every mean and infamous office, and at length dismissed him, in his old age, to freedom and poverty. [7] While these disgraceful stories were circulated, and perhaps exaggerated, in private conversation, the vanity of the favorite was flattered with the most extraordinary honors. In the senate, in the capital, in the provinces, the statues of Eutropius were erected, in brass, or marble, decorated with the symbols of his civil and military virtues, and inscribed with the pompous title of the third founder of Constantinople. He was promoted to the rank of patrician, which began to signify in a popular, and even legal, acceptation, the father of the emperor; and the last year of the fourth century was polluted by the consulship of a eunuch and a slave. This strange and inexpiable prodigy [8] awakened, however, the prejudices of the Romans. The effeminate consul was rejected by the West, as an indelible stain to the annals of the republic; and without invoking the shades of Brutus and Camillus, the colleague of Eutropius, a learned and respectable magistrate, [9] sufficiently represented the different maxims of the two administrations.

[Footnote 3: Barthius, who adored his author with the blind superstition of a commentator, gives the preference to the two books which Claudian composed against Eutropius, above all his other productions, (Baillet Jugemens des Savans, tom. iv. p. 227.) They are indeed a very elegant and spirited satire; and would be more valuable in an historical light, if the invective were less vague and more temperate.]

[Footnote 4: After lamenting the progress of the eunuchs in the Roman palace, and defining their proper functions, Claudian adds,

A fronte recedant. Imperii. —In Eutrop. i. 422.

Yet it does not appear that the eunuchs had assumed any of the efficient offices of the empire, and he is styled only Praepositun sacri cubiculi, in the edict of his banishment. See Cod. Theod. l. leg 17.

Jamque oblita sui, nec sobria divitiis mens In miseras leges hominumque negotia ludit Judicat eunuchus....... Arma etiam violare parat......

Claudian, (i. 229-270,) with that mixture of indignation and humor which always pleases in a satiric poet, describes the insolent folly of the eunuch, the disgrace of the empire, and the joy of the Goths.

Gaudet, cum viderit, hostis, Et sentit jam deesse viros.]

[Footnote 6: The poet's lively description of his deformity (i. 110-125) is confirmed by the authentic testimony of Chrysostom, (tom. iii. p. 384, edit Montfaucon;) who observes, that when the paint was washed away the face of Eutropius appeared more ugly and wrinkled than that of an old woman. Claudian remarks, (i. 469,) and the remark must have been founded on experience, that there was scarcely an interval between the youth and the decrepit age of a eunuch.]

[Footnote 7: Eutropius appears to have been a native of Armenia or Assyria. His three services, which Claudian more particularly describes, were these: 1. He spent many years as the catamite of Ptolemy, a groom or soldier of the Imperial stables. 2. Ptolemy gave him to the old general Arintheus, for whom he very skilfully exercised the profession of a pimp. 3. He was given, on her marriage, to the daughter of Arintheus; and the future consul was employed to comb her hair, to present the silver ewer to wash and to fan his mistress in hot weather. See l. i. 31-137.]

[Footnote 8: Claudian, (l. i. in Eutrop. l—22,) after enumerating the various prodigies of monstrous births, speaking animals, showers of blood or stones, double suns, &c., adds, with some exaggeration,

Omnia cesserunt eunucho consule monstra.

The first book concludes with a noble speech of the goddess of Rome to her favorite Honorius, deprecating the new ignominy to which she was exposed.]

[Footnote 9: Fl. Mallius Theodorus, whose civil honors, and philosophical works, have been celebrated by Claudian in a very elegant panegyric.]

The bold and vigorous mind of Rufinus seems to have been actuated by a more sanguinary and revengeful spirit; but the avarice of the eunuch was not less insatiate than that of the praefect. [10] As long as he despoiled the oppressors, who had enriched themselves with the plunder of the people, Eutropius might gratify his covetous disposition without much envy or injustice: but the progress of his rapine soon invaded the wealth which had been acquired by lawful inheritance, or laudable industry. The usual methods of extortion were practised and improved; and Claudian has sketched a lively and original picture of the public auction of the state. "The impotence of the eunuch," says that agreeable satirist, "has served only to stimulate his avarice: the same hand which in his servile condition, was exercised in petty thefts, to unlock the coffers of his master, now grasps the riches of the world; and this infamous broker of the empire appreciates and divides the Roman provinces from Mount Haemus to the Tigris. One man, at the expense of his villa, is made proconsul of Asia; a second purchases Syria with his wife's jewels; and a third laments that he has exchanged his paternal estate for the government of Bithynia. In the antechamber of Eutropius, a large tablet is exposed to public view, which marks the respective prices of the provinces. The different value of Pontus, of Galatia, of Lydia, is accurately distinguished. Lycia may be obtained for so many thousand pieces of gold; but the opulence of Phrygia will require a more considerable sum. The eunuch wishes to obliterate, by the general disgrace, his personal ignominy; and as he has been sold himself, he is desirous of selling the rest of mankind. In the eager contention, the balance, which contains the fate and fortunes of the province, often trembles on the beam; and till one of the scales is inclined, by a superior weight, the mind of the impartial judge remains in anxious suspense. [11] Such," continues the indignant poet, "are the fruits of Roman valor, of the defeat of Antiochus, and of the triumph of Pompey." This venal prostitution of public honors secured the impunity of future crimes; but the riches, which Eutropius derived from confiscation, were already stained with injustice; since it was decent to accuse, and to condemn, the proprietors of the wealth, which he was impatient to confiscate. Some noble blood was shed by the hand of the executioner; and the most inhospitable extremities of the empire were filled with innocent and illustrious exiles. Among the generals and consuls of the East, Abundantius [12] had reason to dread the first effects of the resentment of Eutropius. He had been guilty of the unpardonable crime of introducing that abject slave to the palace of Constantinople; and some degree of praise must be allowed to a powerful and ungrateful favorite, who was satisfied with the disgrace of his benefactor. Abundantius was stripped of his ample fortunes by an Imperial rescript, and banished to Pityus, on the Euxine, the last frontier of the Roman world; where he subsisted by the precarious mercy of the Barbarians, till he could obtain, after the fall of Eutropius, a milder exile at Sidon, in Phoenicia. The destruction of Timasius [13] required a more serious and regular mode of attack. That great officer, the master-general of the armies of Theodosius, had signalized his valor by a decisive victory, which he obtained over the Goths of Thessaly; but he was too prone, after the example of his sovereign, to enjoy the luxury of peace, and to abandon his confidence to wicked and designing flatterers. Timasius had despised the public clamor, by promoting an infamous dependant to the command of a cohort; and he deserved to feel the ingratitude of Bargus, who was secretly instigated by the favorite to accuse his patron of a treasonable conspiracy. The general was arraigned before the tribunal of Arcadius himself; and the principal eunuch stood by the side of the throne to suggest the questions and answers of his sovereign. But as this form of trial might be deemed partial and arbitrary, the further inquiry into the crimes of Timasius was delegated to Saturninus and Procopius; the former of consular rank, the latter still respected as the father-in-law of the emperor Valens. The appearances of a fair and legal proceeding were maintained by the blunt honesty of Procopius; and he yielded with reluctance to the obsequious dexterity of his colleague, who pronounced a sentence of condemnation against the unfortunate Timasius. His immense riches were confiscated in the name of the emperor, and for the benefit of the favorite; and he was doomed to perpetual exile a Oasis, a solitary spot in the midst of the sandy deserts of Libya. [14] Secluded from all human converse, the master-general of the Roman armies was lost forever to the world; but the circumstances of his fate have been related in a various and contradictory manner. It is insinuated that Eutropius despatched a private order for his secret execution. [15] It was reported, that, in attempting to escape from Oasis, he perished in the desert, of thirst and hunger; and that his dead body was found on the sands of Libya. [16] It has been asserted, with more confidence, that his son Syagrius, after successfully eluding the pursuit of the agents and emissaries of the court, collected a band of African robbers; that he rescued Timasius from the place of his exile; and that both the father and the son disappeared from the knowledge of mankind. [17] But the ungrateful Bargus, instead of being suffered to possess the reward of guilt was soon after circumvented and destroyed, by the more powerful villany of the minister himself, who retained sense and spirit enough to abhor the instrument of his own crimes.

[Footnote 10: Drunk with riches, is the forcible expression of Zosimus, (l. v. p. 301;) and the avarice of Eutropius is equally execrated in the Lexicon of Suidas and the Chronicle of Marcellinus Chrysostom had often admonished the favorite of the vanity and danger of immoderate wealth, tom. iii. p. 381. - certantum saepe duorum Diversum suspendit onus: cum pondere judex Vergit, et in geminas nutat provincia lances. Claudian (i. 192-209) so curiously distinguishes the circumstances of the sale, that they all seem to allude to particular anecdotes.]

[Footnote 12: Claudian (i. 154-170) mentions the guilt and exile of Abundantius; nor could he fail to quote the example of the artist, who made the first trial of the brazen bull, which he presented to Phalaris. See Zosimus, l. v. p. 302. Jerom, tom. i. p. 26. The difference of place is easily reconciled; but the decisive authority of Asterius of Amasia (Orat. iv. p. 76, apud Tillemont, Hist. des Empereurs, tom. v. p. 435) must turn the scale in favor of Pityus.]

[Footnote 13: Suidas (most probably from the history of Eunapius) has given a very unfavorable picture of Timasius. The account of his accuser, the judges, trial, &c., is perfectly agreeable to the practice of ancient and modern courts. (See Zosimus, l. v. p. 298, 299, 300.) I am almost tempted to quote the romance of a great master, (Fielding's Works, vol. iv. p. 49, &c., 8vo. edit.,) which may be considered as the history of human nature.]

[Footnote 14: The great Oasis was one of the spots in the sands of Libya, watered with springs, and capable of producing wheat, barley, and palm-trees. It was about three days' journey from north to south, about half a day in breadth, and at the distance of about five days' march to the west of Abydus, on the Nile. See D'Anville, Description de l'Egypte, p. 186, 187, 188. The barren desert which encompasses Oasis (Zosimus, l. v. p. 300) has suggested the idea of comparative fertility, and even the epithet of the happy island]

[Footnote 15: The line of Claudian, in Eutrop. l. i. 180,

Marmaricus claris violatur caedibus Hammon,

evidently alludes to his persuasion of the death of Timasius. Note: A fragment of Eunapius confirms this account. "Thus having deprived this great person of his life—a eunuch, a man, a slave, a consul, a minister of the bed-chamber, one bred in camps." Mai, p. 283, in Niebuhr. 87—M.]

[Footnote 16: Sozomen, l. viii. c. 7. He speaks from report.]

[Footnote 17: Zosimus, l. v. p. 300. Yet he seems to suspect that this rumor was spread by the friends of Eutropius.]

The public hatred, and the despair of individuals, continually threatened, or seemed to threaten, the personal safety of Eutropius; as well as of the numerous adherents, who were attached to his fortune, and had been promoted by his venal favor. For their mutual defence, he contrived the safeguard of a law, which violated every principal of humanity and justice. [18] I. It is enacted, in the name, and by the authority of Arcadius, that all those who should conspire, either with subjects or with strangers, against the lives of any of the persons whom the emperor considers as the members of his own body, shall be punished with death and confiscation. This species of fictitious and metaphorical treason is extended to protect, not only the illustrious officers of the state and army, who were admitted into the sacred consistory, but likewise the principal domestics of the palace, the senators of Constantinople, the military commanders, and the civil magistrates of the provinces; a vague and indefinite list, which, under the successors of Constantine, included an obscure and numerous train of subordinate ministers. II. This extreme severity might perhaps be justified, had it been only directed to secure the representatives of the sovereign from any actual violence in the execution of their office. But the whole body of Imperial dependants claimed a privilege, or rather impunity, which screened them, in the loosest moments of their lives, from the hasty, perhaps the justifiable, resentment of their fellow-citizens; and, by a strange perversion of the laws, the same degree of guilt and punishment was applied to a private quarrel, and to a deliberate conspiracy against the emperor and the empire. The edicts of Arcadius most positively and most absurdly declares, that in such cases of treason, thoughts and actions ought to be punished with equal severity; that the knowledge of a mischievous intention, unless it be instantly revealed, becomes equally criminal with the intention itself; [19] and that those rash men, who shall presume to solicit the pardon of traitors, shall themselves be branded with public and perpetual infamy. III. "With regard to the sons of the traitors," (continues the emperor,) "although they ought to share the punishment, since they will probably imitate the guilt, of their parents, yet, by the special effect of our Imperial lenity, we grant them their lives; but, at the same time, we declare them incapable of inheriting, either on the father's or on the mother's side, or of receiving any gift or legacy, from the testament either of kinsmen or of strangers. Stigmatized with hereditary infamy, excluded from the hopes of honors or fortune, let them endure the pangs of poverty and contempt, till they shall consider life as a calamity, and death as a comfort and relief." In such words, so well adapted to insult the feelings of mankind, did the emperor, or rather his favorite eunuch, applaud the moderation of a law, which transferred the same unjust and inhuman penalties to the children of all those who had seconded, or who had not disclosed, their fictitious conspiracies. Some of the noblest regulations of Roman jurisprudence have been suffered to expire; but this edict, a convenient and forcible engine of ministerial tyranny, was carefully inserted in the codes of Theodosius and Justinian; and the same maxims have been revived in modern ages, to protect the electors of Germany, and the cardinals of the church of Rome. [20]

[Footnote 18: See the Theodosian Code, l. ix. tit. 14, ad legem Corneliam de Sicariis, leg. 3, and the Code of Justinian, l. ix. tit. viii, viii. ad legem Juliam de Majestate, leg. 5. The alteration of the title, from murder to treason, was an improvement of the subtle Tribonian. Godefroy, in a formal dissertation, which he has inserted in his Commentary, illustrates this law of Arcadius, and explains all the difficult passages which had been perverted by the jurisconsults of the darker ages. See tom. iii. p. 88-111.]

[Footnote 19: Bartolus understands a simple and naked consciousness, without any sign of approbation or concurrence. For this opinion, says Baldus, he is now roasting in hell. For my own part, continues the discreet Heinecclus, (Element. Jur. Civil l. iv. p. 411,) I must approve the theory of Bartolus; but in practice I should incline to the sentiments of Baldus. Yet Bartolus was gravely quoted by the lawyers of Cardinal Richelieu; and Eutropius was indirectly guilty of the murder of the virtuous De Thou.]

[Footnote 20: Godefroy, tom. iii. p. 89. It is, however, suspected, that this law, so repugnant to the maxims of Germanic freedom, has been surreptitiously added to the golden bull.]

Yet these sanguinary laws, which spread terror among a disarmed and dispirited people, were of too weak a texture to restrain the bold enterprise of Tribigild [21] the Ostrogoth. The colony of that warlike nation, which had been planted by Theodosius in one of the most fertile districts of Phrygia, [22] impatiently compared the slow returns of laborious husbandry with the successful rapine and liberal rewards of Alaric; and their leader resented, as a personal affront, his own ungracious reception in the palace of Constantinople. A soft and wealthy province, in the heart of the empire, was astonished by the sound of war; and the faithful vassal who had been disregarded or oppressed, was again respected, as soon as he resumed the hostile character of a Barbarian. The vineyards and fruitful fields, between the rapid Marsyas and the winding Maeander, [23] were consumed with fire; the decayed walls of the cities crumbled into dust, at the first stroke of an enemy; the trembling inhabitants escaped from a bloody massacre to the shores of the Hellespont; and a considerable part of Asia Minor was desolated by the rebellion of Tribigild. His rapid progress was checked by the resistance of the peasants of Pamphylia; and the Ostrogoths, attacked in a narrow pass, between the city of Selgae, [24] a deep morass, and the craggy cliffs of Mount Taurus, were defeated with the loss of their bravest troops. But the spirit of their chief was not daunted by misfortune; and his army was continually recruited by swarms of Barbarians and outlaws, who were desirous of exercising the profession of robbery, under the more honorable names of war and conquest. The rumors of the success of Tribigild might for some time be suppressed by fear, or disguised by flattery; yet they gradually alarmed both the court and the capital. Every misfortune was exaggerated in dark and doubtful hints; and the future designs of the rebels became the subject of anxious conjecture. Whenever Tribigild advanced into the inland country, the Romans were inclined to suppose that he meditated the passage of Mount Taurus, and the invasion of Syria. If he descended towards the sea, they imputed, and perhaps suggested, to the Gothic chief, the more dangerous project of arming a fleet in the harbors of Ionia, and of extending his depredations along the maritime coast, from the mouth of the Nile to the port of Constantinople. The approach of danger, and the obstinacy of Tribigild, who refused all terms of accommodation, compelled Eutropius to summon a council of war. [25] After claiming for himself the privilege of a veteran soldier, the eunuch intrusted the guard of Thrace and the Hellespont to Gainas the Goth, and the command of the Asiatic army to his favorite, Leo; two generals, who differently, but effectually, promoted the cause of the rebels. Leo, [26] who, from the bulk of his body, and the dulness of his mind, was surnamed the Ajax of the East, had deserted his original trade of a woolcomber, to exercise, with much less skill and success, the military profession; and his uncertain operations were capriciously framed and executed, with an ignorance of real difficulties, and a timorous neglect of every favorable opportunity. The rashness of the Ostrogoths had drawn them into a disadvantageous position between the Rivers Melas and Eurymedon, where they were almost besieged by the peasants of Pamphylia; but the arrival of an Imperial army, instead of completing their destruction, afforded the means of safety and victory. Tribigild surprised the unguarded camp of the Romans, in the darkness of the night; seduced the faith of the greater part of the Barbarian auxiliaries, and dissipated, without much effort, the troops, which had been corrupted by the relaxation of discipline, and the luxury of the capital. The discontent of Gainas, who had so boldly contrived and executed the death of Rufinus, was irritated by the fortune of his unworthy successor; he accused his own dishonorable patience under the servile reign of a eunuch; and the ambitious Goth was convicted, at least in the public opinion, of secretly fomenting the revolt of Tribigild, with whom he was connected by a domestic, as well as by a national alliance. [27] When Gainas passed the Hellespont, to unite under his standard the remains of the Asiatic troops, he skilfully adapted his motions to the wishes of the Ostrogoths; abandoning, by his retreat, the country which they desired to invade; or facilitating, by his approach, the desertion of the Barbarian auxiliaries. To the Imperial court he repeatedly magnified the valor, the genius, the inexhaustible resources of Tribigild; confessed his own inability to prosecute the war; and extorted the permission of negotiating with his invincible adversary. The conditions of peace were dictated by the haughty rebel; and the peremptory demand of the head of Eutropius revealed the author and the design of this hostile conspiracy.

[Footnote 21: A copious and circumstantial narrative (which he might have reserved for more important events) is bestowed by Zosimus (l. v. p. 304-312) on the revolt of Tribigild and Gainas. See likewise

[Footnote 21 continued: Socrates, l. vi. c. 6, and Sozomen, l. viii. c. 4. The second book of Claudian against Eutropius, is a fine, though imperfect, piece of history.]

[Footnote 22: Claudian (in Eutrop. l. ii. 237-250) very accurately observes, that the ancient name and nation of the Phrygians extended very far on every side, till their limits were contracted by the colonies of the Bithynians of Thrace, of the Greeks, and at last of the Gauls. His description (ii. 257-272) of the fertility of Phrygia, and of the four rivers that produced gold, is just and picturesque.]

[Footnote 23: Xenophon, Anabasis, l. i. p. 11, 12, edit. Hutchinson. Strabo, l. xii p. 865, edit. Amstel. Q. Curt. l. iii. c. 1. Claudian compares the junction of the Marsyas and Maeander to that of the Saone and the Rhone, with this difference, however, that the smaller of the Phrygian rivers is not accelerated, but retarded, by the larger.]

[Footnote 24: Selgae, a colony of the Lacedaemonians, had formerly numbered twenty thousand citizens; but in the age of Zosimus it was reduced to a small town. See Cellarius, Geograph. Antiq tom. ii. p. 117.]

[Footnote 25: The council of Eutropius, in Claudian, may be compared to that of Domitian in the fourth Satire of Juvenal. The principal members of the former were juvenes protervi lascivique senes; one of them had been a cook, a second a woolcomber. The language of their original profession exposes their assumed dignity; and their trifling conversation about tragedies, dancers, &c., is made still more ridiculous by the importance of the debate.]

[Footnote 26: Claudian (l. ii. 376-461) has branded him with infamy; and Zosimus, in more temperate language, confirms his reproaches. L. v. p. 305.]

[Footnote 27: The conspiracy of Gainas and Tribigild, which is attested by the Greek historian, had not reached the ears of Claudian, who attributes the revolt of the Ostrogoth to his own martial spirit, and the advice of his wife.]

PART II

The bold satirist, who has indulged his discontent by the partial and passionate censure of the Christian emperors, violates the dignity, rather than the truth, of history, by comparing the son of Theodosius to one of those harmless and simple animals, who scarcely feel that they are the property of their shepherd. Two passions, however, fear and conjugal affection, awakened the languid soul of Arcadius: he was terrified by the threats of a victorious Barbarian; and he yielded to the tender eloquence of his wife Eudoxia, who, with a flood of artificial tears, presenting her infant children to their father, implored his justice for some real or imaginary insult, which she imputed to the audacious eunuch. [28] The emperor's hand was directed to sign the condemnation of Eutropius; the magic spell, which during four years had bound the prince and the people, was instantly dissolved; and the acclamations that so lately hailed the merit and fortune of the favorite, were converted into the clamors of the soldiers and people, who reproached his crimes, and pressed his immediate execution. In this hour of distress and despair, his only refuge was in the sanctuary of the church, whose privileges he had wisely or profanely attempted to circumscribe; and the most eloquent of the saints, John Chrysostom, enjoyed the triumph of protecting a prostrate minister, whose choice had raised him to the ecclesiastical throne of Constantinople. The archbishop, ascending the pulpit of the cathedral, that he might be distinctly seen and heard by an innumerable crowd of either sex and of every age, pronounced a seasonable and pathetic discourse on the forgiveness of injuries, and the instability of human greatness. The agonies of the pale and affrighted wretch, who lay grovelling under the table of the altar, exhibited a solemn and instructive spectacle; and the orator, who was afterwards accused of insulting the misfortunes of Eutropius, labored to excite the contempt, that he might assuage the fury, of the people. [29] The powers of humanity, of superstition, and of eloquence, prevailed. The empress Eudoxia was restrained by her own prejudices, or by those of her subjects, from violating the sanctuary of the church; and Eutropius was tempted to capitulate, by the milder arts of persuasion, and by an oath, that his life should be spared. [30] Careless of the dignity of their sovereign, the new ministers of the palace immediately published an edict to declare, that his late favorite had disgraced the names of consul and patrician, to abolish his statues, to confiscate his wealth, and to inflict a perpetual exile in the Island of Cyprus. [31] A despicable and decrepit eunuch could no longer alarm the fears of his enemies; nor was he capable of enjoying what yet remained, the comforts of peace, of solitude, and of a happy climate. But their implacable revenge still envied him the last moments of a miserable life, and Eutropius had no sooner touched the shores of Cyprus, than he was hastily recalled. The vain hope of eluding, by a change of place, the obligation of an oath, engaged the empress to transfer the scene of his trial and execution from Constantinople to the adjacent suburb of Chalcedon. The consul Aurelian pronounced the sentence; and the motives of that sentence expose the jurisprudence of a despotic government. The crimes which Eutropius had committed against the people might have justified his death; but he was found guilty of harnessing to his chariot the sacred animals, who, from their breed or color, were reserved for the use of the emperor alone. [32]

[Footnote 28: This anecdote, which Philostorgius alone has preserved, (l xi. c. 6, and Gothofred. Dissertat. p. 451-456) is curious and important; since it connects the revolt of the Goths with the secret intrigues of the palace.]

[Footnote 29: See the Homily of Chrysostom, tom. iii. p. 381-386, which the exordium is particularly beautiful. Socrates, l. vi. c. 5. Sozomen, l. viii. c. 7. Montfaucon (in his Life of Chrysostom, tom. xiii. p. 135) too hastily supposes that Tribigild was actually in Constantinople; and that he commanded the soldiers who were ordered to seize Eutropius Even Claudian, a Pagan poet, (praefat. ad l. ii. in Eutrop. 27,) has mentioned the flight of the eunuch to the sanctuary.

Suppliciterque pias humilis prostratus ad aras, Mitigat iratas voce tremente nurus,]

[Footnote 30: Chrysostom, in another homily, (tom. iii. p. 386,) affects to declare that Eutropius would not have been taken, had he not deserted the church. Zosimus, (l. v. p. 313,) on the contrary, pretends, that his enemies forced him from the sanctuary. Yet the promise is an evidence of some treaty; and the strong assurance of Claudian, (Praefat. ad l. ii. 46,) Sed tamen exemplo non feriere tuo, may be considered as an evidence of some promise.]

[Footnote 31: Cod. Theod. l. ix. tit. xi. leg. 14. The date of that law (Jan. 17, A.D. 399) is erroneous and corrupt; since the fall of Eutropius could not happen till the autumn of the same year. See Tillemont, Hist. des Empereurs, tom. v. p. 780.]

[Footnote 32: Zosimus, l. v. p. 313. Philostorgius, l. xi. c. 6.]

While this domestic revolution was transacted, Gainas [33] openly revolted from his allegiance; united his forces at Thyatira in Lydia, with those of Tribigild; and still maintained his superior ascendant over the rebellious leader of the Ostrogoths. The confederate armies advanced, without resistance, to the straits of the Hellespont and the Bosphorus; and Arcadius was instructed to prevent the loss of his Asiatic dominions, by resigning his authority and his person to the faith of the Barbarians. The church of the holy martyr Euphemia, situate on a lofty eminence near Chalcedon, [34] was chosen for the place of the interview. Gainas bowed with reverence at the feet of the emperor, whilst he required the sacrifice of Aurelian and Saturninus, two ministers of consular rank; and their naked necks were exposed, by the haughty rebel, to the edge of the sword, till he condescended to grant them a precarious and disgraceful respite. The Goths, according to the terms of the agreement, were immediately transported from Asia into Europe; and their victorious chief, who accepted the title of master-general of the Roman armies, soon filled Constantinople with his troops, and distributed among his dependants the honors and rewards of the empire. In his early youth, Gainas had passed the Danube as a suppliant and a fugitive: his elevation had been the work of valor and fortune; and his indiscreet or perfidious conduct was the cause of his rapid downfall. Notwithstanding the vigorous opposition of the archbishop, he importunately claimed for his Arian sectaries the possession of a peculiar church; and the pride of the Catholics was offended by the public toleration of heresy. [35] Every quarter of Constantinople was filled with tumult and disorder; and the Barbarians gazed with such ardor on the rich shops of the jewellers, and the tables of the bankers, which were covered with gold and silver, that it was judged prudent to remove those dangerous temptations from their sight. They resented the injurious precaution; and some alarming attempts were made, during the night, to attack and destroy with fire the Imperial palace. [36] In this state of mutual and suspicious hostility, the guards and the people of Constantinople shut the gates, and rose in arms to prevent or to punish the conspiracy of the Goths. During the absence of Gainas, his troops were surprised and oppressed; seven thousand Barbarians perished in this bloody massacre. In the fury of the pursuit, the Catholics uncovered the roof, and continued to throw down flaming logs of wood, till they overwhelmed their adversaries, who had retreated to the church or conventicle of the Arians. Gainas was either innocent of the design, or too confident of his success; he was astonished by the intelligence that the flower of his army had been ingloriously destroyed; that he himself was declared a public enemy; and that his countryman, Fravitta, a brave and loyal confederate, had assumed the management of the war by sea and land. The enterprises of the rebel, against the cities of Thrace, were encountered by a firm and well-ordered defence; his hungry soldiers were soon reduced to the grass that grew on the margin of the fortifications; and Gainas, who vainly regretted the wealth and luxury of Asia, embraced a desperate resolution of forcing the passage of the Hellespont. He was destitute of vessels; but the woods of the Chersonesus afforded materials for rafts, and his intrepid Barbarians did not refuse to trust themselves to the waves. But Fravitta attentively watched the progress of their undertaking As soon as they had gained the middle of the stream, the Roman galleys, [37] impelled by the full force of oars, of the current, and of a favorable wind, rushed forwards in compact order, and with irresistible weight; and the Hellespont was covered with the fragments of the Gothic shipwreck. After the destruction of his hopes, and the loss of many thousands of his bravest soldiers, Gainas, who could no longer aspire to govern or to subdue the Romans, determined to resume the independence of a savage life. A light and active body of Barbarian horse, disengaged from their infantry and baggage, might perform in eight or ten days a march of three hundred miles from the Hellespont to the Danube; [38] the garrisons of that important frontier had been gradually annihilated; the river, in the month of December, would be deeply frozen; and the unbounded prospect of Scythia was opened to the ambition of Gainas. This design was secretly communicated to the national troops, who devoted themselves to the fortunes of their leader; and before the signal of departure was given, a great number of provincial auxiliaries, whom he suspected of an attachment to their native country, were perfidiously massacred. The Goths advanced, by rapid marches, through the plains of Thrace; and they were soon delivered from the fear of a pursuit, by the vanity of Fravitta, [38/1] who, instead of extinguishing the war, hastened to enjoy the popular applause, and to assume the peaceful honors of the consulship. But a formidable ally appeared in arms to vindicate the majesty of the empire, and to guard the peace and liberty of Scythia. [39] The superior forces of Uldin, king of the Huns, opposed the progress of Gainas; a hostile and ruined country prohibited his retreat; he disdained to capitulate; and after repeatedly attempting to cut his way through the ranks of the enemy, he was slain, with his desperate followers, in the field of battle. Eleven days after the naval victory of the Hellespont, the head of Gainas, the inestimable gift of the conqueror, was received at Constantinople with the most liberal expressions of gratitude; and the public deliverance was celebrated by festivals and illuminations. The triumphs of Arcadius became the subject of epic poems; [40] and the monarch, no longer oppressed by any hostile terrors, resigned himself to the mild and absolute dominion of his wife, the fair and artful Eudoxia, who was sullied her fame by the persecution of St. John Chrysostom.

[Footnote 33: Zosimus, l. v. p. 313-323,) Socrates, (l. vi. c. 4,) Sozomen, (l. viii. c. 4,) and Theodoret, (l. v. c. 32, 33,) represent, though with some various circumstances, the conspiracy, defeat, and death of Gainas.]

[Footnote 34: It is the expression of Zosimus himself, (l. v. p. 314,) who inadvertently uses the fashionable language of the Christians. Evagrius describes (l. ii. c. 3) the situation, architecture, relics, and miracles, of that celebrated church, in which the general council of Chalcedon was afterwards held.]

[Footnote 35: The pious remonstrances of Chrysostom, which do not appear in his own writings, are strongly urged by Theodoret; but his insinuation, that they were successful, is disproved by facts. Tillemont (Hist. des Empereurs, tom. v. p. 383) has discovered that the emperor, to satisfy the rapacious demands of Gainas, was obliged to melt the plate of the church of the apostles.]

[Footnote 36: The ecclesiastical historians, who sometimes guide, and sometimes follow, the public opinion, most confidently assert, that the palace of Constantinople was guarded by legions of angels.]

[Footnote 37: Zosmius (l. v. p. 319) mentions these galleys by the name of Liburnians, and observes that they were as swift (without explaining the difference between them) as the vessels with fifty oars; but that they were far inferior in speed to the triremes, which had been long disused. Yet he reasonably concludes, from the testimony of Polybius, that galleys of a still larger size had been constructed in the Punic wars. Since the establishment of the Roman empire over the Mediterranean, the useless art of building large ships of war had probably been neglected, and at length forgotten.]

[Footnote 38: Chishull (Travels, p. 61-63, 72-76) proceeded from Gallipoli, through Hadrianople to the Danube, in about fifteen days. He was in the train of an English ambassador, whose baggage consisted of seventy-one wagons. That learned traveller has the merit of tracing a curious and unfrequented route.]

[Footnote 38/1: Fravitta, according to Zosimus, though a Pagan, received the honors of the consulate. Zosim, v. c. 20. On Fravitta, see a very imperfect fragment of Eunapius. Mai. ii. 290, in Niebuhr. 92—M.]

[Footnote 39: The narrative of Zosimus, who actually leads Gainas beyond the Danube, must be corrected by the testimony of Socrates, aud Sozomen, that he was killed in Thrace; and by the precise and authentic dates of the Alexandrian, or Paschal, Chronicle, p. 307. The naval victory of the Hellespont is fixed to the month Apellaeus, the tenth of the Calends of January, (December 23;) the head of Gainas was brought to Constantinople the third of the nones of January, (January 3,) in the month Audynaeus.]

[Footnote 40: Eusebius Scholasticus acquired much fame by his poem on the Gothic war, in which he had served. Near forty years afterwards Ammonius recited another poem on the same subject, in the presence of the emperor Theodosius. See Socrates, l. vi. c. 6.]

After the death of the indolent Nectarius, the successor of Gregory Nazianzen, the church of Constantinople was distracted by the ambition of rival candidates, who were not ashamed to solicit, with gold or flattery, the suffrage of the people, or of the favorite. On this occasion Eutropius seems to have deviated from his ordinary maxims; and his uncorrupted judgment was determined only by the superior merit of a stranger. In a late journey into the East, he had admired the sermons of John, a native and presbyter of Antioch, whose name has been distinguished by the epithet of Chrysostom, or the Golden Mouth. [41] A private order was despatched to the governor of Syria; and as the people might be unwilling to resign their favorite preacher, he was transported, with speed and secrecy in a post-chariot, from Antioch to Constantinople. The unanimous and unsolicited consent of the court, the clergy, and the people, ratified the choice of the minister; and, both as a saint and as an orator, the new archbishop surpassed the sanguine expectations of the public. Born of a noble and opulent family, in the capital of Syria, Chrysostom had been educated, by the care of a tender mother, under the tuition of the most skilful masters. He studied the art of rhetoric in the school of Libanius; and that celebrated sophist, who soon discovered the talents of his disciple, ingenuously confessed that John would have deserved to succeed him, had he not been stolen away by the Christians. His piety soon disposed him to receive the sacrament of baptism; to renounce the lucrative and honorable profession of the law; and to bury himself in the adjacent desert, where he subdued the lusts of the flesh by an austere penance of six years. His infirmities compelled him to return to the society of mankind; and the authority of Meletius devoted his talents to the service of the church: but in the midst of his family, and afterwards on the archiepiscopal throne, Chrysostom still persevered in the practice of the monastic virtues. The ample revenues, which his predecessors had consumed in pomp and luxury, he diligently applied to the establishment of hospitals; and the multitudes, who were supported by his charity, preferred the eloquent and edifying discourses of their archbishop to the amusements of the theatre or the circus. The monuments of that eloquence, which was admired near twenty years at Antioch and Constantinople, have been carefully preserved; and the possession of near one thousand sermons, or homilies has authorized the critics [42] of succeeding times to appreciate the genuine merit of Chrysostom. They unanimously attribute to the Christian orator the free command of an elegant and copious language; the judgment to conceal the advantages which he derived from the knowledge of rhetoric and philosophy; an inexhaustible fund of metaphors and similitudes of ideas and images, to vary and illustrate the most familiar topics; the happy art of engaging the passions in the service of virtue; and of exposing the folly, as well as the turpitude, of vice, almost with the truth and spirit of a dramatic representation.

[Footnote 41: The sixth book of Socrates, the eighth of Sozomen, and the fifth of Theodoret, afford curious and authentic materials for the life of John Chrysostom. Besides those general historians, I have taken for my guides the four principal biographers of the saint. 1. The author of a partial and passionate Vindication of the archbishop of Constantinople, composed in the form of a dialogue, and under the name of his zealous partisan, Palladius, bishop of Helenopolis, (Tillemont, Mem. Eccles. tom. xi. p. 500-533.) It is inserted among the works of Chrysostom. tom. xiii. p. 1-90, edit. Montfaucon. 2. The moderate Erasmus, (tom. iii. epist. Mcl. p. 1331-1347, edit. Lugd. Bat.) His vivacity and good sense were his own; his errors, in the uncultivated state of ecclesiastical antiquity, were almost inevitable. 3. The learned Tillemont, (Mem. Ecclesiastiques, tom. xi. p. 1-405, 547-626, &c. &c.,) who compiles the lives of the saints with incredible patience and religious accuracy. He has minutely searched the voluminous works of Chrysostom himself. 4. Father Montfaucon, who has perused those works with the curious diligence of an *editor, discovered several new homilies, and again reviewed and composed the Life of Chrysostom, (Opera Chrysostom. tom. xiii. p. 91-177.)]*

[Footnote 42: As I am almost a stranger to the voluminous sermons of Chrysostom, I have given my confidence to the two most judicious and moderate of the ecclesiastical critics, Erasmus (tom. iii. p. 1344) and Dupin, (Bibliotheque Ecclesiastique, tom. iii. p. 38:) yet the good taste of the former is sometimes vitiated by an excessive love of antiquity; and the good sense of the latter is always restrained by prudential considerations.]

The pastoral labors of the archbishop of Constantinople provoked, and gradually united against him, two sorts of enemies; the aspiring clergy, who envied his success, and the obstinate sinners, who were offended by his reproofs. When Chrysostom thundered, from the pulpit of St. Sophia, against the degeneracy of the Christians, his shafts were spent among the crowd, without wounding, or even marking, the character of any individual. When he declaimed against the peculiar vices of the rich, poverty might obtain a transient consolation from his invectives; but the guilty were still sheltered by their numbers; and the reproach itself was dignified by some ideas of superiority and enjoyment. But as the pyramid rose towards the summit, it insensibly diminished to a point; and the magistrates, the ministers, the favorite eunuchs, the ladies of the court, [43] the empress Eudoxia herself, had a much larger share of guilt to divide among a smaller proportion of criminals. The personal applications of the audience were anticipated, or confirmed, by the testimony of their own conscience; and the intrepid preacher assumed the dangerous right of exposing both the offence and the offender to the public abhorrence. The secret resentment of the court encouraged the discontent of the clergy and monks of Constantinople, who were too hastily reformed by the fervent zeal of their archbishop. He had condemned, from the pulpit, the domestic females of the clergy of Constantinople, who, under the name of servants, or sisters, afforded a perpetual occasion either of sin or of scandal. The silent and solitary ascetics, who had secluded themselves from the world, were entitled to the warmest approbation of Chrysostom; but he despised and stigmatized, as the disgrace of their holy profession, the crowd of degenerate monks, who, from some unworthy motives of pleasure or profit, so frequently infested the streets of the capital. To the voice of persuasion, the archbishop was obliged to add the terrors of authority; and his ardor, in the exercise of ecclesiastical jurisdiction, was not always exempt from passion; nor was it always guided by prudence. Chrysostom was naturally of a choleric disposition. [44] Although he struggled, according to the precepts of the gospel, to love his private enemies, he indulged himself in the privilege of hating the enemies of God and of the church; and his sentiments were sometimes delivered with too much energy of countenance and expression. He still maintained, from some considerations of health or abstinence, his former habits of taking his repasts alone; and this inhospitable custom, [45] which his enemies imputed to pride, contributed, at least, to nourish the infirmity of a morose and unsocial humor. Separated from that familiar intercourse, which facilitates the knowledge and the despatch of business, he reposed an unsuspecting confidence in his deacon Serapion; and seldom applied his speculative knowledge of human nature to the particular character, either of his dependants, or of his equals.

Conscious of the purity of his intentions, and perhaps of the superiority of his genius, the archbishop of Constantinople extended the jurisdiction of the Imperial city, that he might enlarge the sphere of his pastoral labors; and the conduct which the profane imputed to an ambitious motive, appeared to Chrysostom himself in the light of a sacred and indispensable duty. In his visitation through the Asiatic provinces, he deposed thirteen bishops of Lydia and Phrygia; and indiscreetly declared that a deep corruption of simony and licentiousness had infected the whole episcopal order. [46] If those bishops were innocent, such a rash and unjust condemnation must excite a well-grounded discontent. If they were guilty, the numerous associates of their guilt would soon discover that their own safety depended on the ruin of the archbishop; whom they studied to represent as the tyrant of the Eastern church.

[Footnote 43: The females of Constantinople distinguished themselves by their enmity or their attachment to Chrysostom. Three noble and opulent widows, Marsa, Castricia, and Eugraphia, were the leaders of the persecution, (Pallad. Dialog. tom. xiii. p. 14.) It was impossible that they should forgive a preacher who reproached their affectation to conceal, by the ornaments of dress, their age and ugliness, (Pallad p. 27.) Olympias, by equal zeal, displayed in a more pious cause, has obtained the title of saint. See Tillemont, Mem. Eccles. tom. xi p. 416-440.]

[Footnote 44: Sozomen, and more especially Socrates, have defined the real character of Chrysostom with a temperate and impartial freedom, very offensive to his blind admirers. Those historians lived in the next generation, when party violence was abated, and had conversed with many persons intimately acquainted with the virtues and imperfections of the saint.]

[Footnote 45: Palladius (tom. xiii. p. 40, &c.) very seriously defends the archbishop 1. He never tasted wine. 2. The weakness of his stomach required a peculiar diet. 3. Business, or study, or devotion, often kept him fasting till sunset. 4. He detested the noise and levity of great dinners. 5. He saved the expense for the use of the poor. 6. He was apprehensive, in a capital like Constantinople, of the envy and reproach of partial invitations.]

[Footnote 46: Chrysostom declares his free opinion (tom. ix. hom. iii in Act. Apostol. p. 29) that the number of bishops, who might be saved, bore a very small proportion to those who would be damned.]

This ecclesiastical conspiracy was managed by Theophilus, [47] archbishop of Alexandria, an active and ambitious prelate, who displayed the fruits of rapine in monuments of ostentation. His national dislike to the rising greatness of a city which degraded him from the second to the third rank in the Christian world, was exasperated by some personal dispute with Chrysostom himself. [48] By the private invitation of the empress, Theophilus landed at Constantinople with a stou body of Egyptian mariners, to encounter the populace; and a train of dependent bishops, to secure, by their voices, the majority of a synod. The synod [49] was convened in the suburb of Chalcedon, surnamed the Oak, where Rufinus had erected a stately church and monastery; and their proceedings were continued during fourteen days, or sessions. A bishop and a deacon accused the archbishop of Constantinople; but the frivolous or improbable nature of the forty-seven articles which they presented against him, may justly be considered as a fair and unexceptional panegyric. Four successive summons were signified to Chrysostom; but he still refused to trust either his person or his reputation in the hands of his implacable enemies, who, prudently declining the examination of any particular charges, condemned his contumacious disobedience, and hastily pronounced a sentence of deposition. The synod of the Oak immediately addressed the emperor to ratify and execute their judgment, and charitably insinuated, that the penalties of treason might be inflicted on the audacious preacher, who had reviled, under the name of Jezebel, the empress Eudoxia herself. The archbishop was rudely arrested, and conducted through the city, by one of the Imperial messengers, who landed him, after a short navigation, near the entrance of the Euxine; from whence, before the expiration of two days, he was gloriously recalled.

[Footnote 47: See Tillemont, Mem. Eccles. tom. xi. p. 441-500.]

[Footnote 48: I have purposely omitted the controversy which arose among the monks of Egypt, concerning Origenism and Anthropomorphism; the dissimulation and violence of Theophilus; his artful management of the simplicity of Epiphanius; the persecution and flight of the long, or tall, brothers; the ambiguous support which they received at Constantinople from Chrysostom, &c. &c.]

[Footnote 49: Photius (p. 53-60) has preserved the original acts of the synod of the Oak; which destroys the false assertion, that Chrysostom was condemned by no more than thirty-six bishops, of whom twenty-nine were Egyptians. Forty-five bishops subscribed his sentence. See Tillemont, Mem. Eccles. tom. xi. p. 595. Note: Tillemont argues strongly for the number of thirty-six—M]

The first astonishment of his faithful people had been mute and passive: they suddenly rose with unanimous and irresistible fury. Theophilus escaped, but the promiscuous crowd of monks and Egyptian mariners was slaughtered without pity in the streets of Constantinople. [50] A seasonable earthquake justified the interposition of Heaven; the torrent of sedition rolled forwards to the gates of the palace; and the empress, agitated by fear or remorse, threw herself at the feet of Arcadius, and confessed that the public safety could be purchased only by the restoration of Chrysostom. The Bosphorus was covered with innumerable vessels; the shores of Europe and Asia were profusely illuminated; and the acclamations of a victorious people accompanied, from the port to the cathedral, the triumph of the archbishop; who, too easily, consented to resume the exercise of his functions, before his sentence had been legally reversed by the authority of an ecclesiastical synod. Ignorant, or careless, of the impending danger, Chrysostom indulged his zeal, or perhaps his resentment; declaimed with peculiar asperity against female vices; and condemned the profane honors which were addressed, almost in the precincts of St. Sophia, to the statue of the empress. His imprudence tempted his enemies to inflame the haughty spirit of Eudoxia, by reporting, or perhaps inventing, the famous exordium of a sermon, "Herodias is again furious; Herodias again dances; she once more requires the head of John;" an insolent allusion, which, as a woman and a sovereign, it was impossible for her to forgive. [51] The short interval of a perfidious truce was employed to concert more effectual measures for the disgrace and ruin of the archbishop. A numerous council of the Eastern prelates, who were guided from a distance by the advice of Theophilus, confirmed the validity, without examining the justice, of the former sentence; and a detachment of Barbarian troops was introduced into the city, to suppress the emotions of the people. On the vigil of Easter, the solemn administration of baptism was rudely interrupted by the soldiers, who alarmed the modesty of the naked catechumens, and violated, by their presence, the awful mysteries of the Christian worship. Arsacius occupied the church of St. Sophia, and the archiepiscopal throne. The Catholics retreated to the baths of Constantine, and afterwards to the fields; where they were still pursued and insulted by the guards, the bishops, and the magistrates. The fatal day of the second and final exile of Chrysostom was marked by the conflagration of the cathedral, of the senate-house, and of the adjacent buildings; and this calamity was imputed, without proof, but not without probability, to the despair of a persecuted faction. [52]

[Footnote 50: Palladius owns (p. 30) that if the people of Constantinople had found Theophilus, they would certainly have thrown him into the sea. Socrates mentions (l. vi. c. 17) a battle between the mob and the sailors of Alexandria, in which many wounds were given, and some lives were lost. The massacre of the monks is observed only by the Pagan Zosimus, (l. v. p. 324,) who acknowledges that Chrysostom had a singular talent to lead the illiterate multitude.]

[Footnote 51: See Socrates, l. vi. c. 18. Sozomen, l. viii. c. 20. Zosimus (l. v. p 324, 327) mentions, in general terms, his invectives against Eudoxia. The homily, which begins with those famous words, is rejected as spurious. Montfaucon, tom. xiii. p. 151. Tillemont, Mem. Eccles. tom xi. p. 603.]

[Footnote 52: We might naturally expect such a charge from Zosimus, (l. v. p. 327;) but it is remarkable enough, that it should be confirmed by Socrates, (l. vi. c. 18,) and the Paschal Chronicle, (p. 307.)]

Cicero might claim some merit, if his voluntary banishment preserved the peace of the republic; [53] but the submission of Chrysostom was the indispensable duty of a Christian and a subject. Instead of listening to his humble prayer, that he might be permitted to reside at Cyzicus, or Nicomedia, the inflexible empress assigned for his exile the remote and desolate town of Cucusus, among the ridges of Mount Taurus, in the Lesser Armenia. A secret hope was entertained, that the archbishop might perish in a difficult and dangerous march of seventy days, in the heat of summer, through the provinces of Asia Minor, where he was continually threatened by the hostile attacks of the Isaurians, and the more implacable fury of the monks. Yet Chrysostom arrived in safety at the place of his confinement; and the three years which he spent at Cucusus, and the neighboring town of Arabissus, were the last and most glorious of his life. His character was consecrated by absence and persecution; the faults of his administration were no longer remembered; but every tongue repeated the praises of his genius and virtue: and the respectful attention of the Christian world was fixed on a desert spot among the mountains of Taurus. From that solitude the archbishop, whose active mind was invigorated by misfortunes, maintained a strict and frequent correspondence [54] with the most distant provinces; exhorted the separate congregation of his faithful adherents to persevere in their allegiance; urged the destruction of the temples of Phoenicia, and the extirpation of heresy in the Isle of Cyprus; extended his pastoral care to the missions of Persia and Scythia; negotiated, by his ambassadors, with the Roman pontiff and the emperor Honorius; and boldly appealed, from a partial synod, to the supreme tribunal of a free and general council. The mind of the illustrious exile was still independent; but his captive body was exposed to the revenge of the oppressors, who continued to abuse the name and authority of Arcadius. [55] An order was despatched for the instant removal of Chrysostom to the extreme desert of Pityus: and his guards so faithfully obeyed their cruel instructions, that, before he reached the sea-coast of the Euxine, he expired at Comana, in Pontus, in the sixtieth year of his age. The succeeding generation acknowledged his innocence and merit. The archbishops of the East, who might blush that their predecessors had been the enemies of Chrysostom, were gradually disposed, by the firmness of the Roman pontiff, to restore the honors of that venerable name. [56] At the pious solicitation of the clergy and people of Constantinople, his relics, thirty years after his death, were transported from their obscure sepulchre to the royal city. [57] The emperor Theodosius advanced to receive them as far as Chalcedon; and, falling prostrate on the coffin, implored, in the name of his guilty parents, Arcadius and Eudoxia, the forgiveness of the injured saint. [58]

[Footnote 53: He displays those specious motives (Post Reditum, c. 13, 14) in the language of an orator and a politician.]

[Footnote 54: Two hundred and forty two of the epistles of Chrysostom are still extant, (Opera, tom. iii. p. 528-736.) They are addressed to a great variety of persons, and show a firmness of mind much superior to that of Cicero in his exile. The fourteenth epistle contains a curious narrative of the dangers of his journey.]

[Footnote 55: After the exile of Chrysostom, Theophilus published an enormous and horrible volume against him, in which he perpetually repeats the polite expressions of hostem humanitatis, sacrilegorum principem, immundum daemonem; he affirms, that John Chrysostom had delivered his soul to be adulterated by the devil; and wishes that some further punishment, adequate (if possible) to the magnitude of his crimes, may be inflicted on him. St. Jerom, at the request of his friend Theophilus, translated this edifying performance from Greek into Latin. See Facundus Hermian. Defens. pro iii. Capitul. l. vi. c. 5 published by Sirmond. Opera, tom. ii. p. 595, 596, 597.]

[Footnote 56: His name was inserted by his successor Atticus in the Dyptics of the church of Constantinople, A.D. 418. Ten years afterwards he was revered as a saint. Cyril, who inherited the place, and the passions, of his uncle Theophilus, yielded with much reluctance. See Facund. Hermian. l. 4, c. 1. Tillemont, Mem. Eccles. tom. xiv. p. 277-283.]

[Footnote 57: Socrates, l. vii. c. 45. Theodoret, l. v. c. 36. This event reconciled the Joannites, who had hitherto refused to acknowledge his successors. During his lifetime, the Joannites were respected, by the Catholics, as the true and orthodox communion of Constantinople. Their obstinacy gradually drove them to the brink of schism.]

[Footnote 58: According to some accounts, (Baronius, Annal. Eccles. A.D. 438 No. 9, 10,) the emperor was forced to send a letter of invitation and excuses, before the body of the ceremonious saint could be moved from Comana.]

PART III

Yet a reasonable doubt may be entertained, whether any stain of hereditary guilt could be derived from Arcadius to his successor. Eudoxia was a young and beautiful woman, who indulged her passions, and despised her husband; Count John enjoyed, at least, the familiar confidence of the empress; and the public named him as the real father of Theodosius the younger. [59] The birth of a son was accepted, however, by the pious husband, as an event the most fortunate and honorable to himself, to his family, and to the Eastern world: and the royal infant, by an unprecedented favor, was invested with the titles of Caesar and Augustus. In less than four years afterwards, Eudoxia, in the bloom of youth, was destroyed by the consequences of a miscarriage; and this untimely death confounded the prophecy of a holy bishop, [60] who, amidst the universal joy, had ventured to foretell, that she should behold the long and auspicious reign of her glorious son. The Catholics applauded the justice of Heaven, which avenged the persecution of St. Chrysostom; and perhaps the emperor was the only person who sincerely bewailed the loss of the haughty and rapacious Eudoxia. Such a domestic misfortune afflicted him more deeply than the public calamities of the East; [61] the licentious excursions, from Pontus to Palestine, of the Isaurian robbers, whose impunity accused the weakness of the government; and the earthquakes, the conflagrations, the famine, and the flights of locusts, [62] which the popular discontent was equally disposed to attribute to the incapacity of the monarch. At length, in the thirty-first year of his age, after a reign (if we may abuse that word) of thirteen years, three months, and fifteen days, Arcadius expired in the palace of Constantinople. It is impossible to delineate his character; since, in a period very copiously furnished with historical materials, it has not been possible to remark one action that properly belongs to the son of the great Theodosius.

[Footnote 59: Zosimus, l. v. p. 315. The chastity of an empress should not be impeached without producing a witness; but it is astonishing, that the witness should write and live under a prince whose legitimacy he dared to attack. We must suppose that his history was a party libel, privately read and circulated by the Pagans. Tillemont (Hist. des Empereurs, tom. v. p. 782) is not averse to brand the reputation of Eudoxia.]

[Footnote 60: Porphyry of Gaza. His zeal was transported by the order which he had obtained for the destruction of eight Pagan temples of that city. See the curious details of his life, (Baronius, A.D. 401, No. 17-51,) originally written in Greek, or perhaps in Syriac, by a monk, one of his favorite deacons.]

[Footnote 61: Philostorg. l. xi. c. 8, and Godefroy, Dissertat. p. 457.]

[Footnote 62: Jerom (tom. vi. p. 73, 76) describes, in lively colors, the regular and destructive march of the locusts, which spread a dark cloud, between heaven and earth, over the land of Palestine. Seasonable winds scattered them, partly into the Dead Sea, and partly into the Mediterranean.]

The historian Procopius [63] has indeed illuminated the mind of the dying emperor with a ray of human prudence, or celestial wisdom. Arcadius considered, with anxious foresight, the helpless condition of his son Theodosius, who was no more than seven years of age, the dangerous factions of a minority, and the aspiring spirit of Jezdegerd, the Persian monarch. Instead of tempting the allegiance of an ambitious subject, by the participation of supreme power, he boldly appealed to the magnanimity of a king; and placed, by a solemn testament, the sceptre of the East in the hands of Jezdegerd himself. The royal guardian accepted and discharged this honorable trust with unexampled fidelity; and the infancy of Theodosius was protected by the arms and councils of Persia. Such is the singular narrative of Procopius; and his veracity is not disputed by Agathias, [64] while he presumes to dissent from his judgment, and to arraign the wisdom of a Christian emperor, who, so rashly, though so fortunately, committed his son and his dominions to the unknown faith of a stranger, a rival, and a heathen. At the distance of one hundred and fifty years, this political question might be debated in the court of Justinian; but a prudent historian will refuse to examine the propriety, till he has ascertained the truth, of the testament of Arcadius. As it stands without a parallel in the history of the world, we may justly require, that it should be attested by the positive and unanimous evidence of contemporaries. The strange novelty of the event, which excites our distrust, must have attracted their notice; and their universal silence annihilates the vain tradition of the succeeding age.

[Footnote 63: Procopius, de Bell. Persic. l. i. c. 2, p. 8, edit. Louvre.]

[Footnote 64: Agathias, l. iv. p. 136, 137. Although he confesses the prevalence of the tradition, he asserts, that Procopius was the first who had committed it to writing. Tillemont (Hist. des Empereurs, tom. vi. p. 597) argues very sensibly on the merits of this fable. His criticism was not warped by any ecclesiastical authority: both Procopius and Agathias are half Pagans. Note: See St Martin's article on Jezdegerd, in the Biographie Universelle de Michand—M.]

The maxims of Roman jurisprudence, if they could fairly be transferred from private property to public dominion, would have adjudged to the emperor Honorius the guardianship of his nephew, till he had attained, at least, the fourteenth year of his age. But the weakness of Honorius, and the calamities of his reign, disqualified him from prosecuting this natural claim; and such was the absolute separation of the two monarchies, both in interest and affection, that Constantinople would have obeyed, with less reluctance, the orders of the Persian, than those of the Italian, court. Under a prince whose weakness is disguised by the external signs of manhood and discretion, the most worthless favorites may secretly dispute the empire of the palace; and dictate to submissive provinces the commands of a master, whom they direct and despise. But the ministers of a child, who is incapable of arming them with the sanction of the royal name, must acquire and exercise an independent authority. The great officers of the state and army, who had been appointed before the death of Arcadius, formed an aristocracy, which might have inspired them with the idea of a free republic; and the government of the Eastern empire was fortunately assumed by the praefect Anthemius, [65] who obtained, by his superior abilities, a lasting ascendant over the minds of his equals. The safety of the young emperor proved the merit and integrity of Anthemius; and his prudent firmness sustained the force and reputation of an infant reign. Uldin, with a formidable host of Barbarians, was encamped in the heart of Thrace; he proudly rejected all terms of accommodation; and, pointing to the rising sun, declared to the Roman ambassadors, that the course of that planet should alone terminate the conquest of the Huns. But the desertion of his confederates, who were privately convinced of the justice and liberality of the Imperial ministers, obliged Uldin to repass the Danube: the tribe of the Scyrri, which composed his rear-guard, was almost extirpated; and many thousand captives were dispersed to cultivate, with servile labor, the fields of Asia. [66] In the midst of the public triumph, Constantinople was protected by a strong enclosure of new and more extensive walls; the same vigilant care was applied to restore the fortifications of the Illyrian cities; and a plan was judiciously conceived, which, in the space of seven years, would have secured the command of the Danube, by establishing on that river a perpetual fleet of two hundred and fifty armed vessels. [67]

[Footnote 65: Socrates, l. vii. c. l. Anthemius was the grandson of Philip, one of the ministers of Constantius, and the grandfather of the emperor Anthemius. After his return from the Persian embassy, he was appointed consul and Praetorian praefect of the East, in the year 405 and held the praefecture about ten years. See his honors and praises in Godefroy, Cod. Theod. tom. vi. p. 350. Tillemont, Hist. des Emptom. vi. p. 1. &c.]

[Footnote 66: Sozomen, l. ix. c. 5. He saw some Scyrri at work near Mount Olympus, in Bithynia, and cherished the vain hope that those captives were the last of the nation.]

[Footnote 67: Cod. Theod. l. vii. tit. xvi. l. xv. tit. i. leg. 49.]

But the Romans had so long been accustomed to the authority of a monarch, that the first, even among the females, of the Imperial family, who displayed any courage or capacity, was permitted to ascend the vacant throne of Theodosius. His sister Pulcheria, [68] who was only two years older than himself, received, at the age of sixteen, the title of Augusta; and though her favor might be sometimes clouded by caprice or intrigue, she continued to govern the Eastern empire near forty years; during the long minority of her brother, and after his death, in her own name, and in the name of Marcian, her nominal husband. From a motive either of prudence or religion, she embraced a life of celibacy; and notwithstanding some aspersions on the chastity of Pulcheria, [69] this resolution, which she communicated to her sisters Arcadia and Marina, was celebrated by the Christian world, as the sublime effort of heroic piety. In the presence of the clergy and people, the three daughters of Arcadius [70] dedicated their virginity to God; and the obligation of their solemn vow was inscribed on a tablet of gold and gems; which they publicly offered in the great church of Constantinople. Their palace was converted into a monastery; and all males, except the guides of their conscience, the saints who had forgotten the distinction of sexes, were scrupulously excluded from the holy threshold. Pulcheria, her two sisters, and a chosen train of favorite damsels, formed a religious community: they denounced the vanity of dress; interrupted, by frequent fasts, their simple and frugal diet; allotted a portion of their time to works of embroidery; and devoted several hours of the day and night to the exercises of prayer and psalmody. The piety of a Christian virgin was adorned by the zeal and liberality of an empress. Ecclesiastical history describes the splendid churches, which were built at the expense of Pulcheria, in all the provinces of the East; her charitable foundations for the benefit of strangers and the poor; the ample donations which she assigned for the perpetual maintenance of monastic societies; and the active severity with which she labored to suppress the opposite heresies of Nestorius and Eutyches. Such virtues were supposed to deserve the peculiar favor of the Deity: and the relics of martyrs, as well as the knowledge of future events, were communicated in visions and revelations to the Imperial saint. [71] Yet the devotion of Pulcheria never diverted her indefatigable attention from temporal affairs; and she alone, among all the descendants of the great Theodosius, appears to have inherited any share of his manly spirit and abilities. The elegant and familiar use which she had acquired, both of the Greek and Latin languages, was readily applied to the various occasions of speaking or writing, on public business: her deliberations were maturely weighed; her actions were prompt and decisive; and, while she moved, without noise or ostentation, the wheel of government, she discreetly attributed to the genius of the emperor the long tranquillity of his reign. In the last years of his peaceful life, Europe was indeed afflicted by the arms of war; but the more extensive provinces of Asia still continued to enjoy a profound and permanent repose. Theodosius the younger was never reduced to the disgraceful necessity of encountering and punishing a rebellious subject: and since we cannot applaud the vigor, some praise may be due to the mildness and prosperity, of the administration of Pulcheria.

[Footnote 68: Sozomen has filled three chapters with a magnificent panegyric of Pulcheria, (l. ix. c. 1, 2, 3;) and Tillemont (Memoires Eccles. tom. xv. p. 171-184) has dedicated a separate article to the honor of St. Pulcheria, virgin and empress. Note: The heathen Eunapius gives a frightful picture of the venality and a justice of the court of Pulcheria. Fragm. Eunap. in Mai, ii. 293, in p. 97—M.]

[Footnote 69: Suidas, (Excerpta, p. 68, in Script. Byzant.) pretends, on the credit of the Nestorians, that Pulcheria was exasperated against their founder, because he censured her connection with the beautiful Paulinus, and her incest with her brother Theodosius.]

[Footnote 70: See Ducange, Famil. Byzantin. p. 70. Flaccilla, the eldest daughter, either died before Arcadius, or, if she lived till the year 431, (Marcellin. Chron.,) some defect of mind or body must have excluded her from the honors of her rank.]

[Footnote 71: She was admonished, by repeated dreams, of the place where the relics of the forty martyrs had been buried. The ground had successively belonged to the house and garden of a woman of Constantinople, to a monastery of Macedonian monks, and to a church of St. Thyrsus, erected by Caesarius, who was consul A.D. 397; and the memory of the relics was almost obliterated. Notwithstanding the charitable wishes of Dr. Jortin, (Remarks, tom. iv. p. 234,) it is not easy to acquit Pulcheria of some share in the pious fraud; which must have been transacted when she was more than five-and-thirty years of age.]

The Roman world was deeply interested in the education of its master. A regular course of study and exercise was judiciously instituted; of the military exercises of riding, and shooting with the bow; of the liberal studies of grammar, rhetoric, and philosophy. the most skilful masters of the East ambitiously solicited the attention of their royal pupil; and several noble youths were introduced into the palace, to animate his diligence by the emulation of friendship. Pulcheria alone discharged the important task of instructing her brother in the arts of government; but her precepts may countenance some suspicions of the extent of her capacity, or of the purity of her intentions. She taught him to maintain a grave and majestic deportment; to walk, to hold his robes, to seat himself on his throne, in a manner worthy of a great prince; to abstain from laughter; to listen with condescension; to return suitable answers; to assume, by turns, a serious or a placid countenance: in a word, to represent with grace and dignity the external figure of a Roman emperor. But Theodosius [72] was never excited to support the weight and glory of an illustrious name: and, instead of aspiring to support his ancestors, he degenerated (if we may presume to measure the degrees of incapacity) below the weakness of his father and his uncle. Arcadius and Honorius had been assisted by the guardian care of a parent, whose lessons were enforced by his authority and example. But the unfortunate prince, who is born in the purple, must remain a stranger to the voice of truth; and the son of Arcadius was condemned to pass his perpetual infancy encompassed only by a servile train of women and eunuchs. The ample leisure which he acquired by neglecting the essential duties of his high office, was filled by idle amusements and unprofitable studies. Hunting was the only active pursuit that could tempt him beyond the limits of the palace; but he most assiduously labored, sometimes by the light of a midnight lamp, in the mechanic occupations of painting and carving; and the elegance with which he transcribed religious books entitled the Roman emperor to the singular epithet of Calligraphes, or a fair writer. Separated from the world by an impenetrable veil, Theodosius trusted the persons whom he loved; he loved those who were accustomed to amuse and flatter his indolence; and as he never perused the papers that were presented for the royal signature, the acts of injustice the most repugnant to his character were frequently perpetrated in his name. The emperor himself was chaste, temperate, liberal, and merciful; but these qualities, which can only deserve the name of virtues when they are supported by courage and regulated by discretion, were seldom beneficial, and they sometimes proved mischievous, to mankind. His mind, enervated by a royal education, was oppressed and degraded by abject superstition: he fasted, he sung psalms, he blindly accepted the miracles and doctrines with which his faith was continually nourished. Theodosius devoutly worshipped the dead and living saints of the Catholic church; and he once refused to eat, till an insolent monk, who had cast an excommunication on his sovereign, condescended to heal the spiritual wound which he had inflicted. [73]

[Footnote 72: There is a remarkable difference between the two ecclesiastical historians, who in general bear so close a resemblance. Sozomen (l. ix. c. 1) ascribes to Pulcheria the government of the empire, and the education of her brother, whom he scarcely condescends to praise. Socrates, though he affectedly disclaims all hopes of favor or fame, composes an elaborate panegyric on the emperor, and cautiously suppresses the merits of his sister, (l. vii. c. 22, 42.) Philostorgius (l. xii. c. 7) expresses the influence of Pulcheria in gentle and courtly language. Suidas (Excerpt. p. 53) gives a true character of Theodosius; and I have followed the example of Tillemont (tom. vi. p. 25) in borrowing some strokes from the modern Greeks.]

[Footnote 73: Theodoret, l. v. c. 37. The bishop of Cyrrhus, one of the first men of his age for his learning and piety, applauds the obedience of Theodosius to the divine laws.]

The story of a fair and virtuous maiden, exalted from a private condition to the Imperial throne, might be deemed an incredible romance, if such a romance had not been verified in the marriage of Theodosius. The celebrated Athenais [74] was educated by her father Leontius in the religion and sciences of the Greeks; and so advantageous was the opinion which the Athenian philosopher entertained of his contemporaries, that he divided his patrimony between his two sons, bequeathing to his daughter a small legacy of one hundred pieces of gold, in the lively confidence that her beauty and merit would be a sufficient portion. The jealousy and avarice of her brothers soon compelled Athenais to seek a refuge at Constantinople; and, with some hopes, either of justice or favor, to throw herself at the feet of Pulcheria. That sagacious princess listened to her eloquent complaint; and secretly destined the daughter of the philosopher Leontius for the future wife of the emperor of the East, who had now attained the twentieth year of his age. She easily excited the curiosity of her brother, by an interesting picture of the charms of Athenais; large eyes, a well-proportioned nose, a fair complexion, golden locks, a slender person, a graceful demeanor, an understanding improved by study, and a virtue tried by distress. Theodosius, concealed behind a curtain in the apartment of his sister, was permitted to behold the Athenian virgin: the modest youth immediately declared his pure and honorable love; and the royal nuptials were celebrated amidst the acclamations of the capital and the provinces. Athenais, who was easily persuaded to renounce the errors of Paganism, received at her baptism the Christian name of Eudocia; but the cautious Pulcheria withheld the title of Augusta, till the wife of Theodosius had approved her fruitfulness by the birth of a daughter, who espoused, fifteen years afterwards, the emperor of the West. The brothers of Eudocia obeyed, with some anxiety, her Imperial summons; but as she could easily forgive their unfortunate unkindness, she indulged the tenderness, or perhaps the vanity, of a sister, by promoting them to the rank of consuls and praefects. In the luxury of the palace, she still cultivated those ingenuous arts which had contributed to her greatness; and wisely dedicated her talents to the honor of religion, and of her husband. Eudocia composed a poetical paraphrase of the first eight books of the Old Testament, and of the prophecies of Daniel and Zechariah; a cento of the verses of Homer, applied to the life and miracles of Christ, the legend of St. Cyprian, and a panegyric on the Persian victories of Theodosius; and her writings, which were applauded by a servile and superstitious age, have not been disdained by the candor of impartial criticism. [75] The fondness of the emperor was not abated by time and possession; and Eudocia, after the marriage of her daughter, was permitted to discharge her grateful vows by a solemn pilgrimage to Jerusalem. Her ostentatious progress through the East may seem inconsistent with the spirit of Christian humility; she pronounced, from a throne of gold and gems, an eloquent oration to the senate of Antioch, declared her royal intention of enlarging the walls of the city, bestowed a donative of two hundred pounds of gold to restore the public baths, and accepted the statues, which were decreed by the gratitude of Antioch. In the Holy Land, her alms and pious foundations exceeded the munificence of the great Helena, and though the public treasure might be impoverished by this excessive liberality, she enjoyed the conscious satisfaction of returning to Constantinople with the chains of St. Peter, the right arm of St. Stephen, and an undoubted picture of the Virgin, painted by St. Luke. [76] But this pilgrimage was the fatal term of the glories of Eudocia. Satiated with empty pomp, and unmindful, perhaps, of her obligations to Pulcheria, she ambitiously aspired to the government of the Eastern empire; the palace was distracted by female discord; but the victory was at last decided, by the superior ascendant of the sister of Theodosius. The execution of Paulinus, master of the offices, and the disgrace of Cyrus, Praetorian praefect of the East, convinced the public that the favor of Eudocia was insufficient to protect her most faithful friends; and the uncommon beauty of Paulinus encouraged the secret rumor, that his guilt was that of a successful lover. [77] As soon as the empress perceived that the affection of Theodosius was irretrievably lost, she requested the permission of retiring to the distant solitude of Jerusalem. She obtained her request; but the jealousy of Theodosius, or the vindictive spirit of Pulcheria, pursued her in her last retreat; and Saturninus, count of the domestics, was directed to punish with death two ecclesiastics, her most favored servants. Eudocia instantly revenged them by the assassination of the count; the furious passions which she indulged on this suspicious occasion, seemed to justify the severity of Theodosius; and the empress, ignominiously stripped of the honors of her rank, [78] was disgraced, perhaps unjustly, in the eyes of the world. The remainder of the life of Eudocia, about sixteen years, was spent in exile and devotion; and the approach of age, the death of Theodosius, the misfortunes of her only daughter, who was led a captive from Rome to Carthage, and the society of the Holy Monks of Palestine, insensibly confirmed the religious temper of her mind. After a full experience of the vicissitudes of human life, the daughter of the philosopher Leontius expired, at Jerusalem, in the sixty-seventh year of her age; protesting, with her dying breath, that she had never transgressed the bounds of innocence and friendship. [79]

[Footnote 74: Socrates (l. vii. c. 21) mentions her name, (Athenais, the daughter of Leontius, an Athenian sophist,) her baptism, marriage, and poetical genius. The most ancient account of her history is in John Malala (part ii. p. 20, 21, edit. Venet. 1743) and in the Paschal Chronicle, (p. 311, 312.) Those authors had probably seen original pictures of the empress Eudocia. The modern Greeks, Zonaras, Cedrenus, &c.,

have displayed the love, rather than the talent of fiction. From Nicephorus, indeed, I have ventured to assume her age. The writer of a romance would not have imagined, that Athenais was near twenty eight years old when she inflamed the heart of a young emperor.]

[Footnote 75: Socrates, l. vii. c. 21, Photius, p. 413-420. The Homeric cento is still extant, and has been repeatedly printed: but the claim of Eudocia to that insipid performance is disputed by the critics. See Fabricius, Biblioth. Graec. tom. i. p. 357. The Ionia, a miscellaneous dictionary of history and fable, was compiled by another empress of the name of Eudocia, who lived in the eleventh century: and the work is still extant in manuscript.]

[Footnote 76: Baronius (Annal. Eccles. A.D. 438, 439) is copious and florid, but he is accused of placing the lies of different ages on the same level of authenticity.]

[Footnote 77: In this short view of the disgrace of Eudocia, I have imitated the caution of Evagrius (l. i. c. 21) and Count Marcellinus, (in Chron A.D. 440 and 444.) The two authentic dates assigned by the latter, overturn a great part of the Greek fictions; and the celebrated story of the apple, &c., is fit only for the Arabian Nights, where something not very unlike it may be found.]

[Footnote 78: Priscus, (in Excerpt. Legat. p. 69,) a contemporary, and a courtier, dryly mentions her Pagan and Christian names, without adding any title of honor or respect.]

[Footnote 79: For the two pilgrimages of Eudocia, and her long residence at Jerusalem, her devotion, alms, &c., see Socrates (l. vii. c. 47) and Evagrius, (l. i. c. 21, 22.) The Paschal Chronicle may sometimes deserve regard; and in the domestic history of Antioch, John Malala becomes a writer of good authority. The Abbe Guenee, in a memoir on the fertility of Palestine, of which I have only seen an extract, calculates the gifts of Eudocia at 20,488 pounds of gold, above 800,000 pounds sterling.]

The gentle mind of Theodosius was never inflamed by the ambition of conquest, or military renown; and the slight alarm of a Persian war scarcely interrupted the tranquillity of the East. The motives of this war were just and honorable. In the last year of the reign of Jezdegerd, the supposed guardian of Theodosius, a bishop, who aspired to the crown of martyrdom, destroyed one of the fire-temples of Susa. [80] His zeal and obstinacy were revenged on his brethren: the Magi excited a cruel persecution; and the intolerant zeal of Jezdegerd was imitated by his son Varanes, or Bahram, who soon afterwards ascended the throne. Some Christian fugitives, who escaped to the Roman frontier, were sternly demanded, and generously refused; and the refusal, aggravated by commercial disputes, soon kindled a war between the rival monarchies. The mountains of Armenia, and the plains of Mesopotamia, were filled with hostile armies; but the operations of two successive campaigns were not productive of any decisive or memorable events. Some engagements were fought, some towns were besieged, with various and doubtful success: and if the Romans failed in their attempt to recover the long-lost possession of Nisibis, the Persians were repulsed from the walls of a Mesopotamian city, by the valor of a martial bishop, who pointed his thundering engine in the name of St. Thomas the Apostle. Yet the splendid victories which the incredible speed of the messenger Palladius repeatedly announced to the palace of Constantinople, were celebrated with festivals and panegyrics. From these panegyrics the historians [81] of the age might borrow their extraordinary, and, perhaps, fabulous tales; of the proud challenge of a Persian hero, who was entangled by the net, and despatched by the sword, of Areobindus the Goth; of the ten thousand Immortals, who were slain in the attack of the Roman camp; and of the hundred thousand Arabs, or Saracens, who were impelled by a panic terror to throw themselves headlong into the Euphrates. Such events may be disbelieved or disregarded; but the charity of a bishop,

Acacius of Amida, whose name might have dignified the saintly calendar, shall not be lost in oblivion. Boldly declaring, that vases of gold and silver are useless to a God who neither eats nor drinks, the generous prelate sold the plate of the church of Amida; employed the price in the redemption of seven thousand Persian captives; supplied their wants with affectionate liberality; and dismissed them to their native country, to inform their king of the true spirit of the religion which he persecuted. The practice of benevolence in the midst of war must always tend to assuage the animosity of contending nations; and I wish to persuade myself, that Acacius contributed to the restoration of peace. In the conference which was held on the limits of the two empires, the Roman ambassadors degraded the personal character of their sovereign, by a vain attempt to magnify the extent of his power; when they seriously advised the Persians to prevent, by a timely accommodation, the wrath of a monarch, who was yet ignorant of this distant war. A truce of one hundred years was solemnly ratified; and although the revolutions of Armenia might threaten the public tranquillity, the essential conditions of this treaty were respected near fourscore years by the successors of Constantine and Artaxerxes.

[Footnote 80: Theodoret, l. v. c. 39 Tillemont. Mem. Eccles tom. xii. 356-364. Assemanni, Bibliot. Oriental. tom. iii. p. 396, tom. iv. p. 61. Theodoret blames the rashness of Abdas, but extols the constancy of his martyrdom. Yet I do not clearly understand the casuistry which prohibits our repairing the damage which we have unlawfully committed.]

[Footnote 81: Socrates (l. vii. c. 18, 19, 20, 21) is the best author for the Persian war. We may likewise consult the three Chronicles, the Paschal and those of Marcellinus and Malala.]

Since the Roman and Parthian standards first encountered on the banks of the Euphrates, the kingdom of Armenia [82] was alternately oppressed by its formidable protectors; and in the course of this History, several events, which inclined the balance of peace and war, have been already related. A disgraceful treaty had resigned Armenia to the ambition of Sapor; and the scale of Persia appeared to preponderate. But the royal race of Arsaces impatiently submitted to the house of Sassan; the turbulent nobles asserted, or betrayed, their hereditary independence; and the nation was still attached to the Christian princes of Constantinople. In the beginning of the fifth century, Armenia was divided by the progress of war and faction; [83] and the unnatural division precipitated the downfall of that ancient monarchy. Chosroes, the Persian vassal, reigned over the Eastern and most extensive portion of the country; while the Western province acknowledged the jurisdiction of Arsaces, and the supremacy of the emperor Arcadius. [81/1] After the death of Arsaces, the Romans suppressed the regal government, and imposed on their allies the condition of subjects. The military command was delegated to the count of the Armenian frontier; the city of Theodosiopolis [84] was built and fortified in a strong situation, on a fertile and lofty ground, near the sources of the Euphrates; and the dependent territories were ruled by five satraps, whose dignity was marked by a peculiar habit of gold and purple. The less fortunate nobles, who lamented the loss of their king, and envied the honors of their equals, were provoked to negotiate their peace and pardon at the Persian court; and returning, with their followers, to the palace of Artaxata, acknowledged Chosroes [84/1] for their lawful sovereign. About thirty years afterwards, Artasires, the nephew and successor of Chosroes, fell under the displeasure of the haughty and capricious nobles of Armenia; and they unanimously desired a Persian governor in the room of an unworthy king. The answer of the archbishop Isaac, whose sanction they earnestly solicited, is expressive of the character of a superstitious people. He deplored the manifest and inexcusable vices of Artasires; and declared, that he should not hesitate to accuse him before the tribunal of a Christian emperor, who would punish, without destroying, the sinner. "Our king," continued Isaac, "is too much addicted to licentious pleasures, but he has been purified in the holy waters of baptism. He is a lover of women, but he does not adore the fire or the elements. He may deserve the reproach of lewdness, but he is an undoubted Catholic; and his faith is pure, though his manners are flagitious. I will never consent to abandon my sheep to the rage of devouring wolves; and you would soon repent your rash exchange of the infirmities of a believer, for the specious virtues of a heathen." [85] Exasperated by the firmness of Isaac, the factious nobles accused both the king and the archbishop as the secret adherents of the emperor; and absurdly rejoiced in the sentence of condemnation, which, after a partial hearing, was solemnly pronounced by Bahram himself. The descendants of Arsaces were degraded from the royal dignity, [86] which they had possessed above five hundred and sixty years; [87] and the dominions of the unfortunate Artasires, [87/1] under the new and significant appellation of Persarmenia, were reduced into the form of a province. This usurpation excited the jealousy of the Roman government; but the rising disputes were soon terminated by an amicable, though unequal, partition of the ancient kingdom of Armenia: [87/2] and a territorial acquisition, which Augustus might have despised, reflected some lustre on the declining empire of the younger Theodosius.

[Footnote 82: This account of the ruin and division of the kingdom of Armenia is taken from the third book of the Armenian history of Moses of Chorene. Deficient as he is in every qualification of a good historian, his local information, his passions, and his prejudices are strongly expressive of a native and contemporary. Procopius (de Edificiis, l. iii. c. 1, 5) relates the same facts in a very different manner; but I have extracted the circumstances the most probable in themselves, and the least inconsistent with Moses of Chorene.]

[Footnote 83: The western Armenians used the Greek language and characters in their religious offices; but the use of that hostile tongue was prohibited by the Persians in the Eastern provinces, which were obliged to use the Syriac, till the invention of the Armenian letters by Mesrobes, in the beginning of the fifth century, and the subsequent version of the Bible into the Armenian language; an event which relaxed to the connection of the church and nation with Constantinople.]

[Footnote 84: Moses Choren. l. iii. c. 59, p. 309, and p. 358. Procopius, de Edificiis, l. iii. c. 5. Theodosiopolis stands, or rather stood, about thirty-five miles to the east of Arzeroum, the modern capital of Turkish Armenia. See D'Anville, Geographie Ancienne, tom. ii. p. 99, 100.]

[Footnote 81/1: The division of Armenia, according to M. St. Martin, took place much earlier, A. C. 390. The Eastern or Persian division was four times as large as the Western or Roman. This partition took place during the reigns of Theodosius the First, and Varanes (Bahram) the Fourth. St. Martin, Sup. to Le Beau, iv. 429. This partition was but imperfectly accomplished, as both parts were afterwards reunited under Chosroes, who paid tribute both to the Roman emperor and to the Persian king. v. 439—M.]

[Footnote 84/1: Chosroes, according to Procopius (who calls him Arsaces, the common name of the Armenian kings) and the Armenian writers, bequeathed to his two sons, to Tigranes the Persian, to Arsaces the Roman, division of Armenia, A. C. 416. With the assistance of the discontented nobles the Persian king placed his son Sapor on the throne of the Eastern division; the Western at the same time was united to the Roman empire, and called the Greater Armenia. It was then that Theodosiopolis was built. Sapor abandoned the throne of Armenia to assert his rights to that of Persia; he perished in the struggle, and after a period of anarchy, Bahram V., who had ascended the throne of Persia, placed the last native prince, Ardaschir, son of Bahram Schahpour, on the throne of the Persian division of Armenia. St. Martin, v. 506. This Ardaschir was the Artasires of Gibbon. The archbishop Isaac is called by the Armenians the Patriarch Schag. St. Martin, vi. 29—M.]

[Footnote 85: Moses Choren, l. iii. c. 63, p. 316. According to the institution of St. Gregory, the Apostle of Armenia, the archbishop was always of the royal family; a circumstance which, in some degree, corrected the influence of the sacerdotal character, and united the mitre with the crown.]

[Footnote 86: A branch of the royal house of Arsaces still subsisted with the rank and possessions (as it should seem) of Armenian satraps. See Moses Choren. l. iii. c. 65, p. 321.]

[Footnote 87: Valarsaces was appointed king of Armenia by his brother the Parthian monarch, immediately after the defeat of Antiochus Sidetes, (Moses Choren. l. ii. c. 2, p. 85,) one hundred and thirty years before Christ. Without depending on the various and contradictory periods of the reigns of the last kings, we may be assured, that the ruin of the Armenian kingdom happened after the council of Chalcedon, A.D. 431, (l. iii. c. 61, p. 312;) and under Varamus, or Bahram, king of Persia, (l. iii. c. 64, p. 317,) who reigned from A.D. 420 to 440. See Assemanni, Bibliot. Oriental. tom. iii. p. 396. Note: Five hundred and eighty. St. Martin, ibid. He places this event A. C 429—M—Note: According to M. St. Martin, vi. 32, Vagharschah, or Valarsaces, was appointed king by his brother Mithridates the Great, king of Parthia—M.]

[Footnote 87/1: Artasires or Ardaschir was probably sent to the castle of Oblivion. St. Martin, vi. 31—M.]

[Footnote 87/2: The duration of the Armenian kingdom according to M. St. Martin, was 580 years—M]

CHAPTER XXXIII

CONQUEST OF AFRICA BY THE VANDALS

PART I

DEATH OF HONORIUS—VALENTINIAN III—EMPEROR OF THE EAST—ADMINISTRATION OF HIS MOTHER PLACIDIA—AETIUS AND BONIFACE—CONQUEST OF AFRICA BY THE VANDALS

During a long and disgraceful reign of twenty-eight years, Honorius, emperor of the West, was separated from the friendship of his brother, and afterwards of his nephew, who reigned over the East; and Constantinople beheld, with apparent indifference and secret joy, the calamities of Rome. The strange adventures of Placidia [1] gradually renewed and cemented the alliance of the two empires. The daughter of the great Theodosius had been the captive, and the queen, of the Goths; she lost an affectionate husband; she was dragged in chains by his insulting assassin; she tasted the pleasure of revenge, and was exchanged, in the treaty of peace, for six hundred thousand measures of wheat. After her return from Spain to Italy, Placidia experienced a new persecution in the bosom of her family. She was averse to a marriage, which had been stipulated without her consent; and the brave Constantius, as a noble reward for the tyrants whom he had vanquished, received, from the hand of Honorius himself, the struggling and the reluctant hand of the widow of Adolphus. But her resistance ended with the ceremony of the nuptials: nor did Placidia refuse to become the mother of Honoria and Valentinian the Third, or to assume and exercise an absolute dominion over the mind of her grateful husband. The generous soldier, whose time had hitherto been divided between social pleasure and military service, was taught new lessons of avarice and ambition: he extorted the title of Augustus: and the servant of Honorius was associated to the empire of the West. The death of Constantius, in the seventh month of his reign, instead of diminishing, seemed to inerease the power of Placidia; and the indecent familiarity [2] of her brother, which might be no more than the symptoms of a childish affection, were universally attributed to incestuous love. On a sudden, by some base intrigues of a steward and a nurse, this excessive fondness was converted into an irreconcilable quarrel: the debates of the emperor and his sister were not long confined within the walls of the palace; and as the Gothic soldiers adhered to their queen, the city of Ravenna was agitated with bloody and dangerous tumults, which could only be appeased by the forced or voluntary retreat of Placidia and her children. The royal exiles landed at Constantinople, soon after the marriage of Theodosius, during the festival of the Persian victories. They were treated with kindness and magnificence; but as the statues of the emperor Constantius had been rejected by the Eastern court, the title of Augusta could not decently be allowed to his widow. Within a few months after the arrival of Placidia, a swift messenger announced the death of Honorius, the consequence of a dropsy; but the important secret was not divulged, till the necessary orders had been despatched for the march of a large body of troops to the sea-coast of Dalmatia. The shops and the gates of Constantinople remained shut during seven days; and the loss of a foreign prince, who could neither be esteemed nor regretted, was celebrated with loud and affected demonstrations of the public grief.

[Footnote 1: See vol. iii. p. 296.]

[Footnote 2: It is the expression of Olympiodorus (apud Phetium p. 197;) who means, perhaps, to describe the same caresses which Mahomet bestowed on his daughter Phatemah. Quando, (says the prophet himself,) quando subit mihi desiderium Paradisi, osculor eam, et ingero linguam meam in os ejus. But this sensual indulgence was justified by miracle and mystery; and the anecdote has been communicated to the public by the Reverend Father Maracci in his Version and Confutation of the Koran, tom. i. p. 32.]

While the ministers of Constantinople deliberated, the vacant throne of Honorius was usurped by the ambition of a stranger. The name of the rebel was John; he filled the confidential office of Primicerius, or principal secretary, and history has attributed to his character more virtues, than can easily be reconciled with the violation of the most sacred duty. Elated by the submission of Italy, and the hope of an alliance with the Huns, John presumed to insult, by an embassy, the majesty of the Eastern emperor; but when he understood that his agents had been banished, imprisoned, and at length chased away with deserved ignomiy, John prepared to assert, by arms, the injustice of his claims. In such a cause, the grandson of the great Theodosius should have marched in person: but the young emperor was easily diverted, by his physicians, from so rash and hazardous a design; and the conduct of the Italian expedition was prudently intrusted to Ardaburius, and his son Aspar, who had already signalized their valor against the Persians. It was resolved, that Ardaburius should embark with the infantry; whilst Aspar, at the head of the cavalry, conducted Placidia and her son Valentinian along the sea-coast of the Adriatic. The march of the cavalry was performed with such active diligence, that they surprised, without resistance, the important city of Aquileia: when the hopes of Aspar were unexpectedly confounded by the intelligence, that a storm had dispersed the Imperial fleet; and that his father, with only two galleys, was taken and carried a prisoner into the port of Ravenna. Yet this incident, unfortunate as it might seem, facilitated the conquest of Italy. Ardaburius employed, or abused, the courteous freedom which he was permitted to enjoy, to revive among the troops a sense of loyalty and gratitude; and as soon as the conspiracy was ripe for execution, he invited, by private messages, and pressed the approach of, Aspar. A shepherd, whom the popular credulity transformed into an angel, guided the eastern cavalry by a secret, and, it was thought, an impassable road, through the morasses of the Po: the gates of Ravenna, after a short struggle, were thrown open; and the defenceless tyrant was delivered to the mercy, or rather to the cruelty, of the conquerors. His right hand was first cut off; and, after he had been exposed, mounted on an ass, to the public derision, John was beheaded in the circus of Aquileia. The emperor Theodosius, when he received the news of the victory, interrupted the horse-races; and singing, as he marched through the streets, a suitable psalm, conducted his people from the Hippodrome to the church, where he spent the remainder of the day in grateful devotion. [3]

[Footnote 3: For these revolutions of the Western empire, consult Olympiodor, apud Phot. p. 192, 193, 196, 197, 200; Sozomen, l. ix. c. 16; Socrates, l. vii. 23, 24; Philostorgius, l. xii. c. 10, 11, and Godefroy, Dissertat p. 486; Procopius, de Bell. Vandal. l. i. c. 3, p. 182, 183, in Chronograph, p. 72, 73, and the Chronicles.]

In a monarchy, which, according to various precedents, might be considered as elective, or hereditary, or patrimonial, it was impossible that the intricate claims of female and collateral succession should be clearly defined; [4] and Theodosius, by the right of consanguinity or conquest, might have reigned the sole legitimate emperor of the Romans. For a moment, perhaps, his eyes were dazzled by the prospect of unbounded sway; but his indolent temper gradually acquiesced in the dictates of sound policy. He contented himself with the possession of the East; and wisely relinquished the laborious task of waging a distant and doubtful war against the Barbarians beyond the Alps; or of securing the obedience of the Italians and Africans, whose minds were alienated by the irreconcilable difference of language and interest. Instead of listening to the voice of ambition, Theodosius resolved to imitate the moderation of his grandfather, and to seat his cousin Valentinian on the throne of the West. The royal infant was distinguished at Constantinople by the title of Nobilissimus: he was promoted, before his departure from Thessalonica, to the rank and dignity of Caesar; and after the conquest of Italy, the patrician Helion, by the authority of Theodosius, and in the presence of the senate, saluted Valentinian the Third by the name of Augustus, and solemnly invested him with the diadem and the Imperial purple. [5] By the agreement of the three females who governed the Roman world, the son of Placidia was betrothed to Eudoxia, the daughter of Theodosius and Athenais; and as soon as the lover and his bride had attained the age of puberty, this honorable alliance was faithfully accomplished. At the same time, as a compensation, perhaps, for the expenses of the war, the Western Illyricum was detached from the Italian dominions, and yielded to the throne of Constantinople. [6] The emperor of the East acquired the useful dominion of the rich and maritime province of Dalmatia, and the dangerous sovereignty of Pannonia and Noricum, which had been filled and ravaged above twenty years by a promiscuous crowd of Huns, Ostrogoths, Vandals, and Bavarians. Theodosius and Valentinian continued to respect the obligations of their public and domestic alliance; but the unity of the Roman government was finally dissolved. By a positive declaration, the validity of all future laws was limited to the dominions of their peculiar author; unless he should think proper to communicate them, subscribed with his own hand, for the approbation of his independent colleague. [7]

[Footnote 4: See Grotius de Jure Belli et Pacis, l. ii. c. 7. He has laboriously out vainly, attempted to form a reasonable system of jurisprudence from the various and discordant modes of royal succession, which have been introduced by fraud or force, by time or accident.]

[Footnote 5: The original writers are not agreed (see Muratori, Annali d'Italia tom. iv. p. 139) whether Valentinian received the Imperial diadem at Rome or Ravenna. In this uncertainty, I am willing to believe, that some respect was shown to the senate.]

[Footnote 6: The count de Buat (Hist. des Peup es de l'Europe, tom. vii. p. 292-300) has established the reality, explained the motives, and traced the consequences, of this remarkable cession.]

[Footnote 7: See the first Novel of Theodosius, by which he ratifies and communicates (A.D. 438) the Theodosian Code. About forty years before that time, the unity of legislation had been proved by an exception. The Jews, who were numerous in the cities of Apulia and Calabria, produced a law of the East to justify their exemption from municipal offices, (Cod. Theod. l. xvi. tit. viii. leg. 13;) and the Western emperor was obliged to invalidate, by a special edict, the law, quam constat meis partibus esse damnosam. Cod. Theod. l. xi. tit. i. leg. 158.]

Valentinian, when he received the title of Augustus, was no more than six years of age; and his long minority was intrusted to the guardian care of a mother, who might assert a female claim to the succession of the Western empire. Placidia envied, but she could not equal, the reputation and virtues of the wife and sister of Theodosius, the elegant genius of Eudocia, the wise and successful policy of Pulcheria. The mother of Valentinian was jealous of the power which she was incapable of exercising; [8] she reigned twenty-five years, in the name of her son; and the character of that unworthy emperor gradually countenanced the suspicion that Placidia had enervated his youth by a dissolute education, and studiously diverted his attention from every manly and honorable pursuit. Amidst the decay of military spirit, her armies were commanded by two generals, Aetius [9] and Boniface, [10] who may be deservedly named as the last of the Romans. Their union might have supported a sinking empire; their discord was the fatal and immediate cause of the loss of Africa. The invasion and defeat of Attila have immortalized the fame of Aetius; and though time has thrown a shade over the exploits of his rival, the defence of Marseilles, and the deliverance of Africa, attest the military talents of Count Boniface. In the field of battle, in partial encounters, in single combats, he was still the terror of the Barbarians: the clergy, and particularly his friend Augustin, were edified by the Christian piety which had once tempted him to retire from the world; the people applauded his spotless integrity; the army dreaded his equal and inexorable justice, which may be displayed in a very singular example. A peasant, who complained of the criminal intimacy between his wife and a Gothic soldier, was directed to attend his tribunal the following day: in the evening the count, who had diligently informed himself of the time and place of the assignation, mounted his horse, rode ten miles into the country, surprised the guilty couple, punished the soldier with instant death, and silenced the complaints of the husband by presenting him, the next morning, with the head of the adulterer. The abilities of Aetius and Boniface might have been usefully employed against the public enemies, in separate and important commands; but the experience of their past conduct should have decided the real favor and confidence of the empress Placidia. In the melancholy season of her exile and distress, Boniface alone had maintained her cause with unshaken fidelity; and the troops and treasures of Africa had essentially contributed to extinguish the rebellion. The same rebellion had been supported by the zeal and activity of Aetius, who brought an army of sixty thousand Huns from the Danube to the confines of Italy, for the service of the usurper. The untimely death of John compelled him to accept an advantageous treaty; but he still continued, the subject and the soldier of Valentinian, to entertain a secret, perhaps a treasonable, correspondence with his Barbarian allies, whose retreat had been purchased by liberal gifts, and more liberal promises. But Aetius possessed an advantage of singular moment in a female reign; he was present: he besieged, with artful and assiduous flattery, the palace of Ravenna; disguised his dark designs with the mask of loyalty and friendship; and at length deceived both his mistress and his absent rival, by a subtle conspiracy, which a weak woman and a brave man could not easily suspect. He had secretly persuaded [11] Placidia to recall Boniface from the government of Africa; he secretly advised Boniface to disobey the Imperial summons: to the one, he represented the order as a sentence of death; to the other, he stated the refusal as a signal of revolt; and when the credulous and unsuspectful count had armed the province in his defence, Aetius applauded his sagacity in foreseeing the rebellion, which his own perfidy had excited. A temperate inquiry into the real motives of Boniface would have restored a faithful servant to his duty and to the republic; but the arts of Aetius still continued to betray and to inflame, and the count was urged, by persecution, to embrace the most desperate counsels. The success with which he eluded or repelled the first attacks, could not inspire a vain confidence, that at the head of some loose, disorderly Africans, he should be able to withstand the regular forces of the West, commanded by a rival, whose military character it was impossible for him to despise. After some hesitation, the last struggles of prudence and loyalty, Boniface despatched a trusty friend to the court, or rather to the camp, of Gonderic, king of the Vandals, with the proposal of a strict alliance, and the offer of an advantageous and perpetual settlement.

[Footnote 8: Cassiodorus (Variar. l. xi. Epist. i. p. 238) has compared the regencies of Placidia and Amalasuntha. He arraigns the weakness of the mother of Valentinian, and praises the virtues of his royal mistress. On this occasion, flattery seems to have spoken the language of truth.]

[Footnote 9: Philostorgius, l. xii. c. 12, and Godefroy's Dissertat. p. 493, &c.; and Renatus Frigeridus, apud Gregor. Turon. l. ii. c. 8, in tom. ii. p. 163. The father of Aetius was Gaudentius, an illustrious citizen of the province of Scythia, and master-general of the cavalry; his mother was a rich and noble Italian. From his earliest youth, Aetius, as a soldier and a hostage, had conversed with the Barbarians.]

[Footnote 10: For the character of Boniface, see Olympiodorus, apud Phot. p. 196; and St. Augustin apud Tillemont, Memoires Eccles. tom. xiii. p. 712-715, 886. The bishop of Hippo at length deplored the fall of his friend, who, after a solemn vow of chastity, had married a second wife of the Arian sect, and who was suspected of keeping several concubines in his house.]

[Footnote 11: Procopius (de Bell. Vandal. l. i. c. 3, 4, p. 182-186) relates the fraud of Aetius, the revolt of Boniface, and the loss of Africa. This anecdote, which is supported by some collateral testimony, (see Ruinart, Hist. Persecut. Vandal. p. 420, 421,) seems agreeable to the practice of ancient and modern courts, and would be naturally revealed by the repentance of Boniface.]

After the retreat of the Goths, the authority of Honorius had obtained a precarious establishment in Spain; except only in the province of Gallicia, where the Suevi and the Vandals had fortified their camps, in mutual discord and hostile independence. The Vandals prevailed; and their adversaries were besieged in the Nervasian hills, between Leon and Oviedo, till the approach of Count Asterius compelled, or rather provoked, the victorious Barbarians to remove the scene of the war to the plains of Boetica. The rapid progress of the Vandals soon acquired a more effectual opposition; and the master-general Castinus marched against them with a numerous army of Romans and Goths. Vanquished in battle by an inferior army, Castinus fled with dishonor to Tarragona; and this memorable defeat, which has been represented as the punishment, was most probably the effect, of his rash presumption. [12] Seville and Carthagena became the reward, or rather the prey, of the ferocious conquerors; and the vessels which they found in the harbor of Carthagena might easily transport them to the Isles of Majorca and Minorca, where the Spanish fugitives, as in a secure recess, had vainly concealed their families and their fortunes. The experience of navigation, and perhaps the prospect of Africa, encouraged the Vandals to accept the invitation which they received from Count Boniface; and the death of Gonderic served only to forward and animate the bold enterprise. In the room of a prince not conspicuous for any superior powers of the mind or body, they acquired his bastard brother, the terrible Genseric; [13] a name, which, in the destruction of the Roman empire, has deserved an equal rank with the names of Alaric and Attila. The king of the Vandals is described to have been of a middle stature, with a lameness in one leg, which he had contracted by an accidental fall from his horse. His slow and cautious speech seldom declared the deep purposes of his soul; he disdained to imitate the luxury of the vanquished; but he indulged the sterner passions of anger and revenge. The ambition of Genseric was without bounds and without scruples; and the warrior could dexterously employ the dark engines of policy to solicit the allies who might be useful to his success, or to scatter among his enemies the seeds of hatred and contention. Almost in the moment of his departure he was informed that Hermanric, king of the Suevi, had presumed to ravage the Spanish territories, which he was resolved to abandon.

Impatient of the insult, Genseric pursued the hasty retreat of the Suevi as far as Merida; precipitated the king and his army into the River Anas, and calmly returned to the sea-shore to embark his victorious troops. The vessels which transported the Vandals over the modern Straits of Gibraltar, a channel only twelve miles in breadth, were furnished by the Spaniards, who anxiously wished their departure; and by the African general, who had implored their formidable assistance. [14]

[Footnote 12: See the Chronicles of Prosper and Idatius. Salvian (de Gubernat. Dei, l. vii. p. 246, Paris, 1608) ascribes the victory of the Vandals to their superior piety. They fasted, they prayed, they carried a Bible in the front of the Host, with the design, perhaps, of reproaching the perfidy and sacrilege of their enemies.]

[Footnote 13: Gizericus (his name is variously expressed) statura mediocris et equi casu claudicans, animo profundus, sermone rarus, luxuriae contemptor, ira turbidus, habendi cupidus, ad solicitandas gentes providentissimus, semina contentionum jacere, odia miscere paratus. Jornandes, de Rebus Geticis, c. 33, p. 657. This portrait, which is drawn with some skill, and a strong likeness, must have been copied from the Gothic history of Cassiodorus.]

[Footnote 14: See the Chronicle of Idatius. That bishop, a Spaniard and a contemporary, places the passage of the Vandals in the month of May, of the year of Abraham, (which commences in October,) 2444. This date, which coincides with A.D. 429, is confirmed by Isidore, another Spanish bishop, and is justly preferred to the opinion of those writers who have marked for that event one of the two preceding years. See Pagi Critica, tom. ii. p. 205, &c.]

Our fancy, so long accustomed to exaggerate and multiply the martial swarms of Barbarians that seemed to issue from the North, will perhaps be surprised by the account of the army which Genseric mustered on the coast of Mauritania. The Vandals, who in twenty years had penetrated from the Elbe to Mount Atlas, were united under the command of their warlike king; and he reigned with equal authority over the Alani, who had passed, within the term of human life, from the cold of Scythia to the excessive heat of an African climate. The hopes of the bold enterprise had excited many brave adventurers of the Gothic nation; and many desperate provincials were tempted to repair their fortunes by the same means which had occasioned their ruin. Yet this various multitude amounted only to fifty thousand effective men; and though Genseric artfully magnified his apparent strength, by appointing eighty chinarchs, or commanders of thousands, the fallacious increase of old men, of children, and of slaves, would scarcely have swelled his army to the number of four-score thousand persons. [15] But his own dexterity, and the discontents of Africa, soon fortified the Vandal powers, by the accession of numerous and active allies. The parts of Mauritania which border on the Great Desert and the Atlantic Ocean, were filled with a fierce and untractable race of men, whose savage temper had been exasperated, rather than reclaimed, by their dread of the Roman arms. The wandering Moors, [16] as they gradually ventured to approach the seashore, and the camp of the Vandals, must have viewed with terror and astonishment the dress, the armor, the martial pride and discipline of the unknown strangers who had landed on their coast; and the fair complexions of the blue-eyed warriors of Germany formed a very singular contrast with the swarthy or olive hue which is derived from the neighborhood of the torrid zone. After the first difficulties had in some measure been removed, which arose from the mutual ignorance of their respective language, the Moors, regardless of any future consequence, embraced the alliance of the enemies of Rome; and a crowd of naked savages rushed from the woods and valleys of Mount Atlas, to satiate their revenge on the polished tyrants, who had injuriously expelled them from the native sovereignty of the land.

[Footnote 15: Compare Procopius (de Bell. Vandal. l. i. c. 5, p. 190) and Victor Vitensis, (de Persecutione Vandal. l. i. c. 1, p. 3, edit. Ruinart.) We are assured by Idatius, that Genseric evacuated Spain, cum Vandalis omnibus eorumque familiis; and Possidius (in Vit. Augustin. c. 28, apud Ruinart, p. 427) describes his army as manus ingens immanium gentium Vandalorum et Alanorum, commixtam secum babens Gothorum gentem, aliarumque diversarum personas.]

[Footnote 16: For the manners of the Moors, see Procopius, (de Bell. Vandal. l. ii. c. 6, p. 249;) for their figure and complexion, M. de Buffon, (Histoire Naturelle, tom. iii. p. 430.) Procopius says in general, that the Moors had joined the Vandals before the death of Valentinian, (de Bell. Vandal. l. i. c. 5, p. 190;) and it is probable that the independent tribes did not embrace any uniform system of policy.]

The persecution of the Donatists [17] was an event not less favorable to the designs of Genseric. Seventeen years before he landed in Africa, a public conference was held at Carthage, by the order of the magistrate. The Catholics were satisfied, that, after the invincible reasons which they had alleged, the obstinacy of the schismatics must be inexcusable and voluntary; and the emperor Honorius was persuaded to inflict the most rigorous penalties on a faction which had so long abused his patience and clemency. Three hundred bishops, [18] with many thousands of the inferior clergy, were torn from their churches, stripped of their ecclesiastical possessions, banished to the islands, and proscribed by the laws, if they presumed to conceal themselves in the provinces of Africa. Their numerous congregations, both in cities and in the country, were deprived of the rights of citizens, and of the exercise of religious worship. A regular scale of fines, from ten to two hundred pounds of silver, was curiously ascertained, according to the distinction of rank and fortune, to punish the crime of assisting at a schismatic conventicle; and if the fine had been levied five times, without subduing the obstinacy of the offender, his future punishment was referred to the discretion of the Imperial court. [19] By these severities, which obtained the warmest approbation of St. Augustin, [20] great numbers of Donatists were reconciled to the Catholic Church; but the fanatics, who still persevered in their opposition, were provoked to madness and despair; the distracted country was filled with tumult and bloodshed; the armed troops of Circumcellions alternately pointed their rage against themselves, or against their adversaries; and the calendar of martyrs received on both sides a considerable augmentation. [21] Under these circumstances, Genseric, a Christian, but an enemy of the orthodox communion, showed himself to the Donatists as a powerful deliverer, from whom they might reasonably expect the repeal of the odious and oppressive edicts of the Roman emperors. [22] The conquest of Africa was facilitated by the active zeal, or the secret favor, of a domestic faction; the wanton outrages against the churches and the clergy of which the Vandals are accused, may be fairly imputed to the fanaticism of their allies; and the intolerant spirit which disgraced the triumph of Christianity, contributed to the loss of the most important province of the West. [23]

[Footnote 17: See Tillemont, Memoires Eccles. tom. xiii. p. 516-558; and the whole series of the persecution, in the original monuments, published by Dupin at the end of Optatus, p. 323-515.]

[Footnote 18: The Donatist Bishops, at the conference of Carthage, amounted to 279; and they asserted that their whole number was not less than 400. The Catholics had 286 present, 120 absent, besides sixty four vacant bishoprics.]

[Footnote 19: The fifth title of the sixteenth book of the Theodosian Code exhibits a series of the Imperial laws against the Donatists, from the year 400 to the year 428. Of these the 54th law, promulgated by Honorius, A.D. 414, is the most severe and effectual.]

[Footnote 20: St. Augustin altered his opinion with regard tosthe proper treatment of heretics. His pathetic declaration of pity and indulgence for the Manichaeans, has been inserted by Mr. Locke (vol. iii. p. 469) among the choice specimens of his common-place book. Another philosopher, the celebrated Bayle, (tom. ii. p. 445-496,) has refuted, with superfluous diligence and ingenuity, the arguments by which the bishop of Hippo justified, in his old age, the persecution of the Donatists.]

[Footnote 21: See Tillemont, Mem. Eccles. tom. xiii. p. 586-592, 806. The Donatists boasted of thousands of these voluntary martyrs. Augustin asserts, and probably with truth, that these numbers were much exaggerated; but he sternly maintains, that it was better that some should burn themselves in this world, than that all should burn in hell flames.]

[Footnote 22: According to St. Augustin and Theodoret, the Donatists were inclined to the principles, or at least to the party, of the Arians, which Genseric supported. Tillemont, Mem. Eccles. tom. vi. p. 68.]

[Footnote 23: See Baronius, Annal. Eccles. A.D. 428, No. 7, A.D. 439, No. 35. The cardinal, though more inclined to seek the cause of great events in heaven than on the earth, has observed the apparent connection of the Vandals and the Donatists. Under the reign of the Barbarians, the schismatics of Africa enjoyed an obscure peace of one hundred years; at the end of which we may again trace them by the fight of the Imperial persecutions. See Tillemont, Mem. Eccles. tom. vi. p. 192. &c.]

The court and the people were astonished by the strange intelligence, that a virtuous hero, after so many favors, and so many services, had renounced his allegiance, and invited the Barbarians to destroy the province intrusted to his command. The friends of Boniface, who still believed that his criminal behavior might be excused by some honorable motive, solicited, during the absence of Aetius, a free conference with the Count of Africa; and Darius, an officer of high distinction, was named for the important embassy. [24] In their first interview at Carthage, the imaginary provocations were mutually explained; the opposite letters of Aetius were produced and compared; and the fraud was easily detected. Placidia and Boniface lamented their fatal error; and the count had sufficient magnanimity to confide in the forgiveness of his sovereign, or to expose his head to her future resentment. His repentance was fervent and sincere; but he soon discovered that it was no longer in his power to restore the edifice which he had shaken to its foundations. Carthage and the Roman garrisons returned with their general to the allegiance of Valentinian; but the rest of Africa was still distracted with war and faction; and the inexorable king of the Vandals, disdaining all terms of accommodation, sternly refused to relinquish the possession of his prey. The band of veterans who marched under the standard of Boniface, and his hasty levies of provincial troops, were defeated with considerable loss; the victorious Barbarians insulted the open country; and Carthage, Cirta, and Hippo Regius, were the only cities that appeared to rise above the general inundation.

[Footnote 24: In a confidential letter to Count Boniface, St. Augustin, without examining the grounds of the quarrel, piously exhorts him to discharge the duties of a Christian and a subject: to extricate himself *without delay from his dangerous and guilty situation; and even, if he could obtain the consent of his wife, to embrace a life of celibacy and penance, (Tillemont, Mem. Eccles. tom. xiii. p. 890.) The bishop was intimately connected with Darius, the minister of peace, (Id. tom. xiii. p. 928.)]*

The long and narrow tract of the African coast was filled with frequent monuments of Roman art and magnificence; and the respective degrees of improvement might be accurately measured by the distance from Carthage and the Mediterranean. A simple reflection will impress every thinking mind with the clearest idea of fertility and cultivation: the country was extremely populous; the inhabitants reserved a liberal subsistence for their own use; and the annual exportation, particularly of wheat, was so regular and plentiful, that Africa deserved the name of the common granary of Rome and of mankind. On a sudden the seven fruitful provinces, from Tangier to Tripoli, were overwhelmed by the invasion of the Vandals; whose destructive rage has perhaps been exaggerated by popular animosity, religious zeal, and extravagant declamation. War, in its fairest form, implies a perpetual violation of humanity and justice; and the hostilities of Barbarians are inflamed by the fierce and lawless spirit which incessantly disturbs their peaceful and domestic society. The Vandals, where they found resistance, seldom gave quarter; and the deaths of their valiant countrymen were expiated by the ruin of the cities under whose walls they had fallen. Careless of the distinctions of age, or sex, or rank, they employed every species of indignity and torture, to force from the captives a discovery of their hidden wealth. The stern policy of Genseric justified his frequent examples of military execution: he was not always the master of his own passions, or of those of his followers; and the calamities of war were aggravated by the licentiousness of the Moors, and the fanaticism of the Donatists. Yet I shall not easily be persuaded, that it was the common practice of the Vandals to extirpate the olives, and other fruit trees, of a country where they intended to settle: nor can I believe that it was a usual stratagem to slaughter great numbers of their prisoners before the walls of a besieged city, for the sole purpose of infecting the air, and producing a pestilence, of which they themselves must have been the first victims. [25]

[Footnote 25: The original complaints of the desolation of Africa are contained 1. In a letter from Capreolus, bishop of Carthage, to excuse his absence from the council of Ephesus, (ap. Ruinart, p. 427.) 2. In the life of St. Augustin, by his friend and colleague Possidius, (ap. Ruinart, p. 427.) 3. In the history of the Vandalic persecution, by Victor Vitensis, (l. i. c. 1, 2, 3, edit. Ruinart.) The last picture, which was drawn sixty years after the event, is more expressive of the author's passions than of the truth of facts.]

The generous mind of Count Boniface was tortured by the exquisite distress of beholding the ruin which he had occasioned, and whose rapid progress he was unable to check. After the loss of a battle he retired into Hippo Regius; where he was immediately besieged by an enemy, who considered him as the real bulwark of Africa. The maritime colony of Hippo, [26] about two hundred miles westward of Carthage, had formerly acquired the distinguishing epithet of Regius, from the residence of Numidian kings; and some remains of trade and populousness still adhere to the modern city, which is known in Europe by the corrupted name of Bona. The military labors, and anxious reflections, of Count Boniface, were alleviated by the edifying conversation of his friend St. Augustin; [27] till that bishop, the light and pillar of the Catholic church, was gently released, in the third month of the siege, and in the seventy-sixth year of his age, from the actual and the impending calamities of his country. The youth of Augustin had been stained by the vices and errors which he so ingenuously confesses; but from the moment of his conversion to that of his death, the manners of the bishop of Hippo were pure and austere: and the most conspicuous of his virtues was an ardent zeal against heretics of every denomination; the Manichaeans, the Donatists, and the Pelagians, against whom he waged a perpetual controversy. When the city, some months after his death, was burnt by the Vandals, the library was fortunately saved, which contained his voluminous writings; two hundred and thirty-two separate books or treatises on theological subjects, besides a complete exposition of the psalter and the gospel, and a copious magazine of epistles and homilies. [28] According to the judgment of the most impartial critics, the superficial learning of Augustin was confined to the Latin language; [29] and his style, though sometimes animated by the eloquence of passion, is usually clouded by false and affected rhetoric. But he possessed a strong, capacious, argumentative mind; he boldly sounded the dark abyss of grace, predestination, free will, and original sin; and the rigid system of Christianity which he framed or restored, [30] has been entertained, with public applause, and secret reluctance, by the Latin church. [31]

[Footnote 26: See Cellarius, Geograph. Antiq. tom. ii. part ii. p. 112. Leo African. in Ramusio, tom. i. fol. 70. L'Afrique de Marmol, tom. ii. p. 434, 437. Shaw's Travels, p. 46, 47. The old Hippo Regius was finally destroyed by the Arabs in the seventh century; but a new town, at the distance of two miles, was built with the materials; and it contained, in the sixteenth century, about three hundred families of industrious, but turbulent manufacturers. The adjacent territory is renowned for a pure air, a fertile soil, and plenty of exquisite fruits.]

[Footnote 27: The life of St. Augustin, by Tillemont, fills a quarto volume (Mem. Eccles. tom. xiii.) of more than one thousand pages; and the diligence of that learned Jansenist was excited, on this occasion, by factious and devout zeal for the founder of his sect.]

[Footnote 28: Such, at least, is the account of Victor Vitensis, (de Persecut. Vandal. l. i. c. 3;) though Gennadius seems to doubt whether any person had read, or even collected, all the works of St. Augustin, (see Hieronym. Opera, tom. i. p. 319, in Catalog. Scriptor. Eccles.) They have been repeatedly printed; and Dupin (Bibliotheque Eccles. tom. iii. p. 158-257) has given a large and satisfactory abstract of them as they stand in the last edition of the Benedictines. My personal acquaintance with the bishop of Hippo does not extend beyond the Confessions, and the City of God.]

[Footnote 29: In his early youth (Confess. i. 14) St. Augustin disliked and neglected the study of Greek; and he frankly owns that he read the Platonists in a Latin version, (Confes. vii. 9.) Some modern critics have thought, that his ignorance of Greek disqualified him from expounding the Scriptures; and Cicero or Quintilian would have required the knowledge of that language in a professor of rhetoric.]

[Footnote 30: These questions were seldom agitated, from the time of St. Paul to that of St. Augustin. I am informed that the Greek fathers maintain the natural sentiments of the Semi-Pelagians; and that the orthodoxy of St. Augustin was derived from the Manichaean school.]

[Footnote 31: The church of Rome has canonized Augustin, and reprobated Calvin. Yet as the real difference between them is invisible even to a theological microscope, the Molinists are oppressed by the authority of the saint, and the Jansenists are disgraced by their resemblance to the heretic. In the mean while, the Protestant Arminians stand aloof, and deride the mutual perplexity of the disputants, (see a curious Review of the Controversy, by Le Clerc, Bibliotheque Universelle, tom. xiv. p. 144-398.) Perhaps a reasoner still more independent may smile in his turn, when he peruses an Arminian Commentary on the Epistle to the Romans.]

PART II

By the skill of Boniface, and perhaps by the ignorance of the Vandals, the siege of Hippo was protracted above fourteen months: the sea was continually open; and when the adjacent country had been exhausted by irregular rapine, the besiegers themselves were compelled by famine to relinquish their enterprise. The importance and danger of Africa were deeply felt by the regent of the West. Placidia implored the assistance of her eastern ally; and the Italian fleet and army were reenforced by Asper, who sailed from Constantinople with a powerful armament. As soon as the force of the two empires was united under the command of Boniface, he boldly marched against the Vandals; and the loss of a second battle irretrievably decided the fate of Africa. He embarked with the precipitation of despair; and the people of Hippo were permitted, with their families and effects, to occupy the vacant place of the soldiers, the greatest part of whom were either slain or made prisoners by the Vandals. The count, whose fatal credulity had wounded the vitals of the republic, might enter the palace of Ravenna with some anxiety, which was soon removed by the smiles of Placidia. Boniface accepted with gratitude the rank of patrician, and the dignity of master-general of the Roman armies; but he must have blushed at the sight of those medals, in which he was represented with the name and attributes of victory. [32] The discovery of his fraud, the displeasure of the empress, and the distinguished favor of his rival, exasperated the haughty and perfidious soul of Aetius. He hastily returned from Gaul to Italy, with a retinue, or rather with an army, of Barbarian followers; and such was the weakness of the government, that the two generals decided their private quarrel in a bloody battle. Boniface was successful; but he received in the conflict a mortal wound from the spear of his adversary, of which he expired within a few days, in such Christian and charitable sentiments, that he exhorted his wife, a rich heiress of Spain, to accept Aetius for her second husband. But Aetius could not derive any immediate advantage from the generosity of his dying enemy: he was proclaimed a rebel by the justice of Placidia; and though he attempted to defend some strong fortresses, erected on his patrimonial estate, the Imperial power soon compelled him to retire into Pannonia, to the tents of his faithful Huns. The republic was deprived, by their mutual discord, of the service of her two most illustrious champions. [33]

[Footnote 32: Ducange, Fam. Byzant. p. 67. On one side, the head of Valentinian; on the reverse, Boniface, with a scourge in one hand, and a palm in the other, standing in a triumphal car, which is drawn by four horses, or, in another medal, by four stags; an unlucky emblem! I should doubt whether another example can be found of the head of a subject on the reverse of an Imperial medal. See Science des Medailles, by the Pere Jobert, tom. i. p. 132-150, edit. of 1739, by the haron de la Bastie. Note: Lord Mahon, Life of Belisarius, p. 133, mentions one of Belisarius on the authority of Cedrenus—M.]

[Footnote 33: Procopius (de Bell. Vandal. l. i. c. 3, p. 185) continues the history of Boniface no further than his return to Italy. His death is mentioned by Prosper and Marcellinus; the expression of the latter, that Aetius, the day before, had provided himself with a longer spear, implies something like a regular duel.]

It might naturally be expected, after the retreat of Boniface, that the Vandals would achieve, without resistance or delay, the conquest of Africa. Eight years, however, elapsed, from the evacuation of Hippo to the reduction of Carthage. In the midst of that interval, the ambitious Genseric, in the full tide of apparent prosperity, negotiated a treaty of peace, by which he gave his son Hunneric for a hostage; and consented to leave the Western emperor in the undisturbed possession of the three Mauritanias. [34] This moderation, which cannot be imputed to the justice, must be ascribed to the policy, of the conqueror.

His throne was encompassed with domestic enemies, who accused the baseness of his birth, and asserted the legitimate claims of his nephews, the sons of Gonderic. Those nephews, indeed, he sacrificed to his safety; and their mother, the widow of the deceased king, was precipitated, by his order, into the river Ampsaga. But the public discontent burst forth in dangerous and frequent conspiracies; and the warlike tyrant is supposed to have shed more Vandal blood by the hand of the executioner, than in the field of battle. [35] The convulsions of Africa, which had favored his attack, opposed the firm establishment of his power; and the various seditions of the Moors and Germans, the Donatists and Catholics, continually disturbed, or threatened, the unsettled reign of the conqueror. As he advanced towards Carthage, he was forced to withdraw his troops from the Western provinces; the sea-coast was exposed to the naval enterprises of the Romans of Spain and Italy; and, in the heart of Numidia, the strong inland city of Corta still persisted in obstinate independence. [36] These difficulties were gradually subdued by the spirit, the perseverance, and the cruelty of Genseric; who alternately applied the arts of peace and war to the establishment of his African kingdom. He subscribed a solemn treaty, with the hope of deriving some advantage from the term of its continuance, and the moment of its violation. The vigilance of his enemies was relaxed by the protestations of friendship, which concealed his hostile approach; and Carthage was at length surprised by the Vandals, five hundred and eighty-five years after the destruction of the city and republic by the younger Scipio. [37]

[Footnote 34: See Procopius, de Bell. Vandal. l. i. c 4, p. 186. Valentinian published several humane laws, to relieve the distress of his Numidian and Mauritanian subjects; he discharged them, in a great measure, from the payment of their debts, reduced their tribute to one eighth, and gave them a right of appeal from their provincial magistrates to the praefect of Rome. Cod. Theod. tom. vi. Novell. p. 11, 12.]

[Footnote 35: Victor Vitensis, de Persecut. Vandal. l. ii. c. 5, p. 26. The cruelties of Genseric towards his subjects are strongly expressed in Prosper's Chronicle, A.D. 442.]

[Footnote 36: Possidius, in Vit. Augustin. c. 28, apud Ruinart, p. 428.]

[Footnote 37: See the Chronicles of Idatius, Isidore, Prosper, and Marcellinus. They mark the same year, but different days, for the surprisal of Carthage.]

A new city had arisen from its ruins, with the title of a colony; and though Carthage might yield to the royal prerogatives of Constantinople, and perhaps to the trade of Alexandria, or the splendor of Antioch, she still maintained the second rank in the West; as the Rome (if we may use the style of contemporaries) of the African world. That wealthy and opulent metropolis [38] displayed, in a dependent condition, the image of a flourishing republic. Carthage contained the manufactures, the arms, and the treasures of the six provinces. A regular subordination of civil honors gradually ascended from the procurators of the streets and quarters of the city, to the tribunal of the supreme magistrate, who, with the title of proconsul, represented the state and dignity of a consul of ancient Rome. Schools and gymnasia were instituted for the education of the African youth; and the liberal arts and manners, grammar, rhetoric, and philosophy, were publicly taught in the Greek and Latin languages. The buildings of Carthage were uniform and magnificent; a shady grove was planted in the midst of the capital; the new port, a secure and capacious harbor, was subservient to the commercial industry of citizens and strangers; and the splendid games of the circus and theatre were exhibited almost in the presence of the Barbarians. The reputation of the Carthaginians was not equal to that of their country, and the reproach of Punic faith still adhered to their subtle and faithless character. [39] The habits of trade, and the abuse of luxury, had corrupted their manners; but their impious contempt of monks, and the shameless practice of unnatural lusts, are the two abominations which excite the pious vehemence of Salvian, the preacher of the age. [40] The king of the Vandals severely reformed the vices of a voluptuous people; and the ancient, noble, ingenuous freedom of Carthage (these expressions of Victor are not without energy) was reduced by Genseric into a state of ignominious servitude. After he had permitted his licentious troops to satiate their rage and avarice, he instituted a more regular system of rapine and oppression. An edict was promulgated, which enjoined all persons, without fraud or delay, to deliver their gold, silver, jewels, and valuable furniture or apparel, to the royal officers; and the attempt to secrete any part of their patrimony was inexorably punished with death and torture, as an act of treason against the state. The lands of the proconsular province, which formed the immediate district of Carthage, were accurately measured, and divided among the Barbarians; and the conqueror reserved for his peculiar domain the fertile territory of Byzacium, and the adjacent parts of Numidia and Getulia. [41]

[Footnote 38: The picture of Carthage; as it flourished in the fourth and fifth centuries, is taken from the Expositio totius Mundi, p. 17, 18, in the third volume of Hudson's Minor Geographers, from Ausonius de Claris Urbibus, p. 228, 229; and principally from Salvian, de Gubernatione Dei, l. vii. p. 257, 258.]

[Footnote 39: The anonymous author of the Expositio totius Mundi compares in his barbarous Latin, the country and the inhabitants; and, after stigmatizing their want of faith, he coolly concludes, Difficile autem inter eos invenitur bonus, tamen in multis pauci boni esse possunt P. 18.]

[Footnote 40: He declares, that the peculiar vices of each country were collected in the sink of Carthage, (l. vii. p. 257.) In the indulgence of vice, the Africans applauded their manly virtue. Et illi se magis virilis fortitudinis esse crederent, qui maxime vires foeminei usus probositate fregissent, (p. 268.) The streets of Carthage were polluted by effeminate wretches, who publicly assumed the countenance, the dress, and the character of women, (p. 264.) If a monk appeared in the city, the holy man was pursued with impious scorn and ridicule; de testantibus ridentium cachinnis, (p. 289.)]

[Footnote 41: Compare Procopius de Bell. Vandal. l. i. c. 5, p. 189, 190, and Victor Vitensis, de Persecut Vandal. l. i. c. 4.]

It was natural enough that Genseric should hate those whom he had injured: the nobility and senators of Carthage were exposed to his jealousy and resentment; and all those who refused the ignominious terms, which their honor and religion forbade them to accept, were compelled by the Arian tyrant to embrace the condition of perpetual banishment. Rome, Italy, and the provinces of the East, were filled with a crowd of exiles, of fugitives, and of ingenuous captives, who solicited the public compassion; and the benevolent epistles of Theodoret still preserve the names and misfortunes of Caelestian and Maria. [42] The Syrian bishop deplores the misfortunes of Caelestian, who, from the state of a noble and opulent senator of Carthage, was reduced, with his wife and family, and servants, to beg his bread in a foreign country; but he applauds the resignation of the Christian exile, and the philosophic temper, which, under the pressure of such calamities, could enjoy more real happiness than was the ordinary lot of wealth and prosperity. The story of Maria, the daughter of the magnificent Eudaemon, is singular and interesting. In the sack of Carthage, she was purchased from the Vandals by some merchants of Syria, who afterwards sold her as a slave in their native country. A female attendant, transported in the same ship, and sold in the same family, still continued to respect a mistress whom fortune had reduced to the common level of servitude; and the daughter of Eudaemon received from her grateful affection the domestic services which she had once required from her obedience. This remarkable behavior divulged the real condition of Maria, who, in the absence of the bishop of Cyrrhus, was redeemed from slavery oy the generosity of some soldiers of the garrison. The liberality of Theodoret provided for her decent maintenance; and she passed ten months among the deaconesses of the church; till she was unexpectedly informed, that her father, who had escaped from the ruin of Carthage, exercised an honorable office in one of the Western provinces. Her filial impatience was seconded by the pious bishop: Theodoret, in a letter still extant, recommends Maria to the bishop of Aegae, a maritime city of Cilicia, which was frequented, during the annual fair, by the vessels of the West; most earnestly requesting, that his colleague would use the maiden with a tenderness suitable to her birth; and that he would intrust her to the care of such faithful merchants, as would esteem it a sufficient gain, if they restored a daughter, lost beyond all human hope, to the arms of her afflicted parent.

[Footnote 42: Ruinart (p. 441-457) has collected from Theodoret, and other authors, the misfortunes, real and fabulous, of the inhabitants of Carthage.]

Among the insipid legends of ecclesiastical history, I am tempted to distinguish the memorable fable of the Seven Sleepers; [43] whose imaginary date corresponds with the reign of the younger Theodosius, and the conquest of Africa by the Vandals. [44] When the emperor Decius persecuted the Christians, seven noble youths of Ephesus concealed themselves in a spacious cavern in the side of an adjacent mountain; where they were doomed to perish by the tyrant, who gave orders that the entrance should be firmly secured by the a pile of huge stones. They immediately fell into a deep slumber, which was miraculously prolonged without injuring the powers of life, during a period of one hundred and eighty-seven years. At the end of that time, the slaves of Adolius, to whom the inheritance of the mountain had descended, removed the stones to supply materials for some rustic edifice: the light of the sun darted into the cavern, and the Seven Sleepers were permitted to awake. After a slumber, as they thought of a few hours, they were pressed by the calls of hunger; and resolved that Jamblichus, one of their number, should secretly return to the city to purchase bread for the use of his companions. The youth (if we may still employ that appellation) could no longer recognize the once familiar aspect of his native country; and his surprise was increased by the appearance of a large cross, triumphantly erected over the principal gate of Ephesus. His singular dress, and obsolete language, confounded the baker, to whom he offered an ancient medal of Decius as the current coin of the empire; and Jamblichus, on the suspicion of a secret treasure, was dragged before the judge. Their mutual inquiries produced the amazing discovery, that two centuries were almost elapsed since Jamblichus and his friends had escaped from the rage of a Pagan tyrant. The bishop of Ephesus, the clergy, the magistrates, the people, and, as it is said, the emperor Theodosius himself, hastened to visit the cavern of the Seven Sleepers; who bestowed their benediction, related their story, and at the same instant peaceably expired. The origin of this marvellous fable cannot be ascribed to the pious fraud and credulity of the modern Greeks, since the authentic tradition may be traced within half a century of the supposed miracle. James of Sarug, a Syrian bishop, who was born only two years after the death of the younger Theodosius, has devoted one of his two hundred and thirty homilies to the praise of the young men of Ephesus. [45] Their legend, before the end of the sixth century, was translated from the Syriac into the Latin language, by the care of Gregory of Tours. The hostile communions of the East preserve their memory with equal reverence; and their names are honorably inscribed in the Roman, the Abyssinian, and the Russian calendar. [46] Nor has their reputation been confined to the Christian world. This popular tale, which Mahomet might learn when he drove his camels to the fairs of Syria, is introduced as a divine revelation, into the Koran. [47] The story of the Seven Sleepers has been adopted and adorned by the nations, from Bengal to Africa, who profess the Mahometan religion; [48] and some vestiges of a similar tradition have been discovered in the remote extremities of Scandinavia. [49] This easy and universal belief, so expressive of the sense of mankind, may be ascribed to the genuine merit of the fable itself. We imperceptibly advance from youth to age, without observing the gradual, but incessant, change of human affairs; and even in our larger experience of history, the imagination is accustomed, by a perpetual series of causes and effects, to unite the most distant revolutions. But if the interval between two memorable aeras could be instantly annihilated; if it were possible, after a momentary slumber of two hundred years, to display the new world to the eyes of a spectator, who still retained a lively and recent impression of the old, his surprise and his reflections would furnish the pleasing subject of a philosophical romance. The scene could not be more advantageously placed, than in the two centuries which elapsed between the reigns of Decius and of Theodosius the Younger. During this period, the seat of government had been transported from Rome to a new city on the banks of the Thracian Bosphorus; and the abuse of military spirit had been suppressed by an artificial system of tame and ceremonious servitude. The throne of the persecuting Decius was filled by a succession of Christian and orthodox princes, who had extirpated the fabulous gods of antiquity: and the public devotion of the age was impatient to exalt the saints and martyrs of the Catholic church, on the altars of Diana and Hercules. The union of the Roman empire was dissolved; its genius was humbled in the dust; and armies of unknown Barbarians, issuing from the frozen regions of the North, had established their victorious reign over the fairest provinces of Europe and Africa.

[Footnote 43: The choice of fabulous circumstances is of small importance; yet I have confined myself to the narrative which was translated from the Syriac by the care of Gregory of Tours, (de Gloria Martyrum, l. i. c. 95, in Max. Bibliotheca Patrum, tom. xi. p. 856,) to the Greek acts of their martyrdom (apud Photium, p. 1400, 1401) and to the Annals of the Patriarch Eutychius, (tom. i. p. 391, 531, 532, 535, Vers. Pocock.)]

[Footnote 44: Two Syriac writers, as they are quoted by Assemanni, (Bibliot. Oriental. tom. i. p. 336, 338,) place the resurrection of the Seven Sleepers in the year 736 (A.D. 425) or 748, (A.D. 437,) of the aera of the Seleucides. Their Greek acts, which Photius had read, assign the date of the thirty-eighth year of the reign of Theodosius, which may coincide either with A.D. 439, or 446. The period which had elapsed since the persecution of Decius is easily ascertained; and nothing less than the ignorance of Mahomet, or the legendaries, could suppose an internal of three or four hundred years.]

[Footnote 45: James, one of the orthodox fathers of the Syrian church, was born A.D. 452; he began to compose his sermons A.D. 474; he was made bishop of Batnae, in the district of Sarug, and province of Mesopotamia, A.D. 519, and died A.D. 521. (Assemanni, tom. i. p. 288, 289.) For the homily de Pueris Ephesinis, see p. 335-339: though I could wish that Assemanni had translated the text of James of Sarug, instead of answering the objections of Baronius.]

[Footnote 46: See the Acta Sanctorum of the Bollandists, Mensis Julii, tom. vi. p. 375-397. This immense calendar of Saints, in one hundred and twenty-six years, (1644-1770,) and in fifty volumes in folio, has advanced no further than the 7th day of October. The suppression of the Jesuits has most probably checked an undertaking, which, through the medium of fable and superstition, communicates much historical and philosophical instruction.]

[Footnote 47: See Maracci Alcoran. Sura xviii. tom. ii. p. 420-427, and tom. i. part iv. p. 103. With such an ample privilege, Mahomet has not shown much taste or ingenuity. He has invented the dog (Al Rakim) the Seven Sleepers; the respect of the sun, who altered his course twice a day, that he might not shine into the cavern; and the care of God himself, who preserved their bodies from putrefaction, by turning them to the right and left.]

[Footnote 48: See D'Herbelot, Bibliotheque Orientale, p. 139; and Renaudot, Hist. Patriarch. Alexandrin. p. 39, 40.]

[Footnote 49: Paul, the deacon of Aquileia, (de Gestis Langobardorum, l. i. c. 4, p. 745, 746, edit. Grot.,) who lived towards the end of the eight century, has placed in a cavern, under a rock, on the shore of the ocean, the Seven Sleepers of the North, whose long repose was respected by the Barbarians. Their dress declared them to be Romans and the deacon conjectures, that they were reserved by Providence as the future apostles of those unbelieving countries.]

CHAPTER XXXIV

ATTILA

PART I

THE CHARACTER, CONQUESTS, AND COURT OF ATTILA, KING OF THE HUNS—DEATH OF THEODOSIUS THE YOUNGER—ELEVATION OF MARCIAN TO THE EMPIRE OF THE EAST

The Western world was oppressed by the Goths and Vandals, who fled before the Huns; but the achievements of the Huns themselves were not adequate to their power and prosperity. Their victorious hordes had spread from the Volga to the Danube; but the public force was exhausted by the discord of independent chieftains; their valor was idly consumed in obscure and predatory excursions; and they often degraded their national dignity, by condescending, for the hopes of spoil, to enlist under the banners of their fugitive enemies. In the reign of Attila, [1] the Huns again became the terror of the world; and I shall now describe the character and actions of that formidable Barbarian; who alternately insulted and invaded the East and the West, and urged the rapid downfall of the Roman empire.

[Footnote 1: The authentic materials for the history of Attila, may be found in Jornandes (de Rebus Geticis, c. 34-50, p. 668-688, edit. Grot.) and Priscus (Excerpta de Legationibus, p. 33-76, Paris, 1648.) I have not seen the Lives of Attila, composed by Juvencus Caelius Calanus Dalmatinus, in the twelfth century, or by Nicholas Olahus, archbishop of Gran, in the sixteenth. See Mascou's History of the Germans, ix., and Maffei Osservazioni Litterarie, tom. i. p. 88, 89. Whatever the modern Hungarians have added must be fabulous; and they do not seem to have excelled in the art of fiction. They suppose, that when Attila invaded Gaul and Italy, married innumerable wives, &c., he was one hundred and twenty years of age. Thewrocz Chron. c. i. p. 22, in Script. Hunger. tom. i. p. 76.]

In the tide of emigration which impetuously rolled from the confines of China to those of Germany, the most powerful and populous tribes may commonly be found on the verge of the Roman provinces. The accumulated weight was sustained for a while by artificial barriers; and the easy condescension of the emperors invited, without satisfying, the insolent demands of the Barbarians, who had acquired an eager appetite for the luxuries of civilized life. The Hungarians, who ambitiously insert the name of Attila among their native kings, may affirm with truth that the hordes, which were subject to his uncle Roas, or Rugilas, had formed their encampments within the limits of modern Hungary, [2] in a fertile country, which liberally supplied the wants of a nation of hunters and shepherds. In this advantageous situation, Rugilas, and his valiant brothers, who continually added to their power and reputation, commanded the alternative of peace or war with the two empires. His alliance with the Romans of the West was cemented by his personal friendship for the great Aetius; who was always secure of finding, in the Barbarian camp, a hospitable reception and a powerful support. At his solicitation, and in the name of John the usurper, sixty thousand Huns advanced to the confines of Italy; their march and their retreat were alike expensive to the state; and the grateful policy of Aetius abandoned the possession of Pannonia to his faithful confederates. The Romans of the East were not less apprehensive of the arms of Rugilas, which threatened the provinces, or even the capital. Some ecclesiastical historians have destroyed the Barbarians with lightning and pestilence; [3] but Theodosius was reduced to the more humble expedient of stipulating an annual payment of three hundred and fifty pounds of gold, and of disguising this dishonorable tribute by the title of general, which the king of the Huns condescended to accept. The public tranquillity was frequently interrupted by the fierce impatience of the Barbarians, and the perfidious intrigues of the Byzantine court. Four dependent nations, among whom we may distinguish the Barbarians, disclaimed the sovereignty of the Huns; and their revolt was encouraged and protected by a Roman alliance; till the just claims, and formidable power, of Rugilas, were effectually urged by the voice of Eslaw his ambassador. Peace was the unanimous wish of the senate: their decree was ratified by the emperor; and two ambassadors were named, Plinthas, a general of Scythian extraction, but of consular rank; and the quaestor Epigenes, a wise and experienced statesman, who was recommended to that office by his ambitious colleague.

[Footnote 2: *Hungary has been successively occupied by three Scythian colonies. 1. The Huns of Attila; 2. The Abares, in the sixth century; and, 3. The Turks or Magiars, A.D. 889; the immediate and genuine ancestors of the modern Hungarians, whose connection with the two former is extremely faint and remote. The Prodromus and Notitia of Matthew Belius appear to contain a rich fund of information concerning ancient and modern Hungary. I have seen the extracts in Bibli otheque Ancienne et Moderne, tom. xxii. p. 1-51, and Bibliotheque Raisonnee, tom. xvi. p. 127-175. Note: Mailath (in his Geschichte der Magyaren) considers the question of the origin of the Magyars as still undecided. The old Hungarian chronicles unanimously derived them from the Huns of Attila See note, vol. iv. pp. 341, 342. The later opinion, adopted by Schlozer, Belnay, and Dankowsky, ascribes them, from their language, to the Finnish race. Fessler, in his history of Hungary, agrees with Gibbon in supposing them Turks. Mailath has inserted an ingenious dissertation of Fejer, which attempts to connect them with the Parthians. Vol. i. Ammerkungen p. 50—M.*]

[Footnote 3: *Socrates, l. vii. c. 43. Theodoret, l. v. c. 36. Tillemont, who always depends on the faith of his ecclesiastical authors, strenuously contends (Hist. des Emp. tom. vi. p. 136, 607) that the wars and personages were not the same.*]

The death of Rugilas suspended the progress of the treaty. His two nephews, Attila and Bleda, who succeeded to the throne of their uncle, consented to a personal interview with the ambassadors of Constantinople; but as they proudly refused to dismount, the business was transacted on horseback, in a spacious plain near the city of Margus, in the Upper Maesia. The kings of the Huns assumed the solid benefits, as well as the vain honors, of the negotiation. They dictated the conditions of peace, and each condition was an insult on the majesty of the empire. Besides the freedom of a safe and plentiful market on the banks of the Danube, they required that the annual contribution should be augmented from three hundred and fifty to seven hundred pounds of gold; that a fine or ransom of eight pieces of gold should be paid for every Roman captive who had escaped from his Barbarian master; that the emperor should renounce all treaties and engagements with the enemies of the Huns; and that all the fugitives who had taken refuge in the court or provinces of Theodosius, should be delivered to the justice of their offended sovereign. This justice was rigorously inflicted on some unfortunate youths of a royal race. They were crucified on the territories of the empire, by the command of Attila: and as soon as the king of the Huns had impressed the Romans with the terror of his name, he indulged them in a short and arbitrary respite, whilst he subdued the rebellious or independent nations of Scythia and Germany. [4]

[Footnote 4: See Priscus, p. 47, 48, and Hist. de Peuples de l'Europe, tom. v. i. c. xii, xiii, xiv, xv.]

Attila, the son of Mundzuk, deduced his noble, perhaps his regal, descent [5] from the ancient Huns, who had formerly contended with the monarchs of China. His features, according to the observation of a Gothic historian, bore the stamp of his national origin; and the portrait of Attila exhibits the genuine deformity of a modern Calmuk; [6] a large head, a swarthy complexion, small, deep-seated eyes, a flat nose, a few hairs in the place of a beard, broad shoulders, and a short square body, of nervous strength, though of a disproportioned form. The haughty step and demeanor of the king of the Huns expressed the consciousness of his superiority above the rest of mankind; and he had a custom of fiercely rolling his eyes, as if he wished to enjoy the terror which he inspired. Yet this savage hero was not inaccessible to pity; his suppliant enemies might confide in the assurance of peace or pardon; and Attila was considered by his subjects as a just and indulgent master. He delighted in war; but, after he had ascended the throne in a mature age, his head, rather than his hand, achieved the conquest of the North; and the fame of an adventurous soldier was usefully exchanged for that of a prudent and successful general. The effects of personal valor are so inconsiderable, except in poetry or romance, that victory, even among Barbarians, must depend on the degree of skill with which the passions of the multitude are combined and guided for the service of a single man. The Scythian conquerors, Attila and Zingis, surpassed their rude countrymen in art rather than in courage; and it may be observed that the monarchies, both of the Huns and of the Moguls, were erected by their founders on the basis of popular superstition The miraculous conception, which fraud and credulity ascribed to the virgin-mother of Zingis, raised him above the level of human nature; and the naked prophet, who in the name of the Deity invested him with the empire of the earth, pointed the valor of the Moguls with irresistible enthusiasm. [7] The religious arts of Attila were not less skillfully adapted to the character of his age and country. It was natural enough that the Scythians should adore, with peculiar devotion, the god of war; but as they were incapable of forming either an abstract idea, or a corporeal representation, they worshipped their tutelar deity under the symbol of an iron cimeter. [8] One of the shepherds of the Huns perceived, that a heifer, who was grazing, had wounded herself in the foot, and curiously followed the track of the blood, till he discovered, among the long grass, the point of an ancient sword, which he dug out of the ground and presented to Attila. That magnanimous, or rather that artful, prince accepted, with pious gratitude, this celestial favor; and, as the rightful possessor of the sword of Mars, asserted his divine and indefeasible claim to the dominion of the earth. [9] If the rites of Scythia were practised on this solemn occasion, a lofty altar, or rather pile of fagots, three hundred yards in length and in breadth, was raised in a spacious plain; and the sword of Mars was placed erect on the summit of this rustic altar, which was annually consecrated by the blood of sheep, horses, and of the hundredth captive. [10] Whether human sacrifices formed any part of the worship of Attila, or whether he propitiated the god of war with the victims which he continually offered in the field of battle, the favorite of Mars soon acquired a sacred character, which rended his conquests more easy and more permanent; and the Barbarian princes confessed, in the language of devotion or flattery, that they could not presume to gaze, with a steady eye, on the divine majesty of the king of the Huns. [11] His brother Bleda, who reigned over a considerable part of the nation, was compelled to resign his sceptre and his life. Yet even this cruel act was attributed to a supernatural impulse; and the vigor with which Attila wielded the sword of Mars, convinced the world that it had been reserved alone for his invincible arm. [12] But the extent of his empire affords the only remaining evidence of the number and importance of his victories; and the Scythian monarch, however ignorant of the value of science and philosophy, might perhaps lament that his illiterate subjects were destitute of the art which could perpetuate the memory of his exploits.

[Footnote 5: Priscus, p. 39. The modern Hungarians have deduced his genealogy, which ascends, in the thirty-fifth degree, to Ham, the son of Noah; yet they are ignorant of his father's real name. (De Guignes, Hist. des Huns, tom. ii. p. 297.)]

[Footnote 6: Compare Jornandes (c. 35, p. 661) with Buffon, Hist. Naturelle, tom. iii. p. 380. The former had a right to observe, originis suae sigua restituens. The character and portrait of Attila are probably transcribed from Cassiodorus.]

[Footnote 7: Abulpharag. Pocock, p. 281. Genealogical History of the Tartars, by Abulghazi Bahader Khan, part iii c. 15, part iv c. 3. Vie de Gengiscan, par Petit de la Croix, l. 1, c. 1, 6. The relations of the missionaries, who visited Tartary in the thirteenth century, (see the seventh volume of the Histoire des Voyages,) express the popular language and opinions; Zingis is styled the son of God, &c. &c.]

[Footnote 8: Nec templum apud eos visitur, aut delubrum, ne tugurium quidem culmo tectum cerni usquam potest; sed gladius Barbarico ritu humi figitur nudus, eumque ut Martem regionum quas circumcircant praesulem verecundius colunt. Ammian. Marcellin. xxxi. 2, and the learned Notes of Lindenbrogius and Valesius.]

[Footnote 9: Priscus relates this remarkable story, both in his own text (p. 65) and in the quotation made by Jornandes, (c. 35, p. 662.) He might have explained the tradition, or fable, which characterized this famous sword, and the name, as well as attributes, of the Scythian deity, whom he has translated into the Mars of the Greeks and Romans.]

[Footnote 10: Herodot. l. iv. c. 62. For the sake of economy, I have calculated by the smallest stadium. In the human sacrifices, they cut off the shoulder and arm of the victim, which they threw up into the air, and drew omens and presages from the manner of their falling on the pile]

[Footnote 11: Priscus, p. 65. A more civilized hero, Augustus himself, was pleased, if the person on whom he fixed his eyes seemed unable to support their divine lustre. Sueton. in August. c. 79.]

[Footnote 12: The Count de Buat (Hist. des Peuples de l'Europe, tom. vii. p. 428, 429) attempts to clear Attila from the murder of his brother; and is almost inclined to reject the concurrent testimony of Jornandes, and the contemporary Chronicles.]

If a line of separation were drawn between the civilized and the savage climates of the globe; between the inhabitants of cities, who cultivated the earth, and the hunters and shepherds, who dwelt in tents, Attila might aspire to the title of supreme and sole monarch of the Barbarians. [13] He alone, among the conquerors of ancient and modern times, united the two mighty kingdoms of Germany and Scythia; and those vague appellations, when they are applied to his reign, may be understood with an ample latitude. Thuringia, which stretched beyond its actual limits as far as the Danube, was in the number of his provinces; he interposed, with the weight of a powerful neighbor, in the domestic affairs of the Franks; and one of his lieutenants chastised, and almost exterminated, the Burgundians of the Rhine.

He subdued the islands of the ocean, the kingdoms of Scandinavia, encompassed and divided by the waters of the Baltic; and the Huns might derive a tribute of furs from that northern region, which has been protected from all other conquerors by the severity of the climate, and the courage of the natives. Towards the East, it is difficult to circumscribe the dominion of Attila over the Scythian deserts; yet we may be assured, that he reigned on the banks of the Volga; that the king of the Huns was dreaded, not only as a warrior, but as a magician; [14] that he insulted and vanquished the khan of the formidable Geougen; and that he sent ambassadors to negotiate an equal alliance with the empire of China. In the proud review of the nations who acknowledged the sovereignty of Attila, and who never entertained, during his lifetime, the thought of a revolt, the Gepidae and the Ostrogoths were distinguished by their numbers, their bravery, and the personal merits of their chiefs. The renowned Ardaric, king of the Gepidae, was the faithful and sagacious counsellor of the monarch, who esteemed his intrepid genius, whilst he loved the mild and discreet virtues of the noble Walamir, king of the Ostrogoths. The crowd of vulgar kings, the leaders of so many martial tribes, who served under the standard of Attila, were ranged in the submissive order of guards and domestics round the person of their master. They watched his nod; they trembled at his frown; and at the first signal of his will, they executed, without murmur or hesitation, his stern and absolute commands. In time of peace, the dependent princes, with their national troops, attended the royal camp in regular succession; but when Attila collected his military force, he was able to bring into the field an army of five, or, according to another account, of seven hundred thousand Barbarians. [15]

[Footnote 13: Fortissimarum gentium dominus, qui inaudita ante se potentia colus Scythica et Germanica regna possedit. Jornandes, c. 49, p. 684. Priscus, p. 64, 65. M. de Guignes, by his knowledge of the Chinese, has acquired (tom. ii. p. 295-301) an adequate idea of the empire of Attila.]

[Footnote 14: See Hist. des Huns, tom. ii. p. 296. The Geougen believed that the Huns could excite, at pleasure, storms of wind and rain. This phenomenon was produced by the stone Gezi; to whose magic power the loss of a battle was ascribed by the Mahometan Tartars of the fourteenth century. See Cherefeddin Ali, Hist. de Timur Bec, tom. i. p. 82, 83.]

[Footnote 15: Jornandes, c. 35, p. 661, c. 37, p. 667. See Tillemont, Hist. dea Empereurs, tom. vi. p. 129, 138. Corneille has represented the pride of Attila to his subject kings, and his tragedy opens with these two ridiculous lines:—

Ils ne sont pas venus, nos deux rois! qu'on leur die Qu'ils se font trop attendre, et qu'Attila s'ennuie.

The two kings of the Gepidae and the Ostrogoths are profound politicians and sentimental lovers, and the whole piece exhibits the defects without the genius, of the poet.]

The ambassadors of the Huns might awaken the attention of Theodosius, by reminding him that they were his neighbors both in Europe and Asia; since they touched the Danube on one hand, and reached, with the other, as far as the Tanais. In the reign of his father Arcadius, a band of adventurous Huns had ravaged the provinces of the East; from whence they brought away rich spoils and innumerable captives. [16] They advanced, by a secret path, along the shores of the Caspian Sea; traversed the snowy mountains of Armenia; passed the Tigris, the Euphrates, and the Halys; recruited their weary cavalry with the generous breed of Cappadocian horses; occupied the hilly country of Cilicia, and disturbed the festal songs and dances of the citizens of Antioch. Egypt trembled at their approach; and the monks and pilgrims of the Holy Land prepared to escaped their fury by a speedy embarkation. The memory of this invasion was still recent in the minds of the Orientals. The subjects of Attila might execute, with superior forces, the design which these adventurers had so boldly attempted; and it soon became the subject of anxious conjecture, whether the tempest would fall on the dominions of Rome, or of Persia. Some of the great vassals of the king of the Huns, who were themselves in the rank of powerful princes, had been sent to ratify an alliance and society of arms with the emperor, or rather with the general of the West. They related, during their residence at Rome, the circumstances of an expedition, which they had lately made into the East. After passing a desert and a morass, supposed by the Romans to be the Lake Maeotis, they penetrated through the mountains, and arrived, at the end of fifteen days' march, on the confines of Media; where they advanced as far as the unknown cities of Basic and Cursic. [16/1] They encountered the Persian army in the plains of Media and the air, according to their own expression, was darkened by a cloud of arrows. But the Huns were obliged to retire before the numbers of the enemy. Their laborious retreat was effected by a different road; they lost the greatest part of their booty; and at length returned to the royal camp, with some knowledge of the country, and an impatient desire of revenge. In the free conversation of the Imperial ambassadors, who discussed, at the court of Attila, the character and designs of their formidable enemy, the ministers of Constantinople expressed their hope, that his strength might be diverted and employed in a long and doubtful contest with the princes of the house of Sassan. The more sagacious Italians admonished their Eastern brethren of the folly and danger of such a hope; and convinced them, that the Medes and Persians were incapable of resisting the arms of the Huns; and that the easy and important acquisition would exalt the pride, as well as power, of the conqueror. Instead of contenting himself with a moderate contribution, and a military title, which equalled him only to the generals of Theodosius, Attila would proceed to impose a disgraceful and intolerable yoke on the necks of the prostrate and captive Romans, who would then be encompassed, on all sides, by the empire of the Huns. [17]

[Footnote 16: Alii per Caspia claustra Armeniasque nives, inopino tramite ducti Invadunt Orientis opes: jam pascua fumant Cappadocum, volucrumque parens Argaeus equorum. Jam rubet altus Halys, nec se defendit iniquo Monte Cilix; Syriae tractus vestantur amoeni Assuetumque choris, et laeta plebe canorum, Proterit imbellem sonipes hostilis Orontem. —Claudian, in Rufin. l. ii. 28-35.

See likewise, in Eutrop. l. i. 243-251, and the strong description of Jerom, who wrote from his feelings, tom. i. p. 26, ad Heliodor. p. 200 ad Ocean. Philostorgius (l. ix. c. 8) mentions this irruption.]

[Footnote 16/1: Gibbon has made a curious mistake; Basic and Cursic were the names of the commanders of the Huns. Priscus, edit. Bonn, p. 200—M.]

[Footnote 17: See the original conversation in Priscus, p. 64, 65.]

While the powers of Europe and Asia were solicitous to avert the impending danger, the alliance of Attila maintained the Vandals in the possession of Africa. An enterprise had been concerted between the courts of Ravenna and Constantinople, for the recovery of that valuable province; and the ports of Sicily were already filled with the military and naval forces of Theodosius. But the subtle Genseric, who spread his negotiations round the world, prevented their designs, by exciting the king of the Huns to invade the Eastern empire; and a trifling incident soon became the motive, or pretence, of a destructive war. [18] Under the faith of the treaty of Margus, a free market was held on the Northern side of the Danube, which was protected by a Roman fortress surnamed Constantia. A troop of Barbarians violated the commercial security; killed, or dispersed, the unsuspecting traders; and levelled the fortress with the ground. The Huns justified this outrage as an act of reprisal; alleged, that the bishop of Margus had entered their territories, to discover and steal a secret treasure of their kings; and sternly demanded the guilty prelate, the sacrilegious spoil, and the fugitive subjects, who had escaped from the justice of Attila. The refusal of the Byzantine court was the signal of war; and the Maesians at first applauded the generous firmness of their sovereign. But they were soon intimidated by the destruction of Viminiacum and the adjacent towns; and the people was persuaded to adopt the convenient maxim, that a private citizen, however innocent or respectable, may be justly sacrificed to the safety of his country. The bishop of Margus, who did not possess the spirit of a martyr, resolved to prevent the designs which he suspected. He boldly treated with the princes of the Huns: secured, by solemn oaths, his pardon and reward; posted a numerous detachment of Barbarians, in silent ambush, on the banks of the Danube; and, at the appointed hour, opened, with his own hand, the gates of his episcopal city. This advantage, which had been obtained by treachery, served as a prelude to more honorable and decisive victories. The Illyrian frontier was covered by a line of castles and fortresses; and though the greatest part of them consisted only of a single tower, with a small garrison, they were commonly sufficient to repel, or to intercept, the inroads of an enemy, who was ignorant of the art, and impatient of the delay, of a regular siege. But these slight obstacles were instantly swept away by the inundation of the Huns. [19] They destroyed, with fire and sword, the populous cities of Sirmium and Singidunum, of Ratiaria and Marcianopolis, of Naissus and Sardica; where every circumstance of the discipline of the people, and the construction of the buildings, had been gradually adapted to the sole purpose of defence. The whole breadth of Europe, as it extends above five hundred miles from the Euxine to the Hadriatic, was at once invaded, and occupied, and desolated, by the myriads of Barbarians whom Attila led into the field. The public danger and distress could not, however, provoke Theodosius to interrupt his amusements and devotion, or to appear in person at the head of the Roman legions. But the troops, which had been sent against Genseric, were hastily recalled from Sicily; the garrisons, on the side of Persia, were exhausted; and a military force was collected in Europe, formidable by their arms and numbers, if the generals had understood the science of command, and the soldiers the duty of obedience. The armies of the Eastern empire were vanquished in three successive engagements; and the progress of Attila may be traced by the fields of battle.

The two former, on the banks of the Utus, and under the walls of Marcianopolis, were fought in the extensive plains between the Danube and Mount Haemus. As the Romans were pressed by a victorious enemy, they gradually, and unskilfully, retired towards the Chersonesus of Thrace; and that narrow peninsula, the last extremity of the land, was marked by their third, and irreparable, defeat. By the destruction of this army, Attila acquired the indisputable possession of the field. From the Hellespont to Thermopylae, and the suburbs of Constantinople, he ravaged, without resistance, and without mercy, the provinces of Thrace and Macedonia. Heraclea and Hadrianople might, perhaps, escape this dreadful irruption of the Huns; but the words, the most expressive of total extirpation and erasure, are applied to the calamities which they inflicted on seventy cities of the Eastern empire. [20] Theodosius, his court, and the unwarlike people, were protected by the walls of Constantinople; but those walls had been shaken by a recent earthquake, and the fall of fifty-eight towers had opened a large and tremendous breach. The damage indeed was speedily repaired; but this accident was aggravated by a superstitious fear, that Heaven itself had delivered the Imperial city to the shepherds of Scythia, who were strangers to the laws, the language, and the religion, of the Romans. [21]

[Footnote 18: Priscus, p. 331. His history contained a copious and elegant account of the war, (Evagrius, l. i. c. 17;) but the extracts which relate to the embassies are the only parts that have reached our times. The original work was accessible, however, to the writers from whom we borrow our imperfect knowledge, Jornandes, Theophanes, Count Marcellinus, Prosper-Tyro, and the author of the Alexandrian, or Paschal, Chronicle. M. de Buat (Hist. des Peuples de l'Europe, tom. vii. c. xv.) has examined the cause, the circumstances, and the duration of this war; and will not allow it to extend beyond the year 44.]

[Footnote 19: Procopius, de Edificiis, l. 4, c. 5. These fortresses were afterwards restored, strengthened, and enlarged by the emperor Justinian, but they were soon destroyed by the Abares, who succeeded to the power and possessions of the Huns.]

[Footnote 20: Septuaginta civitates (says Prosper-Tyro) depredatione vastatoe. The language of Count Marcellinus is still more forcible. Pene totam Europam, invasis excisisque civitatibus atque castellis, conrasit.]

[Footnote 21: Tillemont (Hist des Empereurs, tom. vi. p. 106, 107) has paid great attention to this memorable earthquake; which was felt as far from Constantinople as Antioch and Alexandria, and is celebrated by all the ecclesiastical writers. In the hands of a popular preacher, an earthquake is an engine of admirable effect.]

In all their invasions of the civilized empires of the South, the Scythian shepherds have been uniformly actuated by a savage and destructive spirit. The laws of war, that restrain the exercise of national rapine and murder, are founded on two principles of substantial interest: the knowledge of the permanent benefits which may be obtained by a moderate use of conquest; and a just apprehension, lest the desolation which we inflict on the enemy's country may be retaliated on our own. But these considerations of hope and fear are almost unknown in the pastoral state of nations. The Huns of Attila may, without injustice, be compared to the Moguls and Tartars, before their primitive manners were changed by religion and luxury; and the evidence of Oriental history may reflect some light on the short and imperfect annals of Rome. After the Moguls had subdued the northern provinces of China, it was seriously proposed, not in the hour of victory and passion, but in calm deliberate council, to exterminate all the inhabitants of that populous country, that the vacant land might be converted to the pasture of cattle. The firmness of a Chinese mandarin, [22] who insinuated some principles of rational policy into the mind of Zingis, diverted him from the execution of this horrid design. But in the cities of Asia, which yielded to the Moguls, the inhuman abuse of the rights of war was exercised with a regular form of discipline, which may, with equal reason, though not with equal authority, be imputed to the victorious Huns. The inhabitants, who had submitted to their discretion, were ordered to evacuate their houses, and to assemble in some plain adjacent to the city; where a division was made of the vanquished into three parts. The first class consisted of the soldiers of the garrison, and of the young men capable of bearing arms; and their fate was instantly decided they were either enlisted among the Moguls, or they were massacred on the spot by the troops, who, with pointed spears and bended bows, had formed a circle round the captive multitude. The second class, composed of the young and beautiful women, of the artificers of every rank and profession, and of the more wealthy or honorable citizens, from whom a private ransom might be expected, was distributed in equal or proportionable lots. The remainder, whose life or death was alike useless to the conquerors, were permitted to return to the city; which, in the mean while, had been stripped of its valuable furniture; and a tax was imposed on those wretched inhabitants for the indulgence of breathing their native air. Such was the behavior of the Moguls, when they were not conscious of any extraordinary rigor. [23] But the most casual provocation, the slightest motive of caprice or convenience, often provoked them to involve a whole people in an indiscriminate massacre; and the ruin of some flourishing cities was executed with such unrelenting perseverance, that, according to their own expression, horses might run, without stumbling, over the ground where they had once stood. The three great capitals of Khorasan, Maru, Neisabour, and Herat, were destroyed by the armies of Zingis; and the exact account which was taken of the slain amounted to four millions three hundred and forty-seven thousand persons. [24] Timur, or Tamerlane, was educated in a less barbarous age, and in the profession of the Mahometan religion; yet, if Attila equalled the hostile ravages of Tamerlane, [25] either the Tartar or the Hun might deserve the epithet of the Scourge of God. [26]

[Footnote 22: He represented to the emperor of the Moguls that the four provinces, (Petcheli, Chantong, Chansi, and Leaotong,)which he already possessed, might annually produce, under a mild administration,

500,000 ounces of silver, 400,000 measures of rice, and 800,000 pieces of silk. Gaubil, Hist. de la Dynastie des Mongous, p. 58, 59. Yelut chousay (such was the name of the mandarin) was a wise and virtuous minister, who saved his country, and civilized the conquerors. Note: Compare the life of this remarkable man, translated from the Chinese by M. Abel Remusat. Nouveaux Melanges Asiatiques, t. ii. p. 64—M]

[Footnote 23: Particular instances would be endless; but the curious reader may consult the life of Gengiscan, by Petit de la Croix, the Histoire des Mongous, and the fifteenth book of the History of the Huns.]

[Footnote 24: At Maru, 1,300,000; at Herat, 1,600,000; at Neisabour, 1,747,000. D'Herbelot, Bibliotheque Orientale, p. 380, 381. I use the orthography of D'Anville's maps. It must, however, be allowed, that the Persians were disposed to exaggerate their losses and the Moguls to magnify their exploits.]

[Footnote 25: Cherefeddin Ali, his servile panegyrist, would afford us many horrid examples. In his camp before Delhi, Timour massacred 100,000 Indian prisoners, who had smiled when the army of their countrymen appeared in sight, (Hist. de Timur Bec, tom. iii. p. 90.) The people of Ispahan supplied 70,000 human skulls for the structure of several lofty towers, (id. tom. i. p. 434.) A similar tax was levied on the revolt of Bagdad, (tom. iii. p. 370;) and the exact account, which Cherefeddin was not able to procure from the proper officers, is stated by another historian (Ahmed Arabsiada, tom. ii. p. 175, vera Manger) at 90,000 heads.]

[Footnote 26: The ancients, Jornandes, Priscus, &c., are ignorant of this epithet. The modern Hungarians have imagined, that it was applied, by a hermit of Gaul, to Attila, who was pleased to insert it among the titles of his royal dignity. Mascou, ix. 23, and Tillemont, Hist. des Empereurs, tom. vi. p. 143.]

PART II

It may be affirmed, with bolder assurance, that the Huns depopulated the provinces of the empire, by the number of Roman subjects whom they led away into captivity. In the hands of a wise legislator, such an industrious colony might have contributed to diffuse through the deserts of Scythia the rudiments of the useful and ornamental arts; but these captives, who had been taken in war, were accidentally dispersed among the hordes that obeyed the empire of Attila. The estimate of their respective value was formed by the simple judgment of unenlightened and unprejudiced Barbarians. Perhaps they might not understand the merit of a theologian, profoundly skilled in the controversies of the Trinity and the Incarnation; yet they respected the ministers of every religion and the active zeal of the Christian missionaries, without approaching the person or the palace of the monarch, successfully labored in the propagation of the gospel. [27] The pastoral tribes, who were ignorant of the distinction of landed property, must have disregarded the use, as well as the abuse, of civil jurisprudence; and the skill of an eloquent lawyer could excite only their contempt or their abhorrence. [28] The perpetual intercourse of the Huns and the Goths had communicated the familiar knowledge of the two national dialects; and the Barbarians were ambitious of conversing in Latin, the military idiom even of the Eastern empire. [29] But they disdained the language and the sciences of the Greeks; and the vain sophist, or grave philosopher, who had enjoyed the flattering applause of the schools, was mortified to find that his robust servant was a captive of more value and importance than himself. The mechanic arts were encouraged and esteemed, as they tended to satisfy the wants of the Huns. An architect in the service of Onegesius, one of the favorites of Attila, was employed to construct a bath; but this work was a rare example of private luxury; and the trades of the smith, the carpenter, the armorer, were much more adapted to supply a wandering people with the useful instruments of peace and war. But the merit of the physician was received with universal favor and respect: the Barbarians, who despised death, might be apprehensive of disease; and the haughty conqueror trembled in the presence of a captive, to whom he ascribed, perhaps, an imaginary power of prolonging or preserving his life. [30] The Huns might be provoked to insult the misery of their slaves, over whom they exercised a despotic command; [31] but their manners were not susceptible of a refined system of oppression; and the efforts of courage and diligence were often recompensed by the gift of freedom. The historian Priscus, whose embassy is a source of curious instruction, was accosted in the camp of Attila by a stranger, who saluted him in the Greek language, but whose dress and figure displayed the appearance of a wealthy Scythian. In the siege of Viminiacum, he had lost, according to his own account, his fortune and liberty; he became the slave of Onegesius; but his faithful services, against the Romans and the Acatzires, had gradually raised him to the rank of the native Huns; to whom he was attached by the domestic pledges of a new wife and several children. The spoils of war had restored and improved his private property; he was admitted to the table of his former lord; and the apostate Greek blessed the hour of his captivity, since it had been the introduction to a happy and independent state; which he held by the honorable tenure of military service. This reflection naturally produced a dispute on the advantages and defects of the Roman government, which was severely arraigned by the apostate, and defended by Priscus in a prolix and feeble declamation. The freedman of Onegesius exposed, in true and lively colors, the vices of a declining empire, of which he had so long been the victim; the cruel absurdity of the Roman princes, unable to protect their subjects against the public enemy, unwilling to trust them with arms for their own defence; the intolerable weight of taxes, rendered still more oppressive by the intricate or arbitrary modes of collection; the obscurity of numerous and contradictory laws; the tedious and expensive forms of judicial proceedings; the partial administration of justice; and the universal corruption, which increased the influence of the rich, and aggravated the misfortunes of the poor. A sentiment of patriotic sympathy was at length revived in the breast of the fortunate exile; and he lamented, with a flood of tears, the guilt or weakness of those magistrates who had perverted the wisest and most salutary institutions. [32]

[Footnote 27: The missionaries of St. Chrysostom had converted great numbers of the Scythians, who dwelt beyond the Danube in tents and wagons. Theodoret, l. v. c. 31. Photius, p. 1517. The Mahometans, the Nestorians, and the Latin Christians, thought themselves secure of gaining the sons and grandsons of Zingis, who treated the rival missionaries with impartial favor.]

[Footnote 28: The Germans, who exterminated Varus and his legions, had been particularly offended with the Roman laws and lawyers. One of the Barbarians, after the effectual precautions of cutting out the tongue of an advocate, and sewing up his mouth, observed, with much satisfaction, that the viper could no longer hiss. Florus, iv. 12.]

[Footnote 29: Priscus, p. 59. It should seem that the Huns preferred the Gothic and Latin languages to their own; which was probably a harsh and barren idiom.]

[Footnote 30: Philip de Comines, in his admirable picture of the last moments of Lewis XI., (Memoires, l. vi. c. 12,) represents the insolence of his physician, who, in five months, extorted 54,000 crowns, and a rich bishopric, from the stern, avaricious tyrant.]

[Footnote 31: Priscus (p. 61) extols the equity of the Roman laws, which protected the life of a slave. Occidere solent (says Tacitus of the Germans) non disciplina et severitate, sed impetu et ira, ut inimicum, nisi quod impune. De Moribus Germ. c. 25. The Heruli, who were the subjects of Attila, claimed, and exercised, the power of life and death over their slaves. See a remarkable instance in the second book of Agathias]

[Footnote 32: See the whole conversation in Priscus, p. 59-62.]

The timid or selfish policy of the Western Romans had abandoned the Eastern empire to the Huns. [33] The loss of armies, and the want of discipline or virtue, were not supplied by the personal character of the monarch. Theodosius might still affect the style, as well as the title, of Invincible Augustus; but he was reduced to solicit the clemency of Attila, who imperiously dictated these harsh and humiliating conditions of peace. I. The emperor of the East resigned, by an express or tacit convention, an extensive and important territory, which stretched along the southern banks of the Danube, from Singidunum, or Belgrade, as far as Novae, in the diocese of Thrace. The breadth was defined by the vague computation of fifteen [33/1] days' journey; but, from the proposal of Attila to remove the situation of the national market, it soon appeared, that he comprehended the ruined city of Naissus within the limits of his dominions. II. The king of the Huns required and obtained, that his tribute or subsidy should be augmented from seven hundred pounds of gold to the annual sum of two thousand one hundred; and he stipulated the immediate payment of six thousand pounds of gold, to defray the expenses, or to expiate the guilt, of the war. One might imagine, that such a demand, which scarcely equalled the measure of private wealth, would have been readily discharged by the opulent empire of the East; and the public distress affords a remarkable proof of the impoverished, or at least of the disorderly, state of the finances. A large proportion of the taxes extorted from the people was detained and intercepted in their passage, though the foulest channels, to the treasury of Constantinople. The revenue was dissipated by Theodosius and his favorites in wasteful and profuse luxury; which was disguised by the names of Imperial magnificence, or Christian charity. The immediate supplies had been exhausted by the unforeseen necessity of military preparations. A personal contribution, rigorously, but capriciously, imposed on the members of the senatorian order, was the only expedient that could disarm, without loss of time, the impatient avarice of Attila; and the poverty of the nobles compelled them to adopt the scandalous resource of exposing to public auction the jewels of their wives, and the hereditary ornaments of their palaces. [34] III. The king of the Huns appears to have established, as a principle of national jurisprudence, that he could never lose the property, which he had once acquired, in the persons who had yielded either a voluntary, or reluctant, submission to his authority. From this principle he concluded, and the conclusions of Attila were irrevocable laws, that the Huns, who had been taken prisoner in war, should be released without delay, and without ransom; that every Roman captive, who had presumed to escape, should purchase his right to freedom at the price of twelve pieces of gold; and that all the Barbarians, who had deserted the standard of Attila, should be restored, without any promise or stipulation of pardon.

In the execution of this cruel and ignominious treaty, the Imperial officers were forced to massacre several loyal and noble deserters, who refused to devote themselves to certain death; and the Romans forfeited all reasonable claims to the friendship of any Scythian people, by this public confession, that they were destitute either of faith, or power, to protect the suppliant, who had embraced the throne of Theodosius. [35]

[Footnote 33: Nova iterum Orienti assurgit ruina... quum nulla ab Cocidentalibus ferrentur auxilia. Prosper Tyro composed his Chronicle in the West; and his observation implies a censure.]

[Footnote 33/1: Five in the last edition of Priscus. Niebuhr, Byz. Hist. p 147—M]

[Footnote 34: According to the description, or rather invective, of Chrysostom, an auction of Byzantine luxury must have been very productive. Every wealthy house possessed a semicircular table of massy silver such as two men could scarcely lift, a vase of solid gold of the weight of forty pounds, cups, dishes, of the same metal, &c.]

[Footnote 35: The articles of the treaty, expressed without much order or precision, may be found in Priscus, (p. 34, 35, 36, 37, 53, &c.) Count Marcellinus dispenses some comfort, by observing, 1. That Attila himself solicited the peace and presents, which he had formerly refused; and, 2dly, That, about the same time, the ambassadors of India presented a fine large tame tiger to the emperor Theodosius.]

The firmness of a single town, so obscure, that, except on this occasion, it has never been mentioned by any historian or geographer, exposed the disgrace of the emperor and empire. Azimus, or Azimuntium, a small city of Thrace on the Illyrian borders, [36] had been distinguished by the martial spirit of its youth, the skill and reputation of the leaders whom they had chosen, and their daring exploits against the innumerable host of the Barbarians. Instead of tamely expecting their approach, the Azimuntines attacked, in frequent and successful sallies, the troops of the Huns, who gradually declined the dangerous neighborhood, rescued from their hands the spoil and the captives, and recruited their domestic force by the voluntary association of fugitives and deserters. After the conclusion of the treaty, Attila still menaced the empire with implacable war, unless the Azimuntines were persuaded, or compelled, to comply with the conditions which their sovereign had accepted. The ministers of Theodosius confessed with shame, and with truth, that they no longer possessed any authority over a society of men, who so bravely asserted their natural independence; and the king of the Huns condescended to negotiate an equal exchange with the citizens of Azimus. They demanded the restitution of some shepherds, who, with their cattle, had been accidentally surprised. A strict, though fruitless, inquiry was allowed: but the Huns were obliged to swear, that they did not detain any prisoners belonging to the city, before they could recover two surviving countrymen, whom the Azimuntines had reserved as pledges for the safety of their lost companions. Attila, on his side, was satisfied, and deceived, by their solemn asseveration, that the rest of the captives had been put to the sword; and that it was their constant practice, immediately to dismiss the Romans and the deserters, who had obtained the security of the public faith. This prudent and officious dissimulation may be condemned, or excused, by the casuists, as they incline to the rigid decree of St. Augustin, or to the milder sentiment of St. Jerom and St. Chrysostom: but every soldier, every statesman, must acknowledge, that, if the race of the Azimuntines had been encouraged and multiplied, the Barbarians would have ceased to trample on the majesty of the empire. [37]

[Footnote 36: Priscus, p. 35, 36. Among the hundred and eighty-two forts, or castles, of Thrace, enumerated by Procopius, (de Edificiis, l. iv. c. xi. tom. ii. p. 92, edit. Paris,) there is one of the name of Esimontou, whose position is doubtfully marked, in the neighborhood of Anchialus and the Euxine Sea. The name and walls of Azimuntium might subsist till the reign of Justinian; but the race of its brave defenders had been carefully extirpated by the jealousy of the Roman princes]

[Footnote 37: The peevish dispute of St. Jerom and St. Augustin, who labored, by different expedients, to reconcile the seeming quarrel of the two apostles, St. Peter and St. Paul, depends on the solution of an important question, (Middleton's Works, vol. ii. p. 5-20,) which has been frequently agitated by Catholic and Protestant divines, and even by lawyers and philosophers of every age.]

It would have been strange, indeed, if Theodosius had purchased, by the loss of honor, a secure and solid tranquillity, or if his tameness had not invited the repetition of injuries. The Byzantine court was insulted by five or six successive embassies; [38] and the ministers of Attila were uniformly instructed to press the tardy or imperfect execution of the last treaty; to produce the names of fugitives and deserters, who were still protected by the empire; and to declare, with seeming moderation, that, unless their sovereign obtained complete and immediate satisfaction, it would be impossible for him, were it even his wish, to check the resentment of his warlike tribes. Besides the motives of pride and interest, which might prompt the king of the Huns to continue this train of negotiation, he was influenced by the less honorable view of enriching his favorites at the expense of his enemies. The Imperial treasury was exhausted, to procure the friendly offices of the ambassadors and their principal attendants, whose favorable report might conduce to the maintenance of peace. The Barbarian monarch was flattered by the liberal reception of his ministers; he computed, with pleasure, the value and splendor of their gifts, rigorously exacted the performance of every promise which would contribute to their private emolument, and treated as an important business of state the marriage of his secretary Constantius. [39] That Gallic adventurer, who was recommended by Aetius to the king of the Huns, had engaged his service to the ministers of Constantinople, for the stipulated reward of a wealthy and noble wife; and the daughter of Count Saturninus was chosen to discharge the obligations of her country. The reluctance of the victim, some domestic troubles, and the unjust confiscation of her fortune, cooled the ardor of her interested lover; but he still demanded, in the name of Attila, an equivalent alliance; and, after many ambiguous delays and excuses, the Byzantine court was compelled to sacrifice to this insolent stranger the widow of Armatius, whose birth, opulence, and beauty, placed her in the most illustrious rank of the Roman matrons. For these importunate and oppressive embassies, Attila claimed a suitable return: he weighed, with suspicious pride, the character and station of the Imperial envoys; but he condescended to promise that he would advance as far as Sardica to receive any ministers who had been invested with the consular dignity. The council of Theodosius eluded this proposal, by representing the desolate and ruined condition of Sardica, and even ventured to insinuate that every officer of the army or household was qualified to treat with the most powerful princes of Scythia. Maximin, [40] a respectable courtier, whose abilities had been long exercised in civil and military employments, accepted, with reluctance, the troublesome, and perhaps dangerous, commission of reconciling the angry spirit of the king of the Huns. His friend, the historian Priscus, [41] embraced the opportunity of observing the Barbarian hero in the peaceful and domestic scenes of life: but the secret of the embassy, a fatal and guilty secret, was intrusted only to the interpreter Vigilius. The two last ambassadors of the Huns, Orestes, a noble subject of the Pannonian province, and Edecon, a valiant chieftain of the tribe of the Scyrri, returned at the same time from Constantinople to the royal camp. Their obscure names were afterwards illustrated by the extraordinary fortune and the contrast of their sons: the two servants of Attila became the fathers of the last Roman emperor of the West, and of the first Barbarian king of Italy.

[Footnote 38: Montesquieu (Considerations sur la Grandeur, &c. c. xix.) has delineated, with a bold and easy pencil, some of the most striking circumstances of the pride of Attila, and the disgrace of the Romans. He deserves the praise of having read the Fragments of Priscus, which have been too much disregarded.]

[Footnote 39: See Priscus, p. 69, 71, 72, &c. I would fain believe, that this adventurer was afterwards crucified by the order of Attila, on a suspicion of treasonable practices; but Priscus (p. 57) has too plainly distinguished two persons of the name of Constantius, who, from the similar events of their lives, might have been easily confounded.]

[Footnote 40: In the Persian treaty, concluded in the year 422, the wise and eloquent Maximin had been the assessor of Ardaburius, (Socrates, l. vii. c. 20.) When Marcian ascended the throne, the office of Great Chamberlain was bestowed on Maximin, who is ranked, in the public edict, among the four principal ministers of state, (Novell. ad Calc. Cod. Theod. p. 31.) He executed a civil and military commission in the Eastern provinces; and his death was lamented by the savages of Aethiopia, whose incursions he had repressed. See Priscus, p. 40, 41.]

[Footnote 41: Priscus was a native of Panium in Thrace, and deserved, by his eloquence, an honorable place among the sophists of the age. His Byzantine history, which related to his own times, was comprised in seven books. See Fabricius, Bibliot. Graec. tom. vi. p. 235, 236. Notwithstanding the charitable judgment of the critics, I suspect that Priscus was a Pagan. Note: Niebuhr concurs in this opinion. Life of Priscus in the new edition of the Byzantine historians—M]

The ambassadors, who were followed by a numerous train of men and horses, made their first halt at Sardica, at the distance of three hundred and fifty miles, or thirteen days' journey, from Constantinople. As the remains of Sardica were still included within the limits of the empire, it was incumbent on the Romans to exercise the duties of hospitality. They provided, with the assistance of the provincials, a sufficient number of sheep and oxen, and invited the Huns to a splendid, or at least, a plentiful supper. But the harmony of the entertainment was soon disturbed by mutual prejudice and indiscretion. The greatness of the emperor and the empire was warmly maintained by their ministers; the Huns, with equal ardor, asserted the superiority of their victorious monarch: the dispute was inflamed by the rash and unseasonable flattery of Vigilius, who passionately rejected the comparison of a mere mortal with the divine Theodosius; and it was with extreme difficulty that Maximin and Priscus were able to divert the conversation, or to soothe the angry minds, of the Barbarians. When they rose from table, the Imperial ambassador presented Edecon and Orestes with rich gifts of silk robes and Indian pearls, which they thankfully accepted. Yet Orestes could not forbear insinuating that he had not always been treated with such respect and liberality: and the offensive distinction which was implied, between his civil office and the hereditary rank of his colleague seems to have made Edecon a doubtful friend, and Orestes an irreconcilable enemy. After this entertainment, they travelled about one hundred miles from Sardica to Naissus. That flourishing city, which has given birth to the great Constantine, was levelled with the ground: the inhabitants were destroyed or dispersed; and the appearance of some sick persons, who were still permitted to exist among the ruins of the churches, served only to increase the horror of the prospect. The surface of the country was covered with the bones of the slain; and the ambassadors, who directed their course to the north-west, were obliged to pass the hills of modern Servia, before they descended into the flat and marshy grounds which are terminated by the Danube. The Huns were masters of the great river: their navigation was performed in large canoes, hollowed out of the trunk of a single tree; the ministers of Theodosius were safely landed on the opposite bank; and their Barbarian associates immediately hastened to the camp of Attila, which was equally prepared for the amusements of hunting or of war. No sooner had Maximin advanced about two miles [41/1] from the Danube, than he began to experience the fastidious insolence of the conqueror. He was sternly forbid to pitch his tents in a pleasant valley, lest he should infringe the distant awe that was due to the royal mansion. [41/2] The ministers of Attila pressed them to communicate the business, and the instructions, which he reserved for the ear of their sovereign When Maximin temperately urged the contrary practice of nations, he was still more confounded to find that the resolutions of the Sacred Consistory, those secrets (says Priscus) which should not be revealed to the gods themselves, had been treacherously disclosed to the public enemy. On his refusal to comply with such ignominious terms, the Imperial envoy was commanded instantly to depart; the order was recalled; it was again repeated; and the Huns renewed their ineffectual attempts to subdue the patient firmness of Maximin. At length, by the intercession of Scotta, the brother of Onegesius, whose friendship had been purchased by a liberal gift, he was admitted to the royal presence; but, in stead of obtaining a decisive answer, he was compelled to undertake a remote journey towards the north, that Attila might enjoy the proud satisfaction of receiving, in the same camp, the ambassadors of the Eastern and Western empires. His journey was regulated by the guides, who obliged him to halt, to hasten his march, or to deviate from the common road, as it best suited the convenience of the king. The Romans, who traversed the plains of Hungary, suppose that they passed several navigable rivers, either in canoes or portable boats; but there is reason to suspect that the winding stream of the Teyss, or Tibiscus, might present itself in different places under different names. From the contiguous villages they received a plentiful and regular supply of provisions; mead instead of wine, millet in the place of bread, and a certain liquor named camus, which according to the report of Priscus, was distilled from barley. [42] Such fare might appear coarse and indelicate to men who had tasted the luxury of Constantinople; but, in their accidental distress, they were relieved by the gentleness and hospitality of the same Barbarians, so terrible and so merciless in war. The ambassadors had encamped on the edge of a large morass. A violent tempest of wind and rain, of thunder and lightning, overturned their tents, immersed their baggage and furniture in the water, and scattered their retinue, who wandered in the darkness of the night, uncertain of their road, and apprehensive of some unknown danger, till they awakened by their cries the inhabitants of a neighboring village, the property of the widow of Bleda. A bright illumination, and, in a few moments, a comfortable fire of reeds, was kindled by their officious benevolence; the wants, and even the desires, of the Romans were liberally satisfied; and they seem to have been embarrassed by the singular politeness of Bleda's widow, who added to her other favors the gift, or at least the loan, of a sufficient number of beautiful and obsequious damsels. The sunshine of the succeeding day was dedicated to repose, to collect and dry the baggage, and to the refreshment of the men and horses: but, in the evening, before they pursued their journey, the ambassadors expressed their gratitude to the bounteous lady of the village, by a very acceptable present of silver cups, red fleeces, dried fruits, and Indian pepper. Soon after this adventure, they rejoined the march of Attila, from whom they had been separated about six days, and slowly proceeded to the capital of an empire, which did not contain, in the space of several thousand miles, a single city.

[Footnote 41/1: 70 stadia. Priscus, 173—M.]

[Footnote 41/2: He was forbidden to pitch his tents on an eminence because Attila's were below on the plain. Ibid—M.]

[Footnote 42: The Huns themselves still continued to despise the labors of agriculture: they abused the privilege of a victorious nation; and the Goths, their industrious subjects, who cultivated the earth, dreaded their neighborhood, like that of so many ravenous wolves, (Priscus, p. 45.) In the same manner the Sarts and Tadgics provide for their own subsistence, and for that of the Usbec Tartars, their lazy and rapacious sovereigns. See Genealogical History of the Tartars, p. 423 455, &c.]

As far as we may ascertain the vague and obscure geography of Priscus, this capital appears to have been seated between the Danube, the Teyss, and the Carpathian hills, in the plains of Upper Hungary, and most probably in the neighborhood of Jezberin, Agria, or Tokay. [43] In its origin it could be no more than an accidental camp, which, by the long and frequent residence of Attila, had insensibly swelled into a huge village, for the reception of his court, of the troops who followed his person, and of the various multitude of idle or industrious slaves and retainers. [44] The baths, constructed by Onegesius, were the only edifice of stone; the materials had been transported from Pannonia; and since the adjacent country was destitute even of large timber, it may be presumed, that the meaner habitations of the royal village consisted of straw, or mud, or of canvass. The wooden houses of the more illustrious Huns were built and adorned with rude magnificence, according to the rank, the fortune, or the taste of the proprietors. They seem to have been distributed with some degree of order and symmetry; and each spot became more honorable as it approached the person of the sovereign. The palace of Attila, which surpassed all other houses in his dominions, was built entirely of wood, and covered an ample space of ground. The outward enclosure was a lofty wall, or palisade, of smooth square timber, intersected with high towers, but intended rather for ornament than defence. This wall, which seems to have encircled the declivity of a hill, comprehended a great variety of wooden edifices, adapted to the uses of royalty.

A separate house was assigned to each of the numerous wives of Attila; and, instead of the rigid and illiberal confinement imposed by Asiatic jealousy they politely admitted the Roman ambassadors to their presence, their table, and even to the freedom of an innocent embrace. When Maximin offered his presents to Cerca, [44/1] the principal queen, he admired the singular architecture on her mansion, the height of the round columns, the size and beauty of the wood, which was curiously shaped or turned or polished or carved; and his attentive eye was able to discover some taste in the ornaments and some regularity in the proportions. After passing through the guards, who watched before the gate, the ambassadors were introduced into the private apartment of Cerca. The wife of Attila received their visit sitting, or rather lying, on a soft couch; the floor was covered with a carpet; the domestics formed a circle round the queen; and her damsels, seated on the ground, were employed in working the variegated embroidery which adorned the dress of the Barbaric warriors. The Huns were ambitious of displaying those riches which were the fruit and evidence of their victories: the trappings of their horses, their swords, and even their shoes, were studded with gold and precious stones; and their tables were profusely spread with plates, and goblets, and vases of gold and silver, which had been fashioned by the labor of Grecian artists.

The monarch alone assumed the superior pride of still adhering to the simplicity of his Scythian ancestors. [45] The dress of Attila, his arms, and the furniture of his horse, were plain, without ornament, and of a single color. The royal table was served in wooden cups and platters; flesh was his only food; and the conqueror of the North never tasted the luxury of bread.

[Footnote 43: It is evident that Priscus passed the Danube and the Teyss, and that he did not reach the foot of the Carpathian hills. Agria, Tokay, and Jazberin, are situated in the plains circumscribed by this definition. M. de Buat (Histoire des Peuples, &c., tom. vii. p. 461) has chosen Tokay; Otrokosci, (p. 180, apud Mascou, ix. 23,) a learned Hungarian, has preferred Jazberin, a place about thirty-six miles westward of Buda and the Danube. Note: M. St. Martin considers the narrative of Priscus, the only authority of M. de Buat and of Gibbon, too vague to fix the position of Attila's camp. "It is worthy of remark, that in the Hungarian traditions collected by Thwrocz, l. 2, c. 17, precisely on the left branch of the Danube, where Attila's residence was situated, in the same parallel stands the present city of Buda, in Hungarian Buduvur. It is for this reason that this city has retained for a long time among the Germans of Hungary the name of Etzelnburgh or Etzela-burgh, i. e., the city of Attila. The distance of Buda from the place where Priscus crossed the Danube, on his way from Naissus, is equal to that which he traversed to reach the residence of the king of the Huns. I see no good reason for not acceding to the relations of the Hungarian historians." St. Martin, vi. 191—M]

[Footnote 44: The royal village of Attila may be compared to the city of Karacorum, the residence of the successors of Zingis; which, though it appears to have been a more stable habitation, did not equal the size or splendor of the town and abbey of St. Denys, in the 13th century. (See Rubruquis, in the Histoire Generale des Voyages, tom. vii p. 286.) The camp of Aurengzebe, as it is so agreeably described by

Bernier, (tom. ii. p. 217-235,) blended the manners of Scythia with the magnificence and luxury of Hindostan.]

[Footnote 44/1: The name of this queen occurs three times in Priscus, and always in a different form—Cerca, Creca, and Rheca. The Scandinavian poets have preserved her memory under the name of Herkia. St. Martin, vi. 192—M.]

[Footnote 45: When the Moguls displayed the spoils of Asia, in the diet of Toncat, the throne of Zingis was still covered with the original black felt carpet, on which he had been seated, when he was raised to the command of his warlike countrymen. See Vie de Gengiscan, v. c. 9.]

When Attila first gave audience to the Roman ambassadors on the banks of the Danube, his tent was encompassed with a formidable guard. The monarch himself was seated in a wooden chair. His stern countenance, angry gestures, and impatient tone, astonished the firmness of Maximin; but Vigilius had more reason to tremble, since he distinctly understood the menace, that if Attila did not respect the law of nations, he would nail the deceitful interpreter to the cross. and leave his body to the vultures. The Barbarian condescended, by producing an accurate list, to expose the bold falsehood of Vigilius, who had affirmed that no more than seventeen deserters could be found. But he arrogantly declared, that he apprehended only the disgrace of contending with his fugitive slaves; since he despised their impotent efforts to defend the provinces which Theodosius had intrusted to their arms: "For what fortress," (added Attila,) "what city, in the wide extent of the Roman empire, can hope to exist, secure and impregnable, if it is our pleasure that it should be erased from the earth?" He dismissed, however, the interpreter, who returned to Constantinople with his peremptory demand of more complete restitution, and a more splendid embassy.

His anger gradually subsided, and his domestic satisfaction in a marriage which he celebrated on the road with the daughter of Eslam, [45/1] might perhaps contribute to mollify the native fierceness of his temper. The entrance of Attila into the royal village was marked by a very singular ceremony. A numerous troop of women came out to meet their hero and their king. They marched before him, distributed into long and regular files; the intervals between the files were filled by white veils of thin linen, which the women on either side bore aloft in their hands, and which formed a canopy for a chorus of young virgins, who chanted hymns and songs in the Scythian language. The wife of his favorite Onegesius, with a train of female attendants, saluted Attila at the door of her own house, on his way to the palace; and offered, according to the custom of the country, her respectful homage, by entreating him to taste the wine and meat which she had prepared for his reception. As soon as the monarch had graciously accepted her hospitable gift, his domestics lifted a small silver table to a convenient height, as he sat on horseback; and Attila, when he had touched the goblet with his lips, again saluted the wife of Onegesius, and continued his march. During his residence at the seat of empire, his hours were not wasted in the recluse idleness of a seraglio; and the king of the Huns could maintain his superior dignity, without concealing his person from the public view. He frequently assembled his council, and gave audience to the ambassadors of the nations; and his people might appeal to the supreme tribunal, which he held at stated times, and, according to the Eastern custom, before the principal gate of his wooden palace. The Romans, both of the East and of the West, were twice invited to the banquets, where Attila feasted with the princes and nobles of Scythia. Maximin and his colleagues were stopped on the threshold, till they had made a devout libation to the health and prosperity of the king of the Huns; and were conducted, after this ceremony, to their respective seats in a spacious hall. The royal table and couch, covered with carpets and fine linen, was raised by several steps in the midst of the hall; and a son, an uncle, or perhaps a favorite king, were admitted to share the simple and homely repast of

Attila. Two lines of small tables, each of which contained three or four guests, were ranged in order on either hand; the right was esteemed the most honorable, but the Romans ingenuously confess, that they were placed on the left; and that Beric, an unknown chieftain, most probably of the Gothic race, preceded the representatives of Theodosius and Valentinian. The Barbarian monarch received from his cup-bearer a goblet filled with wine, and courteously drank to the health of the most distinguished guest; who rose from his seat, and expressed, in the same manner, his loyal and respectful vows. This ceremony was successively performed for all, or at least for the illustrious persons of the assembly; and a considerable time must have been consumed, since it was thrice repeated as each course or service was placed on the table. But the wine still remained after the meat had been removed; and the Huns continued to indulge their intemperance long after the sober and decent ambassadors of the two empires had withdrawn themselves from the nocturnal banquet. Yet before they retired, they enjoyed a singular opportunity of observing the manners of the nation in their convivial amusements. Two Scythians stood before the couch of Attila, and recited the verses which they had composed, to celebrate his valor and his victories. [45/2] A profound silence prevailed in the hall; and the attention of the guests was captivated by the vocal harmony, which revived and perpetuated the memory of their own exploits; a martial ardor flashed from the eyes of the warriors, who were impatient for battle; and the tears of the old men expressed their generous despair, that they could no longer partake the danger and glory of the field. [46] This entertainment, which might be considered as a school of military virtue, was succeeded by a farce, that debased the dignity of human nature. A Moorish and a Scythian buffoon [46/1] successively excited the mirth of the rude spectators, by their deformed figure, ridiculous dress, antic gestures, absurd speeches, and the strange, unintelligible confusion of the Latin, the Gothic, and the Hunnic languages; and the hall resounded with loud and licentious peals of laughter. In the midst of this intemperate riot, Attila alone, without a change of countenance, maintained his steadfast and inflexible gravity; which was never relaxed, except on the entrance of Irnac, the youngest of his sons: he embraced the boy with a smile of paternal tenderness, gently pinched him by the cheek, and betrayed a partial affection, which was justified by the assurance of his prophets, that Irnac would be the future support of his family and empire. Two days afterwards, the ambassadors received a second invitation; and they had reason to praise the politeness, as well as the hospitality, of Attila. The king of the Huns held a long and familiar conversation with Maximin; but his civility was interrupted by rude expressions and haughty reproaches; and he was provoked, by a motive of interest, to support, with unbecoming zeal, the private claims of his secretary Constantius.

"The emperor" (said Attila) "has long promised him a rich wife: Constantius must not be disappointed; nor should a Roman emperor deserve the name of liar." On the third day, the ambassadors were dismissed; the freedom of several captives was granted, for a moderate ransom, to their pressing entreaties; and, besides the royal presents, they were permitted to accept from each of the Scythian nobles the honorable and useful gift of a horse. Maximin returned, by the same road, to Constantinople; and though he was involved in an accidental dispute with Beric, the new ambassador of Attila, he flattered himself that he had contributed, by the laborious journey, to confirm the peace and alliance of the two nations. [47]

[Footnote 45/1: Was this his own daughter, or the daughter of a person named Escam? (Gibbon has written incorrectly Eslam, an unknown name. The officer of Attila, called Eslas.) In either case the construction is imperfect: a good Greek writer would have introduced an article to determine the sense. Nor is it quite clear, whether Scythian usage is adduced to excuse the polygamy, or a marriage, which would be considered incestuous in other countries. The Latin version has carefully preserved the ambiguity, filiam Escam uxorem. I am not inclined to construe it 'his own daughter' though I have too

little confidence in the uniformity of the grammatical idioms of the Byzantines (though Priscus is one of the best) to express myself without hesitation.—M.]

[Footnote 45/2: This passage is remarkable from the connection of the name of Attila with that extraordinary cycle of poetry, which is found in different forms in almost all the Teutonic languages.]

A Latin poem, de prima expeditione Attilae, Regis Hunnorum, in Gallias, was published in the year 1780, by Fischer at Leipsic. It contains, with the continuation, 1452 lines. It abounds in metrical faults, but is occasionally not without some rude spirit and some copiousness of fancy in the variation of the circumstances in the different combats of the hero Walther, prince of Aquitania. It contains little which can be supposed historical, and still less which is characteristic concerning Attila. It relates to a first expedition of Attila into Europe which cannot be traced in history, during which the kings of the Franks, of the Burgundians, and of Aquitaine, submit themselves, and give hostages to Attila: the king of the Franks, a personage who seems the same with the Hagen of Teutonic romance; the king of Burgundy, his daughter Heldgund; the king of Aquitaine, his son Walther. The main subject of the poem is the escape of Walther and Heldgund from the camp of Attila, and the combat between Walther and Gunthar, king of the Franks. with his twelve peers, among whom is Hagen. Walther had been betrayed while he passed through Worms, the city of the Frankish king. by paying for his ferry over the Rhine with some strange fish, which he had caught during his flight, and which were unknown in the waters of the Rhine. Gunthar was desirous of plundering him of the treasure, which Walther had carried off from the camp of Attila. The author of this poem is unknown, nor can I, on the vague and rather doubtful allusion to Thule, as Iceland, venture to assign its date. It was, evidently, recited in a monastery, as appears by the first line; and no doubt composed there. The faults of metre would point out a late date; and it may have been formed upon some local tradition, as Walther, the hero, seems to have turned monk.

This poem, however, in its character and its incidents, bears no relation to the Teutonic cycle, of which the Nibelungen Lied is the most complete form. In this, in the Heldenbuch, in some of the Danish Sagas. in countess lays and ballads in all the dialects of Scandinavia, appears King Etzel (Attila) in strife with the Burgundians and the Franks. With these appears, by a poetic anachronism, Dietrich of Berne. (Theodoric of Verona,) the celebrated Ostrogothic king; and many other very singular coincidences of historic names, which appear in the poems. (See Lachman Kritik der Sage in his volume of various readings to the Nibelungen; Berlin, 1836, p. 336.)

PART III

I must acknowledge myself unable to form any satisfactory theory as to the connection of these poems with the history of the time, or the period, from which they may date their origin; notwithstanding the laborious investigations and critical sagacity of the Schlegels, the Grimms, of P. E. Muller and Lachman, and a whole host of German critics and antiquaries; not to omit our own countryman, Mr. Herbert, whose theory concerning Attila is certainly neither deficient in boldness nor originality. I conceive the only way to obtain any thing like a clear conception on this point would be what Lachman has begun, (see above,) patiently to collect and compare the various forms which the traditions have assumed, without any preconceived, either mythical or poetical, theory, and, if possible, to discover the original basis of the whole rich and fantastic legend. One point, which to me is strongly in favor of the antiquity of this poetic cycle, is, that the manners are so clearly anterior to chivalry, and to the influence exercised on the poetic literature of Europe by the chivalrous poems and romances. I think I find some traces of that influence in the Latin poem, though strained through the imagination of a monk. The English reader will find an amusing account of the German Nibelungen and Heldenbuch, and of some of the Scandinavian Sagas, in the volume of Northern Antiquities published by Weber, the friend of Sir Walter Scott. Scott himself contributed a considerable, no doubt far the most valuable, part to the work. [46] [46/1] [47]

See also the various German editions of the Nibelungen, to which Lachman, with true German perseverance, has compiled a thick volume of various readings; the Heldenbuch, the old Danish poems by Grimm, the Eddas, &c. Herbert's Attila, p. 510, et seq—M.]

[Footnote 46: If we may believe Plutarch, (in Demetrio, tom. v. p. 24,) it was the custom of the Scythians, when they indulged in the pleasures of the table, to awaken their languid courage by the martial harmony of twanging their bow-strings.]

[Footnote 46/1: The Scythian was an idiot or lunatic; the Moor a regular buffcon—M.]

[Footnote 47: The curious narrative of this embassy, which required few observations, and was not susceptible of any collateral evidence, may be found in Priscus, p. 49-70. But I have not confined myself to the same order; and I had previously extracted the historical circumstances, which were less intimately connected with the journey, and business, of the Roman ambassadors.]

But the Roman ambassador was ignorant of the treacherous design, which had been concealed under the mask of the public faith. The surprise and satisfaction of Edecon, when he contemplated the splendor of Constantinople, had encouraged the interpreter Vigilius to procure for him a secret interview with the eunuch Chrysaphius, [48] who governed the emperor and the empire. After some previous conversation, and a mutual oath of secrecy, the eunuch, who had not, from his own feelings or experience, imbibed any exalted notions of ministerial virtue, ventured to propose the death of Attila, as an important service, by which Edecon might deserve a liberal share of the wealth and luxury which he admired. The ambassador of the Huns listened to the tempting offer; and professed, with apparent zeal, his ability, as well as readiness, to execute the bloody deed; the design was communicated to the master of the offices, and the devout Theodosius consented to the assassination of his invincible enemy. But this perfidious conspiracy was defeated by the dissimulation, or the repentance, of Edecon; and though he might exaggerate his inward abhorrence for the treason, which he seemed to approve, he dexterously assumed the merit of an early and voluntary confession. If we now review the embassy of Maximin, and the behavior of Attila, we must applaud the Barbarian, who respected the laws of hospitality, and generously entertained and dismissed the minister of a prince who had conspired against his life. But the rashness of Vigilius will appear still more extraordinary, since he returned, conscious of his guilt and danger, to the royal camp, accompanied by his son, and carrying with him a weighty purse of gold, which the favorite eunuch had furnished, to satisfy the demands of Edecon, and to corrupt the fidelity of the guards. The interpreter was instantly seized, and dragged before the tribunal of Attila, where he asserted his innocence with specious firmness, till the threat of inflicting instant death on his son extorted from him a sincere discovery of the criminal transaction. Under the name of ransom, or confiscation, the rapacious king of the Huns accepted two hundred pounds of gold for the life of a traitor, whom he disdained to punish. He pointed his just indignation against a nobler object. His ambassadors, Eslaw and Orestes, were immediately despatched to Constantinople, with a peremptory instruction, which it was much safer for them to execute than to disobey. They boldly entered the Imperial presence, with the fatal purse hanging down from the neck of Orestes; who interrogated the eunuch Chrysaphius, as he stood beside the throne, whether he recognized the evidence of his guilt. But the office of reproof was reserved for the superior dignity of his colleague Eslaw, who gravely addressed the emperor of the East in the following words: "Theodosius is the son of an illustrious and respectable parent: Attila likewise is descended from a noble race; and he has supported, by his actions, the dignity which he inherited from his father Mundzuk. But Theodosius has forfeited his paternal honors, and, by consenting to pay tribute has degraded himself to the condition of a slave. It is therefore just, that he should reverence the man whom fortune and merit have placed above him; instead of attempting, like a wicked slave, clandestinely to conspire against his master." The son of Arcadius, who was accustomed only to the voice of flattery, heard with astonishment the severe language of truth: he blushed and trembled; nor did he presume directly to refuse the head of Chrysaphius, which Eslaw and Orestes were instructed to demand. A solemn embassy, armed with full powers and magnificent gifts, was hastily sent to deprecate the wrath of Attila; and his pride was gratified by the choice of Nomius and Anatolius, two ministers of consular or patrician rank, of whom the one was great treasurer, and the other was master-general of the armies of the East. He condescended to meet these ambassadors on the banks of the River Drenco; and though he at first affected a stern and haughty demeanor, his anger was insensibly mollified by their eloquence and liberality. He condescended to pardon the emperor, the eunuch, and the interpreter; bound himself by an oath to observe the conditions of peace; released a great number of captives; abandoned the fugitives and deserters to their fate; and resigned a large territory, to the south of the Danube, which he had already exhausted of its wealth and inhabitants. But this treaty was purchased at an expense which might have supported a vigorous and successful war; and the subjects of Theodosius were compelled to redeem the safety of a worthless favorite by oppressive taxes, which they would more cheerfully have paid for his destruction. [49]

[Footnote 48: M. de Tillemont has very properly given the succession of chamberlains, who reigned in the name of Theodosius. Chrysaphius was the last, and, according to the unanimous evidence of history, the worst of these favorites, (see Hist. des Empereurs, tom. vi. p. 117-119. Mem. Eccles. tom. xv. p. 438.) His partiality for his godfather the heresiarch Eutyches, engaged him to persecute the orthodox party]

[Footnote 49: This secret conspiracy and its important consequences, may be traced in the fragments of Priscus, p. 37, 38, 39, 54, 70, 71, 72. The chronology of that historian is not fixed by any precise date; but the series of negotiations between Attila and the Eastern empire must be included within the three or four years which are terminated, A.D. 450. by the death of Theodosius.]

The emperor Theodosius did not long survive the most humiliating circumstance of an inglorious life. As he was riding, or hunting, in the neighborhood of Constantinople, he was thrown from his horse into the River Lycus: the spine of the back was injured by the fall; and he expired some days afterwards, in the fiftieth year of his age, and the forty-third of his reign. [50] His sister Pulcheria, whose authority had been controlled both in civil and ecclesiastical affairs by the pernicious influence of the eunuchs, was unanimously proclaimed Empress of the East; and the Romans, for the first time, submitted to a female reign. No sooner had Pulcheria ascended the throne, than she indulged her own and the public resentment, by an act of popular justice. Without any legal trial, the eunuch Chrysaphius was executed before the gates of the city; and the immense riches which had been accumulated by the rapacious favorite, served only to hasten and to justify his punishment. [51] Amidst the general acclamations of the clergy and people, the empress did not forget the prejudice and disadvantage to which her sex was exposed; and she wisely resolved to prevent their murmurs by the choice of a colleague, who would always respect the superior rank and virgin chastity of his wife. She gave her hand to Marcian, a senator, about sixty years of age; and the nominal husband of Pulcheria was solemnly invested with the Imperial purple. The zeal which he displayed for the orthodox creed, as it was established by the council of

Chalcedon, would alone have inspired the grateful eloquence of the Catholics. But the behavior of Marcian in a private life, and afterwards on the throne, may support a more rational belief, that he was qualified to restore and invigorate an empire, which had been almost dissolved by the successive weakness of two hereditary monarchs. He was born in Thrace, and educated to the profession of arms; but Marcian's youth had been severely exercised by poverty and misfortune, since his only resource, when he first arrived at Constantinople, consisted in two hundred pieces of gold, which he had borrowed of a friend. He passed nineteen years in the domestic and military service of Aspar, and his son Ardaburius; followed those powerful generals to the Persian and African wars; and obtained, by their influence, the honorable rank of tribune and senator. His mild disposition, and useful talents, without alarming the jealousy, recommended Marcian to the esteem and favor of his patrons; he had seen, perhaps he had felt, the abuses of a venal and oppressive administration; and his own example gave weight and energy to the laws, which he promulgated for the reformation of manners. [52]

[Footnote 50: Theodorus the Reader, (see Vales. Hist. Eccles. tom. iii. p. 563,) and the Paschal Chronicle, mention the fall, without specifying the injury: but the consequence was so likely to happen, and so unlikely to be invented, that we may safely give credit to Nicephorus Callistus, a Greek of the fourteenth century.]

[Footnote 51: Pulcheriae nutu (says Count Marcellinus) sua cum avaritia interemptus est. She abandoned the eunuch to the pious revenge of a son, whose father had suffered at his instigation. Note: Might not the execution of Chrysaphius have been a sacrifice to avert the anger of Attila, whose assassination the eunuch had attempted to contrive?—M.]

[Footnote 52: de Bell. Vandal. l. i. c. 4. Evagrius, l. ii. c. 1. Theophanes, p. 90, 91. Novell. ad Calcem. Cod. Theod. tom. vi. p. 30. The praises which St. Leo and the Catholics have bestowed on Marcian, are diligently transcribed by Baronius, as an encouragement for future princes.]

CHAPTER XXXV

INVASION BY ATTILA

PART I

INVASION OF GAUL BY ATTILA—HE IS REPULSED BY AETIUS AND THE VISIGOTHS—ATTILA INVADES ANDEVACUATES ITALY—THE DEATHS Of ATTILA, AETIUS, AND VALENTINIAN THE THIRD

It was the opinion of Marcian, that war should be avoided, as long as it is possible to preserve a secure and honorable peace; but it was likewise his opinion, that peace cannot be honorable or secure, if the sovereign betrays a pusillanimous aversion to war. This temperate courage dictated his reply to the demands of Attila, who insolently pressed the payment of the annual tribute. The emperor signified to the Barbarians, that they must no longer insult the majesty of Rome by the mention of a tribute; that he was disposed to reward, with becoming liberality, the faithful friendship of his allies; but that, if they presumed to violate the public peace, they should feel that he possessed troops, and arms, and resolution, to repel their attacks. The same language, even in the camp of the Huns, was used by his ambassador Apollonius, whose bold refusal to deliver the presents, till he had been admitted to a personal interview, displayed a sense of dignity, and a contempt of danger, which Attila was not prepared to expect from the degenerate Romans. [1] He threatened to chastise the rash successor of Theodosius; but he hesitated whether he should first direct his invincible arms against the Eastern or the Western empire. While mankind awaited his decision with awful suspense, he sent an equal defiance to the courts of Ravenna and Constantinople; and his ministers saluted the two emperors with the same haughty declaration. "Attila, my lord, and thy lord, commands thee to provide a palace for his immediate reception." [2] But as the Barbarian despised, or affected to despise, the Romans of the East, whom he had so often vanquished, he soon declared his resolution of suspending the easy conquest, till he had achieved a more glorious and important enterprise. In the memorable invasions of Gaul and Italy, the Huns were naturally attracted by the wealth and fertility of those provinces; but the particular motives and provocations of Attila can only be explained by the state of the Western empire under the reign of Valentinian, or, to speak more correctly, under the administration of Aetius. [3]

[Footnote 1: See Priscus, p. 39, 72.]

[Footnote 2: The Alexandrian or Paschal Chronicle, which introduces this haughty message, during the lifetime of Theodosius, may have anticipated the date; but the dull annalist was incapable of inventing the original and genuine style of Attila.]

[Footnote 3: The second book of the Histoire Critique de l'Etablissement de la Monarchie Francoise tom. i. p. 189-424, throws great light on the state of Gaul, when it was invaded by Attila; but the ingenious author, the Abbe Dubos, too often bewilders himself in system and conjecture.]

After the death of his rival Boniface, Aetius had prudently retired to the tents of the Huns; and he was indebted to their alliance for his safety and his restoration. Instead of the suppliant language of a guilty exile, he solicited his pardon at the head of sixty thousand Barbarians; and the empress Placidia confessed, by a feeble resistance, that the condescension, which might have been ascribed to clemency, was the effect of weakness or fear. She delivered herself, her son Valentinian, and the Western empire, into the hands of an insolent subject; nor could Placidia protect the son-in-law of Boniface, the virtuous and faithful Sebastian, [4] from the implacable persecution which urged him from one kingdom to another, till he miserably perished in the service of the Vandals. The fortunate Aetius, who was immediately promoted to the rank of patrician, and thrice invested with the honors of the consulship, assumed, with the title of master of the cavalry and infantry, the whole military power of the state; and he is sometimes styled, by contemporary writers, the duke, or general, of the Romans of the West. His prudence, rather than his virtue, engaged him to leave the grandson of Theodosius in the possession of the purple; and Valentinian was permitted to enjoy the peace and luxury of Italy, while the patrician appeared in the glorious light of a hero and a patriot, who supported near twenty years the ruins of the Western empire. The Gothic historian ingenuously confesses, that Aetius was born for the salvation of the Roman republic; [5] and the following portrait, though it is drawn in the fairest colors, must be allowed to contain a much larger proportion of truth than of flattery. [411] "His mother was a wealthy and noble Italian, and his father Gaudentius, who held a distinguished rank in the province of Scythia, gradually rose from the station of a military domestic, to the dignity of master of the cavalry. Their son, who was enrolled almost in his infancy in the guards, was given as a hostage, first to Alaric, and afterwards to the Huns; [412] and he successively obtained the civil and military honors of the palace, for which he was equally qualified by superior merit. The graceful figure of Aetius was not above the middle stature; but his manly limbs were admirably formed for strength, beauty, and agility; and he excelled in the martial exercises of managing a horse, drawing the bow, and darting the javelin. He could patiently endure the want of food, or of sleep; and his mind and body were alike capable of the most laborious efforts. He possessed the genuine courage that can despise not only dangers, but injuries: and it was impossible either to corrupt, or deceive, or intimidate the firm integrity of his soul." [6] The Barbarians, who had seated themselves in the Western provinces, were insensibly taught to respect the faith and valor of the patrician Aetius. He soothed their passions, consulted their prejudices, balanced their interests, and checked their ambition. [611] A seasonable treaty, which he concluded with Genseric, protected Italy from the depredations of the Vandals; the independent Britons implored and acknowledged his salutary aid; the Imperial authority was restored and maintained in Gaul and Spain; and he compelled the Franks and the Suevi, whom he had vanquished in the field, to become the useful confederates of the republic.

[Footnote 4: Victor Vitensis (de Persecut. Vandal. l. i. 6, p. 8, edit. Ruinart) calls him, acer consilio et strenuus in bello: but his courage, when he became unfortunate, was censured as desperate rashness; and Sebastian deserved, or obtained, the epithet of proeceps, (Sidon. Apollinar Carmen ix. 181.) His adventures in Constantinople, in Sicily, Gaul, Spain, and Africa, are faintly marked in the Chronicles of Marcellinus and Idatius. In his distress he was always followed by a numerous train; since he could ravage the Hellespont and Propontis, and seize the city of Barcelona.]

[Footnote 5: Reipublicae Romanae singulariter natus, qui superbiam Suevorum, Francorumque barbariem immensis caedibus servire Imperio Romano coegisset. Jornandes de Rebus Geticis, c. 34, p. 660.]

[Footnote 4/1: Some valuable fragments of a poetical panegyric on Aetius by Merobaudes, a Spaniard, have been recovered from a palimpsest MS. by the sagacity and industry of Niebuhr. They have been reprinted in the new edition of the Byzantine Historians. The poet speaks in glowing terms of the long (annosa) peace enjoyed under the administration of Aetius. The verses are very spirited. The poet was rewarded by a statue publicly dedicated to his honor in Rome.

Danuvii cum pace redit, Tanaimque furore Exuit, et nigro candentes aethere terras Marte suo caruisse jubet. Dedit otia ferro Caucasus, et saevi condemnant praelia reges. Addidit hiberni famulantia foedera Rhenus Orbis...... Lustrat Aremoricos jam mitior incola saltus; Perdidit et mores tellus, adsuetaque saevo Crimine quaesitas silvis celare rapinas, Discit inexpertis Cererem committere campis; Caesareoque diu manus obluctata labori Sustinet acceptas nostro sub consule leges; Et quamvis Geticis sulcum confundat aratris, Barbara vicinae refugit consortia gentis. —Merobaudes, p. 1]

[Footnote 4/2:—cum Scythicis succumberet ensibus orbis, Telaque Tarpeias premerent Arctoa secures, Hostilem fregit rabiem, pignus quesuperbi Foederis et mundi pretium fuit. Hinc modo voti Rata fides, validis quod dux premat impiger armis Edomuit quos pace puer; bellumque repressit Ignarus quid bella forent. Stupuere feroces In tenero jam membra Getae. Rex ipse, verendum Miratus pueri decus et prudentia fatum Lumina, primaevus dederat gestare furetros, Laudubutque munus librantem et telu gerentem Oblitus quod noster erat Pro nescia regis Corda, feris quanto populis discrimine constet Quod Latium docet arma ducem. —Merobaudes, Panegyr. p. 15—M.]

[Footnote 6: This portrait is drawn by Renetus Profuturus Frigeridus, a contemporary historian, known only by some extracts, which are preserved by Gregory of Tours, (l. ii. c. 8, in tom. ii. p. 163.) It was probably the duty, or at least the interest, of Renatus, to magnify the virtues of Aetius; but he would have shown more dexterity if he had not insisted on his patient, forgiving disposition.]

[Footnote 6/1:

Insessor Libyes, quamvis, fatalibus armis Ausus Elisaei solium rescindere regni, Milibus Arctois Tyrias compleverat arces, Nunc hostem exutus pactis proprioribus arsit

Romanam vincire fidem, Latiosque parentes Adnumerare sib, sociamque intexere prolem. — Merobaudes, p. 12—M.]

From a principle of interest, as well as gratitude, Aetius assiduously cultivated the alliance of the Huns. While he resided in their tents as a hostage, or an exile, he had familiarly conversed with Attila himself, the nephew of his benefactor; and the two famous antagonists appeared to have been connected by a personal and military friendship, which they afterwards confirmed by mutual gifts, frequent embassies, and the education of Carpilio, the son of Aetius, in the camp of Attila. By the specious professions of gratitude and voluntary attachment, the patrician might disguise his apprehensions of the Scythian conqueror, who pressed the two empires with his innumerable armies. His demands were obeyed or eluded. When he claimed the spoils of a vanquished city, some vases of gold, which had been fraudulently embezzled, the civil and military governors of Noricum were immediately despatched to satisfy his complaints: [7] and it is evident, from their conversation with Maximin and Priscus, in the royal village, that the valor and prudence of Aetius had not saved the Western Romans from the common ignominy of tribute. Yet his dexterous policy prolonged the advantages of a salutary peace; and a numerous army of Huns and Alani, whom he had attached to his person, was employed in the defence of Gaul. Two colonies of these Barbarians were judiciously fixed in the territories of Valens and Orleans; [8] and their active cavalry secured the important passages of the Rhone and of the Loire. These savage allies were not indeed less formidable to the subjects than to the enemies of Rome. Their original settlement was enforced with the licentious violence of conquest; and the province through which they marched was exposed to all the calamities of a hostile invasion. [9] Strangers to the emperor or the republic, the Alani of Gaul was devoted to the ambition of Aetius, and though he might suspect, that, in a contest with Attila himself, they would revolt to the standard of their national king, the patrician labored to restrain, rather than to excite, their zeal and resentment against the Goths, the Burgundians, and the Franks.

[Footnote 7: The embassy consisted of Count Romulus; of Promotus, president of Noricum; and of Romanus, the military duke. They were accompanied by Tatullus, an illustrious citizen of Petovio, in the same province, and father of Orestes, who had married the daughter of Count Romulus. See Priscus, p. 57, 65. Cassiodorus (Variar. i. 4) mentions another embassy, which was executed by his father and Carpilio, the son of Aetius; and, as Attila was no more, he could safely boast of their manly, intrepid behavior in his presence.]

[Footnote 8: Deserta Valentinae urbis rura Alanis partienda traduntur. Prosper. Tyronis Chron. in Historiens de France, tom. i. p. 639. A few lines afterwards, Prosper observes, that lands in the ulterior Gaul were assigned to the Alani. Without admitting the correction of Dubos, (tom. i. p. 300,) the reasonable supposition of two colonies or garrisons of Alani will confirm his arguments, and remove his objections.]

[Footnote 9: See Prosper. Tyro, p. 639. Sidonius (Panegyr. Avit. 246) complains, in the name of Auvergne, his native country,

Litorius Scythicos equites tunc forte subacto Celsus Aremorico, Geticum rapiebat in agmen Per terras, Averne, tuas, qui proxima quaedue Discursu, flammis, ferro, feritate, rapinis, Delebant; pacis fallentes nomen inane.

another poet, Paulinus of Perigord, confirms the complaint:—

Nam socium vix ferre queas, qui durior hoste. —See Dubos, tom. i. p. 330.]

The kingdom established by the Visigoths in the southern provinces of Gaul, had gradually acquired strength and maturity; and the conduct of those ambitious Barbarians, either in peace or war, engaged the perpetual vigilance of Aetius. After the death of Wallia, the Gothic sceptre devolved to Theodoric, the son of the great Alaric; [10] and his prosperous reign of more than thirty years, over a turbulent people, may be allowed to prove, that his prudence was supported by uncommon vigor, both of mind and body. Impatient of his narrow limits, Theodoric aspired to the possession of Arles, the wealthy seat of government and commerce; but the city was saved by the timely approach of Aetius; and the Gothic king, who had raised the siege with some loss and disgrace, was persuaded, for an adequate subsidy, to divert the martial valor of his subjects in a Spanish war. Yet Theodoric still watched, and eagerly seized, the favorable moment of renewing his hostile attempts. The Goths besieged Narbonne, while the Belgic provinces were invaded by the Burgundians; and the public safety was threatened on every side by the apparent union of the enemies of Rome. On every side, the activity of Aetius, and his Scythian cavalry, opposed a firm and successful resistance. Twenty thousand Burgundians were slain in battle; and the remains of the nation humbly accepted a dependent seat in the mountains of Savoy. [11] The walls of Narbonne had been shaken by the battering engines, and the inhabitants had endured the last extremities of famine, when Count Litorius, approaching in silence, and directing each horseman to carry behind him two sacks of flour, cut his way through the intrenchments of the besiegers. The siege was immediately raised; and the more decisive victory, which is ascribed to the personal conduct of Aetius himself, was marked with the blood of eight thousand Goths. But in the absence of the patrician, who was hastily summoned to Italy by some public or private interest, Count Litorius succeeded to the command; and his presumption soon discovered that far different talents are required to lead a wing of cavalry, or to direct the operations of an important war. At the head of an army of Huns, he rashly advanced to the gates of Thoulouse, full of careless contempt for an enemy whom his misfortunes had rendered prudent, and his situation made desperate. The predictions of the augurs had inspired Litorius with the profane confidence that he should enter the Gothic capital in triumph; and the trust which he reposed in his Pagan allies, encouraged him to reject the fair conditions of peace, which were repeatedly proposed by the bishops in the name of Theodoric. The king of the Goths exhibited in his distress the edifying contrast of Christian piety and moderation; nor did he lay aside his sackcloth and ashes till he was prepared to arm for the combat. His soldiers, animated with martial and religious enthusiasm, assaulted the camp of Litorius. The conflict was obstinate; the slaughter was mutual. The Roman general, after a total defeat, which could be imputed only to his unskilful rashness, was actually led through the streets of Thoulouse, not in his own, but in a hostile triumph; and the misery which he experienced, in a long and ignominious captivity, excited the compassion of the Barbarians themselves. [12] Such a loss, in a country whose spirit and finances were long since exhausted, could not easily be repaired; and the Goths, assuming, in their turn, the sentiments of ambition and revenge, would have planted their victorious standards on the banks of the Rhone, if the presence of Aetius had not restored strength and discipline to the Romans. [13] The two armies expected the signal of a decisive action; but the generals, who were conscious of each other's force, and doubtful of their own superiority, prudently sheathed their swords in the field of battle; and their reconciliation was permanent and sincere. Theodoric, king of the Visigoths, appears to have deserved the love of his subjects, the confidence of his allies, and the esteem of mankind. His throne was surrounded by six valiant sons, who were educated with equal care in the exercises of the Barbarian camp, and in those of the Gallic schools: from the study of the Roman jurisprudence, they acquired the theory, at least, of law and justice; and the harmonious sense of Virgil contributed to soften the asperity of their native manners. [14] The two daughters of the Gothic king were given in marriage to the eldest sons of the kings of the Suevi and of the Vandals, who reigned in Spain and Africa: but these illustrious alliances were pregnant with guilt and discord. The queen of the Suevi bewailed the death of a husband inhumanly massacred by her brother. The princess of the Vandals was the victim of a jealous tyrant, whom she called her father. The cruel Genseric suspected that his son's wife had conspired to poison him; the supposed crime was punished by the amputation of her nose and ears; and the unhappy daughter of Theodoric was ignominiously returned to the court of Thoulouse in that deformed and mutilated condition. This horrid act, which must seem incredible to a civilized age drew tears from every spectator; but Theodoric was urged, by the feelings of a parent and a king, to revenge such irreparable injuries. The Imperial ministers, who always cherished the discord of the Barbarians, would have supplied the Goths with arms, and ships, and treasures, for the African war; and the cruelty of Genseric might have been fatal to himself, if the artful Vandal had not armed, in his cause, the formidable power of the Huns. His rich gifts and pressing solicitations inflamed the ambition of Attila; and the designs of Aetius and Theodoric were prevented by the invasion of Gaul. [15]

[Footnote 10: Theodoric II., the son of Theodoric I., declares to Avitus his resolution of repairing, or expiating, the faults which his grandfather had committed,—

Quae noster peccavit avus, quem fuscat id unum, Quod te, Roma, capit.

Sidon. Panegyric. Avit. 505.

This character, applicable only to the great Alaric, establishes the genealogy of the Gothic kings, which has hitherto been unnoticed.]

[Footnote 11: The name of Sapaudia, the origin of Savoy, is first mentioned by Ammianus Marcellinus; and two military posts are ascertained by the Notitia, within the limits of that province; a cohort was stationed at Grenoble in Dauphine; and Ebredunum, or Iverdun, sheltered a fleet of small vessels, which commanded the Lake of Neufchatel. See Valesius, Notit. Galliarum, p. 503. D'Anville, Notice de l'Ancienne Gaule, p. 284, 579.]

[Footnote 12: Salvian has attempted to explain the moral government of the Deity; a task which may be readily performed by supposing that the calamities of the wicked are judgments, and those of the righteous, trials.]

[Footnote 13:
—Capto terrarum damna patebant Litorio, in Rhodanum proprios producere fines, Thendoridae fixum; nec erat pugnare necesse, Sed migrare Getis; rabidam trux asperat iram Victor; quod sensit Scythicum sub moenibus hostem Imputat, et nihil estgravius, si forsitan unquam Vincerecontingat, trepido. — Panegyr. Avit. 300, &c.

Sitionius then proceeds, according to the duty of a panegyrist, to transfer the whole merit from Aetius to his minister Avitus.]

[Footnote 14: Theodoric II. revered, in the person of Avitus, the character of his preceptor.

Mihi Romula dudum Per te jura placent; parvumque ediscere jussit Ad tua verba pater, docili quo prisca Maronis Carmine molliret Scythicos mihi pagina mores. —Sidon. Panegyr. Avit. 495 &c.]

[Footnote 15: Our authorities for the reign of Theodoric I. are, Jornandes de Rebus Geticis, c. 34, 36, and the Chronicles of Idatius, and the two Prospers, inserted in the historians of France, tom. i. p. 612-640. To these we may add Salvian de Gubernatione Dei, l. vii. p. 243, 244, 245, and the panegyric of Avitus, by Sidonius.]

The Franks, whose monarchy was still confined to the neighborhood of the Lower Rhine, had wisely established the right of hereditary succession in the noble family of the Merovingians. [16] These princes were elevated on a buckler, the symbol of military command; [17] and the royal fashion of long hair was the ensign of their birth and dignity. Their flaxen locks, which they combed and dressed with singular care, hung down in flowing ringlets on their back and shoulders; while the rest of the nation were obliged, either by law or custom, to shave the hinder part of their head, to comb their hair over the forehead, and to content themselves with the ornament of two small whiskers. [18] The lofty stature of the Franks, and their blue eyes, denoted a Germanic origin; their close apparel accurately expressed the figure of their limbs; a weighty sword was suspended from a broad belt; their bodies were protected by a large shield; and these warlike Barbarians were trained, from their earliest youth, to run, to leap, to swim; to dart the javelin, or battle-axe, with unerring aim; to advance, without hesitation, against a superior enemy; and to maintain, either in life or death, the invincible reputation of their ancestors. [19] Clodion, the first of their long-haired kings, whose name and actions are mentioned in authentic history, held his residence at Dispargum, [20] a village or fortress, whose place may be assigned between Louvain and Brussels. From the report of his spies, the king of the Franks was informed, that the defenceless state of the second Belgic must yield, on the slightest attack, to the valor of his subjects. He boldly penetrated through the thickets and morasses of the Carbonarian forest; [21] occupied Tournay and Cambray, the only cities which existed in the fifth century, and extended his conquests as far as the River Somme, over a desolate country, whose cultivation and populousness are the effects of more recent industry. [22] While Clodion lay encamped in the plains of Artois, [23] and celebrated, with vain and ostentatious security, the marriage, perhaps, of his son, the nuptial feast was interrupted by the unexpected and unwelcome presence of Aetius, who had passed the Somme at the head of his light cavalry. The tables, which had been spread under the shelter of a hill, along the banks of a pleasant stream, were rudely overturned; the Franks were oppressed before they could recover their arms, or their ranks; and their unavailing valor was fatal only to themselves. The loaded wagons, which had followed their march, afforded a rich booty; and the virgin-bride, with her female attendants, submitted to the new lovers, who were imposed on them by the chance of war. This advance, which had been obtained by the skill and activity of Aetius, might reflect some disgrace on the military prudence of Clodion; but the king of the Franks soon regained his strength and reputation, and still maintained the possession of his Gallic kingdom from the Rhine to the Somme. [24] Under his reign, and most probably from the thee enterprising spirit of his subjects, his three capitals, Mentz, Treves, and Cologne, experienced the effects of hostile cruelty and avarice. The distress of Cologne was prolonged by the perpetual dominion of the same Barbarians, who evacuated the ruins of Treves; and Treves, which in the space of forty years had been four times besieged and pillaged, was disposed to lose the memory of her afflictions in the vain amusements of the Circus. [25] The death of Clodion, after a reign of twenty years, exposed his kingdom to the discord and ambition of his two sons. Meroveus, the younger, [26] was persuaded to implore the protection of Rome; he was received at the Imperial court, as the ally of Valentinian, and the adopted son of the patrician Aetius; and dismissed to his native country, with splendid gifts, and the strongest assurances of friendship and support. During his absence, his elder brother had solicited, with equal ardor, the formidable aid of Attila; and the king of the Huns embraced an alliance, which facilitated the passage of the Rhine, and justified, by a specious and honorable pretence, the invasion of Gaul. [27]

[Footnote 16: Reges Crinitos se creavisse de prima, et ut ita dicam nobiliori suorum familia, (Greg. Turon. l. ii. c. 9, p. 166, of the second volume of the Historians of France.) Gregory himself does not mention the Merovingian name, which may be traced, however, to the beginning of the seventh century, as the distinctive appellation of the royal family, and even of the French monarchy. An ingenious critic has deduced the Merovingians from the great Maroboduus; and he has clearly proved, that the prince, who gave his name to the first race, was more ancient than the father of Childeric. See Memoires de l'Academie des Inscriptions, tom. xx. p. 52-90, tom. xxx. p. 557-587.]

[Footnote 17: This German custom, which may be traced from Tacitus to Gregory of Tours, was at length adopted by the emperors of Constantinople. From a MS. of the tenth century, Montfaucon has delineated the representation of a similar ceremony, which the ignorance of the age had applied to King David. See Monumens de la Monarchie Francoise, tom. i. Discours Preliminaire.]

[Footnote 18: Caesaries prolixa... crinium flagellis per terga dimissis, &c. See the Preface to the third volume of the Historians of France, and the Abbe Le Boeuf, (Dissertat. tom. iii. p. 47-79.) This peculiar fashion of the Merovingians has been remarked by natives and strangers; by Priscus, (tom. i. p. 608,) by Agathias, (tom. ii. p. 49,) and by Gregory of Tours, (l. viii. 18, vi. 24, viii. 10, tom. ii. p. 196, 278, 316.)]

[Footnote 19: See an original picture of the figure, dress, arms, and temper of the ancient Franks, in Sidonius Apollinaris, (Panegyr. Majorian. 238-254;) and such pictures, though coarsely drawn, have a real and intrinsic value. Father Daniel (History de la Milice Francoise, tom. i. p. 2-7) has illustrated the description.]

[Footnote 20: Dubos, Hist. Critique, &c., tom. i. p. 271, 272. Some geographers have placed Dispargum on the German side of the Rhine. See a note of the Benedictine Editors, to the Historians of France, tom. ii p. 166.]

[Footnote 21: The Carbonarian wood was that part of the great forest of the Ardennes which lay between the Escaut, or Scheldt, and the Meuse. Vales. Notit. Gall. p. 126.]

[Footnote 22: Gregor. Turon. l. ii. c. 9, in tom. ii. p. 166, 167. Fredegar. Epitom. c. 9, p. 395. Gesta Reg. Francor. c. 5, in tom. ii. p. 544. Vit St. Remig. ab Hincmar, in tom. iii. p. 373.]

[Footnote 23:
—Francus qua Cloio patentes Atrebatum terras pervaserat. —Panegyr. Majorian 213

The precise spot was a town or village, called Vicus Helena; and both the name and place are discovered by modern geographers at Lens See Vales. Notit. Gall. p. 246. Longuerue, Description de la France tom. ii. p. 88.]

[Footnote 24: See a vague account of the action in Sidonius. Panegyr. Majorian 212-230. The French critics, impatient to establish their monarchy in Gaul, have drawn a strong argument from the silence of Sidonius, who dares not insinuate, that the vanquished Franks were compelled to repass the Rhine. Dubos, tom. i. p. 322.]

[Footnote 25: Salvian (de Gubernat. Dei, l. vi.) has expressed, in vague and declamatory language, the misfortunes of these three cities, which are distinctly ascertained by the learned Mascou, Hist. of the Ancient Germans, ix. 21.]

[Footnote 26: Priscus, in relating the contest, does not name the two brothers; the second of whom he had seen at Rome, a beardless youth, with long, flowing hair, (Historians of France, tom. i. p. 607, 608.) The Benedictine Editors are inclined to believe, that they were the sons of some unknown king of the Franks, who reigned on the banks of the Neckar; but the arguments of M. de Foncemagne (Mem. de l'Academie, tom. viii. p. 464) seem to prove that the succession of Clodion was disputed by his two sons, and that the younger was Meroveus, the father of Childeric. Note: The relationship of Meroveus to Clodion is extremely doubtful—By some he is called an illegitimate son; by others merely of his race. Tur ii. c. 9, in Sismondi, Hist. des Francais, i. 177. See Mezeray.]

[Footnote 27: Under the Merovingian race, the throne was hereditary; but all the sons of the deceased monarch were equally entitled to their share of his treasures and territories. See the Dissertations of M. de Foncemagne, in the sixth and eighth volumes of the Memoires de l'Academie.]

PART II

When Attila declared his resolution of supporting the cause of his allies, the Vandals and the Franks, at the same time, and almost in the spirit of romantic chivalry, the savage monarch professed himself the lover and the champion of the princess Honoria. The sister of Valentinian was educated in the palace of Ravenna; and as her marriage might be productive of some danger to the state, she was raised, by the title of Augusta, [28] above the hopes of the most presumptuous subject. But the fair Honoria had no sooner attained the sixteenth year of her age, than she detested the importunate greatness which must forever exclude her from the comforts of honorable love; in the midst of vain and unsatisfactory pomp, Honoria sighed, yielded to the impulse of nature, and threw herself into the arms of her chamberlain Eugenius. Her guilt and shame (such is the absurd language of imperious man) were soon betrayed by the appearances of pregnancy; but the disgrace of the royal family was published to the world by the imprudence of the empress Placidia who dismissed her daughter, after a strict and shameful confinement, to a remote exile at Constantinople. The unhappy princess passed twelve or fourteen years in the irksome society of the sisters of Theodosius, and their chosen virgins; to whose crown Honoria could no longer aspire, and whose monastic assiduity of prayer, fasting, and vigils, she reluctantly imitated. Her impatience of long and hopeless celibacy urged her to embrace a strange and desperate resolution. The name of Attila was familiar and formidable at Constantinople; and his frequent embassies entertained a perpetual intercourse between his camp and the Imperial palace. In the pursuit of love, or rather of revenge, the daughter of Placidia sacrificed every duty and every prejudice; and offered to deliver her person into the arms of a Barbarian, of whose language she was ignorant, whose figure was scarcely human, and whose religion and manners she abhorred. By the ministry of a faithful eunuch, she transmitted to Attila a ring, the pledge of her affection; and earnestly conjured him to claim her as a lawful spouse, to whom he had been secretly betrothed. These indecent advances were received, however, with coldness and disdain; and the king of the Huns continued to multiply the number of his wives, till his love was awakened by the more forcible passions of ambition and avarice. The invasion of Gaul was preceded, and justified, by a formal demand of the princess Honoria, with a just and equal share of the Imperial patrimony. His predecessors, the ancient Tanjous, had often addressed, in the same hostile and peremptory manner, the daughters of China; and the pretensions of Attila were not less offensive to the majesty of Rome. A firm, but temperate, refusal was communicated to his ambassadors. The right of female succession, though it might derive a specious argument from the recent examples of Placidia and Pulcheria, was strenuously denied; and the indissoluble engagements of Honoria were opposed to the claims of her Scythian lover. [29] On the discovery of her connection with the king of the Huns, the guilty princess had been sent away, as an object of horror, from Constantinople to Italy: her life was spared; but the ceremony of her marriage was performed with some obscure and nominal husband, before she was immured in a perpetual prison, to bewail those crimes and misfortunes, which Honoria might have escaped, had she not been born the daughter of an emperor. [30]

[Footnote 28: A medal is still extant, which exhibits the pleasing countenance of Honoria, with the title of Augusta; and on the reverse, the improper legend of Salus Reipublicoe round the monogram of Christ. See Ducange, Famil. Byzantin. p. 67, 73.]

[Footnote 29: See Priscus, p, 39, 40. It might be fairly alleged, that if females could succeed to the throne, Valentinian himself, who had married the daughter and heiress of the younger Theodosius, would have asserted her right to the Eastern empire.]

[Footnote 30: The adventures of Honoria are imperfectly related by Jornandes, de Successione Regn. c. 97, and de Reb. Get. c. 42, p. 674; and in the Chronicles of Prosper and Marcellinus; but they cannot be made consistent, or probable, unless we separate, by an interval of time and place, her intrigue with Eugenius, and her invitation of Attila.]

A native of Gaul, and a contemporary, the learned and eloquent Sidonius, who was afterwards bishop of Clermont, had made a promise to one of his friends, that he would compose a regular history of the war of Attila. If the modesty of Sidonius had not discouraged him from the prosecution of this interesting work, [31] the historian would have related, with the simplicity of truth, those memorable events, to which the poet, in vague and doubtful metaphors, has concisely alluded. [32] The kings and nations of Germany and Scythia, from the Volga perhaps to the Danube, obeyed the warlike summons of Attila. From the royal village, in the plains of Hungary his standard moved towards the West; and after a march of seven or eight hundred miles, he reached the conflux of the Rhine and the Neckar, where he was joined by the Franks, who adhered to his ally, the elder of the sons of Clodion. A troop of light Barbarians, who roamed in quest of plunder, might choose the winter for the convenience of passing the river on the ice; but the innumerable cavalry of the Huns required such plenty of forage and provisions, as could be procured only in a milder season; the Hercynian forest supplied materials for a bridge of boats; and the hostile myriads were poured, with resistless violence, into the Belgic provinces. [33] The consternation of Gaul was universal; and the various fortunes of its cities have been adorned by tradition with martyrdoms and miracles. [34] Troyes was saved by the merits of St. Lupus; St. Servatius was removed from the world, that he might not behold the ruin of Tongres; and the prayers of St. Genevieve diverted the march of Attila from the neighborhood of Paris. But as the greatest part of the Gallic cities were alike destitute of saints and soldiers, they were besieged and stormed by the Huns; who practised, in the example of Metz, [35] their customary maxims of war. They involved, in a promiscuous massacre, the priests who served at the altar, and the infants, who, in the hour of danger, had been providently baptized by the bishop; the flourishing city was delivered to the flames, and a solitary chapel of St. Stephen marked the place where it formerly stood. From the Rhine and the Moselle, Attila advanced into the heart of Gaul; crossed the Seine at Auxerre; and, after a long and laborious march, fixed his camp under the walls of Orleans. He was desirous of securing his conquests by the possession of an advantageous post, which commanded the passage of the Loire; and he depended on the secret invitation of Sangiban, king of the Alani, who had promised to betray the city, and to revolt from the service of the empire. But this treacherous conspiracy was detected and disappointed: Orleans had been strengthened with recent fortifications; and the assaults of the Huns were vigorously repelled by the faithful valor of the soldiers, or citizens, who defended the place. The pastoral diligence of Anianus, a bishop of primitive sanctity and consummate prudence, exhausted every art of religious policy to support their courage, till the arrival of the expected succors. After an obstinate siege, the walls were shaken by the battering rams; the Huns had already occupied the suburbs; and the people, who were incapable of bearing arms, lay prostrate in prayer. Anianus, who anxiously counted the days and hours, despatched a trusty messenger to observe, from the rampart, the face of the distant country. He returned twice, without any intelligence that could inspire hope or comfort; but, in his third report, he mentioned a small cloud, which he had faintly descried at the extremity of the horizon. "It is the aid of God!" exclaimed the bishop, in a tone of pious confidence; and the whole multitude repeated after him, "It is the aid of God." The remote object, on which every eye was fixed, became each moment larger, and more distinct; the Roman and Gothic banners were gradually perceived; and a favorable wind blowing aside the dust, discovered, in deep array, the impatient squadrons of Aetius and Theodoric, who pressed forwards to the relief of Orleans.

[Footnote 31: Exegeras mihi, ut promitterem tibi, Attilae bellum stylo me posteris intimaturum.... coeperam scribere, sed operis arrepti fasce perspecto, taeduit inchoasse. Sidon. Apoll. l. viii. epist. 15, p. 235]

[Footnote 32:
Subito cum rupta tumultu Barbaries totas in te transfuderat Arctos,

Gallia. Pugnacem Rugum comitante Gelono, Gepida trux sequitur; Scyrum Burgundio cogit:

Chunus, Bellonotus, Neurus, Basterna, Toringus,

Bructerus, ulvosa vel quem Nicer abluit unda

Prorumpit Francus. Cecidit cito secta bipenni Hercynia in lintres, et Rhenum texuit alno. Et jam terrificis diffuderat Attila turmis In campos se, Belga, tuos. Panegyr. Avit.]

[Footnote 33: The most authentic and circumstantial account of this war is contained in Jornandes, (de Reb. Geticis, c. 36-41, p. 662-672,) who has sometimes abridged, and sometimes transcribed, the larger history of Cassiodorus. Jornandes, a quotation which it would be superfluous to repeat, may be corrected and illustrated by Gregory of Tours, l. ii. c. 5, 6, 7, and the Chronicles of Idatius, Isidore, and the two Prospers. All the ancient testimonies are collected and inserted in the Historians of France; but the reader should be cautioned against a supposed extract from the Chronicle of Idatius, (among the fragments of Fredegarius, tom. ii. p. 462,) which often contradicts the genuine text of the Gallician bishop.]

[Footnote 34: The ancient legendaries deserve some regard, as they are obliged to connect their fables with the real history of their own times. See the lives of St. Lupus, St. Anianus, the bishops of Metz, Ste. Genevieve, &c., in the Historians of France, tom. i. p. 644, 645, 649, tom. iii. p. 369.]

[Footnote 35: The scepticism of the count de Buat (Hist. des Peuples, tom. vii. p. 539, 540) cannot be reconciled with any principles of reason or criticism. Is not Gregory of Tours precise and positive in his account of the destruction of Metz? At the distance of no more than a hundred years, could he be ignorant, could the people be ignorant of the fate of a city, the actual residence of his sovereigns, the kings of Austrasia? The learned count, who seems to have undertaken the apology of Attila and the Barbarians, appeals to the false Idatius, *parcens Germaniae et Galliae*, and forgets that the true Idatius had explicitly affirmed, *plurimae civitates effractoe*, among which he enumerates Metz.]

The facility with which Attila had penetrated into the heart of Gaul, may be ascribed to his insidious policy, as well as to the terror of his arms. His public declarations were skilfully mitigated by his private assurances; he alternately soothed and threatened the Romans and the Goths; and the courts of Ravenna and Thoulouse, mutually suspicious of each other's intentions, beheld, with supine indifference, the approach of their common enemy. Aetius was the sole guardian of the public safety; but his wisest measures were embarrassed by a faction, which, since the death of Placidia, infested the Imperial palace: the youth of Italy trembled at the sound of the trumpet; and the Barbarians, who, from fear or affection, were inclined to the cause of Attila, awaited with doubtful and venal faith, the event of the war. The patrician passed the Alps at the head of some troops, whose strength and numbers scarcely deserved the name of an army. [36] But on his arrival at Arles, or Lyons, he was confounded by the intelligence, that the Visigoths, refusing to embrace the defence of Gaul, had determined to expect, within their own territories, the formidable invader, whom they professed to despise. The senator Avitus, who, after the honorable exercise of the Praetorian praefecture, had retired to his estate in Auvergne, was persuaded to accept the important embassy, which he executed with ability and success. He represented to Theodoric, that an ambitious conqueror, who aspired to the dominion of the earth, could be resisted only by the firm and unanimous alliance of the powers whom he labored to oppress. The lively eloquence of Avitus inflamed the Gothic warriors, by the description of the injuries which their ancestors had suffered from the Huns; whose implacable fury still pursued them from the Danube to the foot of the Pyrenees. He strenuously urged, that it was the duty of every Christian to save, from sacrilegious violation, the churches of God, and the relics of the saints: that it was the interest of every Barbarian, who had acquired a settlement in Gaul, to defend the fields and vineyards, which were cultivated for his use, against the desolation of the Scythian shepherds. Theodoric yielded to the evidence of truth; adopted the measure at once the most prudent and the most honorable; and declared, that, as the faithful ally of Aetius and the Romans, he was ready to expose his life and kingdom for the common safety of Gaul. [37] The Visigoths, who, at that time, were in the mature vigor of their fame and power, obeyed with alacrity the signal of war; prepared their arms and horses, and assembled under the standard of their aged king, who was resolved, with his two eldest sons, Torismond and Theodoric, to command in person his numerous and valiant people. The example of the Goths determined several tribes or nations, that seemed to fluctuate between the Huns and the Romans. The indefatigable diligence of the patrician gradually collected the troops of Gaul and Germany, who had formerly acknowledged themselves the subjects, or soldiers, of the republic, but who now claimed the rewards of voluntary service, and the rank of independent allies; the Laeti, the Armoricans, the Breones the Saxons, the Burgundians, the Sarmatians, or Alani, the Ripuarians, and the Franks who followed Meroveus as their lawful prince. Such was the various army, which, under the conduct of Aetius and Theodoric, advanced, by rapid marches to relieve Orleans, and to give battle to the innumerable host of Attila. [38]

[Footnote 36:
Vix liquerat Alpes Aetius, tenue, et rarum sine milite ducens Robur, in auxiliis Geticum male credulus agmen Incassum propriis praesumens adfore castris. —Panegyr. Avit. 328, &c.]

[Footnote 37: The policy of Attila, of Aetius, and of the Visigoths, is imperfectly described in the Panegyric of Avitus, and the thirty-sixth chapter of Jornandes. The poet and the historian were both biased by *personal or national prejudices. The former exalts the merit and importance of Avitus; orbis, Avite, salus, &c.! The latter is anxious to show the Goths in the most favorable light. Yet their agreement when they are fairly interpreted, is a proof of their veracity.]*

[Footnote 38: The review of the army of Aetius is made by Jornandes, c. 36, p. 664, edit. Grot. tom. ii. p. 23, of the Historians of France, with the notes of the Benedictine editor. The Loeti were a promiscuous race of Barbarians, born or naturalized in Gaul; and the Riparii, or Ripuarii, derived their name from their post on the three rivers, the Rhine, the Meuse, and the Moselle; the Armoricans possessed the independent cities between the Seine and the Loire. A colony of Saxons had been planted in the diocese of Bayeux; the Burgundians were settled in Savoy; and the Breones were a warlike tribe of Rhaetians, to the east of the Lake of Constance.]

On their approach the king of the Huns immediately raised the siege, and sounded a retreat to recall the foremost of his troops from the pillage of a city which they had already entered. [39] The valor of Attila was always guided by his prudence; and as he foresaw the fatal consequences of a defeat in the heart of Gaul, he repassed the Seine, and expected the enemy in the plains of Chalons, whose smooth and level surface was adapted to the operations of his Scythian cavalry. But in this tumultuary retreat, the vanguard of the Romans and their allies continually pressed, and sometimes engaged, the troops whom Attila had posted in the rear; the hostile columns, in the darkness of the night and the perplexity of the roads, might encounter each other without design; and the bloody conflict of the Franks and Gepidae, in which fifteen thousand [40] Barbarians were slain, was a prelude to a more general and decisive action. The Catalaunian fields [41] spread themselves round Chalons, and extend, according to the vague measurement of Jornandes, to the length of one hundred and fifty, and the breadth of one hundred miles, over the whole province, which is entitled to the appellation of a champaign country. [42] This spacious plain was distinguished, however, by some inequalities of ground; and the importance of a height, which commanded the camp of Attila, was understood and disputed by the two generals. The young and valiant Torismond first occupied the summit; the Goths rushed with irresistible weight on the Huns, who labored to ascend from the opposite side: and the possession of this advantageous post inspired both the troops and their leaders with a fair assurance of victory. The anxiety of Attila prompted him to consult his priests and haruspices. It was reported, that, after scrutinizing the entrails of victims, and scraping their bones, they revealed, in mysterious language, his own defeat, with the death of his principal adversary; and that the Barbarians, by accepting the equivalent, expressed his involuntary esteem for the superior merit of Aetius. But the unusual despondency, which seemed to prevail among the Huns, engaged Attila to use the expedient, so familiar to the generals of antiquity, of animating his troops by a military oration; and his language was that of a king, who had often fought and conquered at their head. [43] He pressed them to consider their past glory, their actual danger, and their future hopes. The same fortune, which opened the deserts and morasses of Scythia to their unarmed valor, which had laid so many warlike nations prostrate at their feet, had reserved the joys of this memorable field for the consummation of their victories. The cautious steps of their enemies, their strict alliance, and their advantageous posts, he artfully represented as the effects, not of prudence, but of fear. The Visigoths alone were the strength and nerves of the opposite army; and the Huns might securely trample on the degenerate Romans, whose close and compact order betrayed their apprehensions, and who were equally incapable of supporting the dangers or the fatigues of a day of battle. The doctrine of predestination, so favorable to martial virtue, was carefully inculcated by the king of the Huns; who assured his subjects, that the warriors, protected by Heaven, were safe and invulnerable amidst the darts of the enemy; but that the unerring Fates would strike their victims in the bosom of inglorious peace. "I myself," continued Attila, "will throw the first javelin, and the wretch who refuses to imitate the example of his sovereign, is devoted to inevitable death." The spirit of the

Barbarians was rekindled by the presence, the voice, and the example of their intrepid leader; and Attila, yielding to their impatience, immediately formed his order of battle. At the head of his brave and faithful Huns, he occupied in person the centre of the line. The nations subject to his empire, the Rugians, the Heruli, the Thuringians, the Franks, the Burgundians, were extended on either hand, over the ample space of the Catalaunian fields; the right wing was commanded by Ardaric, king of the Gepidae; and the three valiant brothers, who reigned over the Ostrogoths, were posted on the left to oppose the kindred tribes of the Visigoths. The disposition of the allies was regulated by a different principle. Sangiban, the faithless king of the Alani, was placed in the centre, where his motions might be strictly watched, and that the treachery might be instantly punished. Aetius assumed the command of the left, and Theodoric of the right wing; while Torismond still continued to occupy the heights which appear to have stretched on the flank, and perhaps the rear, of the Scythian army. The nations from the Volga to the Atlantic were assembled on the plain of Chalons; but many of these nations had been divided by faction, or conquest, or emigration; and the appearance of similar arms and ensigns, which threatened each other, presented the image of a civil war.

[Footnote 39: Aurelianensis urbis obsidio, oppugnatio, irruptio, nec direptio, l. v. Sidon. Apollin. l. viii. Epist. 15, p. 246. The preservation of Orleans might easily be turned into a miracle, obtained and foretold by the holy bishop.]

[Footnote 40: The common editions read xcm but there is some authority of manuscripts (and almost any authority is sufficient) for the more reasonable number of xvm.]

[Footnote 41: Chalons, or Duro-Catalaunum, afterwards Catalauni, had formerly made a part of the territory of Rheims from whence it is distant only twenty-seven miles. See Vales, Notit. Gall. p. 136. D'Anville, Notice de l'Ancienne Gaule, p. 212, 279.]

[Footnote 42: The name of Campania, or Champagne, is frequently mentioned by Gregory of Tours; and that great province, of which Rheims was the capital, obeyed the command of a duke. Vales. Notit. p. 120-123.]

[Footnote 43: I am sensible that these military orations are usually composed by the historian; yet the old Ostrogoths, who had served under Attila, might repeat his discourse to Cassiodorus; the ideas, and even the expressions, have an original Scythian cast; and I doubt, whether an Italian of the sixth century would have thought of the hujus certaminis gaudia.]

The discipline and tactics of the Greeks and Romans form an interesting part of their national manners. The attentive study of the military operations of Xenophon, or Caesar, or Frederic, when they are described by the same genius which conceived and executed them, may tend to improve (if such improvement can be wished) the art of destroying the human species. But the battle of Chalons can only excite our curiosity by the magnitude of the object; since it was decided by the blind impetuosity of Barbarians, and has been related by partial writers, whose civil or ecclesiastical profession secluded them from the knowledge of military affairs. Cassiolorus, however, had familiarly conversed with many Gothic warriors, who served in that memorable engagement; "a conflict," as they informed him, "fierce, various, obstinate, and bloody; such as could not be paralleled either in the present or in past ages." The number of the slain amounted to one hundred and sixty-two thousand, or, according to another account, three hundred thousand persons; [44] and these incredible exaggerations suppose a real and effective loss sufficient to justify the historian's remark, that whole generations may be swept away by the madness of kings, in the space of a single hour. After the mutual and repeated discharge of missile weapons, in which the archers of Scythia might signalize their superior dexterity, the cavalry and infantry of the two armies were furiously mingled in closer combat. The Huns, who fought under the eyes of their king pierced through the feeble and doubtful centre of the allies, separated their wings from each other, and wheeling, with a rapid effort, to the left, directed their whole force against the Visigoths. As Theodoric rode along the ranks, to animate his troops, he received a mortal stroke from the javelin of Andages, a noble Ostrogoth, and immediately fell from his horse. The wounded king was oppressed in the general disorder, and trampled under the feet of his own cavalry; and this important death served to explain the ambiguous prophecy of the haruspices. Attila already exulted in the confidence of victory, when the valiant Torismond descended from the hills, and verified the remainder of the prediction. The Visigoths, who had been thrown into confusion by the flight or defection of the Alani, gradually restored their order of battle; and the Huns were undoubtedly vanquished, since Attila was compelled to retreat. He had exposed his person with the rashness of a private soldier; but the intrepid troops of the centre had pushed forwards beyond the rest of the line; their attack was faintly supported; their flanks were unguarded; and the conquerors of Scythia and Germany were saved by the approach of the night from a total defeat. They retired within the circle of wagons that fortified their camp; and the dismounted squadrons prepared themselves for a defence, to which neither their arms, nor their temper, were adapted. The event was doubtful: but Attila had secured a last and honorable resource. The saddles and rich furniture of the cavalry were collected, by his order, into a funeral pile; and the magnanimous Barbarian had resolved, if his intrenchments should be forced, to rush headlong into the flames, and to deprive his enemies of the glory which they might have acquired, by the death or captivity of Attila. [45]

[Footnote 44: The expressions of Jornandes, or rather of Cassiodorus, are extremely strong. Bellum atrox, multiplex, immane, pertinax, cui simile nulla usquam narrat antiquitas: ubi talia gesta referuntur, ut nihil esset quod in vita sua conspicere potuisset egregius, qui hujus miraculi privaretur aspectu. Dubos (Hist. Critique, tom. i. p. 392, 393) attempts to reconcile the 162,000 of Jornandes with the 300,000 of Idatius and Isidore, by supposing that the larger number included the total destruction of the war, the effects of disease, the slaughter of the unarmed people, &c.]

[Footnote 45: The count de Buat, (Hist. des Peuples, &c., tom. vii. p. 554-573,) still depending on the false, and again rejecting the true, Idatius, has divided the defeat of Attila into two great battles; the former near Orleans, the latter in Champagne: in the one, Theodoric was slain in the other, he was revenged.]

But his enemies had passed the night in equal disorder and anxiety. The inconsiderate courage of Torismond was tempted to urge the pursuit, till he unexpectedly found himself, with a few followers, in the midst of the Scythian wagons. In the confusion of a nocturnal combat, he was thrown from his horse; and the Gothic prince must have perished like his father, if his youthful strength, and the intrepid zeal of his companions, had not rescued him from this dangerous situation. In the same manner, but on the left of the line, Aetius himself, separated from his allies, ignorant of their victory, and anxious for their fate, encountered and escaped the hostile troops that were scattered over the plains of Chalons; and at length reached the camp of the Goths, which he could only fortify with a slight rampart of shields, till the dawn of day. The Imperial general was soon satisfied of the defeat of Attila, who still remained inactive within his intrenchments; and when he contemplated the bloody scene, he observed, with secret satisfaction, that the loss had principally fallen on the Barbarians. The body of Theodoric, pierced with honorable wounds, was discovered under a heap of the slain: is subjects bewailed the death of their king and father; but their tears were mingled with songs and acclamations, and his funeral rites were performed in the face of a vanquished enemy. The Goths, clashing their arms, elevated on a buckler his eldest son Torismond, to whom they justly ascribed the glory of their success; and the new king accepted the obligation of revenge as a sacred portion of his paternal inheritance. Yet the Goths themselves were astonished by the fierce and undaunted aspect of their formidable antagonist; and their historian has compared Attila to a lion encompassed in his den, and threatening his hunters with redoubled fury. The kings and nations who might have deserted his standard in the hour of distress, were made sensible that the displeasure of their monarch was the most imminent and inevitable danger. All his instruments of martial music incessantly sounded a loud and animating strain of defiance; and the foremost troops who advanced to the assault were checked or destroyed by showers of arrows from every side of the intrenchments. It was determined, in a general council of war, to besiege the king of the Huns in his camp, to intercept his provisions, and to reduce him to the alternative of a disgraceful treaty or an unequal combat. But the impatience of the Barbarians soon disdained these cautious and dilatory measures; and the mature policy of Aetius was apprehensive that, after the extirpation of the Huns, the republic would be oppressed by the pride and power of the Gothic nation. The patrician exerted the superior ascendant of authority and reason to calm the passions, which the son of Theodoric considered as a duty; represented, with seeming affection and real truth, the dangers of absence and delay and persuaded Torismond to disappoint, by his speedy return, the ambitious designs of his brothers, who might occupy the throne and treasures of Thoulouse. [46] After the departure of the Goths, and the separation of the allied army, Attila was surprised at the vast silence that reigned over the plains of Chalons: the suspicion of some hostile stratagem detained him several days within the circle of his wagons, and his retreat beyond the Rhine confessed the last victory which was achieved in the name of the Western empire. Meroveus and his Franks, observing a prudent distance, and magnifying the opinion of their strength by the numerous fires which they kindled every night, continued to follow the rear of the Huns till they reached the confines of Thuringia. The Thuringians served in the army of Attila: they traversed, both in their march and in their return, the territories of the Franks; and it was perhaps in this war that they exercised the cruelties which, about fourscore years afterwards, were revenged by the son of Clovis. They massacred their hostages, as well as their captives: two hundred young maidens were tortured with exquisite and unrelenting rage; their bodies were torn asunder by wild horses, or their bones were crushed under the weight of rolling wagons; and their unburied limbs were abandoned on the public roads, as a prey to dogs and vultures. Such were those savage ancestors, whose imaginary virtues have sometimes excited the praise and envy of civilized ages. [47]

[Footnote 46: Jornandes de Rebus Geticis, c. 41, p. 671. The policy of Aetius, and the behavior of Torismond, are extremely natural; and the patrician, according to Gregory of Tours, (l. ii. c. 7, p. 163,) dismissed the prince of the Franks, by suggesting to him a similar apprehension. The false Idatius ridiculously pretends, that Aetius paid a clandestine nocturnal visit to the kings of the Huns and of the Visigoths; from each of whom he obtained a bribe of ten thousand pieces of gold, as the price of an undisturbed retreat.]

[Footnote 47: These cruelties, which are passionately deplored by Theodoric, the son of Clovis, (Gregory of Tours, l. iii. c. 10, p. 190,) suit the time and circumstances of the invasion of Attila. His residence in Thuringia was long attested by popular tradition; and he is supposed to have assembled a couroultai, or diet, in the territory of Eisenach. See Mascou, ix. 30, who settles with nice accuracy the extent of ancient Thuringia, and derives its name from the Gothic tribe of the Therungi]

Neither the spirit, nor the forces, nor the reputation, of Attila, were impaired by the failure of the Gallic expedition In the ensuing spring he repeated his demand of the princess Honoria, and her patrimonial treasures. The demand was again rejected, or eluded; and the indignant lover immediately took the field, passed the Alps, invaded Italy, and besieged Aquileia with an innumerable host of Barbarians. Those Barbarians were unskilled in the methods of conducting a regular siege, which, even among the ancients, required some knowledge, or at least some practice, of the mechanic arts. But the labor of many thousand provincials and captives, whose lives were sacrificed without pity, might execute the most painful and dangerous work. The skill of the Roman artists might be corrupted to the destruction of their country. The walls of Aquileia were assaulted by a formidable train of battering rams, movable turrets, and engines, that threw stones, darts, and fire; [48] and the monarch of the Huns employed the forcible impulse of hope, fear, emulation, and interest, to subvert the only barrier which delayed the conquest of Italy. Aquileia was at that period one of the richest, the most populous, and the strongest of the maritime cities of the Adriatic coast. The Gothic auxiliaries, who appeared to have served under their native princes, Alaric and Antala, communicated their intrepid spirit; and the citizens still remembered the glorious and successful resistance which their ancestors had opposed to a fierce, inexorable Barbarian, who disgraced the majesty of the Roman purple. Three months were consumed without effect in the siege of the Aquileia; till the want of provisions, and the clamors of his army, compelled Attila to relinquish the enterprise; and reluctantly to issue his orders, that the troops should strike their tents the next morning, and begin their retreat. But as he rode round the walls, pensive, angry, and disappointed, he observed a stork preparing to leave her nest, in one of the towers, and to fly with her infant family towards the country. He seized, with the ready penetration of a statesman, this trifling incident, which chance had offered to superstition; and exclaimed, in a loud and cheerful tone, that such a domestic bird, so constantly attached to human society, would never have abandoned her ancient seats, unless those towers had been devoted to impending ruin and solitude. [49] The favorable omen inspired an assurance of victory; the siege was renewed and prosecuted with fresh vigor; a large breach was made in the part of the wall from whence the stork had taken her flight; the Huns mounted to the assault with irresistible fury; and the succeeding generation could scarcely discover the ruins of Aquileia. [50] After this dreadful chastisement, Attila pursued his march; and as he passed, the cities of Altinum, Concordia, and Padua, were reduced into heaps of stones and ashes. The inland towns, Vicenza, Verona, and Bergamo, were exposed to the rapacious cruelty of the Huns. Milan and Pavia submitted, without resistance, to the loss of their wealth; and applauded the unusual clemency which preserved from the flames the public, as well as private, buildings, and spared the lives of the captive multitude. The popular traditions of Comum, Turin, or Modena, may justly be suspected; yet they concur with more authentic evidence to prove, that Attila spread his ravages over the rich plains of modern Lombardy; which are divided by the Po, and bounded by the Alps and Apennine. [51] When he took possession of the royal palace of Milan, he was surprised and offended at the sight of a picture which represented the Caesars seated on their throne, and the princes of Scythia prostrate at their feet. The revenge which Attila inflicted on this monument of Roman vanity, was harmless and ingenious. He commanded a painter to reverse the figures and the attitudes; and the emperors were delineated on the same canvas, approaching in a suppliant posture to empty their bags of tributary gold before the throne of the Scythian monarch. [52] The spectators must have confessed the truth and propriety of the alteration; and were perhaps tempted to apply, on this singular occasion, the well-known fable of the dispute between the lion and the man. [53]

[Footnote 48: *Machinis constructis, omnibusque tormentorum generibus adhibitis.* Jornandes, c. 42, p. 673. In the thirteenth century, the Moguls battered the cities of China with large engines, constructed by the Mahometans or Christians in their service, which threw stones from 150 to 300 pounds weight. In the defence of their country, the Chinese used gunpowder, and even bombs, above a hundred years before they were known in Europe; yet even those celestial, or infernal, arms were insufficient to protect a pusillanimous nation. See Gaubil. Hist. des Mongous, p. 70, 71, 155, 157, &c.]

[Footnote 49: The same story is told by Jornandes, and by Procopius, (de Bell Vandal. l. i. c. 4, p. 187, 188:) nor is it easy to decide which is the original. But the Greek historian is guilty of an inexcusable mistake, in placing the siege of Aquileia after the death of Aetius.]

[Footnote 50: Jornandes, about a hundred years afterwards, affirms, that Aquileia was so completely ruined, ita ut vix ejus vestigia, ut appareant, reliquerint. See Jornandes de Reb. Geticis, c. 42, p. 673. Paul. Diacon. l. ii. c. 14, p. 785. Liutprand, Hist. l. iii. c. 2. The name of Aquileia was sometimes applied to Forum Julii, (Cividad del Friuli,) the more recent capital of the Venetian province. Note: Compare the curious Latin poems on the destruction of Aquileia, published by M. Endlicher in his valuable catalogue of Latin Mss. in the library of Vienna, p. 298, &c.

Repleta quondam domibus sublimibus, ornatis mire, niveis, marmorels, Nune ferax frugum metiris funiculo ruricolarum.

The monkish poet has his consolation in Attila's sufferings in soul and body.

Vindictam tamen non evasit impius destructor tuus Attila sevissimus, Nunc igni simul gehennae et vermibus excruciatur—P. 290—M.]

[Footnote 51: In describing this war of Attila, a war so famous, but so imperfectly known, I have taken for my guides two learned Italians, who considered the subject with some peculiar advantages; Sigonius, de Imperio Occidentali, l. xiii. in his works, tom. i. p. 495-502; and Muratori, Annali d'Italia, tom. iv. p. 229-236, 8vo. edition.]

[Footnote 52: This anecdote may be found under two different articles of the miscellaneous compilation of Suidas.]

[Footnote 53:
Leo respondit, humana, hoc pictum manu: Videres hominem dejectum, si pingere Leones scirent. — Appendix ad Phaedrum, Fab. xxv.

The lion in Phaedrus very foolishly appeals from pictures to the amphitheatre; and I am glad to observe, that the native taste of La Fontaine (l. iii. fable x.) has omitted this most lame and impotent conclusion.]

It is a saying worthy of the ferocious pride of Attila, that the grass never grew on the spot where his horse had trod. Yet the savage destroyer undesignedly laid the foundation of a republic, which revived, in the feudal state of Europe, the art and spirit of commercial industry. The celebrated name of Venice, or Venetia, [54] was formerly diffused over a large and fertile province of Italy, from the confines of Pannonia to the River Addua, and from the Po to the Rhaetian and Julian Alps. Before the irruption of the Barbarians, fifty Venetian cities flourished in peace and prosperity: Aquileia was placed in the most conspicuous station: but the ancient dignity of Padua was supported by agriculture and manufactures; and the property of five hundred citizens, who were entitled to the equestrian rank, must have amounted, at the strictest computation, to one million seven hundred thousand pounds. Many families of Aquileia, Padua, and the adjacent towns, who fled from the sword of the Huns, found a safe, though obscure, refuge in the neighboring islands. [55] At the extremity of the Gulf, where the Adriatic feebly imitates the tides of the ocean, near a hundred small islands are separated by shallow water from the continent, and protected from the waves by several long slips of land, which admit the entrance of vessels through some secret and narrow channels. [56] Till the middle of the fifth century, these remote and sequestered spots remained without cultivation, with few inhabitants, and almost without a name. But the manners of the Venetian fugitives, their arts and their government, were gradually formed by their new situation; and one of the epistles of Cassiodorus, [57] which describes their condition about seventy years afterwards, may be considered as the primitive monument of the republic. [57/1] The minister of Theodoric compares them, in his quaint declamatory style, to water-fowl, who had fixed their nests on the bosom of the waves; and though he allows, that the Venetian provinces had formerly contained many noble families, he insinuates, that they were now reduced by misfortune to the same level of humble poverty. Fish was the common, and almost the universal, food of every rank: their only treasure consisted in the plenty of salt, which they extracted from the sea: and the exchange of that commodity, so essential to human life, was substituted in the neighboring markets to the currency of gold and silver. A people, whose habitations might be doubtfully assigned to the earth or water, soon became alike familiar with the two elements; and the demands of avarice succeeded to those of necessity. The islanders, who, from Grado to Chiozza, were intimately connected with each other, penetrated into the heart of Italy, by the secure, though laborious, navigation of the rivers and inland canals. Their vessels, which were continually increasing in size and number, visited all the harbors of the Gulf; and the marriage which Venice annually celebrates with the Adriatic, was contracted in her early infancy. The epistle of Cassiodorus, the Praetorian praefect, is addressed to the maritime tribunes; and he exhorts them, in a mild tone of authority, to animate the zeal of their countrymen for the public service, which required their assistance to transport the magazines of wine and oil from the province of Istria to the royal city of Ravenna. The ambiguous office of these magistrates is explained by the tradition, that, in the twelve principal islands, twelve tribunes, or judges, were created by an annual and popular election. The existence of the Venetian republic under the Gothic kingdom of Italy, is attested by the same authentic record, which annihilates their lofty claim of original and perpetual independence. [58]

[Footnote 54: Paul the Deacon (de Gestis Langobard. l. ii. c. 14, p. 784) describes the provinces of Italy about the end of the eighth century Venetia non solum in paucis insulis quas nunc Venetias dicimus, constat; sed ejus terminus a Pannoniae finibus usque Adduam fluvium protelatur. The history of that province till the age of Charlemagne forms the first and most interesting part of the Verona (Illustrata, p. 1-388,) in which the marquis Scipio Maffei has shown himself equally capable of enlarged views and minute disquisitions.]

[Footnote 55: This emigration is not attested by any contemporary evidence; but the fact is proved by the event, and the circumstances might be preserved by tradition. The citizens of Aquileia retired to the Isle of Gradus, those of Padua to Rivus Altus, or Rialto, where the city of Venice was afterwards built, &c.]

[Footnote 56: The topography and antiquities of the Venetian islands, from Gradus to Clodia, or Chioggia, are accurately stated in the Dissertatio Chorographica de Italia Medii Aevi. p. 151-155.]

[Footnote 57: Cassiodor. Variar. l. xii. epist. 24. Maffei (Verona Illustrata, part i. p. 240-254) has translated and explained this curious letter, in the spirit of a learned antiquarian and a faithful subject, who considered Venice as the only legitimate offspring of the Roman republic. He fixes the date of the epistle, and consequently the praefecture, of Cassiodorus, A.D. 523; and the marquis's authority has the more weight, as he prepared an edition of his works, and actually published a dissertation on the true orthography of his name. See Osservazioni Letterarie, tom. ii. p. 290-339.]

[Footnote 57/1: The learned count Figliasi has proved, in his memoirs upon the Veneti (Memorie de' Veneti primi e secondi del conte Figliasi, t. vi. Veneziai, 796,) that from the most remote period, this nation, which occupied the country which has since been called the Venetian States or Terra Firma, likewise inhabited the islands scattered upon the coast, and that from thence arose the names of Venetia prima and secunda, of which the first applied to the main land and the second to the islands and lagunes. From the time of the Pelasgi and of the Etrurians, the first Veneti, inhabiting a fertile and pleasant country, devoted themselves to agriculture: the second, placed in the midst of canals, at the mouth of several rivers, conveniently situated with regard to the islands of Greece, as well as the fertile plains of Italy, applied themselves to navigation and commerce. Both submitted to the Romans a short time before the second Punic war; yet it was not till after the victory of Marius over the Cimbri, that their country was reduced to a Roman province. Under the emperors, Venetia Prima obtained more than once, by its calamities, a place in history. But the maritime province was occupied in salt works, fisheries, and commerce. The Romans have considered the inhabitants of this part as beneath the dignity of history, and have left them in obscurity. They dwelt there until the period when their islands afforded a retreat to their ruined and fugitive compatriots. Sismondi. Hist. des Rep. Italiens, v. i. p. 313—G. —Compare, on the origin of Venice, Daru, Hist. de Venise, vol. i. c. I—M.]

[Footnote 58: See, in the second volume of Amelot de la Houssaie, Histoire du Gouvernement de Venise, a translation of the famous Squittinio. This book, which has been exalted far above its merits, is stained, in every line, with the disingenuous malevolence of party: but the principal evidence, genuine and apocryphal, is brought together and the reader will easily choose the fair medium.]

The Italians, who had long since renounced the exercise of arms, were surprised, after forty years' peace, by the approach of a formidable Barbarian, whom they abhorred, as the enemy of their religion, as well as of their republic. Amidst the general consternation, Aetius alone was incapable of fear; but it was impossible that he should achieve, alone and unassisted, any military exploits worthy of his former renown. The Barbarians who had defended Gaul, refused to march to the relief of Italy; and the succors promised by the Eastern emperor were distant and doubtful. Since Aetius, at the head of his domestic troops, still maintained the field, and harassed or retarded the march of Attila, he never showed himself more truly great, than at the time when his conduct was blamed by an ignorant and ungrateful people. [59] If the mind of Valentinian had been susceptible of any generous sentiments, he would have chosen such a general for his example and his guide. But the timid grandson of Theodosius, instead of sharing the dangers, escaped from the sound of war; and his hasty retreat from Ravenna to Rome, from an impregnable fortress to an open capital, betrayed his secret intention of abandoning Italy, as soon as the danger should approach his Imperial person. This shameful abdication was suspended, however, by the spirit of doubt and delay, which commonly adheres to pusillanimous counsels, and sometimes corrects their pernicious tendency. The Western emperor, with the senate and people of Rome, embraced the more salutary resolution of deprecating, by a solemn and suppliant embassy, the wrath of Attila. This important commission was accepted by Avienus, who, from his birth and riches, his consular dignity, the numerous train of his clients, and his personal abilities, held the first rank in the Roman senate. The specious and artful character of Avienus [60] was admirably qualified to conduct a negotiation either of public or private interest: his colleague Trigetius had exercised the Praetorian praefecture of Italy; and Leo, bishop of Rome, consented to expose his life for the safety of his flock. The genius of Leo [61] was exercised and displayed in the public misfortunes; and he has deserved the appellation of Great, by the successful zeal with which he labored to establish his opinions and his authority, under the venerable names of orthodox faith and ecclesiastical discipline. The Roman ambassadors were introduced to the tent of Attila, as he lay encamped at the place where the slow-winding Mincius is lost in the foaming waves of the Lake Benacus, [62] and trampled, with his Scythian cavalry, the farms of Catullus and Virgil. [63] The Barbarian monarch listened with favorable, and even respectful, attention; and the deliverance of Italy was purchased by the immense ransom, or dowry, of the princess Honoria. The state of his army might facilitate the treaty, and hasten his retreat. Their martial spirit was relaxed by the wealth and idolence of a warm climate. The shepherds of the North, whose ordinary food consisted of milk and raw flesh, indulged themselves too freely in the use of bread, of wine, and of meat, prepared and seasoned by the arts of cookery; and the progress of disease revenged in some measure the injuries of the Italians. [64] When Attila declared his resolution of carrying his victorious arms to the gates of Rome, he was admonished by his friends, as well as by his enemies, that Alaric had not long survived the conquest of the eternal city. His mind, superior to real danger, was assaulted by imaginary terrors; nor could he escape the influence of superstition, which had so often been subservient to his designs. [65] The pressing eloquence of Leo, his majestic aspect and sacerdotal robes, excited the veneration of Attila for the spiritual father of the Christians. The apparition of the two apostles, St. Peter and St. Paul, who menaced the Barbarian with instant death, if he rejected the prayer of their successor, is one of the noblest legends of ecclesiastical tradition. The safety of Rome might deserve the interposition of celestial beings; and some indulgence is due to a fable, which has been represented by the pencil of Raphael, and the chisel of Algardi. [66]

[Footnote 59: Sirmond (Not. ad Sidon. Apollin. p. 19) has published a curious passage from the Chronicle of Prosper. Attila, redintegratis viribus, quas in Gallia amiserat, Italiam ingredi per Pannonias intendit; nihil duce nostro Aetio secundum prioris belli opera prospiciente, &c. He reproaches Aetius with neglecting to guard the Alps, and with a design to abandon Italy; but this rash censure may at least be counterbalanced by the favorable testimonies of Idatius and Isidore.]

[Footnote 60: See the original portraits of Avienus and his rival Basilius, delineated and contrasted in the epistles (i. 9. p. 22) of Sidonius. He had studied the characters of the two chiefs of the senate; but he attached himself to Basilius, as the more solid and disinterested friend.]

[Footnote 61: The character and principles of Leo may be traced in one hundred and forty-one original epistles, which illustrate the ecclesiastical history of his long and busy pontificate, from A.D. 440 to 461. See Dupin, Bibliotheque Ecclesiastique, tom. iii. part ii p. 120-165.]

[Footnote 62:
Tardis ingens ubi flexibus errat Mincius, et tenera praetexit arundine ripas—Anne lacus tantos, te Lari maxime, teque Fluctibus, et fremitu assurgens Benace marino.]

[Footnote 63: The marquis Maffei (Verona Illustrata, part i. p. 95, 129, 221, part ii. p. 2, 6) has illustrated with taste and learning this interesting topography. He places the interview of Attila and St. Leo near Ariolica, or Ardelica, now Peschiera, at the conflux of the lake and river; ascertains the villa of Catullus, in the delightful peninsula of Sirmio, and discovers the Andes of Virgil, in the village of Bandes, precisely situate, qua se subducere colles incipiunt, where the Veronese hills imperceptibly slope down into the plain of Mantua. Note: Gibbon has made a singular mistake: the Mincius flows out of the Bonacus at Peschiera, not into it. The interview is likewise placed at Ponte Molino. and at Governolo, at the conflux of the Mincio and the Gonzaga. bishop of Mantua, erected a tablet in the year 1616, in the church of the latter place, commemorative of the event. Descrizione di Verona a de la sua provincia. C. 11, p. 126—M.]

[Footnote 64: *Si statim infesto agmine urbem petiissent, grande discrimen esset: sed in Venetia quo fere tractu Italia mollissima est, ipsa soli coelique clementia robur elanquit. Ad hoc panis usu carnisque coctae, et dulcedine vini mitigatos, &c.* This passage of Florus (iii. 3) is still more applicable to the Huns than to the Cimbri, and it may serve as a commentary on the celestial plague, with which Idatius and Isidore have afflicted the troops of Attila.]

[Footnote 65: The historian Priscus had positively mentioned the effect which this example produced on the mind of Attila. Jornandes, c. 42, p. 673]

[Footnote 66: The picture of Raphael is in the Vatican; the basso (or perhaps the alto) relievo of Algardi, on one of the altars of St. Peter, (see Dubos, Reflexions sur la Poesie et sur la Peinture, tom. i. p. 519, 520.) Baronius (Annal. Eccles. A.D. 452, No. 57, 58) bravely sustains the truth of the apparition; which is rejected, however, by the most learned and pious Catholics.]

Before the king of the Huns evacuated Italy, he threatened to return more dreadful, and more implacable, if his bride, the princess Honoria, were not delivered to his ambassadors within the term stipulated by the treaty. Yet, in the mean while, Attila relieved his tender anxiety, by adding a beautiful maid, whose name was Ildico, to the list of his innumerable wives. [67] Their marriage was celebrated with barbaric pomp and festivity, at his wooden palace beyond the Danube; and the monarch, oppressed with wine and sleep, retired at a late hour from the banquet to the nuptial bed. His attendants continued to respect his pleasures, or his repose, the greatest part of the ensuing day, till the unusual silence alarmed their fears and suspicions; and, after attempting to awaken Attila by loud and repeated cries, they at length broke into the royal apartment. They found the trembling bride sitting by the bedside, hiding her face with her veil, and lamenting her own danger, as well as the death of the king, who had expired during the night. [68] An artery had suddenly burst: and as Attila lay in a supine posture, he was suffocated by a torrent of blood, which, instead of finding a passage through the nostrils, regurgitated into the lungs and stomach. His body was solemnly exposed in the midst of the plain, under a silken pavilion; and the chosen squadrons of the Huns, wheeling round in measured evolutions, chanted a funeral song to the memory of a hero, glorious in his life, invincible in his death, the father of his people, the scourge of his enemies, and the terror of the world. According to their national custom, the Barbarians cut off a part of their hair, gashed their faces with unseemly wounds, and bewailed their valiant leader as he deserved, not with the tears of women, but with the blood of warriors. The remains of Attila were enclosed within three coffins, of gold, of silver, and of iron, and privately buried in the night: the spoils of nations were thrown into his grave; the captives who had opened the ground were inhumanly massacred; and the same Huns, who had indulged such excessive grief, feasted, with dissolute and intemperate mirth, about the recent sepulchre of their king. It was reported at Constantinople, that on the fortunate night on which he expired, Marcian beheld in a dream the bow of Attila broken asunder: and the report may be allowed to prove, how seldom the image of that formidable Barbarian was absent from the mind of a Roman emperor. [69]

[Footnote 67: *Attila, ut Priscus historicus refert, extinctionis suae tempore, puellam Ildico nomine, decoram, valde, sibi matrimonium post innumerabiles uxores... socians.* Jornandes, c. 49, p. 683, 684.

He afterwards adds, (c. 50, p. 686,) *Filii Attilae, quorum per licentiam libidinis poene populus fuit.* Polygamy has been established among the Tartars of every age. The rank of plebeian wives is regulated only by their personal charms; and the faded matron prepares, without a murmur, the bed which is destined for her blooming rival. But in royal families, the daughters of Khans communicate to their sons a prior right. See Genealogical History, p. 406, 407, 408.]

[Footnote 68: The report of her guilt reached Constantinople, where it obtained a very different name; and Marcellinus observes, that the tyrant of Europe was slain in the night by the hand, and the knife, of a woman Corneille, who has adapted the genuine account to his tragedy, describes the irruption of blood in forty bombast lines, and Attila exclaims, with ridiculous fury,

S'il ne veut s'arreter, (his blood.) (Dit-il) on me payera ce qui m'en va couter.]

[Footnote 69: The curious circumstances of the death and funeral of Attila are related by Jornandes, (c. 49, p. 683, 684, 685,) and were probably transcribed from Priscus.]

The revolution which subverted the empire of the Huns, established the fame of Attila, whose genius alone had sustained the huge and disjointed fabric. After his death, the boldest chieftains aspired to the rank of kings; the most powerful kings refused to acknowledge a superior; and the numerous sons, whom so many various mothers bore to the deceased monarch, divided and disputed, like a private inheritance, the sovereign command of the nations of Germany and Scythia. The bold Ardaric felt and represented the disgrace of this servile partition; and his subjects, the warlike Gepidae, with the Ostrogoths, under the conduct of three valiant brothers, encouraged their allies to vindicate the rights of freedom and royalty. In a bloody and decisive conflict on the banks of the River Netad, in Pannonia, the lance of the Gepidae, the sword of the Goths, the arrows of the Huns, the Suevic infantry, the light arms of the Heruli, and the heavy weapons of the Alani, encountered or supported each other; and the victory of the Ardaric was accompanied with the slaughter of thirty thousand of his enemies. Ellac, the eldest son of Attila, lost his life and crown in the memorable battle of Netad: his early valor had raised him to the throne of the Acatzires, a Scythian people, whom he subdued; and his father, who loved the superior merit, would have envied the death of Ellac. [70] His brother, Dengisich, with an army of Huns, still formidable in their flight and ruin, maintained his ground above fifteen years on the banks of the Danube. The palace of Attila, with the old country of Dacia, from the Carpathian hills to the Euxine, became the seat of a new power, which was erected by Ardaric, king of the Gepidae. The Pannonian conquests from Vienna to Sirmium, were occupied by the Ostrogoths; and the settlements of the tribes, who had so bravely asserted their native freedom, were irregularly distributed, according to the measure of their respective strength. Surrounded and oppressed by the multitude of his father's slaves, the kingdom of Dengisich was confined to the circle of his wagons; his desperate courage urged him to invade the Eastern empire: he fell in battle; and his head ignominiously exposed in the Hippodrome, exhibited a grateful spectacle to the people of Constantinople. Attila had fondly or superstitiously believed, that Irnac, the youngest of his sons, was destined to perpetuate the glories of his race. The character of that prince, who attempted to moderate the rashness of his brother Dengisich, was more suitable to the declining condition of the Huns; and Irnac, with his subject hordes, retired into the heart of the Lesser Scythia. They were soon overwhelmed by a torrent of new Barbarians, who followed the same road which their own ancestors had formerly discovered. The Geougen, or Avares, whose residence is assigned by the Greek writers to the shores of the ocean, impelled the adjacent tribes; till at length the Igours of the North, issuing from the cold Siberian regions, which produce the most valuable furs, spread themselves over the desert, as far as the Borysthenes and the Caspian gates; and finally extinguished the empire of the Huns. [71]

[Footnote 70: See Jornandes, de Rebus Geticis, c. 50, p. 685, 686, 687, 688. His distinction of the national arms is curious and important. Nan ibi admirandum reor fuisse spectaculum, ubi cernere erat cunctis, pugnantem Gothum ense furentem, Gepidam in vulnere suorum cuncta tela frangentem, Suevum pede,

Hunnum sagitta praesumere, Alanum gravi Herulum levi, armatura, aciem instruere. I am not precisely informed of the situation of the River Netad.]

[Footnote 71: Two modern historians have thrown much new light on the ruin and division of the empire of Attila; M. de Buat, by his laborious and minute diligence, (tom. viii. p. 3-31, 68-94,) and M. de Guignes, by his extraordinary knowledge of the Chinese language and writers. See Hist. des Huns, tom. ii. p. 315-319.]

Such an event might contribute to the safety of the Eastern empire, under the reign of a prince who conciliated the friendship, without forfeiting the esteem, of the Barbarians. But the emperor of the West, the feeble and dissolute Valentinian, who had reached his thirty-fifth year without attaining the age of reason or courage, abused this apparent security, to undermine the foundations of his own throne, by the murder of the patrician Aetius. From the instinct of a base and jealous mind, he hated the man who was universally celebrated as the terror of the Barbarians, and the support of the republic; [711] and his new favorite, the eunuch Heraclius, awakened the emperor from the supine lethargy, which might be disguised, during the life of Placidia, [72] by the excuse of filial piety. The fame of Aetius, his wealth and dignity, the numerous and martial train of Barbarian followers, his powerful dependants, who filled the civil offices of the state, and the hopes of his son Gaudentius, who was already contracted to Eudoxia, the emperor's daughter, had raised him above the rank of a subject. The ambitious designs, of which he was secretly accused, excited the fears, as well as the resentment, of Valentinian. Aetius himself, supported by the consciousness of his merit, his services, and perhaps his innocence, seems to have maintained a haughty and indiscreet behavior. The patrician offended his sovereign by a hostile declaration; he aggravated the offence, by compelling him to ratify, with a solemn oath, a treaty of reconciliation and alliance; he proclaimed his suspicions, he neglected his safety; and from a vain confidence that the enemy, whom he despised, was incapable even of a manly crime, he rashly ventured his person in the palace of Rome. Whilst he urged, perhaps with intemperate vehemence, the marriage of his son; Valentinian, drawing his sword, the first sword he had ever drawn, plunged it in the breast of a general who had saved his empire: his courtiers and eunuchs ambitiously struggled to imitate their master; and Aetius, pierced with a hundred wounds, fell dead in the royal presence. Boethius, the Praetorian praefect, was killed at the same moment, and before the event could be divulged, the principal friends of the patrician were summoned to the palace, and separately murdered. The horrid deed, palliated by the specious names of justice and necessity, was immediately communicated by the emperor to his soldiers, his subjects, and his allies. The nations, who were strangers or enemies to Aetius, generously deplored the unworthy fate of a hero: the Barbarians, who had been attached to his service, dissembled their grief and resentment: and the public contempt, which had been so long entertained for Valentinian, was at once converted into deep and universal abhorrence. Such sentiments seldom pervade the walls of a palace; yet the emperor was confounded by the honest reply of a Roman, whose approbation he had not disdained to solicit. "I am ignorant, sir, of your motives or provocations; I only know, that you have acted like a man who cuts off his right hand with his left." [73]

[Footnote 71/1: The praises awarded by Gibbon to the character of Aetius have been animadverted upon with great severity. (See Mr. Herbert's Attila. p. 321.) I am not aware that Gibbon has dissembled or palliated any of the crimes or treasons of Aetius: but his position at the time of his murder was certainly that of the preserver of the empire, the conqueror of the most dangerous of the barbarians: it is by no means clear that he was not "innocent" of any treasonable designs against Valentinian. If the early acts of his life, the introduction of the Huns into Italy, and of the Vandals into Africa, were among the proximate causes of the ruin of the empire, his murder was the signal for its almost immediate downfall—M.]

[Footnote 72: Placidia died at Rome, November 27, A.D. 450. She was buried at Ravenna, where her sepulchre, and even her corpse, seated in a chair of cypress wood, were preserved for ages. The empress received many compliments from the orthodox clergy; and St. Peter Chrysologus assured her, that her zeal for the Trinity had been recompensed by an august trinity of children. See Tillemont, Uist. Jer Emp. tom. vi. p. 240.]

[Footnote 73: Aetium Placidus mactavit semivir amens, is the expression of Sidonius, (Panegyr. Avit. 359.) The poet knew the world, and was not inclined to flatter a minister who had injured or disgraced Avitus and Majorian, the successive heroes of his song.]

The luxury of Rome seems to have attracted the long and frequent visits of Valentinian; who was consequently more despised at Rome than in any other part of his dominions. A republican spirit was insensibly revived in the senate, as their authority, and even their supplies, became necessary for the support of his feeble government. The stately demeano of an hereditary monarch offended their pride; and the pleasures of Valentinian were injurious to the peace and honor of noble families. The birth of the empress Eudoxia was equal to his own, and her charms and tender affection deserved those testimonies of love which her inconstant husband dissipated in vague and unlawful amours. Petronius Maximus, a wealthy senator of the Anician family, who had been twice consul, was possessed of a chaste and beautiful wife: her obstinate resistance served only to irritate the desires of Valentinian; and he resolved to accomplish them, either by stratagem or force. Deep gaming was one of the vices of the court: the emperor, who, by chance or contrivance, had gained from Maximus a considerable sum, uncourteously exacted his ring as a security for the debt; and sent it by a trusty messenger to his wife, with an order, in her husband's name, that she should immediately attend the empress Eudoxia. The unsuspecting wife of Maximus was conveyed in her litter to the Imperial palace; the emissaries of her impatient lover conducted her to a remote and silent bed-chamber; and Valentinian violated, without remorse, the laws of hospitality. Her tears, when she returned home, her deep affliction, and her bitter reproaches against a husband whom she considered as the accomplice of his own shame, excited Maximus to a just revenge; the desire of revenge was stimulated by ambition; and he might reasonably aspire, by the free suffrage of the Roman senate, to the throne of a detested and despicable rival. Valentinian, who supposed that every human breast was devoid, like his own, of friendship and gratitude, had imprudently admitted among his guards several domestics and followers of Aetius. Two of these, of Barbarian race were persuaded to execute a sacred and honorable duty, by punishing with death the assassin of their patron; and their intrepid courage did not long expect a favorable moment. Whilst Valentinian amused himself, in the field of Mars, with the spectacle of some military sports, they suddenly rushed upon him with drawn weapons, despatched the guilty Heraclius, and stabbed the emperor to the heart, without the least opposition from his numerous train, who seemed to rejoice in the tyrant's death. Such was the fate of Valentinian the Third, [74] the last Roman emperor of the family of Theodosius. He faithfully imitated the hereditary weakness of his cousin and his two uncles, without inheriting the gentleness, the purity, the innocence, which alleviate, in their characters, the want of spirit and ability. Valentinian was less excusable, since he had passions, without virtues: even his religion was questionable; and though he never deviated into the paths of heresy, he scandalized the pious Christians by his attachment to the profane arts of magic and divination.

[Footnote 74: With regard to the cause and circumstances of the deaths of Aetius and Valentinian, our information is dark and imperfect. Procopius (de Bell. Vandal. l. i. c. 4, p. 186, 187, 188) is a fabulous writer for the events which precede his own memory. His narrative must therefore be supplied and corrected by five or six Chronicles, none of which were composed in Rome or Italy; and which can only *express, in broken sentences, the popular rumors, as they were conveyed to Gaul, Spain, Africa, Constantinople, or Alexandria.]*

As early as the time of Cicero and Varro, it was the opinion of the Roman augurs, that the twelve vultures which Romulus had seen, represented the twelve centuries, assigned for the fatal period of his city. [75] This prophecy, disregarded perhaps in the season of health and prosperity, inspired the people with gloomy apprehensions, when the twelfth century, clouded with disgrace and misfortune, was almost elapsed; [76] and even posterity must acknowledge with some surprise, that the arbitrary interpretation of an accidental or fabulous circumstance has been seriously verified in the downfall of the Western empire. But its fall was announced by a clearer omen than the flight of vultures: the Roman government appeared every day less formidable to its enemies, more odious and oppressive to its subjects. [77] The taxes were multiplied with the public distress; economy was neglected in proportion as it became necessary; and the injustice of the rich shifted the unequal burden from themselves to the people, whom they defrauded of the indulgences that might sometimes have alleviated their misery. The severe inquisition which confiscated their goods, and tortured their persons, compelled the subjects of Valentinian to prefer the more simple tyranny of the Barbarians, to fly to the woods and mountains, or to embrace the vile and abject condition of mercenary servants. They abjured and abhorred the name of Roman citizens, which had formerly excited the ambition of mankind. The Armorican provinces of Gaul, and the greatest part of Spain, were-thrown into a state of disorderly independence, by the confederations of the Bagaudae; and the Imperial ministers pursued with proscriptive laws, and ineffectual arms, the rebels whom they had made. [78] If all the Barbarian conquerors had been annihilated in the same hour, their total destruction would not have restored the empire of the West: and if Rome still survived, she survived the loss of freedom, of virtue, and of honor.

[Footnote 75: This interpretation of Vettius, a celebrated augur, was quoted by Varro, in the xviiith book of his Antiquities. Censorinus, de Die Natali, c. 17, p. 90, 91, edit. Havercamp.]

[Footnote 76: According to Varro, the twelfth century would expire A.D. 447, but the uncertainty of the true aera of Rome might allow some latitude of anticipation or delay. The poets of the age, Claudian (de Bell Getico, 265) and Sidonius, (in Panegyr. Avit. 357,) may be admitted as fair witnesses of the popular opinion.

Jam reputant annos, interceptoque volatu Vulturis, incidunt properatis saecula metis. .... Jam prope fata tui bissenas Vulturis alas Implebant; seis namque tuos, scis, Roma, labores. —See Dubos, Hist. Critique, tom. i. p. 340-346.]

[Footnote 77: The fifth book of Salvian is filled with pathetic lamentations and vehement invectives. His immoderate freedom serves to prove the weakness, as well as the corruption, of the Roman government. His book was published after the loss of Africa, (A.D. 439,) and before Attila's war, (A.D. 451.)]

[Footnote 78: The Bagaudae of Spain, who fought pitched battles with the Roman troops, are repeatedly mentioned in the Chronicle of Idatius. Salvian has described their distress and rebellion in very forcible language. Itaque nomen civium Romanorum... nunc ultro repudiatur ac fugitur, nec vile tamen sed etiam abominabile poene habetur... Et hinc est ut etiam hi quid ad Barbaros non confugiunt, Barbari tamen esse coguntur, scilicet ut est pars magna Hispanorum, et non minima Gallorum.... De Bagaudis nunc mihi sermo est, qui per malos judices et cruentos spoliati, afflicti, necati postquam jus Romanae libertatis amiserant, etiam honorem Romani nominis perdiderunt.... Vocamus rabelles, vocamus perditos quos esse compulimua criminosos. De Gubernat. Dei, l. v. p. 158, 159.]

CHAPTER XXXVI

TOTAL EXTINCTION OF THE WESTERN EMPIRE

PART I

SACK OF ROME BY GENSERIC, KING OF THE VANDALS—HIS NAVAL DEPREDATIONS—SUCCESSION OF THE LAST EMPERORS OF THE WEST, MAXIMUS, AVITUS, MAJORIAN, SEVERUS, ANTHEMIUS, OLYBRIUS, GLYCERIUS, NEPOS, AUGUSTULUS—TOTAL EXTINCTION OF THE WESTERN EMPIRE—REIGN OF ODOACER, THE FIRST BARBARIAN KING OF ITALY

The loss or desolation of the provinces, from the Ocean to the Alps, impaired the glory and greatness of Rome: her internal prosperity was irretrievably destroyed by the separation of Africa. The rapacious Vandals confiscated the patrimonial estates of the senators, and intercepted the regular subsidies, which relieved the poverty and encouraged the idleness of the plebeians. The distress of the Romans was soon aggravated by an unexpected attack; and the province, so long cultivated for their use by industrious and obedient subjects, was armed against them by an ambitious Barbarian. The Vandals and Alani, who followed the successful standard of Genseric, had acquired a rich and fertile territory, which stretched along the coast above ninety days' journey from Tangier to Tripoli; but their narrow limits were pressed and confined, on either side, by the sandy desert and the Mediterranean. The discovery and conquest of the Black nations, that might dwell beneath the torrid zone, could not tempt the rational ambition of Genseric; but he cast his eyes towards the sea; he resolved to create a naval power, and his bold resolution was executed with steady and active perseverance.

The woods of Mount Atlas afforded an inexhaustible nursery of timber: his new subjects were skilled in the arts of navigation and ship-building; he animated his daring Vandals to embrace a mode of warfare which would render every maritime country accessible to their arms; the Moors and Africans were allured by the hopes of plunder; and, after an interval of six centuries, the fleets that issued from the port of Carthage again claimed the empire of the Mediterranean. The success of the Vandals, the conquest of Sicily, the sack of Palermo, and the frequent descents on the coast of Lucania, awakened and alarmed the mother of Valentinian, and the sister of Theodosius. Alliances were formed; and armaments, expensive and ineffectual, were prepared, for the destruction of the common enemy; who reserved his courage to encounter those dangers which his policy could not prevent or elude. The designs of the Roman government were repeatedly baffled by his artful delays, ambiguous promises, and apparent concessions; and the interposition of his formidable confederate, the king of the Huns, recalled the emperors from the conquest of Africa to the care of their domestic safety. The revolutions of the palace, which left the Western empire without a defender, and without a lawful prince, dispelled the apprehensions, and stimulated the avarice, of Genseric. He immediately equipped a numerous fleet of Vandals and Moors, and cast anchor at the mouth of the Tyber, about three months after the death of Valentinian, and the elevation of Maximus to the Imperial throne.

The private life of the senator Petronius Maximus [1] was often alleged as a rare example of human felicity. His birth was noble and illustrious, since he descended from the Anician family; his dignity was supported by an adequate patrimony in land and money; and these advantages of fortune were accompanied with liberal arts and decent manners, which adorn or imitate the inestimable gifts of genius and virtue. The luxury of his palace and table was hospitable and elegant. Whenever Maximus appeared in public, he was surrounded by a train of grateful and obsequious clients; [2] and it is possible that among these clients, he might deserve and possess some real friends. His merit was rewarded by the favor of the prince and senate: he thrice exercised the office of Praetorian praefect of Italy; he was twice invested with the consulship, and he obtained the rank of patrician. These civil honors were not incompatible with the enjoyment of leisure and tranquillity; his hours, according to the demands of pleasure or reason, were accurately distributed by a water-clock; and this avarice of time may be allowed to prove the sense which Maximus entertained of his own happiness. The injury which he received from the emperor Valentinian appears to excuse the most bloody revenge. Yet a philosopher might have reflected, that, if the resistance of his wife had been sincere, her chastity was still inviolate, and that it could never be restored if she had consented to the will of the adulterer. A patriot would have hesitated before he plunged himself and his country into those inevitable calamities which must follow the extinction of the royal house of Theodosius. The imprudent Maximus disregarded these salutary considerations; he gratified his resentment and ambition; he saw the bleeding corpse of Valentinian at his feet; and he heard himself saluted Emperor by the unanimous voice of the senate and people. But the day of his inauguration was the last day of his happiness. He was imprisoned (such is the lively expression of Sidonius) in the palace; and after passing a sleepless night, he sighed that he had attained the summit of his wishes, and aspired only to descend from the dangerous elevation. Oppressed by the weight of the diadem, he communicated his anxious thoughts to his friend and quaestor Fulgentius; and when he looked back with unavailing regret on the secure pleasures of his former life, the emperor exclaimed, "O fortunate Damocles, [3] thy reign began and ended with the same dinner;" a well-known allusion, which Fulgentius afterwards repeated as an instructive lesson for princes and subjects.

[Footnote 1: Sidonius Apollinaris composed the thirteenth epistle of the second book, to refute the paradox of his friend Serranus, who entertained a singular, though generous, enthusiasm for the deceased emperor. This epistle, with some indulgence, may claim the praise of an elegant composition; and it throws much light on the character of Maximus.]

[Footnote 2: Clientum, praevia, pedisequa, circumfusa, populositas, is the train which Sidonius himself (l. i. epist. 9) assigns to another senator of rank]

[Footnote 3:
Districtus ensis cui super impia Cervice pendet, non Siculoe dapes Dulcem elaborabunt saporem: Non avium citharaeque cantus Somnum reducent. —Horat. Carm. iii. 1.

Sidonius concludes his letter with the story of Damocles, which Cicero (Tusculan. v. 20, 21) had so inimitably told.]

The reign of Maximus continued about three months. His hours, of which he had lost the command, were disturbed by remorse, or guilt, or terror, and his throne was shaken by the seditions of the soldiers, the people, and the confederate Barbarians. The marriage of his son Paladius with the eldest daughter of the late emperor, might tend to establish the hereditary succession of his family; but the violence which he offered to the empress Eudoxia, could proceed only from the blind impulse of lust or revenge. His own wife, the cause of these tragic events, had been seasonably removed by death; and the widow of Valentinian was compelled to violate her decent mourning, perhaps her real grief, and to submit to the embraces of a presumptuous usurper, whom she suspected as the assassin of her deceased husband. These suspicions were soon justified by the indiscreet confession of Maximus himself; and he wantonly provoked the hatred of his reluctant bride, who was still conscious that she was descended from a line of emperors. From the East, however, Eudoxia could not hope to obtain any effectual assistance; her father and her aunt Pulcheria were dead; her mother languished at Jerusalem in disgrace and exile; and the sceptre of Constantinople was in the hands of a stranger. She directed her eyes towards Carthage; secretly implored the aid of the king of the Vandals; and persuaded Genseric to improve the fair opportunity of disguising his rapacious designs by the specious names of honor, justice, and compassion. [4] Whatever abilities Maximus might have shown in a subordinate station, he was found incapable of administering an empire; and though he might easily have been informed of the naval preparations which were made on the opposite shores of Africa, he expected with supine indifference the approach of the enemy, without adopting any measures of defence, of negotiation, or of a timely retreat. When the Vandals disembarked at the mouth of the Tyber, the emperor was suddenly roused from his lethargy by the clamors of a trembling and exasperated multitude. The only hope which presented itself to his astonished mind was that of a precipitate flight, and he exhorted the senators to imitate the example of their prince. But no sooner did Maximus appear in the streets, than he was assaulted by a shower of stones; a Roman, or a Burgundian soldier, claimed the honor of the first wound; his mangled body was ignominiously cast into the Tyber; the Roman people rejoiced in the punishment which they had inflicted on the author of the public calamities; and the domestics of Eudoxia signalized their zeal in the service of their mistress. [5]

[Footnote 4: Notwithstanding the evidence of Procopius, Evagrius, Idatius Marcellinus, &c., the learned Muratori (Annali d'Italia, tom. iv. p. 249) doubts the reality of this invitation, and observes, with great truth, "Non si puo dir quanto sia facile il popolo a sognare e spacciar voci false." But his argument, from the interval of time and place, is extremely feeble. The figs which grew near Carthage were produced to the senate of Rome on the third day.]

[Footnote 5: Infidoque tibi Burgundio ductu Extorquet trepidas mactandi principis iras. —Sidon. in Panegyr. Avit. 442.

A remarkable line, which insinuates that Rome and Maximus were betrayed by their Burgundian mercenaries.]

On the third day after the tumult, Genseric boldly advanced from the port of Ostia to the gates of the defenceless city. Instead of a sally of the Roman youth, there issued from the gates an unarmed and venerable procession of the bishop at the head of his clergy. [6] The fearless spirit of Leo, his authority and eloquence, again mitigated the fierceness of a Barbarian conqueror; the king of the Vandals promised to spare the unresisting multitude, to protect the buildings from fire, and to exempt the captives from torture; and although such orders were neither seriously given, nor strictly obeyed, the mediation of Leo was glorious to himself, and in some degree beneficial to his country. But Rome and its inhabitants were delivered to the licentiousness of the Vandals and Moors, whose blind passions revenged the injuries of Carthage. The pillage lasted fourteen days and nights; and all that yet remained of public or private wealth, of sacred or profane treasure, was diligently transported to the vessels of Genseric. Among the spoils, the splendid relics of two temples, or rather of two religions, exhibited a memorable example of the vicissitudes of human and divine things.

Since the abolition of Paganism, the Capitol had been violated and abandoned; yet the statues of the gods and heroes were still respected, and the curious roof of gilt bronze was reserved for the rapacious hands of Genseric. [7] The holy instruments of the Jewish worship, [8] the gold table, and the gold candlestick with seven branches, originally framed according to the particular instructions of God himself, and which were placed in the sanctuary of his temple, had been ostentatiously displayed to the Roman people in the triumph of Titus. They were afterwards deposited in the temple of Peace; and at the end of four hundred years, the spoils of Jerusalem were transferred from Rome to Carthage, by a Barbarian who derived his origin from the shores of the Baltic. These ancient monuments might attract the notice of curiosity, as well as of avarice. But the Christian churches, enriched and adorned by the prevailing superstition of the times, afforded more plentiful materials for sacrilege; and the pious liberality of Pope Leo, who melted six silver vases, the gift of Constantine, each of a hundred pounds weight, is an evidence of the damage which he attempted to repair. In the forty-five years that had elapsed since the Gothic invasion, the pomp and luxury of Rome were in some measure restored; and it was difficult either to escape, or to satisfy, the avarice of a conqueror, who possessed leisure to collect, and ships to transport, the wealth of the capital. The Imperial ornaments of the palace, the magnificent furniture and wardrobe, the sideboards of massy plate, were accumulated with disorderly rapine; the gold and silver amounted to several thousand talents; yet even the brass and copper were laboriously removed. Eudoxia herself, who advanced to meet her friend and deliverer, soon bewailed the imprudence of her own conduct. She was rudely stripped of her jewels; and the unfortunate empress, with her two daughters, the only surviving remains of the great Theodosius, was compelled, as a captive, to follow the haughty Vandal; who immediately hoisted sail, and returned with a prosperous navigation to the port of Carthage. [9] Many thousand Romans of both sexes, chosen for some useful or agreeable qualifications, reluctantly embarked on board the fleet of Genseric; and their distress was aggravated by the unfeeling Barbarians, who, in the division of the booty, separated the wives from their husbands, and the children from their parents. The charity of Deogratias, bishop of Carthage, [10] was their only consolation and support. He generously sold the gold and silver plate of the church to purchase the freedom of some, to alleviate the slavery of others, and to assist the wants and infirmities of a captive multitude, whose health was impaired by the hardships which they had suffered in their passage from Italy to Africa. By his order, two spacious churches were converted into hospitals; the sick were distributed into convenient beds, and liberally supplied with food and medicines; and the aged prelate repeated his visits both in the day and night, with an assiduity that surpassed his strength, and a tender sympathy which enhanced the value of his services. Compare this scene with the field of Cannae; and judge between Hannibal and the successor of St. Cyprian. [11]

[Footnote 6: The apparant success of Pope Leo may be justified by Prosper, and the Historia Miscellan.; but the improbable notion of Baronius A.D. 455, (No. 13) that Genseric spared the three apostolical churches, is not countenanced even by the doubtful testimony of the Liber Pontificalis.]

[Footnote 7: The profusion of Catulus, the first who gilt the roof of the Capitol, was not universally approved, (Plin. Hist. Natur. xxxiii. 18;) but it was far exceeded by the emperor's, and the external gilding of the temple cost Domitian 12,000 talents, (2,400,000 L.) The expressions of Claudian and Rutilius (luce metalli oemula.... fastigia astris, and confunduntque vagos delubra micantia visus) manifestly prove, that this splendid covering was not removed either by the Christians or the Goths, (see Donatus, Roma Antiqua, l. ii. c. 6, p. 125.) It should seem that the roof of the Capitol was decorated with gilt statues, and chariots drawn by four horses.]

[Footnote 8: The curious reader may consult the learned and accurate treatise of Hadrian Reland, de Spoliis Templi Hierosolymitani in Arcu Titiano Romae conspicuis, in 12mo. Trajecti ad Rhenum, 1716.]

[Footnote 9: The vessel which transported the relics of the Capitol was the only one of the whole fleet that suffered shipwreck. If a bigoted sophist, a Pagan bigot, had mentioned the accident, he might have rejoiced that this cargo of sacrilege was lost in the sea.]

[Footnote 10: See Victor Vitensis, de Persecut. Vandal. l. i. c. 8, p. 11, 12, edit. Ruinart. Deogratius governed the church of Carthage only three years. If he had not been privately buried, his corpse would have been torn piecemeal by the mad devotion of the people.]

[Footnote 11: The general evidence for the death of Maximus, and the sack of Rome by the Vandals, is comprised in Sidonius, (Panegyr. Avit. 441-450,) Procopius, (de Bell. Vandal. l. i. c. 4, 5, p. 188, 189, and l. ii. c. 9, p. 255,) Evagrius, (l. ii. c. 7,) Jornandes, (de Reb. Geticis, c. 45, p. 677,) and the Chronicles of Idatius, Prosper, Marcellinus, and Theophanes, under the proper year.]

The deaths of Aetius and Valentinian had relaxed the ties which held the Barbarians of Gaul in peace and subordination. The sea-coast was infested by the Saxons; the Alemanni and the Franks advanced from the Rhine to the Seine; and the ambition of the Goths seemed to meditate more extensive and permanent conquests. The emperor Maximus relieved himself, by a judicious choice, from the weight of these distant cares; he silenced the solicitations of his friends, listened to the voice of fame, and promoted a stranger to the general command of the forces of Gaul.

Avitus, [12] the stranger, whose merit was so nobly rewarded, descended from a wealthy and honorable family in the diocese of Auvergne. The convulsions of the times urged him to embrace, with the same ardor, the civil and military professions: and the indefatigable youth blended the studies of literature and jurisprudence with the exercise of arms and hunting. Thirty years of his life were laudably spent in the public service; he alternately displayed his talents in war and negotiation; and the soldier of Aetius, after executing the most important embassies, was raised to the station of Praetorian praefect of Gaul. Either the merit of Avitus excited envy, or his moderation was desirous of repose, since he calmly retired to an estate, which he possessed in the neighborhood of Clermont. A copious stream, issuing from the mountain, and falling headlong in many a loud and foaming cascade, discharged its waters into a lake about two miles in length, and the villa was pleasantly seated on the margin of the lake. The baths, the porticos, the summer and winter apartments, were adapted to the purposes of luxury and use; and the adjacent country afforded the various prospects of woods, pastures, and meodows. [13] In this retreat, where Avitus amused his leisure with books, rural sports, the practice of husbandry, and the society of his friends, [14] he received the Imperial diploma, which constituted him master-general of the cavalry and infantry of Gaul. He assumed the military command; the Barbarians suspended their fury; and whatever means he might employ, whatever concessions he might be forced to make, the people enjoyed the benefits of actual tranquillity. But the fate of Gaul depended on the Visigoths; and the Roman general, less attentive to his dignity than to the public interest, did not disdain to visit Thoulouse in the character of an ambassador. He was received with courteous hospitality by Theodoric, the king of the Goths; but while Avitus laid the foundations of a solid alliance with that powerful nation, he was astonished by the intelligence, that the emperor Maximus was slain, and that Rome had been pillaged by the Vandals. A vacant throne, which he might ascend without guilt or danger, tempted his ambition; [15] and the Visigoths were easily persuaded to support his claim by their irresistible suffrage. They loved the person of Avitus; they respected his virtues; and they were not insensible of the advantage, as well as honor, of giving an emperor to the West. The season was now approaching, in which the annual assembly of the seven provinces was held at Arles; their deliberations might perhaps be influenced by the presence of Theodoric and his martial brothers; but their choice would naturally incline to the most illustrious of their countrymen. Avitus, after a decent resistance, accepted the Imperial diadem from the representatives of Gaul; and his election was ratified by the acclamations of the Barbarians and provincials. The formal consent of Marcian, emperor of the East, was solicited and obtained; but the senate, Rome, and Italy, though humbled by their recent calamities, submitted with a secret murmur to the presumption of the Gallic usurper.

[Footnote 12: The private life and elevation of Avitus must be deduced, with becoming suspicion, from the panegyric pronounced by Sidonius Apollinaris, his subject, and his son-in-law.]

[Footnote 13: After the example of the younger Pliny, Sidonius (l. ii. c. 2) has labored the florid, prolix, and obscure description of his villa, which bore the name, (Avitacum,) and had been the property of Avitus. The precise situation is not ascertained. Consult, however, the notes of Savaron and Sirmond.]

[Footnote 14: Sidonius (l. ii. epist. 9) has described the country life of the Gallic nobles, in a visit which he made to his friends, whose estates were in the neighborhood of Nismes. The morning hours were spent in the sphoeristerium, or tennis-court; or in the library, which was furnished with Latin authors, profane and religious; the former for the men, the latter for the ladies. The table was twice served, at dinner and supper, with hot meat (boiled and roast) and wine. During the intermediate time, the company slept, took the air on horseback, and need the warm bath.]

[Footnote 15: Seventy lines of panegyric (505-575) which describe the importunity of Theodoric and of Gaul, struggling to overcome the modest reluctance of Avitus, are blown away by three words of an honest historian. Romanum ambisset Imperium, (Greg. Turon. l. ii. c. 1l, in tom. ii. p. 168.)]

Theodoric, to whom Avitus was indebted for the purple, had acquired the Gothic sceptre by the murder of his elder brother Torismond; and he justified this atrocious deed by the design which his predecessor had formed of violating his alliance with the empire. [16] Such a crime might not be incompatible with the virtues of a Barbarian; but the manners of Theodoric were gentle and humane; and posterity may contemplate without terror the original picture of a Gothic king, whom Sidonius had intimately observed, in the hours of peace and of social intercourse. In an epistle, dated from the court of Thoulouse, the orator satisfies the curiosity of one of his friends, in the following description: [17] "By the majesty of his appearance, Theodoric would command the respect of those who are ignorant of his merit; and although he is born a prince, his merit would dignify a private station. He is of a middle stature, his body appears rather plump than fat, and in his well-proportioned limbs agility is united with muscular strength. [18] If you examine his countenance, you will distinguish a high forehead, large shaggy eyebrows, an aquiline nose, thin lips, a regular set of white teeth, and a fair complexion, that blushes more frequently from modesty than from anger. The ordinary distribution of his time, as far as it is exposed to the public view, may be concisely represented. Before daybreak, he repairs, with a small train, to his domestic chapel, where the service is performed by the Arian clergy; but those who presume to interpret his secret sentiments, consider this assiduous devotion as the effect of habit and policy. The rest of the morning is employed in the administration of his kingdom. His chair is surrounded by some military officers of decent aspect and behavior: the noisy crowd of his Barbarian guards occupies the hall of audience; but they are not permitted to stand within the veils or curtains that conceal the council-chamber from vulgar eyes. The ambassadors of the nations are successively introduced: Theodoric listens with attention, answers them with discreet brevity, and either announces or delays, according to the nature of their business, his final resolution. About eight (the second hour) he rises from his throne, and visits either his treasury or his stables. If he chooses to hunt, or at least to exercise himself on horseback, his bow is carried by a favorite youth; but when the game is marked, he bends it with his own hand, and seldom misses the object of his aim: as a king, he disdains to bear arms in such ignoble warfare; but as a soldier, he would blush to accept any military service which he could perform himself. On common days, his dinner is not different from the repast of a private citizen, but every Saturday, many honorable guests are invited to the royal table, which, on these occasions, is served with the elegance of Greece, the plenty of Gaul, and the order and diligence of Italy. [19] The gold or silver plate is less remarkable for its weight than for the brightness and curious workmanship: the taste is gratified without the help of foreign and costly luxury; the size and number of the cups of wine are regulated with a strict regard to the laws of temperance; and the respectful silence that prevails, is interrupted only by grave and instructive conversation. After dinner, Theodoric sometimes indulges himself in a short slumber; and as soon as he wakes, he calls for the dice and tables, encourages his friends to forget the royal majesty, and is delighted when they freely express the passions which are excited by the incidents of play. At this game, which he loves as the image of war, he alternately displays his eagerness, his skill, his patience, and his cheerful temper. If he loses, he laughs; he is modest and silent if he wins. Yet, notwithstanding this seeming indifference, his courtiers choose to solicit any favor in the moments of victory; and I myself, in my applications to the king, have derived some benefit from my losses. [20] About the ninth hour (three o'clock) the tide of business again returns, and flows incessantly till after sunset, when the signal of the royal supper dismisses the weary crowd of suppliants and pleaders. At the supper, a more familiar repast, buffoons and pantomimes are sometimes introduced, to divert, not to offend, the company, by their ridiculous wit: but female singers, and the soft, effeminate modes of music, are severely banished, and such martial tunes as animate the soul to deeds of valor are alone grateful to the ear of Theodoric. He retires from table; and the nocturnal guards are immediately posted at the entrance of the treasury, the palace, and the private apartments."

[Footnote 16: Isidore, archbishop of Seville, who was himself of the blood royal of the Goths, acknowledges, and almost justifies, (Hist. Goth. p. 718,) the crime which their slave Jornandes had basely dissembled, (c 43, p. 673.)]

[Footnote 17: This elaborate description (l. i. ep. ii. p. 2-7) was dictated by some political motive. It was designed for the public eye, and had been shown by the friends of Sidonius, before it was inserted in the collection of his epistles. The first book was published separately. See Tillemont, Memoires Eccles. tom. xvi. p. 264.]

[Footnote 18: I have suppressed, in this portrait of Theodoric, several minute circumstances, and technical phrases, which could be tolerable, or indeed intelligible, to those only who, like the contemporaries of Sidonius, had frequented the markets where naked slaves were exposed to male, (Dubos, Hist. Critique, tom. i. p. 404.)]

[Footnote 19: Videas ibi elegantiam Graecam, abundantiam Gallicanam; celeritatem Italam; publicam pompam, privatam diligentiam, regiam disciplinam.]

[Footnote 20: Tunc etiam ego aliquid obsecraturus feliciter vincor, et mihi tabula perit ut causa salvetur. Sidonius of Auvergne was not a subject of Theodoric; but he might be compelled to solicit either justice or favor at the court of Thoulouse.]

When the king of the Visigoths encouraged Avitus to assume the purple, he offered his person and his forces, as a faithful soldier of the republic. [21] The exploits of Theodoric soon convinced the world that he had not degenerated from the warlike virtues of his ancestors. After the establishment of the Goths in Aquitain, and the passage of the Vandals into Africa, the Suevi, who had fixed their kingdom in Gallicia, aspired to the conquest of Spain, and threatened to extinguish the feeble remains of the Roman dominion. The provincials of Carthagena and Tarragona, afflicted by a hostile invasion, represented their injuries and their apprehensions. Count Fronto was despatched, in the name of the emperor Avitus, with advantageous offers of peace and alliance; and Theodoric interposed his weighty mediation, to declare, that, unless his brother-in-law, the king of the Suevi, immediately retired, he should be obliged to arm in the cause of justice and of Rome. "Tell him," replied the haughty Rechiarius, "that I despise his friendship and his arms; but that I shall soon try whether he will dare to expect my arrival under the walls of Thoulouse." Such a challenge urged Theodoric to prevent the bold designs of his enemy; he passed the Pyrenees at the head of the Visigoths: the Franks and Burgundians served under his standard; and though he professed himself the dutiful servant of Avitus, he privately stipulated, for himself and his successors, the absolute possession of his Spanish conquests. The two armies, or rather the two nations, encountered each other on the banks of the River Urbicus, about twelve miles from Astorga; and the decisive victory of the Goths appeared for a while to have extirpated the name and kingdom of the Suevi. From the field of battle Theodoric advanced to Braga, their metropolis, which still retained the splendid vestiges of its ancient commerce and dignity. [22] His entrance was not polluted with blood; and the Goths respected the chastity of their female captives, more especially of the consecrated virgins: but the greatest part of the clergy and people were made slaves, and even the churches and altars were confounded in the universal pillage. The unfortunate king of the Suevi had escaped to one of the ports of the ocean; but the obstinacy of the winds opposed his flight: he was delivered to his implacable rival; and Rechiarius, who neither desired nor expected mercy, received, with manly constancy, the death which he would probably have inflicted. After this bloody sacrifice to policy or resentment, Theodoric carried his victorious arms as far as Merida, the principal town of Lusitania, without meeting any resistance, except from the miraculous powers of St. Eulalia; but he was stopped in the full career of success, and recalled from Spain before he could provide for the security of his conquests. In his retreat towards the Pyrenees, he revenged his disappointment on the country through which he passed; and, in the sack of Pollentia and Astorga, he showed himself a faithless ally, as well as a cruel enemy. Whilst the king of the Visigoths fought and vanquished in the name of Avitus, the reign of Avitus had expired; and both the honor and the interest of Theodoric were deeply wounded by the disgrace of a friend, whom he had seated on the throne of the Western empire. [23]

[Footnote 21: Theodoric himself had given a solemn and voluntary promise of fidelity, which was understood both in Gaul and Spain.

Romae sum, te duce, Amicus, Principe te, Miles. Sidon. Panegyr. Avit. 511.]

[Footnote 22: Quaeque sinu pelagi jactat se Bracara dives. Auson. de Claris Urbibus, p. 245. —From the design of the king of the Suevi, it is evident that the navigation from the ports of Gallicia to the Mediterranean was known and practised. The ships of Bracara, or Braga, cautiously steered along the coast, without daring to lose themselves in the Atlantic.]

[Footnote 23: This Suevic war is the most authentic part of the Chronicle of Idatius, who, as bishop of Iria Flavia, was himself a spectator and a sufferer. Jornandes (c. 44, p. 675, 676, 677) has expatiated, with pleasure, on the Gothic victory.]

PART II

The pressing solicitations of the senate and people persuaded the emperor Avitus to fix his residence at Rome, and to accept the consulship for the ensuing year. On the first day of January, his son-in-law, Sidonius Apollinaris, celebrated his praises in a panegyric of six hundred verses; but this composition, though it was rewarded with a brass statue, [24] seems to contain a very moderate proportion, either of genius or of truth. The poet, if we may degrade that sacred name, exaggerates the merit of a sovereign and a father; and his prophecy of a long and glorious reign was soon contradicted by the event. Avitus, at a time when the Imperial dignity was reduced to a preeminence of toil and danger, indulged himself in the pleasures of Italian luxury: age had not extinguished his amorous inclinations; and he is accused of insulting, with indiscreet and ungenerous raillery, the husbands whose wives he had seduced or violated. [25] But the Romans were not inclined either to excuse his faults or to acknowledge his virtues. The several parts of the empire became every day more alienated from each other; and the stranger of Gaul was the object of popular hatred and contempt. The senate asserted their legitimate claim in the election of an emperor; and their authority, which had been originally derived from the old constitution, was again fortified by the actual weakness of a declining monarchy. Yet even such a monarchy might have resisted the votes of an unarmed senate, if their discontent had not been supported, or perhaps inflamed, by the Count Ricimer, one of the principal commanders of the Barbarian troops, who formed the military defence of Italy. The daughter of Wallia, king of the Visigoths, was the mother of Ricimer; but he was descended, on the father's side, from the nation of the Suevi; [26] his pride or patriotism might be exasperated by the misfortunes of his countrymen; and he obeyed, with reluctance, an emperor in whose elevation he had not been consulted. His faithful and important services against the common enemy rendered him still more formidable; [27] and, after destroying on the coast of Corsica a fleet of Vandals, which consisted of sixty galleys, Ricimer returned in triumph with the appellation of the Deliverer of Italy. He chose that moment to signify to Avitus, that his reign was at an end; and the feeble emperor, at a distance from his Gothic allies, was compelled, after a short and unavailing struggle to abdicate the purple. By the clemency, however, or the contempt, of Ricimer, [28] he was permitted to descend from the throne to the more desirable station of bishop of Placentia: but the resentment of the senate was still unsatisfied; and their inflexible severity pronounced the sentence of his death He fled towards the Alps, with the humble hope, not of arming the Visigoths in his cause, but of securing his person and treasures in the sanctuary of Julian, one of the tutelar saints of Auvergne. [29] Disease, or the hand of the executioner, arrested him on the road; yet his remains were decently transported to Brivas, or Brioude, in his native province, and he reposed at the feet of his holy patron. [30] Avitus left only one daughter, the wife of Sidonius Apollinaris, who inherited the patrimony of his father-in-law; lamenting, at the same time, the disappointment of his public and private expectations. His resentment prompted him to join, or at least to countenance, the measures of a rebellious faction in Gaul; and the poet had contracted some guilt, which it was incumbent on him to expiate, by a new tribute of flattery to the succeeding emperor. [31]

[Footnote 24: In one of the porticos or galleries belonging to Trajan's library, among the statues of famous writers and orators. Sidon. Apoll. l. ix. epist, 16, p. 284. Carm. viii. p. 350.]

[Footnote 25: Luxuriose agere volens a senatoribus projectus est, is the concise expression of Gregory of Tours, (l. ii. c. xi. in tom. ii. p. 168.) An old Chronicle (in tom. ii. p. 649) mentions an indecent jest of Avitus, which seems more applicable to Rome than to Treves.]

[Footnote 26: Sidonius (Panegyr. Anthem. 302, &c.) praises the royal birth of Ricimer, the lawful heir, as he chooses to insinuate, both of the Gothic and Suevic kingdoms.]

[Footnote 27: See the Chronicle of Idatius. Jornandes (c. xliv. p. 676) styles him, with some truth, virum egregium, et pene tune in Italia ad ex ercitum singularem.]

[Footnote 28: Parcens innocentiae Aviti, is the compassionate, but contemptuous, language of Victor Tunnunensis, (in Chron. apud Scaliger Euseb.) In another place, he calls him, vir totius simplicitatis. This commendation is more humble, but it is more solid and sincere, than the praises of Sidonius]

[Footnote 29: He suffered, as it is supposed, in the persecution of Diocletian, (Tillemont, Mem. Eccles. tom. v. p. 279, 696.) Gregory of Tours, his peculiar votary, has dedicated to the glory of Julian the Martyr an entire book, (de Gloria Martyrum, l. ii. in Max. Bibliot. Patrum, tom. xi. p. 861-871,) in which he relates about fifty foolish miracles performed by his relics.]

[Footnote 30: Gregory of Tours (l. ii. c. xi. p. 168) is concise, but correct, in the reign of his countryman. The words of Idatius, "cadet imperio, caret et vita," seem to imply, that the death of Avitus was violent; but it must have been secret, since Evagrius (l. ii. c. 7) could suppose, that he died of the plaque.]

[Footnote 31: After a modest appeal to the examples of his brethren, Virgil and Horace, Sidonius honestly confesses the debt, and promises payment.

Sic mihi diverso nuper sub Marte cadenti Jussisti placido Victor ut essem animo. Serviat ergo tibi servati lingua poetae, Atque meae vitae laus tua sit pretium. —Sidon. Apoll. Carm. iv. p. 308

See Dubos, Hist. Critique, tom. i. p. 448, &c.]

The successor of Avitus presents the welcome discovery of a great and heroic character, such as sometimes arise, in a degenerate age, to vindicate the honor of the human species. The emperor Majorian has deserved the praises of his contemporaries, and of posterity; and these praises may be strongly expressed in the words of a judicious and disinterested historian: "That he was gentle to his subjects; that he was terrible to his enemies; and that he excelled, in every virtue, all his predecessors who had reigned over the Romans." [32] Such a testimony may justify at least the panegyric of S donius; and we may acquiesce in the assurance, that, although the obsequious orator would have flattered, with equal zeal, the most worthless of princes, the extraordinary merit of his object confined him, on this occasion, within the bounds of truth. [33] Majorian derived his name from his maternal grandfather, who, in the reign of the great Theodosius, had commanded the troops of the Illyrian frontier. He gave his daughter in marriage to the father of Majorian, a respectable officer, who administered the revenues of Gaul with skill and integrity; and generously preferred the friendship of Aetius to the tempting offer of an insidious court. His son, the future emperor, who was educated in the profession of arms, displayed, from his early youth, intrepid courage, premature wisdom, and unbounded liberality in a scanty fortune. He followed the standard of Aetius, contributed to his success, shared, and sometimes eclipsed, his glory, and at last excited the jealousy of the patrician, or rather of his wife, who forced him to retire from the service. [34] Majorian, after the death of Aetius, was recalled and promoted; and his intimate connection with Count Ricimer was the immediate step by which he ascended the throne of the Western empire. During the vacancy that succeeded the abdication of Avitus, the ambitious Barbarian, whose birth excluded him from the Imperial dignity, governed Italy with the title of Patrician; resigned to his friend the conspicuous station of master-general of the cavalry and infantry; and, after an interval of some months, consented to the unanimous wish of the Romans, whose favor Majorian had solicited by a recent victory over the Alemanni. [35] He was invested with the purple at Ravenna: and the epistle which he addressed to the senate, will best describe his situation and his sentiments. "Your election, Conscript Fathers! and the ordinance of the most valiant army, have made me your emperor. [36] May the propitious Deity direct and prosper the counsels and events of my administration, to your advantage and to the public welfare! For my own part, I did not aspire, I have submitted to reign; nor should I have discharged the obligations of a citizen if I had refused, with base and selfish ingratitude, to support the weight of those labors, which were imposed by the republic. Assist, therefore, the prince whom you have made; partake the duties which you have enjoined; and may our common endeavors promote the happiness of an empire, which I have accepted from your hands. Be assured, that, in our times, justice shall resume her ancient vigor, and that virtue shall become, not only innocent, but meritorious. Let none, except the authors themselves, be apprehensive of delations, [37] which, as a subject, I have always condemned, and, as a prince, will severely punish. Our own vigilance, and that of our father, the patrician Ricimer, shall regulate all military affairs, and provide for the safety of the Roman world, which we have saved from foreign and domestic enemies. [38] You now understand the maxims of my government; you may confide in the faithful love and sincere assurances of a prince who has formerly been the companion of your life and dangers; who still glories in the name of senator, and who is anxious that you should never repent the judgment which you have pronounced in his favor." The emperor, who, amidst the ruins of the Roman world, revived the ancient language of law and liberty, which Trajan would not have disclaimed, must have derived those generous sentiments from his own heart; since they were not suggested to his imitation by the customs of his age, or the example of his predecessors. [39]

[Footnote 32: The words of Procopius deserve to be transcribed (de Bell. Vandal. l. i. c. 7, p. 194;) a concise but comprehensive definition of royal virtue.]

[Footnote 33: The Panegyric was pronounced at Lyons before the end of the year 458, while the emperor was still consul. It has more art than genius, and more labor than art. The ornaments are false and trivial; the expression is feeble and prolix; and Sidonius wants the skill to exhibit the principal figure in a strong and distinct light. The private life of Majorian occupies about two hundred lines, 107-305.]

[Footnote 34: She pressed his immediate death, and was scarcely satisfied with his disgrace. It should seem that Aetius, like Belisarius and Marlborough, was governed by his wife; whose fervent piety, though it might work miracles, (Gregor. Turon. l. ii. c. 7, p. 162,) was not incompatible with base and sanguinary counsels.]

[Footnote 35: The Alemanni had passed the Rhaetian Alps, and were defeated in the Campi Canini, or Valley of Bellinzone, through which the Tesin flows, in its descent from Mount Adula to the Lago Maggiore, (Cluver Italia Antiq. tom. i. p. 100, 101.) This boasted victory over nine hundred Barbarians (Panegyr. Majorian. 373, &c.) betrays the extreme weakness of Italy.]

[Footnote 36: Imperatorem me factum, P.C. electionis vestrae arbitrio, et fortissimi exercitus ordinatione agnoscite, (Novell. Majorian. tit. iii. p. 34, ad Calcem. Cod. Theodos.) Sidonius proclaims the unanimous voice of the empire:—

Postquam ordine vobis Ordo omnis regnum dederat; plebs, curia, nules, —Et collega simul. 386.

This language is ancient and constitutional; and we may observe, that the clergy were not yet considered as a distinct order of the state.]

[Footnote 37: Either dilationes, or delationes would afford a tolerable reading, but there is much more sense and spirit in the latter, to which I have therefore given the preference.]

[Footnote 38: Ab externo hoste et a domestica clade liberavimus: by the latter, Majorian must understand the tyranny of Avitus; whose death he consequently avowed as a meritorious act. On this occasion, Sidonius is fearful and obscure; he describes the twelve Caesars, the nations of Africa, &c., that he may escape the dangerous name of Avitus (805-369.)]

[Footnote 39: See the whole edict or epistle of Majorian to the senate, (Novell. tit. iv. p. 34.) Yet the expression, regnum nostrum, bears some taint of the age, and does not mix kindly with the word respublica, which he frequently repeats.]

The private and public actions of Majorian are very imperfectly known: but his laws, remarkable for an original cast of thought and expression, faithfully represent the character of a sovereign who loved his people, who sympathized in their distress, who had studied the causes of the decline of the empire, and who was capable of applying (as far as such reformation was practicable) judicious and effectual remedies to the public disorders. [40] His regulations concerning the finances manifestly tended to remove, or at least to mitigate, the most intolerable grievances. I. From the first hour of his reign, he was solicitous (I translate his own words) to relieve the weary fortunes of the provincials, oppressed by the accumulated weight of indictions and superindictions. [41] With this view he granted a universal amnesty, a final and absolute discharge of all arrears of tribute, of all debts, which, under any pretence, the fiscal officers might demand from the people. This wise dereliction of obsolete, vexatious, and unprofitable claims, improved and purified the sources of the public revenue; and the subject who could now look back without despair, might labor with hope and gratitude for himself and for his country. II. In the assessment and collection of taxes, Majorian restored the ordinary jurisdiction of the provincial magistrates; and suppressed the extraordinary commissions which had been introduced, in the name of the emperor himself, or of the Praetorian praefects. The favorite servants, who obtained such irregular powers, were insolent in their behavior, and arbitrary in their demands: they affected to despise the subordinate tribunals, and they were discontented, if their fees and profits did not twice exceed the sum which they condescended to pay into the treasury. One instance of their extortion would appear incredible, were it not authenticated by the legislator himself. They exacted the whole payment in gold: but they refused the current coin of the empire, and would accept only such ancient pieces as were stamped with the names of Faustina or the Antonines. The subject, who was unprovided with these curious medals, had recourse to the expedient of compounding with their rapacious demands; or if he succeeded in the research, his imposition was doubled, according to the weight and value of the money of former times. [42] III. "The municipal corporations, (says the emperor,) the lesser senates, (so antiquity has justly styled them,) deserve to be considered as the heart of the cities, and the sinews of the republic. And yet so low are they now reduced, by the injustice of magistrates and the venality of collectors, that many of their members, renouncing their dignity and their country, have taken refuge in distant and obscure exile." He urges, and even compels, their return to their respective cities; but he removes the grievance which had forced them to desert the exercise of their municipal functions. They are directed, under the authority of the provincial magistrates, to resume their office of levying the tribute; but, instead of being made responsible for the whole sum assessed on their district, they are only required to produce a regular account of the payments which they have actually received, and of the defaulters who are still indebted to the public. IV. But Majorian was not ignorant that these corporate bodies were too much inclined to retaliate the injustice and oppression which they had suffered; and he therefore revives the useful office of the defenders of cities. He exhorts the people to elect, in a full and free assembly, some man of discretion and integrity, who would dare to assert their privileges, to represent their grievances, to protect the poor from the tyranny of the rich, and to inform the emperor of the abuses that were committed under the sanction of his name and authority.

[Footnote 40: See the laws of Majorian (they are only nine in number, but very long, and various) at the end of the Theodosian Code, Novell. l. iv. p. 32-37. Godefroy has not given any commentary on these additional pieces.]

[Footnote 41: Fessas provincialium varia atque multiplici tributorum exactione fortunas, et extraordinariis fiscalium solutionum oneribus attritas, &c. Novell. Majorian. tit. iv. p. 34.]

[Footnote 42: The learned Greaves (vol. i. p. 329, 330, 331) has found, by a diligent inquiry, that aurei of the Antonines weighed one hundred and eighteen, and those of the fifth century only sixty-eight, English grains. Majorian gives currency to all gold coin, excepting only the Gallic solidus, from its deficiency, not in the weight, but in the standard.]

The spectator who casts a mournful view over the ruins of ancient Rome, is tempted to accuse the memory of the Goths and Vandals, for the mischief which they had neither leisure, nor power, nor perhaps inclination, to perpetrate. The tempest of war might strike some lofty turrets to the ground; but the destruction which undermined the foundations of those massy fabrics was prosecuted, slowly and silently, during a period of ten centuries; and the motives of interest, that afterwards operated without shame or control, were severely checked by the taste and spirit of the emperor Majorian. The decay of the city had gradually impaired the value of the public works. The circus and theatres might still excite, but they seldom gratified, the desires of the people: the temples, which had escaped the zeal of the Christians, were no longer inhabited, either by gods or men; the diminished crowds of the Romans were lost in the immense space of their baths and porticos; and the stately libraries and halls of justice became useless to an indolent generation, whose repose was seldom disturbed, either by study or business. The monuments of consular, or Imperial, greatness were no longer revered, as the immortal glory of the capital: they were only esteemed as an inexhaustible mine of materials, cheaper, and more convenient than the distant quarry. Specious petitions were continually addressed to the easy magistrates of Rome, which stated the want of stones or bricks, for some necessary service: the fairest forms of architecture were rudely defaced, for the sake of some paltry, or pretended, repairs; and the degenerate Romans, who converted the spoil to their own emolument, demolished, with sacrilegious hands, the labors of their ancestors. Majorian, who had often sighed over the desolation of the city, applied a severe remedy to the growing evil. [43] He reserved to the prince and senate the sole cognizance of the extreme cases which might justify the destruction of an ancient edifice; imposed a fine of fifty pounds of gold (two thousand pounds sterling) on every magistrate who should presume to grant such illegal and scandalous license, and threatened to chastise the criminal obedience of their subordinate officers, by a severe whipping, and the amputation of both their hands. In the last instance, the legislator might seem to forget the proportion of guilt and punishment; but his zeal arose from a generous principle, and Majorian was anxious to protect the monuments of those ages, in which he would have desired and deserved to live. The emperor conceived, that it was his interest to increase the number of his subjects; and that it was his duty to guard the purity of the marriage-bed: but the means which he employed to accomplish these salutary purposes are of an ambiguous, and perhaps exceptionable, kind. The pious maids, who consecrated their virginity to Christ, were restrained from taking the veil till they had reached their fortieth year. Widows under that age were compelled to form a second alliance within the term of five years, by the forfeiture of half their wealth to their nearest relations, or to the state. Unequal marriages were condemned or annulled. The punishment of confiscation and exile was deemed so inadequate to the guilt of adultery, that, if the criminal returned to Italy, he might, by the express declaration of Majorian, be slain with impunity. [44]

[Footnote 43: The whole edict (Novell. Majorian. tit. vi. p. 35) is curious. "Antiquarum aedium dissipatur speciosa constructio; et ut aliquid reparetur, magna diruuntur. Hinc jam occasio nascitur, ut etiam unusquisque privatum aedificium construens, per gratiam judicum...... praesumere de publicis locis necessaria, et transferre non dubitet" &c. With equal zeal, but with less power, Petrarch, in the fourteenth century, repeated the same complaints. (Vie de Petrarque, tom. i. p. 326, 327.) If I prosecute this history, I shall not be unmindful of the decline and fall of the city of Rome; an interesting object to which any plan was originally confined.]

[Footnote 44: The emperor chides the lenity of Rogatian, consular of Tuscany in a style of acrimonious reproof, which sounds almost like personal resentment, (Novell. tit. ix. p. 47.) The law of Majorian, which punished obstinate widows, was soon afterwards repealed by his successor Severus, (Novell. Sever. tit. i. p. 37.)]

While the emperor Majorian assiduously labored to restore the happiness and virtue of the Romans, he encountered the arms of Genseric, from his character and situation their most formidable enemy. A fleet of Vandals and Moors landed at the mouth of the Liris, or Garigliano; but the Imperial troops surprised and attacked the disorderly Barbarians, who were encumbered with the spoils of Campania; they were chased with slaughter to their ships, and their leader, the king's brother-in-law, was found in the number of the slain. [45] Such vigilance might announce the character of the new reign; but the strictest vigilance, and the most numerous forces, were insufficient to protect the long-extended coast of Italy from the depredations of a naval war. The public opinion had imposed a nobler and more arduous task on the genius of Majorian. Rome expected from him alone the restitution of Africa; and the design, which he formed, of attacking the Vandals in their new settlements, was the result of bold and judicious policy. If the intrepid emperor could have infused his own spirit into the youth of Italy; if he could have revived in the field of Mars, the manly exercises in which he had always surpassed his equals; he might have marched against Genseric at the head of a Roman army. Such a reformation of national manners might be embraced by the rising generation; but it is the misfortune of those princes who laboriously sustain a declining monarchy, that, to obtain some immediate advantage, or to avert some impending danger, they are forced to countenance, and even to multiply, the most pernicious abuses. Majorian, like the weakest of his predecessors, was reduced to the disgraceful expedient of substituting Barbarian auxiliaries in the place of his unwarlike subjects: and his superior abilities could only be displayed in the vigor and dexterity with which he wielded a dangerous instrument, so apt to recoil on the hand that used it. Besides the confederates, who were already engaged in the service of the empire, the fame of his liberality and valor attracted the nations of the Danube, the Borysthenes, and perhaps of the Tanais. Many thousands of the bravest subjects of Attila, the Gepidae, the Ostrogoths, the Rugians, the Burgundians, the Suevi, the Alani, assembled in the plains of Liguria; and their formidable strength was balanced by their mutual animosities. [46] They passed the Alps in a severe winter. The emperor led the way, on foot, and in complete armor; sounding, with his long staff, the depth of the ice, or snow, and encouraging the Scythians, who complained of the extreme cold, by the cheerful assurance, that they should be satisfied with the heat of Africa. The citizens of Lyons had presumed to shut their gates; they soon implored, and experienced, the clemency of Majorian. He vanquished Theodoric in the field; and admitted to his friendship and alliance a king whom he had found not unworthy of his arms. The beneficial, though precarious, reunion of the greater part of Gaul and Spain, was the effect of persuasion, as well as of force; [47] and the independent Bagaudae, who had escaped, or resisted, the oppression, of former reigns, were disposed to confide in the virtues of Majorian. His camp was filled with Barbarian allies; his throne was supported by the zeal of an affectionate people; but the emperor had foreseen, that it was impossible, without a maritime power, to achieve the conquest of Africa. In the first Punic war, the republic had exerted such incredible diligence, that, within sixty days after the first stroke of the axe had been given in the forest, a fleet of one hundred and sixty galleys proudly rode at anchor in the sea. [48] Under circumstances much less favorable, Majorian equalled the spirit and perseverance of the ancient Romans. The woods of the Apennine were felled; the arsenals and manufactures of Ravenna and Misenum were restored; Italy and Gaul vied with each other in liberal contributions to the public service; and the Imperial navy of three hundred large galleys, with an adequate proportion of transports and smaller vessels, was collected in the secure and capacious harbor of Carthagena in Spain. [49] The intrepid countenance of Majorian animated his troops with a confidence of victory; and, if we might credit the historian Procopius, his courage sometimes hurried him beyond the bounds of prudence. Anxious to explore, with his own eyes, the state of the Vandals, he ventured, after disguising the color of his hair, to visit Carthage, in the character of his own ambassador: and Genseric was afterwards mortified by the discovery, that he had entertained and dismissed the emperor of the Romans. Such an anecdote may be rejected as an improbable fiction; but it is a fiction which would not have been imagined, unless in the life of a hero. [50]

[Footnote 45: Sidon. Panegyr. Majorian, 385-440.]

[Footnote 46: The review of the army, and passage of the Alps, contain the most tolerable passages of the Panegyric, (470-552.) M. de Buat (Hist. des Peuples, &c., tom. viii. p. 49-55) is a more satisfactory commentator, than either Savaron or Sirmond.]

[Footnote 47: It is the just and forcible distinction of Priscus, (Excerpt. Legat. p. 42,) in a short fragment, which throws much light on the history of Majorian. Jornandes has suppressed the defeat and alliance of the Visigoths, which were solemnly proclaimed in Gallicia; and are marked in the Chronicle of Idatius.]

[Footnote 48: Florus, l. ii. c. 2. He amuses himself with the poetical fancy, that the trees had been transformed into ships; and indeed the whole transaction, as it is related in the first book of Polybius, deviates too much from the probable course of human events.]

[Footnote 49:
Iterea duplici texis dum littore classem Inferno superoque mari, cadit omnis in aequor Sylva tibi, &c. — Sidon. Panegyr. Majorian, 441-461.

The number of ships, which Priscus fixed at 300, is magnified, by an indefinite comparison with the fleets of Agamemnon, Xerxes, and Augustus.]

[Footnote 50: Procopius de Bell. Vandal. l. i. c. 8, p. 194. When Genseric conducted his unknown guest into the arsenal of Carthage, the arms clashed of their own accord. Majorian had tinged his yellow locks with a black color.]

PART III

Without the help of a personal interview, Genseric was sufficiently acquainted with the genius and designs of his adversary. He practiced his customary arts of fraud and delay, but he practiced them without success. His applications for peace became each hour more submissive, and perhaps more sincere; but the inflexible Majorian had adopted the ancient maxim, that Rome could not be safe, as long as Carthage existed in a hostile state. The king of the Vandals distrusted the valor of his native subjects, who were enervated by the luxury of the South; [51] he suspected the fidelity of the vanquished people, who abhorred him as an Arian tyrant; and the desperate measure, which he executed, of reducing Mauritania into a desert, [52] could not defeat the operations of the Roman emperor, who was at liberty to land his troops on any part of the African coast. But Genseric was saved from impending and inevitable ruin by the treachery of some powerful subjects, envious, or apprehensive, of their master's success. Guided by their secret intelligence, he surprised the unguarded fleet in the Bay of Carthagena: many of the ships were sunk, or taken, or burnt; and the preparations of three years were destroyed in a single day. [53] After this event, the behavior of the two antagonists showed them superior to their fortune. The Vandal, instead of being elated by this accidental victory, immediately renewed his solicitations for peace. The emperor of the West, who was capable of forming great designs, and of supporting heavy disappointments, consented to a treaty, or rather to a suspension of arms; in the full assurance that, before he could restore his navy, he should be supplied with provocations to justify a second war. Majorian returned to Italy, to prosecute his labors for the public happiness; and, as he was conscious of his own integrity, he might long remain ignorant of the dark conspiracy which threatened his throne and his life. The recent misfortune of Carthagena sullied the glory which had dazzled the eyes of the multitude; almost every description of civil and military officers were exasperated against the Reformer, since they all derived some advantage from the abuses which he endeavored to suppress; and the patrician Ricimer impelled the inconstant passions of the Barbarians against a prince whom he esteemed and hated. The virtues of Majorian could not protect him from the impetuous sedition, which broke out in the camp near Tortona, at the foot of the Alps. He was compelled to abdicate the Imperial purple: five days after his abdication, it was reported that he died of a dysentery; [54] and the humble tomb, which covered his remains, was consecrated by the respect and gratitude of succeeding generations. [55] The private character of Majorian inspired love and respect. Malicious calumny and satire excited his indignation, or, if he himself were the object, his contempt; but he protected the freedom of wit, and, in the hours which the emperor gave to the familiar society of his friends, he could indulge his taste for pleasantry, without degrading the majesty of his rank. [56]

[Footnote 51:

Spoliisque potitus Immensis, robux luxu jam perdidit omne, Quo valuit dum pauper erat. —Panegyr. Majorian, 330.

He afterwards applies to Genseric, unjustly, as it should seem, the vices of his subjects.]

[Footnote 52: He burnt the villages, and poisoned the springs, (Priscus, p. 42.) Dubos (Hist. Critique, tom. i. p. 475) observes, that the magazines which the Moors buried in the earth might escape his destructive search. Two or three hundred pits are sometimes dug in the same place; and each pit contains at least four hundred bushels of corn Shaw's Travels, p. 139.]

[Footnote 53: Idatius, who was safe in Gallicia from the power of Recimer boldly and honestly declares, *Vandali per proditeres admoniti,* &c: i. e. dissembles, however, the name of the traitor.]

[Footnote 54: Procop. de Bell. Vandal. l. i. i. c. 8, p. 194. The testimony of Idatius is fair and impartial: *"Majorianum de Galliis Romam redeuntem, et Romano imperio vel nomini res necessarias ordinantem; Richimer livore percitus, et invidorum consilio fultus, fraude interficit circumventum."* Some read *Suevorum,* and I am unwilling to efface either of the words, as they express the different accomplices who united in the conspiracy against Majorian.]

[Footnote 55: See the Epigrams of Ennodius, No. cxxxv. inter Sirmond. Opera, tom. i. p. 1903. It is flat and obscure; but Ennodius was made bishop of Pavia fifty years after the death of Majorian, and his praise deserves credit and regard.]

[Footnote 56: Sidonius gives a tedious account (l. i. epist. xi. p. 25-31) of a supper at Arles, to which he was invited by Majorian, a short time before his death. He had no intention of praising a deceased emperor: but a casual disinterested remark, "Subrisit Augustus; ut erat, auctoritate servata, cum se communioni dedisset, joci plenus," outweighs the six hundred lines of his venal panegyric.]

It was not, perhaps, without some regret, that Ricimer sacrificed his friend to the interest of his ambition: but he resolved, in a second choice, to avoid the imprudent preference of superior virtue and merit. At his command, the obsequious senate of Rome bestowed the Imperial title on Libius Severus, who ascended the throne of the West without emerging from the obscurity of a private condition. History has scarcely deigned to notice his birth, his elevation, his character, or his death. Severus expired, as soon as his life became inconvenient to his patron; [57] and it would be useless to discriminate his nominal reign in the vacant interval of six years, between the death of Majorian and the elevation of Anthemius. During that period, the government was in the hands of Ricimer alone; and, although the modest Barbarian disclaimed the name of king, he accumulated treasures, formed a separate army, negotiated private alliances, and ruled Italy with the same independent and despotic authority, which was afterwards exercised by Odoacer and Theodoric. But his dominions were bounded by the Alps; and two Roman generals, Marcellinus and Aegidius, maintained their allegiance to the republic, by rejecting, with disdain, the phantom which he styled an emperor. Marcellinus still adhered to the old religion; and the devout Pagans, who secretly disobeyed the laws of the church and state, applauded his profound skill in the science of divination. But he possessed the more valuable qualifications of learning, virtue, and courage; [58] the study of the Latin literature had improved his taste; and his military talents had recommended him to the esteem and confidence of the great Aetius, in whose ruin he was involved. By a timely flight, Marcellinus escaped the rage of Valentinian, and boldly asserted his liberty amidst the convulsions of the Western empire. His voluntary, or reluctant, submission to the authority of Majorian, was rewarded by the government of Sicily, and the command of an army, stationed in that island to oppose, or to attack, the Vandals; but his Barbarian mercenaries, after the emperor's death, were tempted to revolt by the artful liberality of Ricimer. At the head of a band of faithful followers, the intrepid Marcellinus occupied the province of Dalmatia, assumed the title of patrician of the West, secured the love of his subjects by a mild and equitable reign, built a fleet which claimed the dominion of the Adriatic, and alternately alarmed the coasts of Italy and of Africa. [59] Aegidius, the master-general of Gaul, who equalled, or at least who imitated, the heroes of ancient Rome, [60] proclaimed his immortal resentment against the assassins of his beloved master. A brave and numerous army was attached to his standard: and, though he was prevented by the arts of Ricimer, and the arms of the Visigoths, from marching to the gates of Rome, he maintained his independent sovereignty beyond the Alps, and rendered the name of Aegidius, respectable both in peace and war. The Franks, who had punished with exile the youthful follies of Childeric, elected the Roman general for their king: his vanity, rather than his ambition, was gratified by that singular honor; and when the nation, at the end of four years, repented of the injury which they had offered to the Merovingian family, he patiently acquiesced in the restoration of the lawful prince. The authority of Aegidius ended only with his life, and the suspicions of poison and secret violence, which derived some countenance from the character of Ricimer, were eagerly entertained by the passionate credulity of the Gauls. [61]

[Footnote 57: Sidonius (Panegyr. Anthem. 317) dismisses him to heaven:—Auxerat Augustus naturae lege Severus—Divorum numerum. And an old list of the emperors, composed about the time of Justinian, praises his piety, and fixes his residence at Rome, (Sirmond. Not. ad Sidon. p. 111, 112.)]

[Footnote 58: Tillemont, who is always scandalized by the virtues of infidels, attributes this advantageous portrait of Marcellinus (which Suidas has preserved) to the partial zeal of some Pagan historian, (Hist. des Empereurs. tom. vi. p. 330.)]

[Footnote 59: Procopius de Bell. Vandal. l. i. c 6, p. 191. In various circumstances of the life of Marcellinus, it is not easy to reconcile the Greek historian with the Latin Chronicles of the times.]

[Footnote 60: I must apply to Aegidius the praises which Sidonius (Panegyr Majorian, 553) bestows on a nameless master-general, who commanded the rear-guard of Majorian. Idatius, from public report, commends his Christian piety; and Priscus mentions (p. 42) his military virtues.]

[Footnote 61: Greg. Turon. l. ii. c. 12, in tom. ii. p. 168. The Pere Daniel, whose ideas were superficial and modern, has started some objections against the story of Childeric, (Hist. de France, tom. i. Preface Historique, p. lxxvii., &c.:) but they have been fairly satisfied by Dubos, (Hist. Critique, tom. i. p. 460-510,) and by two authors who disputed the prize of the Academy of Soissons, (p. 131-177, 310-339.) With regard to the term of Childeric's exile, it is necessary either to prolong the life of Aegidius beyond the date assigned by the Chronicle of Idatius or to correct the text of Gregory, by reading quarto anno, instead of octavo.]

The kingdom of Italy, a name to which the Western empire was gradually reduced, was afflicted, under the reign of Ricimer, by the incessant depredations of the Vandal pirates. [62] In the spring of each year, they equipped a formidable navy in the port of Carthage; and Genseric himself, though in a very advanced age, still commanded in person the most important expeditions. His designs were concealed with impenetrable secrecy, till the moment that he hoisted sail. When he was asked, by his pilot, what course he should steer, "Leave the determination to the winds, (replied the Barbarian, with pious arrogance;) they will transport us to the guilty coast, whose inhabitants have provoked the divine justice;" but if Genseric himself deigned to issue more precise orders, he judged the most wealthy to be the most criminal. The Vandals repeatedly visited the coasts of Spain, Liguria, Tuscany, Campania, Lucania, Bruttium, Apulia, Calabria, Venetia, Dalmatia, Epirus, Greece, and Sicily: they were tempted to subdue the Island of Sardinia, so advantageously placed in the centre of the Mediterranean; and their arms spread desolation, or terror, from the columns of Hercules to the mouth of the Nile. As they were more ambitious of spoil than of glory, they seldom attacked any fortified cities, or engaged any regular troops in the open field. But the celerity of their motions enabled them, almost at the same time, to threaten and to attack the most distant objects, which attracted their desires; and as they always embarked a sufficient number of horses, they had no sooner landed, than they swept the dismayed country with a body of light cavalry. Yet, notwithstanding the example of their king, the native Vandals and Alani insensibly declined this toilsome and perilous warfare; the hardy generation of the first conquerors was almost extinguished, and their sons, who were born in Africa, enjoyed the delicious baths and gardens which had been acquired by the valor of their fathers. Their place was readily supplied by a various multitude of Moors and Romans, of captives and outlaws; and those desperate wretches, who had already violated the laws of their country, were the most eager to promote the atrocious acts which disgrace the victories of Genseric. In the treatment of his unhappy prisoners, he sometimes consulted his avarice, and sometimes indulged his cruelty; and the massacre of five hundred noble citizens of Zant or Zacynthus, whose mangled bodies he cast into the Ionian Sea, was imputed, by the public indignation, to his latest posterity.

[Footnote 62: The naval war of Genseric is described by Priscus, (Excerpta Legation. p. 42,) Procopius, (de Bell. Vandal. l. i. c. 5, p. 189, 190, and c. 22, p. 228,) Victor Vitensis, (de Persecut. Vandal. l. i. c. 17, and Ruinart, p. 467-481,) and in three panegyrics of Sidonius, whose chronological order is absurdly transposed in the editions both of Savaron and Sirmond. (Avit. Carm. vii. 441-451. Majorian. Carm. v. 327-350, 385-440. Anthem. Carm. ii. 348-386) In one passage the poet seems inspired by his subject, and expresses a strong idea by a lively image:—

Hinc Vandalus hostis Urget; et in nostrum numerosa classe quotannis Militat excidium; conversoque ordine Fati Torrida Caucaseos infert mihi Byrsa furoree]

Such crimes could not be excused by any provocations; but the war, which the king of the Vandals prosecuted against the Roman empire was justified by a specious and reasonable motive. The widow of Valentinian, Eudoxia, whom he had led captive from Rome to Carthage, was the sole heiress of the Theodosian house; her elder daughter, Eudocia, became the reluctant wife of Hunneric, his eldest son; and the stern father, asserting a legal claim, which could not easily be refuted or satisfied, demanded a just proportion of the Imperial patrimony. An adequate, or at least a valuable, compensation, was offered by the Eastern emperor, to purchase a necessary peace. Eudoxia and her younger daughter, Placidia, were honorably restored, and the fury of the Vandals was confined to the limits of the Western empire. The Italians, destitute of a naval force, which alone was capable of protecting their coasts, implored the aid of the more fortunate nations of the East; who had formerly acknowledged, in peace and war, the supremacy of Rome. But the perpetual divisions of the two empires had alienated their interest and their inclinations; the faith of a recent treaty was alleged; and the Western Romans, instead of arms and ships, could only obtain the assistance of a cold and ineffectual mediation. The haughty Ricimer, who had long struggled with the difficulties of his situation, was at length reduced to address the throne of Constantinople, in the humble language of a subject; and Italy submitted, as the price and security to accept a master from the choice of the emperor of the East. [63] It is not the purpose of the present chapter, or even of the present volume, to continue the distinct series of the Byzantine history; but a concise view of the reign and character of the emperor Leo, may explain the last efforts that were attempted to save the falling empire of the West. [64]

[Footnote 63: The poet himself is compelled to acknowledge the distress of Ricimer:—
Praeterea invictus Ricimer, quem publica fata Respiciunt, proprio solas vix Marte repellit Piratam per rura vagum.

Italy addresses her complaint to the Tyber, and Rome, at the solicitation of the river god, transports herself to Constantinople, renounces her ancient claims, and implores the friendship of Aurora, the goddess of the East. This fabulous machinery, which the genius of Claudian had used and abused, is the constant and miserable resource of the muse of Sidonius.]

[Footnote 64: The original authors of the reigns of Marcian, Leo, and Zeno, are reduced to some imperfect fragments, whose deficiencies must be supplied from the more recent compilations of Theophanes, Zonaras, and Cedrenus.]

Since the death of the younger Theodosius, the domestic repose of Constantinople had never been interrupted by war or faction. Pulcheria had bestowed her hand, and the sceptre of the East, on the modest virtue of Marcian: he gratefully reverenced her august rank and virgin chastity; and, after her death, he gave his people the example of the religious worship that was due to the memory of the Imperial saint. [65] Attentive to the prosperity of his own dominions, Marcian seemed to behold, with indifference, the misfortunes of Rome; and the obstinate refusal of a brave and active prince, to draw his sword against the Vandals, was ascribed to a secret promise, which had formerly been exacted from him when he was a captive in the power of Genseric. [66] The death of Marcian, after a reign of seven years, would have exposed the East to the danger of a popular election; if the superior weight of a single family had not been able to incline the balance in favor of the candidate whose interest they supported. The patrician Aspar might have placed the diadem on his own head, if he would have subscribed the Nicene creed. [67] During three generations, the armies of the East were successively commanded by his father, by himself, and by his son Ardaburius; his Barbarian guards formed a military force that overawed the palace and the capital; and the liberal distribution of his immense treasures rendered Aspar as popular as he was powerful. He recommended the obscure name of Leo of Thrace, a military tribune, and the principal steward of his household. His nomination was unanimously ratified by the senate; and the servant of Aspar received the Imperial crown from the hands of the patriarch or bishop, who was permitted to express, by this unusual ceremony, the suffrage of the Deity. [68] This emperor, the first of the name of Leo, has been distinguished by the title of the Great; from a succession of princes, who gradually fixed in the opinion of the Greeks a very humble standard of heroic, or at least of royal, perfection. Yet the temperate firmness with which Leo resisted the oppression of his benefactor, showed that he was conscious of his duty and of his prerogative. Aspar was astonished to find that his influence could no longer appoint a praefect of Constantinople: he presumed to reproach his sovereign with a breach of promise, and insolently shaking his purple, "It is not proper, (said he,) that the man who is invested with this garment, should be guilty of lying." "Nor is it proper, (replied Leo,) that a prince should be compelled to resign his own judgment, and the public interest, to the will of a subject."[69] After this extraordinary scene, it was impossible that the reconciliation of the emperor and the patrician could be sincere; or, at least, that it could be solid and permanent. An army of Isaurians [70] was secretly levied, and introduced into Constantinople; and while Leo undermined the authority, and prepared the disgrace, of the family of Aspar, his mild and cautious behavior restrained them from any rash and desperate attempts, which might have been fatal to themselves, or their enemies. The measures of peace and war were affected by this internal revolution. As long as Aspar degraded the majesty of the throne, the secret correspondence of religion and interest engaged him to favor the cause of Genseric. When Leo had delivered himself from that ignominious servitude, he listened to the complaints of the Italians; resolved to extirpate the tyranny of the Vandals; and declared his alliance with his colleague, Anthemius, whom he solemnly invested with the diadem and purple of the West.

[Footnote 65: St. Pulcheria died A.D. 453, four years before her nominal husband; and her festival is celebrated on the 10th of September by the modern Greeks: she bequeathed an immense patrimony to pious, or, at least, to ecclesiastical, uses. See Tillemont, Memoires Eccles. tom. xv p. 181-184.]

[Footnote 66: See Procopius, de Bell. Vandal. l. i. c. 4, p. 185.]

[Footnote 67: From this disability of Aspar to ascend the throne, it may be inferred that the stain of Heresy was perpetual and indelible, while that of Barbarism disappeared in the second generation.]

[Footnote 68: Theophanes, p. 95. This appears to be the first origin of a ceremony, which all the Christian princes of the world have since adopted and from which the clergy have deduced the most formidable consequences.]

[Footnote 69: Cedrenus, (p. 345, 346,) who was conversant with the writers of better days, has preserved the remarkable words of Aspar.]

[Footnote 70: The power of the Isaurians agitated the Eastern empire in the two succeeding reigns of Zeno and Anastasius; but it ended in the destruction of those Barbarians, who maintained their fierce independences about two hundred and thirty years.]

The virtues of Anthemius have perhaps been magnified, since the Imperial descent, which he could only deduce from the usurper Procopius, has been swelled into a line of emperors. [71] But the merit of his immediate parents, their honors, and their riches, rendered Anthemius one of the most illustrious subjects of the East. His father, Procopius, obtained, after his Persian embassy, the rank of general and patrician; and the name of Anthemius was derived from his maternal grandfather, the celebrated praefect, who protected, with so much ability and success, the infant reign of Theodosius. The grandson of the praefect was raised above the condition of a private subject, by his marriage with Euphemia, the daughter of the emperor Marcian. This splendid alliance, which might supersede the necessity of merit, hastened the promotion of Anthemius to the successive dignities of count, of master-general, of consul, and of patrician; and his merit or fortune claimed the honors of a victory, which was obtained on the banks of the Danube, over the Huns. Without indulging an extravagant ambition, the son-in-law of Marcian might hope to be his successor; but Anthemius supported the disappointment with courage and patience; and his subsequent elevation was universally approved by the public, who esteemed him worthy to reign, till he ascended the throne. [72] The emperor of the West marched from Constantinople, attended by several counts of high distinction, and a body of guards almost equal to the strength and numbers of a regular army: he entered Rome in triumph, and the choice of Leo was confirmed by the senate, the people, and the Barbarian confederates of Italy. [73] The solemn inauguration of Anthemius was followed by the nuptials of his daughter and the patrician Ricimer; a fortunate event, which was considered as the firmest security of the union and happiness of the state. The wealth of two empires was ostentatiously displayed; and many senators completed their ruin, by an expensive effort to disguise their poverty. All serious business was suspended during this festival; the courts of justice were shut; the streets of Rome, the theatres, the places of public and private resort, resounded with hymeneal songs and dances: and the royal bride, clothed in silken robes, with a crown on her head, was conducted to the palace of Ricimer, who had changed his military dress for the habit of a consul and a senator. On this memorable occasion, Sidonius, whose early ambition had been so fatally blasted, appeared as the orator of Auvergne, among the provincial deputies who addressed the throne with congratulations or complaints. [74] The calends of January were now approaching, and the venal poet, who had loved Avitus, and esteemed Majorian, was persuaded by his friends to celebrate, in heroic verse, the merit, the felicity, the second consulship, and the future triumphs, of the emperor Anthemius. Sidonius pronounced, with assurance and success, a panegyric which is still extant; and whatever might be the imperfections, either of the subject or of the composition, the welcome flatterer was immediately rewarded with the praefecture of Rome; a dignity which placed him among the illustrious personages of the empire, till he wisely preferred the more respectable character of a bishop and a saint. [75]

[Footnote 71:
Tali tu civis ab urbe Procopio genitore micas; cui prisca propago Augustis venit a proavis.

The poet (Sidon. Panegyr. Anthem. 67-306) then proceeds to relate the private life and fortunes of the future emperor, with which he must have been imperfectly acquainted.]

[Footnote 72: Sidonius discovers, with tolerable ingenuity, that this disappointment added new lustre to the virtues of Anthemius, (210, &c.,) who declined one sceptre, and reluctantly accepted another, (22, &c.)]

[Footnote 73: The poet again celebrates the unanimity of all orders of the state, (15-22;) and the Chronicle of Idatius mentions the forces which attended his march.]

[Footnote 74: Interveni autem nuptiis Patricii Ricimeris, cui filia perennis Augusti in spem publicae securitatis copulabator. The journey of Sidonius from Lyons, and the festival of Rome, are described with some spirit. L. i. epist. 5, p. 9-13, epist. 9, p. 21.]

[Footnote 75: Sidonius (l. i. epist. 9, p. 23, 24) very fairly states his motive, his labor, and his reward. "Hic ipse Panegyricus, si non judicium, certa eventum, boni operis, accepit." He was made bishop of Clermont, A.D. 471. Tillemont, Mem. Eccles. tom. xvi. p. 750.]

The Greeks ambitiously commend the piety and catholic faith of the emperor whom they gave to the West; nor do they forget to observe, that when he left Constantinople, he converted his palace into the pious foundation of a public bath, a church, and a hospital for old men. [76] Yet some suspicious appearances are found to sully the theological fame of Anthemius. From the conversation of Philotheus, a Macedonian sectary, he had imbibed the spirit of religious toleration; and the Heretics of Rome would have assembled with impunity, if the bold and vehement censure which Pope Hilary pronounced in the church of St. Peter, had not obliged him to abjure the unpopular indulgence. [77] Even the Pagans, a feeble and obscure remnant, conceived some vain hopes, from the indifference, or partiality, of Anthemius; and his singular friendship for the philosopher Severus, whom he promoted to the consulship, was ascribed to a secret project, of reviving the ancient worship of the gods. [78] These idols were crumbled into dust: and the mythology which had once been the creed of nations, was so universally disbelieved, that it might be employed without scandal, or at least without suspicion, by Christian poets. [79] Yet the vestiges of superstition were not absolutely obliterated, and the festival of the Lupercalia, whose origin had preceded the foundation of Rome, was still celebrated under the reign of Anthemius. The savage and simple rites were expressive of an early state of society before the invention of arts and agriculture. The rustic deities who presided over the toils and pleasures of the pastoral life, Pan, Faunus, and their train of satyrs, were such as the fancy of shepherds might create, sportive, petulant, and lascivious; whose power was limited, and whose malice was inoffensive. A goat was the offering the best adapted to their character and attributes; the flesh of the victim was roasted on willow spits; and the riotous youths, who crowded to the feast, ran naked about the fields, with leather thongs in their hands, communicating, as it was supposed, the blessing of fecundity to the women whom they touched. [80] The altar of Pan was erected, perhaps by Evander the Arcadian, in a dark recess in the side of the Palantine hill, watered by a perpetual fountain, and shaded by a hanging grove. A tradition, that, in the same place, Romulus and Remus were suckled by the wolf, rendered it still more sacred and venerable in the eyes of the Romans; and this sylvan spot was gradually surrounded by the stately edifices of the Forum. [81] After the conversion of the Imperial city, the Christians still continued, in the month of February, the annual celebration of the Lupercalia; to which they ascribed a secret and mysterious influence on the genial powers of the animal and vegetable world.

The bishops of Rome were solicitous to abolish a profane custom, so repugnant to the spirit of Christianity; but their zeal was not supported by the authority of the civil magistrate: the inveterate abuse subsisted till the end of the fifth century, and Pope Gelasius, who purified the capital from the last stain of idolatry, appeased by a formal apology, the murmurs of the senate and people. [82]

[Footnote 76: The palace of Anthemius stood on the banks of the Propontis. In the ninth century, Alexius, the son-in-law of the emperor Theophilus, obtained permission to purchase the ground; and ended his days in a monastery which he founded on that delightful spot. Ducange Constantinopolis Christiana, p. 117, 152.]

[Footnote 77: Papa Hilarius... apud beatum Petrum Apostolum, palam ne id fieret, clara voce constrinxit, in tantum ut non ea facienda cum interpositione juramenti idem promitteret Imperator. Gelasius Epistol ad Andronicum, apud Baron. A.D. 467, No. 3. The cardinal observes, with some complacency, that it was much easier to plant heresies at Constantinople, than at Rome.]

[Footnote 78: Damascius, in the life of the philosopher Isidore, apud Photium, p. 1049. Damascius, who lived under Justinian, composed another work, consisting of 570 praeternatural stories of souls, daemons, apparitions, the dotage of Platonic Paganism.]

[Footnote 79: In the poetical works of Sidonius, which he afterwards condemned, (l. ix. epist. 16, p. 285,) the fabulous deities are the principal actors. If Jerom was scourged by the angels for only reading Virgil, the bishop of Clermont, for such a vile imitation, deserved an additional whipping from the Muses.]

[Footnote 80: Ovid (Fast. l. ii. 267-452) has given an amusing description of the follies of antiquity, which still inspired so much respect, that a grave magistrate, running naked through the streets, was not an object of astonishment or laughter.]

[Footnote 81: See Dionys. Halicarn. l. i. p. 25, 65, edit. Hudson. The Roman antiquaries Donatus (l. ii. c. 18, p. 173, 174) and Nardini (p. 386, 387) have labored to ascertain the true situation of the Lupercal.]

[Footnote 82: Baronius published, from the MSS. of the Vatican, this epistle of Pope Gelasius, (A.D. 496, No. 28-45,) which is entitled Adversus Andromachum Senatorem, caeterosque Romanos, qui Lupercalia secundum morem pristinum colenda constituebant. Gelasius always supposes that his adversaries are nominal Christians, and, that he may not yield to them in absurd prejudice, he imputes to this harmless festival all the calamities of the age.]

PART IV

In all his public declarations, the emperor Leo assumes the authority, and professes the affection, of a father, for his son Anthemius, with whom he had divided the administration of the universe. [83] The situation, and perhaps the character, of Leo, dissuaded him from exposing his person to the toils and dangers of an African war. But the powers of the Eastern empire were strenuously exerted to deliver Italy and the Mediterranean from the Vandals; and Genseric, who had so long oppressed both the land and sea, was threatened from every side with a formidable invasion. The campaign was opened by a bold and successful enterprise of the praefect Heraclius. [84] The troops of Egypt, Thebais, and Libya, were embarked, under his command; and the Arabs, with a train of horses and camels, opened the roads of the desert. Heraclius landed on the coast of Tripoli, surprised and subdued the cities of that province, and prepared, by a laborious march, which Cato had formerly executed, [85] to join the Imperial army under the walls of Carthage. The intelligence of this loss extorted from Genseric some insidious and ineffectual propositions of peace; but he was still more seriously alarmed by the reconciliation of Marcellinus with the two empires. The independent patrician had been persuaded to acknowledge the legitimate title of Anthemius, whom he accompanied in his journey to Rome; the Dalmatian fleet was received into the harbors of Italy; the active valor of Marcellinus expelled the Vandals from the Island of Sardinia; and the languid efforts of the West added some weight to the immense preparations of the Eastern Romans. The expense of the naval armament, which Leo sent against the Vandals, has been distinctly ascertained; and the curious and instructive account displays the wealth of the declining empire. The Royal demesnes, or private patrimony of the prince, supplied seventeen thousand pounds of gold; forty-seven thousand pounds of gold, and seven hundred thousand of silver, were levied and paid into the treasury by the Praetorian praefects. But the cities were reduced to extreme poverty; and the diligent calculation of fines and forfeitures, as a valuable object of the revenue, does not suggest the idea of a just or merciful administration. The whole expense, by whatsoever means it was defrayed, of the African campaign, amounted to the sum of one hundred and thirty thousand pounds of gold, about five millions two hundred thousand pounds sterling, at a time when the value of money appears, from the comparative price of corn, to have been somewhat higher than in the present age. [86] The fleet that sailed from Constantinople to Carthage, consisted of eleven hundred and thirteen ships, and the number of soldiers and mariners exceeded one hundred thousand men. Basiliscus, the brother of the empress Vorina, was intrusted with this important command. His sister, the wife of Leo, had exaggerated the merit of his former exploits against the Scythians. But the discovery of his guilt, or incapacity, was reserved for the African war; and his friends could only save his military reputation by asserting, that he had conspired with Aspar to spare Genseric, and to betray the last hope of the Western empire.

[Footnote 83: Itaque nos quibus totius mundi regimen commisit superna provisio.... Pius et triumphator semper Augustus filius noster Anthemius, licet Divina Majestas et nostra creatio pietati ejus plenam Imperii commiserit potestatem, &c..... Such is the dignified style of Leo, whom Anthemius respectfully names, Dominus et Pater meus Princeps sacratissimus Leo. See Novell. Anthem. tit. ii. iii. p. 38, ad calcem Cod. Theod.]

[Footnote 84: The expedition of Heraclius is clouded with difficulties, (Tillemont, Hist. des Empereurs, tom. vi. p. 640,) and it requires some dexterity to use the circumstances afforded by Theophanes, without injury to the more respectable evidence of Procopius.]

[Footnote 85: The march of Cato from Berenice, in the province of Cyrene, was much longer than that of Heraclius from Tripoli. He passed the deep sandy desert in thirty days, and it was found necessary to provide, besides the ordinary supplies, a great number of skins filled with water, and several Psylli, who were supposed to possess the art of sucking the wounds which had been made by the serpents of their native country. See Plutarch in Caton. Uticens. tom. iv. p. 275. Straben Geograph. l. xxii. p. 1193.]

[Footnote 86: The principal sum is clearly expressed by Procopius, (de Bell. Vandal. l. i. c. 6, p. 191;) the smaller constituent parts, which Tillemont, (Hist. des Empereurs, tom. vi. p. 396) has laboriously collected from the Byzantine writers, are less certain, and less important. The historian Malchus laments the public misery, (Excerpt. ex Suida in Corp. Hist. Byzant. p. 58;) but he is surely unjust, when he charges Leo with hoarding the treasures which he extorted from the people. Note: Compare likewise the newly-discovered work of Lydus, de Magistratibus, ed. Hase, Paris, 1812, (and in the new collection of the Byzantines,) l. iii. c. 43. Lydus states the expenditure at 65,000 lbs. of gold, 700,000 of silver. But Lydus exaggerates the fleet to the incredible number of 10,000 long ships, (Liburnae,) and the troops to 400,000 men. Lydus describes this fatal measure, of which he charges the blame on Basiliscus, as the shipwreck of the state.

From that time all the revenues of the empire were anticipated; and the finances fell into inextricable confusion—M.]

Experience has shown, that the success of an invader most commonly depends on the vigor and celerity of his operations. The strength and sharpness of the first impression are blunted by delay; the health and spirit of the troops insensibly languish in a distant climate; the naval and military force, a mighty effort which perhaps can never be repeated, is silently consumed; and every hour that is wasted in negotiation, accustoms the enemy to contemplate and examine those hostile terrors, which, on their first appearance, he deemed irresistible. The formidable navy of Basiliscus pursued its prosperous navigation from the Thracian Bosphorus to the coast of Africa. He landed his troops at Cape Bona, or the promontory of Mercury, about forty miles from Carthage. [87] The army of Heraclius, and the fleet of Marcellinus, either joined or seconded the Imperial lieutenant; and the Vandals who opposed his progress by sea or land, were successively vanquished. [88] If Basiliscus had seized the moment of consternation, and boldly advanced to the capital, Carthage must have surrendered, and the kingdom of the Vandals was extinguished. Genseric beheld the danger with firmness, and eluded it with his veteran dexterity. He protested, in the most respectful language, that he was ready to submit his person, and his dominions, to the will of the emperor; but he requested a truce of five days to regulate the terms of his submission; and it was universally believed, that his secret liberality contributed to the success of this public negotiation. Instead of obstinately refusing whatever indulgence his enemy so earnestly solicited, the guilty, or the credulous, Basiliscus consented to the fatal truce; and his imprudent security seemed to proclaim, that he already considered himself as the conqueror of Africa. During this short interval, the wind became favorable to the designs of Genseric. He manned his largest ships of war with the bravest of the Moors and Vandals; and they towed after them many large barks, filled with combustible materials. In the obscurity of the night, these destructive vessels were impelled against the unguarded and unsuspecting fleet of the Romans, who were awakened by the sense of their instant danger. Their close and crowded order assisted the progress of the fire, which was communicated with rapid and irresistible violence; and the noise of the wind, the crackling of the flames, the dissonant cries of the soldiers and mariners, who could neither command nor obey, increased the horror of the nocturnal tumult. Whilst they labored to extricate themselves from the fire-ships, and to save at least a part of the navy, the galleys of Genseric assaulted them with temperate and disciplined valor; and many of the Romans, who escaped the fury of the flames, were destroyed or taken by the victorious Vandals. Among the events of that disastrous night, the heroic, or rather desperate, courage of John, one of the principal officers of Basiliscus, has rescued his name from oblivion. When the ship, which he had bravely defended, was almost consumed, he threw himself in his armor into the sea, disdainfully rejected the esteem and pity of Genso, the son of Genseric, who pressed him to accept honorable quarter, and sunk under the waves; exclaiming, with his last breath, that he would never fall alive into the hands of those impious dogs. Actuated by a far different spirit, Basiliscus, whose station was the most remote from danger, disgracefully fled In the beginning of the engagement, returned to Constantinople with the loss of more than half of his fleet and army, and sheltered his guilty head in the sanctuary of St. Sophia, till his sister, by her tears and entreaties, could obtain his pardon from the indignant emperor. Heraclius effected his retreat through the desert; Marcellinus retired to Sicily, where he was assassinated, perhaps at the instigation of Ricimer, by one of his own captains; and the king of the Vandals expressed his surprise and satisfaction, that the Romans themselves should remove from the world his most formidable antagonists. [89] After the failure of this great expedition, [891] Genseric again became the tyrant of the sea: the coasts of Italy, Greece, and Asia, were again exposed to his revenge and avarice; Tripoli and Sardinia returned to his obedience; he added Sicily to the number of his provinces; and before he died, in the fulness of years and of glory, he beheld the final extinction of the empire of the West. [90]

[Footnote 87: This promontory is forty miles from Carthage, (Procop. l. i. c. 6, p. 192,) and twenty leagues from Sicily, (Shaw's Travels, p. 89.) Scipio landed farther in the bay, at the fair promontory; see the animated description of Livy, xxix. 26, 27.]

[Footnote 88: Theophanes (p. 100) affirms that many ships of the Vandals were sunk. The assertion of Jornandes, (de Successione Regn.,) that Basiliscus attacked Carthage, must be understood in a very qualified sense]

[Footnote 89: Damascius in Vit. Isidor. apud Phot. p. 1048. It will appear, by comparing the three short chronicles of the times, that Marcellinus had fought near Carthage, and was killed in Sicily.]

[Footnote 891: According to Lydus, Leo, distracted by this and the other calamities of his reign, particularly a dreadful fire at Constantinople, abandoned the palace, like another Orestes, and was preparing to quit Constantinople forever l iii. c. 44, p. 230—M.]

[Footnote 90: For the African war, see Procopius, de Bell. (Vandal. l. i. c. 6, p. 191, 192, 193,) Theophanes, (p. 99, 100, 101,) Cedrenus, (p. 349, 350,) and Zonaras, (tom. ii. l. xiv. p. 50, 51.) Montesquieu (Considerations sur la Grandeur, &c., c. xx. tom. iii. p. 497) has made a judicious observation on the failure of these great naval armaments.]

During his long and active reign, the African monarch had studiously cultivated the friendship of the Barbarians of Europe, whose arms he might employ in a seasonable and effectual diversion against the two empires. After the death of Attila, he renewed his alliance with the Visigoths of Gaul; and the sons of the elder Theodoric, who successively reigned over that warlike nation, were easily persuaded, by the sense of interest, to forget the cruel affront which Genseric had inflicted on their sister. [91] The death of the emperor Majorian delivered Theodoric the Second from the restraint of fear, and perhaps of honor; he violated his recent treaty with the Romans; and the ample territory of Narbonne, which he firmly united to his dominions, became the immediate reward of his perfidy. The selfish policy of Ricimer encouraged him to invade the provinces which were in the possession of Aegidius, his rival; but the active count, by the defence of Arles, and the victory of Orleans, saved Gaul, and checked, during his lifetime, the progress of the Visigoths. Their ambition was soon rekindled; and the design of extinguishing the Roman empire in Spain and Gaul was conceived, and almost completed, in the reign of Euric, who assassinated his brother Theodoric, and displayed, with a more savage temper, superior abilities, both in peace and war. He passed the Pyrenees at the head of a numerous army, subdued the cities of Saragossa and Pampeluna, vanquished in battle the martial nobles of the Tarragonese province, carried his victorious arms into the heart of Lusitania, and permitted the Suevi to hold the kingdom of Gallicia under the Gothic monarchy of Spain. [92] The efforts of Euric were not less vigorous, or less successful, in Gaul; and throughout the country that extends from the Pyrenees to the Rhone and the Loire, Berry and Auvergne were the only cities, or dioceses, which refused to acknowledge him as their master. [93] In the defence of Clermont, their principal town, the inhabitants of Auvergne sustained, with inflexible resolution, the miseries of war, pestilence, and famine; and the Visigoths, relinquishing the fruitless siege, suspended the hopes of that important conquest. The youth of the province were animated by the heroic, and almost incredible, valor of Ecdicius, the son of the emperor Avitus, [94] who made a desperate sally with only eighteen horsemen, boldly attacked the Gothic army, and, after maintaining a flying skirmish, retired safe and victorious within the walls of Clermont. His charity was equal to his courage: in a time of extreme scarcity, four thousand poor were fed at his expense; and his private influence levied an army of Burgundians for the deliverance of Auvergne. From his virtues alone the faithful citizens of Gaul derived any hopes of safety or freedom; and even such virtues were insufficient to avert the impending ruin of their country, since they were anxious to learn, from his authority and example, whether they should prefer the alternative of exile or servitude. [95] The public confidence was lost; the resources of the state were exhausted; and the Gauls had too much reason to believe, that Anthemius, who reigned in Italy, was incapable of protecting his distressed subjects beyond the Alps. The feeble emperor could only procure for their defence the service of twelve thousand British auxiliaries. Riothamus, one of the independent kings, or chieftains, of the island, was persuaded to transport his troops to the continent of Gaul: he sailed up the Loire, and established his quarters in Berry, where the people complained of these oppressive allies, till they were destroyed or dispersed by the arms of the Visigoths. [96]

[Footnote 91: Jornandes is our best guide through the reigns of Theodoric II. and Euric, (de Rebus Geticis, c. 44, 45, 46, 47, p. 675-681.) Idatius ends too soon, and Isidore is too sparing of the information which he might have given on the affairs of Spain. The events that relate to Gaul are laboriously illustrated in the third book of the Abbe Dubos, Hist. Critique, tom. i. p. 424-620.]

[Footnote 92: See Mariana, Hist. Hispan. tom. i. l. v. c. 5. p. 162.]

[Footnote 93: An imperfect, but original, picture of Gaul, more especially of Auvergne, is shown by Sidonius; who, as a senator, and afterwards as a bishop, was deeply interested in the fate of his country. See l. v. epist. 1, 5, 9, &c.]

[Footnote 94: Sidonius, l. iii. epist. 3, p. 65-68. Greg. Turon. l. ii. c. 24, in tom. ii. p. 174. Jornandes, c. 45, p. 675. Perhaps Ecdicius was only the son-in-law of Avitus, his wife's son by another husband.]

[Footnote 95: Si nullae a republica vires, nulla praesidia; si nullae, quantum rumor est, Anthemii principis opes; statuit, te auctore, nobilitas, seu patriaca dimittere seu capillos, (Sidon. l. ii. epist. 1, p. 33.) The last words Sirmond, (Not. p. 25) may likewise denote the clerical tonsure, which was indeed the choice of Sidonius himself.]

[Footnote 96: The history of these Britons may be traced in Jornandes, (c. 45, p. 678,) Sidonius, (l. iii. epistol. 9, p. 73, 74,) and Gregory of Tours, (l. ii. c. 18, in tom. ii. p. 170.) Sidonius (who styles these mercenary troops argutos, armatos, tumultuosos, virtute numero, contul ernio, contumaces) addresses their general in a tone of friendship and familiarity.]

One of the last acts of jurisdiction, which the Roman senate exercised over their subjects of Gaul, was the trial and condemnation of Arvandus, the Praetorian praefect. Sidonius, who rejoices that he lived under a reign in which he might pity and assist a state criminal, has expressed, with tenderness and freedom, the faults of his indiscreet and unfortunate friend. [97] From the perils which he had escaped, Arvandus imbibed confidence rather than wisdom; and such was the various, though uniform, imprudence of his behavior, that his prosperity must appear much more surprising than his downfall. The second praefecture, which he obtained within the term of five years, abolished the merit and popularity of his preceding administration. His easy temper was corrupted by flattery, and exasperated by opposition; he was forced to satisfy his importunate creditors with the spoils of the province; his capricious insolence offended the nobles of Gaul, and he sunk under the weight of the public hatred. The mandate of his disgrace summoned him to justify his conduct before the senate; and he passed the Sea of Tuscany with a favorable wind, the presage, as he vainly imagined, of his future fortunes. A decent respect was still observed for the Proefectorian rank; and on his arrival at Rome, Arvandus was committed to the hospitality, rather than to the custody, of Flavius Asellus, the count of the sacred largesses, who resided in the Capitol. [98] He was eagerly pursued by his accusers, the four deputies of Gaul, who were all distinguished by their birth, their dignities, or their eloquence. In the name of a great province, and according to the forms of Roman jurisprudence, they instituted a civil and criminal action, requiring such restitution as might compensate the losses of individuals, and such punishment as might satisfy the justice of the state. Their charges of corrupt oppression were numerous and weighty; but they placed their secret dependence on a letter which they had intercepted, and which they could prove, by the evidence of his secretary, to have been dictated by Arvandus himself. The author of this letter seemed to dissuade the king of the Goths from a peace with the Greek emperor: he suggested the attack of the Britons on the Loire; and he recommended a division of Gaul, according to the law of nations, between the Visigoths and the Burgundians. [99] These pernicious schemes, which a friend could only palliate by the reproaches of vanity and indiscretion, were susceptible of a treasonable interpretation; and the deputies had artfully resolved not to produce their most formidable weapons till the decisive moment of the contest. But their intentions were discovered by the zeal of Sidonius. He immediately apprised the unsuspecting criminal of his danger; and sincerely lamented, without any mixture of anger, the haughty presumption of Arvandus, who rejected, and even resented, the salutary advice of his friends. Ignorant of his real situation, Arvandus showed himself in the Capitol in the white robe of a candidate, accepted indiscriminate salutations and offers of service, examined the shops of the merchants, the silks and gems, sometimes with the indifference of a spectator, and sometimes with the attention of a purchaser; and complained of the times, of the senate, of the prince, and of the delays of justice. His complaints were soon removed. An early day was fixed for his trial; and Arvandus appeared, with his accusers, before a numerous assembly of the Roman senate. The mournful garb which they affected, excited the compassion of the judges, who were scandalized by the gay and splendid dress of their adversary: and when the praefect Arvandus, with the first of the Gallic deputies, were directed to take their places on the senatorial benches, the same contrast of pride and modesty was observed in their behavior. In this memorable judgment, which presented a lively image of the old republic, the Gauls exposed, with force and freedom, the grievances of the province; and as soon as the minds of the audience were sufficiently inflamed, they recited the fatal epistle. The obstinacy of Arvandus was founded on the strange supposition, that a subject could not be convicted of treason, unless he had actually conspired to assume the purple. As the paper was read, he repeatedly, and with a loud voice, acknowledged it for his genuine composition; and his astonishment was equal to his dismay, when the unanimous voice of the senate declared him guilty of a capital offence. By their decree, he was degraded from the rank of a praefect to the obscure condition of a plebeian, and ignominiously dragged by servile hands to the public prison. After a fortnight's adjournment, the senate was again convened to pronounce the sentence of his death; but while he expected, in the Island of Aesculapius, the expiration of the thirty days allowed by an ancient law to the vilest malefactors, [100] his friends interposed, the emperor Anthemius relented, and the praefect of Gaul obtained the milder punishment of exile and confiscation. The faults of Arvandus might deserve compassion; but the impunity of Seronatus accused the justice of the republic, till he was condemned and executed, on the complaint of the people of Auvergne. That flagitious minister, the Catiline of his age and country, held a secret correspondence with the Visigoths, to betray the province which he oppressed: his industry was continually exercised in the discovery of new taxes and obsolete offences; and his extravagant vices would have inspired contempt, if they had not excited fear and abhorrence. [101]

[Footnote 97: See Sidonius, l. i. epist. 7, p. 15-20, with Sirmond's notes. This letter does honor to his heart, as well as to his understanding. The prose of Sidonius, however vitiated by a false and affected taste, is much superior to his insipid verses.]

[Footnote 98: When the Capitol ceased to be a temple, it was appropriated to the use of the civil magistrate; and it is still the residence of the Roman senator. The jewellers, &c., might be allowed to expose then precious wares in the porticos.]

[Footnote 99: Haec ad regem Gothorum, charta videbatur emitti, pacem cum Graeco Imperatore dissuadens, Britannos super Ligerim sitos impugnari oportere, demonstrans, cum Burgundionibus jure gentium Gallias dividi debere confirmans.]

[Footnote 100: Senatusconsultum Tiberianum, (Sirmond Not. p. 17;) but that law allowed only ten days between the sentence and execution; the remaining twenty were added in the reign of Theodosius.]

[Footnote 101: Catilina seculi nostri. Sidonius, l. ii. epist. 1, p. 33; l. v. epist 13, p. 143; l. vii. epist. vii. p. 185. He execrates the crimes, and applauds the punishment, of Seronatus, perhaps with the indignation of a virtuous citizen, perhaps with the resentment of a personal enemy.]

Such criminals were not beyond the reach of justice; but whatever might be the guilt of Ricimer, that powerful Barbarian was able to contend or to negotiate with the prince, whose alliance he had condescended to accept. The peaceful and prosperous reign which Anthemius had promised to the West, was soon clouded by misfortune and discord. Ricimer, apprehensive, or impatient, of a superior, retired from Rome, and fixed his residence at Milan; an advantageous situation either to invite or to repel the warlike tribes that were seated between the Alps and the Danube. [102] Italy was gradually divided into two independent and hostile kingdoms; and the nobles of Liguria, who trembled at the near approach of a civil war, fell prostrate at the feet of the patrician, and conjured him to spare their unhappy country. "For my own part," replied Ricimer, in a tone of insolent moderation, "I am still inclined to embrace the friendship of the Galatian; [103] but who will undertake to appease his anger, or to mitigate the pride, which always rises in proportion to our submission?" They informed him, that Epiphanius, bishop of Pavia, [104] united the wisdom of the serpent with the innocence of the dove; and appeared confident, that the eloquence of such an ambassador must prevail against the strongest opposition, either of interest or passion. Their recommendation was approved; and Epiphanius, assuming the benevolent office of mediation, proceeded without delay to Rome, where he was received with the honors due to his merit and reputation. The oration of a bishop in favor of peace may be easily supposed; he argued, that, in all possible circumstances, the forgiveness of injuries must be an act of mercy, or magnanimity, or prudence; and he seriously admonished the emperor to avoid a contest with a fierce Barbarian, which might be fatal to himself, and must be ruinous to his dominions. Anthemius acknowledged the truth of his maxims; but he deeply felt, with grief and indignation, the behavior of Ricimer, and his passion gave eloquence and energy to his discourse. "What favors," he warmly exclaimed, "have we refused to this ungrateful man? What provocations have we not endured! Regardless of the majesty of the purple, I gave my daughter to a Goth; I sacrificed my own blood to the safety of the republic. The liberality which ought to have secured the eternal attachment of Ricimer has exasperated him against his benefactor. What wars has he not excited against the empire! How often has he instigated and assisted the fury of hostile nations! Shall I now accept his perfidious friendship? Can I hope that he will respect the engagements of a treaty, who has already violated the duties of a son?" But the anger of Anthemius evaporated in these passionate exclamations: he insensibly yielded to the proposals of Epiphanius; and the bishop returned to his diocese with the satisfaction of restoring the peace of Italy, by a reconciliation, [105] of which the sincerity and continuance might be reasonably suspected. The clemency of the emperor was extorted from his weakness; and Ricimer suspended his ambitious designs till he had secretly prepared the engines with which he resolved to subvert the throne of Anthemius. The mask of peace and moderation was then thrown aside. The army of Ricimer was fortified by a numerous reenforcement of Burgundians and Oriental Suevi: he disclaimed all allegiance to the Greek emperor, marched from Milan to the Gates of Rome, and fixing his camp on the banks of the Anio, impatiently expected the arrival of Olybrius, his Imperial candidate.

[Footnote 102: Ricimer, under the reign of Anthemius, defeated and slew in battle Beorgor, king of the Alani, (Jornandes, c. 45, p. 678.) His sister had married the king of the Burgundians, and he maintained an intimate connection with the Suevic colony established in Pannonia and Noricum.]

[Footnote 103: Galatam concitatum. Sirmond (in his notes to Ennodius) applies this appellation to Anthemius himself. The emperor was probably born in the province of Galatia, whose inhabitants, the Gallo-Grecians, were supposed to unite the vices of a savage and a corrupted people.]

[Footnote 104: Epiphanius was thirty years bishop of Pavia, (A.D. 467-497;) see Tillemont, Mem. Eccles. tom. xvi. p. 788. His name and actions would have been unknown to posterity, if Ennodius, one of his successors, had not written his life; (Sirmond, Opera tom. i. p. 1647-1692;) in which he represents him as one of the greatest characters of the age]

[Footnote 105: Ennodius (p. 1659-1664) has related this embassy of Epiphanius; and his narrative, verbose and turgid as it must appear, illustrates some curious passages in the fall of the Western empire.]

The senator Olybrius, of the Anician family, might esteem himself the lawful heir of the Western empire. He had married Placidia, the younger daughter of Valentinian, after she was restored by Genseric; who still detained her sister Eudoxia, as the wife, or rather as the captive, of his son. The king of the Vandals supported, by threats and solicitations, the fair pretensions of his Roman ally; and assigned, as one of the motives of the war, the refusal of the senate and people to acknowledge their lawful prince, and the unworthy preference which they had given to a stranger. [106] The friendship of the public enemy might render Olybrius still more unpopular to the Italians; but when Ricimer meditated the ruin of the emperor Anthemius, he tempted, with the offer of a diadem, the candidate who could justify his rebellion by an illustrious name and a royal alliance. The husband of Placidia, who, like most of his ancestors, had been invested with the consular dignity, might have continued to enjoy a secure and splendid fortune in the peaceful residence of Constantinople; nor does he appear to have been tormented by such a genius as cannot be amused or occupied, unless by the administration of an empire. Yet Olybrius yielded to the importunities of his friends, perhaps of his wife; rashly plunged into the dangers and calamities of a civil war; and, with the secret connivance of the emperor Leo, accepted the Italian purple, which was bestowed, and resumed, at the capricious will of a Barbarian. He landed without obstacle (for Genseric was master of the sea) either at Ravenna, or the port of Ostia, and immediately proceeded to the camp of Ricimer, where he was received as the sovereign of the Western world. [107]

[Footnote 106: Priscus, Excerpt. Legation p. 74. Procopius de Bell. Vandel l. i. c. 6, p. 191. Eudoxia and her daughter were restored after the death of Majorian. Perhaps the consulship of Olybrius (A.D. 464) was bestowed as a nuptial present.]

[Footnote 107: The hostile appearance of Olybrius is fixed (notwithstanding the opinion of Pagi) by the duration of his reign. The secret connivance of Leo is acknowledged by Theophanes and the Paschal Chronicle. We are ignorant of his motives; but in this obscure period, our ignorance extends to the most public and important facts.]

The patrician, who had extended his posts from the Anio to the Melvian bridge, already possessed two quarters of Rome, the Vatican and the Janiculum, which are separated by the Tyber from the rest of the city; [108] and it may be conjectured, that an assembly of seceding senators imitated, in the choice of Olybrius, the forms of a legal election. But the body of the senate and people firmly adhered to the cause of Anthemius; and the more effectual support of a Gothic army enabled him to prolong his reign, and the public distress, by a resistance of three months, which produced the concomitant evils of famine and pestilence. At length Ricimer made a furious assault on the bridge of Hadrian, or St. Angelo; and the narrow pass was defended with equal valor by the Goths, till the death of Gilimer, their leader. The victorious troops, breaking down every barrier, rushed with irresistible violence into the heart of the city, and Rome (if we may use the language of a contemporary pope) was subverted by the civil fury of Anthemius and Ricimer. [109] The unfortunate Anthemius was dragged from his concealment, and inhumanly massacred by the command of his son-in-law; who thus added a third, or perhaps a fourth, emperor to the number of his victims. The soldiers, who united the rage of factious citizens with the savage manners of Barbarians, were indulged, without control, in the license of rapine and murder: the crowd of slaves and plebeians, who were unconcerned in the event, could only gain by the indiscriminate pillage; and the face of the city exhibited the strange contrast of stern cruelty and dissolute intemperance. [110] Forty days after this calamitous event, the subject, not of glory, but of guilt, Italy was delivered, by a painful disease, from the tyrant Ricimer, who bequeathed the command of his army to his nephew Gundobald, one of the princes of the Burgundians. In the same year all the principal actors in this great revolution were removed from the stage; and the whole reign of Olybrius, whose death does not betray any symptoms of violence, is included within the term of seven months. He left one daughter, the offspring of his marriage with Placidia; and the family of the great Theodosius, transplanted from Spain to Constantinople, was propagated in the female line as far as the eighth generation. [111]

[Footnote 108: Of the fourteen regions, or quarters, into which Rome was divided by Augustus, only one, the Janiculum, lay on the Tuscan side of the Tyber. But, in the fifth century, the Vatican suburb formed a considerable city; and in the ecclesiastical distribution, which had been recently made by Simplicius, the reigning pope, two of the seven regions, or parishes of Rome, depended on the church of St. Peter. See Nardini Roma Antica, p. 67. It would require a tedious dissertation to mark the circumstances, in which I am inclined to depart from the topography of that learned Roman.]

[Footnote 109: Nuper Anthemii et Ricimeris civili furore subversa est. Gelasius in Epist. ad Andromach. apud Baron. A.D. 496, No. 42, Sigonius (tom. i. l. xiv. de Occidentali Imperio, p. 542, 543,) and Muratori (Annali d'Italia, tom. iv. p. 308, 309,) with the aid of a less imperfect Ms. of the Historia Miscella., have illustrated this dark and bloody transaction.]

[Footnote 110: Such had been the saeva ac deformis urbe tota facies, when Rome was assaulted and stormed by the troops of Vespasian, (see Tacit. Hist. iii. 82, 83;) and every cause of mischief had since acquired much additional energy. The revolution of ages may bring round the same calamities; but ages may revolve without producing a Tacitus to describe them.]

[Footnote 111: See Ducange, Familiae Byzantin. p. 74, 75. Areobindus, who appears to have married the niece of the emperor Justinian, was the eighth descendant of the elder Theodosius.]

PART V

Whilst the vacant throne of Italy was abandoned to lawless Barbarians, [112] the election of a new colleague was seriously agitated in the council of Leo. The empress Verina, studious to promote the greatness of her own family, had married one of her nieces to Julius Nepos, who succeeded his uncle Marcellinus in the sovereignty of Dalmatia, a more solid possession than the title which he was persuaded to accept, of Emperor of the West. But the measures of the Byzantine court were so languid and irresolute, that many months elapsed after the death of Anthemius, and even of Olybrius, before their destined successor could show himself, with a respectable force, to his Italian subjects. During that interval, Glycerius, an obscure soldier, was invested with the purple by his patron Gundobald; but the Burgundian prince was unable, or unwilling, to support his nomination by a civil war: the pursuits of domestic ambition recalled him beyond the Alps, [113] and his client was permitted to exchange the Roman sceptre for the bishopric of Salona. After extinguishing such a competitor, the emperor Nepos was acknowledged by the senate, by the Italians, and by the provincials of Gaul; his moral virtues, and military talents, were loudly celebrated; and those who derived any private benefit from his government, announced, in prophetic strains, the restoration of the public felicity. [114] Their hopes (if such hopes had been entertained) were confounded within the term of a single year, and the treaty of peace, which ceded Auvergue to the Visigoths, is the only event of his short and inglorious reign. The most faithful subjects of Gaul were sacrificed, by the Italian emperor, to the hope of domestic security; [115] but his repose was soon invaded by a furious sedition of the Barbarian confederates, who, under the command of Orestes, their general, were in full march from Rome to Ravenna. Nepos trembled at their approach; and, instead of placing a just confidence in the strength of Ravenna, he hastily escaped to his ships, and retired to his Dalmatian principality, on the opposite coast of the Adriatic. By this shameful abdication, he protracted his life about five years, in a very ambiguous state, between an emperor and an exile, till he was assassinated at Salona by the ungrateful Glycerius, who was translated, perhaps as the reward of his crime, to the archbishopric of Milan. [116]

[Footnote 112: *The last revolutions of the Western empire are faintly marked in Theophanes, (p. 102,) Jornandes, (c. 45, p. 679,) the Chronicle of Marcellinus, and the Fragments of an anonymous writer, published by Valesius at the end of Ammianus, (p. 716, 717.) If Photius had not been so wretchedly concise, we should derive much information from the contemporary histories of Malchus and Candidus. See his Extracts, p. 172-179.*]

[Footnote 113: *See Greg. Turon. l. ii. c. 28, in tom. ii. p. 175. Dubos, Hist. Critique, tom. i. p. 613. By the murder or death of his two brothers, Gundobald acquired the sole possession of the kingdom of Burgundy, whose ruin was hastened by their discord.*]

[Footnote 114: *Julius Nepos armis pariter summus Augustus ac moribus. Sidonius, l. v. ep. 16, p. 146. Nepos had given to Ecdicius the title of Patrician, which Anthemius had promised, decessoris Anthemii fidem absolvit. See l. viii. ep. 7, p. 224.*]

[Footnote 115: *Epiphanius was sent ambassador from Nepos to the Visigoths, for the purpose of ascertaining the fines Imperii Italici, (Ennodius in Sirmond, tom. i. p. 1665-1669.) His pathetic discourse concealed the disgraceful secret which soon excited the just and bitter complaints of the bishop of Clermont.*]

[Footnote 116: *Malchus, apud Phot. p. 172. Ennod. Epigram. lxxxii. in Sirmond. Oper. tom. i. p. 1879. Some doubt may, however, be raised on the identity of the emperor and the archbishop.*]

The nations who had asserted their independence after the death of Attila, were established, by the right of possession or conquest, in the boundless countries to the north of the Danube; or in the Roman provinces between the river and the Alps. But the bravest of their youth enlisted in the army of confederates, who formed the defence and the terror of Italy; [117] and in this promiscuous multitude, the names of the Heruli, the Scyrri, the Alani, the Turcilingi, and the Rugians, appear to have predominated. The example of these warriors was imitated by Orestes, [118] the son of Tatullus, and the father of the last Roman emperor of the West. Orestes, who has been already mentioned in this History, had never deserted his country. His birth and fortunes rendered him one of the most illustrious subjects of Pannonia. When that province was ceded to the Huns, he entered into the service of Attila, his lawful sovereign, obtained the office of his secretary, and was repeatedly sent ambassador to Constantinople, to represent the person, and signify the commands, of the imperious monarch. The death of that conqueror restored him to his freedom; and Orestes might honorably refuse either to follow the sons of Attila into the Scythian desert, or to obey the Ostrogoths, who had usurped the dominion of Pannonia. He preferred the service of the Italian princes, the successors of Valentinian; and as he possessed the qualifications of courage, industry, and experience, he advanced with rapid steps in the military profession, till he was elevated, by the favor of Nepos himself, to the dignities of patrician, and master-general of the troops. These troops had been long accustomed to reverence the character and authority of Orestes, who affected their manners, conversed with them in their own language, and was intimately connected with their national chieftains, by long habits of familiarity and friendship. At his solicitation they rose in arms against the obscure Greek, who presumed to claim their obedience; and when Orestes, from some secret motive, declined the purple, they consented, with the same facility, to acknowledge his son Augustulus as the emperor of the West. By the abdication of Nepos, Orestes had now attained the summit of his ambitious hopes; but he soon discovered, before the end of the first year, that the lessons of perjury and ingratitude, which a rebel must inculcate, will be resorted to against himself; and that the precarious sovereign of Italy was only permitted to choose, whether he would be the slave, or the victim, of his Barbarian mercenaries. The dangerous alliance of these strangers had oppressed and insulted the last remains of Roman freedom and dignity. At each revolution, their pay and privileges were augmented; but their insolence increased in a still more extravagant degree; they envied the fortune of their brethren in Gaul, Spain, and Africa, whose victorious arms had acquired an independent and perpetual inheritance; and they insisted on their peremptory demand, that a third part of the lands of Italy should be immediately divided among them. Orestes, with a spirit, which, in another situation, might be entitled to our esteem, chose rather to encounter the rage of an armed multitude, than to subscribe the ruin of an innocent people. He rejected the audacious demand; and his refusal was favorable to the ambition of Odoacer; a bold Barbarian, who assured his fellow-soldiers, that, if they dared to associate under his command, they might soon extort the justice which had been denied to their dutiful petitions. From all the camps and garrisons of Italy, the confederates, actuated by the same resentment and the same hopes, impatiently flocked to the standard of this popular leader; and the unfortunate patrician, overwhelmed by the torrent, hastily retreated to the strong city of Pavia, the episcopal seat of the holy Epiphanites. Pavia was immediately besieged, the fortifications were stormed, the town was pillaged; and although the bishop might labor, with much zeal and some success, to save the property of the church, and the chastity of female captives, the tumult could only be appeased by the execution of Orestes. [119] His brother Paul was slain in an action near Ravenna; and the helpless Augustulus, who could no longer command the respect, was reduced to implore the clemency, of Odoacer.

[Footnote 117: *Our knowledge of these mercenaries, who subverted the Western empire, is derived from Procopius, (de Bell. Gothico, l. i. c. i. p. 308.) The popular opinion, and the recent historians, represent*

Odoacer in the false light of a stranger, and a king, who invaded Italy with an army of foreigners, his native subjects.]

[Footnote 118: Orestes, qui eo tempore quando Attila ad Italiam venit, se illi unxit, ejus notarius factus fuerat. Anonym. Vales. p. 716. He is mistaken in the date; but we may credit his assertion, that the secretary of Attila was the father of Augustulus]

[Footnote 119: See Ennodius, (in Vit. Epiphan. Sirmond, tom. i. p. 1669, 1670.) He adds weight to the narrative of Procopius, though we may doubt whether the devil actually contrived the siege of Pavia, to distress the bishop and his flock.]

That successful Barbarian was the son of Edecon; who, in some remarkable transactions, particularly described in a preceding chapter, had been the colleague of Orestes himself. [119/1] The honor of an ambassador should be exempt from suspicion; and Edecon had listened to a conspiracy against the life of his sovereign. But this apparent guilt was expiated by his merit or repentance; his rank was eminent and conspicuous; he enjoyed the favor of Attila; and the troops under his command, who guarded, in their turn, the royal village, consisted of a tribe of Scyrri, his immediate and hereditary subjects. In the revolt of the nations, they still adhered to the Huns; and more than twelve years afterwards, the name of Edecon is honorably mentioned, in their unequal contests with the Ostrogoths; which was terminated, after two bloody battles, by the defeat and dispersion of the Scyrri. [120] Their gallant leader, who did not survive this national calamity, left two sons, Onulf and Odoacer, to struggle with adversity, and to maintain as they might, by rapine or service, the faithful followers of their exile. Onulf directed his steps towards Constantinople, where he sullied, by the assassination of a generous benefactor, the fame which he had acquired in arms. His brother Odoacer led a wandering life among the Barbarians of Noricum, with a mind and a fortune suited to the most desperate adventures; and when he had fixed his choice, he piously visited the cell of Severinus, the popular saint of the country, to solicit his approbation and blessing. The lowness of the door would not admit the lofty stature of Odoacer: he was obliged to stoop; but in that humble attitude the saint could discern the symptoms of his future greatness; and addressing him in a prophetic tone, "Pursue" (said he) "your design; proceed to Italy; you will soon cast away this coarse garment of skins; and your wealth will be adequate to the liberality of your mind." [121] The Barbarian, whose daring spirit accepted and ratified the prediction, was admitted into the service of the Western empire, and soon obtained an honorable rank in the guards. His manners were gradually polished, his military skill was improved, and the confederates of Italy would not have elected him for their general, unless the exploits of Odoacer had established a high opinion of his courage and capacity. [122] Their military acclamations saluted him with the title of king; but he abstained, during his whole reign, from the use of the purple and diadem, [123] lest he should offend those princes, whose subjects, by their accidental mixture, had formed the victorious army, which time and policy might insensibly unite into a great nation.

[Footnote 119/1: Manso observes that the evidence which identifies Edecon, the father of Odoacer, with the colleague of Orestes, is not conclusive. Geschichte des Ost-Gothischen Reiches, p. 32. But St. Martin inclines to agree with Gibbon, note, vi. 75—M.]

[Footnote 120: Jornandes, c. 53, 54, p. 692-695. M. de Buat (Hist. des Peuples de l'Europe, tom. viii. p. 221-228) has clearly explained the origin and adventures of Odoacer. I am almost inclined to believe that he was the same who pillaged Angers, and commanded a fleet of Saxon pirates on the ocean. Greg. Turon. l. ii. c. 18, in tom. ii. p. 170. 8 Note: According to St. Martin there is no foundation for this conjecture, vii 5—M.]

[Footnote 121: Vade ad Italiam, vade vilissimis nunc pellibus coopertis: sed multis cito plurima largiturus. Anonym. Vales. p. 717. He quotes the life of St. Severinus, which is extant, and contains much unknown and valuable history; it was composed by his disciple Eugippius (A.D. 511) thirty years after his death. See Tillemont, Mem. Eccles. tom. xvi. p. 168-181.]

[Footnote 122: Theophanes, who calls him a Goth, affirms, that he was educated, aursed in Italy, (p. 102;) and as this strong expression will not bear a literal interpretation, it must be explained by long service in the Imperial guards.]

[Footnote 123: Nomen regis Odoacer assumpsit, cum tamen neque purpura nee regalibus uteretur insignibus. Cassiodor. in Chron. A.D. 476. He seems to have assumed the abstract title of a king, without applying it to any particular nation or country. 8 Note: Manso observes that Odoacer never called himself king of Italy, assume the purple, and no coins are extant with his name. Gescnichte Osi Goth. Reiches, p. 36—M.]

Royalty was familiar to the Barbarians, and the submissive people of Italy was prepared to obey, without a murmur, the authority which he should condescend to exercise as the vicegerent of the emperor of the West. But Odoacer had resolved to abolish that useless and expensive office; and such is the weight of antique prejudice, that it required some boldness and penetration to discover the extreme facility of the enterprise. The unfortunate Augustulus was made the instrument of his own disgrace: he signified his resignation to the senate; and that assembly, in their last act of obedience to a Roman prince, still affected the spirit of freedom, and the forms of the constitution. An epistle was addressed, by their unanimous decree, to the emperor Zeno, the son-in-law and successor of Leo; who had lately been restored, after a short rebellion, to the Byzantine throne. They solemnly "disclaim the necessity, or even the wish, of continuing any longer the Imperial succession in Italy; since, in their opinion, the majesty of a sole monarch is sufficient to pervade and protect, at the same time, both the East and the West. In their own name, and in the name of the people, they consent that the seat of universal empire shall be transferred from Rome to Constantinople; and they basely renounce the right of choosing their master, the only vestige that yet remained of the authority which had given laws to the world. The republic (they repeat that name without a blush) might safely confide in the civil and military virtues of Odoacer; and they humbly request, that the emperor would invest him with the title of Patrician, and the administration of the diocese of Italy." The deputies of the senate were received at Constantinople with some marks of displeasure and indignation: and when they were admitted to the audience of Zeno, he sternly reproached them with their treatment of the two emperors, Anthemius and Nepos, whom the East had successively granted to the prayers of Italy. "The first" (continued he) "you have murdered; the second you have expelled; but the second is still alive, and whilst he lives he is your lawful sovereign." But the prudent Zeno soon deserted the hopeless cause of his abdicated colleague. His vanity was gratified by the title of sole emperor, and by the statues erected to his honor in the several quarters of Rome; he entertained a friendly, though ambiguous, correspondence with the patrician Odoacer; and he gratefully accepted the Imperial ensigns, the sacred ornaments of the throne and palace, which the Barbarian was not unwilling to remove from the sight of the people. [124]

[Footnote 124: Malchus, whose loss excites our regret, has preserved (in Excerpt. Legat. p. 93) this extraordinary embassy from the senate to Zeno. The anonymous fragment, (p. /1/,) and the extract from Candidus, (apud Phot. p. 176,) are likewise of some use.]

In the space of twenty years since the death of Valentinian, nine emperors had successively disappeared; and the son of Orestes, a youth recommended only by his beauty, would be the least entitled to the notice of posterity, if his reign, which was marked by the extinction of the Roman empire in the West, did not leave a memorable era in the history of mankind. [125] The patrician Orestes had married the daughter of Count Romulus, of Petovio in Noricum: the name of Augustus, notwithstanding the jealousy of power, was known at Aquileia as a familiar surname; and the appellations of the two great founders, of the city and of the monarchy, were thus strangely united in the last of their successors. [126] The son of Orestes assumed and disgraced the names of Romulus Augustus; but the first was corrupted into Momyllus, by the Greeks, and the second has been changed by the Latins into the contemptible diminutive Augustulus. The life of this inoffensive youth was spared by the generous clemency of Odoacer; who dismissed him, with his whole family, from the Imperial palace, fixed his annual allowance at six thousand pieces of gold, and assigned the castle of Lucullus, in Campania, for the place of his exile or retirement. [127] As soon as the Romans breathed from the toils of the Punic war, they were attracted by the beauties and the pleasures of Campania; and the country-house of the elder Scipio at Liternum exhibited a lasting model of their rustic simplicity. [128] The delicious shores of the Bay of Naples were crowded with villas; and Sylla applauded the masterly skill of his rival, who had seated himself on the lofty promontory of Misenum, that commands, on every side, the sea and land, as far as the boundaries of the horizon. [129] The villa of Marius was purchased, within a few years, by Lucullus, and the price had increased from two thousand five hundred, to more than fourscore thousand, pounds sterling. [130] It was adorned by the new proprietor with Grecian arts and Asiatic treasures; and the houses and gardens of Lucullus obtained a distinguished rank in the list of Imperial palaces. [131] When the Vandals became formidable to the sea-coast, the Lucullan villa, on the promontory of Misenum, gradually assumed the strength and appellation of a strong castle, the obscure retreat of the last emperor of the West. About twenty years after that great revolution, it was converted into a church and monastery, to receive the bones of St. Severinus. They securely reposed, amidst the the broken trophies of Cimbric and Armenian victories,till the beginning of the tenth century; when the fortifications, which might afford a dangerous shelter to the Saracens, were demolished by the people of Naples. [132]

[Footnote 125: The precise year in which the Western empire was extinguished, is not positively ascertained. The vulgar era of A.D. 476 appears to have the sanction of authentic chronicles. But the two dates assigned by Jornandes (c. 46, p. 680) would delay that great event to the year 479; and though M. de Buat has overlooked his evidence, he produces (tom. viii. p. 261-288) many collateral circumstances in support of the same opinion.]

[Footnote 126: See his medals in Ducange, (Fam. Byzantin. p. 81,) Priscus, (Excerpt. Legat. p. 56,) Maffei, (Osservazioni Letterarie, tom. ii p. 314.) We may allege a famous and similar case. The meanest subjects of the Roman empire assumed the illustrious name of Patricius, which, by the conversion of Ireland has been communicated to a whole nation.]

[Footnote 127: Ingrediens autem Ravennam deposuit Augustulum de regno, cujus infantiam misertus concessit ei sanguinem; et quia pulcher erat, tamen donavit ei reditum sex millia solidos, et misit eum intra Campaniam cum parentibus suis libere vivere. Anonym. Vales. p. 716. Jornandes says, (c 46, p. 680,) in Lucullano Campaniae castello exilii poena damnavit.]

[Footnote 128: See the eloquent Declamation of Seneca, (Epist. lxxxvi.) The philosopher might have recollected, that all luxury is relative; and that the elder Scipio, whose manners were polished by study and conversation, was himself accused of that vice by his ruder contemporaries, (Livy, xxix. 19.)]

[Footnote 129: Sylla, in the language of a soldier, praised his peritia castrametandi, (Plin. Hist. Natur. xviii. 7.) Phaedrus, who makes its shady walks (loeta viridia) the scene of an insipid fable, (ii. 5,) has thus described the situation:—

Caesar Tiberius quum petens Neapolim, In Misenensem villam venissit suam; Quae monte summo posita Luculli manu Prospectat Siculum et prospicit Tuscum mare.]

[Footnote 130: From seven myriads and a half to two hundred and fifty myriads of drachmae. Yet even in the possession of Marius, it was a luxurious retirement. The Romans derided his indolence; they soon bewailed his activity. See Plutarch, in Mario, tom. ii. p. 524.]

[Footnote 131: Lucullus had other villa of equal, though various, magnificence, at Baiae, Naples, Tusculum, &c., He boasted that he changed his climate with the storks and cranes. Plutarch, in Lucull. tom. iii. p. 193.]

[Footnote 132: Severinus died in Noricum, A.D. 482. Six years afterwards, his body, which scattered miracles as it passed, was transported by his disciples into Italy. The devotion of a Neapolitan lady invited the saint to the Lucullan villa, in the place of Augustulus, who was probably no more. See Baronius (Annal. Eccles. A.D. 496, No. 50, 51) and Tillemont, (Mem. Eccles. tom. xvi. p. 178-181,) from the original life by Eugippius. The narrative of the last migration of Severinus to Naples is likewise an authentic piece.]

Odoacer was the first Barbarian who reigned in Italy, over a people who had once asserted their just superiority above the rest of mankind. The disgrace of the Romans still excites our respectful compassion, and we fondly sympathize with the imaginary grief and indignation of their degenerate posterity. But the calamities of Italy had gradually subdued the proud consciousness of freedom and glory. In the age of Roman virtue the provinces were subject to the arms, and the citizens to the laws, of the republic; till those laws were subverted by civil discord, and both the city and the province became the servile property of a tyrant. The forms of the constitution, which alleviated or disguised their abject slavery, were abolished by time and violence; the Italians alternately lamented the presence or the absence of the sovereign, whom they detested or despised; and the succession of five centuries inflicted the various evils of military license, capricious despotism, and elaborate oppression. During the same period, the Barbarians had emerged from obscurity and contempt, and the warriors of Germany and Scythia were introduced into the provinces, as the servants, the allies, and at length the masters, of the Romans, whom they insulted or protected. The hatred of the people was suppressed by fear; they respected the spirit and splendor of the martial chiefs who were invested with the honors of the empire; and the fate of Rome had long depended on the sword of those formidable strangers. The stern Ricimer, who trampled on the ruins of Italy, had exercised the power, without assuming the title, of a king; and the patient Romans were insensibly prepared to acknowledge the royalty of Odoacer and his Barbaric successors. The king of Italy was not unworthy of the high station to which his valor and fortune had exalted him: his savage manners were polished by the habits of conversation; and he respected, though a conqueror and a Barbarian, the institutions, and even the prejudices, of his subjects. After an interval of seven years, Odoacer restored the consulship of the West. For himself, he modestly, or proudly, declined an honor which was still accepted by the emperors of the East; but the curule chair was successively filled by eleven of the most illustrious senators; [133] and the list is adorned by the respectable name of Basilius, whose virtues claimed the friendship and grateful applause of Sidonius, his client. [134] The laws of the emperors were strictly enforced, and the civil administration of Italy was still exercised by the Praetorian praefect and his subordinate officers. Odoacer devolved on the Roman magistrates the odious and oppressive task of collecting the public revenue; but he reserved for himself the merit of seasonable and popular indulgence. [135] Like the rest of the Barbarians, he had been instructed in the Arian heresy; but he revered the monastic and episcopal characters; and the silence of the Catholics attest the toleration which they enjoyed. The peace of the city required the interposition of his praefect Basilius in the choice of a Roman pontiff: the decree which restrained the clergy from alienating their lands was ultimately designed for the benefit of the people, whose devotions would have been taxed to repair the dilapidations of the church. [136] Italy was protected by the arms of its conqueror; and its frontiers were respected by the Barbarians of Gaul and Germany, who had so long insulted the feeble race of Theodosius. Odoacer passed the Adriatic, to chastise the assassins of the emperor Nepos, and to acquire the maritime province of Dalmatia. He passed the Alps, to rescue the remains of Noricum from Fava, or Feletheus, king of the Rugians, who held his residence beyond the Danube. The king was vanquished in battle, and led away prisoner; a numerous colony of captives and subjects was transplanted into Italy; and Rome, after a long period of defeat and disgrace, might claim the triumph of her Barbarian master. [137]

[Footnote 133: The consular Fasti may be found in Pagi or Muratori. The consuls named by Odoacer, or perhaps by the Roman senate, appear to have been acknowledged in the Eastern empire.]

[Footnote 134: Sidonius Apollinaris (l. i. epist. 9, p. 22, edit. Sirmond) has compared the two leading senators of his time, (A.D. 468,) Gennadius Avienus and Caecina Basilius. To the former he assigns the specious, to the latter the solid, virtues of public and private life. A Basilius junior, possibly his son, was consul in the year 480.]

[Footnote 135: Epiphanius interceded for the people of Pavia; and the king first granted an indulgence of five years, and afterwards relieved them from the oppression of Pelagius, the Praetorian praefect, (Ennodius in Vit St. Epiphan., in Sirmond, Oper. tom. i. p. 1670-1672.)]

[Footnote 136: See Baronius, Annal. Eccles. A.D. 483, No. 10-15. Sixteen years afterwards the irregular proceedings of Basilius were condemned by Pope Symmachus in a Roman synod.]

[Footnote 137: The wars of Odoacer are concisely mentioned by Paul the Deacon, (de Gest. Langobard. l. i. c. 19, p. 757, edit. Grot.,) and in the two Chronicles of Cassiodorus and Cuspinian. The life of St. Severinus by Eugippius, which the count de Buat (Hist. des Peuples, &c., tom. viii. c. 1, 4, 8, 9) has diligently studied, illustrates the ruin of Noricum and the Bavarian antiquities]

Notwithstanding the prudence and success of Odoacer, his kingdom exhibited the sad prospect of misery and desolation. Since the age of Tiberius, the decay of agriculture had been felt in Italy; and it was a just subject of complaint, that the life of the Roman people depended on the accidents of the winds and waves. [138] In the division and the decline of the empire, the tributary harvests of Egypt and Africa were withdrawn; the numbers of the inhabitants continually diminished with the means of subsistence; and the country was exhausted by the irretrievable losses of war, famine, [139] and pestilence. St. Ambrose has deplored the ruin of a populous district, which had been once adorned with the flourishing cities of Bologna, Modena, Regium, and Placentia. [140] Pope Gelasius was a subject of Odoacer; and he affirms, with strong exaggeration, that in Aemilia, Tuscany, and the adjacent provinces, the human species was almost extirpated. [141] The plebeians of Rome, who were fed by the hand of their master, perished or disappeared, as soon as his liberality was suppressed; the decline of the arts reduced the industrious mechanic to idleness and want; and the senators, who might support with patience the ruin of their country, bewailed their private loss of wealth and luxury. [141/1] One third of those ample estates, to which the ruin of Italy is originally imputed, [142] was extorted for the use of the conquerors. Injuries were aggravated by insults; the sense of actual sufferings was imbittered by the fear of more dreadful evils; and as new lands were allotted to the new swarms of Barbarians, each senator was apprehensive lest the arbitrary surveyors should approach his favorite villa, or his most profitable farm. The least unfortunate were those who submitted without a murmur to the power which it was impossible to resist. Since they desired to live, they owed some gratitude to the tyrant who had spared their lives; and since he was the absolute master of their fortunes, the portion which he left must be accepted as his pure and voluntary gift. [143] The distress of Italy [143/1] was mitigated by the prudence and humanity of Odoacer, who had bound himself, as the price of his elevation, to satisfy the demands of a licentious and turbulent multitude. The kings of the Barbarians were frequently resisted, deposed, or murdered, by their native subjects, and the various bands of Italian mercenaries, who associated under the standard of an elective general, claimed a larger privilege of freedom and rapine. A monarchy destitute of national union, and hereditary right, hastened to its dissolution. After a reign of fourteen years, Odoacer was oppressed by the superior genius of Theodoric, king of the Ostrogoths; a hero alike excellent in the arts of war and of government, who restored an age of peace and prosperity, and whose name still excites and deserves the attention of mankind.

[Footnote 138: Tacit. Annal. iii. 53. The Recherches sur l'Administration des Terres chez les Romains (p. 351-361) clearly state the progress of internal decay.]

[Footnote 139: A famine, which afflicted Italy at the time of the irruption of Odoacer, king of the Heruli, is eloquently described, in prose and verse, by a French poet, (Les Mois, tom. ii. p. 174, 205, edit. in 12 mo.) I am ignorant from whence he derives his information; but I am well assured that he relates some facts incompatible with the truth of history]

[Footnote 140: See the xxxixth epistle of St. Ambrose, as it is quoted by Muratori, sopra le Antichita Italiane, tom. i. Dissert. xxi. p. 354.]

[Footnote 141: Aemilia, Tuscia, ceteraeque provinciae in quibus hominum propenullus exsistit. Gelasius, Epist. ad Andromachum, ap. Baronium, Annal. Eccles. A.D. 496, No. 36.]

[Footnote 141/1: Denina supposes that the Barbarians were compelled by necessity to turn their attention to agriculture. Italy, either imperfectly cultivated, or not at all, by the indolent or ruined proprietors, not only could not furnish the imposts, on which the pay of the soldiery depended, but not even a certain supply of the necessaries of life. The neighboring countries were now occupied by warlike nations; the supplies of corn from Africa were cut off; foreign commerce nearly destroyed; they could not look for supplies beyond the limits of Italy, throughout which the agriculture had been long in a state of progressive but rapid depression. (Denina, Rev. d'Italia t. v. c. i.)—M.]

[Footnote 142: Verumque confitentibus, latifundia perdidere Italiam. Plin. Hist. Natur. xviii. 7.]

[Footnote 143: Such are the topics of consolation, or rather of patience, which Cicero (ad Familiares, lib. ix. Epist. 17) suggests to his friend Papirius Paetus, under the military despotism of Caesar. The argument, however, of "vivere pulcherrimum duxi," is more forcibly addressed to a Roman philosopher, who possessed the free alternative of life or death]

[Footnote 143/1: Compare, on the desolation and change of property in Italy, Manno des Ost-Gothischen Reiches, Part ii. p. 73, et seq—M.]

CHAPTER XXXVII

CONVERSION OF THE BARBARIANS TO CHRISTIANITY

PART I

ORIGIN PROGRESS, AND EFFECTS OF THE MONASTIC LIFE—CONVERSION OF THE BARBARIANS TO CHRISTIANITY AND ARIANISM—PERSECUTION OF THE VANDALS IN AFRICA—EXTINCTION OF ARIANISM AMONG THE BARBARIANS

The indissoluble connection of civil and ecclesiastical affairs has compelled, and encouraged, me to relate the progress, the persecutions, the establishment, the divisions, the final triumph, and the gradual corruption, of Christianity. I have purposely delayed the consideration of two religious events, interesting in the study of human nature, and important in the decline and fall of the Roman empire. I. The institution of the monastic life; [1] and, II. The conversion of the northern Barbarians.

[Footnote 1: The origin of the monastic institution has been laboriously discussed by Thomassin (Discipline de l'Eglise, tom. i. p. 1119-1426) and Helyot, (Hist. des Ordres Monastiques, tom. i. p. 1-66.) These authors are very learned, and tolerably honest, and their difference of opinion shows the subject in its full extent. Yet the cautious Protestant, who distrusts any popish guides, may consult the seventh book of Bingham's Christian Antiquities.]

I. Prosperity and peace introduced the distinction of the vulgar and the Ascetic Christians. [2] The loose and imperfect practice of religion satisfied the conscience of the multitude. The prince or magistrate, the soldier or merchant, reconciled their fervent zeal, and implicit faith, with the exercise of their profession, the pursuit of their interest, and the indulgence of their passions: but the Ascetics, who obeyed and abused the rigid precepts of the gospel, were inspired by the savage enthusiasm which represents man as a criminal, and God as a tyrant. They seriously renounced the business, and the pleasures, of the age; abjured the use of wine, of flesh, and of marriage; chastised their body, mortified their affections, and embraced a life of misery, as the price of eternal happiness. In the reign of Constantine, the Ascetics fled from a profane and degenerate world, to perpetual solitude, or religious society. Like the first Christians of Jerusalem, [3] [311] they resigned the use, or the property of their temporal possessions; established regular communities of the same sex, and a similar disposition; and assumed the names of Hermits, Monks, and Anachorets, expressive of their lonely retreat in a natural or artificial desert. They soon acquired the respect of the world, which they despised; and the loudest applause was bestowed on this Divine Philosophy, [4] which surpassed, without the aid of science or reason, the laborious virtues of the Grecian schools. The monks might indeed contend with the Stoics, in the contempt of fortune, of pain, and of death: the Pythagorean silence and submission were revived in their servile discipline; and they disdained, as firmly as the Cynics themselves, all the forms and decencies of civil society. But the votaries of this Divine Philosophy aspired to imitate a purer and more perfect model. They trod in the footsteps of the prophets, who had retired to the desert; [5] and they restored the devout and contemplative life, which had been instituted by the Essenians, in Palestine and Egypt. The philosophic eye of Pliny had surveyed with astonishment a solitary people, who dwelt among the palm-trees near the Dead Sea; who subsisted without money, who were propagated without women; and who derived from the disgust and repentance of mankind a perpetual supply of voluntary associates. [6]

[Footnote 2: See Euseb. Demonstrat. Evangel., (l. i. p. 20, 21, edit. Graec. Rob. Stephani, Paris, 1545.) In his Ecclesiastical History, published twelve years after the Demonstration, Eusebius (l. ii. c. 17) asserts the Christianity of the Therapeutae; but he appears ignorant that a similar institution was actually revived in Egypt.]

[Footnote 3: Cassian (Collat. xviii. 5.) claims this origin for the institution of the Coenobites, which gradually decayed till it was restored by Antony and his disciples.]

[Footnote 311: It has before been shown that the first Christian community was not strictly coenobitic. See vol. ii—M.]

[Footnote 4: These are the expressive words of Sozomen, who copiously and agreeably describes (l. i. c. 12, 13, 14) the origin and progress of this monkish philosophy, (see Suicer. Thesau, Eccles., tom. ii. p. 1441.) Some modern writers, Lipsius (tom. iv. p. 448. Manuduct. ad Philosoph. Stoic. iii. 13) and La Mothe le Vayer, (tom. ix. de la Vertu des Payens, p. 228-262,) have compared the Carmelites to the Pythagoreans, and the Cynics to the Capucins.]

[Footnote 5: The Carmelites derive their pedigree, in regular succession, from the prophet Elijah, (see the Theses of Beziers, A.D. 1682, in Bayle's Nouvelles de la Republique des Lettres, Oeuvres, tom. i. p. 82, &c., and the prolix irony of the Ordres Monastiques, an anonymous work, tom. i. p. 1-433, Berlin, 1751.) Rome, and the inquisition of Spain, silenced the profane criticism of the Jesuits of Flanders, (Helyot, Hist. des Ordres Monastiques, tom. i. p. 282-300,) and the statue of Elijah, the Carmelite, has been erected in the church of St. Peter, (Voyages du P. Labat tom. iii. p. 87.)]

[Footnote 6: Plin. Hist. Natur. v. 15. Gens sola, et in toto orbe praeter ceteras mira, sine ulla femina, omni venere abdicata, sine pecunia, socia palmarum. Ita per seculorum millia (incredibile dictu) gens aeterna est in qua nemo nascitur. Tam foecunda illis aliorum vitae poenitentia est. He places them just beyond the noxious influence of the lake, and names Engaddi and Massada as the nearest towns. The Laura, and monastery of St. Sabas, could not be far distant from this place. See Reland. Palestin., tom. i. p. 295; tom. ii. p. 763, 874, 880, 890.]

Egypt, the fruitful parent of superstition, afforded the first example of the monastic life. Antony, [7] an illiterate [8] youth of the lower parts of Thebais, distributed his patrimony, [9] deserted his family and native home, and executed his monastic penance with original and intrepid fanaticism. After a long and painful novitiate, among the tombs, and in a ruined tower, he boldly advanced into the desert three days' journey to the eastward of the Nile; discovered a lonely spot, which possessed the advantages of shade and water, and fixed his last residence on Mount Colzim, near the Red Sea; where an ancient monastery still preserves the name and memory of the saint. [10] The curious devotion of the Christians pursued him to the desert; and when he was obliged to appear at Alexandria, in the face of mankind, he supported his fame with discretion and dignity. He enjoyed the friendship of Athanasius, whose doctrine he approved; and the Egyptian peasant respectfully declined a respectful invitation from the emperor Constantine. The venerable patriarch (for Antony attained the age of one hundred and five years) beheld the numerous progeny which had been formed by his example and his lessons. The prolific colonies of monks multiplied with rapid increase on the sands of Libya, upon the rocks of Thebais, and in the cities of the Nile. To the south of Alexandria, the mountain, and adjacent desert, of Nitria, were peopled by five thousand anachorets; and the traveller may still investigate the ruins of fifty monasteries, which were planted in that barren soil by the disciples of Antony. [11] In the Upper Thebais, the vacant island of Tabenne, [12] was occupied by Pachomius and fourteen hundred of his brethren. That holy abbot successively founded nine monasteries of men, and one of women; and the festival of Easter sometimes collected fifty thousand religious persons, who followed his angelic rule of discipline. [13] The stately and populous city of Oxyrinchus, the seat of Christian orthodoxy, had devoted the temples, the public edifices, and even the ramparts, to pious and charitable uses; and the bishop, who might preach in twelve churches, computed ten thousand females and twenty thousand males, of the monastic profession. [14] The Egyptians, who gloried in this marvellous revolution, were disposed to hope, and to believe, that the number of the monks was equal to the remainder of the people; [15] and posterity might repeat the saying, which had formerly been applied to the sacred animals of the same country, That in Egypt it was less difficult to find a god than a man.

[Footnote 7: See Athanas. Op. tom. ii. p. 450-505, and the Vit. Patrum, p. 26-74, with Rosweyde's Annotations. The former is the Greek original the latter, a very ancient Latin version by Evagrius, the friend of St. Jerom.]

[Footnote 8: Athanas. tom. ii. in Vit. St. Anton. p. 452; and the assertion of his total ignorance has been received by many of the ancients and moderns. But Tillemont (Mem. Eccles. tom. vii. p. 666) shows, by some probable arguments, that Antony could read and write in the Coptic, his native tongue; and that he was only a stranger to the Greek letters. The philosopher Synesius (p. 51) acknowledges that the natural genius of Antony did not require the aid of learning.]

[Footnote 9: Aruroe autem erant ei trecentae uberes, et valde optimae, (Vit. Patr. l. v. p. 36.) If the Arura be a square measure, of a hundred Egyptian cubits, (Rosweyde, Onomasticon ad Vit. Patrum, p. 1014, 1015,) and the Egyptian cubit of all ages be equal to twenty-two English inches, (Greaves, vol. i. p. 233,) the arura will consist of about three quarters of an English acre.]

[Footnote 10: The description of the monastery is given by Jerom (tom. i. p. 248, 249, in Vit. Hilarion) and the P. Sicard, (Missions du Levant tom. v. p. 122-200.) Their accounts cannot always be reconciled the father painted from his fancy, and the Jesuit from his experience.]

[Footnote 11: Jerom, tom. i. p. 146, ad Eustochium. Hist. Lausiac. c. 7, in Vit. Patrum, p. 712. The P. Sicard (Missions du Levant, tom. ii. p. 29-79) visited and has described this desert, which now contains four monasteries, and twenty or thirty monks. See D'Anville, Description de l'Egypte, p. 74.]

[Footnote 12: Tabenne is a small island in the Nile, in the diocese of Tentyra or Dendera, between the modern town of Girge and the ruins of ancient Thebes, (D'Anville, p. 194.) M. de Tillemont doubts whether it was an isle; but I may conclude, from his own facts, that the primitive name was afterwards transferred to the great monastery of Bau or Pabau, (Mem. Eccles. tom. vii. p. 678, 688.)]

[Footnote 13: See in the Codex Regularum (published by Lucas Holstenius, Rome, 1661) a preface of St. Jerom to his Latin version of the Rule of Pachomius, tom. i. p. 61.]

[Footnote 14: Rufin. c. 5, in Vit. Patrum, p. 459. He calls it civitas ampla ralde et populosa, and reckons twelve churches. Strabo (l. xvii. p. 1166) and Ammianus (xxii. 16) have made honorable mention of Oxyrinchus, whose inhabitants adored a small fish in a magnificent temple.]

[Footnote 15: Quanti populi habentur in urbibus, tantae paene habentur in desertis multitudines monachorum. Rufin. c. 7, in Vit. Patrum, p. 461. He congratulates the fortunate change.]

Athanasius introduced into Rome the knowledge and practice of the monastic life; and a school of this new philosophy was opened by the disciples of Antony, who accompanied their primate to the holy threshold of the Vatican. The strange and savage appearance of these Egyptians excited, at first, horror and contempt, and, at length, applause and zealous imitation. The senators, and more especially the matrons, transformed their palaces and villas into religious houses; and the narrow institution of six vestals was eclipsed by the frequent monasteries, which were seated on the ruins of ancient temples, and in the midst of the Roman forum. [16] Inflamed by the example of Antony, a Syrian youth, whose name was Hilarion, [17] fixed his dreary abode on a sandy beach, between the sea and a morass, about seven miles from Gaza. The austere penance, in which he persisted forty-eight years, diffused a similar enthusiasm; and the holy man was followed by a train of two or three thousand anachorets, whenever he visited the innumerable monasteries of Palestine. The fame of Basil [18] is immortal in the monastic history of the East. With a mind that had tasted the learning and eloquence of Athens; with an ambition scarcely to be satisfied with the archbishopric of Caesarea, Basil retired to a savage solitude in Pontus; and deigned, for a while, to give laws to the spiritual colonies which he profusely scattered along the coast of the Black Sea. In the West, Martin of Tours, [19] a soldier, a hermit, a bishop, and a saint, established the monasteries of Gaul; two thousand of his disciples followed him to the grave; and his eloquent historian challenges the deserts of Thebais to produce, in a more favorable climate, a champion of equal virtue. The progress of the monks was not less rapid, or universal, than that of Christianity itself. Every province, and, at last, every city, of the empire, was filled with their increasing multitudes; and the bleak and barren isles, from Lerins to Lipari, that arose out of the Tuscan Sea, were chosen by the anachorets for the place of their voluntary exile. An easy and perpetual intercourse by sea and land connected the provinces of the Roman world; and the life of Hilarion displays the facility with which an indigent hermit of Palestine might traverse Egypt, embark for Sicily, escape to Epirus, and finally settle in the Island of Cyprus. [20] The Latin Christians embraced the religious institutions of Rome. The pilgrims, who visited Jerusalem, eagerly copied, in the most distant climates of the earth, the faithful model of the monastic life. The disciples of Antony spread themselves beyond the tropic, over the Christian empire of Aethiopia. [21] The monastery of Banchor, [22] in Flintshire, which contained above two thousand brethren, dispersed a numerous colony among the Barbarians of Ireland; [23] and Iona, one of the Hebrides, which was planted by the Irish monks, diffused over the northern regions a doubtful ray of science and superstition. [24]

[Footnote 16: The introduction of the monastic life into Rome and Italy is occasionally mentioned by Jerom, tom. i. p. 119, 120, 199.]

[Footnote 17: See the Life of Hilarion, by St. Jerom, (tom. i. p. 241, 252.) The stories of Paul, Hilarion, and Malchus, by the same author, are admirably told: and the only defect of these pleasing compositions is the want of truth and common sense.]

[Footnote 18: His original retreat was in a small village on the banks of the Iris, not far from Neo-Caesarea. The ten or twelve years of his monastic life were disturbed by long and frequent avocations. Some critics have disputed the authenticity of his Ascetic rules; but the external evidence is weighty, and they can only prove that it is the work of a real or affected enthusiast. See Tillemont, Mem. Eccles tom. ix. p. 636-644. Helyot, Hist. des Ordres Monastiques tom. i. p. 175-181]

[Footnote 19: See his Life, and the three Dialogues by Sulpicius Severus, who asserts (Dialog. i. 16) that the booksellers of Rome were delighted with the quick and ready sale of his popular work.]

[Footnote 20: When Hilarion sailed from Paraetonium to Cape Pachynus, he offered to pay his passage with a book of the Gospels. Posthumian, a Gallic monk, who had visited Egypt, found a merchant ship bound from Alexandria to Marseilles, and performed the voyage in thirty days, (Sulp. Sever. Dialog. i. 1.) Athanasius, who addressed his Life of St. Antony to the foreign monks, was obliged to hasten the composition, that it might be ready for the sailing of the fleets, (tom. ii. p. 451.)]

[Footnote 21: See Jerom, (tom. i. p. 126,) Assemanni, Bibliot. Orient. tom. iv. p. 92, p. 857-919, and Geddes, Church History of Aethiopia, p. 29-31. The Abyssinian monks adhere very strictly to the primitive institution.]

[Footnote 22: Camden's Britannia, vol. i. p. 666, 667.]

[Footnote 23: All that learning can extract from the rubbish of the dark ages is copiously stated by Archbishop Usher in his Britannicarum Ecclesiarum Antiquitates, cap. xvi. p. 425-503.]

[Footnote 24: This small, though not barren, spot, Iona, Hy, or Columbkill, only two miles in length, aud one mile in breadth, has been distinguished, 1. By the monastery of St. Columba, founded A.D. 566; whose abbot exercised an extraordinary jurisdiction over the bishops of Caledonia; 2. By a classic library, which afforded some hopes of an entire Livy; and, 3. By the tombs of sixty kings, Scots, Irish, and Norwegians, who reposed in holy ground. See Usher (p. 311, 360-370) and Buchanan, (Rer. Scot. l. ii. p. 15, edit. Ruddiman.)]

These unhappy exiles from social life were impelled by the dark and implacable genius of superstition. Their mutual resolution was supported by the example of millions, of either sex, of every age, and of every rank; and each proselyte who entered the gates of a monastery, was persuaded that he trod the steep and thorny path of eternal happiness. [25] But the operation of these religious motives was variously determined by the temper and situation of mankind. Reason might subdue, or passion might suspend, their influence: but they acted most forcibly on the infirm minds of children and females; they were strengthened by secret remorse, or accidental misfortune; and they might derive some aid from the temporal considerations of vanity or interest. It was naturally supposed, that the pious and humble monks, who had renounced the world to accomplish the work of their salvation, were the best qualified for the spiritual government of the Christians. The reluctant hermit was torn from his cell, and seated, amidst the acclamations of the people, on the episcopal throne: the monasteries of Egypt, of Gaul, and of the East, supplied a regular succession of saints and bishops; and ambition soon discovered the secret road which led to the possession of wealth and honors. [26] The popular monks, whose reputation was connected with the fame and success of the order, assiduously labored to multiply the number of their fellow-captives. They insinuated themselves into noble and opulent families; and the specious arts of flattery and seduction were employed to secure those proselytes who might bestow wealth or dignity on the monastic profession. The indignant father bewailed the loss, perhaps, of an only son; [27] the credulous maid was betrayed by vanity to violate the laws of nature; and the matron aspired to imaginary perfection, by renouncing the virtues of domestic life. Paula yielded to the persuasive eloquence of Jerom; [28] and the profane title of mother-in-law of God [29] tempted that illustrious widow to consecrate the virginity of her daughter Eustochium. By the advice, and in the company, of her spiritual guide, Paula abandoned Rome and her infant son; retired to the holy village of Bethlem; founded a hospital and four monasteries; and acquired, by her alms and penance, an eminent and conspicuous station in the Catholic church. Such rare and illustrious penitents were celebrated as the glory and example of their age; but the monasteries were filled by a crowd of obscure and abject plebeians, [30] who gained in the cloister much more than they had sacrificed in the world. Peasants, slaves, and mechanics, might escape from poverty and contempt to a safe and honorable profession; whose apparent hardships are mitigated by custom, by popular applause, and by the secret relaxation of discipline. [31] The subjects of Rome, whose persons and fortunes were made responsible for unequal and exorbitant tributes, retired from the oppression of the Imperial government; and the pusillanimous youth preferred the penance of a monastic, to the dangers of a military, life. The affrighted provincials of every rank, who fled before the Barbarians, found shelter and subsistence: whole legions were buried in these religious sanctuaries; and the same cause, which relieved the distress of individuals, impaired the strength and fortitude of the empire. [32]

[Footnote 25: Chrysostom (in the first tome of the Benedictine edition) has consecrated three books to the praise and defence of the monastic life. He is encouraged, by the example of the ark, to presume that none but the elect (the monks) can possibly be saved (l. i. p. 55, 56.) Elsewhere, indeed, he becomes more merciful, (l. iii. p. 83, 84,) and allows different degrees of glory, like the sun, moon, and stars. In his lively comparison of a king and a monk, (l. iii. p. 116-121,) he supposes (what is hardly fair) that the king will be more sparingly rewarded, and more rigorously punished.]

[Footnote 26: Thomassin (Discipline de l'Eglise tom. i. p. 1426-1469) and Mabillon, (Oeuvres Posthumes, tom. ii. p. 115-158.) The monks were gradually adopted as a part of the ecclesiastical hierarchy.]

[Footnote 27: Dr. Middleton (vol. i. p. 110) liberally censures the conduct and writings of Chrysostom, one of the most eloquent and successful advocates for the monastic life.]

[Footnote 28: Jerom's devout ladies form a very considerable portion of his works: the particular treatise, which he styles the Epitaph of Paula, (tom. i. p. 169-192,) is an elaborate and extravagant panegyric. The exordium is ridiculously turgid: "If all the members of my body were changed into tongues, and if all my limbs resounded with a human voice, yet should I be incapable," &c.]

[Footnote 29: Socrus Dei esse coepisti, (Jerom, tom. i. p. 140, ad Eustochium.) Rufinus, (in Hieronym. Op. tom. iv. p. 223,) who was justly scandalized, asks his adversary, from what Pagan poet he had stolen an expression so impious and absurd.]

[Footnote 30: Nunc autem veniunt plerumque ad hanc professionem servitutis Dei, et ex conditione servili, vel etiam liberati, vel propter hoc a Dominis liberati sive liberandi; et ex vita rusticana et ex opificum exercitatione, et plebeio labore. Augustin, de Oper. Monach. c. 22, ap. Thomassin, Discipline de l'Eglise, tom. iii. p. 1094. The Egyptian, who blamed Arsenius, owned that he led a more comfortable life as a monk than as a shepherd. See Tillemont, Mem. Eccles. tom. xiv. p. 679.]

[Footnote 31: A Dominican friar, (Voyages du P. Labat, tom. i. p. 10,) who lodged at Cadiz in a convent of his brethren, soon understood that their repose was never interrupted by nocturnal devotion; "quoiqu'on ne laisse pas de sonner pour l'edification du peuple."]

[Footnote 32: See a very sensible preface of Lucas Holstenius to the Codex Regularum. The emperors attempted to support the obligation of public and private duties; but the feeble dikes were swept away by the torrent of superstition; and Justinian surpassed the most sanguine wishes of the monks, (Thomassin, tom. i. p. 1782-1799, and Bingham, l. vii. c. iii. p. 253.) Note: The emperor Valens, in *particular, promulgates a law contra ignavise quosdam sectatores, qui desertis civitatum muneribus, captant solitudines secreta, et specie religionis cum coetibus monachorum congregantur. Cad. Theod l. xii. tit. i. leg. 63—G.]*

The monastic profession of the ancients [33] was an act of voluntary devotion. The inconstant fanatic was threatened with the eternal vengeance of the God whom he deserted; but the doors of the monastery were still open for repentance. Those monks, whose conscience was fortified by reason or passion, were at liberty to resume the character of men and citizens; and even the spouses of Christ might accept the legal embraces of an earthly lover. [34] The examples of scandal, and the progress of superstition, suggested the propriety of more forcible restraints. After a sufficient trial, the fidelity of the novice was secured by a solemn and perpetual vow; and his irrevocable engagement was ratified by the laws of the church and state. A guilty fugitive was pursued, arrested, and restored to his perpetual prison; and the interposition of the magistrate oppressed the freedom and the merit, which had alleviated, in some degree, the abject slavery of the monastic discipline. [35] The actions of a monk, his words, and even his thoughts, were determined by an inflexible rule, [36] or a capricious superior: the slightest offences were corrected by disgrace or confinement, extraordinary fasts, or bloody flagellation; and disobedience, murmur, or delay, were ranked in the catalogue of the most heinous sins. [37] A blind submission to the commands of the abbot, however absurd, or even criminal, they might seem, was the ruling principle, the first virtue of the Egyptian monks; and their patience was frequently exercised by the most extravagant trials. They were directed to remove an enormous rock; assiduously to water a barren staff, that was planted in the ground, till, at the end of three years, it should vegetate and blossom like a tree; to walk into a fiery furnace; or to cast their infant into a deep pond: and several saints, or madmen, have been immortalized in monastic story, by their thoughtless and fearless obedience. [38] The freedom of the mind, the source of every generous and rational sentiment, was destroyed by the habits of credulity and submission; and the monk, contracting the vices of a slave, devoutly followed the faith and passions of his ecclesiastical tyrant. The peace of the Eastern church was invaded by a swarm of fanatics, incapable of fear, or reason, or humanity; and the Imperial troops acknowledged, without shame, that they were much less apprehensive of an encounter with the fiercest Barbarians. [39]

[Footnote 33: The monastic institutions, particularly those of Egypt, about the year 400, are described by four curious and devout travellers; Rufinus, (Vit. Patrum, l. ii. iii. p. 424-536,) Posthumian, (Sulp. Sever. Dialog. i.) Palladius, (Hist. Lausiac. in Vit. Patrum, p. 709-863,) and Cassian, (see in tom. vii. Bibliothec. Max. Patrum, his four first books of Institutes, and the twenty-four Collations or Conferences.)]

[Footnote 34: The example of Malchus, (Jerom, tom. i. p. 256,) and the design of Cassian and his friend, (Collation. xxiv. 1,) are incontestable proofs of their freedom; which is elegantly described by Erasmus in his Life of St. Jerom. See Chardon, Hist. des Sacremens, tom. vi. p. 279-300.]

[Footnote 35: See the Laws of Justinian, (Novel. cxxiii. No. 42,) and of Lewis the Pious, (in the Historians of France, tom vi. p. 427,) and the actual jurisprudence of France, in Denissart, (Decisions, &c., tom. iv. p. 855,) &c.]

[Footnote 36: The ancient Codex Regularum, collected by Benedict Anianinus, the reformer of the monks in the beginning of the ninth century, and published in the seventeenth, by Lucas Holstenius, contains thirty different rules for men and women. Of these, seven were composed in Egypt, one in the East, one in Cappadocia, one in Italy, one in Africa, four in Spain, eight in Gaul, or France, and one in England.]

[Footnote 37: The rule of Columbanus, so prevalent in the West, inflicts one hundred lashes for very slight offences, (Cod. Reg. part ii. p. 174.) Before the time of Charlemagne, the abbots indulged themselves in mutilating their monks, or putting out their eyes; a punishment much less cruel than the tremendous vade in pace (the subterraneous dungeon or sepulchre) which was afterwards invented. See an admirable discourse of the learned Mabillon, (Oeuvres Posthumes, tom. ii. p. 321-336,) who, on this occasion, seems to be inspired by the genius of humanity. For such an effort, I can forgive his defence of the holy tear of Vendeme (p. 361-399.)]

[Footnote 38: Sulp. Sever. Dialog. i. 12, 13, p. 532, &c. Cassian. Institut. l. iv. c. 26, 27. "Praecipua ibi virtus et prima est obedientia." Among the Verba seniorum, (in Vit. Patrum, l. v. p. 617,) the fourteenth libel or discourse is on the subject of obedience; and the Jesuit Rosweyde, who published that huge volume for the use of convents, has collected all the scattered passages in his two copious indexes.]

[Footnote 39: Dr. Jortin (Remarks on Ecclesiastical History, vol. iv. p. 161) has observed the scandalous valor of the Cappadocian monks, which was exemplified in the banishment of Chrysostom.] Superstition has often framed and consecrated the fantastic garments of the monks: [40] but their apparent singularity sometimes proceeds from their uniform attachment to a simple and primitive model, which the revolutions of fashion have made ridiculous in the eyes of mankind. The father of the Benedictines expressly disclaims all idea of choice of merit; and soberly exhorts his disciples to adopt the coarse and convenient dress of the countries which they may inhabit. [41] The monastic habits of the ancients varied with the climate, and their mode of life; and they assumed, with the same indifference, the sheep-skin of the Egyptian peasants, or the cloak of the Grecian philosophers. They allowed themselves the use of linen in Egypt, where it was a cheap and domestic manufacture; but in the West they rejected such an expensive article of foreign luxury. [42] It was the practice of the monks either to cut or shave their hair; they wrapped their heads in a cowl to escape the sight of profane objects; their legs and feet were naked, except in the extreme cold of winter; and their slow and feeble steps were supported by a long staff. The aspect of a genuine anachoret was horrid and disgusting: every sensation that is offensive to man was thought acceptable to God; and the angelic rule of Tabenne condemned the salutary custom of bathing the limbs in water, and of anointing them with oil. [43] [431] The austere monks slept on the ground, on a hard mat, or a rough blanket; and the same bundle of palm-leaves served them as a seat in the lay, and a pillow in the night. Their original cells were low, narrow huts, built of the slightest materials; which formed, by the regular distribution of the streets, a large and populous village, enclosing, within the common wall, a church, a hospital, perhaps a library, some necessary offices, a garden, and a fountain or reservoir of fresh water. Thirty or forty brethren composed a family of separate discipline and diet; and the great monasteries of Egypt consisted of thirty or forty families.

[Footnote 40: Cassian has simply, though copiously, described the monastic habit of Egypt, (Institut. l. i.,) to which Sozomen (l. iii. c. 14) attributes such allegorical meaning and virtue.]

[Footnote 41: Regul. Benedict. No. 55, in Cod. Regul. part ii. p. 51.]

[Footnote 42: See the rule of Ferreolus, bishop of Usez, (No. 31, in Cod. Regul part ii. p. 136,) and of Isidore, bishop of Seville, (No. 13, in Cod. Regul part ii. p. 214.)]

[Footnote 43: Some partial indulgences were granted for the hands and feet "Totum autem corpus nemo unguet nisi causa infirmitatis, nec lavabitur aqua nudo corpore, nisi languor perspicuus sit," (Regul. Pachom xcii. part i. p. 78.)]

[Footnote 431: Athanasius (Vit. Ant. c. 47) boasts of Antony's holy horror of clear water, by which his feet were uncontaminated except under dire necessity—M.]

PART II

Pleasure and guilt are synonymous terms in the language of the monks, and they discovered, by experience, that rigid fasts, and abstemious diet, are the most effectual preservatives against the impure desires of the flesh. [44] The rules of abstinence which they imposed, or practised, were not uniform or perpetual: the cheerful festival of the Pentecost was balanced by the extraordinary mortification of Lent; the fervor of new monasteries was insensibly relaxed; and the voracious appetite of the Gauls could not imitate the patient and temperate virtue of the Egyptians. [45] The disciples of Antony and Pachomius were satisfied with their daily pittance, [46] of twelve ounces of bread, or rather biscuit, [47] which they divided into two frugal repasts, of the afternoon and of the evening. It was esteemed a merit, and almost a duty, to abstain from the boiled vegetables which were provided for the refectory; but the extraordinary bounty of the abbot sometimes indulged them with the luxury of cheese, fruit, salad, and the small dried fish of the Nile. [48] A more ample latitude of sea and river fish was gradually allowed or assumed; but the use of flesh was long confined to the sick or travellers; and when it gradually prevailed in the less rigid monasteries of Europe, a singular distinction was introduced; as if birds, whether wild or domestic, had been less profane than the grosser animals of the field. Water was the pure and innocent beverage of the primitive monks; and the founder of the Benedictines regrets the daily portion of half a pint of wine, which had been extorted from him by the intemperance of the age. [49] Such an allowance might be easily supplied by the vineyards of Italy; and his victorious disciples, who passed the Alps, the Rhine, and the Baltic, required, in the place of wine, an adequate compensation of strong beer or cider.

[Footnote 44: St. Jerom, in strong, but indiscreet, language, expresses the most important use of fasting and abstinence: "Non quod Deus universitatis Creator et Dominus, intestinorum nostrorum rugitu, et inanitate ventris, pulmonisque ardore delectetur, sed quod aliter pudicitia tuta esse non possit." (Op. tom. i. p. 32, ad Eustochium.) See the twelfth and twenty-second Collations of Cassian, de Castitate and de Illusionibus Nocturnis.]

[Footnote 45: Edacitas in Graecis gula est, in Gallis natura, (Dialog. i. c. 4 p. 521.) Cassian fairly owns, that the perfect model of abstinence cannot be imitated in Gaul, on account of the aerum temperies, and the qualitas nostrae fragilitatis, (Institut. iv. 11.) Among the Western rules, that of Columbanus is the most austere; he had been educated amidst the poverty of Ireland, as rigid, perhaps, and inflexible as the abstemious virtue of Egypt. The rule of Isidore of Seville is the mildest; on holidays he allows the use of flesh.]

[Footnote 46: "Those who drink only water, and have no nutritious liquor, ought, at least, to have a pound and a half (twenty-four ounces) of bread every day." State of Prisons, p. 40, by Mr. Howard.]

[Footnote 47: See Cassian. Collat. l. ii. 19-21. The small loaves, or biscuit, of six ounces each, had obtained the name of Paximacia, (Rosweyde, Onomasticon, p. 1045.) Pachomius, however, allowed his monks some latitude in the quantity of their food; but he made them work in proportion as they ate, (Pallad. in Hist. Lausiac. c. 38, 39, in Vit. Patrum, l. viii. p. 736, 737.)]

[Footnote 48: See the banquet to which Cassian (Collation viii. 1) was invited by Serenus, an Egyptian abbot.]

[Footnote 49: See the Rule of St. Benedict, No. 39, 40, (in Cod. Reg. part ii. p. 41, 42.) Licet legamus vinum omnino monachorum non esse, sed quia nostris temporibus id monachis persuaderi non potest; he allows them a Roman hemina, a measure which may be ascertained from Arbuthnot's Tables.]

The candidate who aspired to the virtue of evangelical poverty, abjured, at his first entrance into a regular community, the idea, and even the name, of all separate or exclusive possessions. [50] The brethren were supported by their manual labor; and the duty of labor was strenuously recommended as a penance, as an exercise, and as the most laudable means of securing their daily subsistence. [51] The garden and fields, which the industry of the monks had often rescued from the forest or the morass, were diligently cultivated by their hands. They performed, without reluctance, the menial offices of slaves and domestics; and the several trades that were necessary to provide their habits, their utensils, and their lodging, were exercised within the precincts of the great monasteries. The monastic studies have tended, for the most part, to darken, rather than to dispel, the cloud of superstition. Yet the curiosity or zeal of some learned solitaries has cultivated the ecclesiastical, and even the profane, sciences; and posterity must gratefully acknowledge, that the monuments of Greek and Roman literature have been preserved and multiplied by their indefatigable pens. [52] But the more humble industry of the monks, especially in Egypt, was contented with the silent, sedentary occupation of making wooden sandals, or of twisting the leaves of the palm-tree into mats and baskets. The superfluous stock, which was not consumed in domestic use, supplied, by trade, the wants of the community: the boats of Tabenne, and the other monasteries of Thebais, descended the Nile as far as Alexandria; and, in a Christian market, the sanctity of the workmen might enhance the intrinsic value of the work.

[Footnote 50: Such expressions as my book, my cloak, my shoes, (Cassian Institut. l. iv. c. 13,) were not less severely prohibited among the Western monks, (Cod. Regul. part ii. p. 174, 235, 288;) and the rule of Columbanus punished them with six lashes. The ironical author of the Ordres Monastiques, who laughs at the foolish nicety of modern convents, seems ignorant that the ancients were equally absurd.]

[Footnote 51: Two great masters of ecclesiastical science, the P. Thomassin, (Discipline de l'Eglise, tom. iii. p. 1090-1139,) and the P. Mabillon, (Etudes Monastiques, tom. i. p. 116-155,) have seriously examined the manual labor of the monks, which the former considers as a merit and the latter as a duty.]

[Footnote 52: Mabillon (Etudes Monastiques, tom. i. p. 47-55) has collected many curious facts to justify the literary labors of his predecessors, both in the East and West. Books were copied in the ancient monasteries of Egypt, (Cassian. Institut. l. iv. c. 12,) and by the disciples of St. Martin, (Sulp. Sever. in Vit Martin. c. 7, p. 473.) Cassiodorus has allowed an ample scope for the studies of the monks; and we shall not be scandalized, if their pens sometimes wandered from Chrysostom and Augustin to Homer and Virgil.] But the necessity of manual labor was insensibly superseded.

The novice was tempted to bestow his fortune on the saints, in whose society he was resolved to spend the remainder of his life; and the pernicious indulgence of the laws permitted him to receive, for their use, any future accessions of legacy or inheritance. [53] Melania contributed her plate, three hundred pounds weight of silver; and Paula contracted an immense debt, for the relief of their favorite monks; who kindly imparted the merits of their prayers and penance to a rich and liberal sinner. [54] Time continually increased, and accidents could seldom diminish, the estates of the popular monasteries, which spread over the adjacent country and cities: and, in the first century of their institution, the infidel Zosimus has maliciously observed, that, for the benefit of the poor, the Christian monks had reduced a great part of mankind to a state of beggary. [55] As long as they maintained their original fervor, they approved themselves, however, the faithful and benevolent stewards of the charity, which was entrusted to their care. But their discipline was corrupted by prosperity: they gradually assumed the pride of wealth, and at last indulged the luxury of expense. Their public luxury might be excused by the magnificence of religious worship, and the decent motive of erecting durable habitations for an immortal society. But every age of the church has accused the licentiousness of the degenerate monks; who no longer remembered the object of their institution, embraced the vain and sensual pleasures of the world, which they had renounced, [56] and scandalously abused the riches which had been acquired by the austere virtues of their founders. [57] Their natural descent, from such painful and dangerous virtue, to the common vices of humanity, will not, perhaps, excite much grief or indignation in the mind of a philosopher.

[Footnote 53: Thomassin (Discipline de l'Eglise, tom. iii. p. 118, 145, 146, 171-179) has examined the revolution of the civil, canon, and common law. Modern France confirms the death which monks have inflicted on themselves, and justly deprives them of all right of inheritance.]

[Footnote 54: See Jerom, (tom. i. p. 176, 183.) The monk Pambo made a sublime answer to Melania, who wished to specify the value of her gift: "Do you offer it to me, or to God? If to God, He who suspends the mountain in a balance, need not be informed of the weight of your plate." (Pallad. Hist. Lausiac. c. 10, in the Vit. Patrum, l. viii. p. 715.)]

[Footnote 55: Zosim. l. v. p. 325. Yet the wealth of the Eastern monks was far surpassed by the princely greatness of the Benedictines.]

[Footnote 56: The sixth general council (the Quinisext in Trullo, Canon xlvii in Beveridge, tom. i. p. 213) restrains women from passing the night in a male, or men in a female, monastery. The seventh general council (the second Nicene, Canon xx. in Beveridge, tom. i. p. 325) prohibits the erection of double or promiscuous monasteries of both sexes; but it appears from Balsamon, that the prohibition was not effectual. On the irregular pleasures and expenses of the clergy and monks, see Thomassin, tom. iii. p. 1334-1368.]

[Footnote 57: I have somewhere heard or read the frank confession of a Benedictine abbot: "My vow of poverty has given me a hundred thousand crowns a year; my vow of obedience has raised me to the rank of a sovereign prince."—I forget the consequences of his vow of chastity.]

The lives of the primitive monks were consumed in penance and solitude; undisturbed by the various occupations which fill the time, and exercise the faculties, of reasonable, active, and social beings. Whenever they were permitted to step beyond the precincts of the monastery, two jealous companions were the mutual guards and spies of each other's actions; and, after their return, they were condemned to forget, or, at least, to suppress, whatever they had seen or heard in the world. Strangers, who professed the orthodox faith, were hospitably entertained in a separate apartment; but their dangerous conversation was restricted to some chosen elders of approved discretion and fidelity. Except in their presence, the monastic slave might not receive the visits of his friends or kindred; and it was deemed highly meritorious, if he afflicted a tender sister, or an aged parent, by the obstinate refusal of a word or look. [58] The monks themselves passed their lives, without personal attachments, among a crowd which had been formed by accident, and was detained, in the same prison, by force or prejudice.

Recluse fanatics have few ideas or sentiments to communicate: a special license of the abbot regulated the time and duration of their familiar visits; and, at their silent meals, they were enveloped in their cowls, inaccessible, and almost invisible, to each other. [59] Study is the resource of solitude: but education had not prepared and qualified for any liberal studies the mechanics and peasants who filled the monastic communities. They might work: but the vanity of spiritual perfection was tempted to disdain the exercise of manual labor; and the industry must be faint and languid, which is not excited by the sense of personal interest.

[Footnote 58: Pior, an Egyptian monk, allowed his sister to see him; but he shut his eyes during the whole visit. See Vit. Patrum, l. iii. p. 504. Many such examples might be added.]

[Footnote 59: The 7th, 8th, 29th, 30th, 31st, 34th, 57th, 60th, 86th, and 95th articles of the Rule of Pachomius, impose most intolerable laws of silence and mortification.]

According to their faith and zeal, they might employ the day, which they passed in their cells, either in vocal or mental prayer: they assembled in the evening, and they were awakened in the night, for the public worship of the monastery. The precise moment was determined by the stars, which are seldom clouded in the serene sky of Egypt; and a rustic horn, or trumpet, the signal of devotion, twice interrupted the vast silence of the desert. [60] Even sleep, the last refuge of the unhappy, was rigorously measured: the vacant hours of the monk heavily rolled along, without business or pleasure; and, before the close of each day, he had repeatedly accused the tedious progress of the sun. [61] In this comfortless state, superstition still pursued and tormented her wretched votaries. [62] The repose which they had sought in the cloister was disturbed by a tardy repentance, profane doubts, and guilty desires; and, while they considered each natural impulse as an unpardonable sin, they perpetually trembled on the edge of a flaming and bottomless abyss. From the painful struggles of disease and despair, these unhappy victims were sometimes relieved by madness or death; and, in the sixth century, a hospital was founded at Jerusalem for a small portion of the austere penitents, who were deprived of their senses. [63] Their visions, before they attained this extreme and acknowledged term of frenzy, have afforded ample materials of supernatural history. It was their firm persuasion, that the air, which they breathed, was peopled with invisible enemies; with innumerable demons, who watched every occasion, and assumed every form, to terrify, and above all to tempt, their unguarded virtue. The imagination, and even the senses, were deceived by the illusions of distempered fanaticism; and the hermit, whose midnight prayer was oppressed by involuntary slumber, might easily confound the phantoms of horror or delight, which had occupied his sleeping and his waking dreams. [64]

[Footnote 60: The diurnal and nocturnal prayers of the monks are copiously discussed by Cassian, in the third and fourth books of his Institutions; and he constantly prefers the liturgy, which an angel had dictated to the monasteries of Tebennoe.]

[Footnote 61: Cassian, from his own experience, describes the acedia, or listlessness of mind and body, to which a monk was exposed, when he sighed to find himself alone. Saepiusque egreditur et ingreditur cellam, et Solem velut ad occasum tardius properantem crebrius intuetur, (Institut. x. l.)]

[Footnote 62: The temptations and sufferings of Stagirius were communicated by that unfortunate youth to his friend St. Chrysostom. See Middleton's Works, vol. i. p. 107-110. Something similar introduces the life of every saint; and the famous Inigo, or Ignatius, the founder of the Jesuits, (vide d'Inigo de Guiposcoa, tom. i. p. 29-38,) may serve as a memorable example.]

[Footnote 63: Fleury, Hist. Ecclesiastique, tom. vii. p. 46. I have read somewhere, in the Vitae Patrum, but I cannot recover the place that several, I believe many, of the monks, who did not reveal their temptations to the abbot, became guilty of suicide.]

[Footnote 64: See the seventh and eighth Collations of Cassian, who gravely examines, why the demons were grown less active and numerous since the time of St. Antony. Rosweyde's copious index to the Vitae Patrum will point out a variety of infernal scenes. The devils were most formidable in a female shape.]

The monks were divided into two classes: the Coenobites, who lived under a common and regular discipline; and the Anachorets, who indulged their unsocial, independent fanaticism. [65] The most devout, or the most ambitious, of the spiritual brethren, renounced the convent, as they had renounced the world. The fervent monasteries of Egypt, Palestine, and Syria, were surrounded by a Laura, [66] a distant circle of solitary cells; and the extravagant penance of Hermits was stimulated by applause and emulation. [67] They sunk under the painful weight of crosses and chains; and their emaciated limbs were confined by collars, bracelets, gauntlets, and greaves of massy and rigid iron. All superfluous encumbrance of dress they contemptuously cast away; and some savage saints of both sexes have been admired, whose naked bodies were only covered by their long hair. They aspired to reduce themselves to the rude and miserable state in which the human brute is scarcely distinguishable above his kindred animals; and the numerous sect of Anachorets derived their name from their humble practice of grazing in the fields of Mesopotamia with the common herd. [68] They often usurped the den of some wild beast whom they affected to resemble; they buried themselves in some gloomy cavern, which art or nature had scooped out of the rock; and the marble quarries of Thebais are still inscribed with the monuments of their penance. [69] The most perfect Hermits are supposed to have passed many days without food, many nights without sleep, and many years without speaking; and glorious was the man (I abuse that name) who contrived any cell, or seat, of a peculiar construction, which might expose him, in the most inconvenient posture, to the inclemency of the seasons.

[Footnote 65: For the distinction of the Coenobites and the Hermits, especially in Egypt, see Jerom, (tom. i. p. 45, ad Rusticum,) the first Dialogue of Sulpicius Severus, Rufinus, (c. 22, in Vit. Patrum, l. ii. p. 478,) Palladius, (c. 7, 69, in Vit. Patrum, l. viii. p. 712, 758,) and, above all, the eighteenth and nineteenth Collations of Cassian. These writers, who compare the common and solitary life, reveal the abuse and danger of the latter.]

[Footnote 66: Suicer. Thesaur. Ecclesiast. tom. ii. p. 205, 218. Thomassin (Discipline de l'Eglise, tom. i. p. 1501, 1502) gives a good account of these cells. When Gerasimus founded his monastery in the wilderness of Jordan, it was accompanied by a Laura of seventy cells.]

[Footnote 67: Theodoret, in a large volume, (the Philotheus in Vit. Patrum, l. ix. p. 793-863,) has collected the lives and miracles of thirty Anachorets. Evagrius (l. i. c. 12) more briefly celebrates the monks and hermits of Palestine.]

[Footnote 68: Sozomen, l. vi. c. 33. The great St. Ephrem composed a panegyric on these or grazing monks, (Tillemont, Mem. Eccles. tom. viii. p. 292.)]

[Footnote 69: The P. Sicard (Missions du Levant, tom. ii. p. 217-233) examined the caverns of the Lower Thebais with wonder and devotion. The inscriptions are in the old Syriac character, which was used by the Christians of Abyssinia.]

Among these heroes of the monastic life, the name and genius of Simeon Stylites [70] have been immortalized by the singular invention of an aerial penance. At the age of thirteen, the young Syrian deserted the profession of a shepherd, and threw himself into an austere monastery. After a long and painful novitiate, in which Simeon was repeatedly saved from pious suicide, he established his residence on a mountain, about thirty or forty miles to the east of Antioch. Within the space of a mandra, or circle of stones, to which he had attached himself by a ponderous chain, he ascended a column, which was successively raised from the height of nine, to that of sixty, feet from the ground. [71] In this last and lofty station, the Syrian Anachoret resisted the heat of thirty summers, and the cold of as many winters. Habit and exercise instructed him to maintain his dangerous situation without fear or giddiness, and successively to assume the different postures of devotion. He sometimes prayed in an erect attitude, with his outstretched arms in the figure of a cross, but his most familiar practice was that of bending his meagre skeleton from the forehead to the feet; and a curious spectator, after numbering twelve hundred and forty-four repetitions, at length desisted from the endless account. The progress of an ulcer in his thigh [72] might shorten, but it could not disturb, this celestial life; and the patient Hermit expired, without descending from his column. A prince, who should capriciously inflict such tortures, would be deemed a tyrant; but it would surpass the power of a tyrant to impose a long and miserable existence on the reluctant victims of his cruelty. This voluntary martyrdom must have gradually destroyed the sensibility both of the mind and body; nor can it be presumed that the fanatics, who torment themselves, are susceptible of any lively affection for the rest of mankind. A cruel, unfeeling temper has distinguiseed the monks of every age and country: their stern indifference, which is seldom mollified by personal friendship, is inflamed by religious hatred; and their merciless zeal has strenuously administered the holy office of the Inquisition.

[Footnote 70: See Theodoret (in Vit. Patrum, l. ix. p. 848-854,) Antony, (in Vit. Patrum, l. i. p. 170-177,) Cosmas, (in Asseman. Bibliot. Oriental tom. i. p. 239-253,) Evagrius, (l. i. c. 13, 14,) and Tillemont, (Mem. Eccles. tom. xv. p. 347-392.)]

[Footnote 71: The narrow circumference of two cubits, or three feet, which Evagrius assigns for the summit of the column is inconsistent with reason, with facts, and with the rules of architecture. The people who saw it from below might be easily deceived.]

[Footnote 72: I must not conceal a piece of ancient scandal concerning the origin of this ulcer. It has been reported that the Devil, assuming an angelic form, invited him to ascend, like Elijah, into a fiery chariot. The saint too hastily raised his foot, and Satan seized the moment of inflicting this chastisement on his vanity.]

The monastic saints, who excite only the contempt and pity of a philosopher, were respected, and almost adored, by the prince and people. Successive crowds of pilgrims from Gaul and India saluted the divine pillar of Simeon: the tribes of Saracens disputed in arms the honor of his benediction; the queens of Arabia and Persia gratefully confessed his supernatural virtue; and the angelic Hermit was consulted by the younger Theodosius, in the most important concerns of the church and state. His remains were transported from the mountain of Telenissa, by a solemn procession of the patriarch, the master-general of the East, six bishops, twenty-one counts or tribunes, and six thousand soldiers; and Antioch revered his bones, as her glorious ornament and impregnable defence. The fame of the apostles and martyrs was gradually eclipsed by these recent and popular Anachorets; the Christian world fell prostrate before their shrines; and the miracles ascribed to their relics exceeded, at least in number and duration, the spiritual exploits of their lives. But the golden legend of their lives [73] was embellished by the artful credulity of their interested brethren; and a believing age was easily persuaded, that the slightest caprice of an Egyptian or a Syrian monk had been sufficient to interrupt the eternal laws of the universe. The favorites of Heaven were accustomed to cure inveterate diseases with a touch, a word, or a distant message; and to expel the most obstinate demons from the souls or bodies which they possessed. They familiarly accosted, or imperiously commanded, the lions and serpents of the desert; infused vegetation into a sapless trunk; suspended iron on the surface of the water; passed the Nile on the back of a crocodile, and refreshed themselves in a fiery furnace. These extravagant tales, which display the fiction without the genius, of poetry, have seriously affected the reason, the faith, and the morals, of the Christians. Their credulity debased and vitiated the faculties of the mind: they corrupted the evidence of history; and superstition gradually extinguished the hostile light of philosophy and science. Every mode of religious worship which had been practised by the saints, every mysterious doctrine which they believed, was fortified by the sanction of divine revelation, and all the manly virtues were oppressed by the servile and pusillanimous reign of the monks. If it be possible to measure the interval between the philosophic writings of Cicero and the sacred legend of Theodoret, between the character of Cato and that of Simeon, we may appreciate the memorable revolution which was accomplished in the Roman empire within a period of five hundred years.

[Footnote 73: *I know not how to select or specify the miracles contained in the Vitae Patrum of Rosweyde, as the number very much exceeds the thousand pages of that voluminous work. An elegant specimen may be found in the dialogues of Sulpicius Severus, and his Life of St. Martin. He reveres the monks of Egypt; yet he insults them with the remark, that they never raised the dead; whereas the bishop of Tours had restored three dead men to life.*]

II. The progress of Christianity has been marked by two glorious and decisive victories: over the learned and luxurious citizens of the Roman empire; and over the warlike Barbarians of Scythia and Germany, who subverted the empire, and embraced the religion, of the Romans. The Goths were the foremost of these savage proselytes; and the nation was indebted for its conversion to a countryman, or, at least, to a subject, worthy to be ranked among the inventors of useful arts, who have deserved the remembrance and gratitude of posterity. A great number of Roman provincials had been led away into captivity by the Gothic bands, who ravaged Asia in the time of Gallienus; and of these captives, many were Christians, and several belonged to the ecclesiastical order. Those involuntary missionaries, dispersed as slaves in the villages of Dacia, successively labored for the salvation of their masters. The seeds which they planted, of the evangelic doctrine, were gradually propagated; and before the end of a century, the pious work was achieved by the labors of Ulphilas, whose ancestors had been transported beyond the Danube from a small town of Cappadocia.

Ulphilas, the bishop and apostle of the Goths, [74] acquired their love and reverence by his blameless life and indefatigable zeal; and they received, with implicit confidence, the doctrines of truth and virtue which he preached and practised. He executed the arduous task of translating the Scriptures into their native tongue, a dialect of the German or Teutonic language; but he prudently suppressed the four books of Kings, as they might tend to irritate the fierce and sanguinary spirit of the Barbarians. The rude, imperfect idiom of soldiers and shepherds, so ill qualified to communicate any spiritual ideas, was improved and modulated by his genius: and Ulphilas, before he could frame his version, was obliged to compose a new alphabet of twenty-four letters; [741] four of which he invented, to express the peculiar sounds that were unknown to the Greek and Latin pronunciation. [75] But the prosperous state of the Gothic church was soon afflicted by war and intestine discord, and the chieftains were divided by religion as well as by interest. Fritigern, the friend of the Romans, became the proselyte of Ulphilas; while the haughty soul of Athanaric disdained the yoke of the empire and of the gospel The faith of the new converts was tried by the persecution which he excited. A wagon, bearing aloft the shapeless image of Thor, perhaps, or of Woden, was conducted in solemn procession through the streets of the camp; and the rebels, who refused to worship the god of their fathers, were immediately burnt, with their tents and families. The character of Ulphilas recommended him to the esteem of the Eastern court, where he twice appeared as the minister of peace; he pleaded the cause of the distressed Goths, who implored the protection of Valens; and the name of Moses was applied to this spiritual guide, who conducted his people through the deep waters of the Danube to the Land of Promise. [76] The devout shepherds, who were attached to his person, and tractable to his voice, acquiesced in their settlement, at the foot of the Maesian mountains, in a country of woodlands and pastures, which supported their flocks and herds, and enabled them to purchase the corn and wine of the more plentiful provinces. These harmless Barbarians multiplied in obscure peace and the profession of Christianity. [77]

[Footnote 74: On the subject of Ulphilas, and the conversion of the Goths, see Sozomen, l. vi. c. 37. Socrates, l. iv. c. 33. Theodoret, l. iv. c. 37. Philostorg. l. ii. c. 5. The heresy of Philostorgius appears to have given him superior means of information.]

[Footnote 741: This is the Moeso-Gothic alphabet of which many of the letters are evidently formed from the Greek and Roman. M. St. Martin, however contends, that it is impossible but that some written alphabet must have been known long before among the Goths. He supposes that their former letters were those inscribed on the runes, which, being inseparably connected with the old idolatrous superstitions, were proscribed by the Christian missionaries. Everywhere the runes, so common among all the German tribes, disappear after the propagation of Christianity. S. Martin iv. p. 97, 98—M.]

[Footnote 75: A mutilated copy of the four Gospels, in the Gothic version, was published A.D. 1665, and is esteemed the most ancient monument of the Teutonic language, though Wetstein attempts, by some frivolous conjectures, to deprive Ulphilas of the honor of the work. Two of the four additional letters express the W, and our own Th. See Simon, Hist. Critique du Nouveau Testament, tom ii. p. 219-223. Mill. Prolegom p. 151, edit. Kuster. Wetstein, Prolegom. tom. i. p. 114. Note: The Codex Argenteus, found in the sixteenth century at Wenden, near Cologne, and now preserved at Upsal, contains almost the entire four Gospels. The best edition is that of J. Christ. Zahn, Weissenfels, 1805. In 1762 Knettel discovered and published from a Palimpsest MS. four chapters of the Epistle to the Romans: they were reprinted at Upsal, 1763. M. Mai has since that time discovered further fragments, and other remains of Moeso-Gothic literature, from a Palimpsest at Milan. See Ulphilae partium inedi arum in Ambrosianis Palimpsestis ab Ang. Maio repertarum specimen Milan. Ito. 1819—M.]

[Footnote 76: Philostorgius erroneously places this passage under the reign of Constantine; but I am much inclined to believe that it preceded the great emigration.]

[Footnote 77: We are obliged to Jornandes (de Reb. Get. c. 51, p. 688) for a short and lively picture of these lesser Goths. Gothi minores, populus immensus, cum suo Pontifice ipsoque primate Wulfila. The last words, if they are not mere tautology, imply some temporal jurisdiction.]

Their fiercer brethren, the formidable Visigoths, universally adopted the religion of the Romans, with whom they maintained a perpetual intercourse, of war, of friendship, or of conquest. In their long and victorious march from the Danube to the Atlantic Ocean, they converted their allies; they educated the rising generation; and the devotion which reigned in the camp of Alaric, or the court of Thoulouse, might edify or disgrace the palaces of Rome and Constantinople. [78] During the same period, Christianity was embraced by almost all the Barbarians, who established their kingdoms on the ruins of the Western empire; the Burgundians in Gaul, the Suevi in Spain, the Vandals in Africa, the Ostrogoths in Pannonia, and the various bands of mercenaries, that raised Odoacer to the throne of Italy. The Franks and the Saxons still persevered in the errors of Paganism; but the Franks obtained the monarchy of Gaul by their submission to the example of Clovis; and the Saxon conquerors of Britain were reclaimed from their savage superstition by the missionaries of Rome. These Barbarian proselytes displayed an ardent and successful zeal in the propagation of the faith. The Merovingian kings, and their successors, Charlemagne and the Othos, extended, by their laws and victories, the dominion of the cross. England produced the apostle of Germany; and the evangelic light was gradually diffused from the neighborhood of the Rhine, to the nations of the Elbe, the Vistula, and the Baltic. [79]

[Footnote 78: At non ita Gothi non ita Vandali; malis licet doctoribus instituti meliores tamen etiam in hac parte quam nostri. Salvian, de Gubern, Dei, l. vii. p. 243.]

[Footnote 79: Mosheim has slightly sketched the progress of Christianity in the North, from the fourth to the fourteenth century. The subject would afford materials for an ecclesiastical and even philosophical, history]

PART III

The different motives which influenced the reason, or the passions, of the Barbarian converts, cannot easily be ascertained. They were often capricious and accidental; a dream, an omen, the report of a miracle, the example of some priest, or hero, the charms of a believing wife, and, above all, the fortunate event of a prayer, or vow, which, in a moment of danger, they had addressed to the God of the Christians. [80] The early prejudices of education were insensibly erased by the habits of frequent and familiar society, the moral precepts of the gospel were protected by the extravagant virtues of the monks; and a spiritual theology was supported by the visible power of relics, and the pomp of religious worship. But the rational and ingenious mode of persuasion, which a Saxon bishop [81] suggested to a popular saint, might sometimes be employed by the missionaries, who labored for the conversion of infidels. "Admit," says the sagacious disputant, "whatever they are pleased to assert of the fabulous, and carnal, genealogy of their gods and goddesses, who are propagated from each other. From this principle deduce their imperfect nature, and human infirmities, the assurance they were born, and the probability that they will die. At what time, by what means, from what cause, were the eldest of the gods or goddesses produced? Do they still continue, or have they ceased, to propagate? If they have ceased, summon your antagonists to declare the reason of this strange alteration. If they still continue, the number of the gods must become infinite; and shall we not risk, by the indiscreet worship of some impotent deity, to excite the resentment of his jealous superior? The visible heavens and earth, the whole system of the universe, which may be conceived by the mind, is it created or eternal? If created, how, or where, could the gods themselves exist before creation? If eternal, how could they assume the empire of an independent and preexisting world? Urge these arguments with temper and moderation; insinuate, at seasonable intervals, the truth and beauty of the Christian revelation; and endeavor to make the unbelievers ashamed, without making them angry." This metaphysical reasoning, too refined, perhaps, for the Barbarians of Germany, was fortified by the grosser weight of authority and popular consent. The advantage of temporal prosperity had deserted the Pagan cause, and passed over to the service of Christianity. The Romans themselves, the most powerful and enlightened nation of the globe, had renounced their ancient superstition; and, if the ruin of their empire seemed to accuse the efficacy of the new faith, the disgrace was already retrieved by the conversion of the victorious Goths. The valiant and fortunate Barbarians, who subdued the provinces of the West, successively received, and reflected, the same edifying example. Before the age of Charlemagne, the Christian nations of Europe might exult in the exclusive possession of the temperate climates, of the fertile lands, which produced corn, wine, and oil; while the savage idolaters, and their helpless idols, were confined to the extremities of the earth, the dark and frozen regions of the North. [82]

[Footnote 80: To such a cause has Socrates (l. vii. c. 30) ascribed the conversion of the Burgundians, whose Christian piety is celebrated by Orosius, (l. vii. c. 19.)]

[Footnote 81: See an original and curious epistle from Daniel, the first bishop of Winchester, (Beda, Hist. Eccles. Anglorum, l. v. c. 18, p. 203, edit Smith,) to St. Boniface, who preached the gospel among the savages of Hesse and Thuringia. Epistol. Bonifacii, lxvii., in the Maxima Bibliotheca Patrum, tom. xiii. p. 93]

[Footnote 82: The sword of Charlemagne added weight to the argument; but when Daniel wrote this epistle, (A.D. 723,) the Mahometans, who reigned from India to Spain, might have retorted it against the Christians.]

Christianity, which opened the gates of Heaven to the Barbarians, introduced an important change in their moral and political condition. They received, at the same time, the use of letters, so essential to a religion whose doctrines are contained in a sacred book; and while they studied the divine truth, their minds were insensibly enlarged by the distant view of history, of nature, of the arts, and of society. The version of the Scriptures into their native tongue, which had facilitated their conversion, must excite among their clergy some curiosity to read the original text, to understand the sacred liturgy of the church, and to examine, in the writings of the fathers, the chain of ecclesiastical tradition. These spiritual gifts were preserved in the Greek and Latin languages, which concealed the inestimable monuments of ancient learning. The immortal productions of Virgil, Cicero, and Livy, which were accessible to the Christian Barbarians, maintained a silent intercourse between the reign of Augustus and the times of Clovis and Charlemagne. The emulation of mankind was encouraged by the remembrance of a more perfect state; and the flame of science was secretly kept alive, to warm and enlighten the mature age of the Western world.

In the most corrupt state of Christianity, the Barbarians might learn justice from the law, and mercy from the gospel; and if the knowledge of their duty was insufficient to guide their actions, or to regulate their passions, they were sometimes restrained by conscience, and frequently punished by remorse. But the direct authority of religion was less effectual than the holy communion, which united them with their Christian brethren in spiritual friendship. The influence of these sentiments contributed to secure their fidelity in the service, or the alliance, of the Romans, to alleviate the horrors of war, to moderate the insolence of conquest, and to preserve, in the downfall of the empire, a permanent respect for the name and institutions of Rome. In the days of Paganism, the priests of Gaul and Germany reigned over the people, and controlled the jurisdiction of the magistrates; and the zealous proselytes transferred an equal, or more ample, measure of devout obedience, to the pontiffs of the Christian faith. The sacred character of the bishops was supported by their temporal possessions; they obtained an honorable seat in the legislative assemblies of soldiers and freemen; and it was their interest, as well as their duty, to mollify, by peaceful counsels, the fierce spirit of the Barbarians. The perpetual correspondence of the Latin clergy, the frequent pilgrimages to Rome and Jerusalem, and the growing authority of the popes, cemented the union of the Christian republic, and gradually produced the similar manners, and common jurisprudence, which have distinguished, from the rest of mankind, the independent, and even hostile, nations of modern Europe.

But the operation of these causes was checked and retarded by the unfortunate accident, which infused a deadly poison into the cup of Salvation. Whatever might be the early sentiments of Ulphilas, his connections with the empire and the church were formed during the reign of Arianism. The apostle of the Goths subscribed the creed of Rimini; professed with freedom, and perhaps with sincerity, that the Son was not equal, or consubstantial to the Father; [83] communicated these errors to the clergy and people; and infected the Barbaric world with a heresy, [84] which the great Theodosius proscribed and extinguished among the Romans. The temper and understanding of the new proselytes were not adapted to metaphysical subtilties; but they strenuously maintained, what they had piously received, as the pure and genuine doctrines of Christianity. The advantage of preaching and expounding the Scriptures in the Teutonic language promoted the apostolic labors of Ulphilas and his successors; and they ordained a competent number of bishops and presbyters for the instruction of the kindred tribes. The Ostrogoths, the Burgundians, the Suevi, and the Vandals, who had listened to the eloquence of the Latin clergy, [85] preferred the more intelligible lessons of their domestic teachers; and Arianism was adopted as the national faith of the warlike converts, who were seated on the ruins of the Western empire. This irreconcilable difference of religion was a perpetual source of jealousy and hatred; and the reproach of Barbarian was imbittered by the more odious epithet of Heretic. The heroes of the North, who had submitted, with some reluctance, to believe that all their ancestors were in hell, [86] were astonished and exasperated to learn, that they themselves had only changed the mode of their eternal condemnation. Instead of the smooth applause, which Christian kings are accustomed to expect from their royal prelates, the orthodox bishops and their clergy were in a state of opposition to the Arian courts; and their indiscreet opposition frequently became criminal, and might sometimes be dangerous. [87] The pulpit, that safe and sacred organ of sedition, resounded with the names of Pharaoh and Holofernes; [88] the public discontent was inflamed by the hope or promise of a glorious deliverance; and the seditious saints were tempted to promote the accomplishment of their own predictions. Notwithstanding these provocations, the Catholics of Gaul, Spain, and Italy, enjoyed, under the reign of the Arians, the free and peaceful exercise of their religion. Their haughty masters respected the zeal of a numerous people, resolved to die at the foot of their altars; and the example of their devout constancy was admired and imitated by the Barbarians themselves. The conquerors evaded, however, the disgraceful reproach, or confession, of fear, by attributing their toleration to the liberal motives of reason and humanity; and while they affected the language, they imperceptibly imbibed the spirit, of genuine Christianity.

[Footnote 83: The opinions of Ulphilas and the Goths inclined to semi-Arianism, since they would not say that the Son was a creature, though they held communion with those who maintained that heresy. Their apostle represented the whole controversy as a question of trifling moment, which had been raised by the passions of the clergy. Theodoret l. iv. c. 37.]

[Footnote 84: The Arianism of the Goths has been imputed to the emperor Valens: "Itaque justo Dei judicio ipsi eum vivum incenderunt, qui propter eum etiam mortui, vitio erroris arsuri sunt." Orosius, l. vii. c. 33, p. 554. This cruel sentence is confirmed by Tillemont, (Mem. Eccles. tom. vi. p. 604-610,) who coolly observes, "un seul homme entraina dans l'enfer un nombre infini de Septentrionaux, &c." Salvian (de Gubern. Dei, l. v p. 150, 151) pities and excuses their involuntary error.]

[Footnote 85: Orosius affirms, in the year 416, (l. vii. c. 41, p. 580,) that the Churches of Christ (of the Catholics) were filled with Huns, Suevi, Vandals, Burgundians.]

[Footnote 86: Radbod, king of the Frisons, was so much scandalized by this rash declaration of a missionary, that he drew back his foot after he had entered the baptismal font. See Fleury, Hist. Eccles. tom. ix p. 167.]

[Footnote 87: The epistles of Sidonius, bishop of Clermont, under the Visigoths, and of Avitus, bishop of Vienna, under the Burgundians, explain sometimes in dark hints, the general dispositions of the Catholics. The history of Clovis and Theodoric will suggest some particular facts]

[Footnote 88: Genseric confessed the resemblance, by the severity with which he punished such indiscreet allusions. Victor Vitensis, l. 7, p. 10.]

The peace of the church was sometimes interrupted. The Catholics were indiscreet, the Barbarians were impatient; and the partial acts of severity or injustice, which had been recommended by the Arian clergy, were exaggerated by the orthodox writers. The guilt of persecution may be imputed to Euric, king of the Visigoths; who suspended the exercise of ecclesiastical, or, at least, of episcopal functions; and punished the popular bishops of Aquitain with imprisonment, exile, and confiscation. [89] But the cruel and absurd enterprise of subduing the minds of a whole people was undertaken by the Vandals alone. Genseric himself, in his early youth, had renounced the orthodox communion; and the apostate could neither grant, nor expect, a sincere forgiveness. He was exasperated to find that the Africans, who had fled before him in the field, still presumed to dispute his will in synods and churches; and his ferocious mind was incapable of fear or of compassion. His Catholic subjects were oppressed by intolerant laws and arbitrary punishments. The language of Genseric was furious and formidable; the knowledge of his intentions might justify the most unfavorable interpretation of his actions; and the Arians were reproached with the frequent executions which stained the palace and the dominions of the tyrant. Arms and ambition were, however, the ruling passions of the monarch of the sea. But Hunneric, his inglorious son, who seemed to inherit only his vices, tormented the Catholics with the same unrelenting fury which had been fatal to his brother, his nephews, and the friends and favorites of his father; and even to the Arian patriarch, who was inhumanly burnt alive in the midst of Carthage. The religious war was preceded and prepared by an insidious truce; persecution was made the serious and important business of the Vandal court; and the loathsome disease which hastened the death of Hunneric, revenged the injuries, without contributing to the deliverance, of the church. The throne of Africa was successively filled by the two nephews of Hunneric; by Gundamund, who reigned about twelve, and by Thrasimund, who governed the nation about twenty-seven, years. Their administration was hostile and oppressive to the orthodox party. Gundamund appeared to emulate, or even to surpass, the cruelty of his uncle; and, if at length he relented, if he recalled the bishops, and restored the freedom of Athanasian worship, a premature death intercepted the benefits of his tardy clemency. His brother, Thrasimund, was the greatest and most accomplished of the Vandal kings, whom he excelled in beauty, prudence, and magnanimity of soul. But this magnanimous character was degraded by his intolerant zeal and deceitful clemency. Instead of threats and tortures, he employed the gentle, but efficacious, powers of seduction. Wealth, dignity, and the royal favor, were the liberal rewards of apostasy; the Catholics, who had violated the laws, might purchase their pardon by the renunciation of their faith; and whenever Thrasimund meditated any rigorous measure, he patiently waited till the indiscretion of his adversaries furnished him with a specious opportunity. Bigotry was his last sentiment in the hour of death; and he exacted from his successor a solemn oath, that he would never tolerate the sectaries of Athanasius. But his successor, Hilderic, the gentle son of the savage Hunneric, preferred the duties of humanity and justice to the vain obligation of an impious oath; and his accession was gloriously marked by the restoration of peace and universal freedom. The throne of that virtuous, though feeble monarch, was usurped by his cousin Gelimer, a zealous Arian: but the Vandal kingdom, before he could enjoy or abuse his power, was subverted by the arms of Belisarius; and the orthodox party retaliated the injuries which they had endured. [90]

[Footnote 89: Such are the contemporary complaints of Sidonius, bishop of Clermont (l. vii. c. 6, p. 182, &c., edit. Sirmond.) Gregory of Tours who quotes this Epistle, (l. ii. c. 25, in tom. ii. p. 174,) extorts an unwarrantable assertion, that of the nine vacancies in Aquitain, some had been produced by episcopal martyrdoms]

[Footnote 90: The original monuments of the Vandal persecution are preserved in the five books of the history of Victor Vitensis, (de Persecutione Vandalica,) a bishop who was exiled by Hunneric; in the life of St. Fulgentius, who was distinguished in the persecution of Thrasimund (in Biblioth. Max. Patrum, tom. ix. p. 4-16;) and in the first book of the Vandalic War, by the impartial Procopius, (c. 7, 8, p. 196, 197, 198, 199.) Dom Ruinart, the last editor of Victor, has illustrated the whole subject with a copious and learned apparatus of notes and supplement (Paris, 1694.)]

The passionate declamations of the Catholics, the sole historians of this persecution, cannot afford any distinct series of causes and events; any impartial view of the characters, or counsels; but the most remarkable circumstances that deserve either credit or notice, may be referred to the following heads; I. In the original law, which is still extant, [91] Hunneric expressly declares, (and the declaration appears to be correct,) that he had faithfully transcribed the regulations and penalties of the Imperial edicts, against the heretical congregations, the clergy, and the people, who dissented from the established religion. If the rights of conscience had been understood, the Catholics must have condemned their past conduct or acquiesced in their actual suffering. But they still persisted to refuse the indulgence which they claimed. While they trembled under the lash of persecution, they praised the laudable severity of Hunneric himself, who burnt or banished great numbers of Manichaeans; [92] and they rejected, with horror, the ignominious compromise, that the disciples of Arius and of Athanasius should enjoy a reciprocal and similar toleration in the territories of the Romans, and in those of the Vandals. [93] II. The practice of a conference, which the Catholics had so frequently used to insult and punish their obstinate antagonists, was retorted against themselves. [94] At the command of Hunneric, four hundred and sixty-six orthodox bishops assembled at Carthage; but when they were admitted into the hall of audience, they had the mortification of beholding the Arian Cyrila exalted on the patriarchal throne. The disputants were separated, after the mutual and ordinary reproaches of noise and silence, of delay and precipitation, of military force and of popular clamor. One martyr and one confessor were selected among the Catholic bishops; twenty-eight escaped by flight, and eighty-eight by conformity; forty-six were sent into Corsica to cut timber for the royal navy; and three hundred and two were banished to the different parts of Africa, exposed to the insults of their enemies, and carefully deprived of all the temporal and spiritual comforts of life. [95] The hardships of ten years' exile must have reduced their numbers; and if they had complied with the law of Thrasimund, which prohibited any episcopal consecrations, the orthodox church of Africa must have expired with the lives of its actual members. They disobeyed, and their disobedience was punished by a second exile of two hundred and twenty bishops into Sardinia; where they languished fifteen years, till the accession of the gracious Hilderic. [96] The two islands were judiciously chosen by the malice of their Arian tyrants. Seneca, from his own experience, has deplored and exaggerated the miserable state of Corsica, [97] and the plenty of Sardinia was overbalanced by the unwholesome quality of the air. [98] III. The zeal of Generic and his successors, for the conversion of the Catholics, must have rendered them still more jealous to guard the purity of the Vandal faith. Before the churches were finally shut, it was a crime to appear in a Barbarian dress; and those who presumed to neglect the royal mandate were rudely dragged backwards by their long hair. [99] The palatine officers, who refused to profess the religion of their prince, were ignominiously stripped of their honors and employments; banished to Sardinia and Sicily; or condemned to the servile labors of slaves and peasants in the fields of Utica. In the districts which had been peculiarly allotted to the Vandals, the exercise of the Catholic worship was more strictly prohibited; and severe penalties were denounced against the guilt both of the missionary and the proselyte. By these arts, the faith of the Barbarians was preserved, and their zeal was inflamed: they discharged, with devout fury, the office of spies, informers, or executioners; and whenever their cavalry took the field, it was the favorite amusement of the march to defile the churches, and to insult the clergy of the adverse faction. [100] IV. The citizens who had been educated in the luxury of the Roman province, were delivered, with exquisite cruelty, to the Moors of the desert. A venerable train of bishops, presbyters, and deacons, with a faithful crowd of four thousand and ninety-six persons, whose guilt is not precisely ascertained, were torn from their native homes, by the command of Hunneric. During the night they were confined, like a herd of cattle, amidst their own ordure: during the day they pursued their march over the burning sands; and if they fainted under the heat and fatigue, they were goaded, or dragged along, till they expired in the hands of their tormentors. [101] These unhappy exiles, when they reached the Moorish huts, might excite the compassion of a people, whose native humanity was neither improved by reason, nor corrupted by fanaticism: but if they escaped the dangers, they were condemned to share the distress of a savage life. V. It is incumbent on the authors of persecution previously to reflect, whether they are determined to support it in the last extreme. They excite the flame which they strive to extinguish; and it soon becomes necessary to chastise the contumacy, as well as the crime, of the offender. The fine, which he is unable or unwilling to discharge, exposes his person to the severity of the law; and his contempt of lighter penalties suggests the use and propriety of capital punishment. Through the veil of fiction and declamation we may clearly perceive, that the Catholics more especially under the reign of Hunneric, endured the most cruel and ignominious treatment. [102] Respectable citizens, noble matrons, and consecrated virgins, were stripped naked, and raised in the air by pulleys, with a weight suspended at their feet. In this painful attitude their naked bodies were torn with scourges, or burnt in the most tender parts with red-hot plates of iron. The amputation of the ears the nose, the tongue, and the right hand, was inflicted by the Arians; and although the precise number cannot be defined, it is evident that many persons, among whom a bishop [103] and a proconsul [104] may be named, were entitled to the crown of martyrdom. The same honor has been ascribed to the memory of Count Sebastian, who professed the Nicene creed with unshaken constancy; and Genseric might detest, as a heretic, the brave and ambitious fugitive whom he dreaded as a rival. [105] VI. A new mode of conversion, which might subdue the feeble, and alarm the timorous, was employed by the Arian ministers. They imposed, by fraud or violence, the rites of baptism; and punished the apostasy of the Catholics, if they disclaimed this odious and profane ceremony, which scandalously violated the freedom of the will, and the unity of the sacrament. [106] The hostile sects had formerly allowed the validity of each other's baptism; and the innovation, so fiercely maintained by the Vandals, can be imputed only to the example and advice of the Donatists. VII. The Arian clergy surpassed in religious cruelty the king and his Vandals; but they were incapable of cultivating the spiritual vineyard, which they were so desirous to possess. A patriarch [107] might seat himself on the throne of Carthage; some bishops, in the principal cities, might usurp the place of their rivals; but the smallness of their numbers, and their ignorance of the Latin language, [108] disqualified the Barbarians for the ecclesiastical ministry of a great church; and the Africans, after the loss of their orthodox pastors, were deprived of the public exercise of Christianity. VIII. The emperors were the natural protectors of the Homoousian doctrine; and the faithful people of Africa, both as Romans and as Catholics, preferred their lawful sovereignty to the usurpation of the Barbarous heretics. During an interval of peace and friendship, Hunneric restored the cathedral of Carthage; at the intercession of Zeno, who reigned in the East, and of Placidia, the daughter and relict of emperors, and the sister of the queen of the Vandals. [109] But this decent regard was of short duration; and the haughty tyrant displayed his contempt for the religion of the empire, by studiously arranging the bloody images of persecution, in all the principal streets through which the Roman ambassador must pass in his way to the palace. [110] An oath was required from the bishops, who were assembled at Carthage, that they would support the succession of his son Hilderic, and that they would renounce all foreign or transmarine correspondence. This engagement, consistent, as it should seem, with their moral and religious duties, was refused by the more sagacious members [111] of the assembly. Their refusal, faintly colored by the pretence that it is unlawful for a Christian to swear, must provoke the suspicions of a jealous tyrant.

[Footnote 91: Victor, iv. 2, p. 65. Hunneric refuses the name of Catholics to the Homoousians. He describes, as the veri Divinae Majestatis cultores, his own party, who professed the faith, confirmed by more than a thousand bishops, in the synods of Rimini and Seleucia.]

[Footnote 92: Victor, ii, 1, p. 21, 22: Laudabilior... videbatur. In the Mss which omit this word, the passage is unintelligible. See Ruinart Not. p. 164.]

[Footnote 93: Victor, ii. p. 22, 23. The clergy of Carthage called these conditions periculosoe; and they seem, indeed, to have been proposed as a snare to entrap the Catholic bishops.]

[Footnote 94: See the narrative of this conference, and the treatment of the bishops, in Victor, ii. 13-18, p. 35-42 and the whole fourth book p. 63-171. The third book, p. 42-62, is entirely filled by their apology or confession of faith.]

[Footnote 95: See the list of the African bishops, in Victor, p. 117-140, and Ruinart's notes, p. 215-397. The schismatic name of Donatus frequently occurs, and they appear to have adopted (like our fanatics of the last age) the pious appellations of Deodatus, Deogratias, Quidvultdeus, Habetdeum, &c. Note: These names appear to have been introduced by the Donatists—M.]

[Footnote 96: Fulgent. Vit. c. 16-29. Thrasimund affected the praise of moderation and learning; and Fulgentius addressed three books of controversy to the Arian tyrant, whom he styles piissime Rex. Biblioth. Maxim. Patrum, tom. ix. p. 41. Only sixty bishops are mentioned as exiles in the life of Fulgentius; they are increased to one hundred and twenty by Victor Tunnunensis and Isidore; but the number of two hundred and twenty is specified in the Historia Miscella, and a short authentic chronicle of the times. See Ruinart, p. 570, 571.]

[Footnote 97: See the base and insipid epigrams of the Stoic, who could not support exile with more fortitude than Ovid. Corsica might not produce corn, wine, or oil; but it could not be destitute of grass, water, and even fire.]

[Footnote 98: Si ob gravitatem coeli interissent vile damnum. Tacit. Annal. ii. 85. In this application, Thrasimund would have adopted the reading of some critics, utile damnum.]

[Footnote 99: See these preludes of a general persecution, in Victor, ii. 3, 4, 7 and the two edicts of Hunneric, l. ii. p. 35, l. iv. p. 64.]

[Footnote 100: See Procopius de Bell. Vandal. l. i. c. 7, p. 197, 198. A Moorish prince endeavored to propitiate the God of the Christians, by his diligence to erase the marks of the Vandal sacrilege.]

[Footnote 101: See this story in Victor. ii. 8-12, p. 30-34. Victor describes the distress of these confessors as an eye-witness.]

[Footnote 102: See the fifth book of Victor. His passionate complaints are confirmed by the sober testimony of Procopius, and the public declaration of the emperor Justinian. Cod. l. i. tit. xxvii.]

[Footnote 103: Victor, ii. 18, p. 41.]

[Footnote 104: Victor, v. 4, p. 74, 75. His name was Victorianus, and he was a wealthy citizen of Adrumetum, who enjoyed the confidence of the king; by whose favor he had obtained the office, or at least the title, of proconsul of Africa.]

[Footnote 105: Victor, i. 6, p. 8, 9. After relating the firm resistance and dexterous reply of Count Sebastian, he adds, quare alio generis argumento postea bellicosum virum eccidit.]

[Footnote 106: Victor, v. 12, 13. Tillemont, Mem. Eccles. tom. vi. p. 609.]

[Footnote 107: Primate was more properly the title of the bishop of Carthage; but the name of patriarch was given by the sects and nations to their principal ecclesiastic. See Thomassin, Discipline de l'Eglise, tom. i. p. 155, 158.]

[Footnote 108: The patriarch Cyrila himself publicly declared, that he did not understand Latin (Victor, ii. 18, p. 42:) Nescio Latine; and he might converse with tolerable ease, without being capable of disputing or preaching in that language. His Vandal clergy were still more ignorant; and small confidence could be placed in the Africans who had conformed.]

[Footnote 109: Victor, ii. 1, 2, p. 22.]

[Footnote 110: Victor, v. 7, p. 77. He appeals to the ambassador himself, whose name was Uranius.]

[Footnote 111: Astutiores, Victor, iv. 4, p. 70. He plainly intimates that their quotation of the gospel "Non jurabitis in toto," was only meant to elude the obligation of an inconvenient oath. The forty-six bishops who refused were banished to Corsica; the three hundred and two who swore were distributed through the provinces of Africa.]

PART IV

The Catholics, oppressed by royal and military force, were far superior to their adversaries in numbers and learning. With the same weapons which the Greek [112] and Latin fathers had already provided for the Arian controversy, they repeatedly silenced, or vanquished, the fierce and illiterate successors of Ulphilas. The consciousness of their own superiority might have raised them above the arts and passions of religious warfare. Yet, instead of assuming such honorable pride, the orthodox theologians were tempted, by the assurance of impunity, to compose fictions, which must be stigmatized with the epithets of fraud and forgery. They ascribed their own polemical works to the most venerable names of Christian antiquity; the characters of Athanasius and Augustin were awkwardly personated by Vigilius and his disciples; [113] and the famous creed, which so clearly expounds the mysteries of the Trinity and the Incarnation, is deduced, with strong probability, from this African school. [114] Even the Scriptures themselves were profaned by their rash and sacrilegious hands. The memorable text, which asserts the unity of the three who bear witness in heaven, [115] is condemned by the universal silence of the orthodox fathers, ancient versions, and authentic manuscripts. [116] It was first alleged by the Catholic bishops whom Hunneric summoned to the conference of Carthage. [117] An allegorical interpretation, in the form, perhaps, of a marginal note, invaded the text of the Latin Bibles, which were renewed and corrected in a dark period of ten centuries. [118] After the invention of printing, [119] the editors of the Greek Testament yielded to their own prejudices, or those of the times; [120] and the pious fraud, which was embraced with equal zeal at Rome and at Geneva, has been infinitely multiplied in every country and every language of modern Europe.

[Footnote 112: *Fulgentius, bishop of Ruspae, in the Byzacene province, was of a senatorial family, and had received a liberal education. He could repeat all Homer and Menander before he was allowed to study Latin his native tongue, (Vit. Fulgent. c. l.) Many African bishops might understand Greek, and many Greek theologians were translated into Latin.*]

[Footnote 113: *Compare the two prefaces to the Dialogue of Vigilius of Thapsus, (p. 118, 119, edit. Chiflet.) He might amuse his learned reader with an innocent fiction; but the subject was too grave, and the Africans were too ignorant.*]

[Footnote 114: *The P. Quesnel started this opinion, which has been favorably received. But the three following truths, however surprising they may seem, are now universally acknowledged, (Gerard Vossius, tom. vi. p. 516-522. Tillemont, Mem. Eccles. tom. viii. p. 667-671.) 1. St. Athanasius is not the author of the creed which is so frequently read in our churches. 2. It does not appear to have existed within a century after his death. 3. It was originally composed in the Latin tongue, and, consequently in the Western provinces. Gennadius patriarch of Constantinople, was so much amazed by this extraordinary composition, that he frankly pronounced it to be the work of a drunken man. Petav. Dogmat. Theologica, tom. ii. l. vii. c. 8, p. 687.*]

[Footnote 115: *1 John, v. 7. See Simon, Hist. Critique du Nouveau Testament, part i. c. xviii. p. 203-218; and part ii. c. ix. p. 99-121; and the elaborate Prolegomena and Annotations of Dr. Mill and Wetstein to their editions of the Greek Testament. In 1689, the papist Simon strove to be free; in 1707, the Protestant Mill wished to be a slave; in 1751, the Armenian Wetstein used the liberty of his times, and of his sect. Note: This controversy has continued to be agitated, but with declining interest even in the more religious part of the community; and may now be considered to have terminated in an almost general acquiescence of the learned to the conclusions of Porson in his Letters to Travis. See the pamphlets of the late Bishop of Salisbury and of Crito Cantabrigiensis, Dr. Turton of Cambridge—M.*]

[Footnote 116: *Of all the Mss. now extant, above fourscore in number, some of which are more than 1200 years old, (Wetstein ad loc.) The orthodox copies of the Vatican, of the Complutensian editors, of Robert Stephens, are become invisible; and the two Mss. of Dublin and Berlin are unworthy to form an exception. See Emlyn's Works, vol. ii. p 227-255, 269-299; and M. de Missy's four ingenious letters, in tom. viii. and ix. of the Journal Britannique.*]

[Footnote 117: *Or, more properly, by the four bishops who composed and published the profession of faith in the name of their brethren. They styled this text, luce clarius, (Victor Vitensis de Persecut. Vandal. l. iii. c. 11, p. 54.) It is quoted soon afterwards by the African polemics, Vigilius and Fulgentius.*]

[Footnote 118: In the eleventh and twelfth centuries, the Bibles were corrected by Lanfranc, archbishop of Canterbury, and by Nicholas, cardinal and librarian of the Roman church, secundum orthodoxam fidem, (Wetstein, Prolegom. p. 84, 85.) Notwithstanding these corrections, the passage is still wanting in twenty-five Latin Mss., (Wetstein ad loc.,) the oldest and the fairest; two qualities seldom united, except in manuscripts.]

[Footnote 119: The art which the Germans had invented was applied in Italy to the profane writers of Rome and Greece. The original Greek of the New Testament was published about the same time (A.D. 1514, 1516, 1520,) by the industry of Erasmus, and the munificence of Cardinal Ximenes. The Complutensian Polyglot cost the cardinal 50,000 ducats. See Mattaire, Annal. Typograph. tom. ii. p. 2-8, 125-133; and Wetstein, Prolegomena, p. 116-127.]

[Footnote 120: The three witnesses have been established in our Greek Testaments by the prudence of Erasmus; the honest bigotry of the Complutensian editors; the typographical fraud, or error, of Robert Stephens, in the placing a crotchet; and the deliberate falsehood, or strange misapprehension, of Theodore Beza.]

The example of fraud must excite suspicion: and the specious miracles by which the African Catholics have defended the truth and justice of their cause, may be ascribed, with more reason, to their own industry, than to the visible protection of Heaven. Yet the historian, who views this religious conflict with an impartial eye, may condescend to mention one preternatural event, which will edify the devout, and surprise the incredulous. Tipasa, [121] a maritime colony of Mauritania, sixteen miles to the east of Caesarea, had been distinguished, in every age, by the orthodox zeal of its inhabitants. They had braved the fury of the Donatists; [122] they resisted, or eluded, the tyranny of the Arians. The town was deserted on the approach of an heretical bishop: most of the inhabitants who could procure ships passed over to the coast of Spain; and the unhappy remnant, refusing all communion with the usurper, still presumed to hold their pious, but illegal, assemblies. Their disobedience exasperated the cruelty of Hunneric. A military count was despatched from Carthage to Tipasa: he collected the Catholics in the Forum, and, in the presence of the whole province, deprived the guilty of their right hands and their tongues. But the holy confessors continued to speak without tongues; and this miracle is attested by Victor, an African bishop, who published a history of the persecution within two years after the event. [123] "If any one," says Victor, "should doubt of the truth, let him repair to Constantinople, and listen to the clear and perfect language of Restitutus, the sub-deacon, one of these glorious sufferers, who is now lodged in the palace of the emperor Zeno, and is respected by the devout empress." At Constantinople we are astonished to find a cool, a learned, and unexceptionable witness, without interest, and without passion. Aeneas of Gaza, a Platonic philosopher, has accurately described his own observations on these African sufferers. "I saw them myself: I heard them speak: I diligently inquired by what means such an articulate voice could be formed without any organ of speech: I used my eyes to examine the report of my ears: I opened their mouth, and saw that the whole tongue had been completely torn away by the roots; an operation which the physicians generally suppose to be mortal." [124] The testimony of Aeneas of Gaza might be confirmed by the superfluous evidence of the emperor Justinian, in a perpetual edict; of Count Marcellinus, in his Chronicle of the times; and of Pope Gregory the First, who had resided at Constantinople, as the minister of the Roman pontiff. [125] They all lived within the compass of a century; and they all appeal to their personal knowledge, or the public notoriety, for the truth of a miracle, which was repeated in several instances, displayed on the greatest theatre of the world, and submitted, during a series of years, to the calm examination of the senses. This supernatural gift of the African confessors, who spoke without tongues, will command the assent of those, and of those only, who already believe, that their language was pure and orthodox. But the stubborn mind of an infidel, is guarded by secret, incurable suspicion; and the Arian, or Socinian, who has seriously rejected the doctrine of a Trinity, will not be shaken by the most plausible evidence of an Athanasian miracle.

[Footnote 121: Plin. Hist. Natural. v. 1. Itinerar. Wesseling, p. 15. Cellanius, Geograph. Antiq. tom. ii. part ii. p. 127. This Tipasa (which must not be confounded with another in Numidia) was a town of some note since Vespasian endowed it with the right of Latium.]

[Footnote 122: Optatus Milevitanus de Schism. Donatist. l. ii. p. 38.]

[Footnote 123: Victor Vitensis, v. 6, p. 76. Ruinart, p. 483-487.]

[Footnote 124: Aeneas Gazaeus in Theophrasto, in Biblioth. Patrum, tom. viii. p. 664, 665. He was a Christian, and composed this Dialogue (the Theophrastus) on the immortality of the soul, and the resurrection of the body; besides twenty-five Epistles, still extant. See Cave, (Hist. Litteraria, p. 297,) and Fabricius, (Biblioth. Graec. tom. i. p. 422.)]

[Footnote 125: Justinian. Codex. l. i. tit. xxvii. Marcellin. in Chron. p. 45, in Thesaur. Temporum Scaliger. Procopius, de Bell. Vandal. l. i. c. 7. p. 196. Gregor. Magnus, Dialog. iii. 32. None of these witnesses have specified the number of the confessors, which is fixed at sixty in an old menology, (apud Ruinart. p. 486.) Two of them lost their speech by fornication; but the miracle is enhanced by the singular instance of a boy who had never spoken before his tongue was cut out.]

The Vandals and the Ostrogoths persevered in the profession of Arianism till the final ruin of the kingdoms which they had founded in Africa and Italy. The Barbarians of Gaul submitted to the orthodox dominion of the Franks; and Spain was restored to the Catholic church by the voluntary conversion of the Visigoths.

This salutary revolution [126] was hastened by the example of a royal martyr, whom our calmer reason may style an ungrateful rebel. Leovigild, the Gothic monarch of Spain, deserved the respect of his enemies, and the love of his subjects; the Catholics enjoyed a free toleration, and his Arian synods attempted, without much success, to reconcile their scruples by abolishing the unpopular rite of a second baptism. His eldest son Hermenegild, who was invested by his father with the royal diadem, and the fair principality of Boetica, contracted an honorable and orthodox alliance with a Merovingian princess, the daughter of Sigebert, king of Austrasia, and of the famous Brunechild. The beauteous Ingundis, who was no more than thirteen years of age, was received, beloved, and persecuted, in the Arian court of Toledo; and her religious constancy was alternately assaulted with blandishments and violence by Goisvintha, the Gothic queen, who abused the double claim of maternal authority. [127] Incensed by her resistance, Goisvintha seized the Catholic princess by her long hair, inhumanly dashed her against the ground, kicked her till she was covered with blood, and at last gave orders that she should be stripped, and thrown into a basin, or fish-pond. [128] Love and honor might excite Hermenegild to resent this injurious treatment of his bride; and he was gradually persuaded that Ingundis suffered for the cause of divine truth. Her tender complaints, and the weighty arguments of Leander, archbishop of Seville, accomplished his conversion and the heir of the Gothic monarchy was initiated in the Nicene faith by the solemn rites of confirmation. [129] The rash youth, inflamed by zeal, and perhaps by ambition, was tempted to violate the duties of a son and a subject; and the Catholics of Spain, although they could not complain of persecution, applauded his pious rebellion against an heretical father. The civil war was protracted by the long and obstinate sieges of Merida, Cordova, and Seville, which had strenuously espoused the party of Hermenegild He invited the orthodox Barbarians, the Seuvi, and the Franks, to the destruction of his native land; he solicited the dangerous aid of the Romans, who possessed Africa, and a part of the Spanish coast; and his holy ambassador, the archbishop Leander, effectually negotiated in person with the Byzantine court. But the hopes of the Catholics were crushed by the active diligence of the monarch who commanded the troops and treasures of Spain; and the guilty Hermenegild, after his vain attempts to resist or to escape, was compelled to surrender himself into the hands of an incensed father. Leovigild was still mindful of that sacred character; and the rebel, despoiled of the regal ornaments, was still permitted, in a decent exile, to profess the Catholic religion. His repeated and unsuccessful treasons at length provoked the indignation of the Gothic king; and the sentence of death, which he pronounced with apparent reluctance, was privately executed in the tower of Seville. The inflexible constancy with which he refused to accept the Arian communion, as the price of his safety, may excuse the honors that have been paid to the memory of St. Hermenegild. His wife and infant son were detained by the Romans in ignominious captivity; and this domestic misfortune tarnished the glories of Leovigild, and imbittered the last moments of his life.

[Footnote 126: See the two general historians of Spain, Mariana (Hist. de Rebus Hispaniae, tom. i. l. v. c. 12-15, p. 182-194) and Ferreras, (French translation, tom. ii. p. 206-247.) Mariana almost forgets that he is a Jesuit, to assume the style and spirit of a Roman classic. Ferreras, an industrious compiler, reviews his facts, and rectifies his chronology.]

[Footnote 127: Goisvintha successively married two kings of the Visigoths: Athanigild, to whom she bore Brunechild, the mother of Ingundis; and Leovigild, whose two sons, Hermenegild and Recared, were the issue of a former marriage.]

[Footnote 128: Iracundiae furore succensa, adprehensam per comam capitis puellam in terram conlidit, et diu calcibus verberatam, ac sanguins cruentatam, jussit exspoliari, et piscinae immergi. Greg. Turon. l. v. c. 39. in tom. ii. p. 255. Gregory is one of our best originals for this portion of history.]

[Footnote 129: The Catholics who admitted the baptism of heretics repeated the rite, or, as it was afterwards styled, the sacrament, of confirmation, to which they ascribed many mystic and marvellous prerogatives both visible and invisible. See Chardon. Hist. des Sacremens, tom. 1. p. 405-552.]

His son and successor, Recared, the first Catholic king of Spain, had imbibed the faith of his unfortunate brother, which he supported with more prudence and success. Instead of revolting against his father, Recared patiently expected the hour of his death. Instead of condemning his memory, he piously supposed, that the dying monarch had abjured the errors of Arianism, and recommended to his son the conversion of the Gothic nation. To accomplish that salutary end, Recared convened an assembly of the Arian clergy and nobles, declared himself a Catholic, and exhorted them to imitate the example of their prince. The laborious interpretation of doubtful texts, or the curious pursuit of metaphysical arguments, would have excited an endless controversy; and the monarch discreetly proposed to his illiterate audience two substantial and visible arguments,—the testimony of Earth, and of Heaven. The Earth had submitted to the Nicene synod: the Romans, the Barbarians, and the inhabitants of Spain, unanimously professed the same orthodox creed; and the Visigoths resisted, almost alone, the consent of the Christian world. A superstitious age was prepared to reverence, as the testimony of Heaven, the preternatural cures, which were performed by the skill or virtue of the Catholic clergy; the baptismal fonts of Osset in Boetica, [130] which were spontaneously replenished every year, on the vigil of Easter; [131] and the miraculous shrine of St. Martin of Tours, which had already converted the Suevic prince and people of Gallicia. [132] The Catholic king encountered some difficulties on this important change of the national religion. A conspiracy, secretly fomented by the queen-dowager, was formed against his life; and two counts excited a dangerous revolt in the Narbonnese Gaul. But Recared disarmed the conspirators, defeated the rebels, and executed severe justice; which the Arians, in their turn, might brand with the reproach of persecution. Eight bishops, whose names betray their Barbaric origin, abjured their errors; and all the books of Arian theology were reduced to ashes, with the house in which they had been purposely collected. The whole body of the Visigoths and Suevi were allured or driven into the pale of the Catholic communion; the faith, at least of the rising generation, was fervent and sincere: and the devout liberality of the Barbarians enriched the churches and monasteries of Spain. Seventy bishops, assembled in the council of Toledo, received the submission of their conquerors; and the zeal of the Spaniards improved the Nicene creed, by declaring the procession of the Holy Ghost from the Son, as well as from the Father; a weighty point of doctrine, which produced, long afterwards, the schism of the Greek and Latin churches. [133] The royal proselyte immediately saluted and consulted Pope Gregory, surnamed the Great, a learned and holy prelate, whose reign was distinguished by the conversion of heretics and infidels. The ambassadors of Recared respectfully offered on the threshold of the Vatican his rich presents of gold and gems; they accepted, as a lucrative exchange, the hairs of St. John the Baptist; a cross, which enclosed a small piece of the true wood; and a key, that contained some particles of iron which had been scraped from the chains of St. Peter. [134]

[Footnote 130: Osset, or Julia Constantia, was opposite to Seville, on the northern side of the Boetis, (Plin. Hist. Natur. iii. 3:) and the authentic reference of Gregory of Tours (Hist. Francor. l. vi. c. 43, p. 288) deserves more credit than the name of Lusitania, (de Gloria Martyr. c. 24,) which has been eagerly embraced by the vain and superstitious Portuguese, (Ferreras, Hist. d'Espagne, tom. ii. p. 166.)]

[Footnote 131: This miracle was skilfully performed. An Arian king sealed the doors, and dug a deep trench round the church, without being able to intercept the Easter supply of baptismal water.]

[Footnote 132: Ferreras (tom. ii. p. 168-175, A.D. 550) has illustrated the difficulties which regard the time and circumstances of the conversion of the Suevi. They had been recently united by Leovigild to the Gothic monarchy of Spain.]

[Footnote 133: This addition to the Nicene, or rather the Constantinopolitan creed, was first made in the eighth council of Toledo, A.D. 653; but it was expressive of the popular doctrine, (Gerard Vossius, tom. vi. p. 527, de tribus Symbolis.)]

[Footnote 134: See Gregor. Magn. l. vii. epist. 126, apud Baronium, Annal. Eccles. A.D. 559, No. 25, 26.]

The same Gregory, the spiritual conqueror of Britain, encouraged the pious Theodelinda, queen of the Lombards, to propagate the Nicene faith among the victorious savages, whose recent Christianity was polluted by the Arian heresy. Her devout labors still left room for the industry and success of future missionaries; and many cities of Italy were still disputed by hostile bishops. But the cause of Arianism was gradually suppressed by the weight of truth, of interest, and of example; and the controversy, which Egypt had derived from the Platonic school, was terminated, after a war of three hundred years, by the final conversion of the Lombards of Italy. [135]

[Footnote 135: Paul Warnefrid (de Gestis Langobard. l. iv. c. 44, p. 153, edit Grot.) allows that Arianism still prevailed under the reign of Rotharis, (A.D. 636-652.) The pious deacon does not attempt to mark the precise era of the national conversion, which was accomplished, however, before the end of the seventh century.]

The first missionaries who preached the gospel to the Barbarians, appealed to the evidence of reason, and claimed the benefit of toleration. [136] But no sooner had they established their spiritual dominion, than they exhorted the Christian kings to extirpate, without mercy, the remains of Roman or Barbaric superstition. The successors of Clovis inflicted one hundred lashes on the peasants who refused to destroy their idols; the crime of sacrificing to the demons was punished by the Anglo-Saxon laws with the heavier penalties of imprisonment and confiscation; and even the wise Alfred adopted, as an indispensable duty, the extreme rigor of the Mosaic institutions. [137] But the punishment and the crime were gradually abolished among a Christian people; the theological disputes of the schools were suspended by propitious ignorance; and the intolerant spirit which could find neither idolaters nor heretics, was reduced to the persecution of the Jews. That exiled nation had founded some synagogues in the cities of Gaul; but Spain, since the time of Hadrian, was filled with their numerous colonies. [138] The wealth which they accumulated by trade, and the management of the finances, invited the pious avarice of their masters; and they might be oppressed without danger, as they had lost the use, and even the remembrance, of arms. Sisebut, a Gothic king, who reigned in the beginning of the seventh century, proceeded at once to the last extremes of persecution. [139] Ninety thousand Jews were compelled to receive the sacrament of baptism; the fortunes of the obstinate infidels were confiscated, their bodies were tortured; and it seems doubtful whether they were permitted to abandon their native country. The excessive zeal of the Catholic king was moderated, even by the clergy of Spain, who solemnly pronounced an inconsistent sentence: that the sacraments should not be forcibly imposed; but that the Jews who had been baptized should be constrained, for the honor of the church, to persevere in the external practice of a religion which they disbelieved and detested. Their frequent relapses provoked one of the successors of Sisebut to banish the whole nation from his dominions; and a council of Toledo published a decree, that every Gothic king should swear to maintain this salutary edict. But the tyrants were unwilling to dismiss the victims, whom they delighted to torture, or to deprive themselves of the industrious slaves, over whom they might exercise a lucrative oppression. The Jews still continued in Spain, under the weight of the civil and ecclesiastical laws, which in the same country have been faithfully transcribed in the Code of the Inquisition. The Gothic kings and bishops at length discovered, that injuries will produce hatred, and that hatred will find the opportunity of revenge. A nation, the secret or professed enemies of Christianity, still multiplied in servitude and distress; and the intrigues of the Jews promoted the rapid success of the Arabian conquerors. [140]

[Footnote 136: *Quorum fidei et conversioni ita congratulatus esse rex perhibetur, ut nullum tamen cogeret ad Christianismum.... Didiceret enim a doctoribus auctoribusque suae salutis, servitium Christi voluntarium non coactitium esse debere.* Bedae Hist. Ecclesiastic. l. i. c. 26, p. 62, edit. Smith.]

[Footnote 137: See the Historians of France, tom. iv. p. 114; and Wilkins, Leges Anglo-Saxonicae, p. 11, 31. *Siquis sacrificium immolaverit praeter Deo soli morte moriatur.*]

[Footnote 138: The Jews pretend that they were introduced into Spain by the fleets of Solomon, and the arms of Nebuchadnezzar; that Hadrian transported forty thousand families of the tribe of Judah, and ten thousand of the tribe of Benjamin, &c. Basnage, Hist. des Juifs, tom. vii. c. 9, p. 240-256.]

[Footnote 139: Isidore, at that time archbishop of Seville, mentions, disapproves and congratulates, the zeal of Sisebut (Chron. Goth. p. 728.) Barosins (A.D. 614, No. 41) assigns the number of the evidence of Almoin, (l. iv. c. 22;) but the evidence is weak, and I have not been able to verify the quotation, (Historians of France, tom. iii. p. 127.)]

[Footnote 140: Basnage (tom. viii. c. 13, p. 388-400) faithfully represents the state of the Jews; but he might have added from the canons of the Spanish councils, and the laws of the Visigoths, many curious circumstances, essential to his subject, though they are foreign to mine. Note: Compare Milman, Hist. of Jews iii. 256—M]

As soon as the Barbarians withdrew their powerful support, the unpopular heresy of Arius sunk into contempt and oblivion. But the Greeks still retained their subtle and loquacious disposition: the establishment of an obscure doctrine suggested new questions, and new disputes; and it was always in the power of an ambitious prelate, or a fanatic monk, to violate the peace of the church, and, perhaps, of the empire. The historian of the empire may overlook those disputes which were confined to the obscurity of schools and synods. The Manichaeans, who labored to reconcile the religions of Christ and of Zoroaster, had secretly introduced themselves into the provinces: but these foreign sectaries were involved in the common disgrace of the Gnostics, and the Imperial laws were executed by the public hatred. The rational opinions of the Pelagians were propagated from Britain to Rome, Africa, and Palestine, and silently expired in a superstitious age. But the East was distracted by the Nestorian and Eutychian controversies; which attempted to explain the mystery of the incarnation, and hastened the ruin of Christianity in her native land. These controversies were first agitated under the reign of the younger Theodosius: but their important consequences extend far beyond the limits of the present volume. The metaphysical chain of argument, the contests of ecclesiastical ambition, and their political influence on the decline of the Byzantine empire, may afford an interesting and instructive series of history, from the general councils of Ephesus and Chalcedon, to the conquest of the East by the successors of Mahomet.

CHAPTER XXXVIII

REIGN OF CLOVIS

PART I

REIGN AND CONVERSION OF CLOVIS—HIS VICTORIES OVER THE ALEMANNI, BURGUNDIANS, AND VISIGOTHS—ESTABLISHMENT OF THE FRENCH MONARCHY IN GAUL—LAWS OF THE BARBARIANS—STATE OF THE ROMANS—THE VISIGOTHS OF SPAIN—CONQUEST OF BRITAIN BY THE SAXONS

The Gauls, [1] who impatiently supported the Roman yoke, received a memorable lesson from one of the lieutenants of Vespasian, whose weighty sense has been refined and expressed by the genius of Tacitus. [2] "The protection of the republic has delivered Gaul from internal discord and foreign invasions. By the loss of national independence, you have acquired the name and privileges of Roman citizens. You enjoy, in common with yourselves, the permanent benefits of civil government; and your remote situation is less exposed to the accidental mischiefs of tyranny. Instead of exercising the rights of conquest, we have been contented to impose such tributes as are requisite for your own preservation. Peace cannot be secured without armies; and armies must be supported at the expense of the people. It is for your sake, not for our own, that we guard the barrier of the Rhine against the ferocious Germans, who have so often attempted, and who will always desire, to exchange the solitude of their woods and morasses for the wealth and fertility of Gaul. The fall of Rome would be fatal to the provinces; and you would be buried in the ruins of that mighty fabric, which has been raised by the valor and wisdom of eight hundred years. Your imaginary freedom would be insulted and oppressed by a savage master; and the expulsion of the Romans would be succeeded by the eternal hostilities of the Barbarian conquerors." [3] This salutary advice was accepted, and this strange prediction was accomplished. In the space of four hundred years, the hardy Gauls, who had encountered the arms of Caesar, were imperceptibly melted into the general mass of citizens and subjects: the Western empire was dissolved; and the Germans, who had passed the Rhine, fiercely contended for the possession of Gaul, and excited the contempt, or abhorrence, of its peaceful and polished inhabitants. With that conscious pride which the preeminence of knowledge and luxury seldom fails to inspire, they derided the hairy and gigantic savages of the North; their rustic manners, dissonant joy, voracious appetite, and their horrid appearance, equally disgusting to the sight and to the smell. The liberal studies were still cultivated in the schools of Autun and Bordeaux; and the language of Cicero and Virgil was familiar to the Gallic youth. Their ears were astonished by the harsh and unknown sounds of the Germanic dialect, and they ingeniously lamented that the trembling muses fled from the harmony of a Burgundian lyre. The Gauls were endowed with all the advantages of art and nature; but as they wanted courage to defend them, they were justly condemned to obey, and even to flatter, the victorious Barbarians, by whose clemency they held their precarious fortunes and their lives. [4]

[Footnote 1: In this chapter I shall draw my quotations from the Recueil des Historiens des Gaules et de la France, Paris, 1738-1767, in eleven volumes in folio. By the labor of Dom Bouquet, and the other Benedictines, all the original testimonies, as far as A.D. 1060, are disposed in chronological order, and illustrated with learned notes. Such a national work, which will be continued to the year 1500, might provoke our emulation.]

[Footnote 2: Tacit. Hist. iv. 73, 74, in tom. i. p. 445. To abridge Tacitus would indeed be presumptuous; but I may select the general ideas which he applies to the present state and future revelations of Gaul.]

[Footnote 3: Eadem semper causa Germanis transcendendi in Gallias libido atque avaritiae et mutandae sedis amor; ut relictis paludibus et solitudinibus, suis, fecundissimum hoc solum vosque ipsos possiderent.... Nam pulsis Romanis quid aliud quam bella omnium inter se gentium exsistent?]

[Footnote 4: Sidonius Apollinaris ridicules, with affected wit and pleasantry, the hardships of his situation, (Carm. xii. in tom. i. p. 811.)]

As soon as Odoacer had extinguished the Western empire, he sought the friendship of the most powerful of the Barbarians. The new sovereign of Italy resigned to Euric, king of the Visigoths, all the Roman conquests beyond the Alps, as far as the Rhine and the Ocean: [5] and the senate might confirm this liberal gift with some ostentation of power, and without any real loss of revenue and dominion. The lawful pretensions of Euric were justified by ambition and success; and the Gothic nation might aspire, under his command, to the monarchy of Spain and Gaul. Arles and Marseilles surrendered to his arms: he oppressed the freedom of Auvergne; and the bishop condescended to purchase his recall from exile by a tribute of just, but reluctant praise. Sidonius waited before the gates of the palace among a crowd of ambassadors and suppliants; and their various business at the court of Bordeaux attested the power, and the renown, of the king of the Visigoths. The Heruli of the distant ocean, who painted their naked bodies with its coerulean color, implored his protection; and the Saxons respected the maritime provinces of a prince, who was destitute of any naval force. The tall Burgundians submitted to his authority; nor did he restore the captive Franks, till he had imposed on that fierce nation the terms of an unequal peace. The Vandals of Africa cultivated his useful friendship; and the Ostrogoths of Pannonia were supported by his powerful aid against the oppression of the neighboring Huns. The North (such are the lofty strains of the poet) was agitated or appeased by the nod of Euric; the great king of Persia consulted the oracle of the West; and the aged god of the Tyber was protected by the swelling genius of the Garonne. [6] The fortune of nations has often depended on accidents; and France may ascribe her greatness to the premature death of the Gothic king, at a time when his son Alaric was a helpless infant, and his adversary Clovis [7] an ambitious and valiant youth.

[Footnote 5: See Procopius de Bell. Gothico, l. i. c. 12, in tom. ii. p. 81. The character of Grotius inclines me to believe, that he has not substituted the Rhine for the Rhone (Hist. Gothorum, p. 175) without the authority of some Ms.]

[Footnote 6: Sidonius, l. viii. epist. 3, 9, in tom. i. p. 800. Jornandes (de Rebus Geticis, c. 47 p. 680) justifies, in some measure, this portrait of the Gothic hero.]

[Footnote 7: I use the familiar appellation of Clovis, from the Latin Chlodovechus, or Chlodovoeus. But the Ch expresses only the German aspiration, and the true name is not different from Lewis, (Mem. de 'Academie des Inscriptions, tom. xx. p. 68.)]

While Childeric, the father of Clovis, lived an exile in Germany, he was hospitably entertained by the queen, as well as by the king, of the Thuringians. After his restoration, Basina escaped from her husband's bed to the arms of her lover; freely declaring, that if she had known a man wiser, stronger, or more beautiful, than Childeric, that man should have been the object of her preference. [8] Clovis was the offspring of this voluntary union; and, when he was no more than fifteen years of age, he succeeded, by his father's death, to the command of the Salian tribe. The narrow limits of his kingdom were confined to the island of the Batavians, with the ancient dioceses of Tournay and Arras; [10] and at the baptism of Clovis the number of his warriors could not exceed five thousand. The kindred tribes of the Franks, who had seated themselves along the Belgic rivers, the Scheld, the Meuse, the Moselle, and the Rhine, were governed by their independent kings, of the Merovingian race; the equals, the allies, and sometimes the enemies of the Salic prince. But the Germans, who obeyed, in peace, the hereditary jurisdiction of their chiefs, were free to follow the standard of a popular and victorious general; and the superior merit of Clovis attracted the respect and allegiance of the national confederacy. When he first took the field, he had neither gold and silver in his coffers, nor wine and corn in his magazine; [11] but he imitated the example of Caesar, who, in the same country, had acquired wealth by the sword, and purchased soldiers with the fruits of conquest. After each successful battle or expedition, the spoils were accumulated in one common mass; every warrior received his proportionable share; and the royal prerogative submitted to the equal regulations of military law. The untamed spirit of the Barbarians was taught to acknowledge the advantages of regular discipline. [12] At the annual review of the month of March, their arms were diligently inspected; and when they traversed a peaceful territory, they were prohibited from touching a blade of grass. The justice of Clovis was inexorable; and his careless or disobedient soldiers were punished with instant death. It would be superfluous to praise the valor of a Frank; but the valor of Clovis was directed by cool and consummate prudence. [13] In all his transactions with mankind, he calculated the weight of interest, of passion, and of opinion; and his measures were sometimes adapted to the sanguinary manners of the Germans, and sometimes moderated by the milder genius of Rome, and Christianity. He was intercepted in the career of victory, since he died in the forty-fifth year of his age: but he had already accomplished, in a reign of thirty years, the establishment of the French monarchy in Gaul.

[Footnote 8: Greg. l. ii. c. 12, in tom. i. p. 168. Basina speaks the language of nature; the Franks, who had seen her in their youth, might converse with Gregory in their old age; and the bishop of Tours could not wish to defame the mother of the first Christian king.]

[Footnote 9: The Abbe Dubos (Hist. Critique de l'Etablissement de la Monarchie Francoise dans les Gaules, tom. i. p. 630-650) has the merit of defining the primitive kingdom of Clovis, and of ascertaining the genuine number of his subjects.]

[Footnote 10: Ecclesiam incultam ac negligentia civium Paganorum praetermis sam, veprium densitate oppletam, &c. Vit. St. Vedasti, in tom. iii. p. 372. This description supposes that Arras was possessed by the Pagans many years before the baptism of Clovis.]

[Footnote 11: Gregory of Tours (l v. c. i. tom. ii. p. 232) contrasts the poverty of Clovis with the wealth of his grandsons. Yet Remigius (in tom. iv. p. 52) mentions his paternas opes, as sufficient for the redemption of captives.]

[Footnote 12: See Gregory, (l. ii. c. 27, 37, in tom. ii. p. 175, 181, 182.) The famous story of the vase of Soissons explains both the power and the character of Clovis. As a point of controversy, it has been strangely tortured by Boulainvilliers Dubos, and the other political antiquarians.]

[Footnote 13: The duke of Nivernois, a noble statesman, who has managed weighty and delicate negotiations, ingeniously illustrates (Mem. de l'Acad. des Inscriptions, tom. xx. p. 147-184) the political system of Clovis.]

The first exploit of Clovis was the defeat of Syagrius, the son of Aegidius; and the public quarrel might, on this occasion, be inflamed by private resentment. The glory of the father still insulted the Merovingian race; the power of the son might excite the jealous ambition of the king of the Franks. Syagrius inherited, as a patrimonial estate, the city and diocese of Soissons: the desolate remnant of the second Belgic, Rheims and Troyes, Beauvais and Amiens, would naturally submit to the count or patrician: [14] and after the dissolution of the Western empire, he might reign with the title, or at least with the authority, of king of the Romans. [15] As a Roman, he had been educated in the liberal studies of rhetoric and jurisprudence; but he was engaged by accident and policy in the familiar use of the Germanic idiom. The independent Barbarians resorted to the tribunal of a stranger, who possessed the singular talent of explaining, in their native tongue, the dictates of reason and equity. The diligence and affability of their judge rendered him popular, the impartial wisdom of his decrees obtained their voluntary obedience, and the reign of Syagrius over the Franks and Burgundians seemed to revive the original institution of civil society. [16] In the midst of these peaceful occupations, Syagrius received, and boldly accepted, the hostile defiance of Clovis; who challenged his rival in the spirit, and almost in the language, of chivalry, to appoint the day and the field [17] of battle. In the time of Caesar Soissons would have poured forth a body of fifty thousand horse and such an army might have been plentifully supplied with shields, cuirasses, and military engines, from the three arsenals or manufactures of the city. [18] But the courage and numbers of the Gallic youth were long since exhausted; and the loose bands of volunteers, or mercenaries, who marched under the standard of Syagrius, were incapable of contending with the national valor of the Franks. It would be ungenerous without some more accurate knowledge of his strength and resources, to condemn the rapid flight of Syagrius, who escaped, after the loss of a battle, to the distant court of Thoulouse. The feeble minority of Alaric could not assist or protect an unfortunate fugitive; the pusillanimous [19] Goths were intimidated by the menaces of Clovis; and the Roman king, after a short confinement, was delivered into the hands of the executioner. The Belgic cities surrendered to the king of the Franks; and his dominions were enlarged towards the East by the ample diocese of Tongres [20] which Clovis subdued in the tenth year of his reign.

[Footnote 14: M. Biet (in a Dissertation which deserved the prize of the Academy of Soissons, p. 178-226,) has accurately defined the nature and extent of the kingdom of Syagrius and his father; but he too readily allows the slight evidence of Dubos (tom. ii. p. 54-57) to deprive him of Beauvais and Amiens.]

[Footnote 15: I may observe that Fredegarius, in his epitome of Gregory of Tours, (tom. ii. p. 398,) has prudently substituted the name of Patricius for the incredible title of Rex Romanorum.]

[Footnote 16: Sidonius, (l. v. Epist. 5, in tom. i. p. 794,) who styles him the Solon, the Amphion, of the Barbarians, addresses this imaginary king in the tone of friendship and equality. From such offices of arbitration, the crafty Dejoces had raised himself to the throne of the Medes, (Herodot. l. i. c. 96-100.)]

[Footnote 17: Campum sibi praeparari jussit. M. Biet (p. 226-251) has diligently ascertained this field of battle, at Nogent, a Benedictine abbey, about ten miles to the north of Soissons. The ground was marked by a circle of Pagan sepulchres; and Clovis bestowed the adjacent lands of Leully and Coucy on the church of Rheims.]

[Footnote 18: See Caesar. Comment. de Bell. Gallic. ii. 4, in tom. i. p. 220, and the Notitiae, tom. i. p. 126. The three Fabricae of Soissons were, Seutaria, Balistaria, and Clinabaria. The last supplied the complete armor of the heavy cuirassiers.]

[Footnote 19: The epithet must be confined to the circumstances; and history cannot justify the French prejudice of Gregory, (l. ii. c. 27, in tom. ii. p. 175,) ut Gothorum pavere mos est.]

[Footnote 20: Dubos has satisfied me (tom. i. p. 277-286) that Gregory of Tours, his transcribers, or his readers, have repeatedly confounded the German kingdom of Thuringia, beyond the Rhine, and the Gallic city of Tongria, on the Meuse, which was more anciently the country of the Eburones, and more recently the diocese of Liege.]

The name of the Alemanni has been absurdly derived from their imaginary settlement on the banks of the Leman Lake. [21] That fortunate district, from the lake to the Avenche, and Mount Jura, was occupied by the Burgundians. [22] The northern parts of Helvetia had indeed been subdued by the ferocious Alemanni, who destroyed with their own hands the fruits of their conquest. A province, improved and adorned by the arts of Rome, was again reduced to a savage wilderness; and some vestige of the stately Vindonissa may still be discovered in the fertile and populous valley of the Aar. [23] From the source of the Rhine to its conflux with the Mein and the Moselle, the formidable swarms of the Alemanni commanded either side of the river, by the right of ancient possession, or recent victory. They had spread themselves into Gaul, over the modern provinces of Alsace and Lorraine; and their bold invasion of the kingdom of Cologne summoned the Salic prince to the defence of his Ripuarian allies.

Clovis encountered the invaders of Gaul in the plain of Tolbiac, about twenty-four miles from Cologne; and the two fiercest nations of Germany were mutually animated by the memory of past exploits, and the prospect of future greatness. The Franks, after an obstinate struggle, gave way; and the Alemanni, raising a shout of victory, impetuously pressed their retreat. But the battle was restored by the valor, and the conduct, and perhaps by the piety, of Clovis; and the event of the bloody day decided forever the alternative of empire or servitude. The last king of the Alemanni was slain in the field, and his people were slaughtered or pursued, till they threw down their arms, and yielded to the mercy of the conqueror. Without discipline it was impossible for them to rally: they had contemptuously demolished the walls and fortifications which might have protected their distress; and they were followed into the heart of their forests by an enemy not less active, or intrepid, than themselves. The great Theodoric congratulated the victory of Clovis, whose sister Albofleda the king of Italy had lately married; but he mildly interceded with his brother in favor of the suppliants and fugitives, who had implored his protection. The Gallic territories, which were possessed by the Alemanni, became the prize of their conqueror; and the haughty nation, invincible, or rebellious, to the arms of Rome, acknowledged the sovereignty of the Merovingian kings, who graciously permitted them to enjoy their peculiar manners and institutions, under the government of official, and, at length, of hereditary, dukes. After the conquest of the Western provinces, the Franks alone maintained their ancient habitations beyond the Rhine. They gradually subdued, and civilized, the exhausted countries, as far as the Elbe, and the mountains of Bohemia; and the peace of Europe was secured by the obedience of Germany. [24]

[Footnote 21: Populi habitantes juxta Lemannum lacum, Alemanni dicuntur. Servius, ad Virgil. Georgic. iv. 278. Don Bouquet (tom. i. p. 817) has only alleged the more recent and corrupt text of Isidore of Seville.]

[Footnote 22: Gregory of Tours sends St. Lupicinus inter illa Jurensis deserti secreta, quae, inter Burgundiam Alamanniamque sita, Aventicae adja cent civitati, in tom. i. p. 648. M. de Watteville (Hist. de la Confederation Helvetique, tom. i. p. 9, 10) has accurately defined the Helvetian limits of the Duchy of Alemannia, and the Transjurane Burgundy. They were commensurate with the dioceses of Constance and Avenche, or Lausanne, and are still discriminated, in modern Switzerland, by the use of the German, or French, language.]

[Footnote 23: See Guilliman de Rebus Helveticis, l i. c. 3, p. 11, 12. Within the ancient walls of Vindonissa, the castle of Hapsburgh, the abbey of Konigsfield, and the town of Bruck, have successively risen. The philosophic traveller may compare the monuments of Roman conquest of feudal or Austrian tyranny, of monkish superstition, and of industrious freedom. If he be truly a philosopher, he will applaud the merit and happiness of his own times.]

[Footnote 24: Gregory of Tours, (l. ii. 30, 37, in tom. ii. p. 176, 177, 182,) the Gesta Francorum, (in tom. ii. p. 551,) and the epistle of Theodoric, (Cassiodor. Variar. l. ii. c. 41, in tom. iv. p. 4,) represent the defeat of the Alemanni. Some of their tribes settled in Rhaetia, under the protection of Theodoric; whose successors ceded the colony and their country to the grandson of Clovis. The state of the Alemanni under the Merovingian kings may be seen in Mascou (Hist. of the Ancient Germans, xi. 8, &c. Annotation xxxvi.) and Guilliman, (de Reb. Helvet. l. ii. c. 10-12, p. 72-80.)]

Till the thirtieth year of his age, Clovis continued to worship the gods of his ancestors. [25] His disbelief, or rather disregard, of Christianity, might encourage him to pillage with less remorse the churches of a hostile territory: but his subjects of Gaul enjoyed the free exercise of religious worship; and the bishops entertained a more favorable hope of the idolater, than of the heretics. The Merovingian prince had contracted a fortunate alliance with the fair Clotilda, the niece of the king of Burgundy, who, in the midst of an Arian court, was educated in the profession of the Catholic faith. It was her interest, as well as her duty, to achieve the conversion [26] of a Pagan husband; and Clovis insensibly listened to the voice of love and religion. He consented (perhaps such terms had been previously stipulated) to the baptism of his eldest son; and though the sudden death of the infant excited some superstitious fears, he was persuaded, a second time, to repeat the dangerous experiment. In the distress of the battle of Tolbiac, Clovis loudly invoked the God of Clotilda and the Christians; and victory disposed him to hear, with respectful gratitude, the eloquent [27] Remigius, [28] bishop of Rheims, who forcibly displayed the temporal and spiritual advantages of his conversion. The king declared himself satisfied of the truth of the Catholic faith; and the political reasons which might have suspended his public profession, were removed by the devout or loyal acclamations of the Franks, who showed themselves alike prepared to follow their heroic leader to the field of battle, or to the baptismal font. The important ceremony was performed in the cathedral of Rheims, with every circumstance of magnificence and solemnity that could impress an awful sense of religion on the minds of its rude proselytes. [29] The new Constantine was immediately baptized, with three thousand of his warlike subjects; and their example was imitated by the remainder of the gentle Barbarians, who, in obedience to the victorious prelate, adored the cross which they had burnt, and burnt the idols which they had formerly adored. [30] The mind of Clovis was susceptible of transient fervor: he was exasperated by the pathetic tale of the passion and death of Christ; and, instead of weighing the salutary consequences of that mysterious sacrifice, he exclaimed, with indiscreet fury, "Had I been present at the head of my valiant Franks, I would have revenged his injuries." [31] But the savage conqueror of Gaul was incapable of examining the proofs of a religion, which depends on the laborious investigation of historic evidence and speculative theology. He was still more incapable of feeling the mild influence of the gospel, which persuades and purifies the heart of a genuine convert. His ambitious reign was a perpetual violation of moral and Christian duties: his hands were stained with blood in peace as well as in war; and, as soon as Clovis had dismissed a synod of the Gallican church, he calmly assassinated all the princes of the Merovingian race. [32] Yet the king of the Franks might sincerely worship the Christian God, as a Being more excellent and powerful than his national deities; and the signal deliverance and victory of Tolbiac encouraged Clovis to confide in the future protection of the Lord of Hosts. Martin, the most popular of the saints, had filled the Western world with the fame of those miracles which were incessantly performed at his holy sepulchre of Tours. His visible or invisible aid promoted the cause of a liberal and orthodox prince; and the profane remark of Clovis himself, that St.Martin was an expensive friend, [33] need not be interpreted as the symptom of any permanent or rational scepticism. But earth, as well as heaven, rejoiced in the conversion of the Franks. On the memorable day when Clovis ascended from the baptismal font, he alone, in the Christian world, deserved the name and prerogatives of a Catholic king. The emperor Anastasius entertained some dangerous errors concerning the nature of the divine incarnation; and the Barbarians of Italy, Africa, Spain, and Gaul, were involved in the Arian heresy. The eldest, or rather the only, son of the church, was acknowledged by the clergy as their lawful sovereign, or glorious deliverer; and the armies of Clovis were strenuously supported by the zeal and fervor of the Catholic faction. [34]

[Footnote 25: Clotilda, or rather Gregory, supposes that Clovis worshipped the gods of Greece and Rome. The fact is incredible, and the mistake only shows how completely, in less than a century, the national religion of the Franks had been abolished and even forgotten]

[Footnote 26: Gregory of Tours relates the marriage and conversion of Clovis, (l. ii. c. 28-31, in tom. ii. p. 175-178.) Even Fredegarius, or the nameless Epitomizer, (in tom. ii. p. 398-400,) the author of the Gesta Francorum, (in tom. ii. p. 548-552,) and Aimoin himself, (l. i. c. 13, in tom. iii. p. 37-40,) may be heard without disdain. Tradition might long preserve some curious circumstances of these important transactions.]

[Footnote 27: A traveller, who returned from Rheims to Auvergne, had stolen a copy of his declamations from the secretary or bookseller of the modest archbishop, (Sidonius Apollinar. l. ix. epist. 7.) Four epistles of Remigius, which are still extant, (in tom. iv. p. 51, 52, 53,) do not correspond with the splendid praise of Sidonius.]

[Footnote 28: Hincmar, one of the successors of Remigius, (A.D. 845-882,) had composed his life, (in tom. iii. p. 373-380.) The authority of ancient MSS. of the church of Rheims might inspire some confidence, which is destroyed, however, by the selfish and audacious fictions of Hincmar. It is remarkable enough, that Remigius, who was consecrated at the age of twenty-two, (A.D. 457,) filled the episcopal chair seventy-four years, (Pagi Critica, in Baron tom. ii. p. 384, 572.)]

[Footnote 29: A phial (the Sainte Ampoulle of holy, or rather celestial, oil,) was brought down by a white dove, for the baptism of Clovis; and it is still used and renewed, in the coronation of the kings of France. Hincmar (he aspired to the primacy of Gaul) is the first author of this fable, (in tom. iii. p. 377,) whose slight foundations the Abbe de Vertot (Memoires de l'Academie des Inscriptions, tom. ii. p. 619-633) has undermined, with profound respect and consummate dexterity.]

[Footnote 30: Mitis depone colla, Sicamber: adora quod incendisti, incende quod adorasti. Greg. Turon. l. ii. c. 31, in tom. ii. p. 177.]

[Footnote 31: Si ego ibidem cum Francis meis fuissem, injurias ejus vindicassem. This rash expression, which Gregory has prudently concealed, is celebrated by Fredegarius, (Epitom. c. 21, in tom. ii. p. 400,) Ai moin, (l. i. c. 16, in tom. iii. p. 40,) and the Chroniques de St. Denys, (l. i. c. 20, in tom. iii. p. 171,) as an admirable effusion of Christian zeal.]

[Footnote 32: Gregory, (l. ii. c. 40-43, in tom. ii. p. 183-185,) after coolly relating the repeated crimes, and affected remorse, of Clovis, concludes, perhaps undesignedly, with a lesson, which ambition will never hear. "His ita transactis obiit."]

[Footnote 33: After the Gothic victory, Clovis made rich offerings to St. Martin of Tours. He wished to redeem his war-horse by the gift of one hundred pieces of gold, but the enchanted steed could not remove from the stable till the price of his redemption had been doubled. This miracle provoked the king to exclaim, Vere B. Martinus est bonus in auxilio, sed carus in negotio. (Gesta Francorum, in tom. ii. p. 554, 555.)]

[Footnote 34: See the epistle from Pope Anastasius to the royal convert, (in Com. iv. p. 50, 51.) Avitus, bishop of Vienna, addressed Clovis on the same subject, (p. 49;) and many of the Latin bishops would assure him of their joy and attachment.]

Under the Roman empire, the wealth and jurisdiction of the bishops, their sacred character, and perpetual office, their numerous dependants, popular eloquence, and provincial assemblies, had rendered them always respectable, and sometimes dangerous. Their influence was augmented with the progress of superstition; and the establishment of the French monarchy may, in some degree, be ascribed to the firm alliance of a hundred prelates, who reigned in the discontented, or independent, cities of Gaul. The slight foundations of the Armorican republic had been repeatedly shaken, or overthrown; but the same people still guarded their domestic freedom; asserted the dignity of the Roman name; and bravely resisted the predatory inroads, and regular attacks, of Clovis, who labored to extend his conquests from the Seine to the Loire. Their successful opposition introduced an equal and honorable union. The Franks esteemed the valor of the Armoricans [35] and the Armoricans were reconciled by the religion of the Franks. The military force which had been stationed for the defence of Gaul, consisted of one hundred different bands of cavalry or infantry; and these troops, while they assumed the title and privileges of Roman soldiers, were renewed by an incessant supply of the Barbarian youth. The extreme fortifications, and scattered fragments of the empire, were still defended by their hopeless courage. But their retreat was intercepted, and their communication was impracticable: they were abandoned by the Greek princes of Constantinople, and they piously disclaimed all connection with the Arian usurpers of Gaul. They accepted, without shame or reluctance, the generous capitulation, which was proposed by a Catholic hero; and this spurious, or legitimate, progeny of the Roman legions, was distinguished in the succeeding age by their arms, their ensigns, and their peculiar dress and institutions. But the national strength was increased by these powerful and voluntary accessions; and the neighboring kingdoms dreaded the numbers, as well as the spirit, of the Franks. The reduction of the Northern provinces of Gaul, instead of being decided by the chance of a single battle, appears to have been slowly effected by the gradual operation of war and treaty and Clovis acquired each object of his ambition, by such efforts, or such concessions, as were adequate to its real value. His savage character, and the virtues of Henry IV., suggest the most opposite ideas of human nature; yet some resemblance may be found in the situation of two princes, who conquered France by their valor, their policy, and the merits of a seasonable conversion. [36]

[Footnote 35: Instead of an unknown people, who now appear on the text of Procopious, Hadrian de Valois has restored the proper name of the easy correction has been almost universally approved. Yet an unprejudiced reader would naturally suppose, that Procopius means to describe a tribe of Germans in the alliance of Rome; and not a confederacy of Gallic cities, which had revolted from the empire. Note: Compare Hallam's Europe during the Middle Ages, vol i. p. 2, Daru, Hist. de Bretagne vol. i. p. 129—M.]

[Footnote 36: This important digression of Procopius (de Bell. Gothic. l. i. c. 12, in tom. ii. p. 29-36) illustrates the origin of the French monarchy. Yet I must observe, 1. That the Greek historian betrays an inexcusable ignorance of the geography of the West. 2. That these treaties and privileges, which should leave some lasting traces, are totally invisible in Gregory of Tours, the Salic laws, &c.]

The kingdom of the Burgundians, which was defined by the course of two Gallic rivers, the Saone and the Rhone, extended from the forest of Vosges to the Alps and the sea of Marscilles. [37] The sceptre was in the hands of Gundobald. That valiant and ambitious prince had reduced the number of royal candidates by the death of two brothers, one of whom was the father of Clotilda; [38] but his imperfect prudence still permitted Godegesil, the youngest of his brothers, to possess the dependent principality of Geneva. The Arian monarch was justly alarmed by the satisfaction, and the hopes, which seemed to animate his clergy and people after the conversion of Clovis; and Gundobald convened at Lyons an assembly of his bishops, to reconcile, if it were possible, their religious and political discontents. A vain conference was agitated between the two factions. The Arians upbraided the Catholics with the worship of three Gods: the Catholics defended their cause by theological distinctions; and the usual arguments, objections, and replies were reverberated with obstinate clamor; till the king revealed his secret apprehensions, by an abrupt but decisive question, which he addressed to the orthodox bishops. "If you truly profess the Christian religion, why do you not restrain the king of the Franks? He has declared war against me, and forms alliances with my enemies for my destruction. A sanguinary and covetous mind is not the symptom of a sincere conversion: let him show his faith by his works." The answer of Avitus, bishop of Vienna, who spoke in the name of his brethren, was delivered with the voice and countenance of an angel. "We are ignorant of the motives and intentions of the king of the Franks: but we are taught by Scripture, that the kingdoms which abandon the divine law are frequently subverted; and that enemies will arise on every side against those who have made God their enemy. Return, with thy people, to the law of God, and he will give peace and security to thy dominions." The king of Burgundy, who was not prepared to accept the condition which the Catholics considered as essential to the treaty, delayed and dismissed the ecclesiastical conference; after reproaching his bishops, that Clovis, their friend and proselyte, had privately tempted the allegiance of his brother. [39]

[Footnote 37: Regnum circa Rhodanum aut Ararim cum provincia Massiliensi retinebant. Greg. Turon. l. ii. c. 32, in tom. ii. p. 178. The province of Marseilles, as far as the Durance, was afterwards ceded to the Ostrogoths; and the signatures of twenty-five bishops are supposed to represent the kingdom of Burgundy, A.D. 519. (Concil. Epaon, in tom. iv. p. 104, 105.) Yet I would except Vindonissa. The bishop, who lived under the Pagan Alemanni, would naturally resort to the synods of the next Christian kingdom. Mascou (in his four first annotations) has explained many circumstances relative to the Burgundian monarchy.]

[Footnote 38: Mascou, (Hist. of the Germans, xi. 10,) who very reasonably distracts the testimony of Gregory of Tours, has produced a passage from Avitus (epist. v.) to prove that Gundobald affected to deplore the tragic event, which his subjects affected to applaud.]

[Footnote 39: See the original conference, (in tom. iv. p. 99-102.) Avitus, the principal actor, and probably the secretary of the meeting, was bishop of Vienna. A short account of his person and works may be fouud in Dupin, (Bibliotheque Ecclesiastique, tom. v. p. 5-10.)]

PART II

The allegiance of his brother was already seduced; and the obedience of Godegesil, who joined the royal standard with the troops of Geneva, more effectually promoted the success of the conspiracy. While the Franks and Burgundians contended with equal valor, his seasonable desertion decided the event of the battle; and as Gundobald was faintly supported by the disaffected Gauls, he yielded to the arms of Clovis, and hastily retreated from the field, which appears to have been situate between Langres and Dijon. He distrusted the strength of Dijon, a quadrangular fortress, encompassed by two rivers, and by a wall thirty feet high, and fifteen thick, with four gates, and thirty-three towers: [40] he abandoned to the pursuit of Clovis the important cities of Lyons and Vienna; and Gundobald still fled with precipitation, till he had reached Avignon, at the distance of two hundred and fifty miles from the field of battle.

A long siege and an artful negotiation, admonished the king of the Franks of the danger and difficulty of his enterprise. He imposed a tribute on the Burgundian prince, compelled him to pardon and reward his brother's treachery, and proudly returned to his own dominions, with the spoils and captives of the southern provinces. This splendid triumph was soon clouded by the intelligence, that Gundobald had violated his recent obligations, and that the unfortunate Godegesil, who was left at Vienna with a garrison of five thousand Franks, [41] had been besieged, surprised, and massacred by his inhuman brother. Such an outrage might have exasperated the patience of the most peaceful sovereign; yet the conqueror of Gaul dissembled the injury, released the tribute, and accepted the alliance, and military service, of the king of Burgundy. Clovis no longer possessed those advantages which had assured the success of the preceding war; and his rival, instructed by adversity, had found new resources in the affections of his people. The Gauls or Romans applauded the mild and impartial laws of Gundobald, which almost raised them to the same level with their conquerors. The bishops were reconciled, and flattered, by the hopes, which he artfully suggested, of his approaching conversion; and though he eluded their accomplishment to the last moment of his life, his moderation secured the peace, and suspended the ruin, of the kingdom of Burgundy. [42]

[Footnote 40: Gregory of Tours (l. iii. c. 19, in tom. ii. p. 197) indulges his genius, or rather describes some more eloquent writer, in the description of Dijon; a castle, which already deserved the title of a city. It depended on the bishops of Langres till the twelfth century, and afterwards became the capital of the dukes of Burgundy Longuerue Description de la France, part i. p. 280.]

[Footnote 41: The Epitomizer of Gregory of Tours (in tom. ii. p. 401) has supplied this number of Franks; but he rashly supposes that they were cut in pieces by Gundobald. The prudent Burgundian spared the soldiers of Clovis, and sent these captives to the king of the Visigoths, who settled them in the territory of Thoulouse.]

[Footnote 42: In this Burgundian war I have followed Gregory of Tours, (l. ii. c. 32, 33, in tom. ii. p. 178, 179,) whose narrative appears so incompatible with that of Procopius, (de Bell. Goth. l. i. c. 12, in tom. ii. p. 31, 32,) that some critics have supposed two different wars. The Abbe Dubos (Hist. Critique, &c., tom. ii. p. 126-162) has distinctly represented the causes and the events.]

I am impatient to pursue the final ruin of that kingdom, which was accomplished under the reign of Sigismond, the son of Gundobald. The Catholic Sigismond has acquired the honors of a saint and martyr; [43] but the hands of the royal saint were stained with the blood of his innocent son, whom he inhumanly sacrificed to the pride and resentment of a step-mother. He soon discovered his error, and bewailed the irreparable loss. While Sigismond embraced the corpse of the unfortunate youth, he received a severe admonition from one of his attendants: "It is not his situation, O king! it is thine which deserves pity and lamentation." The reproaches of a guilty conscience were alleviated, however, by his liberal donations to the monastery of Agaunum, or St. Maurice, in Vallais; which he himself had founded in honor of the imaginary martyrs of the Thebaean legion. [44] A full chorus of perpetual psalmody was instituted by the pious king; he assiduously practised the austere devotion of the monks; and it was his humble prayer, that Heaven would inflict in this world the punishment of his sins. His prayer was heard: the avengers were at hand: and the provinces of Burgundy were overwhelmed by an army of victorious Franks. After the event of an unsuccessful battle, Sigismond, who wished to protract his life that he might prolong his penance, concealed himself in the desert in a religious habit, till he was discovered and betrayed by his subjects, who solicited the favor of their new masters. The captive monarch, with his wife and two children, was transported to Orleans, and buried alive in a deep well, by the stern command of the sons of Clovis; whose cruelty might derive some excuse from the maxims and examples of their barbarous age. Their ambition, which urged them to achieve the conquest of Burgundy, was inflamed, or disguised, by filial piety: and Clotilda, whose sanctity did not consist in the forgiveness of injuries, pressed them to revenge her father's death on the family of his assassin. The rebellious Burgundians (for they attempted to break their chains) were still permitted to enjoy their national laws under the obligation of tribute and military service; and the Merovingian princes peaceably reigned over a kingdom, whose glory and greatness had been first overthrown by the arms of Clovis. [45]

[Footnote 43: See his life or legend, (in tom. iii. p. 402.) A martyr! how strangely has that word been distorted from its original sense of a common witness. St. Sigismond was remarkable for the cure of fevers]

[Footnote 44: Before the end of the fifth century, the church of St. Maurice, and his Thebaean legion, had rendered Agaunum a place of devout pilgrimage. A promiscuous community of both sexes had introduced some deeds of darkness, which were abolished (A.D. 515) by the regular monastery of Sigismond. Within fifty years, his angels of light made a nocturnal sally to murder their bishop, and his *clergy. See in the Bibliotheque Raisonnee (tom. xxxvi. p. 435-438) the curious remarks of a learned librarian of Geneva.]*

[Footnote 45: Marius, bishop of Avenche, (Chron. in tom. ii. p. 15,) has marked the authentic dates, and Gregory of Tours (l. iii. c. 5, 6, in tom. ii. p. 188, 189) has expressed the principal facts, of the life of Sigismond, and the conquest of Burgundy. Procopius (in tom. ii. p. 34) and Agathias (in tom. ii. p. 49) show their remote and imperfect knowledge.]

The first victory of Clovis had insulted the honor of the Goths. They viewed his rapid progress with jealousy and terror; and the youthful fame of Alaric was oppressed by the more potent genius of his rival. Some disputes inevitably arose on the edge of their contiguous dominions; and after the delays of fruitless negotiation, a personal interview of the two kings was proposed and accepted. The conference of Clovis and Alaric was held in a small island of the Loire, near Amboise. They embraced, familiarly conversed, and feasted together; and separated with the warmest professions of peace and brotherly love. But their apparent confidence concealed a dark suspicion of hostile and treacherous designs; and their mutual complaints solicited, eluded, and disclaimed, a final arbitration. At Paris, which he already considered as his royal seat, Clovis declared to an assembly of the princes and warriors, the pretence, and the motive, of a Gothic war. "It grieves me to see that the Arians still possess the fairest portion of Gaul. Let us march against them with the aid of God; and, having vanquished the heretics, we will possess and divide their fertile provinces." [46] The Franks, who were inspired by hereditary valor and recent zeal, applauded the generous design of their monarch; expressed their resolution to conquer or die, since death and conquest would be equally profitable; and solemnly protested that they would never shave their beards till victory should absolve them from that inconvenient vow. The enterprise was promoted by the public or private exhortations of Clotilda. She reminded her husband how effectually some pious foundation would propitiate the Deity, and his servants: and the Christian hero, darting his battle-axe with a skilful and nervous band, "There, (said he,) on that spot where my Francisca, [47] shall fall, will I erect a church in honor of the holy apostles." This ostentatious piety confirmed and justified the attachment of the Catholics, with whom he secretly corresponded; and their devout wishes were gradually ripened into a formidable conspiracy. The people of Aquitain were alarmed by the indiscreet reproaches of their Gothic tyrants, who justly accused them of preferring the dominion of the Franks: and their zealous adherent Quintianus, bishop of Rodez, [48] preached more forcibly in his exile than in his diocese. To resist these foreign and domestic enemies, who were fortified by the alliance of the Burgundians, Alaric collected his troops, far more numerous than the military powers of Clovis. The Visigoths resumed the exercise of arms, which they had neglected in a long and luxurious peace; [49] a select band of valiant and robust slaves attended their masters to the field; [50] and the cities of Gaul were compelled to furnish their doubtful and reluctant aid. Theodoric, king of the Ostrogoths, who reigned in Italy, had labored to maintain the tranquillity of Gaul; and he assumed, or affected, for that purpose, the impartial character of a mediator. But the sagacious monarch dreaded the rising empire of Clovis, and he was firmly engaged to support the national and religious cause of the Goths.

[Footnote 46: Gregory of Tours (l. ii. c. 37, in tom. ii. p. 181) inserts the short but persuasive speech of Clovis. Valde moleste fero, quod hi Ariani partem teneant Galliarum, (the author of the Gesta Francorum, in tom. ii. p. 553, adds the precious epithet of optimam,) camus cum Dei adjutorio, et, superatis eis, redigamus terram in ditionem nostram.]

[Footnote 47: Tunc rex projecit a se in directum Bipennem suam quod est Francisca, &c. (Gesta Franc. in tom. ii. p. 554.) The form and use of this weapon are clearly described by Procopius, (in tom. ii. p. 37.)

Examples of its national appellation in Latin and French may be found in the Glossary of Ducange, and the large Dictionnaire de Trevoux.]

[Footnote 48: It is singular enough that some important and authentic facts should be found in a Life of Quintianus, composed in rhyme in the old Patois of Rouergue, (Dubos, Hist. Critique, &c., tom. ii. p. 179.)]

[Footnote 49: Quamvis fortitudini vestrae confidentiam tribuat parentum ves trorum innumerabilis multitudo; quamvis Attilam potentem reminiscamini Visigotharum viribus inclinatum; tamen quia populorum ferocia corda longa pace mollescunt, cavete subito in alean aleam mittere, quos constat tantis temporibus exercitia non habere. Such was the salutary, but fruitless, advice of peace of reason, and of Theodoric, (Cassiodor. l. iii. ep. 2.)]

[Footnote 50: Montesquieu (Esprit des Loix, l. xv. c. 14) mentions and approves the law of the Visigoths, (l. ix. tit. 2, in tom. iv. p. 425,) which obliged all masters to arm, and send, or lead, into the field a tenth of their slaves.]

The accidental, or artificial, prodigies which adorned the expedition of Clovis, were accepted by a superstitious age, as the manifest declaration of the divine favor. He marched from Paris; and as he proceeded with decent reverence through the holy diocese of Tours, his anxiety tempted him to consult the shrine of St. Martin, the sanctuary and the oracle of Gaul. His messengers were instructed to remark the words of the Psalm which should happen to be chanted at the precise moment when they entered the church. Those words most fortunately expressed the valor and victory of the champions of Heaven, and the application was easily transferred to the new Joshua, the new Gideon, who went forth to battle against the enemies of the Lord. [51] Orleans secured to the Franks a bridge on the Loire; but, at the distance of forty miles from Poitiers, their progress was intercepted by an extraordinary swell of the River Vigenna or Vienne; and the opposite banks were covered by the encampment of the Visigoths. Delay must be always dangerous to Barbarians, who consume the country through which they march; and had Clovis possessed leisure and materials, it might have been impracticable to construct a bridge, or to force a passage, in the face of a superior enemy. But the affectionate peasants who were impatient to welcome their deliverer, could easily betray some unknown or unguarded ford: the merit of the discovery was enhanced by the useful interposition of fraud or fiction; and a white hart, of singular size and beauty, appeared to guide and animate the march of the Catholic army. The counsels of the Visigoths were irresolute and distracted. A crowd of impatient warriors, presumptuous in their strength, and disdaining to fly before the robbers of Germany, excited Alaric to assert in arms the name and blood of the conquerors of Rome. The advice of the graver chieftains pressed him to elude the first ardor of the Franks; and to expect, in the southern provinces of Gaul, the veteran and victorious Ostrogoths, whom the king of Italy had already sent to his assistance. The decisive moments were wasted in idle deliberation the Goths too hastily abandoned, perhaps, an advantageous post; and the opportunity of a secure retreat was lost by their slow and disorderly motions. After Clovis had passed the ford, as it is still named, of the Hart, he advanced with bold and hasty steps to prevent the escape of the enemy. His nocturnal march was directed by a flaming meteor, suspended in the air above the cathedral of Poitiers; and this signal, which might be previously concerted with the orthodox successor of St. Hilary, was compared to the column of fire that guided the Israelites in the desert. At the third hour of the day, about ten miles beyond Poitiers, Clovis overtook, and instantly attacked, the Gothic army; whose defeat was already prepared by terror and confusion. Yet they rallied in their extreme distress, and the martial youths, who had clamorously demanded the battle, refused to survive the ignominy of flight. The two kings encountered each other in single combat. Alaric fell by the hand of his rival; and the victorious Frank was saved by the goodness of his cuirass, and the vigor of his horse, from the spears of two desperate Goths, who furiously rode against him to revenge the death of their sovereign. The vague expression of a mountain of the slain, serves to indicate a cruel though indefinite slaughter; but Gregory has carefully observed, that his valiant countryman Apollinaris, the son of Sidonius, lost his life at the head of the nobles of Auvergne. Perhaps these suspected Catholics had been maliciously exposed to the blind assault of the enemy; and perhaps the influence of religion was superseded by personal attachment or military honor. [52]

[Footnote 51: This mode of divination, by accepting as an omen the first sacred words, which in particular circumstances should be presented to the eye or ear, was derived from the Pagans; and the Psalter, or Bible, was substituted to the poems of Homer and Virgil. From the fourth to the fourteenth century, these sortes sanctorum, as they are styled, were repeatedly condemned by the decrees of councils, and repeatedly practised by kings, bishops, and saints. See a curious dissertation of the Abbe du Resnel, in the Memoires de l'Academie, tom. xix. p. 287-310]

[Footnote 52: After correcting the text, or excusing the mistake, of Procopius, who places the defeat of Alaric near Carcassone, we may conclude, from the evidence of Gregory, Fortunatus, and the author of the Gesta Francorum, that the battle was fought in campo Vocladensi, on the banks of the Clain, about ten miles to the south of Poitiers. Clovis overtook and attacked the Visigoths near Vivonne, and the victory was decided near a village still named Champagne St. Hilaire. See the Dissertations of the Abbe le Boeuf, tom. i. p. 304-331.]

Such is the empire of Fortune, (if we may still disguise our ignorance under that popular name,) that it is almost equally difficult to foresee the events of war, or to explain their various consequences. A bloody and complete victory has sometimes yielded no more than the possession of the field and the loss of ten thousand men has sometimes been sufficient to destroy, in a single day, the work of ages. The decisive battle of Poitiers was followed by the conquest of Aquitain. Alaric had left behind him an infant son, a bastard competitor, factious nobles, and a disloyal people; and the remaining forces of the Goths were oppressed by the general consternation, or opposed to each other in civil discord. The victorious king of the Franks proceeded without delay to the siege of Angouleme. At the sound of his trumpets the walls of the city imitated the example of Jericho, and instantly fell to the ground; a splendid miracle, which may be reduced to the supposition, that some clerical engineers had secretly undermined the foundations of the rampart. [53] At Bordeaux, which had submitted without resistance, Clovis established his winter quarters; and his prudent economy transported from Thoulouse the royal treasures, which were deposited in the capital of the monarchy. The conqueror penetrated as far as the confines of Spain; [54] restored the honors of the Catholic church; fixed in Aquitain a colony of Franks; [55] and delegated to his lieutenants the easy task of subduing, or extirpating, the nation of the Visigoths. But the Visigoths were protected by the wise and powerful monarch of Italy. While the balance was still equal, Theodoric had perhaps delayed the march of the Ostrogoths; but their strenuous efforts successfully resisted the ambition of Clovis; and the army of the Franks, and their Burgundian allies, was compelled to raise the siege of Arles, with the loss, as it is said, of thirty thousand men. These vicissitudes inclined the fierce spirit of Clovis to acquiesce in an advantageous treaty of peace. The Visigoths were suffered to retain the possession of Septimania, a narrow tract of sea-coast, from the Rhone to the Pyrenees; but the ample province of Aquitain, from those mountains to the Loire, was indissolubly united to the kingdom of France. [56]

[Footnote 53: Angouleme is in the road from Poitiers to Bordeaux; and although Gregory delays the siege, I can more readily believe that he confounded the order of history, than that Clovis neglected the rules of war.]

[Footnote 54: Pyrenaeos montes usque Perpinianum subjecit, is the expression of Rorico, which betrays his recent date; since Perpignan did not exist before the tenth century, (Marca Hispanica, p. 458.) This florid and fabulous writer (perhaps a monk of Amiens—see the Abbe le Boeuf, Mem. de l'Academie, tom. xvii. p. 228-245) relates, in the allegorical character of a shepherd, the general history of his countrymen the Franks; but his narrative ends with the death of Clovis.]

[Footnote 55: The author of the Gesta Francorum positively affirms, that Clovis fixed a body of Franks in the Saintonge and Bourdelois: and he is not injudiciously followed by Rorico, electos milites, atque fortissimos, cum parvulis, atque mulieribus. Yet it should seem that they soon mingled with the Romans of Aquitain, till Charlemagne introduced a more numerous and powerful colony, (Dubos, Hist. Critique, tom. ii. p. 215.)]

[Footnote 56: In the composition of the Gothic war, I have used the following materials, with due regard to their unequal value. Four epistles from Theodoric, king of Italy, (Cassiodor I. iii. epist. 1-4. in tom. iv p. 3-5;) Procopius, (de Bell. Goth. l. i. c 12, in tom. ii. p. 32, 33;) Gregory of Tours, (l. ii. c. 35, 36, 37, in tom. ii. p. 181-183;) Jornandes, (de Reb. Geticis, c. 58, in tom. ii. p. 28;) Fortunatas, (in Vit. St. Hilarii, in tom. iii. p. 380;) Isidore, (in Chron. Goth. in tom. ii. p. 702;) the Epitome of Gregory of Tours, (in tom. ii. p. 401;) the author of the Gesta Francorum, (in tom. ii. p. 553-555;) the Fragments of Fredegarius, (in tom. ii. p. 463;) Aimoin, (l. i. c. 20, in tom. iii. p. 41, 42,) and Rorico, (l. iv. in tom. iii. p. 14-19.)]

After the success of the Gothic war, Clovis accepted the honors of the Roman consulship. The emperor Anastasius ambitiously bestowed on the most powerful rival of Theodoric the title and ensigns of that eminent dignity; yet, from some unknown cause, the name of Clovis has not been inscribed in the Fasti either of the East or West. [57] On the solemn day, the monarch of Gaul, placing a diadem on his head, was invested, in the church of St. Martin, with a purple tunic and mantle. From thence he proceeded on horseback to the cathedral of Tours; and, as he passed through the streets, profusely scattered, with his own hand, a donative of gold and silver to the joyful multitude, who incessantly repeated their acclamations of Consul and Augustus. The actual or legal authority of Clovis could not receive any new accessions from the consular dignity. It was a name, a shadow, an empty pageant; and if the conqueror had been instructed to claim the ancient prerogatives of that high office, they must have expired with the period of its annual duration. But the Romans were disposed to revere, in the person of their master, that antique title which the emperors condescended to assume: the Barbarian himself seemed to contract a sacred obligation to respect the majesty of the republic; and the successors of Theodosius, by soliciting his friendship, tacitly forgave, and almost ratified, the usurpation of Gaul.

[Footnote 57: The Fasti of Italy would naturally reject a consul, the enemy of their sovereign; but any ingenious hypothesis that might explain the silence of Constantinople and Egypt, (the Chronicle of Marcellinus, and the Paschal,) is overturned by the similar silence of Marius, bishop of Avenche, who composed his Fasti in the kingdom of Burgundy. If the evidence of Gregory of Tours were less weighty and positive, (l. ii. c. 38, in tom. ii. p. 183,) I could believe that Clovis, like Odoacer, received the lasting title and honors of Patrician, (Pagi Critica, tom. ii. p. 474, 492.)]

Twenty-five years after the death of Clovis this important concession was more formally declared, in a treaty between his sons and the emperor Justinian. The Ostrogoths of Italy, unable to defend their distant acquisitions, had resigned to the Franks the cities of Arles and Marseilles; of Arles, still adorned with the seat of a Praetorian praefect, and of Marseilles, enriched by the advantages of trade and navigation. [58] This transaction was confirmed by the Imperial authority; and Justinian, generously yielding to the Franks the sovereignty of the countries beyond the Alps, which they already possessed, absolved the provincials from their allegiance; and established on a more lawful, though not more solid, foundation, the throne of the Merovingians. [59] From that era they enjoyed the right of celebrating at Arles the games of the circus; and by a singular privilege, which was denied even to the Persian monarch, the gold coin, impressed with their name and image, obtained a legal currency in the empire. [60] A Greek historian of that age has praised the private and public virtues of the Franks, with a partial enthusiasm, which cannot be sufficiently justified by their domestic annals. [61] He celebrates their politeness and urbanity, their regular government, and orthodox religion; and boldly asserts, that these Barbarians could be distinguished only by their dress and language from the subjects of Rome. Perhaps the Franks already displayed the social disposition, and lively graces, which, in every age, have disguised their vices, and sometimes concealed their intrinsic merit. Perhaps Agathias, and the Greeks, were dazzled by the rapid progress of their arms, and the splendor of their empire. Since the conquest of Burgundy, Gaul, except the Gothic province of Septimania, was subject, in its whole extent, to the sons of Clovis. They had extinguished the German kingdom of Thuringia, and their vague dominion penetrated beyond the Rhine, into the heart of their native forests. The Alemanni, and Bavarians, who had occupied the Roman provinces of Rhaetia and Noricum, to the south of the Danube, confessed themselves the humble vassals of the Franks; and the feeble barrier of the Alps was incapable of resisting their ambition. When the last survivor of the sons of Clovis united the inheritance and conquests of the Merovingians, his kingdom extended far beyond the limits of modern France. Yet modern France, such has been the progress of arts and policy, far surpasses, in wealth, populousness, and power, the spacious but savage realms of Clotaire or Dagobert. [62]

[Footnote 58: Under the Merovingian kings, Marseilles still imported from the East paper, wine, oil, linen, silk, precious stones, spices, &c. The Gauls, or Franks, traded to Syria, and the Syrians were established in Gaul. See M. de Guignes, Mem. de l'Academie, tom. xxxvii. p. 471-475.]

[Footnote 59: This strong declaration of Procopius (de Bell. Gothic. l. iii. cap. 33, in tom. ii. p. 41) would almost suffice to justify the Abbe Dubos.]

[Footnote 60: The Franks, who probably used the mints of Treves, Lyons, and Arles, imitated the coinage of the Roman emperors of seventy-two solidi, or pieces, to the pound of gold. But as the Franks established only a decuple proportion of gold and silver, ten shillings will be a sufficient valuation of their solidus of gold. It was the common standard of the Barbaric fines, and contained forty denarii, or silver three pences. Twelve of these denarii made a solidus, or shilling, the twentieth part of the ponderal and numeral livre, or pound of silver, which has been so strangely reduced in modern France. See La Blanc, Traite Historique des Monnoyes de France, p. 36-43, &c.]

[Footnote 61: Agathias, in tom. ii. p. 47. Gregory of Tours exhibits a very different picture. Perhaps it would not be easy, within the same historical space, to find more vice and less virtue. We are continually shocked by the union of savage and corrupt manners.]

[Footnote 62: M. de Foncemagne has traced, in a correct and elegant dissertation, (Mem. de l'Academie, tom. viii. p. 505-528,) the extent and limits of the French monarchy.]

The Franks, or French, are the only people of Europe who can deduce a perpetual succession from the conquerors of the Western empire. But their conquest of Gaul was followed by ten centuries of anarchy and ignorance. On the revival of learning, the students, who had been formed in the schools of Athens and Rome, disdained their Barbarian ancestors; and a long period elapsed before patient labor could provide the requisite materials to satisfy, or rather to excite, the curiosity of more enlightened times. [63] At length the eye of criticism and philosophy was directed to the antiquities of France; but even philosophers have been tainted by the contagion of prejudice and passion. The most extreme and exclusive systems, of the personal servitude of the Gauls, or of their voluntary and equal alliance with the Franks, have been rashly conceived, and obstinately defended; and the intemperate disputants have accused each other of conspiring against the prerogative of the crown, the dignity of the nobles, or the freedom of the people. Yet the sharp conflict has usefully exercised the adverse powers of learning and genius; and each antagonist, alternately vanquished and victorious has extirpated some ancient errors, and established some interesting truths. An impartial stranger, instructed by their discoveries, their disputes, and even their faults, may describe, from the same original materials, the state of the Roman provincials, after Gaul had submitted to the arms and laws of the Merovingian kings. [64]

[Footnote 63: The Abbe Dubos (Histoire Critique, tom. i. p. 29-36) has truly and agreeably represented the slow progress of these studies; and he observes, that Gregory of Tours was only once printed before the year 1560. According to the complaint of Heineccius, (Opera, tom. iii. Sylloge, iii. p. 248, &c.,) Germany received with indifference and contempt the codes of Barbaric laws, which were published by Heroldus, Lindenbrogius, &c. At present those laws, (as far as they relate to Gaul,) the history of Gregory of Tours, and all the monuments of the Merovingian race, appear in a pure and perfect state, in the first four volumes of the Historians of France.]

[Footnote 64: In the space of [about] thirty years (1728-1765) this interesting subject has been agitated by the free spirit of the count de Boulainvilliers, (Memoires Historiques sur l'Etat de la France, particularly tom. i. p. 15-49;) the learned ingenuity of the Abbe Dubos, (Histoire Critique de l'Etablissement de la Monarchie Francoise dans les Gaules, 2 vols. in 4to;) the comprehensive genius of the president de Montesquieu, (Esprit des Loix, particularly l. xxviii. xxx. xxxi.;) and the good sense and diligence of the Abbe de Mably, (Observations sur l'Histoire de France, 2 vols. 12mo.)]

The rudest, or the most servile, condition of human society, is regulated, however, by some fixed and general rules. When Tacitus surveyed the primitive simplicity of the Germans, he discovered some permanent maxims, or customs, of public and private life, which were preserved by faithful tradition till the introduction of the art of writing, and of the Latin tongue. [65] Before the election of the Merovingian kings, the most powerful tribe, or nation, of the Franks, appointed four venerable chieftains to compose the Salic laws; [66] and their labors were examined and approved in three successive assemblies of the people. After the baptism of Clovis, he reformed several articles that appeared incompatible with Christianity: the Salic law was again amended by his sons; and at length, under the reign of Dagobert, the code was revised and promulgated in its actual form, one hundred years after the establishment of the French monarchy. Within the same period, the customs of the Ripuarians were transcribed and published; and Charlemagne himself, the legislator of his age and country, had accurately studied the two national laws, which still prevailed among the Franks. [67] The same care was extended to their vassals; and the rude institutions of the Alemanni and Bavarians were diligently compiled and ratified by the supreme authority of the Merovingian kings. The Visigoths and Burgundians, whose conquests in Gaul preceded those of the Franks, showed less impatience to attain one of the principal benefits of civilized society. Euric was the first of the Gothic princes who expressed, in writing, the manners and customs of his people; and the composition of the Burgundian laws was a measure of policy rather than of justice; to alleviate the yoke, and regain the affections, of their Gallic subjects. [68] Thus, by a singular coincidence, the Germans framed their artless institutions, at a time when the elaborate system of Roman jurisprudence was finally consummated. In the Salic laws, and the Pandects of Justinian, we may compare the first rudiments, and the full maturity, of civil wisdom; and whatever prejudices may be suggested in favor of Barbarism, our calmer reflections will ascribe to the Romans the superior advantages, not only of science and reason, but of humanity and justice. Yet the laws [68/1] of the Barbarians were adapted to their wants and desires, their occupations and their capacity; and they all contributed to preserve the peace, and promote the improvement, of the society for whose use they were originally established. The Merovingians, instead of imposing a uniform rule of conduct on their various subjects, permitted each people, and each family, of their empire, freely to enjoy their domestic institutions; [69] nor were the Romans excluded from the common benefits of this legal toleration. [70] The children embraced the law of their parents, the wife that of her husband, the freedman that of his patron; and in all causes where the parties were of different nations, the plaintiff or accuser was obliged to follow the tribunal of the defendant, who may always plead a judicial presumption of right, or innocence. A more ample latitude was allowed, if every citizen, in the presence of the judge, might declare the law under which he desired to live, and the national society to which he chose to belong. Such an indulgence would abolish the partial distinctions of victory: and the Roman provincials might patiently acquiesce in the hardships of their condition; since it depended on themselves to assume the privilege, if they dared to assert the character, of free and warlike Barbarians. [71]

[Footnote 65: I have derived much instruction from two learned works of Heineccius, the History, and the Elements, of the Germanic law. In a judicious preface to the Elements, he considers, and tries to excuse the defects of that barbarous jurisprudence.]

[Footnote 66: Latin appears to have been the original language of the Salic law. It was probably composed in the beginning of the fifth century, before the era (A.D. 421) of the real or fabulous Pharamond. The preface mentions the four cantons which produced the four legislators; and many provinces, Franconia, Saxony, Hanover, Brabant, &c., have claimed them as their own. See an excellent Dissertation of Heinecties de Lege Salica, tom. iii. Sylloge iii. p. 247-267. Note: The relative antiquity of the two copies of the Salic law has been contested with great learning and ingenuity. The work of M. Wiarda, History and Explanation of the Salic Law, Bremen, 1808, asserts that what is called the Lex Antiqua, or Vetustior in which many German words are mingled with the Latin, has no claim to superior antiquity, and may be suspected to be more modern. M. Wiarda has been opposed by M. Fuer bach, who maintains the higher age of the "ancient" Code, which has been greatly corrupted by the transcribers. See Guizot, Cours de l'Histoire Moderne, vol. i. sect. 9: and the preface to the useful republication of five of the different texts of the Salic law, with that of the Ripuarian in parallel columns. By E. A. I. Laspeyres, Halle, 1833—M.]

[Footnote 67: Eginhard, in Vit. Caroli Magni, c. 29, in tom. v. p. 100. By these two laws, most critics understand the Salic and the Ripuarian. The former extended from the Carbonarian forest to the Loire, (tom. iv. p. 151,) and the latter might be obeyed from the same forest to the Rhine, (tom. iv. p. 222.)]

[Footnote 68: Consult the ancient and modern prefaces of the several codes, in the fourth volume of the Historians of France. The original prologue to the Salic law expresses (though in a foreign dialect) the genuine spirit of the Franks more forcibly than the ten books of Gregory of Tours.]

[Footnote 69: The Ripuarian law declares, and defines, this indulgence in favor of the plaintiff, (tit. xxxi. in tom. iv. p. 240;) and the same toleration is understood, or expressed, in all the codes, except that of the Visigoths of Spain. Tanta diversitas legum (says Agobard in the ninth century) quanta non solum in regionibus, aut civitatibus, sed etiam in multis domibus habetur. Nam plerumque contingit ut simul eant aut sedeant quinque homines, et nullus eorum communem legem cum altero habeat, (in tom. vi. p. 356.)

He foolishly proposes to introduce a uniformity of law, as well as of faith. Note: It is the object of the important work of M. Savigny, Geschichte des Romisches Rechts in Mittelalter, to show the perpetuity of the Roman law from the 5th to the 12th century—M.]

[Footnote 68/1: The most complete collection of these codes is in the "Barbarorum leges antiquae," by P. Canciani, 5 vols. folio, Venice, 1781-9—M.]

[Footnote 70: Inter Romanos negotia causarum Romanis legibus praecipimus terminari. Such are the words of a general constitution promulgated by Clotaire, the son of Clovis, the sole monarch of the Franks (in tom. iv. p. 116) about the year 560.]

[Footnote 71: This liberty of choice has been aptly deduced (Esprit des Loix, l. xxviii. 2) from the constitution of Lothaire I. (Leg. Langobard. l. ii. tit. lvii. in Codex Lindenbrog. p. 664;) though the example is too recent and partial. From a various reading in the Salic law, (tit. xliv. not. xlv.) the Abbe de Mably (tom. i. p. 290-293) has conjectured, that, at first, a Barbarian only, and afterwards any man, (consequently a Roman,) might live according to the law of the Franks. I am sorry to offend this ingenious conjecture by observing, that the stricter sense (Barbarum) is expressed in the reformed copy of Charlemagne; which is confirmed by the Royal and Wolfenbuttle MSS. The looser interpretation (hominem) is authorized only by the MS. of Fulda, from from whence Heroldus published his edition. See the four original texts of the Salic law in tom. iv. p. 147, 173, 196, 220. Note: Gibbon appears to have doubted the evidence on which this "liberty of choice" rested. His doubts have been confirmed by the researches of M. Savigny, who has not only confuted but traced with convincing sagacity the origin and progress of this error. As a general principle, though liable to some exceptions, each lived according to his native law. Romische Recht. vol. i. p. 123-138—M. Note: This constitution of Lothaire at first related only to the duchy of Rome; it afterwards found its way into the Lombard code. Savigny. p. 138—M.]

PART III

When justice inexorably requires the death of a murderer, each private citizen is fortified by the assurance, that the laws, the magistrate, and the whole community, are the guardians of his personal safety. But in the loose society of the Germans, revenge was always honorable, and often meritorious: the independent warrior chastised, or vindicated, with his own hand, the injuries which he had offered or received; and he had only to dread the resentment of the sons and kinsmen of the enemy, whom he had sacrificed to his selfish or angry passions. The magistrate, conscious of his weakness, interposed, not to punish, but to reconcile; and he was satisfied if he could persuade or compel the contending parties to pay and to accept the moderate fine which had been ascertained as the price of blood. [72] The fierce spirit of the Franks would have opposed a more rigorous sentence; the same fierceness despised these ineffectual restraints; and, when their simple manners had been corrupted by the wealth of Gaul, the public peace was continually violated by acts of hasty or deliberate guilt. In every just government the same penalty is inflicted, or at least is imposed, for the murder of a peasant or a prince. But the national inequality established by the Franks, in their criminal proceedings, was the last insult and abuse of conquest. [73] In the calm moments of legislation, they solemnly pronounced, that the life of a Roman was of smaller value than that of a Barbarian. The Antrustion, [74] a name expressive of the most illustrious birth or dignity among the Franks, was appreciated at the sum of six hundred pieces of gold; while the noble provincial, who was admitted to the king's table, might be legally murdered at the expense of three hundred pieces.

Two hundred were deemed sufficient for a Frank of ordinary condition; but the meaner Romans were exposed to disgrace and danger by a trifling compensation of one hundred, or even fifty, pieces of gold. Had these laws been regulated by any principle of equity or reason, the public protection should have supplied, in just proportion, the want of personal strength. But the legislator had weighed in the scale, not of justice, but of policy, the loss of a soldier against that of a slave: the head of an insolent and rapacious Barbarian was guarded by a heavy fine; and the slightest aid was afforded to the most defenceless subjects. Time insensibly abated the pride of the conquerors and the patience of the vanquished; and the boldest citizen was taught, by experience, that he might suffer more injuries than he could inflict. As the manners of the Franks became less ferocious, their laws were rendered more severe; and the Merovingian kings attempted to imitate the impartial rigor of the Visigoths and Burgundians. [75] Under the empire of Charlemagne, murder was universally punished with death; and the use of capital punishments has been liberally multiplied in the jurisprudence of modern Europe. [76]

[Footnote 72: In the heroic times of Greece, the guilt of murder was expiated by a pecuniary satisfaction to the family of the deceased, (Feithius Antiquitat. Homeric. l. ii. c. 8.) Heineccius, in his preface to the Elements of Germanic Law, favorably suggests, that at Rome and Athens homicide was only punished with exile. It is true: but exile was a capital punishment for a citizen of Rome or Athens.]

[Footnote 73: This proportion is fixed by the Salic (tit. xliv. in tom. iv. p. 147) and the Ripuarian (tit. vii. xi. xxxvi. in tom. iv. p. 237, 241) laws: but the latter does not distinguish any difference of Romans. Yet the orders of the clergy are placed above the Franks themselves, and the Burgundians and Alemanni between the Franks and the Romans.]

[Footnote 74: The Antrustiones, qui in truste Dominica sunt, leudi, fideles, undoubtedly represent the first order of Franks; but it is a question whether their rank was personal or hereditary. The Abbe de Mably (tom. i. p. 334-347) is not displeased to mortify the pride of birth (Esprit, l. xxx. c. 25) by dating the origin of the French nobility from the reign Clotaire II. (A.D. 615.)]

[Footnote 75: See the Burgundian laws, (tit. ii. in tom. iv. p. 257,) the code of the Visigoths, (l. vi. tit. v. in tom. p. 384,) and the constitution of Childebert, not of Paris, but most evidently of Austrasia, (in tom. iv. p. 112.) Their premature severity was sometimes rash, and excessive. Childebert condemned not only murderers but robbers; quomodo sine lege involavit, sine lege moriatur; and even the negligent judge was involved in the same sentence. The Visigoths abandoned an unsuccessful surgeon to the family of his deceased patient, ut quod de eo facere voluerint habeant potestatem, (l. xi. tit. i. in tom. iv. p. 435.)]

[Footnote 76: See, in the sixth volume of the works of Heineccius, the Elementa Juris Germanici, l. ii. p. 2, No. 261, 262, 280-283. Yet some vestiges of these pecuniary compositions for murder have been traced in Germany as late as the sixteenth century.]

The civil and military professions, which had been separated by Constantine, were again united by the Barbarians. The harsh sound of the Teutonic appellations was mollified into the Latin titles of Duke, of Count, or of Praefect; and the same officer assumed, within his district, the command of the troops, and the administration of justice. [77] But the fierce and illiterate chieftain was seldom qualified to discharge the duties of a judge, which required all the faculties of a philosophic mind, laboriously cultivated by experience and study; and his rude ignorance was compelled to embrace some simple, and visible, methods of ascertaining the cause of justice. In every religion, the Deity has been invoked to confirm the truth, or to punish the falsehood of human testimony; but this powerful instrument was misapplied and abused by the simplicity of the German legislators. The party accused might justify his innocence, by producing before their tribunal a number of friendly witnesses, who solemnly declared their belief, or assurance, that he was not guilty. According to the weight of the charge, this legal number of compurgators was multiplied; seventy-two voices were required to absolve an incendiary or assassin: and when the chastity of a queen of France was suspected, three hundred gallant nobles swore, without hesitation, that the infant prince had been actually begotten by her deceased husband. [78] The sin and scandal of manifest and frequent perjuries engaged the magistrates to remove these dangerous temptations; and to supply the defects of human testimony by the famous experiments of fire and water. These extraordinary trials were so capriciously contrived, that, in some cases, guilt, and innocence in others, could not be proved without the interposition of a miracle. Such miracles were really provided by fraud and credulity; the most intricate causes were determined by this easy and infallible method, and the turbulent Barbarians, who might have disdained the sentence of the magistrate, submissively acquiesced in the judgment of God. [79]

[Footnote 77: The whole subject of the Germanic judges, and their jurisdiction, is copiously treated by Heineccius, (Element. Jur. Germ. l. iii. No. 1-72.) I cannot find any proof that, under the Merovingian race, the scabini, or assessors, were chosen by the people. Note: The question of the scabini is treated at considerable length by Savigny. He questions the existence of the scabini anterior to Charlemagne. Before this time the decision was by an open court of the freemen, the boni Romische Recht, vol. i. p. 195. et seq—M.]

[Footnote 78: Gregor. Turon. l. viii. c. 9, in tom. ii. p. 316. Montesquieu observes, (Esprit des Loix. l. xxviii. c. 13,) that the Salic law did not admit these negative proofs so universally established in the Barbaric codes. Yet this obscure concubine (Fredegundis,) who became the wife of the grandson of Clovis, must have followed the Salic law.]

[Footnote 79: Muratori, in the Antiquities of Italy, has given two Dissertations (xxxvii. xxxix.) on the judgments of God. It was expected that fire would not burn the innocent; and that the pure element of water would not allow the guilty to sink into its bosom.]

But the trials by single combat gradually obtained superior credit and authority, among a warlike people, who could not believe that a brave man deserved to suffer, or that a coward deserved to live. [80] Both in civil and criminal proceedings, the plaintiff, or accuser, the defendant, or even the witness, were exposed to mortal challenge from the antagonist who was destitute of legal proofs; and it was incumbent on them either to desert their cause, or publicly to maintain their honor, in the lists of battle. They fought either on foot, or on horseback, according to the custom of their nation; [81] and the decision of the sword, or lance, was ratified by the sanction of Heaven, of the judge, and of the people. This sanguinary law was introduced into Gaul by the Burgundians; and their legislator Gundobald [82] condescended to answer the complaints and objections of his subject Avitus. "Is it not true," said the king of Burgundy to the bishop, "that the event of national wars, and private combats, is directed by the judgment of God; and that his providence awards the victory to the juster cause?" By such prevailing arguments, the absurd and cruel practice of judicial duels, which had been peculiar to some tribes of Germany, was propagated and established in all the monarchies of Europe, from Sicily to the Baltic. At the end of ten centuries, the reign of legal violence was not totally extinguished; and the ineffectual censures of saints, of popes, and of synods, may seem to prove, that the influence of superstition is weakened by its unnatural alliance with reason and humanity. The tribunals were stained with the blood, perhaps, of innocent and respectable citizens; the law, which now favors the rich, then yielded to the strong; and the old, the feeble, and the infirm, were condemned, either to renounce their fairest claims and possessions, to sustain the dangers of an unequal conflict, [83] or to trust the doubtful aid of a mercenary champion. This oppressive jurisprudence was imposed on the provincials of Gaul, who complained of any injuries in their persons and property. Whatever might be the strength, or courage, of individuals, the victorious Barbarians excelled in the love and exercise of arms; and the vanquished Roman was unjustly summoned to repeat, in his own person, the bloody contest which had been already decided against his country. [84]

[Footnote 80: Montesquieu (Esprit des Loix, l. xxviii. c. 17) has condescended to explain and excuse "la maniere de penser de nos peres," on the subject of judicial combats. He follows this strange institution from the age of Gundobald to that of St. Lewis; and the philosopher is some times lost in the legal antiquarian.]

[Footnote 81: In a memorable duel at Aix-la-Chapelle, (A.D. 820,) before the emperor Lewis the Pious, his biographer observes, secundum legem propriam, utpote quia uterque Gothus erat, equestri pugna est, (Vit. Lud. Pii, c. 33, in tom. vi. p. 103.) Ermoldus Nigellus, (l. iii. 543-628, in tom. vi. p. 48-50,) who describes the duel, admires the ars nova of fighting on horseback, which was unknown to the Franks.]

[Footnote 82: In his original edict, published at Lyons, (A.D. 501,) establishes and justifies the use of judicial combat, (Les Burgund. tit. xlv. in tom. ii. p. 267, 268.) Three hundred years afterwards, Agobard, bishop of Lyons, solicited Lewis the Pious to abolish the law of an Arian tyrant, (in tom. vi. p. 356-358.) He relates the conversation of Gundobald and Avitus.]

[Footnote 83: "Accidit, (says Agobard,) ut non solum valentes viribus, sed etiam infirmi et senes lacessantur ad pugnam, etiam pro vilissimis rebus. Quibus foralibus certaminibus contingunt homicidia injusta; et crudeles ac perversi eventus judiciorum." Like a prudent rhetorician, he suppresses the legal privilege of hiring champions.]

[Footnote 84: Montesquieu, (Esprit des Loix, xxviii. c. 14,) who understands why the judicial combat was admitted by the Burgundians, Ripuarians, Alemanni, Bavarians, Lombards, Thuringians, Frisons, and Saxons, is satisfied (and Agobard seems to countenance the assertion) that it was not allowed by the Salic law. Yet the same custom, at least in case of treason, is mentioned by Ermoldus, Nigellus (l. iii. 543, in tom. vi. p. 48,) and the anonymous biographer of Lewis the Pious, (c. 46, in tom. vi. p. 112,) as the "mos antiquus Francorum, more Francis solito," &c., expressions too general to exclude the noblest of their tribes.]

A devouring host of one hundred and twenty thousand Germans had formerly passed the Rhine under the command of Ariovistus. One third part of the fertile lands of the Sequani was appropriated to their use; and the conqueror soon repeated his oppressive demand of another third, for the accommodation of a new colony of twenty-four thousand Barbarians, whom he had invited to share the rich harvest of Gaul. [85] At the distance of five hundred years, the Visigoths and Burgundians, who revenged the defeat of Ariovistus, usurped the same unequal proportion of two thirds of the subject lands. But this distribution, instead of spreading over the province, may be reasonably confined to the peculiar districts where the victorious people had been planted by their own choice, or by the policy of their leader. In these districts, each Barbarian was connected by the ties of hospitality with some Roman provincial. To this unwelcome guest, the proprietor was compelled to abandon two thirds of his patrimony, but the German, a shepherd and a hunter, might sometimes content himself with a spacious range of wood and pasture, and resign the smallest, though most valuable, portion, to the toil of the industrious husbandman. [86] The silence of ancient and authentic testimony has encouraged an opinion, that the rapine of the Franks was not moderated, or disguised, by the forms of a legal division; that they dispersed themselves over the provinces of Gaul, without order or control; and that each victorious robber, according to his wants, his avarice, and his strength, measured with his sword the extent of his new inheritance. At a distance from their sovereign, the Barbarians might indeed be tempted to exercise such arbitrary depredation; but the firm and artful policy of Clovis must curb a licentious spirit, which would aggravate the misery of the vanquished, whilst it corrupted the union and discipline of the conquerors. [86/1] The memorable vase of Soissons is a monument and a pledge of the regular distribution of the Gallic spoils. It was the duty and the interest of Clovis to provide rewards for a successful army, settlements for a numerous people; without inflicting any wanton or superfluous injuries on the loyal Catholics of Gaul. The ample fund, which he might lawfully acquire, of the Imperial patrimony, vacant lands, and Gothic usurpations, would diminish the cruel necessity of seizure and confiscation, and the humble provincials would more patiently acquiesce in the equal and regular distribution of their loss. [87]

[Footnote 85: Caesar de Bell. Gall. l. i. c. 31, in tom. i. p. 213.]

[Footnote 86: The obscure hints of a division of lands occasionally scattered in the laws of the Burgundians, (tit. liv. No. 1, 2, in tom. iv. p. 271, 272,) and Visigoths, (l. x. tit. i. No. 8, 9, 16, in tom. iv. p. 428, 429, 430,) are skillfully explained by the president Montesquieu, (Esprit des Loix, l. xxx. c. 7, 8, 9.) I shall only add, that among the Goths, the division seems to have been ascertained by the judgment of the neighborhood, that the Barbarians frequently usurped the remaining third; and that the Romans might recover their right, unless they were barred by a prescription of fifty years.]

[Footnote 86/1: Sismondi (Hist des Francais, vol. i. p. 197) observes, they were not a conquering people, who had emigrated with their families, like the Goths or Burgundians. The women, the children, the old, had not followed Clovis: they remained in their ancient possessions on the Waal and the Rhine. The adventurers alone had formed the invading force, and they always considered themselves as an army, not as a colony. Hence their laws retained no traces of the partition of the Roman properties. It is curious to observe the recoil from the national vanity of the French historians of the last century. M. Sismondi compares the position of the Franks with regard to the conquered people with that of the Dey of Algiers and his corsair troops to the peaceful inhabitants of that province: M. Thierry (Lettres sur l'Histoire de France, p. 117) with that of the Turks towards the Raias or Phanariotes, the mass of the Greeks—M.]

[Footnote 87: It is singular enough that the president de Montesquieu (Esprit des Loix, l. xxx. c. 7) and the Abbe de Mably (Observations, tom i. p. 21, 22) agree in this strange supposition of arbitrary and private rapine. The Count de Boulainvilliers (Etat de la France, tom. i. p. 22, 23) shows a strong understanding through a cloud of ignorance and prejudice. Note: Sismondi supposes that the Barbarians, if a farm were conveniently situated, would show no great respect for the laws of property; but in general there would have been vacant land enough for the lots assigned to old or worn-out warriors, (Hist. des Francais, vol. i. p. 196.)—M.]

The wealth of the Merovingian princes consisted in their extensive domain. After the conquest of Gaul, they still delighted in the rustic simplicity of their ancestors; the cities were abandoned to solitude and decay; and their coins, their charters, and their synods, are still inscribed with the names of the villas, or rural palaces, in which they successively resided.

One hundred and sixty of these palaces, a title which need not excite any unseasonable ideas of art or luxury, were scattered through the provinces of their kingdom; and if some might claim the honors of a fortress, the far greater part could be esteemed only in the light of profitable farms. The mansion of the long-haired kings was surrounded with convenient yards and stables, for the cattle and the poultry; the garden was planted with useful vegetables; the various trades, the labors of agriculture, and even the arts of hunting and fishing, were exercised by servile hands for the emolument of the sovereign; his magazines were filled with corn and wine, either for sale or consumption; and the whole administration was conducted by the strictest maxims of private economy. [88] This ample patrimony was appropriated to supply the hospitable plenty of Clovis and his successors; and to reward the fidelity of their brave companions who, both in peace and war, were devoted to their persona service. Instead of a horse, or a suit of armor, each companion, according to his rank, or merit, or favor, was invested with a benefice, the primitive name, and most simple form, of the feudal possessions. These gifts might be resumed at the pleasure of the sovereign; and his feeble prerogative derived some support from the influence of his liberality. [88/1] But this dependent tenure was gradually abolished [89] by the independent and rapacious nobles of France, who established the perpetual property, and hereditary succession, of their benefices; a revolution salutary to the earth, which had been injured, or neglected, by its precarious masters. [90] Besides these royal and beneficiary estates, a large proportion had been assigned, in the division of Gaul, of allodial and Salic lands: they were exempt from tribute, and the Salic lands were equally shared among the male descendants of the Franks. [91]

[Footnote 88: See the rustic edict, or rather code, of Charlemagne, which contains seventy distinct and minute regulations of that great monarch (in tom. v. p. 652-657.) He requires an account of the horns and skins of the goats, allows his fish to be sold, and carefully directs, that the larger villas (Capitaneoe) shall maintain one hundred hens and thirty geese; and the smaller (Mansionales) fifty hens and twelve geese. Mabillon (de Re Diplomatica) has investigated the names, the number, and the situation of the Merovingian villas.]

[Footnote 88/1: The resumption of benefices at the pleasure of the sovereign, (the general theory down to his time,) is ably contested by Mr. Hallam; "for this resumption some delinquency must be imputed to the vassal." Middle Ages, vol. i. p. 162. The reader will be interested by the singular analogies with the beneficial and feudal system of Europe in a remote part of the world, indicated by Col. Tod in his splendid work on Raja'sthan, vol. ii p. 129, &c—M.]

[Footnote 89: From a passage of the Burgundian law (tit. i. No. 4, in tom. iv. p. 257) it is evident, that a deserving son might expect to hold the lands which his father had received from the royal bounty of Gundobald. The Burgundians would firmly maintain their privilege, and their example might encourage the Beneficiaries of France.]

[Footnote 90: The revolutions of the benefices and fiefs are clearly fixed by the Abbe de Mably. His accurate distinction of times gives him a merit to which even Montesquieu is a stranger.]

[Footnote 91: See the Salic law, (tit. lxii. in tom. iv. p. 156.) The origin and nature of these Salic lands, which, in times of ignorance, were perfectly understood, now perplex our most learned and sagacious critics. Note: No solution seems more probable, than that the ancient lawgivers of the Salic Franks prohibited females from inheriting the lands assigned to the nation, upon its conquest of Gaul, both in compliance with their ancient usages, and in order to secure the military service of every proprietor. But lands subsequently acquired by purchase or other means, though equally bound to the public defence, were relieved from the severity of this rule, and presumed not to belong to the class of Sallic. Hallam's Middle Ages, vol. i. p. 145. Compare Sismondi, vol. i. p. 196—M.]

In the bloody discord and silent decay of the Merovingian line, a new order of tyrants arose in the provinces, who, under the appellation of Seniors, or Lords, usurped a right to govern, and a license to oppress, the subjects of their peculiar territory. Their ambition might be checked by the hostile resistance of an equal: but the laws were extinguished; and the sacrilegious Barbarians, who dared to provoke the vengeance of a saint or bishop, [92] would seldom respect the landmarks of a profane and defenceless neighbor. The common or public rights of nature, such as they had always been deemed by the Roman jurisprudence, [93] were severely restrained by the German conquerors, whose amusement, or rather passion, was the exercise of hunting. The vague dominion which Man has assumed over the wild inhabitants of the earth, the air, and the waters, was confined to some fortunate individuals of the human species. Gaul was again overspread with woods; and the animals, who were reserved for the use or pleasure of the lord, might ravage with impunity the fields of his industrious vassals. The chase was the sacred privilege of the nobles and their domestic servants. Plebeian transgressors were legally chastised with stripes and imprisonment; [94] but in an age which admitted a slight composition for the life of a citizen, it was a capital crime to destroy a stag or a wild bull within the precincts of the royal forests. [95]

[Footnote 92: Many of the two hundred and six miracles of St. Martin (Greg Turon. in Maxima Bibliotheca Patrum, tom. xi. p. 896-932) were repeatedly performed to punish sacrilege. Audite haec omnes (exclaims the bishop of Tours) protestatem habentes, after relating, how some horses ran mad, that had been turned into a sacred meadow.]

[Footnote 93: Heinec. Element. Jur. German. l. ii. p. 1, No. 8.]

[Footnote 94: Jonas, bishop of Orleans, (A.D. 821-826. Cave, Hist. Litteraria, p. 443,) censures the legal tyranny of the nobles. Pro feris, quas cura hominum non aluit, sed Deus in commune mortalibus ad utendum concessit, pauperes a potentioribus spoliantur, flagellantur, ergastulis detruduntur, et multa alia patiuntur. Hoc enim qui faciunt, lege mundi se facere juste posse contendant. De Institutione Laicorum, l. ii. c. 23, apud Thomassin, Discipline de l'Eglise, tom. iii. p. 1348.]

[Footnote 95: On a mere suspicion, Chundo, a chamberlain of Gontram, king of Burgundy, was stoned to death, (Greg. Turon. l. x. c. 10, in tom. ii. p. 369.) John of Salisbury (Policrat. l. i. c. 4) asserts the rights of nature, and exposes the cruel practice of the twelfth century. See Heineccius, Elem. Jur. Germ. l. ii. p. 1, No. 51-57.]

According to the maxims of ancient war, the conqueror became the lawful master of the enemy whom he had subdued and spared: [96] and the fruitful cause of personal slavery, which had been almost suppressed by the peaceful sovereignty of Rome, was again revived and multiplied by the perpetual hostilities of the independent Barbarians. The Goth, the Burgundian, or the Frank, who returned from a successful expedition, dragged after him a long train of sheep, of oxen, and of human captives, whom he treated with the same brutal contempt. The youths of an elegant form and an ingenuous aspect were set apart for the domestic service; a doubtful situation, which alternately exposed them to the favorable or cruel impulse of passion. The useful mechanics and servants (smiths, carpenters, tailors, shoemakers, cooks, gardeners, dyers, and workmen in gold and silver, &c.) employed their skill for the use, or profit, of their master. But the Roman captives, who were destitute of art, but capable of labor, were condemned, without regard to their former rank, to tend the cattle and cultivate the lands of the Barbarians. The number of the hereditary bondsmen, who were attached to the Gallic estates, was continually increased by new supplies; and the servile people, according to the situation and temper of their lords, was sometimes raised by precarious indulgence, and more frequently depressed by capricious despotism. [97] An absolute power of life and death was exercised by these lords; and when they married their daughters, a train of useful servants, chained on the wagons to prevent their escape, was sent as a nuptial present into a distant country. [98] The majesty of the Roman laws protected the liberty of each citizen, against the rash effects of his own distress or despair. But the subjects of the Merovingian kings might alienate their personal freedom; and this act of legal suicide, which was familiarly practised, is expressed in terms most disgraceful and afflicting to the dignity of human nature. [99] The example of the poor, who purchased life by the sacrifice of all that can render life desirable, was gradually imitated by the feeble and the devout, who, in times of public disorder, pusillanimously crowded to shelter themselves under the battlements of a powerful chief, and around the shrine of a popular saint. Their submission was accepted by these temporal or spiritual patrons; and the hasty transaction irrecoverably fixed their own condition, and that of their latest posterity. From the reign of Clovis, during five successive centuries, the laws and manners of Gaul uniformly tended to promote the increase, and to confirm the duration, of personal servitude. Time and violence almost obliterated the intermediate ranks of society; and left an obscure and narrow interval between the noble and the slave. This arbitrary and recent division has been transformed by pride and prejudice into a national distinction, universally established by the arms and the laws of the Merovingians. The nobles, who claimed their genuine or fabulous descent from the independent and victorious Franks, have asserted and abused the indefeasible right of conquest over a prostrate crowd of slaves and plebeians, to whom they imputed the imaginary disgrace of Gallic or Roman extraction.

[Footnote 96: The custom of enslaving prisoners of war was totally extinguished in the thirteenth century, by the prevailing influence of Christianity; but it might be proved, from frequent passages of Gregory of Tours, &c., that it was practised, without censure, under the Merovingian race; and even Grotius himself, (de Jure Belli et Pacis l. iii. c. 7,) as well as his commentator Barbeyrac, have labored to reconcile it with the laws of nature and reason.]

[Footnote 97: The state, professions, &c., of the German, Italian, and Gallic slaves, during the middle ages, are explained by Heineccius, (Element Jur. Germ. l. i. No. 28-47,) Muratori, (Dissertat. xiv. xv.,) Ducange, (Gloss. sub voce Servi,) and the Abbe de Mably, (Observations, tom. ii. p. 3, &c., p. 237, &c.) Note: Compare Hallam, vol. i. p. 216—M.]

[Footnote 98: Gregory of Tours (l. vi. c. 45, in tom. ii. p. 289) relates a memorable example, in which Chilperic only abused the private rights of a master. Many families which belonged to his domus fiscales in the neighborhood of Paris, were forcibly sent away into Spain.]

[Footnote 99: Licentiam habeatis mihi qualemcunque volueritis disciplinam ponere; vel venumdare, aut quod vobis placuerit de me facere Marculf. Formul. l. ii. 28, in tom. iv. p. 497. The Formula of Lindenbrogius, (p. 559,) and that of Anjou, (p. 565,) are to the same effect Gregory of Tours (l. vii. c. 45, in tom. ii. p. 311) speak of many person who sold themselves for bread, in a great famine.]

The general state and revolutions of France, a name which was imposed by the conquerors, may be illustrated by the particular example of a province, a diocese, or a senatorial family. Auvergne had formerly maintained a just preeminence among the independent states and cities of Gaul. The brave and numerous inhabitants displayed a singular trophy; the sword of Caesar himself, which he had lost when he was repulsed before the walls of Gergovia. [100] As the common offspring of Troy, they claimed a fraternal alliance with the Romans; [101] and if each province had imitated the courage and loyalty of Auvergne, the fall of the Western empire might have been prevented or delayed. They firmly maintained the fidelity which they had reluctantly sworn to the Visigoths, out when their bravest nobles had fallen in the battle of Poitiers, they accepted, without resistance, a victorious and Catholic sovereign. This easy and valuable conquest was achieved and possessed by Theodoric, the eldest son of Clovis: but the remote province was separated from his Austrasian dominions, by the intermediate kingdoms of Soissons, Paris, and Orleans, which formed, after their father's death, the inheritance of his three brothers. The king of Paris, Childebert, was tempted by the neighborhood and beauty of Auvergne. [102] The Upper country, which rises towards the south into the mountains of the Cevennes, presented a rich and various prospect of woods and pastures; the sides of the hills were clothed with vines; and each eminence was crowned with a villa or castle. In the Lower Auvergne, the River Allier flows through the fair and spacious plain of Limagne; and the inexhaustible fertility of the soil supplied, and still supplies, without any interval of repose, the constant repetition of the same harvests. [103] On the false report, that their lawful sovereign had been slain in Germany, the city and diocese of Auvergne were betrayed by the grandson of Sidonius Apollinaris. Childebert enjoyed this clandestine victory; and the free subjects of Theodoric threatened to desert his standard, if he indulged his private resentment, while the nation was engaged in the Burgundian war. But the Franks of Austrasia soon yielded to the persuasive eloquence of their king. "Follow me," said Theodoric, "into Auvergne; I will lead you into a province, where you may acquire gold, silver, slaves, cattle, and precious apparel, to the full extent of your wishes. I repeat my promise; I give you the people and their wealth as your prey; and you may transport them at pleasure into your own country." By the execution of this promise, Theodoric justly forfeited the allegiance of a people whom he devoted to destruction. His troops, reenforced by the fiercest Barbarians of Germany, [104] spread desolation over the fruitful face of Auvergne; and two places only, a strong castle and a holy shrine, were saved or redeemed from their licentious fury. The castle of Meroliac [105] was seated on a lofty rock, which rose a hundred feet above the surface of the plain; and a large reservoir of fresh water was enclosed, with some arable lands, within the circle of its fortifications. The Franks beheld with envy and despair this impregnable fortress; but they surprised a party of fifty stragglers; and, as they were oppressed by the number of their captives, they fixed, at a trifling ransom, the alternative of life or death for these wretched victims, whom the cruel Baroarians were prepared to massacre on the refusal of the garrison. Another detachment penetrated as far as Brivas, or Brioude, where the inhabitants, with their valuable effects, had taken refuge in the sanctuary of St. Julian. The doors of the church resisted the assault; but a daring soldier entered through a window of the choir, and opened a passage to his companions. The clergy and people, the sacred and the profane spoils, were rudely torn from the altar; and the sacrilegious division was made at a small distance from the town of Brioude. But this act of impiety was severely chastised by the devout son of Clovis. He punished with death the most atrocious offenders; left their secret accomplices to the vengeance of St. Julian; released the captives; restored the plunder; and extended the rights of sanctuary five miles round the sepulchre of the holy martyr. [106]

[Footnote 100: When Caesar saw it, he laughed, (Plutarch. in Caesar. in tom. i. p. 409:) yet he relates his unsuccessful siege of Gergovia with less frankness than we might expect from a great man to whom victory was familiar. He acknowledges, however, that in one attack he lost forty-six centurions and seven hundred men, (de Bell. Gallico, l. vi. c. 44-53, in tom. i. p. 270-272.)]

[Footnote 101: Audebant se quondam fatres Latio dicere, et sanguine ab Iliaco populos computare, (Sidon. Apollinar. l. vii. epist. 7, in tom i. p. 799.) I am not informed of the degrees and circumstances of this fabulous pedigree.]

[Footnote 102: Either the first, or second, partition among the sons of Clovis, had given Berry to Childebert, (Greg. Turon. l. iii. c. 12, in tom. ii. p. 192.) Velim (said he) Arvernam Lemanem, quae tanta *jocunditatis gratia refulgere dicitur, oculis cernere,* (l. iii. c. p. 191.) The face of the country was concealed by a thick fog, when the king of Paris made his entry into Clermen.]

[Footnote 103: For the description of Auvergne, see Sidonius, (l. iv. epist. 21, in tom. i. p. 703,) with the notes of Savaron and Sirmond, (p. 279, and 51, of their respective editions.) Boulainvilliers, (Etat de la France, tom. ii. p. 242-268,) and the Abbe de la Longuerue, (Description de la France, part i. p. 132-139.)]

[Footnote 104; *Furorem gentium, quae de ulteriore Rheni amnis parte venerant, superare non poterat,* (Greg. Turon. l. iv. c. 50, in tom. ii. 229.) was the excuse of another king of Austrasia (A.D. 574) for the ravages which his troops committed in the neighborhood of Paris.]

[Footnote 105: From the name and situation, the Benedictine editors of Gregory of Tours (in tom. ii. p. 192) have fixed this fortress at a place named Castel Merliac, two miles from Mauriac, in the Upper Auvergne. In this description, I translate *infra* as if I read *intra*; the two are perpetually confounded by Gregory, or his transcribed and the sense must always decide.]

[Footnote 106: See these revolutions, and wars, of Auvergne, in Gregory of Tours, (l. ii. c. 37, in tom. ii. p. 183, and l. iii. c. 9, 12, 13, p. 191, 192, de Miraculis St. Julian. c. 13, in tom. ii. p. 466.) He frequently betrays his extraordinary attention to his native country.]

PART IV

Before the Austrasian army retreated from Auvergne, Theodoric exacted some pledges of the future loyalty of a people, whose just hatred could be restrained only by their fear. A select band of noble youths, the sons of the principal senators, was delivered to the conqueror, as the hostages of the faith of Childebert, and of their countrymen. On the first rumor of war, or conspiracy, these guiltless youths were reduced to a state of servitude; and one of them, Attalus, [107] whose adventures are more particularly related, kept his master's horses in the diocese of Treves. After a painful search, he was discovered, in this unworthy occupation, by the emissaries of his grandfather, Gregory bishop of Langres; but his offers of ransom were sternly rejected by the avarice of the Barbarian, who required an exorbitant sum of ten pounds of gold for the freedom of his noble captive. His deliverance was effected by the hardy stratagem of Leo, an item belonging to the kitchens of the bishop of Langres. [108] An unknown agent easily introduced him into the same family. The Barbarian purchased Leo for the price of twelve pieces of gold; and was pleased to learn that he was deeply skilled in the luxury of an episcopal table: "Next Sunday," said the Frank, "I shall invite my neighbors and kinsmen. Exert thy art, and force them to confess, that they have never seen, or tasted, such an entertainment, even in the king's house." Leo assured him, that if he would provide a sufficient quantity of poultry, his wishes should be satisfied. The master who already aspired to the merit of elegant hospitality, assumed, as his own, the praise which the voracious guests unanimously bestowed on his cook; and the dexterous Leo insensibly acquired the trust and management of his household. After the patient expectation of a whole year, he cautiously whispered his design to Attalus, and exhorted him to prepare for flight in the ensuing night. At the hour of midnight, the intemperate guests retired from the table; and the Frank's son-in-law, whom Leo attended to his apartment with a nocturnal potation, condescended to jest on the facility with which he might betray his trust. The intrepid slave, after sustaining this dangerous raillery, entered his master's bedchamber; removed his spear and shield; silently drew the fleetest horses from the stable; unbarred the ponderous gates; and excited Attalus to save his life and liberty by incessant diligence. Their apprehensions urged them to leave their horses on the banks of the Meuse; [109] they swam the river, wandered three days in the adjacent forest, and subsisted only by the accidental discovery of a wild plum-tree. As they lay concealed in a dark thicket, they heard the noise of horses; they were terrified by the angry countenance of their master, and they anxiously listened to his declaration, that, if he could seize the guilty fugitives, one of them he would cut in pieces with his sword, and would expose the other on a gibbet. A length, Attalus and his faithful Leo reached the friendly habitation of a presbyter of Rheims, who recruited their fainting strength with bread and wine, concealed them from the search of their enemy, and safely conducted them beyond the limits of the Austrasian kingdom, to the episcopal palace of Langres. Gregory embraced his grandson with tears of joy, gratefully delivered Leo, with his whole family, from the yoke of servitude, and bestowed on him the property of a farm, where he might end his days in happiness and freedom. Perhaps this singular adventure, which is marked with so many circumstances of truth and nature, was related by Attalus himself, to his cousin or nephew, the first historian of the Franks. Gregory of Tours [110] was born about sixty years after the death of Sidonius Apollinaris; and their situation was almost similar, since each of them was a native of Auvergne, a senator, and a bishop. The difference of their style and sentiments may, therefore, express the decay of Gaul; and clearly ascertain how much, in so short a space, the human mind had lost of its energy and refinement. [111]

[Footnote 107: The story of Attalus is related by Gregory of Tours, (l. iii. c. 16, tom. ii. p. 193-195.) His editor, the P. Ruinart, confounds this Attalus, who was a youth (puer) in the year 532, with a friend of Silonius of the same name, who was count of Autun, fifty or sixty years before. Such an error, which cannot be imputed to ignorance, is excused, in some degree, by its own magnitude.]

[Footnote 108: This Gregory, the great grandfather of Gregory of Tours, (in tom. ii. p. 197, 490,) lived ninety-two years; of which he passed forty as count of Autun, and thirty-two as bishop of Langres. According to the poet Fortunatus, he displayed equal merit in these different stations. Nobilis antiqua decurrens prole parentum, Nobilior gestis, nunc super astra manet. Arbiter ante ferox, dein pius ipse sacerdos, Quos domuit judex, fovit amore patris.]

[Footnote 109: As M. de Valois, and the P. Ruinart, are determined to change the Mosella of the text into Mosa, it becomes me to acquiesce in the alteration. Yet, after some examination of the topography. I could defend the common reading.]

[Footnote 110: The parents of Gregory (Gregorius Florentius Georgius) were of noble extraction, (natalibus... illustres,) and they possessed large estates (latifundia) both in Auvergne and Burgundy. He was born in the year 539, was consecrated bishop of Tours in 573, and died in 593 or 595, soon after he had terminated his history. See his life by Odo, abbot of Clugny, (in tom. ii. p. 129-135,) and a new Life in the Memoires de l'Academie, &c., tom. xxvi. p. 598-637.]

[Footnote 111: Decedente atque immo potius pereunte ab urbibus Gallicanis liberalium cultura literarum, &c., (in praefat. in tom. ii. p. 137,) is the complaint of Gregory himself, which he fully verifies by his own work. His style is equally devoid of elegance and simplicity. In a conspicuous station, he still remained a stranger to his own age and country; and in a prolific work (the five last books contain ten years) he has omitted almost every thing that posterity desires to learn. I have tediously acquired, by a painful perusal, the right of pronouncing this unfavorable sentence]

We are now qualified to despise the opposite, and, perhaps, artful, misrepresentations, which have softened, or exaggerated, the oppression of the Romans of Gaul under the reign of the Merovingians.

The conquerors never promulgated any universal edict of servitude, or confiscation; but a degenerate people, who excused their weakness by the specious names of politeness and peace, was exposed to the arms and laws of the ferocious Barbarians, who contemptuously insulted their possessions, their freedom, and their safety. Their personal injuries were partial and irregular; but the great body of the Romans survived the revolution, and still preserved the property, and privileges, of citizens. A large portion of their lands was exacted for the use of the Franks: but they enjoyed the remainder, exempt from tribute; [112] and the same irresistible violence which swept away the arts and manufactures of Gaul, destroyed the elaborate and expensive system of Imperial despotism. The Provincials must frequently deplore the savage jurisprudence of the Salic or Ripuarian laws; but their private life, in the important concerns of marriage, testaments, or inheritance, was still regulated by the Theodosian Code; and a discontented Roman might freely aspire, or descend, to the title and character of a Barbarian. The honors of the state were accessible to his ambition: the education and temper of the Romans more peculiarly qualified them for the offices of civil government; and, as soon as emulation had rekindled their military ardor, they were permitted to march in the ranks, or even at the head, of the victorious Germans. I shall not attempt to enumerate the generals and magistrates, whose names [113] attest the liberal policy of the Merovingians. The supreme command of Burgundy, with the title of Patrician, was successively intrusted to three Romans; and the last, and most powerful, Mummolus, [114] who alternately saved and disturbed the monarchy, had supplanted his father in the station of count of Autun, and left a treasury of thirty talents of gold, and two hundred and fifty talents of silver. The fierce and illiterate Barbarians were excluded, during several generations, from the dignities, and even from the orders, of the church. [115] The clergy of Gaul consisted almost entirely of native provincials; the haughty Franks fell at the feet of their subjects, who were dignified with the episcopal character: and the power and riches which had been lost in war, were insensibly recovered by superstition. [116] In all temporal affairs, the Theodosian Code was the universal law of the clergy; but the Barbaric jurisprudence had liberally provided for their personal safety; a sub-deacon was equivalent to two Franks; the antrustion, and priest, were held in similar estimation: and the life of a bishop was appreciated far above the common standard, at the price of nine hundred pieces of gold. [117] The Romans communicated to their conquerors the use of the Christian religion and Latin language; [118] but their language and their religion had alike degenerated from the simple purity of the Augustan, and Apostolic age. The progress of superstition and Barbarism was rapid and universal: the worship of the saints concealed from vulgar eyes the God of the Christians; and the rustic dialect of peasants and soldiers was corrupted by a Teutonic idiom and pronunciation. Yet such intercourse of sacred and social communion eradicated the distinctions of birth and victory; and the nations of Gaul were gradually confounded under the name and government of the Franks.

[Footnote 112: The Abbe de Mably (tom. p. i. 247-267) has diligently confirmed this opinion of the President de Montesquieu, (Esprit des Loix, l. xxx. c. 13.)]

[Footnote 113: See Dubos, Hist. Critique de la Monarchie Francoise, tom. ii. l. vi. c. 9, 10. The French antiquarians establish as a principle, that the Romans and Barbarians may be distinguished by their names. Their names undoubtedly form a reasonable presumption; yet in reading Gregory of Tours, I have observed Gondulphus, of Senatorian, or Roman, extraction, (l. vi. c. 11, in tom. ii. p. 273,) and Claudius, a Barbarian, (l. vii. c. 29, p. 303.)]

[Footnote 114: Eunius Mummolus is repeatedly mentioned by Gregory of Tours, from the fourth (c. 42, p. 224) to the seventh (c. 40, p. 310) book. The computation by talents is singular enough; but if Gregory attached any meaning to that obsolete word, the treasures of Mummolus must have exceeded 100,000 L. sterling.]

[Footnote 115: See Fleury, Discours iii. sur l'Histoire Ecclesiastique.]

[Footnote 116: The bishop of Tours himself has recorded the complaint of Chilperic, the grandson of Clovis. Ecce pauper remansit Fiscus noster; ecce divitiae nostrae ad ecclesias sunt translatae; nulli penitus nisi soli Episcopi regnant, (l. vi. c. 46, in tom. ii. p. 291.)]

[Footnote 117: See the Ripuarian Code, (tit. xxxvi in tom. iv. p. 241.) The Salic law does not provide for the safety of the clergy; and we might suppose, on the behalf of the more civilized tribe, that they had not foreseen such an impious act as the murder of a priest. Yet Praetextatus, archbishop of Rouen, was assassinated by the order of Queen Fredegundis before the altar, (Greg. Turon. l. viii. c. 31, in tom. ii. p. 326.)]

[Footnote 118: M. Bonamy (Mem. de l'Academie des Inscriptions, tom. xxiv. p. 582-670) has ascertained the Lingua Romana Rustica, which, through the medium of the Romance, has gradually been polished into the actual form of the French language. Under the Carlovingian race, the kings and nobles of France still understood the dialect of their German ancestors.]

The Franks, after they mingled with their Gallic subjects, might have imparted the most valuable of human gifts, a spirit and system of constitutional liberty. Under a king, hereditary, but limited, the chiefs and counsellors might have debated at Paris, in the palace of the Caesars: the adjacent field, where the emperors reviewed their mercenary legions. would have admitted the legislative assembly of freemen and warriors; and the rude model, which had been sketched in the woods of Germany, [119] might have been polished and improved by the civil wisdom of the Romans. But the careless Barbarians, secure of their personal independence, disdained the labor of government: the annual assemblies of the month of March were silently abolished; and the nation was separated, and almost dissolved, by the conquest of Gaul. [120] The monarchy was left without any regular establishment of justice, of arms, or of revenue. The successors of Clovis wanted resolution to assume, or strength to exercise, the legislative and executive powers, which the people had abdicated: the royal prerogative was distinguished only by a more ample privilege of rapine and murder; and the love of freedom, so often invigorated and disgraced by private ambition, was reduced, among the licentious Franks, to the contempt of order, and the desire of impunity. Seventy-five years after the death of Clovis, his grandson, Gontran, king of Burgundy, sent an army to invade the Gothic possessions of Septimania, or Languedoc. The troops of Burgundy, Berry, Auvergne, and the adjacent territories, were excited by the hopes of spoil. They marched, without discipline, under the banners of German, or Gallic, counts: their attack was feeble and unsuccessful; but the friendly and hostile provinces were desolated with indiscriminate rage. The cornfields, the villages, the churches themselves, were consumed by fire: the inhabitants were massacred, or dragged into captivity; and, in the disorderly retreat, five thousand of these inhuman savages were destroyed by hunger or intestine discord. When the pious Gontran reproached the guilt or neglect of their leaders, and threatened to inflict, not a legal sentence, but instant and arbitrary execution, they accused the universal and incurable corruption of the people. "No one," they said, "any longer fears or respects his king, his duke, or his count. Each man loves to do evil, and freely indulges his criminal inclinations. The most gentle correction provokes an immediate tumult, and the rash magistrate, who presumes to censure or restrain his seditious subjects, seldom escapes alive from their revenge." [121] It has been reserved for the same nation to expose, by their intemperate vices, the most odious abuse of freedom; and to supply its loss by the spirit of honor and humanity, which now alleviates and dignifies their obedience to an absolute sovereign. [121/1]

[Footnote 119: Ce beau systeme a ete trouve dans les bois. Montesquieu, Esprit des Loix, l. xi. c. 6.]

[Footnote 120: See the Abbe de Mably. Observations, &c., tom. i. p. 34-56. It should seem that the institution of national assemblies, which are with the French nation, has never been congenial to its temper.]

[Footnote 121: Gregory of Tours (l. viii. c. 30, in tom. ii. p. 325, 326) relates, with much indifference, the crimes, the reproof, and the apology. Nullus Regem metuit, nullus Ducem, nullus Comitem reveretur; et si fortassis alicui ista displicent, et ea, pro longaevitate vitae vestrae, emendare conatur, statim seditio in populo, statim tumultus exoritur, et in tantum unusquisque contra seniorem saeva intentione grassatur, ut vix se credat evadere, si tandem silere nequiverit.]

[Footnote 121/1: This remarkable passage was published in 1779—M.]

The Visigoths had resigned to Clovis the greatest part of their Gallic possessions; but their loss was amply compensated by the easy conquest, and secure enjoyment, of the provinces of Spain. From the monarchy of the Goths, which soon involved the Suevic kingdom of Gallicia, the modern Spaniards still derive some national vanity; but the historian of the Roman empire is neither invited, nor compelled, to pursue the obscure and barren series of their annals. [122] The Goths of Spain were separated from the rest of mankind by the lofty ridge of the Pyrenaean mountains: their manners and institutions, as far as they were common to the Germanic tribes, have been already explained. I have anticipated, in the preceding chapter, the most important of their ecclesiastical events, the fall of Arianism, and the persecution of the Jews; and it only remains to observe some interesting circumstances which relate to the civil and ecclesiastical constitution of the Spanish kingdom.

[Footnote 122: Spain, in these dark ages, has been peculiarly unfortunate. The Franks had a Gregory of Tours; the Saxons, or Angles, a Bede; the Lombards, a Paul Warnefrid, &c. But the history of the Visigoths is contained in the short and imperfect Chronicles of Isidore of Seville and John of Biclar]

After their conversion from idolatry or heresy, the Frank and the Visigoths were disposed to embrace, with equal submission, the inherent evils and the accidental benefits, of superstition. But the prelates of France, long before the extinction of the Merovingian race, had degenerated into fighting and hunting Barbarians. They disdained the use of synods; forgot the laws of temperance and chastity; and preferred the indulgence of private ambition and luxury to the general interest of the sacerdotal profession. [123] The bishops of Spain respected themselves, and were respected by the public: their indissoluble union disguised their vices, and confirmed their authority; and the regular discipline of the church introduced peace, order, and stability, into the government of the state. From the reign of Recared, the first Catholic king, to that of Witiza, the immediate predecessor of the unfortunate Roderic, sixteen national councils were successively convened. The six metropolitans, Toledo, Seville, Merida, Braga, Tarragona, and Narbonne, presided according to their respective seniority; the assembly was composed of their suffragan bishops, who appeared in person, or by their proxies; and a place was assigned to the most holy, or opulent, of the Spanish abbots. During the first three days of the convocation, as long as they agitated the ecclesiastical question of doctrine and discipline, the profane laity was excluded from their debates; which were conducted, however, with decent solemnity. But, on the morning of the fourth day, the doors were thrown open for the entrance of the great officers of the palace, the dukes and counts of the provinces, the judges of the cities, and the Gothic nobles, and the decrees of Heaven were ratified by the consent of the people.

The same rules were observed in the provincial assemblies, the annual synods, which were empowered to hear complaints, and to redress grievances; and a legal government was supported by the prevailing influence of the Spanish clergy. The bishops, who, in each revolution, were prepared to flatter the victorious, and to insult the prostrate labored, with diligence and success, to kindle the flames of persecution, and to exalt the mitre above the crown. Yet the national councils of Toledo, in which the free spirit of the Barbarians was tempered and guided by episcopal policy, have established some prudent laws for the common benefit of the king and people. The vacancy of the throne was supplied by the choice of the bishops and palatines; and after the failure of the line of Alaric, the regal dignity was still limited to the pure and noble blood of the Goths. The clergy, who anointed their lawful prince, always recommended, and sometimes practised, the duty of allegiance; and the spiritual censures were denounced on the heads of the impious subjects, who should resist his authority, conspire against his life, or violate, by an indecent union, the chastity even of his widow. But the monarch himself, when he ascended the throne, was bound by a reciprocal oath to God and his people, that he would faithfully execute this important trust. The real or imaginary faults of his administration were subject to the control of a powerful aristocracy; and the bishops and palatines were guarded by a fundamental privilege, that they should not be degraded, imprisoned, tortured, nor punished with death, exile, or confiscation, unless by the free and public judgment of their peers. [124]

[Footnote 123: Such are the complaints of St. Boniface, the apostle of Germany, and the reformer of Gaul, (in tom. iv. p. 94.) The fourscore years, which he deplores, of license and corruption, would seem to insinuate that the Barbarians were admitted into the clergy about the year 660.]

[Footnote 124: The acts of the councils of Toledo are still the most authentic records of the church and constitution of Spain. The following passages are particularly important, (iii. 17, 18; iv. 75; v. 2, 3, 4, 5, 8; vi. 11, 12, 13, 14, 17, 18; vii. 1; xiii. 2 3 6.) I have found Mascou (Hist. of the Ancient Germans, xv. 29, and Annotations, xxvi. and xxxiii.) and Ferreras (Hist. Generale de l'Espagne, tom. ii.) very useful and accurate guides.]

One of these legislative councils of Toledo examined and ratified the code of laws which had been compiled by a succession of Gothic kings, from the fierce Euric, to the devout Egica. As long as the Visigoths themselves were satisfied with the rude customs of their ancestors, they indulged their subjects of Aquitain and Spain in the enjoyment of the Roman law. Their gradual improvement in arts, in policy, and at length in religion, encouraged them to imitate, and to supersede, these foreign institutions; and to compose a code of civil and criminal jurisprudence, for the use of a great and united people. The same obligations, and the same privileges, were communicated to the nations of the Spanish monarchy; and the conquerors, insensibly renouncing the Teutonic idiom, submitted to the restraints of equity, and exalted the Romans to the participation of freedom. The merit of this impartial policy was enhanced by the situation of Spain under the reign of the Visigoths. The provincials were long separated from their Arian masters by the irreconcilable difference of religion. After the conversion of Recared had removed the prejudices of the Catholics, the coasts, both of the Ocean and Mediterranean, were still possessed by the Eastern emperors; who secretly excited a discontented people to reject the yoke of the Barbarians, and to assert the name and dignity of Roman citizens. The allegiance of doubtful subjects is indeed most effectually secured by their own persuasion, that they hazard more in a revolt, than they can hope to obtain by a revolution; but it has appeared so natural to oppress those whom we hate and fear, that the contrary system well deserves the praise of wisdom and moderation. [125]

[Footnote 125: The Code of the Visigoths, regularly divided into twelve books, has been correctly published by Dom Bouquet, (in tom. iv. p. 273-460.) It has been treated by the President de Montesquieu

(Esprit des Loix, l. xxviii. c. 1) with excessive severity. I dislike the style; I detest the superstition; but I shall presume to think, that the civil jurisprudence displays a more civilized and enlightened state of society, than that of the Burgundians, or even of the Lombards.]

While the kingdom of the Franks and Visigoths were established in Gaul and Spain, the Saxons achieved the conquest of Britain, the third great diocese of the Praefecture of the West. Since Britain was already separated from the Roman empire, I might, without reproach, decline a story familiar to the most illiterate, and obscure to the most learned, of my readers. The Saxons, who excelled in the use of the oar, or the battle-axe, were ignorant of the art which could alone perpetuate the fame of their exploits; the Provincials, relapsing into barbarism, neglected to describe the ruin of their country; and the doubtful tradition was almost extinguished, before the missionaries of Rome restored the light of science and Christianity. The declamations of Gildas, the fragments, or fables, of Nennius, the obscure hints of the Saxon laws and chronicles, and the ecclesiastical tales of the venerable Bede, [126] have been illustrated by the diligence, and sometimes embellished by the fancy, of succeeding writers, whose works I am not ambitious either to censure or to transcribe. [127] Yet the historian of the empire may be tempted to pursue the revolutions of a Roman province, till it vanishes from his sight; and an Englishman may curiously trace the establishment of the Barbarians, from whom he derives his name, his laws, and perhaps his origin.

[Footnote 126: See Gildas de Excidio Britanniae, c. 11-25, p. 4-9, edit. Gale. Nennius, Hist. Britonum, c. 28, 35-65, p. 105-115, edit. Gale. Bede, Hist. Ecclesiast. Gentis Anglorum. i. c. 12-16, p. 49-53. c. 22, p. 58, edit. Smith. Chron. Saxonicum, p. 11-23, &c., edit. Gibson. The Anglo-Saxon laws were published by Wilkins, London, 1731, in folio; and the Leges Wallicae, by Wotton and Clarke, London, 1730, in folio.]

[Footnote 127: The laborious Mr. Carte, and the ingenious Mr. Whitaker, are the two modern writers to whom I am principally indebted. The particular historian of Manchester embraces, under that obscure title, a subject almost as extensive as the general history of England. Note: Add the Anglo-Saxon History of Mr. S. Turner; and Sir F. Palgrave Sketch of the "Early History of England."—M.]

About forty years after the dissolution of the Roman government, Vortigern appears to have obtained the supreme, though precarious command of the princes and cities of Britain. That unfortunate monarch has been almost unanimously condemned for the weak and mischievous policy of inviting [128] a formidable stranger, to repel the vexatious inroads of a domestic foe. His ambassadors are despatched, by the gravest historians, to the coast of Germany: they address a pathetic oration to the general assembly of the Saxons, and those warlike Barbarians resolve to assist with a fleet and army the suppliants of a distant and unknown island. If Britain had indeed been unknown to the Saxons, the measure of its calamities would have been less complete. But the strength of the Roman government could not always guard the maritime province against the pirates of Germany; the independent and divided states were exposed to their attacks; and the Saxons might sometimes join the Scots and the Picts, in a tacit, or express, confederacy of rapine and destruction. Vortigern could only balance the various perils, which assaulted on every side his throne and his people; and his policy may deserve either praise or excuse, if he preferred the alliance of those Barbarians, whose naval power rendered them the most dangerous enemies and the most serviceable allies. Hengist and Horsa, as they ranged along the Eastern coast with three ships, were engaged, by the promise of an ample stipend, to embrace the defence of Britain; and their intrepid valor soon delivered the country from the Caledonian invaders. The Isle of Thanet, a secure and fertile district, was allotted for the residence of these German auxiliaries, and they were supplied, according to the treaty, with a plentiful allowance of clothing and provisions. This favorable reception encouraged five thousand warriors to embark with their families in seventeen vessels, and the infant power of Hengist was fortified by this strong and seasonable reenforcement. The crafty Barbarian suggested to Vortigern the obvious advantage of fixing, in the neighborhood of the Picts, a colony of faithful allies: a third fleet of forty ships, under the command of his son and nephew, sailed from Germany, ravaged the Orkneys, and disembarked a new army on the coast of Northumberland, or Lothian, at the opposite extremity of the devoted land. It was easy to foresee, but it was impossible to prevent, the impending evils. The two nations were soon divided and exasperated by mutual jealousies. The Saxons magnified all that they had done and suffered in the cause of an ungrateful people; while the Britons regretted the liberal rewards which could not satisfy the avarice of those haughty mercenaries. The causes of fear and hatred were inflamed into an irreconcilable quarrel. The Saxons flew to arms; and if they perpetrated a treacherous massacre during the security of a feast, they destroyed the reciprocal confidence which sustains the intercourse of peace and war. [129]

[Footnote 128: This invitation, which may derive some countenance from the loose expressions of Gildas and Bede, is framed into a regular story by Witikind, a Saxon monk of the tenth century, (see Cousin, Hist. de l'Empire d'Occident, tom. ii. p. 356.) Rapin, and even Hume, have too freely used this suspicious evidence, without regarding the precise and probable testimony of Tennius: Iterea venerunt tres Chinlae a exilio pulsoe, in quibus erant Hors et Hengist.]

[Footnote 129: Nennius imputes to the Saxons the murder of three hundred British chiefs; a crime not unsuitable to their savage manners. But we are not obliged to believe (see Jeffrey of Monmouth, l. viii. c. 9-12) that Stonehenge is their monument, which the giants had formerly transported from Africa to Ireland, and which was removed to Britain by the order of Ambrosius, and the art of Merlin. Note: Sir f. Palgrave (Hist. of England, p. 36) is inclined to resolve the whole of these stories, as Niebuhr the older Roman history, into poetry. To the editor they appeared, in early youth, so essentially poetic, as to justify the rash attempt to embody them in an Epic Poem, called Samor, commenced at Eton, and finished before he had arrived at the maturer taste of manhood—M.]

Hengist, who boldly aspired to the conquest of Britain, exhorted his countrymen to embrace the glorious opportunity: he painted in lively colors the fertility of the soil, the wealth of the cities, the pusillanimous temper of the natives, and the convenient situation of a spacious solitary island, accessible on all sides to the Saxon fleets. The successive colonies which issued, in the period of a century, from the mouths of the Elbe, the Weser, and the Rhine, were principally composed of three valiant tribes or nations of Germany; the Jutes, the old Saxons, and the Angles. The Jutes, who fought under the peculiar banner of Hengist, assumed the merit of leading their countrymen in the paths of glory, and of erecting, in Kent, the first independent kingdom. The fame of the enterprise was attributed to the primitive Saxons; and the common laws and language of the conquerors are described by the national appellation of a people, which, at the end of four hundred years, produced the first monarchs of South Britain. The Angles were distinguished by their numbers and their success; and they claimed the honor of fixing a perpetual name on the country, of which they occupied the most ample portion. The Barbarians, who followed the hopes of rapine either on the land or sea, were insensibly blended with this triple confederacy; the Frisians, who had been tempted by their vicinity to the British shores, might balance, during a short space, the strength and reputation of the native Saxons; the Danes, the Prussians, the Rugians, are faintly described; and some adventurous Huns, who had wandered as far as the Baltic, might embark on board the German vessels, for the conquest of a new world. [130] But this arduous achievement was not prepared or executed by the union of national powers. Each intrepid chieftain, according to the measure of his fame and fortunes, assembled his followers; equipped a fleet of three, or perhaps of sixty, vessels; chose the place of the attack; and conducted his subsequent operations according to the events of the war, and the dictates of his private interest. In the invasion of Britain many heroes vanquished and fell; but only seven victorious leaders assumed, or at least maintained, the title of kings. Seven independent thrones, the Saxon Heptarchy, [130/1] were founded by the conquerors, and seven families, one of which has been continued, by female succession, to our present sovereign, derived their equal and sacred lineage from Woden, the god of war. It has been pretended, that this republic of kings was moderated by a general council and a supreme magistrate. But such an artificial scheme of policy is repugnant to the rude and turbulent spirit of the Saxons: their laws are silent; and their imperfect annals afford only a dark and bloody prospect of intestine discord. [131]

[Footnote 130: All these tribes are expressly enumerated by Bede, (l. i. c. 15, p. 52, l. v. c. 9, p. 190;) and though I have considered Mr. Whitaker's remarks, (Hist. of Manchester, vol. ii. p. 538-543,) I do not perceive the absurdity of supposing that the Frisians, &c., were mingled with the Anglo-Saxons.]

[Footnote 130/1: This term (the Heptarchy) must be rejected because an idea is conveyed thereby which is substantially wrong. At no one period were there ever seven kingdoms independent of each other. Palgrave, vol. i. p. 46. Mr. Sharon Turner has the merit of having first confuted the popular notion on this subject. Anglo-Saxon History, vol. i. p. 302—M.]

[Footnote 131: Bede has enumerated seven kings, two Saxons, a Jute, and four Angles, who successively acquired in the heptarchy an indefinite supremacy of power and renown. But their reign was the effect, not of law, but of conquest; and he observes, in similar terms, that one of them subdued the Isles of Man and Anglesey; and that another imposed a tribute on the Scots and Picts. (Hist. Eccles. l. ii. c. 5, p. 83.)]

A monk, who, in the profound ignorance of human life, has presumed to exercise the office of historian, strangely disfigures the state of Britain at the time of its separation from the Western empire. Gildas [132] describes in florid language the improvements of agriculture, the foreign trade which flowed with every tide into the Thames and the Severn the solid and lofty construction of public and private edifices; he accuses the sinful luxury of the British people; of a people, according to the same writer, ignorant of the most simple arts, and incapable, without the aid of the Romans, of providing walls of stone, or weapons of iron, for the defence of their native land. [133] Under the long dominion of the emperors, Britain had been insensibly moulded into the elegant and servile form of a Roman province, whose safety was intrusted to a foreign power. The subjects of Honorius contemplated their new freedom with surprise and terror; they were left destitute of any civil or military constitution; and their uncertain rulers wanted either skill, or courage, or authority, to direct the public force against the common enemy. The introduction of the Saxons betrayed their internal weakness, and degraded the character both of the prince and people. Their consternation magnified the danger; the want of union diminished their resources; and the madness of civil factions was more solicitous to accuse, than to remedy, the evils, which they imputed to the misconduct of their adversaries.

Yet the Britons were not ignorant, they could not be ignorant, of the manufacture or the use of arms; the successive and disorderly attacks of the Saxons allowed them to recover from their amazement, and the prosperous or adverse events of the war added discipline and experience to their native valor.

[Footnote 132: See Gildas de Excidio Britanniae, c. i. p. l. edit. Gale.]

[Footnote 133: Mr. Whitaker (Hist. of Manchester, vol. ii. p. 503, 516) has smartly exposed this glaring absurdity, which had passed unnoticed by the general historians, as they were hastening to more interesting and important events]

While the continent of Europe and Africa yielded, without resistance, to the Barbarians, the British island, alone and unaided, maintained a long, a vigorous, though an unsuccessful, struggle, against the formidable pirates, who, almost at the same instant, assaulted the Northern, the Eastern, and the Southern coasts. The cities which had been fortified with skill, were defended with resolution; the advantages of ground, hills, forests, and morasses, were diligently improved by the inhabitants; the conquest of each district was purchased with blood; and the defeats of the Saxons are strongly attested by the discreet silence of their annalist. Hengist might hope to achieve the conquest of Britain; but his ambition, in an active reign of thirty-five years, was confined to the possession of Kent; and the numerous colony which he had planted in the North, was extirpated by the sword of the Britons. The monarchy of the West Saxons was laboriously founded by the persevering efforts of three martial generations. The life of Cerdic, one of the bravest of the children of Woden, was consumed in the conquest of Hampshire, and the Isle of Wight; and the loss which he sustained in the battle of Mount Badon, reduced him to a state of inglorious repose. Kenric, his valiant son, advanced into Wiltshire; besieged Salisbury, at that time seated on a commanding eminence; and vanquished an army which advanced to the relief of the city. In the subsequent battle of Marlborough, [134] his British enemies displayed their military science. Their troops were formed in three lines; each line consisted of three distinct bodies, and the cavalry, the archers, and the pikemen, were distributed according to the principles of Roman tactics. The Saxons charged in one weighty column, boldly encountered with their shord swords the long lances of the Britons, and maintained an equal conflict till the approach of night. Two decisive victories, the death of three British kings, and the reduction of Cirencester, Bath, and Gloucester, established the fame and power of Ceaulin, the grandson of Cerdic, who carried his victorious arms to the banks of the Severn.

[Footnote 134: At Beran-birig, or Barbury-castle, near Marlborough. The Saxon chronicle assigns the name and date. Camden (Britannia, vol. i. p. 128) ascertains the place; and Henry of Huntingdon (Scriptores pest Bedam, p. 314) relates the circumstances of this battle. They are probable and characteristic; and the historians of the twelfth century might consult some materials that no longer exist.]

After a war of a hundred years, the independent Britons still occupied the whole extent of the Western coast, from the wall of Antoninus to the extreme promontory of Cornwall; and the principal cities of the inland country still opposed the arms of the Barbarians. Resistance became more languid, as the number and boldness of the assailants continually increased. Winning their way by slow and painful efforts, the Saxons, the Angles, and their various confederates, advanced from the North, from the East, and from the South, till their victorious banners were united in the centre of the island. Beyond the Severn the Britons still asserted their national freedom, which survived the heptarchy, and even the monarchy, of the Saxons. The bravest warriors, who preferred exile to slavery, found a secure refuge in the mountains of Wales: the reluctant submission of Cornwall was delayed for some ages; [135] and a band of fugitives acquired a settlement in Gaul, by their own valor, or the liberality of the Merovingian kings. [136] The Western angle of Armorica acquired the new appellations of Cornwall, and the Lesser Britain; and the vacant lands of the Osismii were filled by a strange people, who, under the authority of their counts and bishops, preserved the laws and language of their ancestors. To the feeble descendants of Clovis and Charlemagne, the Britons of Armorica refused the customary tribute, subdued the neighboring dioceses of Vannes, Rennes, and Nantes, and formed a powerful, though vassal, state, which has been united to the crown of France. [137]

[Footnote 135: Cornwall was finally subdued by Athelstan, (A.D. 927-941,) who planted an English colony at Exeter, and confined the Britons beyond the River Tamar. See William of Malmsbury, l. ii., in the Scriptores post Bedam, p. 50. The spirit of the Cornish knights was degraded by servitude: and it should seem, from the Romance of Sir Tristram, that their cowardice was almost proverbial.]

[Footnote 136: The establishment of the Britons in Gaul is proved in the sixth century, by Procopius, Gregory of Tours, the second council of Tours, (A.D. 567,) and the least suspicious of their chronicles and lives of saints. The subscription of a bishop of the Britons to the first council of Tours, (A.D. 461, or rather 481,) the army of Riothamus, and the loose declamation of Gildas, (alii transmarinas petebant regiones, c. 25, p. 8,) may countenance an emigration as early as the middle of the fifth century. Beyond that era, the Britons of Armorica can be found only in romance; and I am surprised that Mr. Whitaker (Genuine History of the Britons, p. 214-221) should so faithfully transcribe the gross ignorance of Carte, whose venial errors he has so rigorously chastised.]

[Footnote 137: The antiquities of Bretagne, which have been the subject even of political controversy, are illustrated by Hadrian Valesius, (Notitia Galliarum, sub voce Britannia Cismarina, p. 98-100.) M. D'Anville, (Notice de l'Ancienne Gaule, Corisopiti, Curiosolites, Osismii, Vorganium, p. 248, 258, 508, 720, and Etats de l'Europe, p. 76-80,) Longuerue, (Description de la France, tom. i. p. 84-94,) and the Abbe de Vertot, (Hist. Critique de l'Etablissement des Bretons dans les Gaules, 2 vols. in 12 mo., Paris, 1720.) I may assume the merit of examining the original evidence which they have produced. Note: Compare Gallet, Memoires sur la Bretagne, and Daru, Histoire de Bretagne. These authors appear to me to establish the point of the independence of Bretagne at the time that the insular Britons took refuge in their country, and that the greater part landed as fugitives rather than as conquerors. I observe that M. Lappenberg (Geschichte von England, vol. i. p. 56) supposes the settlement of a military colony formed of British soldiers, (Milites limitanei, laeti,) during the usurpation of Maximus, (381, 388,) who gave their name and peculiar civilization to Bretagne. M. Lappenberg expresses his surprise that Gibbon here rejects the authority which he follows elsewhere—M.]

PART V

In a century of perpetual, or at least implacable, war, much courage, and some skill, must have been exerted for the defence of Britain. Yet if the memory of its champions is almost buried in oblivion, we need not repine; since every age, however destitute of science or virtue, sufficiently abounds with acts of blood and military renown. The tomb of Vortimer, the son of Vortigern, was erected on the margin of the sea-shore, as a landmark formidable to the Saxons, whom he had thrice vanquished in the fields of Kent. Ambrosius Aurelian was descended from a noble family of Romans; [138] his modesty was equal to his valor, and his valor, till the last fatal action, [139] was crowned with splendid success. But every British name is effaced by the illustrious name of Arthur, [140] the hereditary prince of the Silures, in South Wales, and the elective king or general of the nation. According to the most rational account, he defeated, in twelve successive battles, the Angles of the North, and the Saxons of the West; but the declining age of the hero was imbittered by popular ingratitude and domestic misfortunes. The events of his life are less interesting than the singular revolutions of his fame. During a period of five hundred years the tradition of his exploits was preserved, and rudely embellished, by the obscure bards of Wales and Armorica, who were odious to the Saxons, and unknown to the rest of mankind. The pride and curiosity of the Norman conquerors prompted them to inquire into the ancient history of Britain: they listened with fond credulity to the tale of Arthur, and eagerly applauded the merit of a prince who had triumphed over the Saxons, their common enemies. His romance, transcribed in the Latin of Jeffrey of Monmouth, and afterwards translated into the fashionable idiom of the times, was enriched with the various, though incoherent, ornaments which were familiar to the experience, the learning, or the fancy, of the twelfth century. The progress of a Phrygian colony, from the Tyber to the Thames, was easily ingrafted on the fable of the Aeneid; and the royal ancestors of Arthur derived their origin from Troy, and claimed their alliance with the Caesars. His trophies were decorated with captive provinces and Imperial titles; and his Danish victories avenged the recent injuries of his country. The gallantry and superstition of the British hero, his feasts and tournaments, and the memorable institution of his Knights of the Round Table, were faithfully copied from the reigning manners of chivalry; and the fabulous exploits of Uther's son appear less incredible than the adventures which were achieved by the enterprising valor of the Normans. Pilgrimage, and the holy wars, introduced into Europe the specious miracles of Arabian magic. Fairies and giants, flying dragons, and enchanted palaces, were blended with the more simple fictions of the West; and the fate of Britain depended on the art, or the predictions, of Merlin. Every nation embraced and adorned the popular romance of Arthur, and the Knights of the Round Table: their names were celebrated in Greece and Italy; and the voluminous tales of Sir Lancelot and Sir Tristram were devoutly studied by the princes and nobles, who disregarded the genuine heroes and historians of antiquity. At length the light of science and reason was rekindled; the talisman was broken; the visionary fabric melted into air; and by a natural, though unjust, reverse of the public opinion, the severity of the present age is inclined to question the existence of Arthur. [141]

[Footnote 138: Bede, who in his chronicle (p. 28) places Ambrosius under the reign of Zeno, (A.D. 474-491,) observes, that his parents had been "purpura induti;" which he explains, in his ecclesiastical history, by "regium nomen et insigne ferentibus," (l. i. c. 16, p. 53.) The expression of Nennius (c. 44, p. 110, edit. Gale) is still more singular, "Unus de consulibus gentis Romanicae est pater meus."]

[Footnote 139: By the unanimous, though doubtful, conjecture of our antiquarians, Ambrosius is confounded with Natanleod, who (A.D. 508) lost his own life, and five thousand of his subjects, in a battle against Cerdic, the West Saxon, (Chron. Saxon. p. 17, 18.)]

[Footnote 140: As I am a stranger to the Welsh bards, Myrdhin, Llomarch, and Taliessin, my faith in the existence and exploits of Arthur principally rests on the simple and circumstantial testimony of Nennius. (Hist. Brit. c. 62, 63, p. 114.) Mr. Whitaker, (Hist. of Manchester, vol. ii. p. 31-71) had framed an interesting, and even probable, narrative of the wars of Arthur: though it is impossible to allow the reality of the round table. Note: I presume that Gibbon means Llywarch Hen, or the Aged—The Elegies of this Welsh prince and bard have been published by Mr. Owen; to whose works and in the Myvyrian Archaeology, slumbers much curious information on the subject of Welsh tradition and poetry. But the Welsh antiquarians have never obtained a hearing from the public; they have had no Macpherson to compensate for his corruption of their poetic legends by forcing them into popularity—See also Mr. Sharon Turner's Essay on the Welsh Bards—M.]

[Footnote 141: The progress of romance, and the state of learning, in the middle ages, are illustrated by Mr. Thomas Warton, with the taste of a poet, and the minute diligence of an antiquarian. I have derived much instruction from the two learned dissertations prefixed to the first volume of his History of English Poetry. Note: These valuable dissertations should not now be read without the notes and preliminary essay of the late editor, Mr. Price, which, in point of taste and fulness of information, are worthy of accompanying and completing those of Warton—M.]

Resistance, if it cannot avert, must increase the miseries of conquest; and conquest has never appeared more dreadful and destructive than in the hands of the Saxons; who hated the valor of their enemies, disdained the faith of treaties, and violated, without remorse, the most sacred objects of the Christian worship. The fields of battle might be traced, almost in every district, by monuments of bones; the fragments of falling towers were stained with blood; the last of the Britons, without distinction of age or sex, was massacred, [142] in the ruins of Anderida; [143] and the repetition of such calamities was frequent and familiar under the Saxon heptarchy. The arts and religion, the laws and language, which the Romans had so carefully planted in Britain, were extirpated by their barbarous successors. After the destruction of the principal churches, the bishops, who had declined the crown of martyrdom, retired with the holy relics into Wales and Armorica; the remains of their flocks were left destitute of any spiritual food; the practice, and even the remembrance, of Christianity were abolished; and the British clergy might obtain some comfort from the damnation of the idolatrous strangers. The kings of France maintained the privileges of their Roman subjects; but the ferocious Saxons trampled on the laws of Rome, and of the emperors. The proceedings of civil and criminal jurisdiction, the titles of honor, the forms of office, the ranks of society, and even the domestic rights of marriage, testament, and inheritance, were finally suppressed; and the indiscriminate crowd of noble and plebeian slaves was governed by the traditional customs, which had been coarsely framed for the shepherds and pirates of Germany. The language of science, of business, and of conversation, which had been introduced by the Romans, was lost in the general desolation. A sufficient number of Latin or Celtic words might be assumed by the Germans, to express their new wants and ideas; [144] but those illiterate Pagans preserved and established the use of their national dialect. [145] Almost every name, conspicuous either in the church or state, reveals its Teutonic origin; [146] and the geography of England was universally inscribed with foreign characters and appellations. The example of a revolution, so rapid and so complete, may not easily be found; but it will excite a probable suspicion, that the arts of Rome were less deeply rooted in Britain than in Gaul or Spain; and that the native rudeness of the country and its inhabitants was covered by a thin varnish of Italian manners.

[Footnote 142: Hoc anno (490) Aella et Cissa obsederunt Andredes-Ceaster; et interfecerunt omnes qui id incoluerunt; adeo ut ne unus Brito ibi superstes fuerit, (Chron. Saxon. p. 15;) an expression more dreadful in its simplicity, than all the vague and tedious lamentations of the British Jeremiah.]

[Footnote 143: Andredes-Ceaster, or Anderida, is placed by Camden (Britannia, vol. i. p. 258) at Newenden, in the marshy grounds of Kent, which might be formerly covered by the sea, and on the edge of the great forest (Anderida) which overspread so large a portion of Hampshire and Sussex.]

[Footnote 144: Dr. Johnson affirms, that few English words are of British extraction. Mr. Whitaker, who understands the British language, has discovered more than three thousand, and actually produces a long and various catalogue, (vol. ii. p. 235-329.) It is possible, indeed, that many of these words may have been imported from the Latin or Saxon into the native idiom of Britain. Note: Dr. Prichard's very curious researches, which connect the Celtic, as well as the Teutonic languages with the Indo-European class, make it still more difficult to decide between the Celtic or Teutonic origin of English words—See Prichard on the Eastern Origin of the Celtic Nations Oxford, 1831—M.]

[Footnote 145: In the beginning of the seventh century, the Franks and the Anglo-Saxons mutually understood each other's language, which was derived from the same Teutonic root, (Bede, l. i. c. 25, p. 60.)]

[Footnote 146: After the first generation of Italian, or Scottish, missionaries, the dignities of the church were filled with Saxon proselytes.]

This strange alteration has persuaded historians, and even philosophers, that the provincials of Britain were totally exterminated; and that the vacant land was again peopled by the perpetual influx, and rapid increase, of the German colonies. Three hundred thousand Saxons are said to have obeyed the summons of Hengist; [147] the entire emigation of the Angles was attested, in the age of Bede, by the solitude of their native country; [148] and our experience has shown the free propagation of the human race, if they are cast on a fruitful wilderness, where their steps are unconfined, and their subsistence is plentiful. The Saxon kingdoms displayed the face of recent discovery and cultivation; the towns were small, the villages were distant; the husbandry was languid and unskilful; four sheep were equivalent to an acre of the best land; [149] an ample space of wood and morass was resigned to the vague dominion of nature; and the modern bishopric of Durham, the whole territory from the Tyne to the Tees, had returned to its primitive state of a savage and solitary forest. [150] Such imperfect population might have been supplied, in some generations, by the English colonies; but neither reason nor facts can justify the unnatural supposition, that the Saxons of Britain remained alone in the desert which they had subdued. After the sanguinary Barbarians had secured their dominion, and gratified their revenge, it was their interest to preserve the peasants as well as the cattle, of the unresisting country. In each successive revolution, the patient herd becomes the property of its new masters; and the salutary compact of food and labor is silently ratified by their mutual necessities. Wilfrid, the apostle of Sussex, [151] accepted from his royal convert the gift of the Vpeninsula of Selsey, near Chichester, with the persons and property of its inhabitants, who then amounted to eighty-seven families. He released them at once from spiritual and temporal bondage; and two hundred and fifty slaves of both sexes were baptized by their indulgent master. The kingdom of Sussex, which spread from the sea to the Thames, contained seven thousand families; twelve hundred were ascribed to the Isle of Wight; and, if we multiply this vague computation, it may seem probable, that England was cultivated by a million of servants, or villains, who were attached to the estates of their arbitrary landlords. The indigent Barbarians were often tempted to sell their children, or themselves into perpetual, and even foreign, bondage; [152] yet the special exemptions which were granted to national slaves, [153] sufficiently declare that they were much less numerous than the strangers and captives, who had lost their liberty, or changed their masters, by the accidents of war. When time and religion had mitigated the fierce spirit of the Anglo-Saxons, the laws encouraged the frequent practice of manumission; and their subjects, of Welsh or Cambrian extraction, assumed the respectable station of inferior freemen, possessed of lands, and entitled to the rights of civil society. [154] Such gentle treatment might secure the allegiance of a fierce people, who had been recently subdued on the confines of Wales and Cornwall. The sage Ina, the legislator of Wessex, united the two nations in the bands of domestic alliance; and four British lords of Somersetshire may be honorably distinguished in the court of a Saxon monarch. [155]

[Footnote 147: Carte's History of England, vol. i. p. 195. He quotes the British historians; but I much fear, that Jeffrey of Monmouth (l. vi. c. 15) is his only witness.]

[Footnote 148: Bede, Hist. Ecclesiast. l. i. c. 15, p. 52. The fact is probable, and well attested: yet such was the loose intermixture of the German tribes, that we find, in a subsequent period, the law of the Angli and Warini of Germany, (Lindenbrog. Codex, p. 479-486.)]

[Footnote 149: See Dr. Henry's useful and laborious History of Great Britain, vol. ii. p. 388.]

[Footnote 150: Quicquid (says John of Tinemouth) inter Tynam et Tesam fluvios extitit, sola eremi vastitudo tunc temporis fuit, et idcirco nullius ditioni servivit, eo quod sola indomitorum et sylvestrium animalium spelunca et habitatio fuit, (apud Carte, vol. i. p. 195.) From bishop Nicholson (English Historical Library, p. 65, 98) I understand that fair copies of John of Tinemouth's ample collections are preserved in the libraries of Oxford, Lambeth, &c.]

[Footnote 151: See the mission of Wilfrid, &c., in Bede, Hist. Eccles. l. iv. c. 13, 16, p. 155, 156, 159.]

[Footnote 152: From the concurrent testimony of Bede (l. ii. c. 1, p. 78) and William of Malmsbury, (l. iii. p. 102,) it appears, that the Anglo-Saxons, from the first to the last age, persisted in this unnatural practice. Their youths were publicly sold in the market of Rome.]

[Footnote 153: According to the laws of Ina, they could not be lawfully sold beyond the seas.]

[Footnote 154: The life of a Wallus, or Cambricus, homo, who possessed a hyde of land, is fixed at 120 shillings, by the same laws (of Ina, tit. xxxii. in Leg. Anglo-Saxon. p. 20) which allowed 200 shillings for a free Saxon, 1200 for a Thane, (see likewise Leg. Anglo-Saxon. p. 71.) We may observe, that these legislators, the West Saxons and Mercians, continued their British conquests after they became Christians. The laws of the four kings of Kent do not condescend to notice the existence of any subject Britons.]

[Footnote 155: See Carte's Hist. of England, vol. i. p. 278.]

The independent Britons appear to have relapsed into the state of original barbarism, from whence they had been imperfectly reclaimed. Separated by their enemies from the rest of mankind, they soon became an object of scandal and abhorrence to the Catholic world. [156] Christianity was still professed in the mountains of Wales; but the rude schismatics, in the form of the clerical tonsure, and in the day of the celebration of Easter, obstinately resisted the imperious mandates of the Roman pontiffs. The use of the Latin language was insensibly abolished, and the Britons were deprived of the art and learning which Italy communicated to her Saxon proselytes. In Wales and Armorica, the Celtic tongue, the native idiom of the West, was preserved and propagated; and the Bards, who had been the companions of the Druids, were still protected, in the sixteenth century, by the laws of Elizabeth. Their chief, a respectable officer of the courts of Pengwern, or Aberfraw, or Caermarthen, accompanied the king's servants to war: the monarchy of the Britons, which he sung in the front of battle, excited their courage, and justified their depredations; and the songster claimed for his legitimate prize the fairest heifer of the spoil. His subordinate ministers, the masters and disciples of vocal and instrumental music, visited, in their respective circuits, the royal, the noble, and the plebeian houses; and the public poverty, almost exhausted by the clergy, was oppressed by the importunate demands of the bards. Their rank and merit were ascertained by solemn trials, and the strong belief of supernatural inspiration exalted the fancy of the poet, and of his audience. [157] The last retreats of Celtic freedom, the extreme territories of Gaul and Britain, were less adapted to agriculture than to pasturage: the wealth of the Britons consisted in their flocks and herds; milk and flesh were their ordinary food; and bread was sometimes esteemed, or rejected, as a foreign luxury. Liberty had peopled the mountains of Wales and the morasses of Armorica; but their populousness has been maliciously ascribed to the loose practice of polygamy; and the houses of these licentious barbarians have been supposed to contain ten wives, and perhaps fifty children. [158] Their disposition was rash and choleric; they were bold in action and in speech; [159] and as they were ignorant of the arts of peace, they alternately indulged their passions in foreign and domestic war. The cavalry of Armorica, the spearmen of Gwent, and the archers of Merioneth, were equally formidable; but their poverty could seldom procure either shields or helmets; and the inconvenient weight would have retarded the speed and agility of their desultory operations. One of the greatest of the English monarchs was requested to satisfy the curiosity of a Greek emperor concerning the state of Britain; and Henry II. could assert, from his personal experience, that Wales was inhabited by a race of naked warriors, who encountered, without fear, the defensive armor of their enemies. [160]

[Footnote 156: At the conclusion of his history, (A.D. 731,) Bede describes the ecclesiastical state of the island, and censures the implacable, though impotent, hatred of the Britons against the English nation, and the Catholic church, (l. v. c. 23, p. 219.)]

[Footnote 157: Mr. Pennant's Tour in Wales (p. 426-449) has furnished me with a curious and interesting account of the Welsh bards. In the year 1568, a session was held at Caerwys by the special command of Queen Elizabeth, and regular degrees in vocal and instrumental music were conferred on fifty-five minstrels. The prize (a silver harp) was adjudged by the Mostyn family.]

[Footnote 158: Regio longe lateque diffusa, milite, magis quam credibile sit, referta. Partibus equidem in illis miles unus quinquaginta generat, sortitus more barbaro denas aut amplius uxores. This reproach of William of Poitiers (in the Historians of France, tom. xi. p. 88) is disclaimed by the Benedictine editors.]

[Footnote 159: Giraldus Cambrensis confines this gift of bold and ready eloquence to the Romans, the French, and the Britons. The malicious Welshman insinuates that the English taciturnity might possibly be the effect of their servitude under the Normans.]

[Footnote 160: The picture of Welsh and Armorican manners is drawn from Giraldus, (Descript. Cambriae, c. 6-15, inter Script. Camden. p. 886-891,) and the authors quoted by the Abbe de Vertot, (Hist. Critique tom. ii. p. 259-266.)]

By the revolution of Britain, the limits of science, as well as of empire, were contracted. The dark cloud, which had been cleared by the Phoenician discoveries, and finally dispelled by the arms of Caesar, again settled on the shores of the Atlantic, and a Roman province was again lost among the fabulous Islands of the Ocean. One hundred and fifty years after the reign of Honorius, the gravest historian of the times [161] describes the wonders of a remote isle, whose eastern and western parts are divided by an antique wall, the boundary of life and death, or, more properly, of truth and fiction. The east is a fair country, inhabited by a civilized people: the air is healthy, the waters are pure and plentiful, and the earth yields her regular and fruitful increase. In the west, beyond the wall, the air is infectious and mortal; the ground is covered with serpents; and this dreary solitude is the region of departed spirits, who are transported from the opposite shores in substantial boats, and by living rowers. Some families of fishermen, the subjects of the Franks, are excused from tribute, in consideration of the mysterious office which is performed by these Charons of the ocean. Each in his turn is summoned, at the hour of midnight, to hear the voices, and even the names, of the ghosts: he is sensible of their weight, and he feels himself impelled by an unknown, but irresistible power. After this dream of fancy, we read with astonishment, that the name of this island is Brittia; that it lies in the ocean, against the mouth of the Rhine, and less than thirty miles from the continent; that it is possessed by three nations, the Frisians, the Angles, and the Britons; and that some Angles had appeared at Constantinople, in the train of the French ambassadors. From these ambassadors Procopius might be informed of a singular, though not improbable, adventure, which announces the spirit, rather than the delicacy, of an English heroine. She had been betrothed to Radiger, king of the Varni, a tribe of Germans who touched the ocean and the Rhine; but the perfidious lover was tempted, by motives of policy, to prefer his father's widow, the sister of Theodebert, king of the Franks. [162] The forsaken princess of the Angles, instead of bewailing, revenged her disgrace. Her warlike subjects are said to have been ignorant of the use, and even of the form, of a horse; but she boldly sailed from Britain to the mouth of the Rhine, with a fleet of four hundred ships, and an army of one hundred thousand men. After the loss of a battle, the captive Radiger implored the mercy of his victorious bride, who generously pardoned his offence, dismissed her rival, and compelled the king of the Varni to discharge with honor and fidelity the duties of a husband. [163] This gallant exploit appears to be the last naval enterprise of the Anglo-Saxons. The arts of navigation, by which they acquired the empire of Britain and of the sea, were soon neglected by the indolent Barbarians, who supinely renounced all the commercial advantages of their insular situation. Seven independent kingdoms were agitated by perpetual discord; and the British world was seldom connected, either in peace or war, with the nations of the Continent. [164]

[Footnote 161: See Procopius de Bell. Gothic. l. iv. c. 20, p. 620-625. The Greek historian is himself so confounded by the wonders which he relates, that he weakly attempts to distinguish the islands of Britia and Britain, which he has identified by so many inseparable circumstances.]

[Footnote 162: Theodebert, grandson of Clovis, and king of Austrasia, was the most powerful and warlike prince of the age; and this remarkable adventure may be placed between the years 534 and 547, the extreme terms of his reign. His sister Theudechildis retired to Sens, where she founded monasteries, and distributed alms, (see the notes of the Benedictine editors, in tom. ii. p. 216.) If we may credit the praises of Fortunatus, (l. vi. carm. 5, in tom. ii. p. 507,) Radiger was deprived of a most valuable wife.]

[Footnote 163: Perhaps she was the sister of one of the princes or chiefs of the Angles, who landed in 527, and the following years, between the Humber and the Thames, and gradually founded the kingdoms of East Anglia and Mercia. The English writers are ignorant of her name and existence: but Procopius may have suggested to Mr. Rowe the character and situation of Rodogune in the tragedy of the Royal Convert.]

[Footnote 164: In the copious history of Gregory of Tours, we cannot find any traces of hostile or friendly intercourse between France and England except in the marriage of the daughter of Caribert, king of Paris, quam regis cujusdam in Cantia filius matrimonio copulavit, (l. ix. c. 28, in tom. ii. p. 348.) The bishop of Tours ended his history and his life almost immediately before the conversion of Kent.]

I have now accomplished the laborious narrative of the decline and fall of the Roman empire, from the fortunate age of Trajan and the Antonines, to its total extinction in the West, about five centuries after the Christian era. At that unhappy period, the Saxons fiercely struggled with the natives for the possession of Britain: Gaul and Spain were divided between the powerful monarchies of the Franks and Visigoths, and the dependent kingdoms of the Suevi and Burgundians: Africa was exposed to the cruel persecution of the Vandals, and the savage insults of the Moors: Rome and Italy, as far as the banks of the Danube, were afflicted by an army of Barbarian mercenaries, whose lawless tyranny was succeeded by the reign of Theodoric the Ostrogoth. All the subjects of the empire, who, by the use of the Latin language, more particularly deserved the name and privileges of Romans, were oppressed by the disgrace and calamities of foreign conquest; and the victorious nations of Germany established a new system of manners and government in the western countries of Europe. The majesty of Rome was faintly represented by the princes of Constantinople, the feeble and imaginary successors of Augustus. Yet they continued to reign over the East, from the Danube to the Nile and Tigris; the Gothic and Vandal kingdoms of Italy and Africa were subverted by the arms of Justinian; and the history of the Greek emperors may still afford a long series of instructive lessons, and interesting revolutions.

PART VI

The Greeks, after their country had been reduced into a province, imputed the triumphs of Rome, not to the merit, but to the fortune, of the republic. The inconstant goddess, who so blindly distributes and resumes her favors, had now consented (such was the language of envious flattery) to resign her wings, to descend from her globe, and to fix her firm and immutable throne on the banks of the Tyber. [1000] A wiser Greek, who has composed, with a philosophic spirit, the memorable history of his own times, deprived his countrymen of this vain and delusive comfort, by opening to their view the deep foundations of the greatness of Rome. [2000] The fidelity of the citizens to each other, and to the state, was confirmed by the habits of education, and the prejudices of religion. Honor, as well as virtue, was the principle of the republic; the ambitious citizens labored to deserve the solemn glories of a triumph; and the ardor of the Roman youth was kindled into active emulation, as often as they beheld the domestic images of their ancestors. [3000] The temperate struggles of the patricians and plebeians had finally established the firm and equal balance of the constitution; which united the freedom of popular assemblies, with the authority and wisdom of a senate, and the executive powers of a regal magistrate. When the consul displayed the standard of the republic, each citizen bound himself, by the obligation of an oath, to draw his sword in the cause of his country, till he had discharged the sacred duty by a military service of ten years. This wise institution continually poured into the field the rising generations of freemen and soldiers; and their numbers were reenforced by the warlike and populous states of Italy, who, after a brave resistance, had yielded to the valor and embraced the alliance, of the Romans. The sage historian, who excited the virtue of the younger Scipio, and beheld the ruin of Carthage, [4000] has accurately described their military system; their levies, arms, exercises, subordination, marches, encampments; and the invincible legion, superior in active strength to the Macedonian phalanx of Philip and Alexander. From these institutions of peace and war Polybius has deduced the spirit and success of a people, incapable of fear, and impatient of repose. The ambitious design of conquest, which might have been defeated by the seasonable conspiracy of mankind, was attempted and achieved; and the perpetual violation of justice was maintained by the political virtues of prudence and courage. The arms of the republic, sometimes vanquished in battle, always victorious in war, advanced with rapid steps to the Euphrates, the Danube, the Rhine, and the Ocean; and the images of gold, or silver, or brass, that might serve to represent the nations and their kings, were successively broken by the iron monarchy of Rome. [5000]

[Footnote 1000: Such are the figurative expressions of Plutarch, (Opera, tom. ii. p. 318, edit. Wechel,) to whom, on the faith of his son Lamprias, (Fabricius, Bibliot. Graec. tom. iii. p. 341,) I shall boldly impute the malicious declamation. The same opinions had prevailed among the Greeks two hundred and fifty years before Plutarch; and to confute them is the professed intention of Polybius, (Hist. l. i. p. 90, edit. Gronov. Amstel. 1670.)]

[Footnote 2000: See the inestimable remains of the sixth book of Polybius, and many other parts of his general history, particularly a digression in the seventeenth book, in which he compares the phalanx and the legion.]

[Footnote 3000: Sallust, de Bell. Jugurthin. c. 4. Such were the generous professions of P. Scipio and Q. Maximus. The Latin historian had read and most probably transcribes, Polybius, their contemporary and friend.]

[Footnote 4000: While Carthage was in flames, Scipio repeated two lines of the Iliad, which express the destruction of Troy, acknowledging to Polybius, his friend and preceptor, (Polyb. in Excerpt. de Virtut. et Vit. tom. ii. p. 1455-1465,) that while he recollected the vicissitudes of human affairs, he inwardly applied them to the future calamities of Rome, (Appian. in Libycis, p. 136, edit. Toll.)]

[Footnote 5000: See Daniel, ii. 31-40. "And the fourth kingdom shall be strong as iron; forasmuch as iron breaketh in pieces and subdueth all things." The remainder of the prophecy (the mixture of iron and clay) was accomplished, according to St. Jerom, in his own time. Sicut enim in principio nihil Romano Imperio fortius et durius, ita in fine rerum nihil imbecillius; quum et in bellis civilibus et adversus diversas nationes, aliarum gentium barbararum auxilio indigemus, (Opera, tom. v. p. 572.)]

The rise of a city, which swelled into an empire, may deserve, as a singular prodigy, the reflection of a philosophic mind. But the decline of Rome was the natural and inevitable effect of immoderate greatness. Prosperity ripened the principle of decay; the causes of destruction multiplied with the extent of conquest; and as soon as time or accident had removed the artificial supports, the stupendous fabric yielded to the pressure of its own weight. The story of its ruin is simple and obvious; and instead of inquiring why the Roman empire was destroyed, we should rather be surprised that it had subsisted so long. The victorious legions, who, in distant wars, acquired the vices of strangers and mercenaries, first oppressed the freedom of the republic, and afterwards violated the majesty of the purple. The emperors, anxious for their personal safety and the public peace, were reduced to the base expedient of corrupting the discipline which rendered them alike formidable to their sovereign and to the enemy; the vigor of the military government was relaxed, and finally dissolved, by the partial institutions of Constantine; and the Roman world was overwhelmed by a deluge of Barbarians.

The decay of Rome has been frequently ascribed to the translation of the seat of empire; but this History has already shown, that the powers of government were divided, rather than removed. The throne of Constantinople was erected in the East; while the West was still possessed by a series of emperors who held their residence in Italy, and claimed their equal inheritance of the legions and provinces. This dangerous novelty impaired the strength, and fomented the vices, of a double reign: the instruments of an oppressive and arbitrary system were multiplied; and a vain emulation of luxury, not of merit, was introduced and supported between the degenerate successors of Theodosius. Extreme distress, which unites the virtue of a free people, imbitters the factions of a declining monarchy. The hostile favorites of Arcadius and Honorius betrayed the republic to its common enemies; and the Byzantine court beheld with indifference, perhaps with pleasure, the disgrace of Rome, the misfortunes of Italy, and the loss of the West. Under the succeeding reigns, the alliance of the two empires was restored; but the aid of the Oriental Romans was tardy, doubtful, and ineffectual; and the national schism of the Greeks and Latins was enlarged by the perpetual difference of language and manners, of interests, and even of religion. Yet the salutary event approved in some measure the judgment of Constantine. During a long period of decay, his impregnable city repelled the victorious armies of Barbarians, protected the wealth of Asia, and commanded, both in peace and war, the important straits which connect the Euxine and Mediterranean Seas. The foundation of Constantinople more essentially contributed to the preservation of the East, than to the ruin of the West.

As the happiness of a future life is the great object of religion, we may hear without surprise or scandal, that the introduction or at least the abuse, of Christianity had some influence on the decline and fall of the Roman empire. The clergy successfully preached the doctrines of patience and pusillanimity: the active virtues of society were discouraged; and the last remains of military spirit were buried in the cloister: a large portion of public and private wealth was consecrated to the specious demands of charity and devotion; and the soldiers' pay was lavished on the useless multitudes of both sexes, who could only plead the merits of abstinence and chastity. [511] Faith, zeal, curiosity, and the more earthly passions of malice and ambition, kindled the flame of theological discord; the church, and even the state, were distracted by religious factions, whose conflicts were sometimes bloody, and always implacable; the attention of the emperors was diverted from camps to synods; the Roman world was oppressed by a new species of tyranny; and the persecuted sects became the secret enemies of their country. Yet party spirit, however pernicious or absurd, is a principle of union as well as of dissension. The bishops, from eighteen hundred pulpits, inculcated the duty of passive obedience to a lawful and orthodox sovereign; their frequent assemblies, and perpetual correspondence, maintained the communion of distant churches; and the benevolent temper of the gospel was strengthened, though confined, by the spiritual alliance of the Catholics. The sacred indolence of the monks was devoutly embraced by a servile and effeminate age; but if superstition had not afforded a decent retreat, the same vices would have tempted the unworthy Romans to desert, from baser motives, the standard of the republic. Religious precepts are easily obeyed, which indulge and sanctify the natural inclinations of their votaries; but the pure and genuine influence of Christianity may be traced in its beneficial, though imperfect, effects on the Barbarian proselytes of the North. If the decline of the Roman empire was hastened by the conversion of Constantine, his victorious religion broke the violence of the fall, and mollified the ferocious temper of the conquerors.

[Footnote 511: It might be a curious speculation, how far the purer morals of the genuine and more active Christians may have compensated, in the population of the Roman empire, for the secession of such numbers into inactive and unproductive celibacy—M.]

This awful revolution may be usefully applied to the instruction of the present age. It is the duty of a patriot to prefer and promote the exclusive interest and glory of his native country: but a philos may be permitted to enlarge his views, and to consider Europe as one great republic whose various inhabitants have obtained almost the same level of politeness and cultivation. The balance of power will continue to fluctuate, and the prosperity of our own, or the neighboring kingdoms, may be alternately exalted or depressed; but these partial events cannot essentially injure our general state of happiness, the system of arts, and laws, and manners, which so advantageously distinguish, above the rest of mankind, the Europeans and their colonies. The savage nations of the globe are the common enemies of civilized society; and we may inquire, with anxious curiosity, whether Europe is still threatened with a repetition of those calamities, which formerly oppressed the arms and institutions of Rome. Perhaps the same reflections will illustrate the fall of that mighty empire, and explain the probable causes of our actual security.

I. The Romans were ignorant of the extent of their danger, and the number of their enemies. Beyond the Rhine and Danube, the Northern countries of Europe and Asia were filled with innumerable tribes of hunters and shepherds, poor, voracious, and turbulent; bold in arms, and impatient to ravish the fruits of industry. The Barbarian world was agitated by the rapid impulse of war; and the peace of Gaul or Italy was shaken by the distant revolutions of China. The Huns, who fled before a victorious enemy, directed their march towards the West; and the torrent was swelled by the gradual accession of captives and allies. The flying tribes who yielded to the Huns assumed in their turn the spirit of conquest; the endless column of Barbarians pressed on the Roman empire with accumulated weight; and, if the foremost were destroyed, the vacant space was instantly replenished by new assailants. Such formidable emigrations can no longer issue from the North; and the long repose, which has been imputed to the decrease of population, is the happy consequence of the progress of arts and agriculture. Instead of some rude villages, thinly scattered among its woods and morasses, Germany now produces a list of two thousand three hundred walled towns: the Christian kingdoms of Denmark, Sweden, and Poland, have been successively established; and the Hanse merchants, with the Teutonic knights, have extended their colonies along the coast of the Baltic, as far as the Gulf of Finland. From the Gulf of Finland to the Eastern Ocean, Russia now assumes the form of a powerful and civilized empire. The plough, the loom, and the forge, are introduced on the banks of the Volga, the Oby, and the Lena; and the fiercest of the Tartar hordes have been taught to tremble and obey. The reign of independent Barbarism is now contracted to a narrow span; and the remnant of Calmucks or Uzbecks, whose forces may be almost numbered, cannot seriously excite the apprehensions of the great republic of Europe. [6000] Yet this apparent security should not tempt us to forget, that new enemies, and unknown dangers, may possibly arise from some obscure people, scarcely visible in the map of the world, The Arabs or Saracens, who spread their conquests from India to Spain, had languished in poverty and contempt, till Mahomet breathed into those savage bodies the soul of enthusiasm.

[Footnote 6000: *The French and English editors of the Genealogical History of the Tartars have subjoined a curious, though imperfect, description of their present state. We might question the independence of the Calmucks, or Eluths, since they have been recently vanquished by the Chinese, who, in the year 1759, subdued the Lesser Bucharia, and advanced into the country of Badakshan, near the source of the Oxus, (Memoires sur les Chinois, tom. i. p. 325-400.) But these conquests are precarious, nor will I venture to insure the safety of the Chinese empire.*]

II. The empire of Rome was firmly established by the singular and perfect coalition of its members. The subject nations, resigning the hope, and even the wish, of independence, embraced the character of Roman citizens; and the provinces of the West were reluctantly torn by the Barbarians from the bosom of their mother country. [7000] But this union was purchased by the loss of national freedom and military spirit; and the servile provinces, destitute of life and motion, expected their safety from the mercenary troops and governors, who were directed by the orders of a distant court. The happiness of a hundred millions depended on the personal merit of one or two men, perhaps children, whose minds were corrupted by education, luxury, and despotic power. The deepest wounds were inflicted on the empire during the minorities of the sons and grandsons of Theodosius; and, after those incapable princes seemed to attain the age of manhood, they abandoned the church to the bishops, the state to the eunuchs, and the provinces to the Barbarians. Europe is now divided into twelve powerful, though unequal kingdoms, three respectable commonwealths, and a variety of smaller, though independent, states: the chances of royal and ministerial talents are multiplied, at least, with the number of its rulers; and a Julian, or Semiramis, may reign in the North, while Arcadius and Honorius again slumber on the thrones of the South. The abuses of tyranny are restrained by the mutual influence of fear and shame; republics have acquired order and stability; monarchies have imbibed the principles of freedom, or, at least, of moderation; and some sense of honor and justice is introduced into the most defective constitutions by the general manners of the times. In peace, the progress of knowledge and industry is accelerated by the emulation of so many active rivals: in war, the European forces are exercised by temperate and undecisive contests. If a savage conqueror should issue from the deserts of Tartary, he must repeatedly vanquish the robust peasants of Russia, the numerous armies of Germany, the gallant nobles of France, and the intrepid freemen of Britain; who, perhaps, might confederate for their common defence. Should the victorious Barbarians carry slavery and desolation as far as the Atlantic Ocean, ten thousand vessels would transport beyond their pursuit the remains of civilized society; and Europe would revive and flourish in the American world, which is already filled with her colonies and institutions. [8000]

[Footnote 7000: The prudent reader will determine how far this general proposition is weakened by the revolt of the Isaurians, the independence of Britain and Armorica, the Moorish tribes, or the Bagaudae of Gaul and Spain, (vol. i. p. 328, vol. iii. p. 315, vol. iii. p. 372, 480.)]

[Footnote 8000: America now contains about six millions of European blood and descent; and their numbers, at least in the North, are continually increasing. Whatever may be the changes of their political situation, they must preserve the manners of Europe; and we may reflect with some pleasure, that the English language will probably be diffused ever an immense and populous continent.]

III. Cold, poverty, and a life of danger and fatigue, fortify the strength and courage of Barbarians. In every age they have oppressed the polite and peaceful nations of China, India, and Persia, who neglected, and still neglect, to counterbalance these natural powers by the resources of military art. The warlike states of antiquity, Greece, Macedonia, and Rome, educated a race of soldiers; exercised their bodies, disciplined their courage, multiplied their forces by regular evolutions, and converted the iron, which they possessed, into strong and serviceable weapons. But this superiority insensibly declined with their laws and manners; and the feeble policy of Constantine and his successors armed and instructed, for the ruin of the empire, the rude valor of the Barbarian mercenaries. The military art has been changed by the invention of gunpowder; which enables man to command the two most powerful agents of nature, air and fire. Mathematics, chemistry, mechanics, architecture, have been applied to the service of war; and the adverse parties oppose to each other the most elaborate modes of attack and of defence. Historians may indignantly observe, that the preparations of a siege would found and maintain a flourishing colony; [9000] yet we cannot be displeased, that the subversion of a city should be a work of cost and difficulty; or that an industrious people should be protected by those arts, which survive and supply the decay of military virtue. Cannon and fortifications now form an impregnable barrier against the Tartar horse; and Europe is secure from any future irruptions of Barbarians; since, before they can conquer, they must cease to be barbarous. Their gradual advances in the science of war would always be accompanied, as we may learn from the example of Russia, with a proportionable improvement in the arts of peace and civil policy; and they themselves must deserve a place among the polished nations whom they subdue.

[Footnote 9000: On avoit fait venir (for the siege of Turin) 140 pieces de canon; et il est a remarquer que chaque gros canon monte revient a environ ecus: il y avoit 100,000 boulets; 106,000 cartouches d'une facon, et 300,000 d'une autre; 21,000 bombes; 27,700 grenades, 15,000 sacs a terre, 30,000 instruments pour la pionnage; 1,200,000 livres de poudre. Ajoutez a ces munitions, le plomb, le fer, et le fer-blanc, les cordages, tout ce qui sert aux mineurs, le souphre, le salpetre, les outils de toute espece. Il est certain que les frais de tous ces preparatifs de destruction suffiroient pour fonder et pour faire fleurir la plus aombreuse colonie. Voltaire, Siecle de Louis XIV. c. xx. in his Works. tom. xi. p. 391.]

Should these speculations be found doubtful or fallacious, there still remains a more humble source of comfort and hope. The discoveries of ancient and modern navigators, and the domestic history, or tradition, of the most enlightened nations, represent the human savage, naked both in body and mind and destitute of laws, of arts, of ideas, and almost of language. [1001] From this abject condition, perhaps the primitive and universal state of man, he has gradually arisen to command the animals, to fertilize the earth, to traverse the ocean and to measure the heavens. His progress in the improvement and exercise of his mental and corporeal faculties [1101] has been irregular and various; infinitely slow in the beginning, and increasing by degrees with redoubled velocity: ages of laborious ascent have been followed by a moment of rapid downfall; and the several climates of the globe have felt the vicissitudes of light and darkness. Yet the experience of four thousand years should enlarge our hopes, and diminish our apprehensions: we cannot determine to what height the human species may aspire in their advances towards perfection; but it may safely be presumed, that no people, unless the face of nature is changed, will relapse into their original barbarism. The improvements of society may be viewed under a threefold aspect. 1. The poet or philosopher illustrates his age and country by the efforts of a single mind; but those superior powers of reason or fancy are rare and spontaneous productions; and the genius of Homer, or Cicero, or Newton, would excite less admiration, if they could be created by the will of a prince, or the lessons of a preceptor. 2. The benefits of law and policy, of trade and manufactures, of arts and sciences, are more solid and permanent: and many individuals may be qualified, by education and discipline, to promote, in their respective stations, the interest of the community. But this general order is the effect of skill and labor; and the complex machinery may be decayed by time, or injured by violence.

3. Fortunately for mankind, the more useful, or, at least, more necessary arts, can be performed without superior talents, or national subordination: without the powers of one, or the union of many. Each village, each family, each individual, must always possess both ability and inclination to perpetuate the use of fire [1201] and of metals; the propagation and service of domestic animals; the methods of hunting and fishing; the rudiments of navigation; the imperfect cultivation of corn, or other nutritive grain; and the simple practice of the mechanic trades. Private genius and public industry may be extirpated; but these hardy plants survive the tempest, and strike an everlasting root into the most unfavorable soil. The splendid days of Augustus and Trajan were eclipsed by a cloud of ignorance; and the Barbarians subverted the laws and palaces of Rome. But the scythe, the invention or emblem of Saturn, [1301] still continued annually to mow the harvests of Italy; and the human feasts of the Laestrigons [1401] have never been renewed on the coast of Campania.

[Footnote 1001: It would be an easy, though tedious, task, to produce the authorities of poets, philosophers, and historians. I shall therefore content myself with appealing to the decisive and authentic testimony of Diodorus Siculus, (tom. i. l. i. p. 11, 12, l. iii. p. 184, &c., edit. Wesseling.) The Icthyophagi, who in his time wandered along the shores of the Red Sea, can only be compared to the natives of New Holland, (Dampier's Voyages, vol. i. p. 464-469.) Fancy, or perhaps reason, may still suppose an extreme and absolute state of nature far below the level of these savages, who had acquired some arts and instruments.]

[Footnote 1101: See the learned and rational work of the president Goguet, de l'Origine des Loix, des Arts, et des Sciences. He traces from facts, or conjectures, (tom. i. p. 147-337, edit. 12mo.,) the first and most difficult steps of human invention.]

[Footnote 1201: It is certain, however strange, that many nations have been ignorant of the use of fire. Even the ingenious natives of Otaheite, who are destitute of metals, have not invented any earthen vessels capable of sustaining the action of fire, and of communicating the heat to the liquids which they contain.]

[Footnote 1301: Plutarch. Quaest. Rom. in tom. ii. p. 275. Macrob. Saturnal. l. i. c. 8, p. 152, edit. London. The arrival of Saturn (of his religious worship) in a ship, may indicate, that the savage coast of Latium was first discovered and civilized by the Phoenicians.]

[Footnote 1401: In the ninth and tenth books of the Odyssey, Homer has embellished the tales of fearful and credulous sailors, who transformed the cannibals of Italy and Sicily into monstrous giants.]

Since the first discovery of the arts, war, commerce, and religious zeal have diffused, among the savages of the Old and New World, these inestimable gifts: they have been successively propagated; they can never be lost. We may therefore acquiesce in the pleasing conclusion, that every age of the world has increased, and still increases, the real wealth, the happiness, the knowledge, and perhaps the virtue, of the human race. [1501]

[Footnote 1501: The merit of discovery has too often been stained with avarice, cruelty, and fanaticism; and the intercourse of nations has produced the communication of disease and prejudice. A singular exception is due to the virtue of our own times and country. The five great voyages, successively undertaken by the command of his present Majesty, were inspired by the pure and generous love of science and of mankind. The same prince, adapting his benefactions to the different stages of society, has founded his school of painting in his capital; and has introduced into the islands of the South Sea the vegetables and animals most useful to human life.]

EDWARD GIBBON – A SHORT BIOGRAPHY

Edward Gibbon was born on 8th May, 1737, the son of Edward and Judith Gibbon at Lime Grove, in the town of Putney, Surrey. He had six siblings, all of whom died in infancy. His grandfather, also named Edward, had lost everything as a result of the South Sea Bubble collapse in 1720, but eventually regained much of his wealth, so that Gibbon's father was able to inherit a substantial estate.

As a youth, Gibbon's health was under constant threat. He described himself as "a puny child, neglected by my Mother, starved by my nurse". At age nine, he was sent to Dr. Woddeson's school at Kingston-upon-Thames, shortly after which his mother died. He was then moved to the Westminster School boarding house, owned by his adored "Aunt Kitty", Catherine Porten.

By 1751, Gibbon's reading was already extensive and certainly pointed toward his future pursuits having covered such works as Laurence Echard's Roman History (1713), William Howell's An Institution of General History (1680–85), and several of the 65 volumes of the acclaimed Universal History from the Earliest Account of Time (1747–1768).

Following a stay at Bath, at age 15, in 1752 to improve his health, Gibbon was sent by his father to Magdalen College, Oxford, where he was enrolled as a gentleman-commoner (a rank of student above commoners i.e. normal students who paid the normal rate for tuition and boarding but below noblemen. They paid double the tuition fee and enjoyed more privileges). He was ill-suited, however, to the college atmosphere and later rued his 14 months there as the "most idle and unprofitable" of his life. Because of his autobiography, it used to be thought that his penchant for "theological controversy" (his aunt's influence) fully bloomed when he came under the spell of the deist or rationalist theologian Conyers Middleton, the author of Free Inquiry into the Miraculous Powers (1749). In that tract, Middleton denied the validity of such powers; Gibbon promptly objected, or so the argument used to run. The product of that disagreement, with some assistance from the work of Catholic Bishop Jacques-Bénigne Bossuet, and that of the Elizabethan Jesuit Robert Parsons, yielded the most memorable event of his time at Oxford: his conversion to Roman Catholicism on 8th June 1753. He was further 'corrupted' by the 'free thinking' deism of the playwright/poet couple David and Lucy Mallet; and finally Gibbon's father, already deeply in despair, had had enough.

However, this story has fallen somewhat into disrepute only being introduced to the final draft of Gibbon's "Memoirs" in 1792–93. There are also other accounts as to why Gibbons may have given a new 'backstory' to his conversion.

Within weeks of his conversion, the Gibbons was removed from Oxford and sent to live under the care and tutelage of Daniel Pavillard, Reformed pastor of Lausanne in Switzerland.

Here he made great friendships with Jacques Georges Deyverdun (the French-language translator of Goethe's The Sorrows of Young Werther), and John Baker Holroyd (later Lord Sheffield).

Just a year and a half later, after his father threatened to disinherit him, on Christmas Day, 1754, he reconverted to Protestantism. "The various articles of the Romish creed," he wrote, "disappeared like a dream".

He remained in Lausanne for five intellectually productive years, a period that greatly enriched Gibbon's already immense aptitude for scholarship and erudition: he read Latin literature; travelled throughout Switzerland studying its cantons' constitutions; and studied the works of Hugo Grotius, Samuel von Pufendorf, John Locke, Pierre Bayle, and Blaise Pascal.

He also met the one love in his life: the daughter of the pastor of Crassy; Suzanne Curchod. As the two developed an ever-closer relationship; Gibbon raised the question of marriage, but ultimately wedlock was out of the question, blocked both by his father's staunch disapproval and Curchod's refusal to leave Switzerland.

Gibbon returned to England in August 1758 to face his father. There was to be no refusal of his wishes. Gibbon put it rather poetically: "I sighed as a lover, I obeyed as a son." He proceeded to cut off all contact with Suzanne, even as she vowed to wait for him.

Upon his return to England, Gibbon published his first book, Essai sur l'Étude de la Littérature in 1761, which produced an initial taste of celebrity and distinguished him, in Paris at least, as a man of letters.

Interestingly to add to his interests and talents he had, from 1759 to 1770, served on active duty and then in reserve with the South Hampshire militia, his deactivation in December 1762 coinciding with the militia's dispersal after the Seven Years' War.

In 1763, he began as many men of privilege of class then did to round out and embellish their education on the Grand Tour, which included a visit to Rome. In his autobiography Gibbon vividly records his rapture when he finally neared "the great object of my pilgrimage": ...at the distance of twenty-five years I can neither forget nor express the strong emotions which agitated my mind as I first approached and entered the eternal City. After a sleepless night, I trod, with a lofty step the ruins of the Forum; each memorable spot where Romulus stood, or Tully spoke, or Caesar fell, was at once present to my eye; and several days of intoxication were lost or enjoyed before I could descend to a cool and minute investigation.

And it was here that Gibbon first conceived the idea of composing a history of the city, later extended to the entire empire, a moment known to history as the Capitoline vision: "It was at Rome, on the 15th of October 1764, as I sat musing amidst the ruins of the Capitol, while the barefooted fryars were singing

Vespers in the temple of Jupiter, that the idea of writing the decline and fall of the City first started to my mind".

In June 1765, Gibbon returned to his father's house. He would remain there for the following five years until his father's death. He always considered this span of time as the worst of his life. He busied himself with various writing projects which failed to reach fruition. His first historical narrative, the History of Switzerland, was neither published nor finished. Gibbon had become too self-critical and abandoned the work a mere 60 pages in.

His second work, Memoires Litteraires de la Grande Bretagne, in two volumes, described both the literary and the social conditions of England at the time. When published it failed to gain any traction.

With the death of his father and the settling of the estate Gibbon had enough of a legacy to be free of any financial problems. He moved to Bentinck Street in London and began to live the life that suited him. He joined a number of clubs, including Dr. Johnson's Literary Club. He succeeded Oliver Goldsmith at the Royal Academy as 'professor in ancient history' (honorary but nonetheless prestigious). And he was writing. The work for which he would gain worldwide fame was under way.

But still other interests would divert his attention.

In late 1774, he was initiated a freemason of the Premier Grand Lodge of England. That same year he was returned to Parliament for the seat of Liskeard in Cornwall through the intervention of his relative and patron, Edward Eliot. Gibbon became a typical backbencher, mute and indifferent to his responsibilities, apart from routinely voting for the Whig Administration.

After several rewrites usually brought on by self-doubt and seven years of work the first volume of The History of the Decline and Fall of the Roman Empire, was published on 17th February 1776.

It was an immediate success. Within a year it had gone through three editions and the royalties were very handsome indeed.

Further volumes followed quickly and with the same measure of success; Volumes II and III were published on 1st March 1781, and volume IV was released in June 1784. Volumes V and VI were completed during a second Lausanne sojourn (September 1783 to August 1787) where Gibbon reunited with his friend Deyverdun. By early 1787, he was "straining for the goal" and with great relief the project was finished in June. Gibbon later wrote: "It was on the day, or rather the night, of 27th June 1787, between the hours of eleven and twelve, that I wrote the last lines of the last page in a summer-house in my garden...I will not dissemble the first emotions of joy on the recovery of my freedom, and perhaps the establishment of my fame. But my pride was soon humbled, and a sober melancholy was spread over my mind by the idea that I had taken my everlasting leave of an old and agreeable companion, and that, whatsoever might be the future date of my history, the life of the historian must be short and precarious".

Volumes V, and VI finally reached the press in May 1788, their publication having been delayed since March, so it could coincide with a dinner party on the 8th celebrating Gibbon's 51st birthday.

Praise came from all directions. Leading it were such contemporary luminaries as Adam Smith, Lord Camden, and Horace Walpole. Smith remarked that Gibbon's triumph had positioned him "at the very head of Europe's literary tribe."

In November of that year, he was elected a Fellow of the Royal Society, the main proposer being his good friend Lord Sheffield.

But the high-water mark had been reached and for Gibbon the following years were of sorrow and increasing health problems.

In 1789 he returned to Lausanne only to learn of and be "deeply affected" by the death of Deyverdun, who had willed Gibbon his home, La Grotte. He resided there with little commotion, took in the local society, received a visit from Sheffield in 1791, and "shared the common abhorrence" of the French Revolution.

In a letter to Lord Sheffield on 5th February 1791, Gibbon praised Burke's Reflections on the Revolution in France: "Burke's book is a most admirable medicine against the French disease, which has made too much progress even in this happy country. I admire his eloquence, I approve his politics, I adore his chivalry, and I can even forgive his superstition...The French spread so many lyes about the sentiments of the English nation, that I wish the most considerable men of all parties and descriptions would join in some public act declaring themselves satisfied with, and resolved to support, our present constitution."

In 1793, word came of Lady Sheffield's death; Gibbon immediately left Lausanne and set sail to comfort a grieving but composed Sheffield. But for Gibbon too, time was failing. His health began to fail critically in December, and at the turn of the new year, he was in rapid decline.

Gibbon is believed to have suffered from an extreme case of scrotal swelling, probably a hydrocele testis, a condition in which the scrotum swell with fluid in a compartment overlying either testicle. In an age when close-fitting clothes were fashionable, his condition led to a chronic and disfiguring inflammation that left Gibbon a lonely figure. As his condition worsened, he underwent numerous procedures to alleviate the condition, but with no enduring success. In early January, the last of a series of three operations caused an unremitting peritonitis to set in and spread, from which he died.

Edward Gibbon, the "English giant of the Enlightenment" finally succumbed at 12:45 pm, 16 January 1794 at age 56. He was buried in the Sheffield Mausoleum attached to the north transept of the Church of St Mary and St Andrew, Fletching, East Sussex.

EDWARD GIBBON – A CONCISE BIBLIOGRAPHY

Essai sur l'Étude de la Littérature (1761)
Critical Observations on the Sixth Book of Vergil's 'The Aeneid' (1770)
The History of the Decline and Fall of the Roman Empire (Vol I, 1776; Vols. II, III, 1781; Vols. IV, V, VI, 1788–1789)
A Vindication of some passages in the fifteenth and sixteenth chapters of the History of the Decline and Fall of the Roman Empire (1779)
Mémoire Justificatif pour servir de Réponse à l'Exposé, etc. de la Cour de France (1779)

Mémoires Littéraires de la Grande-Bretagne. co-author: Georges Deyverdun (2 vols: vol. 1, 1767; vol. 2, 1768)
Miscellaneous Works of Edward Gibbon, Esq., ed. John Lord Sheffield (2 vols., 1796; 5 vols., 1814; 3 vols., 1815) Includes Memoirs of the Life and Writings of Edward Gibbon, Esq.
Autobiographies of Edward Gibbon, ed. John Murray (1896). Edward Gibbon's complete memoirs (six drafts) from the original manuscripts.
The Private Letters of Edward Gibbon, 2 vols., ed. Rowland E. Prothero (1896)
The works of Edward Gibbon (Volume 3, 1906)
Gibbon's Journal to 28 January 1763, ed. D.M. Low (1929)
Le Journal de Gibbon à Lausanne, ed. Georges A. Bonnard (1945)
Miscellanea Gibboniana, eds. G.R. de Beer, L. Junod, G.A. Bonnard (1952)
The Letters of Edward Gibbon, 3 vols., ed. J.E. Norton (1956). vol. 1: 1750–1773; vol. 2: 1774–1784; vol. 3: 1784–1794. cited as 'Norton, Letters'
Gibbon's Journey from Geneva to Rome, ed. G.A. Bonnard (1961) Journal
Edward Gibbon: Memoirs of My Life, ed. G.A. Bonnard (1969; 1966). portions of Edward Gibbon's memoirs arranged chronologically, omitting repetition.
The English Essays of Edward Gibbon, ed. Patricia Craddock (1972)

www.ingramcontent.com/pod-product-compliance
Lightning Source LLC
Chambersburg PA
CBHW050122170426
43197CB00011B/1675